The
Bible Knowledge
Commentary

ACTS & EPISTLES

The
Bible Knowledge Commentary

ACTS & EPISTLES

John F. Walvoord and Roy B. Zuck
GENERAL EDITORS

DAVID C COOK

transforming lives together

THE BIBLE KNOWLEDGE COMMENTARY: ACTS & EPISTLES
Published by David C Cook
4050 Lee Vance Drive
Colorado Springs, CO 80918 U.S.A.

David C Cook U.K., Kingsway Communications
Eastbourne, East Sussex BN23 6NT, England

The graphic circle C logo is a registered trademark of David C Cook.

The website addresses recommended throughout this book are offered as a resource
to you. These websites are not intended in any way to be or imply an endorsement
on the part of David C Cook, nor do we vouch for their content.

Unless otherwise noted, all Scripture quotations are taken from the Holy Bible, New
International Version®, NIV®. Copyright © 1973, 1978 by Biblica, Inc.™ Used by
permission of Zondervan. All rights reserved worldwide. www.zondervan.com.
The authors have added italics to Scripture quotations for emphasis.

LCCN 2017955580
ISBN 978-0-8307-7268-1
eISBN 978-0-8307-7287-2

Cover Design: Nick Lee
Cover Photo: Getty Images

Printed in the United States of America
First Edition 2018

1 2 3 4 5 6 7 8 9 10

010818

CONTENTS

PREFACE

The Bible Knowledge Commentary series is an exposition of the Scriptures written and edited solely by Dallas Seminary faculty members. It is designed for pastors, laypersons, Bible teachers, serious Bible students, and others who want a comprehensive but brief and reliable commentary on the entire Bible.

Why another Bible commentary when so many commentaries are already available? Several features make this series a distinctive Bible study tool.

The Bible Knowledge Commentary series is written by faculty members of one school: Dallas Theological Seminary. This commentary interprets the Scriptures consistently from the grammatical-historical approach and from the pretribulational, premillennial perspective, for which Dallas Seminary is well known. At the same time, the authors often present various views of passages where differences of opinion exist within evangelical scholarship.

Additionally, this commentary has features that not all commentaries include. (a) In their comments on the biblical text, the writers discuss how the purpose of the book unfolds, how each part fits with the whole and with what precedes and follows it. This helps readers see why the biblical authors chose the material they did as their words were guided by the Holy Spirit's inspiration. (b) Problem passages, puzzling Bible-time customs, and alleged contradictions are carefully considered and discussed. (c) Insights from modern conservative biblical scholarship are incorporated in this series. (d) Many Hebrew, Aramaic, and Greek words, important to the understanding of certain passages, are discussed. These words are transliterated for the benefit of readers not proficient in the biblical languages. Yet those who do know these languages will also appreciate these comments. (e) Throughout the series, dozens of maps, charts, and diagrams are included; they are placed conveniently with the Bible passages being discussed, not at the end of each book. (f) Numerous cross references to related or parallel passages are included with the discussions on many passages.

The material on each Bible book includes an *Introduction* (discussion of items such as authorship, date, purpose, unity, style, unique features), *Outline, Commentary,* and *Bibliography.* In the *Commentary* section, summaries of entire sections of the text are given, followed by detailed comments on the passage verse by verse and often phrase by phrase. All words quoted from the New International Version of the Bible appear in boldface type, as do the verse numbers at the beginning of paragraphs. The *Bibliography* entries, suggested for further study, are not all endorsed in their entirety by the authors and editors. The writers and editors have listed both works they have consulted and others which would be useful to readers.

Personal pronouns referring to Deity are capitalized, which often helps make it clear that the commentator is writing about a Member of the Trinity. The word LORD is the English translation of the Hebrew YHWH, often rendered *Yahweh* in English. *Lord* translates *'Ădōnāy.* When the two names stand together as a compound name of God, they are rendered "Sovereign LORD," as in the NIV.

The New Testament Consulting Editor, Dr. Stanley D. Toussaint, has added to the quality of this commentary by reading the manuscripts and offering helpful suggestions. His work is greatly appreciated. We also express thanks to Lloyd Cory, Victor Books Reference Editor, to Barbara Williams, whose careful editing enhanced the material appreciably, to hardworking Production Coordinator Myrna Jean Hasse, and to the many manuscript typists at Scripture Press and Dallas Theological Seminary for their diligence.

This commentary series is an exposition of the Bible, an explanation of the text of Scripture, based on careful exegesis. It is not primarily a devotional commentary, or an exegetical work giving details of lexicology, grammar, and syntax with extensive discussion of critical matters pertaining to textual and background data. May this commentary deepen your insight into the Scriptures, as you seek to have "the eyes of your heart ... enlightened" (Eph. 1:18) by the teaching ministry of the Holy Spirit.

This book is designed to enrich your understanding and appreciation of the Scriptures, God's inspired, inerrant Word, and to motivate you "not merely [to] listen to the Word" but also to "do what it says" (James 1:22) and "also ... to teach others" (2 Tim. 2:2).

John F. Walvoord
Roy B. Zuck

Editors

John F. Walvoord, B.A., M.A., TH.M., Th.D., D.D., Litt.D.
Chancellor Emeritus
Professor Emeritus of Systematic Theology

Roy B. Zuck, A.B., Th.M., Th.D.
Senior Professor Emeritus of Bible Exposition
Editor, *Bibliotheca Sacra*

Consulting Editors

Old Testament
Kenneth L. Barker, B.A., Th.M., Ph.D.
Writer, Lewisville, Texas

Eugene H. Merrill, B.A., M.A., M.Phil., Ph.D.
Distinguished Professor of Old Testament Studies

New Testament
Stanley D. Toussaint, B.A., Th.M., Th.D.
Senior Professor Emeritus of Bible Exposition

Series Contributing Authors

Walter L. Baker, B.A., Th.M., D.D.
Associate Professor Emeritus of World
Missions and Intercultural Studies
Obadiah

Craig Blaising, B.S. Th.M., Th.D., Ph.D.
Professor of Christian Theology Southern
Baptist Theological Seminary Louisville,
Kentucky
Malachi

J. Ronald Blue, B.A., Th.M.
President Emeritus CAM International
Dallas, Texas
Habakkuk

Sid S. Buzzell, B.S., Th.M., Ph.D.
Professor of Bible Exposition Colorado
Christian University Lakewood,
Colorado
Proverbs

Donald K. Campbell, B.A., Th.M., Th.D.
President Emeritus
Professor Emeritus of Bible Exposition
Joshua

**Robert B. Chisholm, Jr., B.A., M. Div.,
Th.M., Th.D.**
Professor of Old Testament Studies
Hosea, Joel

Thomas L. Constable, B.A., Th.M., Th.D.
Chairman and Senior Professor of Bible
Exposition
1 and 2 Kings

Jack S. Deere, B.A., Th.M., Th.D.
Associate Senior Pastor Trinity
Fellowship Church Amarillo, Texas
Deuteronomy, Song of Songs

Charles H. Dyer, B.A., Th.M., Th.D.
Provost and Senior Vice-President of
Education
Moody Bible Institute Chicago, Illinois
Jeremiah, Lamentations, Ezekiel

Gene A. Getz, B.A., M.A., Ph.D.
Senior Pastor
Fellowship Bible Church, North Plano,
Texas
Nehemiah

Donald R. Glenn, B.S., M.A., Th.M.
Chairman and Senior Professor of Old Testament Studies
Ecclesiastes

John D. Hannah, B.S., Th.M., Th.D.
Chairman and Distinguished Professor of Historical Theology
Exodus, Jonah, Zephaniah

Elliott E. Johnson, B.S., Th.M., Th.D.
Senior Professor of Bible Exposition
Nahum

F. Duane Lindsey, B.A., B.D., Th.M., Th.D.
Former Registrar, Research Librarian, and Assistant Professor of Systematic Theology
Leviticus, Judges, Haggai, Zechariah

John A. Martin, B.A., Th.M., Th.D.
Provost
Robert Wesleyan College
Rochester, New York
Ezra, Esther, Isaiah, Micah

Eugene H. Merrill, B.A., M.A., M.Phil., Ph.D.
Distinguished Professor of Old Testament Studies
Numbers, 1 and 2 Samuel, 1 and 2 Chronicles

J. Dwight Pentecost, B.A., Th.M., Th.D.
Distinguished Professor Emeritus of Bible Exposition
Daniel

John W. Reed, B.A., M.A., M.Div., Ph.D.
Director of D.Min. Studies
Senior Professor Emeritus of Pastoral Ministries
Ruth

Allen P. Ross, B.A., M.A., M.Div., Ph.D.
Professor of Old Testament Studies
Trinity Evangelical Episcopal Seminary
Ambridge, Pennsylvania
Genesis, Psalms

Donald R. Sunukjian, B.A., Th.M., Th.D., Ph.D.
Professor of Christian Ministry and Leadership
Talbot School of Theology La Mirada, California
Amos

Roy B. Zuck, B.A., Th.M., Th.D.
Editor, Bibliotheca Sacra
Senior Professor of Bible Exposition
Job

*Authorial information based on original edition of the Bible Knowledge Commentary set. At the time of the commentary's first printing, each author was a faculty member of Dallas Theological Seminary.

Abbreviations

A. *General*

act.	active	n., nn.	note(s)
Akk.	Akkadian	n.d.	no date
Apoc.	Apocrypha	neut.	neuter
Aram.	Aramaic	n.p.	no publisher, no place of
ca.	*circa,* about		publication
cf.	*confer,* compare	no.	number
chap., chaps.	chapter(s)	NT	New Testament
comp.	compiled, compilation,	OT	Old Testament
	compiler	p., pp.	page(s)
ed.	edited, edition, editor	par., pars.	paragraph(s)
eds.	editors	part.	participle
e.g.	*exempli gratia,* for example	pass.	passive
Eng.	English	perf.	perfect
et al.	*et alii,* and others	pl.	plural
fem.	feminine	pres.	present
Gr.	Greek	q.v.	*quod vide,* which see
Heb.	Hebrew	Sem.	Semitic
ibid.	*ibidem,* in the same place	sing.	singular
i.e.	*id est,* that is	s.v.	*sub verbo,* under the word
imper.	imperative	trans.	translation, translator,
imperf.	imperfect		translated
lit.	literal, literally	viz.	*videlicet,* namely
LXX	Septuagint	vol., vols.	volume(s)
marg.	margin, marginal reading	v., vv.	verse(s)
masc.	masculine	vs.	versus
ms., mss.	manuscript(s)	Vul.	Vulgate
MT	Masoretic text		

B. *Abbreviations of Books of the Bible*

Gen.	Ruth	Job	Lam.	Jonah
Ex.	1, 2 Sam.	Ps., Pss. (pl.)	Ezek.	Micah
Lev.	1, 2 Kings	Prov.	Dan.	Nahum
Num.	1, 2 Chron.	Ecc.	Hosea	Hab.
Deut.	Ezra	Song	Joel	Zeph.
Josh.	Neh.	Isa.	Amos	Hag.
Jud.	Es.	Jer.	Obad.	Zech.
				Mal.

Matt.	Acts	Eph.	1, 2 Tim.	James
Mark	Rom.	Phil.	Titus	1, 2 Peter
Luke	1, 2 Cor.	Col.	Phile.	1, 2, 3 John
John	Gal.	1, 2 Thes.	Heb.	Jude
				Rev.

C. *Abbreviations of Bible Versions, Translations, and Paraphrases*

ASV	American Standard Version
JB	Jerusalem Bible
KJV	King James Version
NASB	New American Standard Bible
NEB	New English Bible
NIV	New International Version
NKJV	New King James Version
Ph.	New Testament in Modern English (J.B. Phillips)
RSV	Revised Standard Version
Sco.	New Scofield Reference Bible
Wms.	The New Testament (Charles B. Williams)

11

Transliterations

Hebrew

Consonants

א – '	ד – $\underline{d}$	י – y	ס – s	ר – r
ב – b	ה – h	כ – k	ע – '	שׂ – ś
ב – $\underline{b}$	ו – w	כ – $\underline{k}$	פ – p	שׁ – š
ג – g	ז – z	ל – l	פ – $\underline{p}$	ת – t
ג – $\underline{g}$	ח – ḥ	מ – m	צ – ṣ	ת – $\underline{t}$
ד – $\underline{d}$	ט – ṭ	נ – n	ק – q	

Daghesh forte is represented by doubling the letter.

Vocalization

בָה – bâh	בָ – bā	בָ – bo[1]	בְ – bĕ
בוֹ – bô	בֹ – bō	בֻ – bu[1]	בְ – b'
בוּ – bû	בֻ – bū	בֶ – be	בָה – bāh
בֵי – bê	בֵ – bē	בִי – bi[1]	בָא – bā'
בֶי – bè	בִ – bī	בַ – bă	בֵה – bēh
בִי – bî	בַ – ba	בָ – bŏ	בֶה – beh

[1] In closed syllables

Greek

α, ᾳ	— a	ξ	— x	γγ	— ng
β	— b	ο	— o	γκ	— nk
γ	— g	π	— p	γξ	— nx
δ	— d	ρ	— r	γχ	— nch
ε	— e	σ, ς	— s	αἰ	— ai
ζ	— z	τ	— t	αὐ	— au
η, ῃ	— ē	υ	— y	εἰ	— ei
θ	— th	φ	— ph	εὐ	— eu
ι	— i	χ	— ch	ηὐ	— ēu
κ	— k	ψ	— ps	οἰ	— oi
λ	— l	ω, ῳ	— ō	οὐ	— ou
μ	— m	ῥ	— rh	υἱ	— hui
ν	— n	ʽ	— h		

Groupings of New Testament Books

I. **History**
   A. Four Gospels
   B. Acts

II. **Epistles**
   A. Pauline

   Journey Epistles $\begin{cases} \text{Galatians} \\ \text{1 and 2 Thessalonians} \\ \text{1 and 2 Corinthians} \\ \text{Romans} \end{cases}$

   Prison Epistles $\begin{cases} \text{Ephesians} \\ \text{Philippians} \\ \text{Colossians} \\ \text{Philemon} \end{cases}$

   Pastoral Epistles $\begin{cases} \text{1 Timothy} \\ \text{Titus} \\ \text{2 Timothy} \end{cases}$

   B. General

   Hebrew Christians $\begin{cases} \text{Hebrews} \\ \text{James} \end{cases}$

   Others $\begin{cases} \text{1 and 2 Peter} \\ \text{1, 2, and 3 John} \\ \text{Jude} \end{cases}$

III. **Visions**
   Revelation

ACTS

Stanley D. Toussaint

INTRODUCTION

Among the New Testament writings, Acts stands out as singular and unique. This claim is made on the basis of several considerations. For one, it is the only historical sequel to the four Gospels in the canonical writings. No other narrative in the New Testament continues the accounts given by the four evangelists.

Furthermore, this book forms a background and setting for most of Paul's writings. Bruce writes, "But it is Luke that we have to thank for the coherent record of Paul's apostolic activity. Without [Acts], we should be incalculably poorer. Even with it, there is much in Paul's letters that we have difficulty in understanding; how much more there would be if we had no Book of Acts" (F.F. Bruce, *Commentary on the Book of the Acts*, p. 27).

The Book of Acts gives today's Christians basic information and insights into the early church. Luke portrays the tensions, persecutions, frustrations, theological problems, and hopes confronting the neophyte bride of Christ. How great would be the church's lack without the material in Acts!

In addition, Acts marks the transition from the work of God provincially among the Jews to His establishment of the universal church. In a real sense the reader goes from Jerusalem to the uttermost part of the world in these 28 chapters.

Besides all these, Acts presents a stimulating challenge to every Christian today. The zeal, the faith, the joy, the commitment, and the obedience of those early saints is an example to all believers. It is crucial for followers of Jesus Christ to be as intimately acquainted with this book as possible. As Rackham affirms, "We can hardly overestimate the importance of the Acts of the Apostles" (Richard Belward Rackham, *The Acts of the Apostles*, p. xiii).

Title of the Book. The earliest extant evidence for the name "Acts" is found in an anti-Marcionite Prologue to the Gospel of Luke, a work dated between A.D. 150 and 180. How or why it received this title is open to speculation.

It must be conceded that "Acts" is not an accurate title because the book by no means contains all the acts of all the apostles. Only Peter and Paul are emphasized. The great Apostle John is mentioned, but none of his words are recorded. The death of John's brother James is given in one brief sentence (Acts 12:2).

The work more accurately could be titled "Certain Acts of Certain Apostles." However, the title "The Acts of the Apostles" is so well established it identifies this work of Luke very well.

Purpose of Acts. Under the inspiration of the Holy Spirit Luke certainly had a purpose in writing. What was he intending to accomplish? To put it another way,

Miracles by Peter and Paul	
Peter	
Acts 3:1-11	Healed a man lame from birth
5:15-16	Peter's shadow healed people
5:17	Success caused Jewish jealousy
8:9-24	Dealt with Simon, a sorcerer
9:36-41	Raised Dorcas to life
Paul	
14:8-18	Healed a man lame from birth
19:11-12	Handkerchiefs and aprons from Paul healed people
13:45	Success caused Jewish jealousy
13:6-11	Dealt with Bar-Jesus, a sorcerer
20:9-12	Raised Eutychus to life

15

why did he select the materials he chose for the book? To this question there are two answers.

On the one hand some say the primary purpose is a historical one; on the other hand some say the goal is apologetic, that is, it is a written defense. All acknowledge there are subsidiary ends, but the question revolves around its primary purpose.

The view that the purpose of Acts is a Pauline apologetic is buttressed by the amazing set of parallels between Peter and Paul (see chart "Miracles by Peter and Paul").

Perhaps Luke intended in this way to defend Paul's apostleship; Paul certainly did not rate behind Peter in power and authority. This may also account for the *three* accounts of Paul's conversion (chaps. 9; 22; 26). But though there are striking parallels between Peter's and Paul's ministries, the vindication of Paul's apostleship can hardly be the book's primary purpose. There is just too much in the book that would be extraneous to this goal. How does the appointment of the Seven in Acts 6 or the detailed description of the shipwreck in Acts 27 further that end?

Most recognize that Acts shows the universality of Christianity. Is this its primary purpose? The gospel goes to Samaritans, the Ethiopian eunuch, Cornelius, Gentiles at Antioch, poor and wealthy, educated and uneducated, women and men, the high and lofty as well as those in humble positions. This approach also helps explain the emphasis on the Jerusalem Council described in Acts 15. However, this again does not explain certain elements in the book such as the choice of Matthias in Acts 1 or the selection of the Seven in Acts 6.

The question remains, what is the primary purpose of Acts? F.F. Bruce, a representative of those who believe the goal is an apologetic one, affirms, "Luke is, in fact, one of the first Christian apologists. In that particular type of apologetic which is addressed to the secular authorities to establish the law-abiding character of Christianity he is absolutely the pioneer" (Bruce, *Acts*, p. 24; cf. F.J. Foakes Jackson and Kirsopp Lake, eds., *The Beginnings of Christianity*, vol. 2, *Prolegomena II: Criticism*. Grand Rapids: Baker Book House, 1979, pp.

177-87). There is much in Acts to substantiate the idea that the book was written to defend Christianity before Roman rulers.

The persecution in Acts is always religious except in two locations—Philippi (chap. 16) and Ephesus (chap. 19). In both of these the opposition was due to vested interests. In every other case the persecutions arose from Jewish sources.

It may be debated, however, whether the primary purpose of Acts is apologetic, even though much in the book substantiates that view. Why include the shipwreck of Acts 27, for instance? Another objection to the concept of an apologetic purpose is the close association of Luke's Gospel with Acts. It is patently clear that Luke-Acts is a two-part work; Acts 1:1 is evidence enough of this. Acts, then, can hardly be apologetic in its primary purpose because there is little in the Gospel of Luke which reveals such an intention.

By far the most popular view of the purpose of Acts is the one which states that it is a historical one. According to this approach Luke's goal was to record the spread of the gospel message from Jerusalem to Judea to Samaria and to the ends of the earth (1:8). Barclay asserts, "Luke's great aim was to show the expansion of Christianity, to show how that religion which began in a little corner of Palestine had in a little more than 30 years reached Rome" (William Barclay, *The Acts of the Apostles*, p. xvii). This explains the transition from a Jewish ministry to a Gentile one, and from Peter to Paul. In addition, this view suits the historical outlook of Acts 1:1 with Luke 1:1-4. The prologue of Luke 1:1-4 is that of a historian like Herodotus, Thucydides, or Polybius. It is quite clear that Luke was writing history in both books.

But is Luke only a historiographer? Luke-Acts is history but it is also intensely theological and especially eschatological. The Book of Acts opens with an eschatological question (1:6) and concludes with eschatological terminology ("the kingdom of God," 28:31). In addition there is a stress on God's sovereignty. In spite of intense opposition of every kind, the Word of God spreads and people respond. Nothing can stop the steady growth of Christianity. The purpose of the Book of Acts may be stated as follows: *To explain with the Gospel of Luke the orderly and sovereignly directed progress of the kingdom message from Jews to Gentiles, and from Jerusalem to Rome.* In Luke's Gospel the question is answered, "If Christianity has its roots in the Old Testament and in Judaism, how did it become a worldwide religion?" The Book of Acts continues in the vein of the Gospel of Luke to answer the same problem.

Alongside this worldwide progression there is an emphasis on eschatology in both Luke and Acts. The prophetic expression *kingdom of God* occurs in Luke 32 times and in Acts 6 times besides the allusions to God's kingdom in 1:6 and 20:25 (cf. 1:3; 8:12; 14:22; 19:8; 28:23, 31). In addition there are many references to eschatology in other terminology and by inference (1:11; 2:19-21, 34-35; 3:19-25; 6:14; 10:42; 13:23-26, 32-33; 15:15-18; 17:3, 7, 31; 20:24-25, 32; 21:28; 23:6; 24:15-17, 21, 25; 26:6-8, 18; 28:20). Obviously, the church in the present Age is heavily accented, but the church also is seen as an heir of the kingdom. It may be concluded, then, that Luke shows how the kingdom message moved from mostly Jews to mostly Gentiles and from Jerusalem to Rome.

This progression is directed in an orderly and sovereign way. One theme that runs as a heavy cord in the fabric of the book is God's sovereignty. In spite of strong opposition, under the Lord's direction the Word of the Lord grew and spread. Thus the purpose of Luke in writing Acts is to show how it is God's intention for His millennial kingdom to include a population of believers taken from Jews and Gentiles during this Age.

If this purpose statement is accepted, it does not rule out the previous suggestions. It includes both Peter and Paul as prime characters, Peter the minister to the circumcised, and Paul to the uncircumcised. The universality of the gospel is part of Luke's emphasis in both his Gospel and here in Acts. Certainly the progression of the book, declared in 1:8, fits into this statement. All of these contribute to the overall purpose of Luke in penning this work.

Sources Luke May Have Used. Under the inspiration of the Holy Spirit Luke probably used a number of sources. First and primary were his own personal experiences. This is most clearly seen in the "we" sections of Acts (16:10-40; 20:5-28:31). A second source of information would have been Paul, with whom Luke spent much time. The apostle's conversion and his experiences in ministry undoubtedly would have been discussed by the two in their time together. A third source is seen in the other witnesses whom Luke contacted (cf. 20:4-5; 21:15-19). In Acts 21:18-19 James is mentioned as being one with whom Luke met. James certainly would have been able to convey information about the very first chapters in Acts! In fact, the early chapters of Acts seem to betray an Aramaic source. Furthermore, while Paul was incarcerated for two years in Caesarea (24:27), Luke would have been free to carry out thorough investigative work in Palestine (Luke 1:2-3). Having carefully researched eyewitness accounts, Luke, by the Spirit's direction, penned the Book of Acts.

Date of the Book. The writing of Acts must have taken place before the destruction of Jerusalem in A.D. 70. Certainly an event of such magnitude would not have been ignored. This is especially true in light of one of the basic themes of the book: God's turning to the Gentiles from the Jews because of the Jews' rejection of Jesus Christ.

Luke scarcely would have omitted an account of Paul's death, traditionally dated from A.D. 66-68, if it had occurred before he wrote Acts.

Nor did Luke mention the Neronian persecutions which began after the great fire of Rome in A.D. 64.

Furthermore, a defense of Christianity before Nero by using the Book of Acts to appeal to what lower officials had ruled regarding Paul would have had little point at the time of the Neronian antagonism. At that time Nero was so intent on destroying the church, the defense set forth in Acts would have had little effect in dissuading him.

The date usually accepted by conservative scholars for the writing of Acts is around A.D. 60-62. Accordingly the place of writing would be Rome or possibly both Caesarea and Rome. At the time of writing Paul's release was either imminent or had just taken place.

Outline of the Book. The outline used in this study is the result of using two keys in Acts. The first and most obvious one is the theme verse, Acts 1:8, "But you will receive power when the Holy Spirit comes on you; and you will be My witnesses in Jerusalem, and in all Judea and Samaria, and to the ends of the earth."

The second key is the use Luke makes of "progress reports" which are sprinkled throughout the book (cf. 2:47; 6:7; 9:31; 12:24; 16:5; 19:20; 28:30-31). Because Luke does not use a precise formula there is some debate as to the location of other progress reports (cf. 2:41; 4:31; 5:42; 8:25, 40; etc.). However, these other statements either do not have the same sense of summary or they lack finality.

The beautiful correlation of these two factors—the key verse of Acts 1:8 and the seven progress reports—form the basis of the following outline.

OUTLINE

I. The Witness in Jerusalem (1:1–6:7)
   A. The expectation of the chosen (chaps. 1–2)
      1. The introduction (1:1-5)
      2. The internment at Jerusalem (1:6-26)
      3. The inception of the church (chap. 2)
   Progress report no. 1: "And the Lord added to their number daily those who were being saved" (2:47).
   B. The expansion of the church at Jerusalem (3:1–6:7)
      1. Opposition to the church (3:1–4:31)
      2. Correction in the church (4:32–5:11)
      3. Progression in the church (5:12-42)
      4. Administration in the church (6:1-7)
   Progress report no. 2: "So the Word of God spread. The number of disciples in Jerusalem increased rapidly" (6:7).

II. The Witness in all Judea and Samaria (6:8–9:31)
   A. The martyrdom of Stephen (6:8–8:1a)
      1. The arrest of Stephen (6:8–7:1)
      2. The address of Stephen (7:2-53)
      3. The attack on Stephen (7:54–8:1a)
   B. The ministry of Philip (8:1b-40)
      1. In Samaria (8:1b-25)
      2. To the Ethiopian eunuch (8:26-40)
   C. The message of Saul (9:1-31)
      1. The conversion of Saul (9:1-19a)
      2. The conflicts of Saul (9:19b-31)
   Progress report no. 3: "Then the church throughout Judea, Galilee, and Samaria . . . was strengthened; and [it was] encouraged by the Holy Spirit, it grew in numbers, living in the fear of the Lord" (9:31).

III. The Witness to the Extremity of the Earth (9:32–28:31)
   A. The extension of the church to Antioch (9:32–12:24)
      1. The preparation of Peter for a universal gospel (9:32–10:48)
      2. The preparation of the apostles for a universal gospel (11:1-18)
      3. The preparation of the church at Antioch for a universal gospel (11:19-30)
      4. The persecution of the church at Jerusalem (12:1-24)
   Progress report no. 4: "But the Word of God continued to increase and spread" (12:24).
   B. The extension of the church in Asia Minor (12:25–16:5)
      1. The call and dedication of Barnabas and Saul (12:25–13:3)
      [First missionary journey, chaps. 13–14]
      2. The circuit in Asia Minor (13:4–14:28)
      3. The conference at Jerusalem (15:1-35)
      4. The confirmation of the churches in Asia Minor (15:36–16:5)
      [Second missionary journey, 15:36–18:22]

Progress report no. 5: "So the churches were strengthened in the faith and grew daily in numbers" (16:5).

C. The extension of the church in the Aegean area (16:6–19:20)
1. The call to Macedonia (16:6-10)
2. The conflicts in Macedonia (16:11–17:15)
3. The crusade in Achaia (17:16–18:18)
4. The conclusion of the second missionary journey (18:19-22)
5. The conquest of Ephesus (18:23–19:20)
  [Third missionary journey, 18:23–21:16]

Progress report no. 6: "In this way the Word of the Lord spread widely and grew in power" (19:20).

D. The extension of the church to Rome (19:21–28:31)
1. The completion of the third journey (19:21–21:16)
2. The captivity at Jerusalem (21:17–23:32)
3. The captivity at Caesarea (23:33–26:32)
4. The captivity at Rome (chaps. 27–28)

Progress report no. 7: "Paul . . . welcomed all who came to see him. Boldly and without hindrance he preached the kingdom of God and taught about the Lord Jesus Christ" (28:30-31).

COMMENTARY

I. The Witness in Jerusalem (1:1–6:7)

A. The expectation of the chosen (chaps. 1–2)

1. THE INTRODUCTION (1:1-5)

1:1-2. In the first two verses of this book Luke looked back to his Gospel. **Theophilus** may have been Luke's patron who financed the writing of Luke and Acts. At any rate he was a believer in Christ. These two books would confirm and instruct Theophilus, as well as the church of Christ, in the faith (cf. Luke 1:1-4).

The verb **began** indicates that Acts continues the account of the ministry and teaching Christ began on earth. He is still working and teaching through His people today.

The reference to the Lord's Ascension in Acts 1:2 looks back to Luke 24:51.

Two commandments were given by the Lord before He returned to heaven: (1) the apostolic band was to remain in Jerusalem (Acts 1:4; cf. Luke 24:49); (2) they were to go into the world as witnesses (Acts 1:8; cf. Luke 10:4; 24:47). These **instructions** may have seemed contradictory but they were to be obeyed sequentially.

1:3. The Lord's post-resurrection appearances attested the reality of the Resurrection. Christ **gave many convincing proofs** of this. The word "proofs" (*tekmēriois*) occurs only here in the New Testament and looks at demonstrable evidence in contrast with evidence provided by witnesses. In other words, the Resurrection was proven by touch, sight, and feel (cf. Luke 24:39-40; 1 John 1:1).

For **40 days** after His resurrection the Lord **appeared** to the apostles and discussed **the kingdom of God** with **them.** What is meant by this term? God has always ruled over the world and especially in Israel (Dan. 2:47; 4:3, 25-26, 32, 34-37; 5:21; 6:25-27; Pss. 5:2; 84:3; 89:6-18; 103; etc.). However, a time is coming, commonly called the Millennium, when God will burst into human history in a spectacular way to establish His rule on earth. This is what is meant by the term "kingdom of God" (cf. comments on Matt. 3:2; 13:10-16). Though this topic was the subject of much of the Lord's teaching and preaching before the Cross, He saw fit to discuss it further during His 40 days of post-resurrection ministry.

1:4. The promised **gift** from the **Father,** also anticipated in Luke 24:49, was quite obviously the Holy Spirit (cf. Acts 1:5; John 14:16; 15:26; 16:7).

1:5. Indeed **John** had predicted a Spirit baptism by the Lord Jesus. The greatness of Christ was seen in the fact that John identified people with himself by **water** baptism; Christ Jesus would join His followers to Himself by **the Holy Spirit.** The word **baptized,** which normally means "dipped or immersed," here has the idea of "uniting with" (cf. 1 Cor. 10:1-2). The Lord made the same prediction of Spirit baptism that John made (Matt. 3:11; Mark 1:8; cf. Acts 11:16).

2. THE INTERNMENT AT JERUSALEM (1:6-26)

a. The Ascension (1:6-11)

1:6. The disciples' question, **Lord are You at this time going to restore the kingdom to Israel?** is most illuminating. The sentence is introduced by the connective **so** (*men oun*), which associates the thought of verse 6 with verse 5. In the disciples' minds the outpouring of the Holy Spirit and the coming of the promised kingdom were closely associated. And well they should be, because the Old Testament frequently joined the two (cf. Isa. 32:15-20; 44:3-5; Ezek. 39:28-29; Joel 2:28–3:1; Zech. 12:8-10). When Christ told the disciples of the soon-coming Spirit baptism, they immediately concluded that the restoration of Israel's kingdom was near in time (cf. comments on "restore" in Acts 3:21).

1:7. Some conclude from the Lord's response that the apostles had a false concept of the kingdom. But this is wrong. Christ did not accuse them of this. If the followers of the Lord Jesus had an incorrect view, this would have been the time for Him to correct it. The fact is, Christ taught the coming of an earthly, literal kingdom (cf. Matt. 19:28; Luke 19:11-27; 22:28-30). Acts 1:3 states that the Lord instructed the disciples about the kingdom; He certainly gave them the right impression as to its character and future coming. What Jesus discussed here (v. 7) was the *time* of the coming of the kingdom. The Greek word for **times** (*chronous*) basically describes duration of times, and the word for **dates** (*kairous*) refers to both length of times and kinds of times (as in, e.g., "hard times"). The disciples were **not . . . to know** either the times or the critical periods **the Father** had **set by His . . . authority.** Later, further revelation would be made concerning these (cf. 1 Thes. 5:1).

1:8. This verse contrasts (*alla,* **but**) with verse 7. Instead of knowing the times or dates, the apostles were to be Christ's witnesses **to the ends of the earth.** This they were to do after they had been supernaturally empowered by **the Holy Spirit.**

The meaning of the clause **you will be My witnesses** is subject to question. Is

this a command, or is it a simple statement of fact? Grammatically the words may be taken either way, but because of 10:42 (cf. 4:20) it is clearly an imperative in the future tense.

Probably "the ends (sing., 'end' in the Gr. text) of the earth" looks to Rome, the proud center of world civilization in the Apostolic Age, a significant distance from Jerusalem (more than 1,400 miles, as the crow flies).

1:9-11. These verses describe the Lord's Ascension but they also anticipate His return. He will come back in **a cloud,** bodily, in view of people (Rev. 1:7), and to the Mount of Olives (Zech. 14:4)—**the same way** the apostles saw **Him** go.

The Ascension of Christ marked the conclusion of His ministry on earth in His bodily presence. It also exalted Him to the right hand of the Father (Acts 2:33-36; 5:30-31; Heb. 1:3; 8:1; 12:2). At the same time the Ascension meant that the continuing work of Christ on earth was now placed in the hands of His disciples (Acts 1:1-2, 8).

It was imperative that the Ascension occur so that the promised Comforter could come (cf. John 14:16, 26; 15:26; 16:7; Acts 2:33-36). The Holy Spirit would empower the disciples as they ministered the gospel and waited for the kingdom.

b. The supplication in the Upper Room (1:12-14)

1:12-14. A **Sabbath Day's walk** was about 3,000 feet or a bit more than half a mile (cf. Ex. 16:29; Num. 35:5). **The Mount of Olives** is this short distance east of Jerusalem.

The apostles were gathered **upstairs.** Large groups normally would meet in upper stories because the largest rooms were upstairs (cf. Acts 20:8-9). The lower stories had smaller rooms so that their walls would bear the weight of the upper stories.

The **prayer** (1:14) may be specific prayer for the promise referred to in verse 4. In the Greek "prayer" has the article. The disciples were following the instruction suggested by Jesus (Luke 11:13). However, since the day of Pentecost, it is not necessary for Christians to pray for the Holy Spirit (cf. Rom. 8:9).

Evidently the Lord's resurrection led to the conversion of the **brothers** of Jesus

SERMONS AND SPEECHES IN ACTS

| Speakers | | | Occasions and/or | | |
Peter	Paul	Others	Hearers	Cities	References
1. Peter			Selection of successor to Judas	Jerusalem	1:16-22
2. Peter			Signs on the day of Pentecost	Jerusalem	2:14-36
3. Peter			Healing of lame man in the temple	Jerusalem	3:12-26
4. Peter			Before the Sanhedrin for preaching the resurrection of Christ	Jerusalem	4:8-12
		Gamaliel	Before the Sanhedrin, regarding Peter and others	Jerusalem	5:35-39
		Stephen	Before the Sanhedrin, after Stephen was arrested	Jerusalem	7:2-53
5. Peter			At Cornelius' house, to present the gospel to Gentiles there	Caesarea	10:34-43
6. Peter			Defense to the church about what happened in Caesarea	Jerusalem	11:4-17
	1. Paul		Sabbath sermon to Jews in the synagogue	Antioch of Pisidia	13:16-41
	2. Paul and Barnabas		Crowd who wanted to worship them	Lystra	14:15-17
7. Peter			Church council	Jerusalem	15:7-11
		James	Church council	Jerusalem	15:13-21
	3. Paul		Athenians on Mars' Hill	Athens	17:22-31
		Demetrius	Workmen who were disturbed at Paul's preaching	Ephesus	19:25-27
		Town clerk	Riot at Ephesus	Ephesus	19:35-40
	4. Paul		Gathering of Ephesian elders	Miletus	20:18-35
	5. Paul		Mob of people who tried to kill Paul	Jerusalem	22:1-21
	6. Paul		Defense before the Sanhedrin	Jerusalem	23:1-6
	7. Paul		Defense before Felix	Caesarea	24:10-21
	8. Paul		Defense before Festus	Caesarea	25:8, 10-11
	9. Paul		Defense before Herod Agrippa II	Caesarea	26:1-23
	10. Paul		Shipmates in a violent storm	Mediterranean Sea, between Crete and Malta	27:21-26
	11. Paul		Testimony to Jewish leaders	Rome	28:17-20, 25-28

(cf. John 7:5; 1 Cor. 15:7). If so, this is the only recorded appearance Christ made to unsaved people after His resurrection.

c. The completion of the apostolate (1:15-26)

1:15. Peter, leader of the apostolic band, **stood up among the** group of some **120** who were **gathered together in** Jerusalem. Obviously there were far more followers elsewhere (cf. 1 Cor. 15:6).

1:16-17. Peter's allusion to the Old Testament shows his high view of the Scriptures. The Psalms were inspired by **the Holy Spirit** speaking **through the mouth of David.** Peter's assessment was that **the Scripture had to be fulfilled.** The verb "had to" is from *dei,* which is used of logical or divine necessity.

Peter said that David prophesied of **Judas.** But when did David discuss Judas Iscariot? Certainly he did not refer to him directly or name him. In the Psalms the Messiah is anticipated as the ideal King; therefore the royal psalms, which discuss the King of Israel, often anticipate Christ. Likewise the enemies of the royal psalmist became the enemies of the Messiah. Therefore Judas was predicted in Psalms 69:25 and 109:8 as Acts 1:20 states. Both of these psalms are royal imprecatory psalms (cf. Ps. 41:9).

1:18-19. Though **Judas** himself did not personally buy **a field,** he did so indirectly. The priests used the betrayal money Judas flung into the temple to make this purchase in Judas' name (Matt. 27:3-10).

The account of Judas' violent end in Acts 1:18 seems to contradict Matthew 27:5, which starkly says he "hanged himself." One explanation is that Judas' **intestines** quickly became swollen and distended after he hanged himself, so he **burst open.** Another explanation, more probable, is that Judas hanged himself over a cliff and the rope or branch of the tree he was using broke. When he fell to the rocks below, he "burst open."

Akeldama is Aramaic for **Field of Blood.** The exact location of that field is unknown, but traditionally it is believed to be near the Greek Orthodox Church and Convent of Saint Oniprius, where the Valley of Hinnom joins the Kidron Valley, southeast of Jerusalem (see map).

LOCATION OF AKELDAMA

1:20. On Peter's quotation of Psalms 69:25 and 109:8 in reference to Judas, see comments on Acts 1:16-17.

1:21. Once again (cf. v. 16) Luke used the verb *dei,* translated **it is necessary,** to show logical or divine necessity. Interestingly the apostolate saw fit to replace the vacancy left by Judas, but later when the Apostle James died (12:2) no record was given of a successor being appointed. Evidently it was necessary to replace Judas' position because he had vacated his place of promise, referred to in Matthew 19:28. There **the Lord** promised the apostles they would sit on 12 thrones reigning over Christ's kingdom of Israel when He returns to reign on Planet Earth (cf. Rev. 21:14).

1:22. The importance of the Resurrection is seen in the requirement that the replacement **must** be **a witness . . . of His resurrection.** The resurrection of the Lord **Jesus** is a cornerstone of the Christian faith (cf. 1 Cor. 15).

1:23-26. With **two men** to choose from, **Joseph** (alias **Barsabbas** and **Justus**) and **Matthias,** the apostles did two things: **they prayed** (acknowledging the Lord's omniscience; cf. Ps 139:1-6; John 2:25;

4:29) and **they drew lots.** Probably the two names were written on stones placed in a container. When the stones were shaken out of the container, the first stone to fall out was considered the Lord's choice.

This is the last time in the Bible lots were said to be used to determine God's will. A couple of observations are in order. First, no moral question was involved here. It was a matter of making a choice between two men who were apparently equally qualified. Second, this procedure may have come from Proverbs 16:33 which says the decision of lots is from the Lord.

Some feel the choice of Matthias was a wrong one. It is contended that this was a poor method of choosing and Paul should have filled the vacancy left by Judas' apostasy. However, those who believe Matthias was a proper selection argue that Matthew 19:28 is Jewish in its orientation and Paul was to minister to Gentiles (Gal. 2:9). Furthermore Luke, Paul's friend and companion, acknowledged the Twelve as an official group (Acts 2:14; 6:2). Finally, there is no sense or spirit of censure in the Acts account on the selection of Matthias.

3. THE INCEPTION OF THE CHURCH
  (CHAP. 2)

a. *The descent of the Holy Spirit (2:1-13)*

2:1. The day of Pentecost was an annual feast that followed the Feast of Firstfruits by a week of weeks (i.e., seven weeks, or 49 days) and therefore also was called the Feast of Weeks (cf. Lev. 23:15-22). The name "Pentecost," of Greek derivation, means 50 because it was the 50th day after the Firstfruits feast (Lev. 23:16).

Where the followers of Christ were gathered at this time is not definitely known. Luke simply wrote, **They were all together in one place.** Perhaps they were in the temple precincts. However, the place is called a "house" (Acts 2:2), an unlikely designation for the temple, though it may be referred to as a house (cf. 7:47). If they were not assembled at the temple, they must have been near it (cf. 2:6).

2:2-3. The references to "wind" and "fire" are significant. The word for "Spirit" (*pneuma*) is related to *pnoē,* the word translated "wind" here. It also

means breath. Both nouns—"spirit" and "wind" or "breath"—are from the verb *pneō,* "to blow, to breathe." The **sound like the blowing of a violent wind . . . from heaven** points to the power of the Holy Spirit and the fullness of His coming.

The **tongues of fire** portray the presence of God. Several times in the Old Testament God displayed Himself in the form of flames (Gen. 15:17; Ex. 3:2-6; 13:21-22; 19:18; 40:38; cf. Matt. 3:11; Luke 3:16).

No believer there was exempt from this experience, for the flames **separated and came to rest on each of them.**

2:4. The filling **with the Holy Spirit** is separate from the baptism of the Spirit. The Spirit's baptism occurs once for each believer at the moment of salvation (cf. 11:15-16; Rom. 6:3; 1 Cor. 12:13; Col. 2:12), but the Spirit's filling may occur not only at salvation but also on a number of occasions after salvation (Acts 4:8, 31; 6:3, 5; 7:55; 9:17; 13:9, 52).

An evidence of the baptism of the Holy Spirit was **other tongues** (*heterais glōssais;* cf. 11:15-16). These were undoubtedly spoken living languages; the word used in 2:6, 8 is *dialektō,* which means "language" and not ecstatic utterance. This gives insight into what is meant by "tongues" in chapters 2; 10; 19; and in 1 Corinthians 12–14.

This event marked the beginning of the church. Up to this point the church was anticipated (Matt. 16:18). The church is constituted a body by means of Spirit baptism (1 Cor. 12:13). The first occurrence of the baptism of the Spirit therefore must indicate the inauguration of the church. Of course Acts 2:1-4 does not state that Spirit baptism took place at Pentecost. However, 1:5 anticipates it and 11:15-16 refers back to it as having occurred at Pentecost. The church, therefore, came into existence then.

2:5-13. Jews of the "diaspora" (dispersion; cf. James 1:1; 1 Peter 1:1) **were . . . in Jerusalem** for the feast. Perhaps they were bilingual, speaking both Greek and their native languages. They were dumbfounded to hear Jews from Galilee speaking the languages of peoples surrounding the Mediterranean Sea.

It is a question whether only the Twelve spoke in **tongues** or all 120.

Several factors support the idea of only the Twelve being involved in this phenomenon: (1) They are referred to as **Galileans** (Acts 2:7; cf. 1:11-13). (2) Peter stood up with "the Eleven" (2:14). (3) The nearest antecedent of "they" in verse 1 is the "apostles" in 1:26. However, a problem with this view is that the number of languages listed in 2:9-11 is more than 12. But one apostle could have spoken more than one language, in sequence. Still it is possible that all 120 spoke in tongues. Since the majority of them were from Galilee they could have been called Galileans. The references to the Twelve would have indicated they were the leaders of the 120.

The topic the people discussed in all these languages was **the wonders of God.** It seems they were praising God. Their message was not one of repentance; it was not the gospel.

Unable to explain this miracle away, the Jewish unbelievers were puzzled, and some resorted to scoffing and asserted, **They have had too much wine.** The word "wine" (*gleukous*) means new sweet wine.

b. The discourse of Peter (2:14-40)

This sermon has basically one theme: Jesus is the Messiah and Lord (v. 36). Peter's discourse may be outlined as follows:

I. This is the fulfillment of prophecy (vv. 15-21)
    A. A defense (v. 15)
    B. An explanation (vv. 16-21)
II. Jesus is the Messiah (vv. 22-32)
    A. His works attest that He is the Messiah (v. 22)
    B. His resurrection attests that He is the Messiah (vv. 23-32)
III. Jesus, the glorified Messiah, poured forth the Holy Spirit (vv. 33-36)
IV. Application (vv. 37-40)

2:14-15. Peter began with a rebuttal of their accusation of drunkenness. It was **only 9 in the morning** (lit., "the third hour of the day"; days began at 6 A.M.), far too early for a group of revelers to be inebriated!

2:16-21. Instead of being drunk the believers were experiencing what was described in Joel 2. In Peter's words, **This is what was spoken by the Prophet Joel.** This clause does not mean, "This is *like*

that"; it means Pentecost fulfilled what Joel had described. However, the prophecies of Joel quoted in Acts 2:19-20 were not fulfilled. The implication is that the remainder would be fulfilled if Israel would repent. This aspect of contingency is discussed more fully in the comments on 3:19-23.

2:22. Jesus' **miracles,** Peter said, were God's way of verifying Jesus' claims **to you,** the Jews (cf. 1 Cor. 1:22; 14:22).

2:23. The point of this verse is clear: the Crucifixion was no accident. It was in **God's set purpose** (*boulē*, "plan") and was God's determined will, not merely His inclination. It was a divine necessity (cf. 4:28). When Peter referred to **you,** he meant Jews; and by **wicked men** he perhaps meant Gentiles because the word "wicked" means lawless (*anomōn*). Both Gentiles and Jews were implicated in Christ's **death.** Many times the apostles accused the Jews of crucifying Jesus (2:23, 36; 3:15; 4:10; 5:30; 7:52; 10:39; 13:28), though the apostles also held the Gentiles culpable (2:23; 4:27; cf. Luke 23:24-25).

2:24. The resurrection of the Lord is a basic doctrine in Acts (v. 32; 3:15, 26; 4:10; 5:30; 10:40; 13:30, 33-34, 37; 17:31; 26:23). Here is another indication that He is the Messiah for **it was impossible for death to keep its hold on Him** (John 20:9).

2:25-35. These verses include four proofs of the Lord's resurrection and Ascension: (a) The prophecy of Psalm 16:8-11 and the presence of David's **tomb** (Acts 2:25-31), (b) the witnesses of the Resurrection (v. 32), (c) the supernatural events of Pentecost (v. 33), and (d) the Ascension of David's greater Son (Ps. 110:1; Acts 2:34-35).

The word translated **grave** in verses 27 and 31 is *hadēs*, which means either the grave (as here) or the underworld of departed spirits.

Peter's point is that since **David,** the **patriarch** and prophet **was** dead and **buried,** he could not have been referring to himself in Psalm 16:8-11; hence he was writing about **the Christ** ("Messiah") and His **resurrection.** The **oath** (Acts 2:30) looks back to Psalm 132:11 (cf. 2 Sam. 7:15-16). **God . . . raised . . . Jesus to life,** and **exalted** Him (cf. Acts 3:13; Phil. 2:9) **to** the **Father's right hand** (cf. Acts 5:30-31; Eph. 1:20; Col. 3:1; Heb. 1:3; 8:1; 10:12; 12:2; 1 Peter 3:22). Thus Jesus had the authority to send **the promised Holy Spirit** (Acts 1:5, 8; John 14:16, 26; 15:26; 16:7), whose presence was evidenced by what they saw ("tongues of fire," Acts 2:3) and heard ("a violent wind," v. 2), and the apostles speaking in other languages (vv. 4, 6, 8, 11).

Just as David was not speaking of himself in Psalm 16:8-11, so in Psalm 110:1 he was not speaking of himself. David was not resurrected (Acts 2:29, 31) nor **did he ascend to heaven** (v. 34). **The Lord** is Yahweh God who spoke **to my** (David's) **Lord,** who is Christ, God's Son.

On five occasions in Acts some of the apostles said they were **witnesses of** the resurrected Christ (v. 32; 3:15; 5:32; 10:39-41; 13:30-31). They knew whereof they spoke!

2:36. Here is the conclusion of Peter's argument. The noun **Lord,** referring to **Christ,** probably is a reference to Yahweh. The same word *kyrios* is used of **God** in verses 21, 34, and 39 (cf. Phil. 2:9). This is a strong affirmation of Christ's deity.

2:37. Verses 37-40 contain the application of Peter's sermon. The verb **cut** (*katenygēsan*) means "to strike or prick violently, to stun." The convicting work of the Spirit (cf. John 16:8-11) in their hearts was great.

Their question had a ring of desperation about it (cf. Acts 16:30). If the Jews had crucified their Messiah and He was now exalted, what was left for them to do? **What** could and must they **do?**

2:38-39. Peter's answer was forthright. First they were to **repent.** This verb (*metanoēsate*) means "change your outlook," or "have a change of heart; reverse the direction of your life." This obviously results in a change of conduct, but the emphasis is on the mind or outlook. The Jews had rejected Jesus; now they were to trust in Him. Repentance was repeatedly part of the apostles' message in Acts (v. 38; 3:19; 5:31; 8:22; 11:18; 13:24; 17:30; 19:4; 20:21; 26:20).

A problem revolves around the command "be baptized" and its connection with the remainder of 2:38. There are several views: (1) One is that both repentance and baptism result in remission of sins. In this view, baptism is essential for salvation. The problem with this interpretation is that elsewhere in Scripture forgiveness of sins is based on

faith alone (John 3:16, 36; Rom. 4:1-17; 11:6; Gal. 3:8-9; Eph. 2:8-9; etc.). Furthermore Peter, the same speaker, later promised forgiveness of sins on the basis of faith alone (Acts 5:31; 10:43; 13:38; 26:18).

(2) A second interpretation translates 2:38, "Be baptized . . . on the basis of the remission of your sins." The preposition used here is *eis* which, with the accusative case, may mean "on account of, on the basis of." It is used in this way in Matthew 3:11; 12:41; and Mark 1:4. Though it is possible for this construction to mean "on the basis of," this is not its normal meaning; *eis* with the accusative case usually describes purpose or direction.

(3) A third view takes the clause **and be baptized, every one of you, in the name of Jesus Christ** as parenthetical. Several factors support this interpretation: (a) The verb makes a distinction between singular and plural verbs and nouns. The verb "repent" is plural and so is the pronoun "your" in the clause **so that your sins may be forgiven** (lit., "unto the remission of your sins," *eis aphesin tōn hamartiōn hymōn*). Therefore the verb "repent" must go with the purpose of forgiveness of sins. On the other hand the imperative "be baptized" is singular, setting it off from the rest of the sentence. (b) This concept fits with Peter's proclamation in Acts 10:43 in which the same expression "sins may be forgiven" (*aphesin hamartiōn*) occurs. There it is granted on the basis of faith alone. (c) In Luke 24:47 and Acts 5:31 the same writer, Luke, indicates that repentance results in remission of sins.

The gift of the Holy Spirit is God's **promise** (cf. 1:5, 8; 2:33) to those who turn to the Lord, including Jews and their descendants and those **who are far off,** that is, Gentiles (cf. Eph. 2:13, 17, 19). Acts 2:38-39 put together the human side of salvation ("repent") and the divine side (**call** means "to elect"; cf. Rom. 8:28-30).

2:40. Peter's **words** in this verse look back to verses 23 and 36. Israel was guilty of a horrendous sin; individual Jews could be spared from God's judgment on that **generation** if they would repent (cf. Matt. 21:41-44; 22:7; 23:34–24:2). They would be set apart to Christ and His church if only they would be disassociated from Israel.

*c. The description of the first church
(2:41-47)*

2:41. Three thousand who believed **were baptized,** thus displaying their identification with Christ. This group of people immediately joined the fellowship of believers.

2:42. The activity of this early church was twofold. The believers first continued steadfastly (*proskarterountes,* "persisting in or continuing in"; cf. 1:14; 2:46; 6:4; 8:13; 10:7; Rom. 12:12; 13:6; Col. 4:2) in **the apostles' teaching** or doctrine. The second was **fellowship,** which is defined as **the breaking of bread and . . . prayer.** The omission of "and" between "fellowship" and "to the breaking of bread and to prayer" indicates the last two activities are appositional to fellowship.

Perhaps the breaking of bread included both the Lord's Table and a common meal (cf. Acts 2:46; 20:7; 1 Cor. 10:16; 11:23-25; Jude 12).

2:43. Wonders (*terata,* "miracles evoking awe") **and miraculous signs** (*sēmeia,* "miracles pointing to a divine truth") authenticated the veracity of **the apostles** (cf. 2 Cor. 12:12; Heb. 2:3-4). The apostles performed many such "signs and wonders" (Acts 4:30; 5:12; 6:8; 8:6, 13; 14:3; 15:12). Christ too had performed many "wonders" and "signs"—and also "miracles" (*dynameis,* "works of power").

2:44-45. The **selling** of property and the common possession of the proceeds may imply that the early church expected the Lord to return soon and establish His kingdom. This may explain why the practice was not continued. Holding **everything in common** was not socialism or communism because it was voluntary (cf. 4:32, 34-35; 5:4). Also their goods were not evenly distributed but were given to meet needs as they arose.

2:46-47. The activities described in verses 42-47 would tend to separate the church from traditional Judaism even though **every day** (cf. v. 47) **they continued** (*proskarterountes;* cf. v. 42) **to meet together in the temple courts.**

One of the subthemes of Acts is joy, because a victorious church is a joyful one. This is seen in verses 46-47 and numerous other times (5:41; 8:8, 39; 11:23; 12:14; 13:48, 52; 14:17; 15:3, 31; 16:34; 21:17). In their fellowship they **broke bread in their homes and ate together** (cf. 2:42) with joy. (The word **praising** [*ainountes*] is used only nine times in the NT, seven of them by Luke: Luke 2:13, 20; 19:37; 24:53; Acts 2:47; 3:8-9; Rom. 15:11; Rev. 19:5).

With the first of seven summary progress reports (cf. Acts 6:7; 9:31; 12:24; 16:5; 19:20; 28:30-31) Luke brought this section of Acts to a close: each day others **were being saved.** The church grew rapidly right from the start!

B. The expansion of the church at Jerusalem (3:1-6:7)

1. OPPOSITION TO THE CHURCH (3:1-4:31)

a. The occasion (chap. 3)

3:1. Apparently there were several times for **prayer** at the Jerusalem **temple**—9 A.M., 12 noon, and 3 P.M. Perhaps the hour of 3 P.M. is stated here because it helps explain 4:3.

3:2. The description of **a man crippled from birth** emphasizes his hopeless condition. He was more than 40 years old (4:22). People **carried** him **every day to the temple gate** named **Beautiful** so that he could **beg.** This may have been the eastern gate of the temple area that led from the court of the Gentiles into the women's court.

3:3-11. God's supernatural healing of the crippled man through **Peter and John** (v. 7), together with his exuberant response (v. 8), attracted a crowd amazed **(filled with wonder and amazement)** at what had taken place. They ran and assembled at **Solomon's Colonnade,** a portico of columns running the length of the east side of the outer court (cf. 5:12). Two other cripples were healed in Acts (9:32-34; 14:8-10).

3:12. Peter assessed the situation and used it as an opportunity to preach. His message included: (a) an explanation (vv. 12-16) and (b) an exhortation (vv. 17-26).

3:13-15. Peter attributed the power for healing to **Jesus,** here described as God's **Servant** (cf. v. 26; 4:27, 30). This term recalls the title "Servant of Yahweh" in Isaiah 42:1; 49:6-7; 52:13; 53:11. Interestingly forms of the verb **handed . . . over** (*paradidōmi*) are used twice in Isaiah 53:12 in the Septuagint. This lowly Servant (cf. Phil. 2:6-8) was exalted (glorified; cf. John 12:23; 17:1; Acts 2:33; Phil. 2:9; Heb. 1:3-4, 8) by the God of the Jews' ancestors, Abraham, Isaac, and Jacob (cf. Gen. 32:9; Ex. 3:6, 16; Matt. 22:32; Mark 12:26; Luke 20:37; Acts 7:32). Peter emphasized with sledgehammer effect three contradictions in the people's conduct (3:13-15). First, he said the Jews demanded Christ's death when Pilate . . . had decided to let Him go. Second, the Jews disowned the Holy and Righteous One and demanded the release of a murderer. Third, Israel killed the Author of life but God raised Him from the dead. Peter's titles of Christ are interesting: "His Servant Jesus," "the Holy and Righteous One" (cf. Heb. 7:26), and "the Author of life" (cf. John 10:10). In the third title the irony is strong: they *killed* the Author of *life* but He was raised to *life* from the dead! (On Jesus' resurrection, see comments on Acts 2:24. On witnesses of the Resurrection, see 2:32.)

3:16. The crippled man's healing came because of his faith in the name of Jesus. Faith was also evident in many of those whom Jesus healed (e.g., Mark 5:34; 10:52; Luke 17:19). In Bible times a person's name represented him and his characteristics. In Acts, Luke spoke of "the name" (of Jesus) at least 33 times (cf. Acts 2:21, 38; 3:6, 16; 4:7, 10, 12, 17-18; 5:28, 40-41; etc.).

3:17-18. Peter's exhortation begins here. The people with their leaders (cf. Luke 23:13) had acted in ignorance (cf. Acts 17:30; Eph. 4:18; 1 Peter 1:14) in the sense that they did not recognize who Jesus really is. So God gave them further opportunity to repent. Though they crucified Him in ignorance, the suffering of Christ fulfilled Old Testament prophecies (cf. Acts 17:3; 26:23).

3:19-21. Peter's exhortation, as in his Pentecost sermon (2:38), was to repent. Was Peter saying here that if Israel repented, God's kingdom would have come to earth? This must be answered in the affirmative for several reasons: (1) The word restore (3:21) is related to the word "restore" in 1:6. In 3:21 it is in its noun form (*apokatastaseōs*), and in 1:6 it is a verb (*apokathistaneis*). Both occurrences anticipate the restoration of the kingdom to Israel (cf. Matt. 17:11; Mark 9:12). (2) The concept of restoration parallels regeneration when it is used of the

kingdom (cf. Isa. 65:17; 66:22; Matt. 19:28; Rom. 8:20-22). (3) The purpose clauses are different in Acts 3:19 and 20. In verse 19 a so that translates *pros to* (some mss. have *eis to*) with the infinitive. This points to a near purpose. The two occurrences of that in verses 19b and 20 are translations of a different construction (*hopōs* with subjunctive verbs), and refer to more remote purposes. Thus repentance would result in forgiveness of sins, the near purpose (v. 19a). Then if Israel as a whole would repent, a second more remote goal, the coming of the kingdom (times of refreshing at the second coming of Christ) would be fulfilled. (4) The sending of the Christ, that is, Messiah (v. 20) meant the coming of the kingdom. (5) The Old Testament "foretold these days" (v. 24; cf. v. 21). The Old Testament prophets did not predict the church; to them it was a mystery (Rom. 16:25; Eph. 3:1-6). But the prophets often spoke of the messianic golden age, that is, the Millennium.

This offer of salvation and of the Millennium pointed both to God's graciousness and to Israel's unbelief. On the one hand God was giving the Jews an opportunity to repent after the sign of Christ's resurrection. They had refused the "pre-Cross" Jesus; now they were being offered a post-Resurrection Messiah. On the other hand Peter's words underscore Israel's rejection. They had been given the sign of Jonah but still they refused to believe (cf. Luke 16:31). In a real sense this message confirmed Israel's unbelief.

Some Bible scholars oppose the view that the kingdom was offered by Peter. They do so on the basis of several objections: (1) Since God knew Israel would reject the offer, it was not a legitimate offer. But it was as genuine as the presentation of the gospel to any nonelect person. (2) This puts kingdom truth in the Church Age. However, church truth is found before the church began at Pentecost (cf. Matt. 16:18; 18:17; John 10:16; 14:20). (3) This view leads to ultradispensationalism. But this is not a necessary consequence if this offer is seen as *a transition within the Church Age.* Acts must be seen as a hinge book, a transition work bridging the work of Christ on earth with His work through the church on earth.

In conclusion, Acts 3:17-21 shows that Israel's repentance was to have had two purposes: (1) for *individual* Israelites there was forgiveness of sins, and (2) for *Israel as a nation* her Messiah would return to reign.

3:22-23. Here Jesus is portrayed as the "New Testament Moses" in fulfillment of Deuteronomy 18:15-19 (cf. John 6:14). Christ will come not only with deliverance as Moses did, but He will also judge as Moses did (cf. Lev. 23:29 with Deut. 18:19; also cf. Num. 14:26-35).

3:24-25. Peter's mention of **Samuel** as the next prophet after Moses (cf. 13:20) clearly implies that Joshua did not fulfill Deuteronomy 18:15.

All the prophets (cf. Acts 3:18, 21) in one way or another wrote about **these days,** that is, the Messianic Age. The Jews were **heirs of the prophets** of **the** Abrahamic **Covenant** given to **Abraham** (Gen. 12:2-3; 15:18-21; 17:1-8; 22:18) and confirmed to the Jews' **fathers** (e.g., Isaac [Gen. 26:41]). The Jews then could be blessed if they, like Abraham, believed (cf. Rom. 3:28-29; 4:3; Gal. 3:6-7). In fact **all peoples** would **be blessed** through Abraham (cf. Gen. 12:3; Rom. 4:12, 16; Gal. 3:29; Eph. 3:6).

3:26. Jesus, God's **Servant** (cf. v. 13; 4:27, 30), was **sent . . . first to you,** that is, to the Jews. This chronological pattern was followed throughout the Gospels and Acts (cf., e.g., Matt. 10:5; Acts 13:46; Rom. 1:16). The reason for this is that the establishing of the kingdom depended and still depends on Israel's response (cf. Matt. 23:39; Rom. 11:26).

b. The incarceration (4:1-22)

4:1-2. Involved in this apprehension of Peter, John, and the healed man (v. 14), were **the priests and the captain of the temple guard and the Sadducees.** Since the captain of the temple guard was responsible for maintaining order in the temple, it is no surprise that he, along with the priests and Sadducees, interrupted **Peter and John** in order to disband the mob (cf. 3:11).

The priests were primarily Sadducees in their religious affiliation (5:17); so the principal accusers were Sadducees. These people were distinguished by several characteristics: (a) a disbelief in a bodily resurrection and a denial of the existence of angels or spirits (23:8); (b) loyalty to the Roman government; (c) a desire to maintain the status quo; (d) an association with the wealthy class; and (e) adherence only to the Pentateuch. The Sadducees **were greatly disturbed** by Peter and John's preaching **because** it directly opposed the Sadducees' denial of **the resurrection** and would also shake the establishment.

4:3. The two apostles were incarcerated overnight **because it was** already **evening,** that is, late afternoon (cf. 3 P.M. in 3:1), too late for a trial.

4:4. One of the subthemes of Acts is the growth of God's Word in spite of opposition. Like a juggernaut the message irresistibly moved ahead. Two leading apostles were bound, but the Word of God cannot be bound! (Cf. 28:30-31; Phil. 1:12-14.)

Annas' Family

ANNAS
High priest, A.D. 6-15.
Appointed by
Quirinius, governor of
Syria; deposed by
Valerius Gratus,
procurator of Judea

SON: ELEAZAR High priest, A.D. 16-17	SON: JONATHAN (possibly "John" in Acts 4:6) High priest, A.D. 36-37	SON: THEOPHILUS High priest, A.D. 37-41		SON: MATTHIAS High priest, A.D. 42	SON: ANNAS High priest, A.D. 61	SON-IN-LAW: CAIAPHAS High priest, A.D. 18-36. Also called Joseph, his personal name. Appointed by Valerius Gratus. Deposed by Procurator Vitellius. A Sadducee
		GRANDSON: MATTHIAS High priest, A.D. 65-66				

4:5-6. Luke's careful description of the Jewish leaders underscores the pomp and power of this assembly. Simple fishermen were in the midst of the highest leaders in the land! **The rulers, elders, and teachers of the Law** included the Sanhedrin, the Jewish supreme court (cf. v. 15). **Annas** was Caiaphas' father-in-law. Annas had been **high priest** from A.D. 6 to 15, and was deposed. His son-in-law **Caiaphas** was priest from A.D. 18 to 36. But apparently Annas, being something of a priestly statesman, was still thought of by the Jews as their high priest. (See the chart on Annas' family. Cf. comments on Luke 3:2; John 18:13; Acts 7:1.) The assembly had examined Jesus on trial; now, ironically, they were facing two of Jesus' prominent—and bold—followers! Nothing is known of the **John** and **Alexander** mentioned here.

4:7-10. When **Peter and John** were **brought before** the Sanhedrin, and were asked the basis of their authority, **Peter,** the spokesman, was **filled with the Holy Spirit** (cf. 2:4). This is Peter's fourth speech already in the Book of Acts! Speaking with irony, he said, in effect, "Are we on trial for doing a good deed to a cripple?" The miracle was done not in their power, but **by the name of Jesus Christ** (cf. 3:16; 4:7, 12, 17-18). Though they had **crucified** Jesus, **God** had **raised** Him **from the dead** (cf. 2:23-24; 3:15).

4:11. The One who healed the cripple was **the Stone** which the **builders rejected.** Here Peter quoted Psalm 118:22. The background of this verse is disputed. The rejected stone (Ps. 118) may be (a) an actual building stone, (b) the nation of Israel, or (c) David. Or it may also be a proverb with no specific application. Most probably, to David the rejected stone in Psalm 118:22 meant Israel, a nation spurned by other nations. At any rate, the verse finds its ultimate fulfillment in Christ Jesus who is the "ideal" Israel (cf. Isa. 5:1-7; Matt. 2:15; 21:42; Mark 12:10; Luke 20:17; 1 Peter 2:7). The rejected Stone (Christ rejected by the nation in their crucifying Him) is **the Capstone,** the resurrected Lord.

4:12. The word **salvation** goes back to Psalm 118 which Peter had just quoted, for it is a prominent theme there. Verses 22-29 in that psalm anticipate millennial

deliverance. In Acts 4:12 Peter was speaking not only of individual justification, but also of national salvation, predicted in Psalm 118.

The rulers were thus put on the defense! They had rejected the only Savior of Israel and they were preventing the completion of God's building. Thus no other way of salvation is available to people (cf. John 14:6; 1 Tim. 2:5).

4:13-14. The authorities **were astonished** (cf. 3:10) that **Peter and John . . . unschooled** (*agrammatoi,* "illiterate") and **ordinary** (*idiōtai*) **men,** spoke with such **courage.** Courage (*parrēsia,* "boldness" or "courage to speak openly and frankly") is another theme prominent in Acts (2:29; 4:13, 29, 31; 28:31; cf. the verb "to speak boldly" in 9:27-28; 13:46; 14:3; 18:26; 19:8; 26:26). The Sanhedrin, realizing that Peter and John **had been with** Jesus (cf. John 7:15), were silenced. The apostles were thus experiencing what Christ had promised (Matt. 10:19-20; Luke 12:11-12; 21:12-15).

4:15-17. Significantly the authorities could not and did not **deny** the reality of the **miracle.** They deliberately refused to mention the word "Jesus"; they referred to Him as **this name** (cf. the high priest's same refusal in 5:28).

Perhaps Luke obtained this information about what went on behind the closed doors from someone such as Nicodemus or Paul. Even though Paul was not a Sadducee, he probably would have had access to such information.

The Sanhedrin, the supreme court and administrative body of the Jews, consisted of 71 members, including the high priest. Most of them were Sadducees. In Acts this was the first of four times some of Jesus' followers were brought before the Sanhedrin (cf. Peter and the apostles, 5:27; Stephen, 6:12; and Paul, 22:30).

4:18-22. When **Peter and John** were **commanded . . . not to speak or teach at all in the name of Jesus,** they rejoined that they must **obey** God **rather than** human authorities (cf. 5:29). They were simply being witnesses as Christ had commanded them (1:8). The authorities threatened them (apparently with punishment if they continued to preach Jesus) and released them. They were afraid **to**

punish them then **because all the people were praising God** (cf. 3:9; 5:26).

c. The supplication (4:23-31)

Three movements may be discerned in this prayer of the early church: (1) God is sovereign (v. 24). (2) God's plan includes believers' facing opposition against the Messiah (vv. 25-28). (3) Because of these things they petitioned God to grant them boldness to preach (vv. 29-30).

4:23-24. Interestingly the believers (Peter and John's **own people**), faced with persecution, acknowledged God's **sovereign** creative power.

4:25-27. The words **by the Holy Spirit through the mouth of . . . David** point up, as do many passages, the divine inspiration of Scripture through human agents (cf. 28:25). Acts 4:25-26 contains a quotation from Psalm 2:1-2, which is prophetic of the Tribulation. In a *preliminary* sense Peter saw the opposition to the Messiah, God's **Anointed One** (*tou Christou*; cf. "anointed," Acts 4:27)—predicted by David in Psalm 2—as fulfilled in the early church. The parallels are obvious.

Nations (*ethnē*, Acts 4:25) compare with **Gentiles** (*ethnesin*, v. 27); **peoples** (*laoi*, v. 25) compare with **people of Israel** (*laois Israēl*, v. 27); **kings** (v. 26) compare with **Herod** (v. 27); and **rulers** (v. 26) compare with **Pontius Pilate** (v. 27).

4:28-30. Just as God's sovereign **power and will had decided beforehand** that Christ should be opposed, so now Peter and John prayed for God's power to be manifested in **great boldness** for the apostolic church. They also petitioned the Lord for supernatural ability **to heal** and to **perform miraculous signs** (*sēmeia*; cf. 2:43) **and wonders** (*terata*; cf. 2:43) **through the name of . . . Jesus.**

4:31. The Lord's answer to the believers' prayer for boldness was preceded by a shaking of their **meeting** place. The answer also included a supernatural filling **with the Holy Spirit** (cf. v. 8). When Luke, as here, used a verb form to refer to believers being filled with the Spirit, he usually said the filling was bestowed sovereignly by God. This is in distinction to the imperative in Ephesians 5:18 which states that Christians are responsible for being Spirit-filled.

2. CORRECTION IN THE CHURCH (4:32–5:11)

a. The division of goods (4:32-37)

Luke had two reasons for including this passage here. For one thing he used it to introduce Barnabas to his readers. A common technique of Luke was to introduce a character quickly in a minor role and then later bring him on stage in a major role. This he did with Barnabas.

Luke's second purpose in these verses was to show how Barnabas and the rest of the church contrasted with Ananias and Sapphira (chap. 5). The generosity of the church and especially Barnabas differed markedly from the selfishness of that husband-wife team.

4:32-35. **The believers were** unified not only spiritually (**one in heart and mind**) but also materially (cf. 2:44-45 and comments there). Their selling of their goods was voluntary and the distribution was according to **need.** The Lord answered their prayer for boldness (4:29) for **the apostles** kept on testifying of Christ's **resurrection. Grace** (v. 33) is one of numerous times that word occurs in Acts (e.g., 6:8; 11:23; 13:43; 14:3, 26; 15:11, 40; 18:27; 20:24, 32; etc.).

4:36-37. Joseph was nicknamed **Barnabas which means Son of Encouragement,** evidently because of his character and ability to encourge those who were downhearted.

How could **a Levite** own property as Barnabas did? Were not Levites prohibited from owning property? (Num. 18:20, 24) The answer may be that whereas the Levites were not to hold land in Israel, they could own land elsewhere. Apparently Barnabas, being **from** the island of **Cyprus,** owned land there. It is also possible that his wife owned land in Israel and that they together sold it. Most probably the restriction in Numbers 18:20, 24 was no longer observed, as seen in the case of Jeremiah (cf. Jer. 1:1; 32:6-15).

b. The deceit of Ananias and Sapphira (5:1-11)

This story is reminiscent of Achan in Joshua 7 (cf. Num. 15:32-36; 16:1-35).

5:1-2. The sin of **Ananias** and **his wife Sapphira** is explained in verses 3-4, 9. They could have retained the proceeds from their sale **of property,** of course, but in collusion with each other they had lied, saying they had given all the money when actually they had given only a **part of the money.**

The phrase **the apostles' feet** is the same as in 4:35, 37 and throws Ananias' action into bold contrast with Barnabas' action.

5:3. In response **Peter** accused **Ananias** by saying, **Satan has . . . filled your heart.** The verb translated "filled" is *eplērōsen*, from *plēroō*, which here has the idea of control or influence. The same verb is used in the command, "Be filled with the Spirit" (Eph. 5:18). Ananias, a believer, was influenced by Satan, not the Spirit! The fact that Peter asked, **How is it. . . ?** implies that Satan had gained control because Ananias had not dealt with some previous sin in his life.

5:4. Peter referred to Ananias' lying "to the Holy Spirit" (v. 3); now Peter referred to his lying **to God.** This is an affirmation of the Holy Spirit's deity.

The fact that believers had the right to keep their money shows that this was not Christian socialism. It was a free-will arrangement for the support of the church, used only temporarily because evidently the early church expected Christ to come in their generation.

5:5-6. When Ananias heard this, he fell down and died. As Peter wrote later, judgment begins "with the family of God" (1 Peter 4:17). This is a case of "sin that leads to death" (1 John 5:16). This discipline was severe because it was an example, as Achan was an example to Israel (cf. 1 Cor. 10:6).

5:7-10. Then **Sapphira,** not aware of her husband's sudden death, also lied about the amount they **got for the land.**

Peter accused Sapphira of agreeing with Ananias **to test the Spirit of the Lord.** "To test the Holy Spirit" is to see how much one can get away with before He judges; it means to presume on Him, to see if He will perform His Word, or to stretch Him to the limits of judgment (cf. Deut. 6:16; Matt. 4:7).

5:11. As a result of the discipline of this couple, **all** the believers and unbelievers **who heard about** it felt **great fear,** a consequence already stated in verse 5 and repeated here for emphasis (cf. 19:17).

The purpose of this account in the narrative is manifold: (1) It revealed God's displeasure with sin, particularly dishonesty, in His body, the church. (2) It marked the church off as distinct from Israel, for such discipline was not seen in Israel. The word **church** (used here for the first time in Acts) refers to the universal church here and in 9:31 and 20:28, and to local congregations in 11:26 and 13:1. (3) It indicated God was at work in this new group.

3. PROGRESSION IN THE CHURCH (5:12-42)

a. The authentication of the apostles (5:12-16)

This paragraph prepares readers for what follows. Such activity could hardly go unnoticed!

5:12. Once again **the apostles** were used by God to perform **many miraculous signs and wonders** (cf. comments on 2:43). Interestingly the regular meeting place of the early Jerusalem church was in the temple at **Solomon's Colonnade,** where people gathered after they had heard of the lame man's healing (3:11).

5:13. This verse probably means that no hypocrite or unbeliever **dared joined them.** The case of Ananias and Sapphira frightened them too much!

The words **no one else** are literally, "none of the rest" (*tōn loipōn oudeis*). The words "the rest" are used of the lost (trans. "others" in Luke 8:10; cf. Rom. 11:7; Eph. 2:3; 1 Thes. 4:13; 5:6).

5:14. In spite of the reluctance of the unsaved to join the group of believers, **more and more men and women believed in the Lord and were added to their number.** Rapid numerical growth was a phenomenon of the early church (cf. 2:41, 47; 4:4; 6:1, 7; 9:31).

5:15-16. Miraculous signs (cf. v. 12) confirmed the Word of God in the midst of the young church. This shows God's sovereign sanction of the church, following His discipline of it. Many people revealed not only their confidence in the apostles to heal, but also their superstition. They thought it was **Peter's shadow** itself which fell **on the sick** that would heal **them.**

The apostles' divinely given power to heal and to exorcise demons accords with the Lord's promise to them (Matt. 10:8; Mark 16:17-18).

b. The second detention and release of the apostles (5:17-20)

5:17-20. After this second apprehension and incarceration of **the apostles**—apparently all 12 of them—God supernaturally released them and commanded them by means of **an angel** to continue the public proclamation (**in the temple courts,** near the church's gathering place; cf. v. 12) of **the full message of this new life** (lit., "all the words of this life," an unusual way to refer to the gospel). In Acts this is the first of three miraculous jail miracles (cf. Peter, 12:6-10; Paul and Silas, 16:26-27).

c. The examination and defense of the apostles (5:21-32)

5:21a. The obedience of the apostles to the angel's directive (v. 20) is evident. Though their sleep was abbreviated the preceding night, **at daybreak they entered the temple courts** (cf. v. 20).

5:21b-25. The facts recorded in these verses are filled with irony: (1) **The guards** were carefully keeping empty **jail** cells secured (vv. 21b-23). (2) The highest powers **of Israel** were gathered to judge prisoners they did not have. (3) While the frenzied leaders were deliberating as to what had happened to **the men** who had been in their custody, they were told the apostles were preaching in the **courts** of the **temple. The captain of the temple guard and the chief priests** (cf. 4:1) **were puzzled** (*diēporoun,* lit., "were perplexed," or "were at a loss") as to how to explain the **locked** but empty cells. Perhaps they also wondered **what would come of** them for losing their prisoners! (Cf. 16:27-28.)

5:26-27. The captain and the jail **officers** carefully recaptured **the apostles** (without using **force,** for fear of arousing the anger of the populace) and **brought the apostles . . . before the Sanhedrin** for questioning. (On the Sanhedrin, see comments on 4:15; cf. 6:12; 22:30.)

5:28. Use of the pronoun **this** twice underscores the high priest's reluctance to pronounce the name of Jesus (cf. "this name," 4:17). Obviously his hatred of Christ Jesus was great!

5:29. Here **Peter** reiterated a basic principle already affirmed in 4:19-20. The converse is also true: Christians are to **obey** their governments unless it is a sin to do so (cf. Rom. 13:1-7; 1 Peter 2:13-17).

5:30-31. This response by Peter and the apostles about Jesus' resurrection must have infuriated the Sadducees (cf. 4:1-2; 5:17; 23:8). Yet it was the same message Peter, once again the apostles' spokesman, had preached before: (a) they had **killed** Jesus, but **God . . . raised** Him **from the dead** (cf. 2:23-24, 36; 3:15; 4:10); (b) they could have **forgiveness of sins** (cf. 2:38; 10:43; 13:38; 26:18) by turning to Him in **repentance** (cf. 2:38; 3:16; 4:12; 8:22).

5:32. The apostles were well aware of their responsibility for they asserted, **We are witnesses of these things** (*rhēmatōn,* "words, sayings," or "things"). Furthermore, **the Holy Spirit** was corroborating their testimony by supernaturally enabling them to preach with boldness and to perform miracles. This same Spirit is **given to** all who believe in Christ (Rom. 8:9).

d. The liberation of the apostles (5:33-42)

5:33. The fury of the leaders toward the apostles could have been expected. The leaders **wanted to put them to death.** Their opposition followed the same pattern as their hostility to the Lord a few weeks earlier. Characteristically opposition grows, and so it did here.

5:34-35. The venerated **Gamaliel,** a **Pharisee** and **teacher,** influenced **the Sanhedrin** not to oppose the apostles. He spoke not from sympathy for the church, but from insight into God's sovereign working on earth (cf. v. 39).

5:36. Nothing is known of this **Theudas** with his **400** insurrectionists, whose cause came to naught. Though Josephus, a Jewish historian of the first century, described a rebellion led by a Theudas, that insurrection was later and much larger. Furthermore, that rebellion *followed* the one led by the Judas described in verse 37.

5:37. The insurrection led by **Judas the Galilean** was Gamaliel's second illustration. Josephus gave a rather full account of this movement which led to the execution of Judas, but also spawned further rebellion.

5:38-39. Here is the conclusion and main thrust of Gamaliel's speech. Seeing what would come of this movement would tell them if it were **of human origin** or **from God.** Interestingly this speech was, in one sense, an apologetic for the church of Jesus Christ given by a representative of the church's enemies: to try to stop God's work would be like **fighting against God!**

5:40. Not considering it adequate simply to admonish **the apostles,** the council **had them flogged and ordered them not to speak in the name of Jesus** (on Jesus' "name" see comments on 3:16). The flogging was evidently punishment for the apostles' disobedience to their earlier prohibition (cf. 4:18, 21; 5:28).

5:41-42. In spite of the bloody beating, **the apostles left the Sanhedrin, rejoicing.** Here again the theme of joy is evident in the Book of Acts (cf. comments on 2:46-47). A victorious church rejoices in God's working in spite of persecution—and even on account of it, as here. The apostles were honored to be **suffering disgrace for the name** (on "the name" see 3:16; cf. 1 Peter 4:14, 16). Later, Peter encouraged Christians to "rejoice" when they would "participate" in sufferings on behalf of Christ (1 Peter 4:13; cf. 1 Peter 2:18-21; 3:8-17).

Luke's object in writing Acts 5:17-42 was to show how Israel as a nation was continuing down its tragic path of rejecting Jesus as its Messiah.

4. ADMINISTRATION IN THE CHURCH (6:1-7)

6:1. The Grecian Jews could not speak Aramaic, the native tongue of Jews living in Israel. They probably were reared outside the land and were bilingual, speaking both Greek and their native tongues (cf. 2:5-11). Probably Gentile proselytes to Judaism who later became Christians were also in this group. The native Jews were also bilingual in that they spoke Aramaic and Greek (cf. 21:40). In the Jewish world tensions existed between the Grecian Jews and **the Aramaic-speaking** Jews; tragically these strains were brought into the church.

6:2. The **tables** (*trapezais*) may refer to tables used for serving food or to money tables, that is, banks. Probably it was used here to refer to the place where funds and supplies were administered for the widows.

The Twelve recognized their proper priorities in **the ministry of the Word of God** and prayer (cf. v. 4).

6:3-4. The apostles mentioned three qualifications for those who would be enlisted to serve: they must (a) **be full of the Spirit and** (b) be full of **wisdom** (cf. v. 10). In addition they were to (c) be **known** for these things, that is, the previous two qualifications were to be their reputations. All three were necessary for the handling of finances. (Faith, v. 5, is not another qualification, for belief is simply the means of being filled with the Holy Spirit.)

Selecting **seven men** may go back to the tradition in Jewish communities where seven respected men managed the public business in an official council.

By choosing these seven, the Twelve could **give** their **attention to prayer and the ministry of the Word** (cf. v. 2).

6:5. The suggestion of the Twelve **pleased the whole group** of the disciples. Significantly all seven men had Greek names, implying they were Hellenists. **Nicolas,** the last one named, was not even a Jew but was **a convert to Judaism** and then to Christianity. The early church evidently felt the problem of the unintentional neglect of Grecian Jewish widows would be best solved by the Hellenistic Jews; certainly they would not neglect the Aramaic-speaking widows.

The introduction of these seven (cf. 21:8) prepares readers for the ministries of **Stephen** and **Philip,** the first two men listed. Furthermore, the reference to Grecian Jews looks ahead to the wider spread of the gospel outside the circle of Jerusalem and Judea. (Nothing else is known about the other four: **Procorus, Nicanor, Timon, Parmenas.**)

6:6. Though the Christian community selected the Seven, they were commissioned by **the apostles.** This was done by prayer and the laying on of **hands.** The practice of laying hands on others was a gesture signifying commissioning and granting of authority (cf. 8:17-19; 13:3; 19:6; 1 Tim. 4:14; 5:22; Heb. 6:2).

Were these the first deacons? Which church office is in view here? Three answers are given to these questions.

(1) Some say these were the first deacons. Several factors are used to support this viewpoint. First, the office of deacon is assumed in Paul's letters (cf. Phil. 1:1). If Acts 6:1-6 is not an account

of their beginning, it is argued, when and where did deacons originate? Second, several words related to deacon (*diakonos*) are found here: "distribution" (lit., "service") in verse 1 is *diakonia*, and "to wait" in verse 2 is *diakonein*. However, these men were never called "deacons" (*diakonoi*) as such. Much later they were called "the Seven" (21:8). Furthermore, the words "distribution" and "wait" do not seem to have a technical sense here. These words in the Greek New Testament are commonly used in a nonspecialized sense.

(2) Others hold that these were precursors to the office of elder. This is not a common interpretation, but it gains its support from 11:30, which refers to relief money being given to the elders. If deacons handled these funds earlier (chap. 6), it is argued, they must have later become the elders (chap. 11). However, the office of elder has its origin in the Jewish synagogue.

(3) A third view is that these seven men held a temporary position for the purpose of meeting a specific need. This seems to be the best approach for a couple of reasons. First, these men were chosen for a particular task, not an overall one. Second, they were in a temporary responsibility because of the communal nature of the church at Jerusalem. Even so, these men do illustrate the role and function of the office of deacons.

6:7. This verse contains another of Luke's progress reports. The church was rapidly growing in numbers (cf. 2:41, 47; 4:4; 5:14; 6:1; 9:31), with even many Jewish **priests** becoming believers (**obedient to the faith;** cf. Rom. 1:5). With the appointment of these men, readers are prepared for the work of Stephen and Philip and the proclamation of the gospel outside Jerusalem.

II. The Witness in All Judea and Samaria (6:8–9:31)

A. The martyrdom of Stephen (6:8–8:1a)

1. THE ARREST OF STEPHEN (6:8–7:1)

Stephen's ministry, arrest, and trial are strikingly similar to the Lord's.

6:8. Like Christ and the apostles, **Stephen** was **full of God's grace and power** (cf. 4:33; Luke 2:40, 52). Interestingly Stephen was "full of" or controlled by five factors: the Spirit, wisdom, faith, grace, power (Acts 6:3, 5, 8). What an outstanding leader! Furthermore, he **did great wonders and miraculous signs** (cf. 2:22; Luke 24:19; also cf. Acts 2:43). These evidences of God's grace were in addition to his responsibilities in the daily ministration to the widows.

6:9-11. The Synagogue of the Freedmen was perhaps comprised of those who themselves or whose forebears had been set free from being prisoners of war or from slavery. Precisely who they were is not known for sure.

The members of this synagogue were from three divergent areas—North Africa (**Cyrene and Alexandria** were two of its leading cities), **Asia** (the western portion of modern-day Turkey), and **Cilicia.** Possibly this was the assembly Paul attended because Tarsus was located in the province of Cilicia.

Besides being one of the Seven and a wonder-worker, Stephen was also a skilled debater. His opponents **could not stand up against his wisdom or the Spirit by which he spoke** (cf. "full of the Spirit and wisdom" in v. 3 and "full of . . . the Holy Spirit" in v. 5 and 7:55).

To remove Stephen, the men of the synagogue covertly induced men to make an accusation against him. Like those who complained against the Lord Jesus, they charged **Stephen** with **blasphemy** (cf. Matt. 26:65).

6:12-14. These words were sufficient to arouse the laity and leaders to apprehend **Stephen** and accuse **him before the Sanhedrin.** This is the third of four times in Acts when the Lord's followers stood before this Jewish court; the others were Peter and John (4:15), Peter and the apostles (5:27), and Paul (22:30).

The **false witnesses** were not necessarily outright liars. Stephen had probably said the things they accused him of; however, they misrepresented the intentions and imports of his statements (cf. Matt. 26:61; Mark 14:58; John 2:19). The Lord Himself predicted the destruction of the temple (Matt. 24:1-2; Mark 13:1-2; Luke 21:5-6), though He never said *He* would do it. The other half of the allegation against Stephen involved the temporary nature of the Mosaic system. Undoubtedly he saw the theological implications of justification by faith and the fulfillment of the Law in Christ. Furthermore, if the gospel was for the whole world (Acts 1:8), the Law had to be a temporary arrangement.

6:15. All . . . the Sanhedrin—all 71 of them—**looked intently at Stephen** to see his response. **They saw that his face was like** that **of an angel.** Evidently his face glowed with glory (cf. Moses' face, Ex. 34:29, 35).

7:1. The high priest mentioned here possibly is Caiaphas, the same one who presided over the trials of the Lord (Matt. 26:57; Mark 14:54; Luke 22:53; John 18:13, 24; cf. comments on Acts 4:5-6).

2. THE ADDRESS OF STEPHEN (7:2-53)

7:2-53. This is the longest recorded message in Acts, which shows the importance Luke attached to it. Stephen, a Grecian Jew, by his life and words prepared the way for the gospel to reach outside the pale of Judaism.

But what did Stephen say in this powerful discourse that resulted in his death? Though he touched on the accusations made against him, Stephen did not give a legal defense of himself. Rather, he set forth Israel's past history and God's past workings in order to vindicate Christianity.

In this discourse three ideas run like cords through its fabric:

1. *There is progress and change in God's program.* God was creative and innovative in His dealings with humans and particularly with Israel. Stephen developed this thought in five points: (a) The promise to **Abraham** (vv. 2-8). From working with the entire human race, the Lord sovereignly called Abraham, father of the Jews, from **Mesopotamia** to the land of promise, and gave him 12 great-grandsons who became the progenitors of Israel's 12 tribes. (b) The sojourn of **Joseph** (vv. 9-16). This move to **Egypt** was the fulfillment of God's prediction recorded in verses 6-7. It too was a radical change for Jacob's descendants. (c) The deliverance under **Moses** (vv. 17-43). A major portion of Stephen's discourse pertained to **Moses** and the Exodus, another important aspect of Israel's history. (d) The building of **the tabernacle** (vv. 44-46). Constructing the tabernacle so that it was portable implied it was

temporary. (It was called **the tabernacle of Testimony** because it testified to God's presence among them.) (e) The construction of the temple (vv. 47-50). Even the temple was to be a symbol of God's presence and not the very home of God.

In God's workings with the nation from Abraham to Solomon there was innovation and change. The point is clear: If God changed so many things in Israel's history, who is to say that the Law and the temple were permanent?

2. *The blessings of God are not limited to the land of Israel and the temple area.* Some of Israel's greatest favors were bestowed apart from the temple and the land.

Stephen gave four examples: (a) Israel's patriarchs and leaders were blessed *outside* the land. **Abraham** was called in Mesopotamia and given promises **before he lived in Haran** (vv. 2-5). In **Egypt . . . Joseph** found favor with **Pharaoh** because **God was with him** (vv. 9-10). **Moses** was commissioned by God in **Midian** (vv. 29-34). To substantiate the fact that God blessed Moses while he was in Midian, Stephen carefully recounted that **two sons** were born to Moses there. (b) The Law itself was given outside the land: Moses **was in the congregation in the desert** (v. 38). (c) The tabernacle was built in the desert. The tabernacle was **with them in the desert** (v. 44). In fact the Jews **brought it with them when they took the land** (v. 45). (d) Even the temple, though in the land, was not to be limited in its theology. How could the temple be God's dwelling place when the Scripture declares, **Heaven is My throne, and the earth is My footstool?** (v. 49; Isa. 66:1)

3. *Israel in its past always evidenced a pattern of opposition to God's plans and His men.* This is the main point of Stephen's discourse, as its climax affirms (Acts 7:51-53). **You are just like your fathers: You always resist the Holy Spirit!** This theme is seen throughout the message, but there are some definite specifics. (a) Instead of going directly from Mesopotamia to the Promised Land, **Abraham** tarried in Haran (vv. 2-4). (b) **Joseph** was **sold** by his brothers into slavery in **Egypt** (v. 9). (c) **Moses** was rejected by the Israelites (vv. 23-29). It is highly significant that both Joseph and Moses were not accepted until their *second* appearances

(vv. 13, 35-36). The parallel with Christ could not have escaped Stephen's hearers. (d) Israel rejected true worship by turning to idols (vv. 39-43). Her blatant unbelief was seen in idolatry, a sin which the Jews of the Apostolic Age particularly abhorred. As a result God judged the nation by sending her into Exile in Babylon (v. 43). (e) The people of Israel missed the point of the temple (vv. 48-50). The strong and clear assertion of Stephen (v. 48) implies that the Jews believed the temple was God's dwelling place on earth, the Jewish counterpart to Mount Olympia. Indeed the temple was to be a place of worship and prayer; but it was not God's home (cf. 1 Kings 8:23-53).

Stephen's three main points in this discourse fit together. Since there is progression in God's program and since His blessings are not limited to the temple, Israel had better be careful not to "resist" (Acts 7:51) His workings as they had in the past. They would withstand God's purpose by refusing to see His work in the church and His blessing outside the borders of Israel. This defense related specifically to the accusation made against Stephen in 6:11-14.

A chronological problem exists in 7:6, where Stephen said Israel would be **enslaved and mistreated 400 years.** For in Galatians 3:17 Paul implied that the period of time from the Abrahamic promise in Genesis 15:13-16 to Mount Sinai was 430 years. The difference between the 400 and 430 years can easily be accounted for by understanding that Stephen used round numbers. Another explanation is that the 400 years was the actual time of bondage whereas the 430 years described the time from the confirming of the covenant in Genesis 35:9-15 to the Exodus, which occurred in 1446 B.C. The main problem, however, is the time Israel spent in bondage in Egypt. If Galatians 3:17 means it was 430 years from the promise given to Abraham (Gen. 15) to the Exodus, the time in Egypt would then be 215 years. However, if Acts 7:6 is taken at face value the bondage was 400 years. Perhaps the best solution is to say Paul was looking at *periods* of time. The promises were given to Abraham, Isaac, and Jacob. These three patriarchs were all recipients of God's promise. The promise was reconfirmed in

Genesis 46:1-4 to Jacob at Beersheba as he was on his way to Egypt. From that point (the end of God's giving promises to the patriarchs) to the Exodus was 400 years. (Cf. Harold W. Hoehner, "The Duration of the Egyptian Bondage," *Bibliotheca Sacra* 126. October–December 1969:306-16.)

Another apparent discrepancy in Stephen's discourse is in Acts 7:14. Stephen stated that **75** persons were in Jacob's **family,** but the Hebrew text has "70" in both Genesis 46:27 and Exodus 1:5. In both places the Septuagint has 75. It is commonly said that Stephen, a Greek-speaking Jew, would have used the Septuagint and therefore was making only an "honest" mistake. This difficulty, however, can be resolved in other ways. One of the most widely accepted solutions is to recognize that the Hebrew text includes Jacob, Joseph, and Joseph's two sons, Ephraim and Manasseh (a total of 70), but that the Septuagint omits Jacob and Joseph but includes Joseph's seven grandchildren (mentioned in 1 Chron. 7:14-15, 20-25). This is supported by the Hebrew in Genesis 46:8-26 which enumerates 66 names, omitting Jacob, Joseph, and Joseph's two sons. Another solution is that the Septuagint's 75 includes the 66 plus the 9 wives of Jacob's 12 sons (Judah's and Simeon's wives had died and Joseph's wife was in Egypt).

Acts 7:16 contains another apparent discrepancy. Stephen's words imply that **Jacob** was buried **at Shechem** whereas the Old Testament clearly affirms that he and his wife Leah (and his parents Isaac and Rebekah and his grandparents Abraham and Sarah) were interred in the Cave of Machpelah at Hebron (Gen. 49:29–50:13). However, the bodies buried at Shechem did not include Jacob but did include those of Joseph and his brothers. Joseph was buried first in Egypt but was reburied in Shechem (Gen. 50:26; Ex. 13:19; Josh. 24:32). True, Joshua 24:32 refers only to Joseph's bones, but evidently his brothers were also buried at Shechem (though Josephus states otherwise). The pronoun **their** (Acts 7:16), then, does not include Abraham, Isaac, and Jacob, but looks back to the words **our fathers** in verse 15 and refers to Joseph and his brothers.

Stephen's phrase, **the tomb that Abraham had bought from the sons of**

Hamor at Shechem (v. 16), presents another problem. Actually Jacob, not Abraham, bought the plot of ground (Gen. 33:19). This may be explained by saying that Abraham in a sense did purchase the property in the person of his grandson. Abraham would be given title to Shechem through Jacob.

This favorable allusion to Shechem, the "capital" of the Samaritans, would not please Stephen's audience. But his reference to Samaria prepares readers for the next step in the outreach of the gospel (Acts 8).

3. THE ATTACK ON STEPHEN (7:54–8:1A)

7:54-56. The response of the religious authorities to Stephen's message was easily predictable: **They were furious** (cf. 5:33) **and gnashed their teeth at him.**

Instead of being intimidated, **Stephen, full of the Holy Spirit** (cf. 6:3, 5, 10), **saw the glory of God, and Jesus standing at the right hand of God.** The Lord Jesus normally is seated at the Father's right hand (Ps. 110:1; Rom. 8:34; Col. 3:1; Heb. 1:3, 13; 8:1; 10:12; 12:2; 1 Peter 3:22). The standing position may imply that the Lord Christ was standing to welcome Stephen.

Acts 7:56 is a climactic verse in this chapter for several reasons. First, it repeats the claim Christ made at His trial before the high priest (Mark 14:62). Just as His claim resulted in His being accused of blasphemy, so also these words brought a violent response toward Stephen. Second, the term **Son of Man** is filled with significance. This is the last time it is used in the New Testament and it is the only time in the Gospels and Acts when it is not spoken by the Lord Jesus. This expression, Son of Man, shows that Jesus is the Messiah for it comes from Daniel 7:13-14. It is definitely eschatological. (See additional comments on "the Son of Man" at Mark 8:31.) Third, Acts 7:56 combines two great messianic passages—Daniel 7:13-14 and Psalm 110:1. Daniel 7:13-14 emphasizes the universal aspect of the Lord's rule. He is not simply a Jewish ruler; He is Savior of the world. Psalm 110:1 presents the Messiah as being at God's **right hand.** Besides stressing power and position, this also shows acceptance. Christ is therefore the Mediator (cf. 1 Tim. 2:5), thus proving

that people have access to God by means other than the temple and its priests.

7:57-58. The response of the Sanhedrin was immediate and violent. They quickly saw the theological implications of Stephen's doctrine—Israel was guilty; the Law was temporary; the temple must be done away—so they **dragged him out of the city and began to stone him.** Blasphemy was to be punished by death (Lev. 24:16). The Jews' martyring Stephen is ironic because these forefathers, having worshiped "Moloch" (Acts 7:43), should have been put to death, according to Moses (Lev. 20:2).

A young theologue **named Saul** agreed that Stephen should be stoned. **The witnesses laid their clothes at** his **feet.** This meant Saul was giving his approval by guarding their clothes (Acts 8:1; 22:20).

7:59-60. In words reminiscent of the Lord's, **Stephen** committed his **spirit** to the **Lord** and **prayed** for his enemies (cf. Luke 23:34, 46). Luke recorded the fact of his death by simply writing, **he fell asleep.** For a Christian, his body (not his soul) sleeps in death (cf. John 11:11; 1 Thes. 4:13, 15).

8:1a. The words **giving approval** (*syneudokōn*) indicate active approval, not just passive consent (cf. Rom. 1:32). This gives fuller meaning to Saul's deed in Acts 7:58.

B. *The ministry of Philip (8:1b-40)*

1. IN SAMARIA (8:1B-25)

a. *The persecution of the church (8:1b-3)*

Chapter 8 is closely linked with chapters 6 and 7. The *subject* of persecution begun in 6 is continued in 8. Furthermore, the *personality* of Saul, introduced in 7, is also found in 8. There is a close connection between Philip (chap. 8) and Stephen (chaps. 6–7) because both belonged to the Seven (6:5). Even the order of their two names in 6:5 is followed in the sequence of the narrative in 6:8–8:40.

8:1b. On that day indicates that the **persecution of the church** was signaled by Stephen's martyrdom. It implies that Jewish leaders approved of Stephen's execution. Israel was in the process of confirming its tragic choice to reject Jesus as her Messiah.

The fact that **all the Jerusalem** believers **except the apostles were scattered throughout Judea and Samaria** was God's method of fulfilling the mandate of 1:8. The word "scattered" (*diesparēsan*), also used in 8:4, comes from the verb *speirō*, used to refer to sowing seed (Matt. 6:26; 13:3-4, 18; 25:24, 26; Luke 8:5; 12:24; etc.) This statement also prepares the way for the ministry of Philip in Samaria (Acts 8:4-25).

Though Luke refers to "all," he could not have included everyone, for the church continued on in Jerusalem. From the context it may be concluded that the primary objects of persecution were the Greek-speaking Jews. They would have been easily identifiable and would have been associated with Stephen.

Why the apostles did not leave the city is not stated. Perhaps their sense of obligation to the church in Jerusalem kept them there. The Jerusalem church undoubtedly became more Jewish with the evacuation of people who would be more sympathetic with Stephen. At the same time this persecution deepened the cleavage between the church and Judaism.

8:2-3. These verses contrast sharply with each other. **Godly men buried Stephen and mourned deeply for him.** On the other hand **Saul began to destroy the church.** The word for "destroy" (*elymaineto*, used only here in the NT) appears in the Septuagint in Psalm 79:13 (80:13 in Eng. texts) about wild boars that destroy (NIV, "ravage") a vineyard. Saul's zeal was so great against Christians that it was as if he were wildly raging against them (cf. Acts 9:1, 13). In violence **he dragged off men and women** (cf. 9:29; 22:4-5) and beat them (22:19; 26:11). This caused havoc in Jerusalem (9:21). Saul's own later imprisonment as an apostle *for* Christ contrasted with his imprisoning these followers!

Stephen's martyrdom together with the ensuing persecution of the church confirmed Israel's unbelief and her obstinate refusal to accept Jesus as her Redeemer.

b. The proclamation of the message (8:4-8)

8:4. In the Greek this verse begins with "therefore on the other hand" (*men oun*, not trans. in the NIV). Because of persecution believers were **scattered** (cf. v. 1) and **the Word** of God spread (cf. Rom. 8:28; 2 Cor. 2:14; Phil. 1:12-14). This is another evidence of God's sovereign control; in spite of opposition the Word of God grew (cf. Acts 12:24; 19:20).

8:5. Philip, a Grecian Jew and therefore more broadminded than Aramaic-speaking Jews in Israel (cf. 6:1), went to the Samaritans. Samaria is north of Jerusalem, but Luke said Philip **went down** because **Samaria** is lower in elevation than Jerusalem. The significance of Philip's ministry in this unnamed city is seen when Matthew 10:5-6; Luke 9:52-54; and John 4:9 are compared with Acts 8:5.

8:6-7. Philip's proclamation of Christ was confirmed by **miraculous signs** (*sēmeia*; cf. v. 13) so that **they all paid close attention to what he said.** The miracles (casting out **evil spirits,** i.e., demons, and healing **paralytics and cripples** [cf. 3:1-10]) authenticated his message (cf. 2:43).

8:8. Once again the gospel resulted in **great joy** (cf. comments on 2:46-47).

c. The professions of faith (8:9-13)

8:9-10. Many traditions revolve around **Simon** the sorcerer. It is alleged: (a) that he was the founder of the Gnostic heresies, (b) that he went to Rome and perverted Christian doctrine there, and (c) that he became involved in a miracle contest with Peter and lost. At any rate, this Simon of Samaria did practice **sorcery in the city** and amazed **all the people of Samaria.** Because of his "sorcery," the ability to exercise control over nature and/or people by means of demonic power, **people** called him **the Great Power.** They may or may not have thought of him as possessing deity. At any rate Simon **boasted that he was someone great,** and the people of Samaria believed him. Furthermore, he accepted their adulation.

8:11-12. Simon's **magic** means his sorcery, his demonic powers (the Gr. words for "practiced sorcery" and "magic" are related). When **Philip** came to Samaria, **he preached the good news of the kingdom of God and the name** (cf. 3:16) **of Jesus Christ.** The term "the kingdom of God" refers to the coming kingdom (cf. 1:3, 6). "The name of Jesus

Christ" looks to His position as Messiah (cf. 8:5, "the Christ," lit., the Messiah). In other words, the message meant that some Samaritans would become heirs of the Millennium by faith in Jesus, the Messiah.

As an evidence of their faith the Samaritans **were baptized, both men and women** (cf. "men and women" in v. 3). The contrasts and comparisons between Simon and Philip are striking. Both performed miracles, Simon by demonic power and Philip by divine power. Simon boasted and welcomed acclaim to himself, but Philip proclaimed Christ. People were amazed at Simon's magic, but people were converted to Christ by Philip's ministry.

8:13. Amazingly **Simon himself believed and was baptized.** Now rather than people following Simon, **he followed Philip!** His response must have had a profound effect on his own followers.

Was Simon saved? Luke did not specify this clearly, so it is difficult to be dogmatic. But seven facts suggest that Simon probably was not born again: (1) The verb "believe" (*pisteuō*) does not always refer to saving faith. Simon's faith could have been like that of the demons in James 2:19, merely intellectual assent. (2) Furthermore, faith based on signs is not a trustworthy faith (cf. John 2:23-25; 4:48). (3) In addition, Luke never stated that Simon received the Holy Spirit (Acts 8:17-18). (4) Simon continued to have a self-centered interest in the display of miraculous power (vv. 18-19). (5) The verb "repent" (*metanoeō*) used in verse 22 is normally addressed to lost people. (6) The word "perish" (*eis apōleian*) employed in verse 20 is strong. It is related to the word "perish" in John 3:16. (7) The description of Simon in Acts 8:23 is a better description of a lost man than of one who is saved (cf. Deut. 29:18). Still one cannot be dogmatic on this point. The Lord knows those who are His (2 Tim. 2:19).

d. The proof of the work (8:14-17)

8:14-17. It was necessary for **the apostles in Jerusalem** to commission **Peter and John to** Samaria for several reasons. Normally **the Holy Spirit** baptizes, indwells, and seals at the moment of faith, but in this instance the delay served several purposes: (1) Peter and John's prayer (for bestowing of **the Holy Spirit**) and their laying **on of hands** (resulting in the coming of the Spirit) confirmed Philip's ministry among the Samaritans. This authenticated this new work to the Jerusalem apostles. (2) Also this confirmed Philip's ministry to the Samaritans. This message Philip had preached was validated by the coming of the Spirit, a mark of the coming kingdom (cf. v. 12; Jer. 31:31-34; Ezek. 36:23-27; Joel 2:28-32). (3) Perhaps the most important aspect of God's withholding the Spirit till apostolic representatives came from the Jerusalem church was to prevent schism. Because of the natural propensity of division between Jews and Samaritans it was essential for **Peter and John** to welcome the Samaritan believers officially into the church. The contrast between John's attitude here and in Luke 9:52-54 is significant.

e. The perversion of the truth (8:18-24)

8:18-19. The clause **Simon saw that the Spirit was given** implies there was some external manifestation to evidence the coming of **the Holy Spirit.** Possibly it was speaking in tongues, though the Scripture does not say so (cf. 2:4; 10:45-46; 19:6).

The term *simony*, which is the buying or selling of things considered religious or sacred such as an ecclesiastical office, comes from Simon's desire to purchase the **ability** to impart the Holy Spirit to others.

Luke's purpose in including this incident with Simon was to show the superiority of Christianity over the occult and demoniacs. Several times this kind of conflict took place in Acts, and Christ was always the Victor (13:6-12; 16:16-18; 19:13-20; 28:1-6).

8:20. Peter's response to Simon's request was one of outrage. **May your money perish with you!**

The reason for such strong language was Simon's failure to understand grace, the free nature of God's salvation and blessings. Peter explained his strong language by saying, **You thought you could buy the gift of God with money!**

8:21-22. The language of this verse, **You have no part or share in this**

ministry (*logō*, "word, matter"), implies Simon was not a Christian. (For similar terminology see Deut. 12:12; 14:27. Just as the Levites had no inheritance in the Promised Land, so also Simon had no portion in the matter of salvation.) The adverb **perhaps** does not mean **God** is reluctant to forgive sin. The question was whether Simon would **repent of** his heart's intention.

8:23-24. The allusion to **bitterness** (lit., "gall of bitterness," *cholēn pikrias*) seems to refer to Deuteronomy 29:18, which speaks of idolatry and bitter apostasy (cf. Heb. 12:15). **Simon** had been captivated by false doctrine and sin. Simon's response may have been genuine or simply an outcry of fear. At least he was apprehensive about the outcome of his tragic request (Acts 8:18-19).

f. The promotion of the work (8:25)

8:25. **Peter and John** were so convinced of God's working among the Samaritans that when they **returned to Jerusalem** they too shared **the gospel** with Samaritans, in fact, **in many Samaritan villages.** This was a remarkable thing for these Jewish apostles to do!

2. TO THE ETHIOPIAN EUNUCH (8:26-40)

a. The command (8:26)

8:26. Though Luke gave no record of God's commanding **Philip** to preach to the Samaritans (v. 5), God did sovereignly direct Philip toward Gaza (see the map at Acts 9). The highway is referred to as **the desert road.** The expression may refer to a desert road or a desert city. Ancient Gaza was destroyed in 93 B.C. and the city was rebuilt nearer the Mediterranean in 57 B.C. The old city was called Desert Gaza. The Greek for the angel's command could be translated, "Arise and **go to the south to the road . . . that goes down from Jerusalem to Gaza.** This is desert." This reference to the road in 8:36 may imply that the road, not the city, was in a deserted area.

b. The contact (8:27-30)

8:27. The **Ethiopian eunuch** is described rather fully as **an important official in charge of all the treasury of Candace, queen of the Ethiopians.** "Ethiopia" here refers not to modern-day Ethiopia but to ancient Nubia, the region

from Aswan in southern Egypt to Khartoum, Sudan. Candace was a title given to the queen-mother, as Pharaoh was used of the king of Egypt. Governmental power rested in the hands of Candace, for the royal son, worshiped as an offspring of the sun, was therefore above such mundane activities as ruling over a nation. Rulership was therefore vested with the queen-mother. The fact that **this** eunuch **had gone to Jerusalem to worship** is interesting. The Law prohibited eunuchs from entering the Lord's assembly (Deut. 23:1). However, Isaiah 56:3-5 predicts great blessing for eunuchs in the Millennial Age. Evidently this eunuch was a worshiper of Yahweh though not a full-fledged proselyte.

8:28-30. The eunuch's wealth is revealed in the simple description **sitting in his chariot.** As this finance officer was riding, he was **reading** from **the Book of Isaiah.** Since it was customary to read aloud, **Philip** could have easily **heard the** portion of Scripture the eunuch was **reading** (v. 30). Interestingly **Philip** was guided first by an angel (v. 26) and then by **the Holy Spirit** (v. 29).

c. The conversion (8:31-35)

8:31-35. The quotation from Isaiah 53:7-8 was perplexing to the eunuch. Welcoming the opportunity to have **Philip** explain the passage, **he invited** the apostle into his chariot. The Ethiopian knew the passage described an individual, but was it Isaiah **or someone else?** **Philip** seized the opportunity to present **the good news about Jesus** from Isaiah 53 (cf. John 5:39).

d. The consequences (8:36-40)

8:36-39. The first consequence of Philip's evangelization was the eunuch's conversion. His response, **Why shouldn't I be baptized?** indicates that **water** baptism was the seal of a personal decision to trust in Christ (cf. Matt. 28:19). The second result was joy, for **the eunuch . . . went on his way rejoicing.** A third result was a further outreach of the gospel to one who was neither Jew nor Samaritan, but a Gentile (African) worshiper of Yahweh who was not a full-fledged proselyte to Judaism. Possibly the eunuch was uncircumcised. (As indicated in the NIV marg., Acts 8:37 is included only in late Gr. mss. and therefore was probably not in the original ms.)

When the baptism was completed the Spirit of the Lord suddenly took Philip away, and the eunuch did not see him again. Whatever happened to the Ethiopian eunuch after that is unknown.

8:40. Philip, however, appeared at Azotus. This city is the same as Ashdod, an ancient Philistine capital. As he traveled to Caesarea he proclaimed the gospel in all the towns along the way (see Azotus and Caesarea on the map at chap. 9). Evidently Philip then settled in Caesarea for he was still there about 20 years later (cf. 21:8). Significantly an evangelist may be resident or itinerary; Philip carried on both types of ministries.

The area around Azotus and Caesarea was later visited by Peter (9:32-43). Even though Philip the evangelist resided in Caesarea, the Lord called Peter from Joppa to give the gospel to Cornelius in Caesarea (chaps. 10–11).

C. The message of Saul (9:1-31)

The conversion of Saul (Paul) is believed by some to be the most important event in the church since Pentecost. Luke certainly considered Saul's conversion significant for he recorded it three times in Acts (chaps. 9, 22, 26).

The record of Saul's conversion at this juncture prepares readers for the gospel going to Gentiles (chap. 10). The apostle to the Gentiles (Gal. 2:8; Eph. 3:8) was preceded in this ministry by Peter's evangelization of Cornelius and his household.

The account of Saul's Damascus Road experience may be recorded here also to relate it to Stephen's martyrdom. Stephen's discourse seemed to have spurred Saul to renewed efforts to stamp out Christianity (Acts 8:1-3). If the doctrine propagated by Stephen was correct, then the Law was in jeopardy. So Saul, zealous as he was, went on persecuting the church (cf. Gal. 1:13; Phil. 3:6).

But Saul the persecutor was about to become Paul the apostle of Jesus Christ! His background and qualifications suited him eminently for the work to which God had called him: (1) He knew the Jewish culture and language well (Acts 21:40; Phil. 3:5). (2) Because he was reared in Tarsus he was well acquainted with the

Greek culture and its philosophies (Acts 17:22-31; Titus 1:12). (3) He possessed all the privileges of a Roman citizen (Acts 16:37; 22:23-29; 25:10-12). (4) He was trained and skilled in Jewish theology (Gal. 1:14). (5) Because he was capable in a secular trade he was able to support himself (Acts 18:3; 1 Cor. 9:4-18; 2 Cor. 11:7-11; 1 Thes. 2:9; 2 Thes. 3:8). (6) God gave him zeal, leadership qualities, and theological insight.

1. THE CONVERSION OF SAUL (9:1-19A)

a. The conviction of Saul (9:1-9)

9:1a. The adverb still looks back to 8:3. While the gospel was reaching farther outside of Jerusalem, Saul was continuing his relentless persecution of the church.

9:1b-2. So great was Saul's hatred for the church that he went to the high priest and asked him for letters to the synagogues in Damascus. Damascus (see its location on the map) was not under the control of Judea, Galilee, or the Decapolis. What jurisdiction would the high priest have over synagogues in Damascus? This is usually answered by saying Rome recognized the right of extradition when the high priest in Jerusalem demanded it. But this can also be explained in another way. At that time Damascus may have been under the Nabatean king, Aretas IV (cf. 2 Cor. 11:32-33). In order to gain favor with the anti-Roman Jews, Aretas, who hated the Romans, would have conceded this favor to the high priest.

The mention of "synagogues in Damascus" indicates that Christianity was still closely associated with Judaism (in James 2:2 the word "meeting" renders the Gr. synagōgēn, "synagogue"). Mention of Damascus shows that Christianity had spread rapidly.

Strangely, Saul referred to Christianity as the Way, a term used only in Acts (19:9, 23; 22:4; 24:14, 22).

9:3-4. Saul both heard the voice of the Lord Jesus and saw Him (cf. 9:17, 27; 22:14; 26:16; 1 Cor. 9:1; 15:8). Though there is no explicit statement of Saul's seeing Christ, it is implicit in the reference to a light from heaven. It was fundamental to Saul's apostleship that he saw the resurrected Lord (cf. 1 Cor. 9:1).

The question, Why do you persecute Me? (cf. Acts 9:5) is filled with signif-

PALESTINE, SYRIA, CILICIA, AND CYPRUS

icance for it shows the union of Christ with His church. The Lord did not ask, "Why do you persecute My church?" The reference to "Me" gave Saul his first glimpse into the great doctrine of Christians being in Christ. This same truth was implied earlier by Luke when he wrote that the Lord continues His work on earth in the church (1:1). Also Ananias' lie to Peter was a lie to the Holy Spirit (5:3). Luke, with Paul, saw Christ and the church as the Head and its body.

9:5. Some interpret "Lord" in Saul's question, **Who are You, Lord?** (*kyrie*) as "Sir." It is possible for this noun to have this meaning, as it does in Matthew 13:27; 27:63; John 4:11; Acts 10:4; and elsewhere. However, there is too much that is supernatural in this passage to use the mere human vocative, "Sir." Even though **Saul** did not immediately recognize this One as Jesus, he must have acknowledged a supernatural being. Jesus then identified Himself to Saul: **I am Jesus** (cf. 9:17).

The words, "It is hard for thee to kick against the pricks" (KJV), are not in the better and earlier Greek manuscripts. But this statement *is* found in Acts 26:14.

9:6. The resurrected Lord commanded Saul, **Go into the city and you will be told what you must do.** This does

not mean that Ananias (v. 10) taught Saul the doctrine of justification, as some claim. Instead, Saul was told he must proclaim the gospel, which would involve suffering (vv. 15-16; 22:10, 15; 26:16-20). The Lord Himself gave Saul the truth of justification by faith on the Damascus Road; Acts 26:18 is clear on that point (cf. Gal. 1:11-12).

9:7. An apparent discrepancy stands between verse 7 and 22:9. In 9:7 Luke recorded that **the men** who traveled **with Saul . . . heard the sound** (*phōnēs*), but in 22:9 Luke wrote that "they did not understand the voice" (*phōnēn*). Literally, that clause in 22:9 may be translated, "They did not hear the sound." The NIV correctly translates the verse, because the verb "to hear" with the genitive case may mean "to hear a sound" and with the accusative case "to hear with understanding." The genitive case is employed in 9:7, and the accusative is used in 22:9. So the travelers with Saul heard the sound (9:7) but did not understand what Christ said (22:9).

9:8. If Saul's "thorn in the flesh" was eye trouble (cf. comments on 2 Cor. 12:7), this may have been the prelude of it. At any rate there is a sharp contrast between **Saul** in Acts 9:1 and 8. One moment he was storming up the road, determined to capture and imprison Christians. Soon thereafter he was **led** like a child **by the hand into Damascus.** God's grace is often displayed in great powerful acts and in apparent catastrophes.

9:9. The **three days** of blindness, fasting, and praying (v. 11) were a time of waiting. Saul still had not received the message God had promised him (v. 6).

b. The contrition of Saul (9:10-19a)

9:10-14. By means of **a vision** God instructed a reluctant **Ananias** to **restore** Saul's **sight.** He was to go to **Saul** where he was staying with a man named **Judas** whose **house** was **on Straight Street.** It was one of the two parallel streets that ran from the western to the eastern wall. The first reference to Saul's birthplace— **Tarsus**—is given in verse 11 (see the map; cf. comments on v. 30).

Interestingly believers were first called **saints** in the Book of Acts here (v. 13). The church is comprised of "set-apart ones" (*hagiois*; cf. "saints" in Rom.

1:1; Eph. 1:1; Phil. 1:1). From Acts 9:14 it is evident that the news of Saul's coming to persecute believers in Damascus had preceded his arrival, and **Ananias** feared what Saul might do.

9:15. The Lord assured **Ananias . . . This man is My chosen instrument to carry My name before the Gentiles and their kings and before the people of Israel.** Saul was to become Paul, the apostle to the uncircumcised (Rom. 11:13; Gal. 2:2, 7-8; Eph. 3:8), including kings (cf. Governor Felix [Acts 24:1-23], Governor Porcius Festus [24:27-25:12], King Herod Agrippa II [25:13-26:32], and possibly Emperor Nero [25:11]). The apostle, of course, also ministered to "the people of Israel" (cf. 9:20; 13:5, 14; 14:1; 17:2, 10, 17; 18:4, 19; 19:8; 26:17-20; Rom. 1:16). How amazing that the one who persecuted Christians so violently should himself be transformed into a witness of the gospel—and such a dynamic, forceful witness at that!

9:16. The partial fulfillment of this prediction is seen in Saul's inventory of his suffering (2 Cor. 11:23-27).

Three times in as many verses the conversation between Ananias and the Lord included the word **name** (Acts 9:14-16; cf. 3:16).

9:17. Brother Saul—what words of encouragement these must have been to **Saul!** The first recorded man to call Saul a Christian brother was **Ananias.** A more complete statement of Ananias' words is given in 22:14-16. Ananias' apprehension of Saul was turned to love for Saul because of the Lord's directive. Ananias identified with Saul by **placing his hands on** him.

Saul's being **filled with the Holy Spirit** clearly followed his conversion (cf. 4:8, 31; Eph. 5:18).

9:18. In his healing from his blindness **something like scales fell from Saul's eyes, and he could see again.** The word "scales" (*lepides,* from the verb *lepō,* "to peel") was used of the scales of fish and crocodiles. As in several previous conversions recorded in Acts, water baptism followed conversion (8:12, 38).

After this event Ananias disappeared from the narrative and is not mentioned again except in chapter 22 where Paul recounted his own conversion.

9:19a. The three days without food or drink, in addition to the shock of his "exposure" to the resurrected Christ, left Saul weak. However, several things helped him regain **his strength:** his encounter with Ananias, his healing, his filling with the Spirit, his water baptism, and his **taking some food.**

2. THE CONFLICTS OF SAUL (9:19B-31)

a. *The confession of Saul (9:19b-22)*

9:19b-20. After only a few **days with the** Christians **in Damascus** Saul **began to preach in the synagogues that Jesus is the Son of God.** Preaching to Jews in their synagogues was also his strategy on his missionary journeys (the first journey—13:5, 14; 14:1; the second journey—17:2, 10, 17; 18:4; the third journey—18:19; 19:8). Acts 9:20 includes the only occurrence of the phrase "Son of God" in Acts. On the Damascus Road the first thing Saul learned was who Jesus is.

9:21. The Jews **were astonished.** This response is understandable. The Greek verb *existanto* is literally, "they were beside themselves; they were struck out of their senses"; several other people had the same response to Jesus (Mark 2:12; 5:42; 6:51). This word is used in Acts five times (2:7; 8:13; 9:21; 10:45; 12:16). Saul's intense persecution campaign had **raised havoc in Jerusalem** (cf. 8:3; 22:19; 26:11).

9:22. Saul used his theological training to good advantage in pressing home the truth that the Lord **Jesus is the** Messiah. He had gone to **Damascus** to persecute the church; he ended up preaching Jesus. What a contrast! What grace! No wonder the Damascus **Jews** were **baffled** (*synechynnen,* "bewildered, confused," from *syncheō,* used in the NT only in 2:6; 9:22; 21:27, 31).

b. *The conspiracies against Saul (9:23-31)*

(1) In Damascus. **9:23-25.** One of the themes in Acts, underscored in this paragraph, is the Jewish leaders' opposition to the gospel. It is clear from 2 Corinthians 11:32-33 that this was a joint effort of the Jews and the governor under King Aretas (a Nabatean), though the Jews were the prime movers. Saul's **followers,** aware that **the Jews conspired to kill him . . . lowered him in a basket outside the wall** since **the city gates** were guarded. Saul's plans for persecuting Christians in Damascus took a strange

turn; he had entered the city blind and left in a basket! Ironically *he* became the object of persecution.

The reference to "followers" (*mathē-tai*, lit., "disciples") shows that Saul was already having a fruitful ministry. He was a gifted leader.

Luke in compressing the narrative omits Saul's brief sojourn into Arabia, mentioned by Paul in Galatians 1:17. Probably this occurred between Acts 9:22 and 23. The purpose of Paul's time in Arabia is unknown. Possibly he went there to evangelize, but the area was sparsely populated and it was Saul's strategy to go to populous metropolitan centers. He may have left Damascus to reduce the church's persecution. Or, more probably, he went to Arabia to meditate and study.

(2) In Jerusalem (9:26-30). **9:26-28. Saul** had left **Jerusalem** an inveterate enemy of Christianity to persecute the church **in Damascus;** but in God's sovereign grace he joined the believers and preached the gospel in that very city. He joined the work in Jerusalem, but the believers there refused to trust him (cf. Ananias' similar fear, v. 13). In Damascus Saul needed a friend, Ananias; in Jerusalem he needed another, **Barnabas.** He whose name means "Son of Encouragement" (4:36) proved to be that for Saul. Barnabas is seen in Acts on four other occasions. (a) 11:22-24; (b) 11:30; 12:25; (c) 13:1-2, 50; 14:12; (d) 15:2, 12, 22, 25, 37. The believers in Jerusalem, convinced by Barnabas that Saul had in fact been converted, allowed **Saul** to stay **with them.** In Damascus he **preached fearlessly in the name of Jesus,** and in **Jerusalem** he was **speaking boldly in the name of the Lord** (cf. comments on "boldly" in 4:31).

9:29. Saul **talked and debated with the Grecian Jews,** thus continuing the work of Stephen (cf. 6:8-10). Evidently Saul's debating ability proved to be too much for the Grecian Jews as they attempted to assassinate him.

9:30. The brothers (cf. v. 17) at Jerusalem then escorted Saul **to Caesarea,** the seaport about 65 miles away by road, **and sent him** to his hometown, **Tarsus.** An ancient city, then over 4,000 years old, Tarsus was an intellectual city in the Roman Empire. (For a brief survey of

significant events in Tarsus' history, see V. Gilbert Beers, *The Victor Handbook of Bible Knowledge.* Wheaton, Ill.: Scripture Press Publications, Victor Books, 1981, p. 555.)

Saul's movements in chapter 9 may be summarized as follows:
1. Jerusalem (vv. 1-2)
2. Damascus (vv. 3-22)
3. Arabia (Gal. 1:17)
4. Damascus (Acts 9:23-25; Gal. 1:17; 2 Cor. 11:32-33)
5. Jerusalem (Acts 9:26-29; Gal. 1:18-20)
6. Caesarea (Acts 9:30)
7. Tarsus (v. 30; Gal. 1:21-24)

(3) The conclusion. **9:31.** In the phrase **the church throughout Judea, Galilee, and Samaria** the word "church" is singular. Luke was obviously speaking of the universal church as it was dispersed in the Holy Land.

So strong was Jewish antagonism to Saul and his ministry that after he left the area the church **enjoyed a time of peace.**

The church was still confined to Jews, half-Jews (the Samaritans), and proselytes to Judaism who became Christians (with the one exception of the eunuch from Ethiopia, 8:26-40). But all was in readiness for the extension of the church to a new segment of the world's population.

With this third of seven progress reports on the spiritual and numerical growth of the church (cf. 2:47; 6:7; 12:24; 16:5; 19:20; 28:30-31), Luke brought this section of his book to a conclusion.

III. The Witness to the Extremity of the Earth (9:32-28:31)

A. The extension of the church to Antioch (9:32-12:24)

1. THE PREPARATION OF PETER FOR A UNIVERSAL GOSPEL (9:32-10:48)

a. Peter at Lydda (9:32-35)

9:32-35. **Peter** was last mentioned in 8:25 when he was returning to Jerusalem from Samaria with John. Peter was involved in an itinerant mission around Judea which brought him to **Lydda.** Lydda, mentioned only here in the New Testament, is today called Lod; Israel's international airport is just north of the city. Peter later carried on an extensive traveling ministry, evident from 1 Corinthians 9:5. This is also implied from the addressees of his first epistle (1 Peter 1:1). Philip had preceded Peter to the area in and around Caesarea (Acts 8:40).

The miraculous healing of **Aeneas, a paralytic who had been bedridden for eight years,** was the occasion for many to come to faith in Christ. Three times in Acts, Luke used the words **turned to the Lord** to refer to salvation (9:35; 11:21; 15:19). The gospel was beginning to attract a wider audience, for many in this coastal region were Gentiles. **Sharon** is the fertile plain along the coast of Palestine, about 10 miles wide and 50 miles long. Lydda was on the southeastern edge of the plain. This miracle was Peter's second healing of a cripple (cf. 3:1-10; also cf. 14:8-10).

b. Peter at Joppa (9:36-43)

9:36-38. While **Peter was** at **Lydda,** a well-beloved Christian woman (a disciple) in **Joppa** by the name of **Dorcas . . . died.** Her name means "gazelle" in Greek as does its counterpart **Tabitha** in Aramaic. She was known for her help to **the poor.** Because the cities of **Lydda** and **Joppa** are only about 12 miles apart **two men were sent** from Joppa to call Peter. (For a brief statement on Joppa's history see Beers, *The Victor Handbook of Bible Knowledge,* p. 559.) No one had been raised from the dead in the early church so far as the records of Acts declare, but the faith of the believers was so great they expected the Lord to use Peter to resurrect Dorcas.

9:39-41. When **Peter** arrived, he **sent** the weeping **widows** and other believers out of the **upstairs . . . room,** prayed **on his knees** for Dorcas, and commanded her to arise (cf. Mark 5:41). To avoid ceremonial defilement (cf. Lev. 21:1; Num. 5:2; 9:6-10; 19:11), **Peter** did not touch her until after God restored her to life.

9:42-43. **This** miracle, like previous ones, led **many** to believe **in the Lord** (2:43, 47; 4:4; 5:12, 14; 8:6; 9:33-35). After this miracle **Peter** remained **in Joppa for some time** (lit., "sufficient days") **with a tanner named Simon.** His house was "by the sea" (10:6).

This passage (9:32-43) shows the excellent preparation given Peter for his ensuing experience with Cornelius.

(1) Two outstanding miracles confirmed his ministry; God was with him in a special way. (2) He was ministering in an area that was partially Gentile. (3) His living in the home of Simon the tanner was significant. Tanners were considered to be ceremonially unclean because they were constantly in contact with the skins of dead animals (Lev. 11:40).

c. Peter and Cornelius (chap. 10)

The importance of this event is seen in the fact that Luke recounts it three times—here in Acts 10, again in chapter 11, and finally in 15:6-9. The geographic extension of the gospel in Acts is an initial fulfillment of Jesus' words in Matthew 8:11: "Many will come from the east and the west, and will take their places . . . in the kingdom of heaven."

(1) The vision of Cornelius (10:1-8). **10:1.** By separate visions both Peter and **Cornelius** were prepared for this momentous happening. Cornelius and his vision are described first. Cornelius was a **centurion,** a Roman officer in charge of 100 soldiers, in **the Italian Regiment,** consisting of 600 soldiers. In the New Testament centurions are consistently viewed in a favorable light (cf. Matt. 8:5-10; 27:54; Mark 15:44-45; Acts 22:25-26; 23:17-18; 27:6, 43). Centurion Cornelius became one of the first Gentiles after Pentecost to hear the good news of Jesus Christ's forgiveness.

10:2. From the description of Cornelius as **devout** (*eusebēs*, used only here and in v. 7; 2 Peter 2:9) **and God-fearing** ("righteous and God-fearing," Acts 10:22), it can be inferred he was not a full-fledged proselyte to Judaism (he had not been circumcised, 11:3), but he did worship Yahweh. Evidently he attended the synagogue and to the best of his knowledge and ability followed the Old Testament Scriptures. Nevertheless, he had not entered into New Testament salvation (cf. 11:14).

10:3-6. The time reference, **3 in the afternoon,** may refer to a Jewish time of prayer (cf. 3:1). If so, the Lord approached Cornelius by means of **an angel** while he was at prayer (cf. 10:9). Later Cornelius called this angel "a man in shining clothes" (v. 30). **Cornelius** responded to **the angel** by asking, **What is it, Lord?** Perhaps "Lord" (*kyrie*) here means "Sir" (cf. comments on 9:5). This soldier's piety was evidenced by his **prayers** and his generous giving **to the poor** (cf. 10:2). The angel instructed him to send for **Simon . . . Peter** at the home of **Simon the tanner** (cf. 9:43).

10:7. When the angel who spoke to him had gone, the centurion **called** three of his men—two **servants** and a military aide, also **a devout man** (*eusebē*; cf. v. 2). Undoubtedly these three had been influenced by Cornelius' devotion.

10:8. He told them everything that had happened. Related to the Greek participle used here (*exēgēsamenos*) is the English noun "exegesis." The verb means he "explained" everything.

The three went off **to Joppa,** some 33 miles south of Caesarea (v. 24), to bring Peter back to Cornelius.

(2) The vision of Peter (10:9-16). **10:9.** That **Peter** prayed morning and evening may be assumed, for those were normal times of prayer. In addition he prayed at **noon.** Prayer three times a day was not commanded in the Scriptures, but Peter followed the example of pious men before him (cf. Ps. 55:17; Dan. 6:10). Peter **went up to the** (flat) **roof to pray;** this would have given him privacy.

10:10-12. While **hungry,** Peter **fell into a trance** in which God gave him a vision of a **sheet** coming **down to earth** with **all kinds of . . . animals . . . reptiles . . . and birds.**

10:13-14. When God commanded Peter to **eat** of these animals, his response was, **Surely not, Lord!** Significantly his refusal ("surely not") was *mēdamōs,* a more polite and subjective term than *oudamōs* ("by no means," used only in Matt. 2:6). This was the third time in Peter's career that he directly refused God's will (cf. Matt. 16:23; John 13:8).

Peter knew from the Law that he should not eat **unclean** animals (Lev. 11). But could he not have killed and **eaten** the clean animals and left the unclean? Probably Peter understood the command to include them all. Or possibly the large sheet contained only unclean animals.

10:15. Do not call anything impure that God has made clean. This rebuttal gives Mark 7:14-23 more meaning (cf. 1 Tim. 4:4). It is generally recognized that Mark wrote down Peter's words. In retrospect Peter must have recognized

that Jesus as the Messiah cleansed all goods from ceremonial defilement.

10:16. Why did Peter refuse **three times** to eat the unclean foods? For one thing, this indicated emphasis. But more than that it revealed certainty and truth. Here was one place where Peter was being scrupulous beyond the will of God. His intentions were good, but he was being disobedient. Also, was there some link here with Peter's threefold denial (John 18:17, 25-27) and with his three affirmations of his love for the Lord? (John 21:15-17)

(3) The visit of the messengers (10:17-23a). **10:17-22.** In marvelous timing and by the coordination of the sovereign God the three messengers and **Peter** met. **The** Holy **Spirit,** who told Peter about the arrival of the **three men,** may have been the One whose unidentified voice Peter heard earlier (vv. 13, 15).

The men . . . from Cornelius spoke highly of him (cf. vv. 2, 4) and conveyed to **Peter** their purpose in coming.

10:23a. Then Peter invited the men into the house to be his guests. Since Peter had been waiting for his noon meal (cf. v. 10), he undoubtedly now shared it with his visitors. Perhaps he was already beginning to discern the lesson of his vision!

(4) The visitation of Gentiles (10:23b-43). **10:23b.** By the time **Peter** and his guests finished lunch it must have been too late to start back to Caesarea that day. **The next day** they began the almost-two-day trip. (Cornelius' emissaries had left Caesarea after 3 P.M. one day [vv. 3, 8] and arrived at noon two days later [vv. 9, 19]. Cf. "four days ago" in v. 30.)

Peter took with him **some of the brothers from Joppa.** The two-by-two motif is common in the Gospels and Acts; Christian workers often went out by twos. In this debatable situation at least six people accompanied Peter (11:12). So there would be seven witnesses to attest to what would transpire.

10:24. Cornelius was so confident that Peter would come and he was so expectant of Peter's message that he **called together his relatives and close friends.**

10:25-26. When **Peter** arrived, **Cornelius** prostrated himself before the apostle in worship. The verb *prosekynēsen* means "he worshiped" and is here translated **in reverence. Peter,** refusing this kind of obeisance, urged Cornelius to **stand up,** for, **he said, I am only a man myself.**

10:27-29. Peter was well aware of the consequences of his fellowshiping with Gentiles in their homes (cf. 11:2-3), but he had learned the lesson of the vision well. The command to eat unclean animals meant he was **not** to **call any man impure or unclean.** So he **came without** protest.

10:30-33. After **Cornelius** recounted the circumstances that brought **Peter** to his house he said, **Now we are all here in the presence of God to listen to everything the Lord has commanded you to tell us.** What a divinely prepared audience!

10:34-35. These words of **Peter** were revolutionary. They swept away the prejudice and indoctrination of generations of Judaism. However, Gentile salvation certainly was a doctrine known in the Old Testament (cf. Jonah; Gen. 12:3). In the Old Testament the Jews were God's Chosen People, the special recipients of His promises and revelation. Here Peter stated that God's program was reaching out to the world through the church.

There is considerable debate about Peter's words that God **accepts men from every nation who fear Him and do what is right.** This does not teach salvation by works because a person's first responsibility before God is to fear Him, which is tantamount to trusting Him and reverencing Him. It is the New Testament parallel to Micah 6:8. Furthermore, God's acceptance of such people refers to His welcoming them to a right relationship by faith in Christ (cf. Acts 11:14).

10:36-37. Peter then outlined the career of **Christ** (vv. 36-43), the sovereign **Lord of all,** through whom **God sent ... the good news of peace.** Bible students have often observed how this parallels the Gospel of Mark almost perfectly. Mark began with John's **baptism** and traced the ministry of the Lord Jesus from **Galilee** to **Judea** to Jerusalem and finally to the Crucifixion, Resurrection, and the Great Commission.

10:38. The word *Messiah* means "Anointed One"; so when Peter said,

God anointed Jesus of Nazareth he was saying, "God declared Him the Messiah" (cf. Isa. 61:1-3; Luke 4:16-21; Acts 4:27). This declaration occurred at the Lord's baptism (cf. Matt. 3:16-17; Mark 1:9-11; Luke 3:21-22; John 1:32-34). Isaiah spoke of the Anointed One performing great deeds (Isa. 61:1-3), and as Peter declared, **He went around doing good and healing all who were under the power of the devil.**

10:39-41. Peter affirmed that he and his associates were personal eyewitnesses of all Jesus **did. They,** that is, **the Jews ... killed Him by hanging Him on a tree,** an ignominious form of execution. Earlier Peter had told Jews **in Jerusalem,** "You killed the Author of life" (3:15); to the rulers he said, "You crucified" Him (4:10); and to the Sanhedrin he replied, "You killed" Him "by hanging Him on a tree" (5:30). And Stephen too told the Sanhedrin, "You . . . have murdered Him" (7:52). On five occasions in Acts, the apostles said they were **witnesses** of the resurrected Christ (2:32; 3:15; 5:32; 10:41; 13:30-31). After Christ's resurrection the disciples **ate and drank with Him** (cf. John 21:13). This was proof that the resurrected Lord Jesus was no bodiless phantom and it explains how Christ was **seen** (Acts 10:40).

10:42-43. Peter made it clear that Christ's ministry results either in judgment (v. 42) or salvation (v. 43). The key phrase is, **Everyone who believes in Him.** This Greek construction consists of a present participle with an article, which is almost the equivalent of a noun (in this case "every believer in Him"). The key element in salvation is faith, belief in Christ. This message of **forgiveness of sins** (cf. 2:38; 5:31; 13:38; 26:18) **through** faith in the Messiah was spoken of by the prophets (e.g., Isa. 53:11; Jer. 31:34; Ezek. 36:25-26).

(5) The vindication by the Spirit (10:44-48). **10:44-45.** Peter's message was rapidly concluded by the sovereign interruption of **the Holy Spirit** who **came on all** those **who heard** Peter's **message** about Jesus and believed. **The** six (cf. v. 23; 11:12) **circumcised believers ... were astonished** (*exestēsan;* "they were beside themselves"; cf. 9:21) at this evidence of equality of **Gentiles** with Jewish believers.

10:46. The sign which God used to validate the reality of Gentile salvation was **speaking in tongues.** (For the significance of tongues-speaking in Acts, see the comments on 19:1-7.)

10:47-48. Peter quickly discerned at least three theological implications of what had happened: (1) He could not argue with God (11:17). (2) Cornelius and his household, though uncircumcised (11:3), were **baptized** because they had believed in **Christ,** as evidenced by their receiving **the Holy Spirit.** The order of these events was believing in Christ, receiving the Holy Spirit, speaking in tongues, and being baptized in water. (3) The reality of Cornelius' conversion was confirmed by Peter's staying with him several **days,** probably to instruct him more fully in his newfound faith.

2. THE PREPARATION OF THE APOSTLES FOR A UNIVERSAL GOSPEL (11:1-18)

a. The accusation (11:1-3)

11:1-2. The response on the part of Jewish Christians was mixed. The expression **circumcised believers** (also used in 10:45) evidently describes Christians who still held to the Law of Moses (cf. 15:5; 21:20; Gal. 2:12).

11:3. The accusation lodged against Peter was that he **went into the house of uncircumcised men and ate with them.** The primary problem was not his preaching to Gentiles but his eating with them (cf. Mark 2:16; Luke 15:2; Gal. 2:12). This gives even greater significance to Peter's vision (Acts 10:9-16). Eating with someone was a mark of acceptance and fellowship (cf. 1 Cor. 5:11). This problem could have caused a serious break in the church.

b. The answer (11:4-17)

11:4-14. Peter recounted to the circumcised believers in Jerusalem briefly what had occurred (cf. chap. 10), including his **vision** (11:5-7), his response to it (vv. 8-10), and the trip to Cornelius' **house** (vv. 11-14).

11:15-16. In recounting what happened next, Peter made an important identification of the day of Pentecost with the Lord's prediction of **Spirit** baptism (1:4-5). Luke did not state specifically in chapter 2 that Pentecost was that fulfillment, but Peter here pointedly said so by

the phrase **at the beginning** (cf. 10:47, "just as we have," and 11:17, "the same gift as He gave us"). The Church Age, then, began on the day of Pentecost.

11:17. Peter's defense did not rest on what he himself did, but on what *God* did. God had made no distinction between Jew and Gentile, so how could Peter?

c. The acquittal (11:18)

11:18. With Peter the saints recognized that the conversion of **Gentiles** was initiated by **God** and that they should not stand in His way. This response had two ensuing and significant results. First, it preserved the unity of the body of Christ, the church. Second, it drove a huge wedge between Church-Age believers and temple-worshipers in Jerusalem. Before this the common Jewish people looked on Christians with favor (cf. 2:47; 5:13, 26), but soon thereafter the Jews opposed the church. This antagonism is attested by Israel's response to the execution of James (12:2-3; cf. 12:11). Perhaps this concourse with Gentiles was a starting point of the Jewish opposition.

3. THE PREPARATION OF THE CHURCH AT ANTIOCH FOR A UNIVERSAL GOSPEL (11:19-30)

a. The cosmopolitan nature of the church (11:19-21)

This is a crucial hinge in the Acts account. For the first time the church actively proselytized Gentiles. The Samaritans of chapter 8 were partly Jewish; the Ethiopian eunuch on his own was reading Isaiah 53 on his return from Jerusalem; and even Cornelius took the initiative in seeking the gospel from Peter's lips. But here the church took the first steps to take the message to uncircumcised Greeks.

11:19. The narrative reaches back to **Stephen** (8:1-2) to point to still another result of his martyrdom. His death had helped move the gospel into Samaria (cf. the similarity between 8:4 and 11:19). Also Stephen's death had incited Saul to persecute the church more vigorously (8:3) and he consequently was converted (9:1-30). Now a third result from Stephen's martyrdom was the spreading of the gospel to Gentile lands (**Phoenicia, Cyprus, and Antioch**).

11:20. The reference to **Antioch** in Syria prepares the reader for the importance of this city in the subsequent narrative. This city, one of many bearing the same name, was the third largest in the Roman Empire behind Rome and Alexandria. Located on the Orontes River 15 miles inland, it was known as Antioch on the Orontes. Beautifully situated and carefully planned, it was a commercial center and the home of a large Jewish community. In spite of the fact that it was a vile city, with gross immorality and ritual prostitution as part of its temple worship, the church at Antioch was destined to become the base of operations for Paul's missionary journeys. The Roman satirist, Juvenal, complained, "The sewage of the Syrian Orontes has for long been discharged into the Tiber." By this he meant that Antioch was so corrupt it was impacting Rome, more than 1,300 miles away.

This amazing step forward for the gospel to the Gentiles (**Greeks** at Antioch) was accomplished by unnamed helpers of the faith. Nevertheless this was a bold and critical move by these believers from **Cyprus,** the island not too far from Antioch, **and Cyrene,** a city in North Africa (cf. Matt. 27:32; Acts 2:10; 6:9; 13:1).

11:21. The clause **believed and turned to the Lord** does not necessarily refer to two separate actions. The Greek construction (an aorist participle with an aorist finite verb) often indicates that the two actions are simultaneous. This clause, then, means, "in believing, they turned to the Lord."

b. The confirmation of the church (11:22-26)

11:22. Such an important move on the part of **the church** could not escape the attention of the mother church in **Jerusalem.** Earlier the Jerusalem apostles sent Peter and John to check up on Philip's ministry in Samaria. Now the Jerusalem saints **sent Barnabas** all the way **to Antioch,** over 300 miles north. The selection of that delegate was of crucial importance; and Barnabas was a wise choice for several reasons. First, he, like some of these Christian ambassadors, was from Cyprus (4:36; 11:20). Second, he

was a generous man (4:37) and therefore thoughtful of others. Third, he was a gracious gentleman as attested by his nickname (4:36) and Luke's testimony about him (11:24).

11:23. Barnabas could not escape the conclusion that **God** was genuinely at work in Antioch, and as Luke often noted there was the response of joy. True to his nickname, Son of Encouragement (4:36), he **encouraged** the believers (cf. 14:22). (Barnabas is also mentioned in 9:27; 11:25, 30; 12:25; 13:1-2, 7, 43, 46, 50; 14:3, 12, 14, 20; 15:2, 12, 22, 25, 35-37, 39; 1 Cor. 9:6; Gal. 2:1, 9, 13; Col. 4:10.)

11:24. Three things were said about Barnabas: **he was a good man,** he was **full of the Holy Spirit, and** he was full of **faith** (Stephen too was full of faith and the Holy Spirit; 6:5). Luke wrote this description of Barnabas *after* the confrontation between Paul and Barnabas, recorded in 15:39. Since Luke was Paul's traveling companion, this statement about Barnabas must have been Paul's assessment as well.

11:25. The work in Antioch grew to such proportions **Barnabas** needed aid, and he could think of no one better suited for the work than **Saul** who was living in **Tarsus** (cf. 9:30). Possibly some of the sufferings and persecutions Paul described in 2 Corinthians 11:23-27 took place while he was in Tarsus. This may also be where Paul had the revelation described in 2 Corinthians 12:1-4. Based on Acts 22:17-21, some think that Saul was already ministering to Gentiles when Barnabas contacted him to bring him to Antioch.

11:26. Barnabas and Saul ministered a full year in Antioch, teaching great numbers of people. The church was continuing to grow numerically (cf. 2:41, 47; 4:4; 5:14; 6:1; 9:31; 11:21, 24).

Jesus' disciples were first called Christians at Antioch. The ending "-ian" means "belonging to the party of"; thus "Christians" were those of Jesus' party. The word "Christians" is used only two other times in the New Testament: in 26:28 and 1 Peter 4:16. The significance of the name, emphasized by the word order in the Greek text, is that people recognized Christians as a distinct group. The church was more and more being separated from Judaism.

c. The charity of the church (11:27-30)

11:27. Believers from Jerusalem with the gift of prophecy **came down from Jerusalem to Antioch.** (Though going north, they went "down" because Jerusalem is on a much higher elevation than Antioch.)

11:28. Agabus, also mentioned again in 21:10-11, prophesied **that a severe famine would spread over the entire Roman world.** This was actually a series of severe famines that struck various sections of the Roman Empire **during the reign of** Emperor **Claudius** (A.D. 41–54.) This same Claudius later expelled Jews from Rome (18:2). (See the list of Roman emperors at Luke 2:1.)

11:29-30. The Christians at Antioch, **each according to his ability** (cf. 1 Cor. 16:2; 2 Cor. 9:7), sent money to the believers **in Judea.** This expression of love undoubtedly bound the two churches together (cf. Rom. 15:27).

When **Barnabas and Saul** brought the gift to Judea, they gave the **gift to the elders.** This is the first mention of church elders in Acts and significantly they received finances. Evidently they had ultimate oversight over all aspects of the ministry. Later Paul and his companions presented the offering of the churches of Achaia, Macedonia, and Asia Minor to the elders of the Jerusalem church. This may have happened when Paul arrived in Jerusalem (Acts 21:18; though this verse doesn't refer to offering money).

Though there is some question about it, this famine visit in 11:27-30 is probably the same one referred to in Galatians 2:1-10.

4. THE PERSECUTION OF THE CHURCH AT JERUSALEM (12:1-24)

The purpose of this section of Acts is to confirm Israel's rejection of the Messiah. Luke has skillfully woven this theme throughout the entire book and it can be seen up to this point in 4:1-30 (esp. 4:29); 5:17-40; 6:11–8:3; 9:1-2, 29. This animosity of Israel set the stage for the first missionary journey.

a. The martyrdom of James (12:1-2)

12:1-2. Artfully, Luke contrasted the love of the church at Antioch for the saints at Jerusalem with the coldhearted enmity of **Herod** and the Jews for **the church.**

The Herod mentioned here is Agrippa I, a ruler popular with the Jews for he was partly Jewish, being of Hasmonean descent. His kingdom covered basically the same area as that of his grandfather Herod the Great. He was known for doing everything possible to curry the favor of the Jews, so he found it politically expedient to arrest Christians and to execute **James, the brother of John.** Herod Agrippa I died in A.D. 44. His son, Herod Agrippa II, was king of Judea from A.D. 50–70. Paul was on trial before Agrippa II and his sister Bernice (25:13–26:32). (See the chart on the Herods at Luke 1:5.)

b. The imprisonment and escape of Peter (12:3-19)

This incident clearly indicates that the church was an identifiable group which had become hated and despised by the Jews.

12:3-4. The execution of James **pleased the Jews** so Herod apprehended and incarcerated **Peter . . . during the Feast of Unleavened Bread.** This seven-day spring feast followed immediately after the Passover. **Herod intended to bring** out Peter **for public trial after the Passover.** The "Passover" here referred to the combined eight-day festival, the Passover itself followed by the seven days of unleavened bread. For at least two reasons Herod would find it expedient to execute Peter. First, Peter was known as the leader of the church, and second, he had fraternized with Gentiles.

Herod made certain that Peter's imprisonment was secure by **handing him over to be guarded by four squads of four soldiers each!** Probably this means two were chained to Peter, one on each side and two were standing guard outside (cf. vv. 6, 10). The four squads probably were each on guard for six hours each. Evidently the authorities remembered Peter's earlier escape (cf. 5:19-24) and Herod did not want that to happen again.

12:5. So Peter was kept in prison, but the church was earnestly praying to God for him. The contrast is obvious: Peter was bound, but prayer was loosed!

12:6. Peter was so trusting the Lord that he was sound asleep the **night before** his **trial** (cf. 1 Peter 2:23; 5:7). He did not fear for his life because Christ had said he would live to an old age (John 21:18).

12:7-10. This is the second time **an angel** helped Peter escape (cf. 5:17-20). Awakening **Peter**, the angel told him to get dressed **and follow** him **out of the prison.** Supernaturally God caused **the chains** to fall **off** his **wrists,** kept the guards asleep, and opened **the iron gate.**

12:11. One of the subthemes of Acts is the outreach of the gospel in spite of opposition. This is seen in Peter's release. When **Peter came to himself,** braced by the night air, he acknowledged God's deliverance for him **from** Herod and the Jews. He now knew this was no vision (v. 9).

12:12. This verse introduces the reader to John **Mark** who figures prominently in Paul's first missionary journey. Evidently his mother **Mary** was a woman of prominence and means. Probably her house was a principal meeting place of the church, so it must have been spacious. Because John Mark's father is not named, Mary may have been a widow. This same Mark is considered to be the writer of the Gospel bearing his name (cf. Mark 14:51-52; 1 Peter 5:13).

12:13-17. The story of Peter's unsuspected arrival at John Mark's home is filled with humor and human interest. Joy in the Book of Acts is also evident here in the **servant girl . . . Rhoda** who answered Peter's knock and **recognized** his **voice.** Though the saints were praying earnestly (v. 5) for Peter's release, they did not expect an answer so soon! When Rhoda insisted, **Peter is at the door!** they replied, **You're out of your mind. It must be his angel.** This statement implies a belief in personal angels, that is, angels who are assigned to individuals (cf. Dan. 10:21; Matt. 18:10). It also suggests a belief that an angel may look like the person with whom he is identified!

When they **saw** Peter, **they were astonished** (*exestēsan;* cf. 9:21). Peter's mention of **James** indicates that James had a place of prominence in the Jerusalem church. Quite clearly this James was the Lord's half brother.

After making himself known to the brothers, Peter **left for another place.** Where this was is not known. It is possible, because of 1 Peter 1:1, to say he went to Asia Minor. Later Peter was at Antioch of Syria (Gal. 2:11). Paul referred to Peter's itinerant ministry (1 Cor. 1:12; 9:5).

12:18-19. After an investigation of Peter's escape, **Herod . . . cross-examined the guards and** ruthlessly **ordered** their executions. Herod no doubt justified such harshness by reasoning that guards whose prisoners escape are irresponsible and unreliable. Yet Herod lost 16 guards by his actions (cf. v. 4). **Herod** then left **Judea** to stay for **a while** in **Caesarea,** the capital of the Roman province of Judea, from which Roman governors governed the nation.

c. The death of Herod Agrippa I (12:20-23)

12:20-23. Tyre and Sidon were in Herod's dominion and for some reason had incurred his wrath. Because these cities **depended on** Galilee for grain, they desired to make **peace** with Herod Agrippa. Probably they bribed **Blastus, a trusted personal servant of the king,** to work out a reconciliation. **On the appointed day** when **Herod** was delivering a speech, **the people** honored him as **a god,** and the Lord **God** judged him with death. This was in A.D. 44. This account parallels that given by Josephus in his *Antiquities of the Jews* (19. 8. 2). After Herod's death, Felix and Festus, successively, were the governors of Judea.

Three of Herod's children figure prominently in the later narrative of Acts—Drusilla, the wife of Felix (24:24-26); Bernice (25:13, 23), and Herod Agrippa II (25:13–26:32).

d. The prosperity of the church (12:24)

12:24. But the Word of God continued to increase and spread (cf. similar wording in 6:7; 13:49; 19:20). In spite of opposition and persecution the Lord sovereignly prospered the work of His church. With this progress report Luke brought another section of his work to a conclusion (cf. 2:47; 6:7; 9:31; 12:24; 16:5; 19:20; 28:30-31). From Antioch the gospel message was now ready to go to Asia Minor.

PAUL'S FIRST MISSIONARY JOURNEY

MILES

0   100   200   300

B. The extension of the church in Asia Minor (12:25–16:5)

1. THE CALL AND DEDICATION OF BARNABAS AND SAUL (12:25–13:3)

12:25. After depositing the famine relief money with the elders at **Jerusalem** (11:27-30), **Barnabas and Saul** returned to Antioch. They took **with them John . . . Mark** (cf. 13:5), a cousin of Barnabas (Col. 4:10) from Jerusalem (Acts 12:12).

[First missionary journey, chaps. 13–14]

13:1. The church at Antioch now became the base of operation for Saul's ministry. Jerusalem was still the mother church, but the missionary church was Antioch on the Orontes River. Furthermore, Peter was no longer the central figure; Saul became that.

The diversity in the backgrounds of the leaders of the church at Antioch shows the cosmopolitan nature of the church. **Barnabas** was a Jew from Cyprus (4:36). **Simeon** was also a Jew, but his Latin nickname **Niger** not only indicates he was of dark complexion but also that he moved in Roman circles. He could be the Simon of Cyrene who carried Christ's cross (Matt. 27:32; Mark 15:21), but this is highly debatable. **Lucius** was from **Cyrene** in North Africa (cf. Acts 11:20). **Manaen** had high contacts for he **had been** reared **with Herod the tetrarch,** actually Herod Antipas, who beheaded John the Baptist and who treated the Lord so shamefully at His trial (see the chart on the Herod family at Luke 1:5). One in that court (Manaen) became a disciple; the other (Herod) an antagonist! At the end of the list, for he was last on this scene, was **Saul,** a Jew trained in Rabbinical schools. Despite their variegated backgrounds, these men functioned as one.

Perhaps the name of Barnabas appears first in the list because as the delegate from the mother church in Jerusalem he held the priority position.

13:2. Evidently God made His will known by means of the "prophets" in the church (cf. v. 1). Frequently in Acts **the Holy Spirit** gave directives to God's leaders (e.g., 8:29; 10:19; 13:4). Here He directed the five, **while they were worshiping . . . and fasting,** to **set apart for Him Barnabas and Saul.** Once again the principle of two men working together is underscored. The verb "set apart" (*aphorizō*) is used of three separations in Saul's life—at his birth he was separated to God (Gal. 1:15); at his conversion he was set apart for the gospel (Rom. 1:1); and in Antioch he was separated for a specific service (Acts 13:2).

13:3. The church leaders **placed their hands on** Barnabas and Saul **and sent them off.** The laying on of hands identified the church with their ministry and acknowledged God's direction for them (cf. Ananias' identifying himself with Saul by laying hands on him, 9:17). Two of the choicest were sent on this significant mission.

2. THE CIRCUIT IN ASIA MINOR (13:4–14:28)

a. At Cyprus (13:4-12)

13:4. Directed **by the Holy Spirit** (cf. v. 2) they first **went down to Seleucia,** a seaport 16 miles from Antioch, **and sailed from there to Cyprus.** This island, known in the Old Testament as Kittim (Gen. 10:4), was the homeland of Barnabas (Acts 4:36). This implies Barnabas was the leader of the party (cf. the order of names in 13:2, 7).

13:5. Salamis was the largest city in the eastern half of Cyprus. Evidently a large number of Jews resided there, for Barnabas and Saul **proclaimed** God's **Word . . . in the . . . synagogues,** not "a" synagogue.

There was wisdom in going to these religious centers: (1) It gave priority in that generation to the Jews receiving the gospel first (cf. Rom. 1:16; Acts 13:46; 17:2; 18:4, 19; 19:8). (2) Gentiles in the synagogues would be a fruitful field for sowing the gospel because they would already be acquainted with the Old Testament and its anticipation of the Messiah.

John Mark, a cousin of Barnabas (Col. 4:10), **was with them as their helper** (cf. Acts 12:25). What is meant by the term "helper" (*hypēretēn*) is debated. Probably he instructed new converts, assisted in baptisms (cf. 1 Cor. 1:14-17), and helped in any way he could.

13:6. The results of the ministry in Salamis are unstated. **Paphos,** 100 miles southwest of Salamis and the seat of the provincial government, was their next point of ministry. What took place here is of great significance in the progression of the gospel to Gentiles.

At Paphos, Barnabas and Saul **met a Jewish sorcerer and false prophet named Bar-Jesus.** The word "sorcerer" (*magos*) could describe a counselor or honorable gentleman (e.g., the "Magi" in Matt. 2:1, 7, 16) or it could refer to a fraudulent wizard, as here. It is related to the verb "practice sorcery" (*mageuō*) used of Simon (Acts 8:9).

13:7. It so happened that Bar-Jesus **was an attendant of the proconsul, Sergius Paulus.** This sorcerer was greatly threatened by the **intelligent** proconsul's interest in the gospel. Proconsuls were governors appointed by the Roman senate; procurators, on the other hand, were appointed by the emperor. Three Judea procurators are mentioned in the New Testament: Pontius Pilate (A.D. 26–36), Antonius Felix (A.D. 52–59?), and Porcius Festus (A.D. 59–62).

13:8. The sorcerer . . . tried to turn the proconsul from the faith.

The name **Elymas** is something of a problem. Probably it is a Semitic word meaning "sorcerer," which was given or taken by him as a nickname.

13:9. At this juncture **Saul,** now for the first time **called Paul,** stepped to the fore and assumed leadership. He probably was more aggressive and also knew Gentile minds better than Barnabas. From this point on Paul was the leader and his name preceded Barnabas' name except when they were in Jerusalem (15:12, 25) and in 14:14.

Furthermore, the Roman name Paul was used from here on; the Jewish name Saul was used only when he in his personal testimonies referred to his former life (22:7; 26:14).

13:10. In Aramaic, Bar-Jesus means "Son of Jesus." But Paul told him that instead of being a son of Jesus ("Jesus" means "Yahweh is salvation"), Elymas was **a child** (*huie,* lit., "son") **of the devil.** Paul lashed at him with strong language: Bar-Jesus was **an enemy of everything that is right** (lit., "righteousness"), he was **full of . . . deceit** (*dolou*) **and trickery** (*rhadiourgias,* "unscrupulous mischief, work that easily deceives," used only here in the NT) and **perverting the right ways of the Lord.** Sorcery, exercising power by the help and control of demons, had led

him into all kinds of deception of others and distortion of the truth. The occult is indeed dangerous.

This is the second of four incidents of conflict with and victory over demonic powers in the Book of Acts (cf. 8:9-23; 16:16-18; 19:13-17).

13:11-12. In judgment Paul inflicted a temporary blindness on Elymas. This is the first of Paul's recorded miracles and it was performed in conflict with a Jew over giving the gospel to a Gentile.

Seeing this miracle, Sergius Paulus' interest in the Word of God (v. 7) blossomed into genuine faith in Christ. Interestingly the Greek names of this **proconsul** and of the apostle were the same: Paulus.

This incident is significant for three reasons: (1) It marks the beginning of Paul's leadership in this journey; verse 13 refers to "Paul and his companions." (2) From this point on the ministry took on an even more decidedly Gentile slant. (3) It is filled with figurative nuances. A Gentile with the name Paul accepted the message while a Jew opposed it. The Jews' blindness pictured the judicial blinding of Israel (cf. 28:26-27). Luke by this means emphasized the transitional nature of the Book of Acts. On one hand Gentiles became the primary object of the gospel, and on the other God temporarily turned from the Jews and thus judged them.

b. At Pisidian Antioch (13:13-52)

(1) The defection of John Mark. **13:13.** Barnabas' greatness is displayed by his willingness to let Paul be the leader. So **Paul and his companions sailed to Perga in Pamphylia.** But **John** (i.e., John Mark) **left them** and returned **to Jerusalem.** What caused Mark to desert is open to speculation: (1) Perhaps he was disillusioned with the change in leadership. After all, Barnabas, the original leader, was John Mark's cousin. (2) The new emphasis on Gentiles may have been too much of an adjustment for a Palestinian Jew like Mark. (3) Possibly he was afraid of the dangerous road over the Taurus Mountains to Antioch which Paul was determined to travel. (4) There is some evidence Paul became quite ill in Perga, possibly with malaria, as the city of Perga was subject to malarial infections.

Furthermore, Paul preached to the people of Galatia "because of an illness" (Gal. 4:13). The missionary party may have gone inland to higher ground to avoid the ravages of malaria and Mark in discouragement over this may have returned home. (5) Some think Mark was homesick. His mother may have been a widow (Acts 12:12); perhaps Mark became lonesome for her and home. Whatever the reason, Paul considered it a defection and a fault (cf. 15:38).

(2) The discourse on the first Sabbath (13:14-41). **13:14.** This Antioch was actually in Phrygia but was known as **Pisidian Antioch** because it was so near Pisidia. Like other cities—such as Lystra, Troas, Philippi, and Corinth—Antioch was a Roman colony. Paul visited these cities because they were located at strategic points.

13:15. The first opportunity for Paul and Barnabas to preach came in **the synagogue.** In the Sabbath service it was customary to read two portions of the Old Testament—one **from the Law** (the Pentateuch) **and** one from **the Prophets.** "The Law and the Prophets" means the entire Old Testament (cf. Matt. 5:17; 7:12; 11:13; 22:40; Luke 16:16; Acts 24:14; 28:23; Rom. 3:21). Evidently Paul and Barnabas had made themselves known to the **rulers** of the synagogue before the meeting. After the Scripture reading they were invited to share **a message of encouragement for the people.**

13:16-25. Paul seized the opportunity to present the fulfillments of Old Testament expectations of the Messiah in Jesus. Luke recorded a number of "sample sermons" of Paul in Acts (cf. 14:15-17; 17:22-31; 20:18-35). This, the first recorded discourse of Paul and the most completely preserved, illustrated how Paul preached to an audience grounded in the Old Testament.

The message may be divided into three parts by the three occurrences of direct address (13:16, 26, 38) and outlined as follows: (1) the anticipation of and preparation for **the coming of** the Messiah (vv. 16-25), (2) the rejection, crucifixion, and resurrection of the Lord Jesus (vv. 26-37), and (3) the application and appeal (vv. 38-41).

The apostle began with the vocatives, **Men of Israel and you Gentiles who worship God** (v. 16). This address embraced both Jews and Gentiles. Probably the Gentiles were not full-fledged converts to Judaism. And yet, though they revered the Yahweh of Israel (cf. vv. 26, 43), they did not have New Testament salvation. (The phrase trans. "devout converts to Judaism" in v. 43 should be trans. "worshipers." It refers to pagan worshipers but not full-fledged proselytes to Judaism. In Acts the phrase is used in almost a technical sense.)

In surveying the history of Israel, Paul mentioned the key events and people: the **stay in Egypt** (v. 17), the Exodus (v. 17), the **40**-year wilderness sojourn (v. 18), the Conquest and possession of Palestine (v. 19; the **seven nations in Canaan** which God **overthrew** are

PAUL'S EPISTLES, WRITTEN ON HIS JOURNEYS AND DURING HIS IMPRISONMENTS

Epistle	Number of Epistles	Journeys and Imprisonments
GALATIANS	1	After his first missionary journey
1 THESSALONIANS	2	On his second missionary journey
2 THESSALONIANS		
1 CORINTHIANS	3	On his third missionary journey
2 CORINTHIANS		
ROMANS		
EPHESIANS	4	During his first imprisonment
PHILIPPIANS		
COLOSSIANS		
PHILEMON		
1 TIMOTHY	3	Before and during his second
TITUS		imprisonment
2 TIMOTHY		

listed in Deut. 7:1), the period of the **Judges** (Acts 13:20), and the monarchy under **Saul** and **David** (vv. 21–22). Mention of **David** made an easy transition to refer to **the Savior Jesus** (v. 23) and to His harbinger **John** the Baptist (vv. 24-25). (Cf. Stephen's message in 7:2-47.) The **450 years** (13:20) includes the oppression in Egypt (400 years), the wilderness sojourn (40 years), and the Conquest of Canaan under Joshua (10 years).

13:26-37. Paul, like Peter (2:23, 36; 3:15; 4:10; 5:30; 10:39) and Stephen (7:52), directly blamed the Jews for killing **Jesus.** His resurrection, frequently spoken of by His followers in Acts, was witnessed **for many days.** This is the fifth time in Acts that the apostles stated that they were **witnesses** of the resurrection of Jesus Christ (2:32; 3:15; 5:32; 10:39-41; 13:30-31).

Do the words **by raising up Jesus** (v. 33) refer to His resurrection or to His exaltation? It probably refers to the latter for several reasons: (1) When the Resurrection is mentioned in the next verse it is explained as being **from the dead.** (2) The same verb "raise up" (*anistēmi*) is used in the sense of elevation in 3:22, 26; 7:37 ("send," NIV). (3) A synonym (*egeirō*) is used in 13:22 to refer to David's promotion to kingship. (4) The primary reason for taking it to refer to Jesus' exaltation is the meaning of **Psalm** 2:7. This Old Testament passage, quoted by Paul (Acts 13:33), described the anointing of the King, which will find its ultimate fulfillment in the Millennium.

Paul confirmed the fact of Jesus' resurrection from the dead by quoting from Isaiah 55:3 and Psalm 16:10 (Acts 13:34-35). Earlier Peter had argued similarly from Psalm 16:10 (see comments on Acts 2:25-32).

13:38-39. Forgiveness of sins was mentioned frequently by the apostles in Acts (cf. 2:38; 5:31; 26:18). Acts 13:39 gives the thesis of Paul's Epistle to the Galatians, which was probably written shortly after his first missionary journey and before the Jerusalem Council (Acts 15). (See the chart "Paul's Epistles, Written on His Journeys and during His Imprisonments.")

13:40-41. Habakkuk 1:5, quoted in Acts 13:41, is an appropriate warning against impending judgment. Judah, the prophet had said, would fall to Babylon (Hab. 1:6), which would be God's doings. Here Paul left unnamed the source of the judgment on the unbelieving Jews in his day. Paul's warning: believe or be judged.

(3) The disputation on the second Sabbath (13:42-52). **13:42-43.** The leaders were interested in Paul's message and desired to hear more. Some were disposed to accept the gospel; **Paul and Barnabas . . . urged them to continue in the grace of God.**

13:44-45. On the next Sabbath . . . the Jews (i.e., Jewish leaders), moved by **jealousy . . . talked abusively against what Paul was saying** ("abusively" renders the Gr. participle *blasphēmountes*).

13:46. To combat this Jewish opposition **Paul and Barnabas answered them boldly, We had to speak the Word of God to you first.** Apostolic preaching was noted for its boldness (cf. comments on 4:13).

It was necessary that the apostles go to the Jews first for a number of reasons. First, the coming of the earthly kingdom depended on Israel's response to the coming of Christ (cf. Matt. 23:39; Rom. 11:26). Second, only after Israel rejected the gospel could Paul devote himself to the Gentiles. Third, the message of Jesus is fundamentally Jewish in that the Old Testament, the Messiah, and the promises are all Jewish. (On "the Jew first," cf. Acts 3:26; Rom. 1:16.)

So Paul turned **to the Gentiles** in Antioch. This pattern was repeated in city after city until Paul reached Rome (cf. Acts 13:50-51; 14:2-6; 17:5, 13-15; 18:6; 19:8-9). There for the final time in the book the Apostle Paul turned from Jews to Gentiles (28:23-28).

13:47. In thus turning to the Gentiles Paul and Barnabas saw an outworking of the prophecy of Isaiah 49:6, **I have made you a light to the Gentiles.** This Old Testament passage has at least three applications—to Israel (Isa. 49:3), to Christ (Luke 2:29-32), and to Paul, the apostle to the Gentiles.

13:48. The Gentiles rejoiced in this turn of events **and all who were appointed for eternal life believed.** It is difficult to miss the doctrine of God's election here; the words "were appointed" come from the verb *tassō*, a military word meaning "to arrange" or "to assign." Luke used it here to show that God's elective decree included Gentiles.

13:49-51. The good news was shared so that **the Word of the Lord spread through the whole region** (cf. 6:7; 12:24; 19:20). But **the Jews** had contacts in high places and used these to stir **up persecution against Paul and Barnabas,** who in conformity with the Lord's instruction (Matt. 10:14) **shook the dust from their feet in protest** and left the city.

13:52. Joy was again a fruit of the gospel (cf. v. 48; 2:46). In addition they **were filled . . . with the Holy Spirit** (cf. 2:4).

c. At Iconium (14:1-6)

14:1-2. This paragraph (vv. 1-6) confirms the events which occurred in Pisidian Antioch. The Spirit of God was clearly prospering the apostles' ministry, as evidenced by their preaching **so effectively that a great number of Jews and Gentiles believed.** But again there was opposition (cf. growth and opposition in 13:49-50). The result of that opposition is seen in 14:6.

14:3. The NIV renders the connective *oun* (normally trans. "therefore") with the word **So.** This conjunction is a bit of a problem. It may suggest that the time in which the opposition arose (v. 2) provided further opportunity for preaching. Or it may indicate that the opposition was an evidence of God's working in the hearts of the people (cf. 1 Cor. 16:8-9), thus leading to further preaching. Probably the latter is to be preferred.

Again apostolic boldness is evident (cf. Acts 4:13; 13:46).

The reference to **miraculous signs and wonders** was further confirmation of God's endorsement of this ministry (cf. 2:43; 4:30; 5:12; 6:8; 8:6, 13; 15:12). Later Paul referred to these miracles to validate the reality of the gospel among the Galatians (Gal. 3:5). This, of course, assumes the South Galatian view of the term "Galatia" in that epistle. (See the *Introduction* to Gal. for a discussion of the South and North Galatian views.) On the confirming nature of miracles, see comments on 2 Corinthians 12:12 and Hebrews 2:3-4.

14:4. The apostolic band was referred to as **apostles.** And so they were,

for the word means "those sent with authority as representatives of another," and these men had been sent out by the church of Antioch on the Orontes River (13:3) with the church's authority.

14:5-6. When Paul and Barnabas learned of **a plot . . . to mistreat . . . and stone them,** they **fled to . . . Lystra and Derbe,** cities of Lycaonia. Luke's accuracy as a historian has been vindicated here. Though Iconium was also a **Lycaonian** city its citizens were primarily Phrygian. In location and nature Lystra and Derbe were Lycaonian (cf. "Lycaonian language," v. 11).

d. At Lystra (14:7-20a)

(1) The superstition of the Gentiles (14:7-18). **14:7.** Paul and Barnabas did not go to Lystra and Derbe simply to escape persecution; they also went to preach the gospel. The verbal construction **they continued to preach the good news** emphasizes continuity of action over a period of time.

14:8. Lystra, a Roman colony, was the home of at least one hopeless cripple. The dire circumstances of this man are seen in the repeated idea: **crippled in his feet . . . lame from birth . . . had never walked.** Apparently there was no Jewish synagogue in Lystra, so God used a different thrust, the healing of this helpless cripple, to bring the gospel to these people. This is the third time in Acts a cripple was healed (3:1-10; 9:33-35).

14:9-10. Paul's healing of this infirm man closely parallels Peter's healing in chapter 3. In each case the cripple was lame from birth (3:2; 14:8); both Peter and **Paul** gazed at the one **to be healed** (3:4; 14:9); and both healed men responded by jumping and walking (3:8; 14:10). This shows Paul was equal to Peter in his apostleship (cf. *Introduction*).

14:11-13. The response of the **Lycaonian** folk was one of pagan credulity. Because the people spoke in their native **language,** Paul and Barnabas could not understand what they were saying. Attributing deity to **Barnabas** and **Paul** probably can be traced to a legend about **Zeus** and **Hermes** visiting an aged Lystrian couple named Philemon and Baucis, who were abundantly rewarded for their hospitality.

Zeus was the chief god and Hermes the messenger equivalent to the Roman gods Jupiter and Mercury, respectively. Why then would Barnabas be referred to as Zeus when Paul was the leader? The answer is that Paul was the spokesman and would therefore be called Hermes and Barnabas, the more retiring of the two, would be seen as Zeus, the dignified, behind-the-scenes god.

In one spontaneous movement **the priest of Zeus . . . brought bulls and wreaths to the city gates** so the people could **offer sacrifices** to Paul and Barnabas. The wreaths were woolen garlands placed on the sacrificial animals.

14:14. When **the** two **apostles** discerned what was happening, they were horrified. **Their** tearing of **clothes** was a way of showing strong aversion to blasphemy. Usually rips were made four or five inches into the neckline of the garment.

14:15-18. This message, evidently preached by both apostles (pl. verb in the Gr.) is another sample sermon. It illustrates how these early preachers approached superstitious heathen. By contrast, the first of Paul's messages demonstrated how he preached to those well acquainted with the Old Testament (cf. 13:16-41).

After disclaiming their own deity, they urged their hearers **to turn from** their cultic gods **to the** one true and **living God.** This God, Creator of all, is therefore supreme over all (cf. 17:24; Rom. 1:19-20). He is recognizable not only from His creating **rain** and **crops** but also by His beneficial providence in giving **food** and **joy.**

Some interpret Acts 14:16 to mean that God will not judge the heathen who lived before the Apostolic Age. However, verse 16 must be taken with verse 17. Up to the time of the church, God gave no direct revelation to the **nations** (i.e., Gentiles) so they were responsible only for their reactions to the general revelation discernible in Creation (cf. comments on 17:27, 30 and Rom. 1:18-20).

(2) The stoning of Paul. **14:19-20a.** Once again some **Jews** proved to be enemies of the gospel of grace, and turned **the crowd,** which had just tried to make Paul and Barnabas gods, against them so **they stoned Paul.** This is the

second of five times a crowd was incited because of Paul's ministry (cf. 13:50; 16:19-22; 17:5-8, 13; 19:25-34). Whether or not Paul was **dead** is not stated; probably he was unconscious and at death's door (cf. 2 Cor. 12:2-4). At any rate his recovery was so rapid as to be miraculous. The reference to Paul's stoning (2 Cor. 11:25) undoubtedly had this incident in view (cf. 2 Tim. 3:11).

e. At Derbe (14:20b-21a)

14:20b-21a. The apostles' ministry here, in the most remote and easterly of the cities reached in Asia Minor on this journey, was successful. The gospel met no great opposition and **a large number of disciples** were **won** over to the Lord Jesus (cf. 20:4).

f. The return to Antioch of Syria (14:21b-28)

14:21b-22. Tarsus, Paul's hometown, was only about 160 miles farther on from Derbe, but the two apostles retraced their steps in Asia Minor in order to confirm the churches so recently established.

By warning and by promise, Paul and Barnabas strengthened (cf. 15:32, 41) and encouraged the believers. Previously Barnabas had encouraged the believers in Antioch of Syria (11:23). The warning consisted of a prediction of many **hardships** and the promise was the anticipation of entering the **kingdom of God.** The latter term certainly describes the eschatological reign of Christ on earth.

14:23. The believers were given not only edification but also organization. **Paul and Barnabas appointed elders for them in each church.** These elders were not novices in the faith (1 Tim. 3:6); they were probably Jews who came out of the synagogues where they had been steeped in the Scriptures. Thus elders from the synagogues became elders in the churches.

14:24-28. When the apostles returned **to Antioch** (retracing their steps through the provinces of **Pisidia** and **Pamphylia** and preaching **in Perga;** cf. 13:13-14), they gave to **the** sending church a full report of **all that God had done.** The clause, **how He had opened the door of faith to the Gentiles,** is most important: (a) It shows the gospel had gone to Gentiles. (b) It was a "by-faith" message and not by works of the Law. (c) God did it, for He opened the door.

Thus ends the first missionary journey which lasted between one and two years and in which Paul and Barnabas traversed more than 700 miles by land and 500 miles by sea. But more than that, it demolished the wall between Jews and Gentiles (cf. Eph. 2:14-16). The two apostles had been committed by the church at Antioch to God's grace (cf. Acts 15:40) and they saw His grace at work (cf. "grace" in 13:43; 14:3).

Probably Paul wrote the Book of Galatians from Antioch shortly after his first missionary journey and before the Jerusalem Council (Acts 15).

3. THE CONFERENCE AT JERUSALEM (15:1-35)

a. The dissension concerning circumcision (15:1-2)

15:1-2. The men who came down from Judea to Antioch may well be the same ones referred to in Galatians 2:12. They insisted circumcision was essential for justification. Perhaps they based their theology on such passages as Genesis 17:14 and Exodus 12:48-49.

At any rate, they were sure to cause a severe schism in the church, so their teaching brought Paul and Barnabas into sharp dispute and debate with them.

The men from Judea were dogmatic in their doctrine in spite of the fact they had no authority from the church in Jerusalem. How they explained the case of Cornelius (Acts 10) or the work of Barnabas (11:22-24) is left unstated. Perhaps they felt Cornelius' case was unique and the believers in Antioch in chapter 11 were too insignificant to use as examples. Now the movement was becoming overwhelming and this was their way of protesting.

The church at Antioch felt it was wise to discuss the matter with the apostles and elders in Jerusalem. So they commissioned Paul and Barnabas for the task and wisely sent some other believers along as witnesses. These witnesses would protect Paul and Barnabas against being accused of distorting the facts.

b. The discussion concerning circumcision (15:3-12)

15:3-4. As the men in the delegation made their way to Jerusalem they reported the good news of Gentile conversions to the brethren in Phoenicia and Samaria. Once again the response of a believing church was joy! (cf. 2:46) Furthermore, the church in Jerusalem with its leaders welcomed Paul and Barnabas; this was scarcely the response of the antagonists.

15:5. The issue was stated forthrightly by the believing Pharisees. Significantly circumcision also involved keeping the whole Old Testament Law as Paul later wrote (Gal. 5:3). The method of justification ultimately determines the method of sanctification (cf. Col. 2:6).

15:6-9. The apostles and elders met to consider this question. In addition many other believers were present (cf. vv. 12, 22).

The problem was no small one; there was much discussion (zēteseōs, meaning "inquiry, debate, questioning"; trans. "debate" in v. 2; "controversies" in 1 Tim. 6:4; "arguments" in 2 Tim. 2:23 and Titus 3:9). Peter wisely permitted this to continue for a time lest the impression be given that the results were a foregone conclusion. The date of this council is generally taken to be A.D. 49. When Peter referred to God's choice of Cornelius some time ago he was looking back about 10 years (Acts 10:1–11:18). The issue of whether to accept Gentiles was settled then and there. This was evidenced, Peter said, because God gave the Holy Spirit to them (10:44-46) just as He did to the Jews (2:4; 11:15). So God made no distinction between believing Jews and Gentiles. All are accepted by faith.

15:10. Requiring Gentiles to be circumcised to obey the Mosaic Law would have had two results: (a) the Jews would test (peirazete) God (cf. Deut. 6:16) and (b) they would put on the necks of the disciples an unbearable yoke (cf. Matt. 23:4). To "test" God is to see how far one can go with God (cf. Acts 5:9). Putting a yoke on the disciples' necks was an appropriate way to state the second result, for "taking the yoke" was used to describe Gentile proselytes coming into Judaism. It spoke of an obligation.

In discussing the question Peter referred not only to Gentiles but also to all believers coming under the Law. The term "disciples" was used of both Jews and Gentiles.

15:11. The statement, **We are saved, just as they are,** is amazing. A Jew under the Law would say the opposite and in reverse order ("they are saved as we are"), but one who knew God's **grace,** as Peter did, would not say that. Salvation for anyone—Jew or Gentile—is by God's grace (v. 11) and is by faith (v. 9; cf. Gal. 2:16; Eph. 2:8).

15:12. Barnabas and Paul, who next addressed the assembly, described **the miraculous signs and wonders** (*sēmeia* and *terata*; cf. 2:43 [see comments there]; 5:12; 6:8; 8:6, 13; 14:3) that **God had done among the Gentiles through them.** These would especially convince the Jews (cf. 1 Cor. 1:22) so **they listened** in silence. This response implied they would not argue against the testimonies of Peter, Paul, and Barnabas.

c. The decision concerning circumcision (15:13-29)

15:13-14. James, evidently the head of the church at Jerusalem, then took the floor and issued a summary statement. He was Jesus' half brother and wrote the Epistle of James.

He began by discussing Peter's experience (Acts 10). In referring to Peter as **Simon,** James used a name which would be logical in its setting in Jerusalem (actually the Gr. has *Symeōn,* an even more Jewish spelling, used only here and in 2 Peter 1:1 in the NT).

The phrase **at first** is crucial because it affirmed that Paul and Barnabas were not the first to go to **the Gentiles.** As Peter had already said (Acts 15:7-11) the question had actually been settled in principle (chaps. 10–11) *before* Paul and Barnabas went on their first journey.

15:15-18. Quite properly the council desired more than the testimony of experience. They wanted to know how it corresponded with the witness of the Scriptures. This was the ultimate test.

To prove that Gentile salvation apart from circumcision was an Old Testament doctrine, James quoted from Amos 9:11-12. Several problems are involved in this quotation.

One problem involves the text. James here quoted a text similar to the Septuagint (the Gr. OT) that differs from the Hebrew text. The Hebrew of Amos 9:12 may be translated, "That they may possess the remnant of Edom and all the nations who are called by My name." But James used the noun **of men** (or "of mankind"), not "Edom," and the verb **seek,** not "possess."

The Hebrew consonants for "Edom" and for "Adam" are identical (*'dm*). The confusion in the vowels (added much later) is easy to understand. The only distinction in the Hebrew between "possess" (*yāraš*) and "seek" (*dāraš*) is in one consonant. The text James used may well represent the original.

Another problem, the major one, involves interpretation. What did Amos mean when he wrote these verses, and how did James use the passage? Several observations need to be noted before the passage is interpreted: (1) James did not say Amos 9:11-12 was *fulfilled* in the church; he simply asserted that what was happening in the church was **in** full **agreement** with the Old Testament **prophets.** (2) The word "prophets" is plural, implying that the quotation from Amos was representative of what the prophets in general affirmed. (3) James' main point is clear: Gentile salvation apart from the Law does not contradict the Old Testament prophets. (4) The words **After this** are neither in the Masoretic text nor the Septuagint; both have "in that day." Any interpretation of the passage must consider these factors.

Bible students interpret these verses in one of three ways. Those who hold to amillennial theology say the rebuilt house (*skēnēn,* "tent") of David is the church which God is using to preach to the Gentiles. While this view at first appears plausible, several factors oppose it. (1) The verb **return** (*anastrepsō*) used in Acts 15:16 means an actual return. Luke used it only in 5:22 ("went back") and here (he did not use it in his Gospel); in both occurrences it describes a literal, bodily return. Since God's Son has not yet returned bodily, this rebuilding has not taken place. (2) Christ's present ministry in heaven is not associated with the Davidic throne elsewhere in the New Testament. He is now seated at the right hand of God (Ps. 110:1; Rom. 8:34; Col. 3:1; Heb. 1:3; 8:1; 10:12; 12:2; 1 Peter 3:22). When He returns He will sit on David's throne (2 Sam. 7:16; Ps. 89:4; Matt. 19:28; 25:31). (3) The church was a mystery, a truth not revealed to Old Testament saints (Rom. 16:25; Eph. 3:5-6;

Col. 1:24-27); so the church would not be referred to in Amos.

A second view of the passage is commonly held by premillenarians. According to this view there are four chronological movements in this passage: the present Church Age ("taking from the Gentiles a people for Himself," Acts 15:14), the return of Christ to Israel (v. 16a), the establishing of the Davidic kingdom (v. 16b), and the turning of Gentiles to God (v. 17). While this does interpret these verses in a logical fashion, this approach has some difficulties. (1) The quotation begins with the words "After this." Premillenarians assert James used this phrase to suit his interpretation of the passage. But since the quotation begins with "after this" James must be quoting the sense of Amos 9:11. Therefore this phrase looks back, not to Acts 15:14, but to Amos 9:8-10, which describes the Tribulation ("a time of trouble for Jacob," Jer. 30:7). (2) If the temporal phrase "after this" refers to the present Age in Amos 9:11, Amos would then have predicted the church in the Old Testament.

A third view, also premillennial, may be more plausible. James simply asserted that Gentiles will be saved in the Millennium when Christ will return **and rebuild David's fallen tent,** that is, restore the nation Israel. Amos said nothing about Gentiles needing to be circumcised. Several factors support this interpretation: (1) This fits the purpose of the council. If Gentiles will be saved in the Kingdom Age (the Millennium), why should they become Jewish proselytes by circumcision in the Church Age? (2) This approach suits the meaning of "in that day" in Amos 9:11. After the Tribulation (Amos 9:8-10) God will establish the messianic kingdom (Amos 9:11-12). James (Acts 15:16) interpreted "in that day" to mean that "at the time when" God does one (the Tribulation) He will then do the other. In that sense James could say "After this." (3) This interpretation gives significance to the word "first" in verse 14. Cornelius and his household were among the first Gentiles to become members of Christ's body, the church. Gentile salvation will culminate in great blessing for them in the Millennium (cf. Rom. 11:12). (4) A number of prophets predicted Gentile salvation in the Millennium, as James stated in Acts 15:15 (e.g., Isa. 42:6; 60:3; Mal. 1:11).

15:19-21. As a result of this theological discussion James set forth a practical decision. It was his considered **judgment** (*krinō,* lit., "I judge") that the church **should not make it difficult** (*parenochlein,* "to annoy"; used only here in the NT) **for the Gentiles.** This parallels in thought the sentiments of Peter expressed in verse 10. **Instead** (*alla,* "but," a strong adversative conjunction) James suggested they draft a letter affirming an ethic which would not offend those steeped in the Old Testament.

The Gentiles were **to abstain from** three items: (a) **food polluted by idols,** (b) **sexual immorality,** and (c) **the meat of strangled animals and . . . blood.** Many Bible teachers say these are only ceremonial matters. The food polluted by idols is explained in verse 29 as "food sacrificed to idols" (cf. 21:25). This then, it is argued, looks at the same problem Paul discussed (1 Cor. 8–10). The abstinence from sexual immorality is explained as referring to the marriage laws of Leviticus 18:6-20. The prohibition against eating blood is taken to refer to Leviticus 17:10-14. All three prohibitions according to this interpretation look back to the Jewish *ceremonial* Law.

However, it seems better to take these as moral issues. The reference to food polluted by idols should be taken in the sense of Revelation 2:14, 20. It was a usual practice among Gentiles to use an idol's temple for banquets and celebrations. Paul also condemned the practice of Christians participating in these (1 Cor. 10:14-22). Fornication was such a common sin among the Gentiles that it was an accepted practice. The problem of immorality even persisted among Christians all too often, as is witnessed by the New Testament injunctions against it (cf. 1 Cor. 6:12-18, where Paul was evidently answering arguments in favor of immorality). The third prohibition goes back further than Leviticus 17; it looks back to Genesis 9, where God established the Noahic Covenant, a "contract" still in effect today. There God gave people the privilege of eating flesh but the blood was to be drained from it.

All three prohibitions in Acts 15:20 are best taken in an ethical or moral sense. If this be so, they are still the responsibility of Christians today, even to the point of not eating blood sausage and raw meat. By not attending temple banquets, or being involved in fornication, or eating meat with blood in it, the Gentile Christians would be maintaining high moral standards and would keep from offending their Jewish brothers. There were Jews in every city who would be offended by Christians not following these strictures. These Israelites were well acquainted with these moral issues.

15:22. The whole church (cf. v. 12) was permitted to express itself on this issue. Interestingly two witnesses were delegated to attend **Paul and Barnabas** for the protection of both sides (v. 2). They would "confirm by word of mouth" what was written (v. 27). No one could claim there were poor communications about this delicate issue.

Silas was one of these **two men.** This is in keeping with Luke's style of bringing someone on the scene unobtrusively who later becomes a main character (cf. v. 40). These two **leaders,** also "prophets" (v. 32), may have represented two groups in the Jerusalem church—**Judas,** probably a brother of Joseph (cf. 1:23), for the Hebrew section; and Silas, a Roman citizen (cf. 16:37), for the Hellenists.

15:23-29. The **letter,** sent by **the apostles and elders,** confirmed the findings of the council. The church's admiration for **Barnabas and Paul** is evidenced by the words **our dear friends** and their acknowledging that Paul and Barnabas had **risked their lives for the name** (cf. comments on 3:16) **of our Lord Jesus Christ** (cf. 13:50; 14:5, 19). Significantly the letter referred **to the Holy Spirit** as the "Prime Mover" in this discernment of truth.

d. The delegation among the Gentiles (15:30-35)

15:30-35. The contingent from Jerusalem together with Judas and Silas **went down to Antioch** (Antioch is on a lower elevation than Jerusalem) **and delivered the letter.** The brothers in Antioch were encouraged by the letter, and also by **Judas and Silas,** the **prophets,** who encouraged the church still further and strengthened them by a lengthy message.

The saints in Antioch appreciated the ministry of Judas and Silas and **sent** them **off** with blessings. The word **peace** expressed a desire for well-being in all areas of their lives.

Verse 34 is omitted by several important Greek manuscripts. Perhaps a scribe added it later to explain the choice of Silas (v. 40).

In the following months **Paul and Barnabas** continued to minister to the saints **in Antioch.**

4. THE CONFIRMATION OF THE CHURCHES IN ASIA MINOR (15:36-16:5)

[Second missionary journey, 15:36-18:22]

a. The contention between Paul and Barnabas (15:36-41)

15:36-41. Later when **Paul** proposed **to Barnabas** a return trip to confirm the churches established on their first journey, **Barnabas wanted to take . . . Mark with them. Paul** disagreed with this suggestion because Mark **had deserted them** earlier, **in Pamphylia** (cf. 13:13). The argument became **such a sharp disagreement** (*paroxysmos*, "provoking, stirring up, arousing," the root of the Eng. "paroxysm") **that they parted company.** The Lord overruled in this dissension for through it two missionary journeys instead of one were formed—one to **Cyprus** with **Barnabas** and **Mark,** and the other to **Syria and Cilicia** and ultimately Europe with **Paul** and **Silas.** Probably both Paul and Barnabas were right in their assessments of Mark. It may have been too soon for Mark to venture out with such a pro-Gentile apostle as Paul, but Barnabas certainly and correctly saw good raw material in his cousin Mark (cf. Col. 4:10; 2 Tim. 4:11; Phile. 24; 1 Peter 5:13). Paul later spoke of Barnabas in positive terms (1 Cor. 9:6; Col. 4:10). The Apostle Paul owed much to Barnabas and it appears they remained friends despite their contention over Mark.

Neither Mark nor Barnabas are seen again in the Book of Acts; the same is true of Peter following the Jerusalem Council (Acts 15).

Paul's choice of Silas, whose Roman name (in Gr.) was Sylvanus (2 Cor. 1:19; 1 Thes. 1:1; 2 Thes. 1:1; 1 Peter 5:12), was a wise one: (1) He was an official repre-

PAUL'S SECOND MISSIONARY JOURNEY

sentative of the Jerusalem church in taking to Antioch the decree of the Jerusalem Council (Acts 15:22). (2) He was a Roman citizen (16:37). (3) He was a prophet (15:32). (4) The church at Antioch knew him well, so both Paul and Silas were **commended by the brothers to the grace of the Lord.** (5) Because Silas served as Peter's amanuensis, it may be concluded he was skilled in the Greek language (cf. 1 Peter 5:12). The ministry of Paul and Silas involved their **strengthening the churches** (cf. Acts 14:22; 15:32).

b. The conscription of Timothy (16:1-5)

16:1-3. Timothy, whose home was **Lystra,** was of mixed parentage; his **mother was** Jewish and his **father was a Greek.** Probably Timothy had been converted under Paul's ministry during the apostle's first visit to Lystra (cf. 1 Tim. 1:2). Some suggest he had been led to the Lord by his grandmother Lois and his mother Eunice (2 Tim. 1:5). At any rate, he became Paul's protegé. Because of Timothy's good reputation (Acts 16:2) **Paul wanted to take him along on the journey,** probably as a helper as Mark had been. There was a problem, however. The Jews to whom Paul would be preaching the gospel would be offended if a man with a Jewish mother was uncircumcised. So Timothy was **circumcised.** Apparently he had been uncircumcised because of his father's influence.

This appears to contradict Paul's thinking in Galatians 2:3-5 where he refused to let Titus be circumcised. The situations, however, were different. In Galatians 2 the issue was the method of justification; here it was a question of not giving offense (cf. 1 Cor. 9:19-23). The Jerusalem Council, of course, had determined circumcision was not necessary for salvation (Acts 15:10-11, 19). In Acts 16 Paul acted as he did for the sake of the ministry; it was a wise move.

16:4. As they traveled from town to town, they delivered the decisions reached by the Jerusalem Council (15:23-29). Assuming Paul wrote Galatians after the first missionary journey, but before the Jerusalem Council, the report of the decision would be strong confirmation of the gospel which he preached and about which he wrote.

16:5. With another "progress report" (cf. *Introduction*), Luke brought

another section of his book to a close. The word **strengthened** (*estereounto,* "being made solid or firm") differs from its synonym *epistērizō* ("to strengthen"; 14:22; 15:32, 41).

C. The extension of the church in the Aegean area (16:6–19:20)

1. THE CALL TO MACEDONIA (16:6-10)

16:6-7. God's guidance was at first negative. Evidently the missionary party first attempted to go to the western **province of Asia** whose leading city was Ephesus. So they went **throughout the region of Phrygia and Galatia** (cf. 18:23). Possibly this should be understood as the Phrygian region of Galatia. **They** then proceeded north to eastern **Mysia and tried to enter Bithynia, but** again they were prevented from doing so by **the Spirit of Jesus.** How these hindrances were accomplished is not stated. It may have been circumstances, a word of prophecy, a vision, or some other phenomenon. At any rate, God planned for people in both Ephesus and Bithynia to hear the gospel at a later time (cf. 18:19-21, 24–19:41; 1 Peter 1:1).

16:8-9. Finally, at **Troas,** a seaport city on the Aegean Sea near the ancient site of Troy, God gave positive direction by means of a **night . . . vision** to **Paul. Macedonia** was a Roman senatorial province, corresponding roughly to northern Greece today.

16:10. The first of the **we** sections begins here in Acts, indicating that Luke joined the party of Paul, Silas, and Timothy. The how, why, and precise location of Luke's joining the group are left unstated.

2. THE CONFLICTS IN MACEDONIA (16:11–17:15)

a. At Philippi (16:11-40)

(1) The conversion of Lydia (16:11-15). **16:11.** The journey **from Troas** to **Samothrace** and **to Neapolis,** the seaport city for Philippi, was a rapid one, implying that the wind was with them (cf. 20:6 where the trip in the opposite direction took five days).

16:12. From Neapolis the missionaries **traveled** the 10 miles on the Via Egnatia, the Egnatian Road **to Philippi,** which Luke described as **a Roman colony and the leading city of that district of**

Macedonia. Quite clearly Luke displayed pride in the city he came to love. Some say he grew up and attended medical school there. Philippi, originally named Crenides ("Fountains"), was taken by Philip of Macedon and renamed after him. In 168 B.C. Philippi became a Roman possession. After Mark Antony and Octavian defeated Brutus and Cassius, the assassins of Julius Caesar, near Philippi in 42 B.C., the city was made into a Roman colony. This gave it special privileges (e.g, fewer taxes) but more importantly it became like a "transplanted" Rome (cf. comments on Philippi in the *Introduction* to Phil.). The primary purpose of colonies was military, for the Roman leaders felt it wise to have Roman citizens and sympathizers settled in strategic locations. So Octavian (who became Caesar Augustus, the first Roman emperor, in 27 B.C.) settled more colonists (primarily former soldiers) at Philippi after his defeat of Antony at Actium, on Greece's west coast, in 31 B.C.

16:13. The Jewish population at Philippi must have been limited, for there was no synagogue there; 10 Jewish males were required for a synagogue. **A place of prayer** (cf. v. 16), which may have been a place in the open air or a simple building, was located by the Gangites **River** about a mile and one-half west of town.

To the women . . . gathered there, the missionaries presented the gospel.

16:14. Lydia was a seller of **purple cloth.** This purple color came from a shellfish, the murex, or from the root of a plant. She was from **Thyatira,** a city known for its commerce in Asia Minor (cf. comments on Thyatira in Rev. 2:18-29). She **was a worshiper of God,** a term used for Gentiles (e.g., Cornelius [Acts 10:2] and those in Thessalonica [17:4] and Athens [17:17]) who were not proselytes to Judaism but who did worship Yahweh. Even so, they were not in the New Testament church, the body of Christ. **The Lord opened her heart** (cf. Luke 24:45) **to respond to Paul's message.** Again Luke stressed the sovereignty of God in salvation (cf. Acts 13:48).

16:15. Lydia was then **baptized,** apparently soon after her faith in Christ. **The members of her household** probably refer to servants as well as to her children, if she was a widow. Other persons in the New Testament who along with their "household" members came to Christ include Cornelius (10:24, 44), the Philippian jailer (16:31), Crispus (18:8), Aristobulus (Rom. 16:10), Narcissus (Rom. 16:11), and Stephanas (1 Cor. 1:16).

That she was a woman of considerable means is evidenced by the size of her **house.** It would have to be ample enough to house four men as well as her household without embarrassment (cf. Acts 16:40).

(2) The deliverance of the soothsayer. **16:16-18.** Some men were exploiting a demon-possessed **slave girl** for her ability to predict the future. The English words, **a spirit by which she predicted the future,** translate two Greek words, "a spirit, a python." This concept goes back to the Greek city of Delphi where the god Apollo was believed to be embodied in a python snake. The original priestess at Delphi was purported to be possessed by Apollo and thereby able to predict the future; therefore anyone possessed by the python spirit could foretell coming events. No doubt an actual demon gave such a person predictive powers. Demons took advantage of people's worship of false gods (cf. 17:23; 1 Cor. 10:20).

The **girl** attached herself to **Paul and the** others and was **shouting** (imperf. tense) who they were (**servants of the Most High God**) and what they preached (**the way to be saved**). Though her statements were true, the gospel of Christ would be damaged by an association with a demon-possessed slave girl. So after **many days . . . Paul** exorcised the demon, speaking directly **to the spirit.** (Other cases of victory over the occult in Acts are recorded in 8:9-24; 13:6-12; 19:13-20.)

(3) The conversion of the jailer (16:19-34). **16:19-21.** Each Roman colony was governed by two leaders called *douviri* in Latin. The term **magistrates** translates *stratēgois,* the Greek equivalent for the Latin word.

The charge of the slave girl's **owners** against **Paul and Silas** was obviously prejudicial. Shortly before this incident the Emperor Claudius had expelled the Jews from Rome (18:2). Philippi, a Roman colony, would have caught this flavor of anti-Semitism. This also helps explain why Timothy and Luke were not taken before the authorities. Timothy was a half-Gentile (16:1) and Luke was probably a Gentile.

Furthermore, Paul and Silas were accused of disrupting the **city . . . by advocating customs unlawful for . . . Romans to accept or practice.** Rome permitted the peoples of its colonies to have their own religions but not to proselytize Roman citizens. The civil leaders could not distinguish between Judaism and Christianity (cf. 18:14-15), so they would see the preaching of Paul and Silas as a flagrant infraction of imperial law.

16:22. Impelled by **the crowd . . . the magistrates ordered them to be stripped and beaten.** The verb translated "beaten" is from *rhabdizō,* which means "to beat with a rod." This was one of the three beatings Paul referred to in 2 Corinthians 11:25, the only other place where this verb occurs in the New Testament.

16:23-24. Paul and Silas were **severely flogged** and then **thrown into prison.** What a reception in the first European city where they preached the gospel! **The jailer** with his strict **orders** was not going to take any chances so **he put them in the inner cell** (possibly a dungeon, at least the most secure cell) **and fastened their feet in stocks.**

16:25. Paul and Silas singing in the inner prison gives special significance to the theme of joy in Acts (cf. Ps. 42:8; "at night His song is with me"). Their **praying and singing** was heard not only by God but also by **the other prisoners.**

16:26. This supernatural deliverance reminds the reader of the parallel experiences of Peter (cf. 5:18-20; 12:3-11). This was certainly an unusual midnight experience in a **prison**—the earth quaking, the **prison** shaking, **doors** flying **open . . . chains** falling off.

16:27-28. Because **the jailer** was responsible for any escaped **prisoners** (cf. 12:19), **he drew his sword . . . to kill himself. But Paul,** seeing what was about to happen, reassured him that the prisoners had not **escaped.** Perhaps the other prisoners were so impressed with the God of Paul and Silas that they did not dare flee!

16:29-30. Going into Paul and Silas' cell, **the jailer . . . trembling . . . asked, Men, what must I do to be saved?** This question was filled with significance. He

must have understood what he was asking. Undoubtedly he had heard the story of the slave girl and how she had announced these men to be servants of God with the message of salvation (v. 17). Possibly also the prayers and singing of **Paul and Silas** (v. 25) had reached his ears. The awesome earthquake with the subsequent opportunity for the prisoners to escape and Paul's reassuring words all moved him to ask for the way of salvation.

16:31-32. Verse 31 is a key passage on the message of faith. All that is needed for justification is faith **in the Lord Jesus.** The jailer had asked what he should do. The answer was that he need perform no works; he only needed to **believe** in Jesus who is the Lord.

The words **and your household** mean those members of **his house** who were of sufficient age to believe would be saved (cf. v. 34) as they trusted Christ. Each member had to believe to be saved.

16:33. The jailer . . . washed the **wounds** of Paul and Silas (cf. v. 23)—an amazing thing for a jailer to do for his prisoners. Then by water baptism **he and all his family** gave testimony to the washing away of their sins.

16:34. The jailer took the former prisoners home and fed them! And his **family** was joyful. Once again the evidence of the victorious gospel was joy.

(4) The deliverance of Paul and Silas (16:35-40). **16:35-36.** Apparently **the jailer** brought **Paul** and **Silas** back to prison. What prompted **the magistrates** to change their minds is left unstated. Perhaps the earthquake jarred their senses, or maybe on further reflection they realized how unjust they had been.

16:37-40. Paul's demand that the magistrates **escort** him and Silas **out of prison** appears to be vindictive. But it probably was designed to spare the young church in Philippi from further harassment. It certainly would place the believers in a far more secure position before the officials.

But why did **Paul** wait so long to mention his **Roman** citizenship? Perhaps the uproar at the trial (vv. 19-22) kept him from being heard. Or maybe Paul purposely waited till the most propitious time to give out this information. Born a

Roman citizen (22:28), Paul had certain rights, including a public hearing. And no Roman citizen was supposed to be scourged.

In only two places in Acts was Paul harmed or threatened by Gentiles—in Philippi and in Ephesus (19:23-41). In both instances people were losing money in vested interests and in each case Paul was vindicated by a Roman official. **After their prison release, Paul and Silas . . . met with the** believers at **Lydia's house** (cf. 16:15).

With Paul's departure the first **we** section ends, indicating Luke remained on at Philippi (cf. **they** in 16:40).

b. At Thessalonica (17:1-9)

17:1. The journey from Philippi to Thessalonica was about 100 miles with **Amphipolis and Apollonia** at approximately 30-mile intervals on the Via Egnatia. Evidently there were no Jewish synagogues in the two towns where Paul did not stop. A **synagogue** provided an excellent point of contact for the gospel (cf. v. 10) so Paul remained at **Thessalonica,** modern Saloniki, to preach.

17:2. The reference to **three Sabbath days** does not mean the missionary band stayed only three weeks in Thessalonica. Paul carried on the work with a Jewish emphasis for three Sabbaths and then turned to Gentiles and ministered to them for some weeks after that. This was the situation for three reasons: (1) The Philippian church sent money to Paul at least twice during this visit (Phil. 4:15-16), implying a longer lapse of time than three weeks. (2) In addition, Paul supported himself by manual labor (1 Thes. 2:9; 2 Thes. 3:7-10). This may indicate that considerable time elapsed before the aid from Philippi arrived. (3) Most of the converts at Thessalonica were not from the synagogue but were Gentiles steeped in idolatry (cf. 1 Thes. 1:9).

17:3-4. Paul and Silas' ministry in presenting the crucified and resurrected Jesus as **the Christ** (the Messiah) met with response: **some . . . Jews,** many **Godfearing Greeks** (cf. 16:14, where the same Greek word is used of Lydia, who is called "a worshiper of God"; cf. the same word in 17:17), **and not a few prominent women** (cf. v. 12). The gospel message

was received by people of various nationalities and social positions.

17:5. Luke evidently included this incident to reemphasize the continued Jewish rejection. Jason probably had provided lodging for **Paul and Silas. The Jews were** intent on finding Paul and Silas **in order to bring them out to the crowd.** Thessalonica was a free city which meant it was sovereign in its local affairs and not subject to provincial administration in such matters. Besides local rulers, Thessalonica also had its own local assembly called the *dēmos,* the word translated "crowd" here (see the NIV marg.; cf. 19:30 ["crowd"], 33 ["people"] where the noun also occurs).

17:6-7. Because the mob could **not find** Paul and Silas **they** grabbed **Jason and some other** believers and accused them **before the city officials** (*politarchas,* lit., "city rulers"). In Macedonian cities these magistrates formed the city council. The charge was specifically against **Jason** (possibly a relative of Paul; cf. Rom. 16:21) for harboring men who had **caused trouble all over the world**—obviously an exaggeration—and defied **Caesar's decrees, saying that there is another King, One called Jesus.** This latter accusation is significant for it shows Jews were behind the whole mob scene (cf. Acts 17:5); only they would have known enough about Paul's theology to make such a charge. (Jews also accused Jesus of claiming to be "a king"; Luke 23:2.) Furthermore it reflects Paul's proclamation. As the Thessalonian Epistles indicate, Paul proclaimed that the messianic kingdom will be established at the return of Christ (1 Thes. 3:13; 5:1-11; 2 Thes. 1:5-10; 2:14; cf. Luke 23:2; John 18:33-37).

17:8-9. The crowd and the politarchs **were** in **turmoil** (*etaraxan,* "agitated, disturbed, troubled"; cf. John 11:33; Acts 16:20) probably because they could not find Paul and Silas (17:6), the source of the city's problem. Probably the bondposting was to guarantee that Paul and Silas would leave town and not return. If more trouble arose, **Jason and the others** would lose their money. This may explain why Paul was prohibited from returning (1 Thes. 2:18). In spite of this, the Christians at Thessalonica kept on boldly proclaiming the gospel (1 Thes. 1:7-10; cf. 2:14-16).

ACTS

c. At Berea (17:10-15)

17:10. Under cover of **night** (cf. Paul's other nighttime escape; 9:25) **the brothers sent Paul and Silas away to Berea.** Perhaps Timothy accompanied them or he may have joined them at Berea later (cf. 17:14). Berea was about 46 miles southwest of Thessalonica on the eastern slopes of a mountain. Berea was also on the way to Achaia, the province that corresponds to southern Greece today. Sopater was from Berea (20:4). As usual, Paul and Silas **went to the . . . synagogue** (cf. 17:2, 17; 18:4, 19; 19:8).

17:11-12. The Berean Jews **were of more noble character than the Thessalonians. They** welcomed Paul's **message with great eagerness and examined the Scriptures every day to see if what Paul said was true.** This differed from the Jews in Thessalonica only some of whom believed (v. 4), whereas most of them were jealous of Paul and stirred up trouble. The Bereans' interest in the Word resulted in many conversions of both Jews and Greeks. Interestingly **prominent . . .women** in both Thessalonica and Berea received Christ (vv. 4, 12).

17:13-14. Once again Jewish unbelievers (from **Thessalonica**) forced the expulsion of **Paul. Stirring** is from the same Greek word used in verse 8 to speak of being "in turmoil." **Silas and Timothy** remained **at Berea** to help establish the fledgling church, while **Paul** went on south.

17:15. Whether **Paul** went **to Athens** by boat or by land is not known. In either case some brothers **accompanied** Paul to guarantee his safe arrival. Paul told the friends to instruct **Silas and Timothy to join him** in Athens **as soon as possible.** It is clear from 1 Thessalonians 3:1-2, 6 that Silas and Timothy did rejoin Paul at Athens. Silas likewise was commissioned by Paul to leave Athens and then meet him at Corinth (cf. Acts 18:1-5).

3. THE CRUSADE IN ACHAIA (17:16-18:18)

a. At Athens (17:16-34)

17:16. The glory of Greece in the fifth and fourth centuries B.C. was fading in Paul's day and even **Athens,** the proud center of Hellenism, was past its bloom. Even so, it was still a vital cultural center with a world-famous university. Many of its famous buildings were built during the days of its leader Pericles (461-429 B.C.). Beautiful as were the architecture and art forms, Paul could not enjoy them because **he was greatly distressed to see that the city was full of idols.** The art of Athens was a reflection of its worship. The intellectual capital of the world was producing idolatry.

17:17. In this city Paul waged spiritual warfare on two fronts, **the synagogue** and **the marketplace.** In the synagogue he no doubt used his normal approach, proving from the Old Testament Scriptures that Jesus is the Messiah (cf. vv. 2-3). In that synagogue were **Jews** and **God-fearing** Gentiles (cf. v. 4). In the marketplace (*agora,* the center of civic life) where philosophers debated and presented their views, Paul **reasoned . . . with those who happened to be there.**

17:18. The primary antagonists of Paul in the *agora* were the **Epicurean and Stoic philosophers.** The Epicureans, who followed Epicurus (341-270 B.C.), said the chief end of man was pleasure and happiness. This pleasure, they believed, is attained by avoiding excesses and the fear of death, by seeking tranquility and freedom from pain, and by loving mankind. They believed that if gods exist they do not become involved in human events.

The Stoics, on the other hand, were followers of Zeno (ca. 320-ca. 250 B.C.) and got their name from the painted portico or *stoa,* where they traditionally taught in Athens. Pantheistic in their view, they felt a great "Purpose" was directing history. Man's responsibility was to fit himself and align himself with this Purpose through tragedy and triumph. Quite obviously this outlook, while it produced certain noble qualities, also resulted in inordinate pride and self-sufficiency.

When these philosophers encountered Paul, they **began to dispute with him. Some of them asked, What is this babbler trying to say?** "Dispute" is *syneballon* (lit., "to throw with," i.e., to toss ideas back and forth). This differs slightly from what Paul did in the synagogues. There he reasoned (*dielegeto,* "discussed, conversed," v. 17; cf. the same word in v. 2; 18:4, 19; 19:8). The word translated "babbler" is *spermologos* (lit., "seed-picker"). It described someone who, like a bird picking up seeds, took some learning here and some there and then passed it off as his own. **Others remarked, He seems to be advocating foreign gods.** This response was due to their inability to grasp Paul's doctrine of Christ and **the Resurrection;** it was totally foreign to their thinking (cf. 17:31-32).

17:19-21. Areopagus, literally, "Hill of Ares," was the **meeting** place of the Council of the Areopagus, the supreme body for judicial and legislative matters in Athens. In the Apostolic Age its power had been reduced to oversight over religion and education.

There is some question as to where this council met in Paul's time. Some think it met on the traditional Mars Hill behind the *agora* and immediately west of the Acropolis. Others say it met in the Stoa Basileios, a building in the *agora.* The council wanted to know about Paul's **new teaching,** which was **strange** to their **ears.** In Athens, the ancient world's intellectual center, **the Athenians and** foreign residents loved **to** debate **the latest ideas.** This openness gave Paul an opportunity to preach his message.

17:22. Beginning with this verse (and continuing through v. 31) is another of Paul's "sample sermons" (cf. 13:16-41; 14:15-18; 20:18-35). This one shows how Paul addressed intellectual pagans. The thrust of his message is clear: the Creator God, who has revealed Himself in Creation, has now commanded all to repent, for everyone must give an account to Jesus Christ whom God raised from the dead.

Paul's discourse includes three parts: (a) the introduction (17:22-23), (b) the unknown God (vv. 24-29), and (c) the message from God (vv. 30-31).

Paul began wisely by acknowledging they were **very religious.** These two words translate the Greek *deisidaimonesterous* from *deidō* ("to fear or revere"), *daimōn* ("deities, evil spirits"), and *stereos* ("firm, hard"). The idea is that the Athenians were firm and rigid in their reverencing of their deities. This was a carefully chosen word. Hearing it, the **men of Athens** would have thought of their deities or gods. But Paul subtly implied that their deities were evil spirits or demons, not gods. Behind idols are demons (cf. comments on 16:16).

17:23. The Athenians, who feared they might overlook venerating some deity they did not know about, dedicated an altar TO AN UNKNOWN GOD. When Paul referred to this, he did not emphasize the **altar** but their ignorance of the true God.

17:24. Because **God** made **everything,** He is supreme over all—**the Lord of heaven and earth** (cf. 14:15; cf. Ps. 24:1). Such a great God **does not live** in humanly constructed **temples,** as the Athenians assumed their Greek gods did (cf. Stephen's words in Acts 7:48-50).

17:25. God is above human temples, but **He** is also self-sufficient and **is not** sustained **by human** provisions. This truth would appeal to the Epicureans who believed that what god or gods existed were above human events.

The last part of the verse, dealing with God's providing people with **life** (cf. v. 28) and material needs (cf. 14:17), suited the Stoic philosophy of aligning their lives with the "Purpose" of the Cosmos. Paul was thus beginning where his listeners were and was leading them from their inadequate concepts of the truth.

17:26. From one man refers back to Adam. This would be a blow to Athenian pride; they were sourced in the same original Creation as everyone else! One purpose of this Creation was to populate the planet (Gen. 1:28).

This sovereign God has omnipotently decreed the history (**the times**) **and** boundaries (**the exact places**) for the nations (cf. Deut. 32:8). Greece was not the only **nation on earth!**

17:27. One of God's purposes in revealing Himself in Creation and history is that people **would seek Him** (cf. Rom. 1:19-20). Though sovereign (Acts 17:24), He is also immanent and not so **far** removed that **He** cannot be found.

17:28. To buttress his point Paul apparently quoted from Epimenides, the Cretan poet (whom Paul also quoted later in Titus 1:12): **For in Him we live** (cf. Acts 17:25), **and move, and have our being.** Also Paul quoted the poet Aratus, from Paul's homeland Cilicia: **We are His offspring.** This second quotation was from Aratus' work *Phainomena.* All people—Athenians along with all others—are God's offspring, not in the sense that they are all His redeemed children or in the sense that they all possess an element of deity, but in the sense that they are created by God and receive their very life and breath from Him (v. 25). The Athenians' very creation and continued existence depended on this one God whom they did not know! No such claim could ever be made of any of the scores of false gods worshiped by the Greeks.

17:29. The conclusion is inevitable: since humans have been created by God, **the divine Being,** He cannot possibly be in the form of an idol, **an image** conceived and constructed by man (cf. Rom. 1:22-23). ("Divine being" translates *theion,* lit., "divine nature," used frequently in classical Gr., but in the NT only here and in 2 Peter 1:3-4). This would be a revolutionary concept to the Athenians, whose city was "full of idols" (Acts 17:16) and "objects of worship" (v. 23).

17:30. God overlooked human ignorance revealed in idol-making, that is, He was patient. Though people are under His wrath (Rom. 1:18) and are without excuse because of natural revelation (Rom. 1:19-20), God "in His forbearance (*anochē,* 'holding back, delay') left the sins committed beforehand unpunished" (Rom. 3:25). This parallels Acts 14:16, "In the past, He let all nations go their way" (cf. comments there). All through time the Gentiles were responsible for the general revelation given to them; now with the worldwide proclamation of the gospel, the Gentiles are also responsible to special revelation. That response is to obey God's command **to repent** of their sins.

17:31. At this point Paul introduced a distinctively Christian viewpoint. His reference to **the Man** clearly looks to Daniel 7:13-14 which speaks of the Son of Man. This One, **appointed** by God the Father, **will judge the world with justice** (cf. John 5:22). The authentication of Christ's person and work was His resurrection. Here again the resurrection of Jesus was preached. The idea of resurrection (cf. Acts 17:18, 32) was incompatible with Greek philosophy. The Greeks wanted to get rid of their bodies, not take them on again! A personal judgment was also unpalatable to Greeks. The gospel message struck at the center of the Athenians' needs.

Interestingly Paul (vv. 30-31) discussed the topics of sin ("to repent"), righteousness ("justice"), and judgment ("He will judge"), the same areas in which Jesus said the Holy Spirit would convict people (John 16:5-11).

17:32-34. To a Greek it was nonsense to believe a dead man could be raised from the grave to live forever, so **some of them sneered. Others** with more discretion **said** they wanted **to hear** Paul **again on this subject.** As a result **a few men became followers of Paul and believed,** including even **Dionysius,** an **Areopagus** member (i.e., a council **member;** cf. comments on v. 19), and **a woman named Damaris.** Other women converts in Acts include Lydia (16:14-15), a few prominent women in Thessalonica (17:4), and a number of prominent Greek women in Berea (v. 12).

Was Paul's ministry at Athens a failure? This is difficult to assess. There is no record of a church being founded in Athens. Paul later referred to the household of Stephanas (1 Cor. 16:15) in Corinth as "the first converts" (lit., "firstfruits") of Achaia. (Athens was in Achaia.) How could this be if some were converted in Athens, as Acts 17:34 asserts? Probably the solution is found in thinking of Stephanas as the firstfruits "of a church" in Achaia. Also possibly the term "firstfruits" can be used of more than one person.

If no church was begun in Athens, the failure was not in Paul's message or method but in the hardness of the Athenians' hearts.

b. At Corinth (18:1-18)

18:1. Without explaining the circumstances Luke simply stated, **After this, Paul left Athens and went to Corinth.** The cities of Athens and Corinth, though only 50 miles apart, were quite different. Athens was noted for its culture and learning, Corinth for its commerce and profligacy. Corinth was located just south of a narrow isthmus which joined the peninsula called Peloponnesus to Achaia to the north. Land trade moving north and south went through Corinth as did sea trade going east and west. Corinth possessed two seaport cities—Lechaeum two miles to the west on the Gulf of Corinth which opened to the Adriatic Sea, and Cenchrea, seven miles to the southeast which brought trade from the Aegean Sea. The southern tip of the Peloponnesus Peninsula was dangerous for ocean travel, so ships would put into port at one of Corinth's seaports and have their cargoes carried across to the other side of the isthmus for shipping there.

In 146 B.C. the Romans razed Corinth. However, its strategic location would not permit the city to die. It was rebuilt a century later in 46 B.C.

As one would expect from a city supported by commerce and travelers, Corinth was marked by profligate and licentious living. It was a center for the worship of Aphrodite, the goddess of love, who promoted immorality in the name of religion.

Politically, Corinth was a Roman colony and capital of the province of Achaia.

Some insights into Paul's emotions as he came to Corinth are seen in 1 Corinthians 2:1-5. His acknowledged weakness, fear, and much trembling may have been due to several factors: (1) He came alone. (2) The difficulties he had faced since coming to Macedonia may have filled him with apprehension as to what would happen in Corinth (cf. Acts 18:9-10). (3) Even in a world hardened to profligacy Corinth held a reputation for its sexual license.

The fact that Paul came to Corinth alone *may* account for his having baptized some people in that city, a practice he normally delegated to others (cf. 1 Cor. 1:14-17).

18:2. In Corinth Paul met **Aquila and his wife Priscilla.** Aquila was **a Jew,** originally from **Pontus,** a province in northeast Asia Minor south of the Black Sea. Displaced from Rome because of an edict in A.D. 49 or 50 from **Claudius** for **all the Jews to leave Rome,** Aquila and Priscilla had come to Corinth to ply their trade. (Claudius reigned from A.D. 41 to 54; see the list of Roman emperors at Luke 2:1.) Suetonius (A.D. 69?–140), a biographer of Roman emperors, described what may have been the occasion for such a decree. In his *Life of Claudius* (25. 4) he referred to the constant riots of the Jews at the instigation of Chrestus.

Possibly the name Chrestus is a reference to Christ.

Whether Aquila and Priscilla were Christians before they met Paul is not known. Because Aquila was called "a Jew" did not mean he knew Christ (cf. Apollos, a Jew; Acts 18:24). Nor can it be argued that Paul lived with them because they were believers; he stayed with them because they were tentmakers (v. 3).

Several times Priscilla's name is given before Aquila's (vv. 18-19, 26; Rom. 16:3). This *may* be due to her noble family background.

18:3. Their mutual trade was **tent-making.** The term used here is *skēnopoioi,* which some say includes working in leather. Perhaps leather was used in the tents as was goat's hair, for which Paul's home province of Cilicia was well known.

As is still common in the Middle East, a workman's shop was downstairs and his living quarters upstairs.

18:4. Once again Paul, according to his custom, began his work of evangelism **in the synagogue** (cf. 9:20; 13:5, 14; 14:1; 17:2, 10, 17; 18:19; 19:8).

18:5. With the arrival of **Silas and Timothy . . . from Macedonia** (cf. 17:14-15), **Paul devoted himself exclusively to preaching.** The verb translated "devoted . . . exclusively" is *syneicheto* (from *synechō*) which here in the passive means "to be constrained." Several factors about Silas and Timothy's arrival encouraged Paul: (1) The pair evidently brought financial aid from Macedonia (cf. 2 Cor. 11:9; Phil 4:15). Because of this monetary gift it was no longer necessary for Paul to pursue a trade and he could give himself totally to the work of the gospel. (2) The good news about the steadfastness of the Thessalonian church refreshed Paul (cf. 1 Thes. 3:6-8). (3) Their companionship would have been an encouragement to the apostle.

His message was the same as the one he learned on the Damascus Road: **Jesus is the Christ,** that is, the Messiah (cf. Acts 2:36; 3:18, 20; 17:3; 18:28).

18:6. Once again is seen the pattern of Jewish opposition to the gospel, followed by Paul's subsequent turning **to the Gentiles** (cf. 13:7-11, 46; 14:2-6; 17:5; 19:8-9; 28:23-28).

Paul's shaking **out his clothes** parallels Paul's and Barnabas' shaking dust

PAUL'S THIRD MISSIONARY JOURNEY

MILES

0   100   200   300

from their feet (13:51). When Paul said, **Your blood be on your own heads,** he was referring to their destruction and their own **responsibility** for it (cf. Ezek. 33:1-6).

18:7-8. After **Paul left the synagogue,** he found a fortunate location for preaching the gospel to the assembly of the saints **next door** in **the house of Titius Justus.** He was probably a Gentile, for he is called **a worshiper of God** (cf. 16:14; 17:4). In addition, **Crispus, the synagogue ruler,** with **his** family **believed.** He would have been well acquainted with the Old Testament Scriptures, and his conversion undoubtedly was an impetus for **many** more **Corinthians** to be converted.

18:9-11. Some threatening circumstances must have prompted this **vision** from **the Lord.** Perhaps this was God's response to Paul's vow (cf. v. 18 and the comments made there). The Lord urged **Paul** to **keep on** ministering in Corinth, assuring him that **no . . . harm** would come. No doubt **Paul** welcomed this word because of recent attacks against him in other cities (cf. 17:5, 13) and in Corinth itself (18:6). Paul obediently followed the Lord's direction and **stayed for a year and a half** (cf. v. 18), second only in length to his two to three years in Ephesus (19:10; 20:31).

Interestingly the word used for **people** in 18:10 is *laos,* often used of God's people Israel. Quite clearly, the Lord's plans for the world meant that the church temporarily was to take the place of His Chosen People, the Jews (cf. Rom. 11:11-21).

18:12. Verses 12-17 form a critical point in Luke's apologetic. It is important first because of who **Gallio** was, a Roman **proconsul,** governor **of Achaia.** Any judgment pronounced by him would establish legal precedent. Furthermore, Gallio was a brother of Seneca (4 B.C.?–A.D. 65), a philosopher of great influence in Rome.

The unbelieving **Jews** were not about to stop opposing **Paul** (cf. v. 6). They **united** and **brought him into court.**

18:13-15. The Jews **charged** Paul with **persuading the people to worship God in ways contrary to the** Roman **law.** Rome did not permit the propagation of

new religions. Judaism was an accepted and established belief. These Jews were saying in effect that Christianity was a new and different cult, distinct from Judaism.

However, **Gallio** saw it differently. To him Christianity came under the aegis of Judaism and therefore was not a **matter** to be settled in a civil court. This decision was crucial for it was tantamount to legitimatizing Christianity in the eyes of Roman law.

18:16-17. The spontaneous outburst of violence against **Sosthenes, the synagogue ruler,** betrayed the spirit of anti-Semitism that lay just beneath the veneer of society in Corinth. The Gentiles in Corinth wanted nothing of the Jews' contentions. Sosthenes had evidently become ruler of the synagogue in place of Crispus and had led in the Jews' charge against Paul. He may well be the same Sosthenes who was later converted to Christianity and was referred to in 1 Corinthians 1:1.

Such a minor incident was of **no concern** to **Gallio.** Though there was violence, he was unconcerned about religious matters.

18:18. The actual length of Paul's stay **in Corinth** is unclear because the 18 months (v. 11) may be dated from the time of Paul's vision (vv. 9-10) or it may include all of Paul's **time** in Corinth (from v. 5 on).

Paul then **left** Corinth, heading for his sending church, Antioch on the Orontes River in **Syria. But before he left he had his hair cut off at Cenchrea,** Corinth's southeastern port, **because of a vow he had taken.** When Paul made this vow is unstated. He may have made it when he left Troas for Macedonia, or at the beginning of his ministry at Corinth, or more likely, before the Lord gave him the vision (vv. 9-10). During the vow Paul would have let his hair grow. Now the time of the Nazirite vow was over (after about a year and a half), and Paul got a haircut at Cenchrea (cf. Num. 6:1-21).

Josephus wrote about some Jews who immediately after a misfortune, shaved their heads and refused to offer sacrifices for 30 days (*Jewish Wars* 2.15. 1). If this is the case Paul would have cut his hair at the beginning of his vow. But this is somewhat improbable because there is no mention of an illness or other affliction (unless 2 Cor. 12:7-9 fits in here).

While Paul was at Corinth he penned 1 and 2 Thessalonians (see the chart at Acts 13:38-39).

4. THE CONCLUSION OF THE SECOND MISSIONARY JOURNEY (18:19-22)

18:19. Priscilla and Aquila accompanied **Paul** as far as **Ephesus.** Evidently Silas and Timothy remained in Macedonia and Achaia to oversee the churches there. Why Priscilla and Aquila moved to Ephesus is not known. Probably it was for the sake of the gospel.

As in every city where there was a **synagogue** Paul **went** in **and reasoned with the Jews** (cf. 9:20; 13:5, 14; 14:1; 17:2, 10, 17; 18:4; 19:8).

18:20-21. Unlike the obstinate refusal of the Jews in other synagogues to believe, those in **Ephesus** desired further interchange with Paul. However, he was more inclined to press on homeward. Some Greek manuscripts add that Paul's desire to go to Jerusalem in haste was to keep a feast. If this is accurate, probably Paul wanted to observe the Passover.

18:22. After landing **at Caesarea** on the Palestinian coast—a voyage of about 500 miles from Ephesus—Paul **went up** (to Jerusalem) **and greeted the church and then went down to Antioch.** "Going up" and "going down" are almost technical terms that refer to going to and leaving Jerusalem's higher elevation.

5. THE CONQUEST OF EPHESUS (18:23-19:20)

[Third missionary journey, 18:23-21:16]

a. The initiation of Paul's third journey (18:23)

18:23. With great brevity Luke covered the first part of the apostle's third missionary journey. Obviously Luke's aim was to emphasize Paul's ministry in Ephesus. On Paul's way to Ephesus he ministered in **Galatia and Phrygia** (cf. 16:6), **strengthening all the disciples.** No doubt many of them were converts from his second missionary journey. For this reason the incident of 18:24-28 is used to introduce Paul's work in Ephesus.

b. The instruction of Apollos (18:24-28)

This episode (18:24-28) and the following (19:1-7) underscore the transitional nature of this phase of church history. It may be assumed from 19:1-7 that Apollos had not received Christian baptism and probably had not received the Holy Spirit.

This section of Acts also indicates that Christianity is the logical outgrowth of the Old Testament and of John the Baptist's ministry. In fact, the message of Paul is superior to that of the spiritual giant John the Baptist. Though John's message had reached as far as Alexandria and Ephesus, John's work was brought to fruition only in Christ.

18:24. What took place in verses 24-28 occurred after Paul left **Ephesus**

SPEAKING IN TONGUES IN ACTS

PASSAGE	TONGUES-SPEAKERS	AUDIENCE	RELATED TO SALVATION	PURPOSE
2:1-4	The 12 Apostles and others	Unsaved Jews	After salvation	To validate (for Jews) the fulfillment of Joel 2
10:44-47	Gentiles (Cornelius and his household)	Saved Jews (Peter and others) who doubted God's plan	The same time as salvation	To validate (for Jews) God's acceptance of Gentiles
19:1-7	About 12 Old Testament believers	Jews who needed confirmation of the message	The same time as salvation	To validate (for Jews) Paul's message

(v. 21) and before he returned (19:1). During this interval a church had been started, probably under the influence of Aquila and Priscilla. To this church came the gifted **Apollos** from **Alexandria** in northern Africa. As **a Jew**, he knew the **Scriptures**, that is, the Old Testament, well.

18:25. His doctrine regarding **Jesus** was accurate but deficient. Probably this means Apollos did not know about the Holy Spirit's baptism. John's **baptism** symbolized cleansing by God because of repentance toward God (cf. 19:4). But Christian baptism pictures union with Christ in His death, burial, and resurrection by means of Spirit baptism (cf. Rom. 6:3-10; 1 Cor. 12:13; Gal. 3:27; Col. 2:12).

18:26. Rather than correct Apollos publicly, **Priscilla and Aquila . . . invited him to their home and explained to him the way of God** (cf. "the way of the Lord," v. 25) **more adequately.**

18:27-28. Armed with this new doctrine **Apollos** crossed the Aegean Sea **to Achaia** (probably at Corinth) where he was mightily used. **He vigorously refuted the Jews** demonstrating **from the Scriptures** (which he knew well, v. 24), **that Jesus is the** Messiah. This was Paul's approach as well (v. 5). So forceful was Apollos' ministry that factious believers at Corinth formed an Apollos party (1 Cor. 1:12). There is no indication that Apollos promoted such a faction and Paul nowhere held him accountable for it.

c. The influence of the gospel (19:1-20)

(1) With the 12 (19:1-7). **19:1-2. Ephesus** became Paul's base of operation during his third missionary journey. Ephesus was the home of the Temple of Artemis, one of the seven wonders of the ancient world. The temple, according to its ruins, was 239' wide and 418' long, four times the size of the Parthenon in Athens! As a commercial center, Ephesus was the leading city of the province of Asia. Its present-day extensive ruins reveal the glory of its past. However, the Caÿster River silted its harbor full and the site was later abandoned. During Paul's time the city was approaching its zenith.

Arriving in this metropolitan area from **the interior** road (perhaps a shorter route than others), **Paul . . . found some disciples.** What Luke meant by the term

"disciples" is unclear. Normally Luke used it of Christians; it may have that meaning here because Paul's question included the words **when you believed** (i.e., believed in Jesus Christ).

The answer of these disciples is also enigmatic. When they said, **No, we have not even heard that there is a Holy Spirit,** they probably meant they had not heard He had been given or was being given. A similar construction is used in the Greek in John 7:39. Furthermore, John the Baptist had clearly predicted the coming work of the Holy Spirit (Matt. 3:11; Mark 1:8; Luke 3:16; cf. John 1:32-33).

19:3-4. Like Apollos (18:25) these Ephesian disciples knew only of **John's baptism,** a sign **of repentance** toward God (Matt. 3:2, 6, 8, 11; Mark 1:4-5; Luke 3:8). Paul told them that John pointed to Jesus Christ as **the One** in whom they should **believe** (Matt. 3:11-12; Mark 1:7-8; Luke 3:16-17).

19:5. This is the only place in the New Testament that refers to anyone being rebaptized. Quite clearly, John's ministry was anticipatory; Christ is the fulfillment of all things.

19:6. The laying on of **hands** may have been in conjunction with the baptism or more probably afterward. As a result **the Holy Spirit came on these disciples and they spoke in tongues and prophesied.** The subject of tongues in Acts confirms Paul's statement that tongues "are a sign . . . for unbelievers" (cf. comments on 1 Cor. 14:22). The purpose of tongues was to overcome unbelief. The accompanying chart compares the usages of tongues-speaking in Acts and points up its purpose.

It should also be noted that the reception of the Holy Spirit in Acts does not follow any set pattern. He came into believers before baptism (Acts 10:44), at the time of or after baptism (8:12-16; 19:6), and by the laying on of apostolic hands (8:17; 19:6). Yet Paul declared (Rom. 8:9) that anyone without the Holy Spirit is not a Christian. Quite obviously the transitional Book of Acts is not to be used as a doctrinal source on how to receive the Holy Spirit (cf. comments on tongues, 1 Cor. 13:8–14:25).

19:7. The reference to **12 men** does not imply, as some have suggested, that the church is the new Israel. If there is any significance to the number, it is that this fullness of the Spirit is yet to be experienced by Israel (cf. Ezek. 36:26-27; Joel 2:28-32; Zech. 12:10-14).

(2) In the synagogue. **19:8.** In accord with his promise (18:21) **Paul** did return to the Ephesus **synagogue and spoke boldly there for three months.** Three months in a synagogue without a riot was something of a record for Paul. Perhaps the cosmopolitan nature of Ephesus caused the Jews there to be more tolerant. On the apostles' boldness, see comments on 4:13.

The topic of his discussion was **the kingdom of God** which obviously included the person and work of Christ but also must have anticipated His millennial reign (cf. 1:3, 6).

(3) In the school of Tyrannus (19:9-12). **19:9.** Once again the old pattern of Jewish opposition arose (cf. 18:6). This time the Jews **publicly maligned the Way** (on "the Way," cf. 9:2; 19:23; 22:4; 24:14, 22). **So Paul left them.**

After he led the believers out of the synagogue he taught **daily in the lecture hall of Tyrannus.** Apparently Tyrannus made his lecture hall available to traveling teachers. One Greek manuscript adds that the school was available from 11 A.M. to 4 P.M., when most people would have their noon meal and an afternoon "siesta." This tradition is probably correct. The rest of each day Paul worked with his own hands (20:34).

19:10. Paul ministered in Ephesus **for two years.** But according to Acts 20:31, he was there for three years. Since it was customary to count part of a unit of time as a whole, his ministry was actually between two and three years.

So effective was this work that the gospel emanated throughout **the province of Asia,** on the west coast of modern-day Turkey. During this time the churches at Colosse, Laodicea, and Hierapolis were founded (Col. 4:13). Some believe all seven churches of Revelation 2-3 were started at this time, but this cannot be asserted dogmatically.

19:11-12. These feats of **Paul** parallel the **miracles** of Peter in 5:15-16. Quite clearly God's hand of blessing and endorsement was on Paul. Apparently the **handkerchiefs and aprons** were tangible

symbols of God's power through His apostle; these objects had no magical powers in themselves. Certainly this is no basis for people trying to repeat such miracles today. As seen many times in Acts, miracles confirmed the work of the apostles (2:43; 4:30; 5:12; 6:8; 8:6, 13; 14:3; 15:12; cf. 2 Cor. 12:12; Heb. 2:3-4).

The mention of **evil spirits** bridges this portion with the next incident (Acts 19:13-20).

(4) With exorcism and sorcery (19:13-20). One of the themes of Acts is the victory of Christ over occultism (cf. 8:9-24; 13:6-12; 16:16-18). This incident is another example of His power over demons.

19:13. Some itinerant Jewish exorcists who obviously used a variety of chants and methods **tried to invoke Jesus' name** over **demon-possessed** people.

19:14. Sceva is said to be **a Jewish chief priest.** But perhaps he merely claimed to be, and Luke simply recorded his boast. Or Sceva may have actually been a chief priest whose **seven sons** had gone astray into exorcism.

19:15. Some significance may be attached to the variation in the verbs for "know" used here by **the evil spirit** (i.e., the demon). He said, **Jesus I know** (*ginōskō*, "to know by interaction and experience"), **and** he added, **Paul I know about** (*epistamai*, "to know about, to understand"). **But** the demon did not know Sceva's sons.

19:16. Instead of being exorcised of this demon, **the** possessed **man** became supernaturally strong and overcame **all** seven (*amphoterōn* normally means "both" but may also signify "all"), **beating** them. The seven **ran out of the house naked and bleeding.** Demons can sometimes cause those they possess to have unusual physical power (cf. Mark 5:3-4).

19:17-18. The result was **fear** (or awe, *phobos*) on the part of both **Jews and** Gentiles (cf. 5:5), and **high** esteem for Jesus' **name** (in contrast with the attempted use of His name for exorcism; cf. 19:13). **Many** Christians had also been involved in sorcery and spiritism and they **openly confessed their evil deeds.** The noun translated "deeds" is *praxeis*, which probably describes magical spells and formulas. Giving out these secrets would cause them to lose their power.

19:19. Furthermore, many publicly **burned** their manuals of **sorcery**. In sorcery, people by the assistance of demons sought to gain power over others. The word translated **drachmas** is actually *argyriou* and simply means "silver"; consequently the value of the coins is unknown. But **50,000** silver coins was a large sum.

19:20. The cleansed church became a powerful and growing church. (The spreading of God's **Word** is also mentioned in 6:7; 12:24; 13:49.) With this sixth "progress report" Luke brought another section of his book to a conclusion (cf. 2:47; 6:7; 9:31; 12:24; 16:5; 28:30-31).

D. *The extension of the church to Rome (19:21–28:31)*

1. THE COMPLETION OF THE THIRD JOURNEY (19:21-21:16)

a. *The disturbance at Ephesus (19:21-41)*

19:21. This verse sets the tone for the remainder of the book. Paul's sights were now set on **Rome** (via **Jerusalem**) with the ultimate goal of reaching Spain (Rom. 1:15; 15:22-24). Luke made no reference to Spain because one of his purposes in writing Acts was to trace the spread of the gospel up to Paul's being in Rome, center of the Roman world. Several have observed how Luke's Gospel focuses *in* on Jerusalem, whereas Acts emphasizes the message going *out* from Jerusalem to Rome. These two cities seem to be the focal points of Luke-Acts.

The NIV simply says **Paul decided** whereas the Greek has *etheto ho Paulos en tō pneumati*, "Paul purposed in the spirit." This may mean Paul's own spirit or the Holy Spirit. Since the verb means "purposed," not "was led," it may refer to Paul's human spirit.

First, however, he desired to visit the churches of **Macedonia and Achaia.** The purposes of this itinerary were (a) to confirm the churches and (b) to take up an offering for the saints in Jerusalem.

19:22. Timothy, who was last seen with Paul in Corinth (18:5), once again came on the scene. He **and Erastus** were **sent . . . to Macedonia,** evidently to prepare for Paul's coming. Paul also mentioned Erastus in 2 Timothy 4:20.

19:23-24. Before Paul's departure and as an incentive for him to leave Ephesus there was a riot. On the words **the Way,** see comments on 9:2.

In only two incidents recorded in Acts did Gentiles oppose Paul: (a) here and (b) in the case of the Philippian fortune-teller (16:16-24). In both cases the opposition was because of vested monetary interests.

Actually two goddesses in Asia Minor were named **Artemis.** The one, a goddess worshiped in Greek culture whose counterpart in Rome was Diana, was the virgin goddess of the hunt. The other was Artemis of the Ephesians, a many-breasted goddess of fertility. Probably the original "statue" was a meteorite that resembled a woman with many breasts (cf. 19:35).

Silver **craftsmen** made statues (**silver shrines**) of this Ephesian goddess, but because of the power of the gospel their business had gone bad.

19:25-27. Demetrius (v. 24), a silversmith, assembled the other craftsmen and appealed to them on the basis of both business (**our trade will lose its good name**) and religion (**the temple of the great goddess Artemis will be discredited**). The appeal on the basis of the cult of Artemis was obviously hypocritical; his concern was simply financial. Artemis was worshiped in many cities besides Ephesus. Obviously Paul's view **that man-made** idols are not **gods** would ruin their thriving idol-making **business.**

19:28-29. The silversmiths, enraged at Paul by Demetrius' speech, instigated a riot and **rushed** to **the** Ephesian **theater,** the largest place for an assembly of people in the city, capable of seating 25,000. As tokens of opposition **the people seized Gaius and Aristarchus** (cf. 20:4). Gaius was a common name; so it is doubtful this is the same man mentioned in Romans 16:23 and 1 Corinthians 1:14. Aristarchus is also mentioned in Acts 20:4 and 27:2. Evidently the two escaped with little or no injury.

19:30-31. These verses are important not only for what they directly state but also for what they imply. **Paul** was eager to defend the gospel, ready to take on his opponents! But the Christians did **not let him. Even some of the officials of the province** would not let him get caught in the riot. They were *Asiarchs* (lit., "rulers of Asia"), in charge of the community's political and religious welfare. They would be on good terms with Rome and therefore would evidence Christianity's good standing with the government.

19:32-34. Luke's sense of humor is seen in this passage. Ironically **most of the people did not even know why they were there.** Because **the Jews** were monotheists and strongly opposed to idols, they thrust **Alexander to the front** in order to issue a disclaimer. The reduction in Artemis' idol business was not their fault! However, anti-Semitism took over, the mob refused to listen to **a Jew,** and **they** chanted in frenzy **for about two hours, Great is Artemis of the Ephesians!**

19:35-39. The term **city clerk** (*grammateus,* lit., "scribe") does not do justice to this man's position. Actually he was the chief executive officer of the city. When he appeared, the people listened.

He first appealed to the position of **Ephesus** as **the guardian of** Artemis' **temple** and to **her** heaven-sent **image.** The latter assertion may be a subtle rebuttal of the statement (v. 26, "manmade gods are no gods at all"). Artemis, he argued, was *not* man-made. So why should they be concerned with Paul's preaching? Second, the town clerk asserted the innocence of Gaius and Aristarchus, thereby exonerating Paul as well (v. 37). Third, he pointed out the legal methods of obtaining a hearing— through **the courts . . . proconsuls,** and **a legal assembly** (vv. 38-39). *This* assembly was not legal.

19:40-41. Finally, the unnamed official warned of the political implications of the **commotion** in the city. They would be hard-pressed to give Rome a legitimate explanation of this riot, and the city could be deprived of some of its liberties because of it. So Paul was cleared of any misdeeds, religious or political.

While Paul was at Ephesus, he wrote 1 Corinthians as well as an earlier letter to the Corinthians that is not part of the biblical canon (cf. 1 Cor. 5:9). In addition he made a third visit to Corinth which is unrecorded in Acts (cf. 2 Cor. 12:14; 13:1; see "Contacts and Correspondence" in the *Introduction* to 2 Cor.).

b. The departure from Macedonia and Achaia (20:1-6)

20:1-2. This segment of the third missionary journey is covered briefly by Luke. Second Corinthians 2:12-13; 7:5-7 gives further information about Paul's stop at Troas for evangelistic purposes and of his desire to see Titus for a report on the Corinthian church. Subsequently Paul went to **Macedonia** (cf. Acts 19:21), met Titus, and wrote 2 Corinthians.

During this time Paul probably ministered as far as Illyricum, corresponding roughly to modern-day Yugoslavia (Rom. 15:19; cf. 2 Cor. 10:13).

20:3. During the apostle's **three**-month stay in Achaia he wrote Romans (cf. Rom. 15:23–16:2) from Corinth.

The **plot** by **the Jews . . . against** Paul was evidently to assassinate him on board ship and dispose of his body at sea. Somehow the insidious plan became known to Paul and **he decided** not to go directly to the eastern Mediterranean but **to go back through Macedonia.** Possibly he had wanted to be in Jerusalem for Passover; now the best he could hope for would be Pentecost (Acts 20:16).

20:4-6. The mention of these seven men implies what is stated elsewhere: Paul was concerned for the collection for the saints in Jerusalem. As representatives of various churches they carried funds. Three men were from Macedonia (**Sopater . . . Aristarchus, and Secundus**) and four were from Asia Minor (**Gaius . . . Timothy . . . Tychicus** [cf. Eph. 6:21; Col. 4:7; 2 Tim. 4:12; Titus 3:12], **and Trophimus** [cf. Acts 21:29; 2 Tim. 4:20]). Their rendezvous point was **Troas.** In Acts 19:29 Gaius is said to be "from Macedonia," whereas in 20:4 he is said to be **from Derbe.** Probably these are two different men (cf. a third Gaius, from Corinth; 1 Cor. 1:14).

In Acts 20:5-6 Luke resumed another **we** section. Luke was left at **Philippi** in chapter 16 and evidently remained there until this point. Then he rejoined the party to accompany Paul to Jerusalem. **The Feast of Unleavened Bread** was in the spring. They made the 150-mile trip from Philippi to Troas in **five days.**

c. The discourse at Troas (20:7-12)

20:7. This is the clearest verse in the New Testament which indicates that Sunday was the normal meeting day of the apostolic church. Paul stayed in Troas for seven days (v. 6) and the church met **on the first day of the week.** Luke's method of counting days here was not Jewish, which measures from sundown to sundown, but Roman, which counted from midnight to midnight. This can be stated dogmatically because "daylight" (v. 11) was **the next day** (v. 7).

Probably the church met at night because most people had to work during the day. Because Paul was leaving them, possibly for the final time, he prolonged his discourse **until midnight**.

20:8-10. The presence of **many lamps** would contribute to a soporific atmosphere because the lamps consumed oxygen. Probably crowded conditions exacerbated the condition.

A young man named Eutychus (lit., "fortunate") proved to be true to his name. Luke, the physician, affirmed that Eutychus **was picked up dead** after he had fallen from a **third-story** window. It was normal for the larger rooms to be on the top floor of a building (see comments on 1:13). After the manner of Elijah and Elisha (1 Kings 17:21; 2 Kings 4:34-35), **Paul** embraced Eutychus and the young man came **alive**.

20:11-12. As part of the meal they participated in the Lord's Supper (**broke bread and ate;** cf. v. 7), and the meeting continued until dawn. Eutychus, **the** fortunate **young man** (cf. vv. 9-10), was taken **home alive**.

d. The discourse at Miletus (20:13-38)

20:13-15. Evidently **Paul** remained in Troas longer than he originally planned (v. 7). To compensate for the delay he sent the rest of the party **on ahead**. The journey across land from Troas to **Assos** is much shorter than by sea. By this arrangement Paul was able to stay a bit longer in Troas. They sailed from Assos **to Mitylene . . . Chios . . . Samos** and **Miletus**. The voyage to the last three stops took one **day** each.

20:16-17. Paul avoided a stop in Ephesus because **he was in a hurry to reach Jerusalem, if possible, by the day of Pentecost.** He knew it would take far too long to say good-bye to his many friends in Ephesus. **Miletus** was some 30 miles by land south of **Ephesus,** so he **sent** for the Ephesian church's **elders** to come there. Evidently his ship had a layover of several days in the port of Miletus.

20:18. Here begins another "sample sermon" of Paul (cf. 13:16-41; 14:15-17; 17:22-31), this one given to Christian leaders, men he loved deeply. This discourse has three parts: (a) a review of Paul's *past* three-year's ministry in Ephesus (20:18-21), (b) a description of the *present* situation (vv. 22-27), and (c) the *future* responsibilities of the Ephesian elders (vv. 28-35).

20:19. In Ephesus, as elsewhere, **the Jews** had plotted against Paul, though the riot recorded in Acts 19 emphasizes opposition from Gentiles. Here Luke referred to **the plots** by the Jews, but he did not detail them (cf. Paul's words in 1 Cor. 15:30-32; 16:9; 2 Cor. 1:8-10).

20:20. Paul's ministry **from house to house** (cf. 2:46) is contrasted with his public ministry and probably refers to house churches. If so, each elder was possibly the overseer of a house church. Paul both preached and **taught**.

20:21. In the Greek the words **repentance** and **faith** are joined together by one article. This may imply that these two words stress two aspects of trust in Christ (cf. 2:38). When a person places his faith in Christ, he is then turning from (repenting of) his former unbelief. This is the same message for **both Jews and Greeks** (i.e., Gentiles; cf. 19:10; Gal. 3:28).

20:22. Here Paul began to describe present circumstances (vv. 22-27). The NIV words, **compelled by the Spirit,** are literally, "bound in the Spirit" (*dedemenos . . . tō pneumati*). Probably this refers to the Holy Spirit's guidance in the apostle's life (cf. Luke 2:27; 4:1; Acts 8:29; 10:19; 11:12; 16:6-7). Paul's reason for **going to Jerusalem,** though not stated, evidently was to take the offering from churches to the poor saints in Jerusalem (24:17; cf. comments on 21:12-14).

20:23. Already Paul had been warned by **the Holy Spirit**—that is, evidently by people with the Spirit-given gift of prophecy—**that prison and hardships** awaited him in Jerusalem. He anticipated troubles in Jerusalem when he wrote Romans 15:30-31. Yet he was determined to go there (cf. Acts 19:21; 20:16).

20:24-25. When these verses are read together, it becomes clear that the **preaching** of **the kingdom** and **the gospel of God's grace** are related. God's work of grace enables believing Gentiles to have both the privilege of salvation and of entering the Lord's millennial reign.

Because of the warning to Paul (v. 23) he concluded that the Ephesian elders would not **see** him **again.** The NIV translation, **none of you,** is a bit strong. The Greek refers to "all" of them (as a group) not seeing Paul again (lit., "all of you [as a group] will never see me again"). He did not say no *one* of them would see him again (cf. the pl. verb in v. 38). His ambition was to **finish the race,** which later he said he did (2 Tim. 4:7).

20:26-27. In conformity with Ezekiel 33:1-6, Paul declared himself to be **innocent of the blood of all men** in Ephesus (cf. comments on Acts 18:6). He preached to "all men" (cf. "all the Jews and Greeks . . . in the province of Asia," 19:10). And the content of His preaching was all of God's **will** (*boulēn,* "purpose, plan"; cf. 2:23; 4:28; 13:36; Eph. 1:11; Heb. 6:17). Interestingly Paul used several words in referring to his role in communicating the gospel: (a) "preach" (Acts 20:20) and **proclaim** (v. 27), both from *anangellō* ("proclaim, announce"); (b) "taught" (from *didaskō,* "teach," v. 20); (c) "declared" (v. 21) and "testifying" (v. 24), both from *diamartyromai* ("solemnly bear witness to"); (d) **declare** (*martyromai,* "testify," v. 26).

20:28. In verses 28-35 Paul turned to the future responsibilities of the elders in Ephesus. First, they were to **guard** (*prosechete,* "attend to" in the sense of taking care of) themselves **and all the flock.** Significantly before they could provide for the flock they had to care for their own spiritual well-being.

Here the elders are described as **overseers** (*episkopous,* from the verb *episkopeō,* "to look for, to care for"). The term "elders" has primarily Jewish antecedents and stresses the dignity of the office, whereas "overseers" is mainly Greek in its derivation and emphasizes the responsibility of the office, namely, "to look after" others.

The value of the flock, over which the elders were to **be shepherds** (*poimainein,* pres. tense infinitive; cf. 1 Peter 5:2), is underscored by Paul's calling it **the church of God** (i.e., the church that is owned by God) and by his referring to its purchase (cf. Ps. 74:2) by **His own blood.**

Nowhere does the Bible speak of the blood of God the Father. The Greek here can read "by the blood of His own," that is, His own Son. The Greek word for **bought** means "acquired, obtained."

20:29-31. These verses explain the need for the command to elders to guard themselves and the flock (v. 28). False teachers, called **savage wolves,** would enter **the flock,** or even some of their **own** would **distort the truth.** This warning is attested by subsequent references to the church at Ephesus (1 Tim. 1:6-7, 19-20; 4:1-7; 2 Tim. 1:15; 2:17-18; 3:1-9; Rev. 2:1-7). Again Paul urged the leaders, **Be on your guard!** He had repeatedly warned them of the danger of doctrinal error. In fact he had done so **with tears** (cf. Acts 20:19).

20:32. Paul then committed them first **to God** and then **to the Word of His grace.** Though trust in God is essential, it must be accompanied by obedience to His Word. This will lead to edification (it will **build you up**) and to **an inheritance among all those who are sanctified** (cf. 26:18; Eph. 1:18; Col. 1:12; 1 Peter 1:4).

20:33-34. Paul worked to provide for himself and for others (cf. 18:3; Eph. 4:28).

20:35. Hard work also enabled Paul to **help the weak** (cf. 1 Thes. 5:14). **The words** of the Lord, **It is more blessed to give than to receive,** are not found in the four Gospels. They represent an oral tradition passed on to the early church.

20:36-38. The elders' deep love for Paul is displayed here. The remainder of the trip to Jerusalem (21:1-25) is filled with details of such expressions of love for Paul. Why did Luke linger on these points? He did this to contrast the response to Paul in Gentile lands with that of the Jews in Jerusalem.

e. The dissuasions from Miletus to Jerusalem (21:1-16)

21:1. Each of these stops—from **Cos** to **Rhodes** to **Patara**—evidently represented one day's **sea** journey (cf. 20:13-15).

21:2. Rather than remain on board a boat which put into port each evening Paul boarded **a ship** which evidently was larger and would make the journey **to Phoenicia** with no stops.

21:3-4. Going **south** of **Cyprus** they **landed at Tyre where** the **ship was to unload its cargo,** a task which took a week (v. 4). The persecution of the early church in Jerusalem had scattered the believers to Phoenicia (11:19), so Paul sought out believers there.

Through the Spirit the believers at Tyre **urged Paul not to go on to Jerusalem.** In view of the phrase, "through the Spirit," was Paul wrong in pursuing his course to Jerusalem? Probably he was not violating God's will for several reasons: (1) Acts 20:22 and 21:14 imply it was God's will for Paul to continue on to Jerusalem (cf. 19:21). (2) The comfort given by God (23:11) implies Paul had not stubbornly refused the Lord's will. (3) In 23:1 Paul declared he had lived in all good conscience to that day.

Probably, then, the words "through the Spirit" (21:4) mean they knew through the Spirit that Paul would suffer in Jerusalem (cf. 20:23); therefore, concerned for his safety, they tried to dissuade him.

21:5-6. This was Paul's first contact with this church at Tyre, and yet after only one week there was a strong bond of love. The departure scene is not as poignant as the one at Miletus (20:37), but it was meaningful.

21:7. The ship then proceeded 20 miles south to **Ptolemais,** modern Acre or Akko, for **a** one-day stop. Probably the church there began as a result of the persecutions mentioned in 11:19, as did the church in **Tyre.**

21:8-9. The 40-mile trip to **Caesarea** may have been by land or by sea; probably it was the latter because the overland route was rather difficult and the port at Caesarea was commodious.

Paul's host there was **Philip the evangelist.** He was **one of the Seven** (cf. 6:1-5) who ministered to widows in Jerusalem. His evangelistic work was described in chapter 8. Evidently he had settled in Caesarea (cf. 8:40), even though it was the most Roman city in Israel, and had lived there for some 20 years when Paul arrived.

He had four unmarried (*parthenoi,* lit., "virgins") **daughters who had the gift of prophecy.** This spiritual gift, evident in the early church, was not limited to men (cf. 1 Cor. 11:5). Their apparent silence in view of all the other prophecies regarding Paul's suffering in Jerusalem is surprising.

21:10-11. Agabus, a prophet introduced in 11:28, **came down from Judea,** evidently from Jerusalem, for it was his home and Caesarea was in the province of Judea. Dramatically he illustrated how Paul would be bound in Jerusalem. Prophets often symbolized their predictions (cf. 1 Kings 11:29-31; Isa. 20:2-4; Jer. 13:1-7; Ezek. 4). The fact that Paul would be imprisoned was known by several including Paul himself (Acts 20:23).

21:12-14. After **the people** heard that prophecy, they **pleaded with Paul not to go up to Jerusalem** (cf. v. 4). Even Luke joined in the plea, as indicated by the use of **we** here. But the apostle **would not be dissuaded.**

Though Luke did not say so, apparently one reason this trip to **Jerusalem** was important to Paul was that he was taking an offering to the Jerusalem believers (cf. 24:17; Rom. 15:25-27; 1 Cor. 16:1-4; 2 Cor. 8:13-14; 9:12-13; Gal. 2:10). **Paul** wanted to make this presentation of money in order to fortify one of his basic doctrines, the unity of Jew and Gentile in Christ (Eph. 2:11-22; 3:6).

21:15-16. The distance **from Caesarea to Jerusalem** is about 65 miles, a two-day journey by horse. Some think **the home of Mnason** was at a halfway point **where** Paul and his party may have spent the night. More probably, Mnason was a resident of Jerusalem. Interestingly Mnason was **from Cyprus,** the island where Barnabas was born.

2. THE CAPTIVITY AT JERUSALEM (21:17–23:32)

a. *The detention of Paul (21:17-36)*

(1) The vow of Paul (21:17-26). **21:17-19.** As soon as possible **Paul and** his party had an audience with **James,** head of the church at Jerusalem (cf. 15:13-21), and with **all** that church's **elders.** Luke only mentioned Paul's report of **what God had done among the Gentiles through his ministry** (cf. 14:27). Obviously Paul at this point also turned the large offering for the saints at Jerusalem (24:17) over to James in the presence of the elders. Probably because Luke's emphasis was on the gospel going from the Jews to the Gentiles, he omitted this matter of money.

THE TEMPLE AREA

ANTONIA FORTRESS

PORTICO

COURT OF THE GENTILES

SACRED ENCLOSURE

PORTICO

COURT OF PRIESTS WITH ALTAR

TREASURY (WOMENS' COURT)

SOLOMON'S PORCH

THE HOLY OF HOLIES

THE HOLY PLACE

COURT OF ISRAEL

COURT OF THE GENTILES

ROYAL PORTICO

21:20-21. When the leaders of the Jerusalem church **heard** of Paul's ministry among the Gentiles, **they praised God.** Undoubtedly included in this was thanksgiving for the Gentile offering to the believing Jews in Jerusalem (see comments on vv. 12-14).

While there was rejoicing over Paul's report, there was also apprehension about Paul's reputation among believing **Jews** who were **zealous for the Law.** A patently false report had gone out concerning Paul. It was true **Paul** taught **Gentiles** that it was religiously inconsequential whether they circumcised their sons or not and he did not teach them Jewish customs. However, he never taught **Jews . . . not to circumcise their** sons or to disregard Jewish **customs.**

21:22-24. James and the elders suggested that Paul **join in** the **purification rites** of **four men** who had taken a **vow** and **pay their expenses.** This was for the purpose of placating Jewish believers. Whether Paul's actions accomplished this is left unstated. That was beside Luke's purpose.

The details of this vow are unknown; it can only be surmised exactly what Paul was to do. The four men evidently had a Nazirite vow. At the conclusion of their vow some costly sacrifices were required

of each man (cf. Num. 6:13-17). These men evidently were too poor to pay for them. Paul was asked to underwrite the expense of their sacrifices and thereby display his sympathy with the zealots of **the Law.**

Was Paul wrong in entering into this arrangement, which was a specific part of the Law? For several reasons it may be said he was not: (1) Paul himself had previously taken a Nazirite vow (Acts 18:18). (2) Later he unashamedly referred to this incident before Felix (24:17-18). (3) This action on Paul's part only confirmed one of the principles of his ministry which was to become like a Jew to win the Jews, and to become like one under the Law to win those under it (1 Cor. 9:20). (4) One of Paul's goals for the Jerusalem trip, along with relief of the poor, was the unifying of Jews and Gentiles. (5) Paul was not denying the finished work of Christ by offering animal sacrifices. The epistles Paul had already written by this time (Gal., 1 and 2 Thes., 1 and 2 Cor., Rom.) make it clear that such a denial was incomprehensible. He must have looked on these sacrifices as memorials. After all, this will be the significance of millennial sacrifices (Ezek. 43:18–46:24; Mal. 1:11; 3:3-4). (6) Paul later asserted he did not violate his own conscience (Acts 23:1).

21:25-26. The decision of the Jerusalem Council was once again iterated (cf. 15:20, 29). The elders assured **Paul** that their plan (mentioned in 21:23-24) did not conflict with the council's earlier **decision.** Paul then followed the elders' suggestion **and purified himself** with **the four men** (vv. 23-24). This did not conflict with Paul's teaching that Jews and Gentiles cannot be brought under the Law to be saved. This was a matter of Jewish custom, not of salvation or of sanctification.

(2) The violence of the people (21:27-36). **21:27.** This opposition to Paul came not from believers but from unbelieving Jews. A riot was instigated by **some Jews from the province of Asia,** a place where the gospel had enjoyed great success. These men, in Jerusalem for the Feast of Pentecost, immediately recognized their old nemesis in **the temple** and incited **the whole crowd and seized him.** This is the sixth time a crowd was incited

because of Paul's ministry (14:19; 16:19-22; 17:5-8, 13; 19:25-34).

21:28-29. The patently false charges they brought against Paul were similar to those raised against Stephen (6:11, 13-14). When they accused Paul of bringing **Greeks into the temple area** they were assuming a falsehood. Such an act in Jewish eyes would have **defiled** their **holy place.** Gentiles were permitted into the court of the Gentiles but no farther. Two inscriptions have been found on a balustrade separating the court of the Gentiles from the rest of the temple area. These warned Gentiles they would have themselves to blame for their deaths which would certainly ensue if they would proceed beyond the barrier (cf. Eph. 2:14).

So deep was this feeling that the Romans gave permission to Jews to fulfill this death sentence, even if the intruder was a Roman citizen.

21:30. The whole city was galvanized into action; they seized **Paul** and **dragged him from the temple.** Here the "temple" evidently refers to the court of the men. After they had brought Paul out, **immediately the gates were shut** so that no one could proceed beyond the court of the Gentiles and thus defile the temple.

21:31-32. Adjoining the temple area to the northwest was the Fortress of Antonia with two flights of steps leading into the outer court of the temple (see the sketch of the temple area and the fortress). **Troops** were stationed there, and more were added during Jewish feast days. They were part of the Roman Tenth Legion. **The commander** of the troops at the fortress, Claudius Lysias (cf. 23:26), **at once took some officers and soldiers and ran down to the crowd.** "Commander" is *chiliarchos*, leader of a thousand soldiers (25:23). The "officers" (*hekatontarchas*, lit., "rulers of hundreds" or centurions) indicates at least 200 **soldiers** were involved since the noun is plural.

21:33-36. These men rescued **Paul,** who was promptly **arrested** (*epelabeto*, "laid hold of," the same verb trans. "seizing" in v. 30) by **the commander** who **ordered him to be bound with two chains.** So great was the confusion and **violence** Paul **had to be carried by the soldiers. The crowd . . . kept shouting, Away with him!** In the same city a crowd

had shouted similar words against the Lord Jesus (Luke 23:18; John 19:15).

b. The defense of Paul (21:37–23:10)

(1) Before the mob (21:37-22:29). **21:37-38. The commander,** surprised that **Paul** could **speak Greek,** had supposed the apostle to be an **Egyptian** insurrectionist who had not yet been apprehended by the Romans. Evidently this Egyptian rebel was unable or refused to speak Greek.

Josephus wrote of an Egyptian impostor who claimed to be a prophet. He said this Egyptian had gathered 30,000 followers (Luke with accuracy states **4,000;** Josephus had a tendency to inflate numbers) and in A.D. 54 came to the Mount of Olives promising his adherents that the walls of Jerusalem would collapse at his command. Instead, the Roman army promptly marched on them, killed some and captured others, while the remainder were scattered. The Egyptian escaped.

Undoubtedly the people of Israel would have liked to lay their hands on this character who had caused so much trouble. When Lysias saw the riot in the temple, he assumed the center of the attention was this Egyptian and that the Jews were venting their wrath on him.

21:39-40. Paul assured the commander he was **a Jew** (with rights to be in the temple) and also **a citizen of Tarsus,** where he learned Greek. Tarsus was a city which enjoyed a good reputation, particularly for being an educational center. As yet Paul had not revealed his Roman citizenship (cf. 22:23-29).

When **Paul** was granted **permission to speak to** the mob, he addressed **them in Aramaic,** the common language of Palestinian Jews, used throughout the Middle East at that time. He **stood on the** stairs of the fortress overlooking **the crowd** below.

Paul's defense was in three parts: (a) his conduct before his conversion (22:1-5), (b) his conversion (22:6-16), and (c) his commission to minister (22:17-21).

22:1. The vocatives **Brothers and fathers** with which Paul began his speech are those Stephen used (7:2). Stephen's speech and martyrdom had a lasting impression on Paul! (cf. 8:1)

22:2. When they heard him speak to them in Aramaic, they quieted down.

Undoubtedly the Jews in the land were pleased if not surprised that a Jew of the Dispersion, as **Paul** was, could speak Aramaic as well as Greek. So they settled down and listened.

22:3-9. How much of Paul's rearing took place in Jerusalem (cf. 26:4) is not known. The verb translated **brought up** is from *anatrephō*, which may also mean "educate." One of his mentors was the beloved and esteemed **Gamaliel** (cf. 5:34).

Paul's point here is obvious. He had been thoroughly committed to **the Law** and to stamping out Christianity. On the **Way**, see comments on 9:2 (cf. 19:9, 23; 22:4; 24:14). His determination was so deep that only a radically supernatural transformation could change his viewpoint. He recounted the events of his conversion (22:6-9; cf. 9:1-6).

22:10-11. The statement, **There you will be told all that you have been assigned to do** (cf. 9:6), looks ahead to Paul's future ministry and anticipates his words in 22:14-15.

22:12-13. The Jewish viewpoint of this address is seen in Paul's description of **Ananias. He was a devout observer of the Law and highly respected by all the Jews living there.** These facts about him are not given in Acts 9. **Brother** reflects the same outlook seen in 22:5 where Jews in Damascus were called the "brothers" of the Jews in Jerusalem.

22:14-15. The reference to seeing Christ, **the Righteous One,** is important because it qualified Paul to be an apostle (cf. 1 Cor. 9:1; 15:8). The term "Righteous One" was also used by Stephen (Acts 7:52). The **all men** to whom Paul was to present the gospel included Gentiles, kings, and Jews (9:15).

22:16. Two questions revolve about this verse. First, when was Paul saved—on the Damascus Road or at Judas' house? Several factors suggest he was saved on the Damascus Road: (1) The gospel was presented to him directly by Christ (Gal. 1:11-12), not later by Ananias. (2) Already (Acts 22:10) Paul said he had submitted in faith to Christ. (3) Paul was filled with the Spirit *before* his baptism with water (9:17-18). (4) The Greek aorist participle, *epikalesamenos*, translated **calling on His name** refers either to action which is simultaneous with or before that of the main verb. Here Paul's calling on Christ's name (for salvation) preceded his water

baptism. The participle may be translated, "having called on His name."

Second, what then do the words **wash your sins away** mean? Do they teach that salvation comes by water baptism? Because Paul was already cleansed spiritually (see comments in preceding par.), these words must refer to the symbolism of baptism. Baptism is a picture of God's inner work of washing away sin (cf. 1 Cor. 6:11; 1 Peter 3:21).

22:17-18. Paul's departure from **Jerusalem,** according to 9:29-30, was because of the advice of Christian brothers. Actually a combination of divine revelation (22:17-18) and human direction led Paul to go to Tarsus.

22:19-20. Paul's rejoinder to the **Lord** shows he thought the Jews would be impressed by the radical change in his life; after all, he had been most zealous in persecuting believers (8:3; 9:2; 22:4-5; 26:11), even taking part in the martyrdom of **Stephen** (7:58; 8:1).

22:21-22. When **Paul** mentioned his commission to preach **to the Gentiles,** the mob was moved to instant rage and violence. Preaching to Gentiles could not have caused such a response because the religious authorities of Israel had preached to Gentiles (cf. Matt. 23:15). Paul's message that infuriated the mob was that Jews and Gentiles were equal without the Law of Moses (cf. Eph. 2:11-22; 3:2-6; Gal. 3:28).

This response is important to the argument of the Book of Acts. It indicates the Jews in Jerusalem had irrevocably refused the gospel of Jesus Christ and had sealed their fate. Less than 20 years later in A.D. 70 the city of Jerusalem became rubble and ruin (cf. Matt. 24:1-2; 21:41; 22:7). This, of course, does not mean Israel will not be restored in the future (cf. Rom. 11:26).

22:23-24. The people in the mob **threw off their cloaks and flung dust into the air** as expressions of intense anger. **The commander** who could not understand Aramaic was confused by everything that was going on. He was determined to get to the bottom of it all, even if it meant flogging **Paul.**

This flogging is different from Paul's beating with rods at Philippi and on two other occasions (2 Cor. 11:25; Acts 16:22-23). Nor was it the same as the Jewish 39 lashes administered with the long whips, a punishment Paul had received five times (2 Cor. 11:24). The Roman scourge was inflicted with shorter whips embedded with pieces of metal or bones and attached to a strong wooden handle. It could kill a man or leave him permanently crippled. This was the punishment Christ received (Matt. 27:26), leaving Him unable to carry His cross.

22:25-27. By law **a Roman citizen** not proven **guilty** of a crime could not be flogged. **Paul** called the centurion's attention to this fact by a question. When this was reported **to the commander** he was incredulous that Paul in his circumstances, the object of such hatred by the Jews, could be **a Roman citizen.**

22:28. During the reign of Emperor Claudius (A.D. 41–54; see the chart on Roman emperors at Luke 2:1) it was possible to purchase Roman **citizenship.** Those in government who sold this privilege could feather their nests with the bribery money. In contrast with **the commander . . . Paul** was **born a citizen** because his parents were citizens.

22:29. **The commander,** knowing **he had put Paul . . . in chains,** was fearful that Rome would learn he had violated Roman law. The chains probably were those that would hold him for flogging. Paul as a citizen was in chains at a later time (26:29).

Could not anyone avoid flogging by simply claiming to be a Roman citizen? Perhaps; but if a person falsely claimed to be a citizen, he was liable to the death penalty.

(2) Before the Sanhedrin (22:30–23:10). **22:30.** By this time **the commander** knew the accusations against Paul were Jewish (cf. vv. 23-29), and the best way to unearth these was to have a hearing before **the Sanhedrin.** If the prisoner was found innocent he could be released, but if the charges were valid the case could be remitted to the procurator, the Roman governor (cf. 23:26-30).

23:1-2. The setting for this brief trial is given here. After Paul claimed **all good conscience** in his ministry (cf. 24:16; 1 Cor. 4:4), **the high priest Ananias ordered those standing near Paul to strike him on the mouth.** Ananias' response is in keeping with what is known about him from Josephus, who

described him as insolent, hot-tempered, profane, and greedy. Ironically, at the beginning of Paul's ministry another Ananias helped him receive his sight.

23:3-5. Paul's outburst was triggered by the high priest's illegal command. How could the priest **violate the Law** while sitting as **judge** over one who supposedly had transgressed **the Law?** Jewish **law** presumed the accused to be innocent until proven guilty. Like a **whitewashed wall,** Ananias looked all right on the outside but was weak and deteriorating inwardly. Jesus too in His trials was struck on the mouth and challenged the legality of it (John 18:20-23).

Paul's statement, **Brothers, I did not realize that he was the high priest,** presents a problem. This could hardly be because of poor eyesight because Paul had "looked straight (*atenisas,* lit., "looked intently') at the Sanhedrin" (Acts 23:1). Paul's words could be irony in which he was saying he *could* not recognize such a violent man as priest. However, the word "brothers" (v. 5) renders this interpretation improbable. Possibly there was such confusion the **high priest** was not identifiable. Certainly he was not wearing his priestly garments. It is also probable Paul did not know Ananias personally because the apostle had not had contact with the Sanhedrin for many years. The high priesthood changed hands frequently (see the chart on Annas' family at 4:5-6).

At any rate, Paul recognized the position of the high priest even if he did not respect the priest as a person.

23:6-9. In such a scene justice was impossible. Recognizing this, **Paul** changed his tactics completely and stated his **hope in the resurrection of the dead** along with **the Pharisees** (on this hope, cf. 24:15; 26:6-7; 28:20). This immediately disrupted the proceedings because it started an argument **between the Pharisees and the Sadducees** (cf. 4:1-2). By using this clever tactic, Paul divided his enemy. Amazingly the **Pharisees** defended Paul, a fellow **Pharisee.**

23:10. Paul was in more danger in the midst of the Jews than he was in a Roman prison. So again he was brought up the steps to **the** army **barracks** at the Antonia Fortress (cf. 21:35).

ACTS

c. The danger to Paul (23:11-32)

23:11. The importance of this vision was not only in its comfort and encouragement (cf. 18:9-10) but also in the confirmation it gave of Paul's plans to go to Rome. The gospel of Christ would literally go from **Jerusalem** to **Rome** by means of the Apostle **Paul**. This was the fourth vision **the Lord** gave Paul (cf. 9:4-6; 16:9; 18:9-10).

23:12-13. So great was the hatred for Paul, **the very next morning . . . 40 fanatical Jews formed a conspiracy and bound themselves with an oath not to eat or drink until they had killed** him (cf. the crowd's efforts to kill him; 21:31). The verb for taking an oath is *anathematizō* (whence the Eng. "anathema"), which means a person binds himself under a curse if he does not fulfill his oath. Presumably these men were later released from this oath by lawyers because Paul's circumstances changed through a dramatic series of events.

23:14-15. The complicity of **the chief priests and elders** in this plot reveals both their lack of a legitimate case against Paul and their base characters. The fanatic zeal of the 40 men is also seen because a number of them would certainly be killed in overcoming Paul's guards, should their plan be carried out.

23:16-22. Paul's unnamed nephew somehow **heard** about the **plot** of the 40 and was able to get to **the barracks** to tell **Paul** and then **the commander.** Many unresolved questions come to mind. Was Paul's nephew a Christian? How did he secure this information? Did Paul's **sister** live in Jerusalem? If Paul had relatives living in Jerusalem, why did he not stay with them?

The nephew was a **young man** (vv. 17-19, 22). This Greek word *neanias*, used in verse 17, was earlier used of Paul (7:58) and Eutychus (20:9). It may refer to a man in his twenties or thirties. (*Neaniskos*, a synonym of *neanios*, is used in 23:18 and 22. In v. 19 the NIV has "young man" but the Gr. does not.) When the fortress **commander** heard of this plan, he **cautioned** Paul's nephew not to **tell anyone** he had **reported this.**

23:23-24. The commander decided to get Paul away from this danger spot. So he made every possible provision for Paul's security in his escape. First, he sent

Paul in the company of more than 470 men—**two . . . centurions . . . 200 soldiers** (a centurion was over 100), **70 horsemen, and 200 spearmen.** Second, they began the journey under cover of nightfall at **9 P.M.** In addition, **Caesarea** would be a far more secure place, not as subject to a riot as was Jerusalem. For the third time(!) Paul left a city surreptitiously, at night (cf. Damascus, 9:25; Thessalonica, 17:10).

23:25-30. When a prisoner was forwarded to a superior, the subordinate officer was required to accompany the subject with a written statement of the case.

This **letter** from **Claudius Lysias** presents the essentials of the case. The commander bent the truth in saying he **rescued Paul** (v. 27) because he actually learned from a subordinate that Paul was a Roman citizen (22:26). He also discreetly omitted any reference to his preparing to have Paul flogged (cf. 22:25, 29).

The importance of this document is seen in 23:29 where the commander declared Paul to be innocent. Compare similar comments by Gallio (18:14-15), the city executive of Ephesus (19:40), Pharisees (23:9), Festus (25:25), and Herod Agrippa II (26:31-32).

23:31-32. The journey to **Antipatris** from Jerusalem was more than 35 miles. This must have been a forced march because they arrived by **the next day.** The terrain from Jerusalem to Lydda or Joppa (modern-day Lod; cf. 9:32-43), seven or eight miles before Antipatris, was difficult and would provide suitable cover for an ambush party. Once the entourage was in Antipatris **the soldiers** were no longer needed. The remaining 27 miles to Caesarea could be traversed with less danger.

3. THE CAPTIVITY AT CAESAREA (23:33-26:32)

a. Paul's defense before Felix (23:33-24:27)

23:33-35. When the cavalry and Paul **arrived,** Felix held a minor preliminary interrogation. Felix was the procurator (**governor**) of Judea about A.D. 52-58. He is one of three Roman procurators mentioned in the New Testament. The others are Pontius Pilate (A.D. 26-36) and Porcius Festus (A.D. 58-62). Felix married Drusilla (24:24), a sister of Herod Agrippa

86

II, the Agrippa in 25:13–26:32. (See the chart on the Herods at Luke 1:5.)

After Felix learned Paul **was from Cilicia he** determined to **hear the case.** Evidently a case could be tried in the province of the accused or in the province in which his alleged crime took place. The question actually involved "**what** sort of (*poias*) **province**" Paul was from. At this time Cilicia was not a full province but was under the legate of Syria, for whom Felix was a deputy. The legate would not want to be bothered with such a small case as this. Furthermore, Felix would not want to incur the Jews' wrath by forcing them to present their case against Paul in his hometown Tarsus, a city so far away. Felix could make only one decision and that was to hear the case. But witnesses against Paul would have to be present (cf. Acts 23:30).

24:1. The high priest himself **went down to Caesarea** as well as **some of the elders** of the Sanhedrin. They had hired an attorney (*rhētoros*, "a public speaker, orator," used only here in the NT), **Tertullus,** who was to present the case **before** Felix.

24:2-4. The lawyer spent almost as much time on his introduction as he did on the specific charges against **Paul.** His description of **Felix** was obviously fawning flattery, for Felix was known for his violent use of repressive force and corrupt self-aggrandizement. Felix had been a slave, won his freedom, and curried favor with the imperial court. Tacitus, a Roman historian, bitingly summed up Felix's character with the terse comment, "He exercised royal power with the mind of a slave."

24:5-8. The accusations were three: (1) Paul was a worldwide **troublemaker, stirring up riots** everywhere. (2) **He** was **a** leader **of the Nazarene sect.** (3) He attempted **to desecrate the temple.**

The first charge had political overtones because Rome desired to maintain order throughout its empire.

The second charge was also concerned with the government because Tertullus made it appear that Christianity was divorced from the Jewish religion. Rome permitted Judaism as a *religio licita* (a legal religion), but it would not tolerate any new religions. By describing Christianity as a "sect" (*haireseōs*, "faction,

party, school"; whence the Eng. "heresy") of the Nazarenes, the attorney made Paul's faith appear to be cultic and bizarre.

Desecrating the temple also had political overtones because the Romans had given the Jews permission to execute any Gentile who went inside the barrier of the temple (cf. 21:28). At this point Tertullus modified the original charge made in 21:28. There Paul was accused of bringing a Gentile (Trophimus the Ephesian) into the temple courts; here Paul is said to have attempted desecration. The truth was severely damaged in the clause **so we seized him,** the implication being they took Paul to arrest him. (The NIV marg. gives some words that are added in vv. 6-8 in a few less-reliable Gr. mss.)

24:9-10. After **the Jews** had agreed to the veracity of their prosecuting attorney's charges, **Paul** was given an opportunity to answer.

His introduction was much shorter and truthful. He implied Felix knew the situation in Judea well enough to make an accurate decision.

24:11. Paul gave several points in his own defense. First, he had not been in **Jerusalem** long enough to instigate a riot. In fact one of his purposes for being in Jerusalem was **to worship,** to observe the Feast of Pentecost (20:16). Another reason was developed in 24:17-18.

24:12-13. Second, even Paul's calumniators could **not** cite an instance when he instigated a riot in the city.

24:14-16. Third, he worshiped **the God of** Israel in full conformity **with the Law and . . . the Prophets** (cf. 26:22; 28:23). (On the term "the Law and the Prophets" see Matt. 5:17.) Furthermore his faith was not in **a** sect but in Christianity, which was known as **the Way** (cf. Acts 9:2; 19:9, 23; 22:4; 24:22). His **hope** in the **resurrection** (cf. 23:6; 26:6-7) was **the same** as that of his accusers (Paul assumed a number of them were Pharisees). By this Paul meant Christianity was an outgrowth of the Old Testament. Further, Paul **always** sought **to keep** his **conscience clear** (cf. 23:1). "Clear" translates *aproskopon* (lit., "not causing to stumble, or not offending"), used only two other times in the New Testament, both by Paul (1 Cor. 10:32; Phil. 1:10).

24:17. This is the only time in Acts Paul's goal of bringing an offering to Jerusalem from the Gentile churches is mentioned. Luke did not stress this because it was not a major factor in his argument. However, it was most important to Paul as is evidenced by his frequent allusions to it in his epistles (Rom. 15:25-28; 1 Cor. 16:1-4; 2 Cor. 8:13-14; 9:12-13; Gal. 2:10).

What did Paul mean when he said he went **to Jerusalem . . . to present offerings?** Perhaps he meant he "entered the temple to present offerings" (cf. Acts 24:18). But more probably he meant he offered thank offerings for God's blessings on his ministry.

24:18. Again Paul affirmed that he was not the instigator of a **disturbance** (cf. v. 12); his accusers were!

24:19-21. Finally, Paul said his genuine accusers were not present, the **Jews from the province of Asia** who made the original false allegations and incited the riot in the temple (cf. 21:27). Since **the Sanhedrin** had not found him guilty (23:1-9), Tertullus' speech did not really contain any legitimate charges.

24:22. How **Felix** knew about Christianity can only be surmised. Probably he heard about it from Drusilla, his wife, who was a daughter of Herod Agrippa I and a sister of Herod Agrippa II. Because she was a Jewess (v. 24) she would know about **the Way.** Besides this, Felix could scarcely have ruled in Judea for several years without learning something about the faith of the early church.

Rather than make a decision which would have been unfavorable to the religious authorities he **adjourned the proceedings.** He said, **When Lysias the commander comes . . . I will decide your case.** Whether Claudius Lysias (cf. 23:25-30) ever came to Caesarea or not was beside the point; the case had been postponed indefinitely.

24:23. Felix, evidently aware of Paul's innocence, granted him a limited amount of **freedom** as a prisoner under the guardianship of **the centurion.** Later another centurion gave Paul similar freedom in Sidon (27:3).

24:24-26. Felix must have taken a brief trip **with his wife, Drusilla.** When they returned, Felix **sent for Paul** who **spoke about faith in Christ Jesus.** Felix was brought under conviction when **Paul discoursed on righteousness, self-control, and the judgment to come.** Well he should, for his marriage to Drusilla was his third and he had to break up another marriage to secure her. His regime was marked by injustices that contrasted with the righteousness of God. And he was a man grossly lacking in self-control.

The duplicity and greed of Felix is seen in his desire to be bribed by **Paul.**

24:27. To placate **the Jews,** Felix **left Paul in prison** even though he knew Paul was innocent. **Felix** eventually lost his position because he was cruelly intemperate in putting down a Jewish and Gentile conflict in Caesarea.

b. Paul's defense before Festus (25:1-12)

25:1. This section (vv. 1-12) is crucial because in it Paul appealed to Caesar. It sets the direction for the remainder of the book and also shows how the apostle reached Rome.

Little is known of Porcius **Festus,** Roman procurator of Judea, A.D. 58-62, but what history discloses is favorable. His desire to rule well is attested by his going to Jerusalem **three days after arriving in the province.** No doubt he had heard of the volatile nature of that city!

25:2-3. One item heavy on the minds of the religious authorities was a trial for **Paul.** They knew their case was so weak that the only way they could rid themselves of him was by **ambush** while he was being **transferred** from Caesarea **to Jerusalem.**

25:4-5. Evidently **Festus** felt their request was unreasonable so he promised to reopen the case in **Caesarea.** Paul was already there and Festus was returning **there.**

25:6-7. The scene of previous trials repeated itself. Luke added, however, that the **charges** were **many** and **serious.**

25:8-9. After **Paul** briefly and categorically denied the allegations against him, **Festus** asked the prisoner if he would be **willing to go . . . to Jerusalem** for another **trial.** Festus had changed his mind on this (cf. vv. 4-5), apparently feeling this would be a suitable compromise to placate **the Jews.** Also he was realizing he did not know how to handle this kind of religious case (v. 20).

25:10. Paul would have nothing to do with this switch for several reasons: (1) The journey from Caesarea to Jerusalem would be most dangerous. The 40 Jews who two years before (cf. 24:27) had taken an oath to murder Paul (23:13-14) would probably have gotten out of their oath somehow by then, but they would still want to kill Paul. (2) The possibility of a fair trial in Jerusalem was remote. (3) He had already languished as a prisoner in Caesarea for some two years.

The charges brought against Paul were civil (they said he had done **wrong to the Jews**); therefore the present **court** where Festus represented Caesar, was the proper one.

25:11. The charges were serious enough to demand a **death** penalty. If the accusations were **true,** Paul said, he was willing **to die.** He interpreted Festus' suggestion that he go to Jerusalem (v. 9) as tantamount to delivering Paul over to the **Jews,** even though the trial would be conducted by Festus.

25:12. There is some debate as to whether **Festus** was legally bound to remand the case **to Caesar** (Nero, who reigned from A.D. 54–68), or if he could have chosen to handle the case himself. If Festus had decided to hear the case and made a negative decision, Paul could still have appealed to Caesar. But Festus probably had no alternative but to transfer the case to Rome. So **after he had conferred with his council,** he announced that in view of Paul's appeal, he must go **to Caesar.**

c. Paul's defense before Agrippa II (25:13–26:32)

25:13. The **King Agrippa** referred to here was Agrippa II, son of Herod Agrippa I (12:1) and a great-grandson of Herod the Great (Matt. 2:1). (See the chart on the Herods at Luke 1:5.) At this time he was a young man of about 30 years of age and the ruler of territories northeast of Palestine with the title of King. Because he was a friend of the Roman imperial family he was awarded the privilege of appointing the Jewish high priest and also had been made the custodian of the temple treasury. His background made him eminently qualified to hear Paul; he was well acquainted with the Jews' religion (cf. Acts 25:26-27).

Agrippa II and his sister **Bernice,** came to **Caesarea to pay their respects to Festus.** Though Bernice had a tendency to support the Jews she lived a profligate life. She had an incestuous relationship with Agrippa, her brother.

25:14-21. Festus reviewed his dealings with **Paul's case** which had been **left** to him by **Felix.** Festus frankly confessed he was incapable of handling the case (v. 20). In particular he did not understand Paul's insistence on the resurrection of Christ (v. 19).

25:22. The rehearsal of the situation had its desired effect on **Agrippa.** The Herodian family was useful to Rome for its knowledge of Jewish affairs and Agrippa's insights would be helpful **to Festus.**

25:23-24. The petty King **Agrippa** and his sister **Bernice** used this occasion to display their position, clothes, and ceremony. Luke undoubtedly was contrasting the lowly prisoner **Paul** in the audience room with Agrippa and Bernice and **the high-ranking officers and the leading men of the city.** Because five cohorts (each cohort had a thousand soldiers) were stationed at Caesarea, five high-ranking officers were there (*chiliarchoi,* lit., "commanders of a thousand"; cf. 21:31). **Festus** told **Agrippa** that the Jews urged that Paul should die.

25:25-27. The statement in verse 25 is significant because it shows that Festus, like Felix before him, **found** Paul **had done nothing deserving of death** (cf. 23:9, 29; 26:31).

It would look bad for Festus **to send** Paul to Caesar with no clear **charges against him.** Festus believed that **Agrippa,** with his knowledge of Jewish customs and laws, could help Festus **write** out some charges that would be specific enough for Caesar Nero to consider.

Two interesting terms for Roman royalty are found in this chapter, the first of which is *Sebastos* meaning "revered" or "august" and used in the New Testament only in 25:21, 25; 27:1. In chapter 25 it is translated "Emperor" and in 27:1 it is rendered "Imperial."

The other term is *kyrios* meaning "lord." In 25:26 "the lord" is translated **His Majesty.** Both Augustus and Tiberius refused this title for themselves because they felt it exalted them too highly;

however, by the time Paul made his appeal to Caesar, Nero was on the throne and "lord" was used much more commonly of the Caesar. Though Nero did accept the title of "lord," he had not yet gone to the excesses that characterized his reign later. At this juncture Nero was reputed to be a fair-minded ruler.

26:1. Paul had already made **his defense** to Festus (25:6-12), so now the apostle directed his address to **Agrippa.** Furthermore, the purpose of this speech was for Agrippa's information.

The motioning of the **hand** was evidently after the manner of orators of that time. This speech has a number of parts: (1) complimentary remarks (26:2-3), (2) Paul's early life in Judaism (vv. 4-8), (3) his zeal in opposing Christianity (vv. 9-11), (4) his conversion and commission (vv. 12-18), (5) his ministry (vv. 19-23), (6) his verbal jousts with Festus and Agrippa (vv. 24-29).

26:2-3. Paul was sincere in these compliments because he knew **Agrippa** was indeed **well acquainted with all the Jewish customs and controversies,** in addition to being a practicing Jew.

In contrast with Tertullus who promised a brief speech before Felix (24:4), Paul implied his defense might be more lengthy. This is the climax of all Paul's defenses recorded in Acts (cf. 22:1-21; 23:1-8; 24:10-21; 25:6-11).

26:4-8. In summary, Paul asserted that from his early **life he lived . . . according to** and for the **hope** of Israel (vv. 6-7; cf. 23:6; 24:15; 28:20). (On his living **in Jerusalem,** see 22:3.) He stated that this hope involved the resurrection from **the dead.** This is why Christ quoted Moses (Ex. 3:6) to defend the doctrine of the Resurrection (Matt. 22:32). Because Yahweh is the God of Abraham, Isaac, and Jacob, people must be resurrected in order to receive the promise God made to them. Likewise the promises made to the Jews demand they be resurrected in the coming Messianic Age.

Paul's reference to the **12 tribes** of Israel shows the error of British-Israelism with its "10 lost tribes of Israel" (cf. Matt. 19:28; Luke 22:30; James 1:1; Rev. 7:4-8; 21:12).

26:9-11. Besides being committed to Judaism, Paul had also been fanatic in his opposition to Christianity (cf. 8:3; 9:2; 22:4-5, 19). His casting votes **against** imprisoned Christians does not necessarily mean Paul was a member of the Sanhedrin. It may simply mean he agreed with the Sanhedrin's action (cf. 8:1; 22:20).

When Paul apprehended Christians he **tried to force them to blaspheme,** that is, to recant their belief in Jesus.

26:12-18. As Paul recounted his conversion (cf. 9:1-19; 22:1-21) he once again told of the **light . . . brighter than the** noonday sun (22:6). For the first time the reader is informed that the language of the heavenly **voice** was **Aramaic,** though it was implied because the spelling of Saul's name in 9:4 and 22:7 was Aramaic.

Some believe that the statement, **It is hard for you to kick against the goads,** means Paul had guilt feelings and was violating his conscience in persecuting believers in Christ. However, Paul wrote later that in spite of his blaspheming, violence, and persecution of the church he was shown mercy because he was acting in ignorance and unbelief (1 Tim. 1:13). Kicking the goads evidently referred to the futility of his persecuting the church.

The statement of Paul's commission (Acts 26:18) closely resembled the work of the Messiah, predicted in Isaiah 35:5; 42:7, 16; 61:1. As a representative of the Lord **Jesus** Christ, Paul did figuratively what the Lord Jesus will someday do on earth literally. Spiritually Paul had led many **from the darkness** of sin (John 3:19; 2 Cor. 4:4; Eph. 4:18; 5:8; Col. 1:13) **to light** in Christ (John 12:36; 2 Cor. 4:6; Eph. 5:8; Col. 1:12; 1 Thes. 5:5). This salvation releases from Satan's **power** (John 8:44; Heb. 2:14) and gives **forgiveness of sins** (Acts 2:38; 5:31; 10:43; 13:38; Eph. 1:7; Col. 1:14) and a spiritual inheritance (Rom. 8:17; Col. 1:12) with **those who are sanctified,** that is, those who are positionally set apart to God by His redeeming work (cf. 1 Cor. 1:30; Heb. 10:10; 13:12).

26:19-23. Paul's statement in verse 20 is something of a problem. He said he had **preached** to **those in Damascus, then to those in Jerusalem and in all Judea.** But Paul wrote the Galatians he was unknown in the churches of Judea (Gal. 1:22). Many have felt that there was an early textual corruption and that the Greek text should read, "To those in

PAUL'S JOURNEY TO ROME

MILES

0   100   200   300

Damascus, then to those in Jerusalem, and throughout every country, both to Jews and Gentiles." Admittedly the present Greek text is rough (it changes from the dative case to the accusative), but this textual emendation is extremely speculative and unnecessary.

Probably Paul first summarized his ministry to the Jews and then described his work among **Gentiles.** He affirmed much the same in Acts 26:17-18. In other words Paul's statement here is not to be taken in strict chronological sequence but as a general overview of his ministry. First, he preached to Jews and then to Gentiles, in conformity with 1:8. Both groups needed to **repent and turn to God.** Frequently in Acts the apostles spoke of repentance (2:38; 3:19; 5:31; 8:22; 11:18; 13:24; 17:30; 19:4; 20:21).

Furthermore, Paul asserted, his message was a fulfillment of Old Testament prophecies (26:22; cf. 24:14; 28:23), concerning the death and resurrection of the Messiah. Frequently in Acts, the apostles also spoke of Christ's resurrection.

26:24-29. Festus, with his Greek outlook, thought the doctrine of the Resurrection was impossible (cf. 17:32; 23:6-7), so he **interrupted** Paul, though the apostle had already made his primary points. Festus said that Paul was **out of** his **mind,** that his education was **driving** him **insane.**

But **Paul** clearly asserted his sanity and then turned once again to **Agrippa. None of this**—that is, Christ's death and resurrection and the beginning of the church—could have **escaped** Agrippa's attention. He was well-schooled in Judaism, and Christianity was no esoteric secret society.

Finally Paul pressed the issue with a forthright question, **King Agrippa, do you believe the prophets?** (cf. 26:22) **I know you do** (cf. Paul's witness to Felix, 24:24).

Now Agrippa was in a corner. If he accepted the prophets he would be forced to admit Christ Jesus fulfilled them. His only escape was to parry the question with an interrogative of his own.

The NIV translation of 26:28 catches the spirit of Agrippa's question well. It was probably a joking rebuttal of Paul.

Paul took his response seriously, for he loved people for the Lord's sake. Even if it took a **long** time to win Agrippa to Christ, Paul was willing to take the time. He replied that he prayed that Agrippa and **all who** were **listening to** him would **become** like him (i.e., a Christian), **except for these chains.** (This is the first mention of chains on Paul since 22:29.) So Paul's defense came to a conclusion.

26:30-32. Already others had said Paul was innocent: Pharisees (23:9); Claudius Lysias, the commander in Jerusalem (23:29); and Governor **Festus** (25:25). Now **Agrippa,** a man of power, well-trained in Judaism and sympathetic with Jews, stated, **This man could have been set free, if he had not appealed to Caesar.**

4. THE CAPTIVITY AT ROME (CHAPS. 27-28)

a. The sea journey (chap. 27)

Why did Luke go into such lengthy detail about the voyage from Caesarea to Rome? There is no easy answer. (1) It may simply be a device to emphasize Paul's journey to and his arrival at Rome. As the Gospel writers stressed the Lord's final approach to Jerusalem and His last days there to heighten the impact of His death and resurrection, so Luke climaxed his Luke-Acts work with the proclamation of the gospel of the kingdom to Gentiles in the Roman capital.

(2) Luke may have used the example of great ancient epics of his day which commonly employed the theme of a storm and shipwreck. This would parallel the modern use of a chase scene in a movie or television drama. The problem with this view is a simple one. How does this contribute to Luke's purpose in writing? Simply following the example of ancient epics would not really add to the book.

(3) Possibly the writer desired to show a parallel with Jonah and his storm (Jonah 1:4-15). After Jonah lived through the storm by miraculous means he preached to a large Gentile capital city. The comparison with Paul is obvious.

(4) The purpose of this account is to show God's sovereign protection and direction in Paul's ministry. It was God's will for the apostle to minister the gospel in Rome.

(5) It was Luke's intention to show Paul's leadership and thereby to underscore the fact that God's program had

become primarily Gentile and therefore Paul was God's man of the hour. In the account Paul certainly does come off as the one who is in control even in the spheres of ocean travel and shipwreck.

(6) Some think the story is something of an allegory. In the Old Testament the sea was portrayed as an enemy; so here it figures opposition to the spread of the gospel. In spite of all antagonism the good news of the kingdom will survive and will ultimately reach its predetermined goal. But this is so allegorical it is a highly improbable view.

The answer to the question of Luke's great emphasis on the journey to Rome may be a combination of answers 1, 3, 4, and 5, though it is difficult to be dogmatic.

27:1. Who and how many **other prisoners** accompanied **Paul** to Rome is an unanswered question. Nor is the reader informed as to why the others were being taken to the capital city.

The **centurion . . . Julius, who** is a primary character in this account, **belonged to the Imperial Regiment,** an honorary title given to certain troops. "Imperial" translates *Sebastēs,* meaning "revered" (cf. comments on 25:25). A "centurion" commanded 100 soldiers (cf. 10:1; 21:32 ["officers" in NIV]; 22:25-26; 23:17, 23; 24:23).

Use of the pronoun **we** indicates Luke accompanied Paul on this journey.

27:2-3. Adramyttium, the home base of the **ship,** was east-southeast of Troas in northwest Asia Minor. Evidently the ship was making its last journey to its base before the stormy winter sailing season set in. Apparently the centurion wanted to find a ship bound for Rome along the way or to get to the Egnatian Road and use it to transport the prisoners.

Aristarchus evidently accompanied Paul to be his helper. Aristarchus stayed with Paul during his Roman incarceration (Col. 4:10; Phile. 24).

Interestingly **Paul** had **friends** in **Sidon,** the ship's first port of call after leaving Caesarea. The **kindness** of this centurion is mindful of another centurion's kindness (Acts 24:23).

27:4-8. The information in these verses points up the difficulty of sailing from east to west in the Mediterranean Sea. **The** prevailing **winds** blew from the

west so the ships would sail to the east **of Cyprus** and proceed with **difficulty** along the southwest coast of Asia Minor and to the east **of Crete.** When Paul sailed in the opposite direction, the ship took a more direct route (21:1-3).

In **Myra,** a port city on the south coast of Asia Minor, **the centurion found an Alexandrian ship sailing for Italy.** This was a grain ship (27:38) large enough to carry 276 passengers (v. 37). Egypt was Rome's breadbasket. The grain ships would commonly sail north to Asia Minor and then make their way west across the Mediterranean using the islands for as much protection as they could obtain from them.

Paul's journey on this second ship took him from Myra toward the island of **Cnidus** and then southwest to the south side of Crete, **to a place called Fair Havens.** The Cretans were known for their laziness and depravity (Titus 1:12). Later Paul wrote to Titus to appoint elders for that island's churches (Titus 1:5).

27:9-12. The Fast referred to here was probably the Day of Atonement which occurred in late September to early October. After that time of year the unsettled weather patterns over the Mediterranean Sea made sailing hazardous. In those days sea traffic ceased by early November.

Paul was perhaps included in the ship's council because of his experiences in travel (cf. 2 Cor. 11:25, "three times I was shipwrecked") and his natural leadership. Contrary to Paul's advice **the majority** (Acts 27:11) **decided** it best to **sail on** to a more commodious **harbor** and to **winter there.** The authority rested ultimately in the hands of **the centurion** because grain ships were considered to be in government service. So they sailed along the southern coast of **Crete.** They hoped to **reach** the harbor of **Phoenix.**

27:13-17. Once caught by a sudden **Northeaster,** a **hurricane**-like **wind,** they could not remain in the protection **of** Crete and **were driven** helplessly into the open sea. **Cauda,** a **small island** 25 miles south of Crete, provided a brief respite from the teeth of the wind. While they were south of the island they hauled in **the lifeboat** which was normally pulled in tow but now was probably full of water.

What is meant by **they passed ropes under the ship itself to hold it together** is not positively clear. It probably means the sailors encircled the boat with ropes so that the beams would not separate and leak more water from the pressure of the sea and storm.

The sandbars of Syrtis were located off Libya of North Africa. The Greek word translated sea anchor is *skeuos* and literally means "vessel" or "equipment," so it could refer to any gear. Probably, however, it was an anchor.

27:18-26. The storm raged on; so the next day they threw the cargo overboard and the day after that the ship's tackle. So awesome was the storm that after many days, they gave up all hope of getting out of the situation alive.

The passengers and probably also the crew had gone . . . without food for a number of days. Perhaps the storm had destroyed much of the supplies; some evidently were seasick; and perhaps many were too discouraged to eat (cf. v. 33). After Paul reminded them of the advice he gave earlier at Crete (cf. v. 10), he encouraged them with a message from God. This was not the first time a vision had lifted Paul's spirits (cf. 18:9-10; 23:11); in fact, in the Jerusalem vision (23:11) God promised Paul not only safety there but ultimately a safe journey to Rome. Here too God (through an angel) promised that Paul would stand trial before Caesar. Twice Paul urged his shipmates (all 275 of them; cf. 27:37) to keep up their courage (vv. 22, 25). The verb "to keep up one's courage" (*euthymeō*) is used only three times in the New Testament—twice here and in James 5:13 ("to be happy"). The verb has the idea of having good feelings or being in good spirits. Even as a prisoner Paul did not hesitate to make known his faith in God.

27:27-32. The Adriatic Sea was a term used in New Testament times of the sea not only between Italy and Greece but also south of Italy and Sicily to Malta. After two weeks in the storm the sailors finally sensed they were coming to some land. The water was becoming shallower (from 120 feet to 90 feet). Their soundings were made by throwing into the water a line with lead on it (*bolisantes*, "took soundings," is lit., "heaving the lead") and thereby judging the water's depth. As they came into even shallower water they dropped four anchors. Paul warned the centurion that the sailors attempting to escape needed to stay with the ship (cf. v. 24). The soldiers cut . . . the lifeboat loose which meant that all aboard could only depend on the Lord God for deliverance.

27:33-35. Because of Paul's confidence in the Lord to keep them all safe (v. 24), he encouraged them to eat (vv. 33-34). He then took some bread, unashamedly thanked God for it, and broke it and started eating. Though this sounds like an observance of the Lord's Table, it probably was not. Most of those 276 people were not Christians. Rather it was a public testimony by Paul of his faith in the God and Father of the Lord Jesus as well as a practical expedient of eating in order to muster strength for the ordeal ahead.

27:36. Two problems were mentioned in verse 33—the people had "gone without food" for a fortnight and also had "been in constant suspense." But now they were all encouraged (lit., "they became of good spirits," *euthymoi*; cf. vv. 22, 25) and ate some food themselves— solving the two problems in verse 33.

27:37-38. This grain ship not only carried cargo but also had 276 passengers and crew members. The number of prisoners (v. 42) is not stated. This was not an excessively large ship, for Josephus wrote about a ship which he boarded to Italy which carried 600 passengers.

27:39-40. Seeing a bay with a sandy beach at dawn, they decided to try running the ship aground. They cut away the anchors and rudders . . . hoisted the foresail, and headed for the beach. The word "rudders" (*pēdaliōn*) literally describes the blades of oars and refers to paddle rudders extending from the sides of the ship. These were tied while the ship was at anchor.

27:41. The ship struck a sandbar which the sailors had not seen. Because of the beating of the waves, the back of the ship was broken to pieces while the bow was stuck in the sand.

27:42-44. Because soldiers were accountable with their own lives for any prisoners who escaped (cf. 12:19; 16:27) they planned to kill the prisoners to prevent any of them from swimming away and escaping. For the soldiers this was simply a matter of self-preservation.

The centurion, however, wanted to spare Paul's life. He saw the value and trustworthiness of this prisoner and so forestalled the soldiers' plan. Obviously God was sovereignly at work to spare Paul for ministry at Rome and to guarantee the fulfillment of his prediction (v. 24). In the cold rain (28:2) the passengers (soldiers and prisoners) and crewmen who could swim were urged to swim ashore, while the rest held onto the ship's debris.

As Paul had predicted, the ship was lost (27:22), they ran aground on an island (v. 26), and no one perished (v. 22).

b. The sojourn at Malta (28:1-10)

28:1-2. They were shipwrecked on **Malta**, a small **island** 60 miles south of Sicily. Malta had good harbors and was ideally located for trade. In two weeks the storm had carried them 600 miles west of Fair Havens, Crete. **The islanders** translates *hoi barbaroi* (lit., "the barbarians"), a Greek term used to refer to non-Greek-speaking people. This does not mean the people were savages or uncultured, but that their civilization was not Greek-oriented. They **showed . . . unusual** hospitality to the victims of the shipwreck, building them a fire and welcoming them.

28:3. Because the weather was cold (v. 2) a snake would be stiff and lethargic. Of course the heat of **the fire** would drive **a viper** from the flames and also make it more active.

28:4-6. Seeing that **Paul** was bitten by **the snake the islanders** concluded he was **a murderer**, now getting **justice.** But when he was unaffected by the viper's bite (with not even any swelling of his hand), the islanders superstitiously **said** that Paul **was a god.** No doubt Paul's response to this, though not recorded, was similar to his reaction at Lystra (14:8-18).

28:7-10. Publius took **Paul** and others (**us** included Luke) to his **estate . . . for three days.** One benefit of Paul's ministry was the healing of Publius' **father** (who had **fever and dysentery**) and **the rest of the sick on the island.** Interestingly Paul, besides not being harmed by the viper, was used by God to heal others. No wonder the islanders **honored** the shipwrecked men **in many**

ways, even giving them **supplies** before they set sail three months later (v. 11). These supplies were no doubt given in gratitude for Paul's services.

c. The summation of service at Rome (28:11-31)

28:11. Since the crew and passengers left Crete in October or November ("after the Fast," 27:9) and were in the storm two weeks, their **three** months' stay on Malta brought them through the winter into February or March. In that time they saw another **ship** docked at the island. Because **it was** of **Alexandrian** origin, it too was probably a grain ship (cf. 27:6, 38) from Egypt that had spent the three months of winter, when it was too dangerous to sail, at a seaport on Malta. Probably it was at the Valletta harbor.

The twin gods Castor and Pollux on the ship's figurehead were the heavenly twin sons of Zeus and Leda according to Greek mythology; supposedly they brought good fortune to mariners. If their constellation, Gemini, was seen during a storm it was an omen of good luck. Possibly Luke included this detail to contrast the superstition of the people of Malta, Rome, Greece, and Egypt with Christianity.

28:12-14. The journey was carefully traced by Luke: from Malta to **Syracuse,** Sicily; to **Rhegium** (today Reggio) on the "toe" of Italy; to **Puteoli** (today Pozzuoli), 152 miles south of Rome; and finally **to Rome** itself. Puteoli was an important commercial seaport halfway between Rhegium and Rome. At Puteoli Paul and his companions **found some brothers.** This is significant because it shows that the gospel had already spread from Rome to this Italian seaport. No doubt a church had been planted in Rome by Roman Jews who had gone to the Pentecost feast, heard Peter's sermon, were saved, and returned home with the good news (2:10). Paul accepted the believers' invitation to **spend a week with them.** Perhaps the centurion was in charge of unloading the ship or else had to spend a week in Puteoli on some other business.

28:15. The Christians at Rome soon **heard** of Paul's **coming,** so **they traveled as far as the Forum of Appius** (a market town 43 miles from Rome) **and the Three Taverns** (33 miles from Rome) **to meet**

him and his companions. The noun *apantēsin*, translated as an infinitive "to meet," was used in Greek literature of an entourage coming out of a city to meet an official going to the city. It is also used in 1 Thessalonians 4:17, which speaks of believers being "caught up . . . to meet (*apantēsin*) the Lord in the air." Like an entourage, believers will go up at the Rapture into the clouds to meet Jesus, their Savior and Lord, coming from heaven to take them to Himself. Paul looked forward to joining that group.

At the sight of these men Paul thanked God and was encouraged (lit., "received courage," *tharsos*; the verb *tharseō* is used in the LXX of people in distress who were then encouraged; cf. comments on Mark 6:50). At last God was bringing Paul to Rome. And the welcome of fellow believers, whom he had never met, uplifted his soul. So they proceeded on the Appian Way, "the queen of the long roads," to the city of Rome.

28:16. Because he was a trusted prisoner, **Paul was allowed to live by himself, with a soldier to guard him.** Paul's residence was in a rented house (v. 30).

28:17-20. The climax of the book is found in these closing verses (vv. 17, 24) which speak of another rejection of the gospel and of Paul's taking the message to Gentiles (v. 28).

As usual **Paul** first spoke with **the Jews** (cf. 9:20; 13:5, 14; 14:1; 17:2, 10, 17; 18:4, 19; 19:8). In this case **he called . . . the leaders** to meet with him because he could not go to their synagogues.

In his presentation Paul made several significant points: (1) He was innocent of damaging **the Jews** or their **customs** (28:17). (2) The Roman authorities in Judea thought Paul was innocent (v. 18; cf. 23:29; 25:25; 26:31-32). (3) Paul's only recourse was **to appeal to Caesar** because the Jews refused to deal with Paul justly (28:19; cf. 25:11). (4) This fourth point is a major one: he was not pressing charges against Israel; he only wanted to be acquitted (28:19). (5) His primary objective in calling the leaders was to **talk with** them about **the hope of Israel.** This term and concept was used by Paul a number of times in the last part of Acts (cf. 23:6; 24:15; 26:6-7). The hope of Israel was more than a resurrection; it meant

fulfillment of the Old Testament promises to Israel (cf. 26:6-7). Paul firmly believed Jesus is the Messiah of Israel who will return someday and establish Himself as the King of Israel and Lord of the nations (cf. 1:6).

28:21-22. The response of the leaders was ambivalent: they said they knew nothing about Paul and their only reports about Christianity **(this sect)** were negative. One wonders if they were being truthful. How could Jewish leaders be unaware of Jews in Rome who had become Christians and also of the existence of tensions between the church and Judaism in Jerusalem? It is quite possible they had heard nothing of Paul, but they probably knew more than they acknowledged about Christianity. They were interested in hearing Paul's **views** since they knew **that people** were **talking against** his message.

28:23-24. In the Jewish leaders' second meeting with **Paul,** they were much more definitive in their responses to the gospel. This time they **came in even larger numbers.** The discussion was also longer. All day long Paul spoke of **the kingdom of God and tried to convince them about Jesus from the Law of Moses and from the Prophets** (cf. 24:14; 26:22).

The term "kingdom of God" includes the death and resurrection of Christ as its basis but also looks ahead to Christ's reign on earth. It is clearly eschatological in significance (cf. 1:3-6; 8:12; 14:22; 19:8; 20:25; Luke 1:33; 4:43; 6:20; 7:28; 8:1, 10; 9:2, 11, 27, 60, 62; 10:9, 11; 11:2, 20; 12:31-32; 13:18, 20, 28-29; 14:15; 16:16; 17:20-21; 18:16-17, 24-25, 29-30; 19:11; 21:31; 22:16, 18, 29-30; 23:42, 51). To the Jews the concept of the Messiah dying for sins as an atonement and the teaching of justification by faith as the way of entering the kingdom sounded strange.

The Jews were divided in their responses. **Some were convinced . . . but others** refused to **believe** (Acts 28:24). In Greek the verb "convinced" is in the imperfect tense and may be rendered, "began to be convinced," that is, they were not fully convinced. The same verb, used in verse 23, is translated, "tried to convince."

28:25-27. The disagreement **among** the Jewish leaders in Rome about Paul's message showed that they were not amenable to the gospel. With prophetic insight **Paul** applied the words of **Isaiah** (6:9-10) to his own contemporaries. Obstinate refusal to believe results in **calloused** hearts, deafened **ears,** and spiritually blinded **eyes.** This had happened to Israel both in Isaiah's day and in Paul's (cf. Rom. 11:7-10). Interestingly Paul ascribed Isaiah's words to the inspiration of **the Holy Spirit** (cf. Acts 4:25).

28:28. At the climax of this book and now for the final time the gospel focus was turned toward **Gentiles.** From Jerusalem to Rome most Jews rejected it and in city after city the message was then directed tó non-Jews. Now in the capital of the Roman world the same phenomenon occurred; so it will be until the fullness of Gentiles comes (Rom. 11:19-26).

28:29. Some Greek manuscripts add, "After he said this, the Jews left, arguing vigorously among themselves" (NIV marg.). Probably this verse should not be included in the text, though this undoubtedly was their response (cf. v. 25).

28:30-31. These verses are Luke's final "progress report" (cf. 2:47; 6:7; 9:31; 12:24; 16:5; 19:20). With freedom **in his own rented** quarters Paul . . . **preached** God's **kingdom.** This eschatological expression indicates not only that Jews and Gentiles alike are justified by faith but also that Gentiles with Jews will participate in the millennial kingdom (cf. comments on 28:23).

One question commonly raised pertains to Paul's activities after this two-year captivity. What happened? Perhaps no charges were filed in Rome and Paul was released. The Jews would know they had no case against Paul outside of Judea and so would be reluctant to argue their cause in Rome.

Probably Paul returned to the provinces of Macedonia, Achaia, and Asia and then turned west to Spain according to his original plans (Rom. 15:22-28). Then he ministered once more in the Aegean area where he was taken prisoner, removed to Rome, and executed.

During this two-year period Paul wrote what are commonly called his "Prison Epistles"—Ephesians, Colossians, Philemon, and Philippians (see the chart "Paul's Epistles, Written on His Journeys and During His Imprisonments," at Acts 13:16-25).

While Paul was in Rome during this incarceration the gospel was not bound. **He** spoke **boldly** (cf. comments on Acts 4:13). The last word in the Greek text of Acts is the adverb *akōlytōs* which means **without hindrance.** Men may bind the preachers, but the gospel cannot be chained!

And so it was that the kingdom message under God's sovereign control went from Jew to Gentile, and from Jerusalem to Rome.

BIBLIOGRAPHY

Alexander, Joseph Addison. *Commentary on the Acts of the Apostles.* New York: Charles Scribner, 1875. Reprint (2 vols. in 1). Grand Rapids: Zondervan Publishing House, n.d.

Barclay, William. *The Acts of the Apostles.* Philadelphia: Westminster Press, 1953.

Bruce, F.F. *Commentary on the Book of the Acts.* The New International Commentary on the New Testament. Grand Rapids: Wm. B. Eerdmans Publishing Co., 1954.

Dunnett, Walter M. *The Book of Acts.* Grand Rapids: Baker Book House, 1981.

Harrison, Everett F. *Acts: The Expanding Church.* Chicago: Moody Press, 1975.

Hiebert, D. Edmond. *Personalities around Paul.* Chicago: Moody Press, 1973.

Jensen, Irving L. *Acts: An Inductive Study.* Chicago: Moody Press, 1968.

Kent, Homer A., Jr. *Jerusalem to Rome: Studies in the Book of Acts.* Grand Rapids: Baker Book House, 1972.

Longenecker, Richard N. "The Acts of the Apostles." In *The Expositor's Bible Commentary,* vol. 9. Grand Rapids: Zondervan Publishing House, 1981.

Lumby, J. Rawson. *The Acts of the Apostles.* Cambridge: At the University Press, 1882.

Marshall, I. Howard. *The Acts of the Apostles: An Introduction and Commentary.* The Tyndale New Testament Commentaries. Grand Rapids: Wm. B. Eerdmans Publishing Co., 1980.

Morgan, G. Campbell. *The Acts of the Apostles*. New York: Fleming H. Revell Co., 1924.

Neil, William. *Acts*. New Century Bible Commentary Series. Rev. ed. Grand Rapids: Wm. B. Eerdmans Publishing Co., 1981.

Rackham, Richard Belward. *The Acts of the Apostles: An Exposition*. London: Methuen & Co., 1901. Reprint. Grand Rapids: Baker Book House, 1978.

Ryrie, Charles Caldwell. *The Acts of the Apostles*. Everyman's Bible Commentary. Chicago: Moody Press, 1967.

Thomas, W.H. Griffith. *Outline Studies in the Acts of the Apostles*. Grand Rapids: Wm. B. Eerdmans Publishing Co., 1956.

KEY PLACES IN PAUL'S MINISTRY

MILES

0   100   200   300

Places and Dates of the Writings
of the New Testament Epistles

Decade	Books	Places	Dates
A.D. 40–49	James	Jerusalem	A.D. 45–48
	Galatians	Antioch of Syria	40–49, after Paul's first missionary journey
50–59	1 Thessalonians	Corinth	50–54, in Paul's second missionary journey
	2 Thessalonians	Corinth	50–54, in Paul's second missionary journey
	1 Corinthians	Ephesus	About 56, in Paul's third missionary journey
	2 Corinthians	Macedonia	About 56, in Paul's third missionary journey
	Romans	Corinth	57, in Paul's third missionary journey
60–69	Ephesians	Rome	60
	1 John	Ephesus	60–65
	2 John	Ephesus	Early 60s
	3 John	Ephesus	Early 60s
	Philippians	Rome	60–61
	Colossians	Rome	60–62
	Philemon	Rome	60–62
	1 Timothy	Macedonia?	63–66
	Titus	Macedonia?	63–66
	1 Peter	Rome?	64
	Jude	?	67–80
	2 Timothy	Rome	67
	2 Peter	Rome?	67–68
	Hebrews	?	68–69

ROMANS

John A. Witmer

INTRODUCTION

This letter is the premier example of the epistolary form of writing, not only in the Pauline body of material and in the New Testament but also in all of ancient literature. It stands first in every list of the Apostle Paul's writings though it was not first in time of composition. This bears witness to the importance of the work both in its theme and in its content. It may also reflect the significance of the location of the letter's first readers, the imperial capital of Rome. In addition a possible tie grows out of the fact that the Book of Acts ends with Paul in Rome so that his letter to the Romans follows naturally in the order of Bible books.

Authorship. That Paul is the author of this letter is denied by almost no one. Even the ancient heretics admitted Romans was written by Paul. So do the modern (19th century and later) radical German critics, who deny many other facts in the Scriptures. Paul identified himself as the author by name, of course (1:1); but that is no guarantee of the acceptance of his authorship, since he did that in all his letters, including those for which his authorship is questioned or denied. In Romans Paul referred to himself by name only once, in contrast with several of his other letters; but a number of other internal details support Paul's authorship. He claimed to be of the tribe of Benjamin (11:1; cf. Phil. 3:5). He sent greetings to Priscilla and Aquila (Rom. 16:3), whom Paul had met in Corinth (Acts 18:2-3) and left in Ephesus (Acts 18:18-19) on his second missionary journey. Paul referred to his journey to Jerusalem with the love gift from the churches in Macedonia and Achaia (Rom. 15:25-27), facts confirmed in the Book of Acts (19:21; 20:1-5; 21:15, 17-19) and the epistles to the Corinthians (1 Cor. 16:1-5; 2 Cor. 8:1-12; 9:1-5). And Paul mentioned

several times his intention to visit Rome (Rom. 1:10-13, 15; 15:22-32), a fact also confirmed in the Book of Acts (19:21). These confirming coincidences between Romans and Acts in particular support Paul as the author of this letter.

Unity. Acceptance of the unity and integrity of Romans is another matter, however. A number of critics from Marcion to the present have questioned chapters 15 and 16 or parts of both as belonging to the letter. Chapter 16 is a special target, in part because of Paul's greetings to Priscilla and Aquila (v. 3), who were last seen settled in Ephesus (Acts 18:19, 26). But the couple had previously lived in Italy (Acts 18:2) and had left only because of an imperial decree. Their return to Rome when circumstances permitted is reasonable. The major Greek manuscripts support the unity of the letter, a position endorsed by the overwhelming consensus of scholarship.

Recipients. A valid question does exist concerning the identity of the recipients of this letter. Paul simply addressed it "to all in Rome who are loved by God and called to be saints" (Rom. 1:7); he did not address it to "the church in Rome." That a church did exist in Rome is obvious, because Paul sent greetings to the church that met in the home of Aquila and Priscilla (16:5). Probably several churches were in Rome; perhaps this multiplicity of churches is why Paul addressed the letter to "the saints" instead of to "the church."

Were these believers in Rome Jews or Gentiles in ethnic background? The answer is both. Aquila, for example, was a Jew (Acts 18:2), as were Andronicus, Junias, and Herodion, all three identified as Paul's relatives (Rom. 16:7, 11). According to Josephus and others a large Jewish colony lived in Rome (cf. Acts

ROMANS

28:17-28). But Rome was a Gentile city, the capital of a Gentile empire in which all Jews, believing and unbelieving, formed a small minority. In addition, though Paul never failed to witness and to minister to Jews, his calling from God was to be "the apostle to the Gentiles" (Rom. 11:13; cf. 15:16). So it is reasonable to conclude that his readers were mostly Gentile in background.

This conclusion is supported by evidence in the letter. Paul addressed Jews directly (2:17), and he included Jewish Christians with himself when he spoke of "Abraham, our forefather" (4:1, 12). On the other hand Paul directly said, "I am talking to you Gentiles" (11:13). Several additional passages indicate that Gentile Christians made up a segment of his readers (11:17-31; 15:14-16). In fact the implication from 1:5, 13 is that Paul considered the Christian community in Rome predominantly Gentile.

Since the Apostle Paul had not yet visited Rome, how had the Christian faith been introduced to the city? Apparently no other apostle had yet reached Rome, in the light of Paul's stated purpose to be a pioneer missionary and to open virgin territory to the gospel (15:20). In particular, it is evident that Peter was not in Rome at that time because Paul expressed no greetings to him, a grievous error if Peter indeed were there.

Perhaps a partial answer to the founding of the church at Rome is the fact that "visitors from Rome" (Acts 2:10) were in the crowd that witnessed the miracle of Pentecost and heard Peter's sermon. Some of them probably were among the 3,000 converts that day and returned to Rome as believers in Jesus Christ to propagate their faith. Other believers migrated to Rome through the years since Pentecost, for Rome was a magnet that drew people from all over the empire for business and other reasons. Aquila and Priscilla are good examples. They had lived in Italy before (Acts 18:2), and undoubtedly returned as soon as circumstances permitted. Phoebe (Rom. 16:1-2), apparently the courier of this letter, is another example. She did not go to Rome primarily to deliver Paul's letter; she delivered Paul's letter because she was making a trip to Rome. In fact, Phoebe's planned trip to Rome was undoubtedly the specific occasion for

Paul's writing this letter. Humanly speaking, Paul seized this opportunity to communicate with a group of Christians he was deeply interested in and planned to visit as soon as possible.

Just as Paul's absence of greeting to Peter in chapter 16 is evidence that Peter was not in Rome at the time, so his numerous greetings to individuals (28 persons are named or referred to, plus several groups) reveal the impact of Paul's ministry on the establishment and the development of the church in Rome. Many of the believers there were Paul's converts or associates in other parts of the empire. As a result Paul had a proprietary interest in the Christian community of Rome. He considered the church there one of his, as this letter bears witness.

Place and Date. Though Paul never named the city, it is obvious that he wrote this letter from Corinth, Cenchrea (16:1) being its eastern harbor. The letter was written at the close of Paul's third missionary journey during the "three months" he was in Greece (Acts 20:3) just before his return to Jerusalem with the offering from the churches of Macedonia and Achaia for the poor believers there (Rom. 15:26). After leaving Corinth, Paul was in Philippi during the Passover and the Feast of Unleavened Bread (Acts 20:6) and desired to reach Jerusalem by Pentecost (Acts 20:16). The letter was written, therefore, in the late winter or early spring of A.D. 57 or 58.

Purposes. While Phoebe's projected trip to Rome (Rom. 16:2) was undoubtedly the specific occasion for Paul's writing this letter, he had several objectives in writing. The most obvious was to announce his plans to visit Rome after his return to Jerusalem (15:24, 28-29; cf. Acts 19:21) and to prepare the Christian community there for his coming. The believers in Rome had been on Paul's heart and prayer list for a long time (Rom. 1:9-10) and his desire to visit them and to minister to them, unfulfilled to this point, was finally about to be satisfied (1:11-15; 15:22-23, 29, 32). Therefore Paul wanted to inform them of his plans and to have them anticipate and pray for their fulfillment (15:30-32).

A second purpose Paul had for writing this letter was to present a complete and detailed statement of the gospel message he proclaimed. Paul was eager "to preach the gospel also to you who are at Rome" (1:15) and he wanted them to know what it was. As a result in this letter Paul accomplished what Jude desired to do, "to write to you about the salvation we share" (Jude 3). Perhaps Jude was kept from doing this because Paul already had, for Romans certainly is a very full and logical presentation of the Triune Godhead's plan of salvation for human beings, from its beginning in man's condemnation in sin to its consummation in their sharing eternity in God's presence, conformed to the image of God's Son, the Lord Jesus Christ.

A third purpose for writing this letter is not as obvious as the first two. It is related to the tension between the Jewish and the Gentile segments in the Christian community at Rome and a possible conflict between them. Paul was hounded in his ministry by the Judaizers, who followed him from city to city and sought to lead his converts away from liberty in the gospel (Gal. 5:1). The letter to the Galatians is Paul's classic though not his only response to the Judaizers. Their attacks on Paul incorporated physical violence about the time this letter to the Romans was written (Acts 20:3). Whether the Judaizers had reached Rome before Paul or not, the Jew-versus-Gentile issue looms large in this letter. Paul did not take sides, but he carefully set forth both sides of the question. On the one hand he emphasized the historical and chronological priority of the Jews—"first for the Jew, then for the Gentile" (Rom. 1:16; cf. 2:9-10). He also stressed the "advantage . . . in being a Jew" (3:1-2; 9:4-5). On the other hand he pointed out that "since there is only one God" (3:30), He is the God of the Gentiles as well as the God of the Jews (3:29). As a result "Jews and Gentiles alike are all under sin" (3:9) and alike are saved by faith in the Lord Jesus Christ and His redemptive and propitiatory sacrifice. Furthermore, in order to bring believing Gentiles into His program of salvation, extending His grace to all human beings, God temporarily halted His specific program for Israel as a chosen nation, since that nation through its official leaders and as a whole had rejected in unbelief God's Son as the Messiah. During this period God contin-

ues to have a believing "remnant chosen by grace" (11:5) "until the full number of the Gentiles has come in" (11:25) and God takes up again and fulfills His promises to Israel as a nation.

Related to the Jewish-Gentile tension that runs throughout this letter is a muted but definite undertone that questions God's goodness and wisdom and justice as seen in His plan of salvation. No complaints against God are voiced, but they are implied. As a result this letter to the Romans is more than an exposition of Paul's "gospel of God's grace" (Acts 20:24), a declaration of God's plan of salvation for all human beings by grace through faith. It is a theodicy, an apologetic for God, a defense and vindication of God's nature and His plan for saving people. It sets God forth "to be just and the One who justifies the man who has faith in Jesus" (Rom. 3:26). It exults in "the depth of the riches of the wisdom and knowledge of God" (11:33) and challenges the readers, "Let God be true, and every man a liar" (3:4).

Theme. Growing out of Paul's three purposes for writing this letter (especially the latter two purposes), is the theme of the work. In the simplest and most general terms it is "the gospel" (1:16). More specifically it is "a righteousness from God" which "is revealed" in that gospel and is understood and appropriated "by faith from first to last" (1:17). This "righteousness from God" is first the righteousness God Himself possesses and manifests in all His actions; and second, it is the righteousness that God gives to human beings by grace through faith. This involves an imputed righteous standing before God (justification) and an imparted righteous practice and a progressively transformed lifestyle, the latter due to the regenerating and indwelling Holy Spirit of God (regeneration and sanctification). Practice is consummated and conformed to standing (glorification) when a believer in Jesus Christ through death and resurrection or through translation—"our adoption as sons, the redemption of our bodies" (8:23)—stands in the presence of God "conformed to the likeness of His Son" (8:29). God's program of salvation for people will not fail because it is His work, and "He who began a good work in you will carry it on to completion until the day of Christ Jesus" (Phil. 1:6).

OUTLINE

COMMENTARY

I. Introductory Matters (1:1-17)

A. Epistolary greetings (1:1-7)

The customary formula for letters in ancient times included (a) naming and identifying the author, (b) naming and

Paul's Introductions to His Epistles

Epistle	Paul's Titles	Paul's Companions	Addressees	Greetings
Romans	Paul, a *servant* of Christ Jesus, called to be an *apostle* and set apart for the gospel	—	To all in Rome who are loved by God and called to be *saints*	*Grace and peace* to you from God our Father and from the Lord Jesus Christ.
1 Corinthians	Paul, called to be an *apostle* of Christ Jesus by *the will of God*	*our brother* Sosthenes	To the *church of God* in Corinth, to those *sanctified* . . . together with all those everywhere who call on the name of our Lord Jesus Christ.	*Grace and peace* to you from God our Father and the Lord Jesus Christ.
2 Corinthians	Paul an *apostle* of Christ Jesus *by the will of God*	Timothy *our brother*	To the *church of God* in Corinth, together with all the *saints* throughout Achaia	*Grace and peace* to you from God our Father and the Lord Jesus Christ.
Galatians	Paul an *apostle*—sent not from men nor by man, but by Jesus Christ and God the Father, who raised Him from the dead	and all the *brothers* with me	To the *churches* in Galatia	*Grace and peace* to you from God our Father and the Lord Jesus Christ.
Ephesians	Paul, an *apostle* of Christ Jesus *by the will of God*	—	To the *saints* in Ephesus, the faithful in Christ Jesus	*Grace and peace* to you from God our Father and the Lord Jesus Christ.
Philippians	Paul . . . *servants* of Christ Jesus	Timothy	To all the *saints* in Christ Jesus at Philippi	*Grace and peace* to you from God our Father and the Lord Jesus Christ.
Colossians	Paul, an *apostle* of Christ Jesus *by the will of God*	Timothy *our brother*	To the *holy* and faithful brothers in Christ at Colosse	*Grace and peace* to you from God our Father.
1 Thessalonians	Paul	Silas and Timothy	To the *church* of the Thessalonians *in God the* Father and the Lord Jesus Christ	*Grace and peace* to you.
2 Thessalonians	Paul	Silas and Timothy	To the *church* of the Thessalonians *in God* our Father and the Lord Jesus Christ	*Grace and peace* to you from God the Father and the Lord Jesus Christ.
1 Timothy	Paul, an *apostle* of Christ Jesus by the command of God our Savior and of Christ Jesus our hope	—	To Timothy, my true son in the faith	*Grace, mercy, and peace* from God the Father and Christ Jesus our Lord.
2 Timothy	Paul, an *apostle* of Christ Jesus *by the will of God,* according to the promise of life that is in Christ Jesus	—	To Timothy, my dear son	*Grace, mercy, and peace* from God the Father and Christ Jesus our Lord.
Titus	Paul, a *servant* of God and an *apostle* of Jesus Christ	—	To Titus, my true son in our common faith	*Grace and peace* from God the Father and Christ Jesus our Savior.
Philemon	Paul, a *prisoner* of Christ Jesus	Timothy *our brother*	To Philemon our dear friend and fellow worker, to Apphia our sister, to Archippus our fellow soldier, and to the church that meets in your home	*Grace* to you *and peace* from God our Father and the Lord Jesus Christ.

identifying the recipient, and (c) a word of salutation. Paul followed this formula in this letter to the Romans despite the lengthy digression precipitated by the word "gospel." The same formula is used in all the New Testament letters except Hebrews and 1 John. (See the chart, "Paul's Introductions to His Epistles.")

1:1. Paul identified himself first as **a servant of Christ Jesus.** "Servant" *(doulos)* means slave, a person owned by another. Paul wore this title gladly (Gal. 1:10; Titus 1:1), reveling in the Old Testament picture of a slave who in love binds himself to his master for life (Ex. 21:2-6).

Paul also identified himself as **an apostle**—one sent with delegated authority (cf. Matt. 10:1-2)—a position to which he was **called.** (Lit., the Gr. is, "a called apostle.") This calling was from God (Acts 9:15; Gal. 1:1), though it was acknowledged by men (Gal. 2:7-9). It involved being **set apart** (from *aphorizō*; cf. Acts 13:2) **for the gospel of God,** the message of good news from God that centered on "His Son" (Rom. 1:2, 9) which Paul was "eager to preach" (v. 15) without shame (v. 16). This setting apart did not keep Paul from making tents to support himself and his companions (Acts 20:34; 1 Thes. 2:9; 2 Thes. 3:8) nor from mingling freely with all levels of pagan society. It was a setting apart to something—a commitment and dedication, not from things in isolation like the Pharisees. (Interestingly the word "Pharisee" means "separated one" in the sense of being isolated and segregated.)

1:2. The phrase **Holy Scriptures** refers obviously to the Old Testament and occurs only here in the New Testament (2 Tim. 3:15 uses different Gr. words for "holy" and "Scriptures"). Paul did not quote any **prophets** where **the gospel** was **promised,** but Philip's use of Isaiah 53:7-8 with the Ethiopian eunuch is a good example (Acts 8:30-35; cf. Luke 24:25-27, 45-47).

1:3-4. God's good news concerns **His Son,** identified as **Jesus Christ our Lord.** This asserts Christ's deity as basic to His person and prior to His Incarnation, since His identification with David's line "came to be," a literal rendering of the participle *genomenou*, translated **was.** He was genuinely **human** too, as His tie

with **David** and **His resurrection from the dead** show. That resurrection **declared** Him **to be the Son of God** because it validated His claims to deity and His predictions that He would rise from the dead (John 2:18-22; Matt. 16:21). This declaration was made **through** (lit., "in accord with") **the Spirit of holiness.** This is the Holy Spirit, and not, as some have suggested, Christ's human spirit.

1:5-7. Paul's ministry from Jesus was **among all the Gentiles,** which included the Romans, whom Paul addressed not as a church but as individual believers. Paul was the human agent (from and **for** Christ he **received grace and apostleship,** i.e., "the grace of apostleship"; cf. 12:3; 15:15) but the calling (God's summons to salvation; cf. 8:28, 30) came from the Lord and set his readers apart as "saints." **Obedience** and **faith** are often linked (cf. 15:18; 16:26; also cf. 1 Peter 1:2). Just as Paul was a "called" apostle, so the believers **in Rome** were **called to belong to Jesus Christ** (lit., "called of Jesus Christ") and **called to be saints** (lit., "called saints").

Paul's salutation like that in all his epistles, expressed the desire that they enjoy God's **grace and peace.**

B. Establishing rapport (1:8-15)

1:8-15. Paul made a practice of beginning his letters with a word of thanks to **God,** a specific prayer, and a personal message to the recipients. For the Romans he rejoiced that news of their **faith** had spread **all over the world,** a hyperbole meaning throughout the Roman Empire. His constant intercession for them (vv. 9-10) had the new note of petition for his projected visit, a heart-desire of long standing that finally was definitely on Paul's agenda (v. 10; cf. 15:23-24). This visit would be **mutually** beneficial spiritually; he desired to minister for three purposes: (a) to the strengthening of the Romans (1:11; to **impart . . . some spiritual gift** means either to exercise his own spiritual gift on their behalf or to bestow on them spiritual favors, i.e., blessings); (b) to see some spiritual fruit (**a harvest,** v. 13) **among** them and, in turn, (c) to be strengthened by them (v. 12). In this sense Paul's ministry at Rome would be the same as in **other** centers of the empire.

As a result of his "apostleship" (v. 5) to the Gentiles Paul felt obligated (lit., "I am a debtor") to the entire human race to proclaim God's good news (vv. 14-15). The word translated non-Greeks is literally, "barbarians," all other human beings from the viewpoint of the Greeks (cf. Col. 3:11). Parallel to it is the word foolish (*anoētois*; cf. Titus 3:3) in the next couplet, which has the significance of uncultured. Paul's sense of debt to the Gentile world produced an eagerness (I am so eager, Rom. 1:15) to evangelize it, including Rome, capital of the empire.

C. Emphasizing theme (1:16-17)

1:16. Paul's eagerness to evangelize sprang also from his estimate of his message, the gospel. (This is the fourth of five times Paul used the word "gospel" in these opening verses: vv. 1, 9, 15-17.) Many consider this the theme of the letter, which it is in one sense. At least Paul gladly proclaimed it as God's panacea for mankind's spiritual need. He identified it as the infinite resources (*dynamis*, "spiritual ability") of God applied toward the goal of salvation in the life of everyone who believes regardless of racial background. He recognized, however, a priority for the Jew expressed in the word first, which has sufficient textual support here and is unquestioned in 2:9-10.

Because the Jews were God's Chosen People (11:1), the custodians of God's revelation (3:2), and the people through whom Christ came (9:5), they have a preference of privilege expressed historically in a chronological priority. As the Lord Jesus stated it, "Salvation is from the Jews" (John 4:22). In Paul's ministry he sought out the Jews first in every new city (Acts 13:5, 14; 14:1; 17:2, 10, 17; 18:4, 19; 19:8). Three times he responded to their rejection of his message by turning to the Gentiles (Acts 13:46; 18:6; 28:25-28; cf. comments on Eph. 1:12). Today evangelism of the world must include the Jews, but the priority of the Jews has been fulfilled.

1:17. The theme of the letter is expressed in the phrase a righteousness from God is revealed. The subjective genitive (lit., "of God") identifies this as a righteousness that God provides for people on the basis of and in response to faith in the gospel (cf. 3:22). (NIV's by

faith from first to last renders the Gr. *ek pisteōs eis pistin*, lit., "out of faith in reference to faith.") Such a righteousness is totally unachieveable by human efforts. This righteousness is not God's personal attribute, however, since it comes "from God," it is consistent with His nature and standard. Robertson happily calls it "a God kind of righteousness" (A.T. Robertson, *Word Pictures in the New Testament*. Nashville: Broadman Press, 1943, 4:327). In response to faith this righteousness is imputed by God in justification and imparted progressively in regeneration and sanctification, culminating in glorification when standing and state become identical. "Righteousness" and "justify," though seemingly unrelated in English, are related in Greek. "Righteousness" is *dikaiosynē*, and "justify" is *dikaioō*. Paul used the noun many times in his epistles, including 28 times in Romans (1:17; 3:21-22, 25-26; 4:3, 5-6, 9, 11, 13, 22; 5:17, 21; 6:13, 16, 18-20; 8:10; 9:30; 10:3-6 [twice in v. 3], 10; 14:17). And Paul used the Greek verb 15 times in Romans (2:13; 3:4, 20, 24, 26, 28, 30; 4:2, 5; 5:1, 9; 6:7; 8:30 [twice], 33). To justify a person is to declare him forensically (legally) righteous. "Declared righteous" is the way the NIV translates *dikaioō* in 2:13 and 3:20 and "freed" is NIV's rendering in 6:7.

Paul's closing words in 1:17, The righteous will live by faith, are a quotation from Habakkuk 2:4, also quoted in Galatians 3:11 and Hebrews 10:38. As a result of faith (cf. "believes" in Rom. 1:16) in Christ, a person is declared "righteous" (cf. 3:22) and is given eternal life. What a marvelous work of God!

II. God's Righteousness Revealed in Condemnation (1:18-3:20)

The first step in the revelation of the righteousness that God provides for people by faith is to set forth their need for it because they are under God's judgment. The human race stands condemned before God and is helpless and hopeless apart from God's grace.

A. Condemnation against pagan humanity (1:18-32)

This section looks at the human race prior to the call of Abram and the establishment of a special people of God. This situation persisted in the pagan world of the Gentiles as distinct from the Jews.

1. REASONS FOR CONDEMNATION (1:18-23)

God never condemns without just cause. Here three bases are stated for His judgment of the pagan world.

a. For suppressing God's truth (1:18)

1:18. This verse serves as a topic sentence for this entire section. In addition, it stands in contrastive parallel to verse 17. The continuing revelation (the verb **is being revealed** is in the pres. tense) of **the wrath of God** is an expression of His personal righteousness (which also "is being revealed," Gr., v. 17) and its opposition to human sinfulness. Therefore people need the continuing revelation of "a righteousness from God" (v. 17) that He provides. God's wrath is directed **against all the godlessness** (*asebeian*, "lack of proper reverence for God") **and wickedness** (*adikian*, "unrighteousness") **of men,** not against the men as such. (God's wrath will also be revealed in the future; cf. 2:5.) God hates sin and judges it, but loves sinners and desires their salvation.

Failure to give God His due inevitably results in failure to treat people, created by God in His image, the right way. Conversely, people (in their unrighteousness toward others) continue to **suppress** (*katechontōn*, lit., "holding down") **the truth** (cf. 1:25; 2:8) concerning both God and man. People had God's truth but suppressed it, refusing to heed it. And these wicked ones did this in an attitude of **wickedness** (*en adikia*). This suppression of the truth is Paul's first reason for God's condemnation of the pagan world.

b. For ignoring God's revelation (1:19-20)

These verses declare that knowledge concerning God is available to all. This knowledge is called natural revelation because it is seen in the created world, is accessible to the entire human race, and is not soteriological, dealing with salvation effected by Christ.

1:19. Paul called this knowledge **plain** (*phaneron*), which means visible or clear. This is true **because God has made it plain** (*ephanerōsen*, the verb related to the noun *phaneron*). Some scholars

translate the phrase **to them** as "in them," insisting that verse 19 is speaking of the knowledge of God within the being of man through conscience and religious consciousness. Preferable is the position that verse 19 states the fact of natural revelation and verse 20 explains the process. One support for this view is the word "for" which begins verse 20 and indicates a tie between the verses.

1:20. "What may be known about God" (v. 19) is now called **God's invisible qualities** and identified as **His eternal power and divine nature.** Since "God is spirit" (John 4:24), all His qualities are invisible to physical eyes and can be **understood** by the human mind only as they are reflected in **what has been made,** that is, in God's creative work. The self-existent God, however, is the Creator of all things, and therefore **since the Creation of the world** His "invisible qualities" **have been clearly seen.** Paul may have intended a play on words between the noun translated "invisible qualities" (*aorata*) and the verb translated "clearly seen" (*kathoratai*) because they share a common Greek root. Both the verb "clearly seen" and the participle "being understood" are in the present tense, which emphasizes the continuous nature of the action. The word *theiotēs*, translated "divine nature," occurs only here in the New Testament and embraces the properties which make God God. Creation, which people see, reveals God's unseen character—the all-powerful Deity. An Old Testament parallel to these verses is Psalm 19:1-6.

Paul's conclusion to this description of natural revelation is important—**men are without excuse.** The witness to God in nature is so clear and so constant that ignoring it is indefensible. Their condemnation is based not on their rejecting Christ of whom they have not heard, but on their sinning against the light they have.

c. For perverting God's glory (1:21-23)

1:21. This reason for God's condemnation of the pagan world builds on the preceding one just as that one built on the first. The relationship is seen in the use of the same Greek connective (*dioti*) at the beginning of verses 19 and 21, in the latter translated **for.** People's suppression of the truth is seen in their rejecting the clear evidence of God as the sovereign Creator and their perversion of that knowledge into idolatry.

The clause **although they knew God** refers to an original experiential knowledge of God such as Adam and Eve had both before and after the Fall. How long this knowledge of God continued before it was perverted is not stated, but God was known by people. This fact makes human actions all the more reprehensible. One would suppose that to know God would be to honor Him, but these people **neither glorified Him as God nor gave thanks to Him.** They turned from the very purpose for which God made them: to glorify Him for His Person and thank Him for His works. With such willful rebellion against God it is little wonder that **their thinking became futile** (*emataiōthēsan*, lit., "became worthless, purposeless"; cf. Eph. 4:17) **and their foolish** (*asynetos*, "morally senseless"; cf. Rom. 1:31) **hearts were darkened** (cf. Eph. 4:18). When truth is rejected, in time the ability to recognize and to receive truth is impaired (cf. John 3:19-20).

1:22-23. When the true Source of wisdom is rejected (cf. Ps. 111:10), people's claim **to be wise** is an idle boast. Progressively **they became fools** (*emōranthēsan*, lit., "became stupid"), a reality demonstrated by the worship as gods of idols in the forms of people **and animals** (cf. Rom. 1:25). The ultimate irony in humanity's refusal to glorify the true **God** is the insanity or stupidity of idolatry described in Isaiah 44:9-20. Man's refusal to acknowledge and glorify God leads to a downward path: first, worthless thinking; next, moral insensitivity; and then, religious stupidity (seen in idol-worship).

2. RESULTS OF CONDEMNATION (1:24-32)

In a real sense the results of God's condemnation on rebellious humanity are nothing more than the natural consequences of suppressing truth, ignoring revelation, and perverting God's glory. However, God did more than simply let nature take its course. God acted to abandon (the thrice-mentioned "gave them over" [vv. 24, 26, 28] is *paredōken*, "abandoned") people to expressions of a corrupt lifestyle that deserved God's wrath and the sentence of death (v. 32).

a. Abandoned to fornication (1:24-25)

1:24. One aspect of mankind's corruption (to which **God** actively let people go) was **sexual** profligacy. The frequency of live-in lovers, wife-swapping, and group sex parties today only confirms this result of God's abandonment. Sex within marriage is a holy gift from God, but otherwise sex is **impurity** (lit., "uncleanness") and **the degrading of . . . bodies** by using them contrary to God's intent.

1:25. In a sense this verse repeats the truth of verse 23, but it expresses more. **The truth of God** is not only the truth concerning God but also God's truth concerning all things, including mankind. This truth is that people are creatures of God and can find true fulfillment only in worshiping and obediently serving God **the Creator. A lie** (lit., "the lie") on the other hand says that the creature—angelic (Isa. 14:13-14; John 8:44) or human (Gen. 3:4-5)—can exist independent of God, self-sufficient, self-directing, and self-fulfilling. Mankind made himself his god in place of the true God. Because God the Creator **is forever praised** (in contrast with creatures who are undeserving of worship), Paul added **Amen.** This word transliterates in both Greek and English the Hebrew word meaning "so let it be." As an affirmation, not a wish, it places approval on what has just been said (cf. comments on 2 Cor. 1:20).

b. Abandoned to sexual perversion (1:26-27)

1:26-27. Also **God gave them over to shameful lusts** (lit., "passions of disgrace"). This involved, as the text states, both sexes engaging in homosexual instead of heterosexual relationships. **Women** deliberately **exchanged natural relations** (with men in marriage) **for unnatural ones** (with other women). This is the second "exchange" the unregenerate made (cf. v. 25). **Men . . . were inflamed with lust** (*orexei*, "sexual lust," used only here in the NT and differing from the more common word for lust in v. 26).

The words translated **women** and **men** in these verses are the sexual words "females" and "males." Contemporary homosexuals insist that these verses mean that it is perverse for a heterosexual male or female to engage in homosexual relations but it is not perverse for a homosexual male or female to do so since homosexuality is such a person's natural preference. This is strained exegesis unsupported by the Bible. The only natural sexual relationship the Bible recognizes is a heterosexual one (Gen. 2:21-24; Matt. 19:4-6) within marriage. All homosexual relations constitute sexual **perversion** and are subject to God's judgment. Such lustful and **indecent acts** have within them the seeds of punishment (**due penalty**).

c. Abandoned to depraved lifestyle (1:28-32)

1:28. Pagan humanity's rebellion also included the rejection of **the knowledge** (*epignōsei*, "full knowledge"; cf. v. 32) **of God.** In a sense they put God out of their minds. God's responding judgment was abandonment (cf. vv. 24, 26) **to a depraved** (*adokimon*, "disapproved") **mind,** which expressed itself in attitudes and actions that **ought not to be done** (lit., "what is unfitting or improper," a technical Stoic word).

1:29-31. The mental vacuum created by dismissing God was **filled** (the perf. tense implies filled full) **with** four forms of active sin: **wickedness** (*adikia*; cf. v. 18), **evil** (*ponēria*), **greed, and depravity** (*kakia*, "badness or malice"). These four in turn express themselves in 17 more specific types of wickedness. The first two, **envy** and **murder,** sound much alike in Greek: *phthonou* and *phonou*. Also the four vices in verse 31 each begin with the Greek letter alpha ("a" in Eng.).

1:32. This whole pattern of evil becomes the lifestyle of people who **continue to do** (pres. tense implies continuing or habitual action) **these very things** in open defiance of God, a defiance aggravated (a) by fully knowing (*epignontes*; cf. v. 28) that **such things deserve death** and (b) by encouraging others in the same lifestyle. Such extremity of human rebellion against God fully warrants **God's** condemnation.

B. Condemnation according to divine standards (2:1-16)

1. TRUTHFULNESS (2:1-4)

2:1. In any generalization such as the preceding blanket indictment of pagan humanity (1:18-32) exceptions to the rule

always exist. Obviously some pagans had high ethical standards and moral lifestyles and condemned the widespread moral corruption of their contemporaries. In addition the Jews morally stood in sharp contrast with the pagan world around them and freely condemned the Gentiles. Both groups of moralists might conclude that God's condemnation did not apply to them because of their higher planes of living. But Paul insisted that they also stood condemned because they were doing **the same things** for which they judged others.

Therefore, Paul declared, **at whatever point you judge the other, you are condemning yourself.** Everyone in the entire human race has turned away from God and commits sins even though there are differences of frequency, extent, and degree. In addition the entire human race, especially moral pagans and the Jews, stood condemned before God (and **have no excuse** [cf. 1:20]) because God's judgment is based on three divine standards—truth (2:2-4), impartiality (vv. 5-11), and Jesus Christ Himself (vv. 12-16)—which are absolute and infinite, condemning every person.

2:2-3. The first divine standard of judgment is **truth.** Nowhere in Scripture is God identified as "Truth" as He is as "Spirit" (John 4:24), "Light" (1 John 1:5) and "Love" (1 John 4:8, 16), though Jesus did call Himself "the Truth" (John 14:6). But God is called "the God of truth" (Ps. 31:5; Isa. 65:16). Truth—absolute, infinite truth—is unquestionably one of God's essential attributes. As a result when **God's judgment** of people is declared to be **based on** (lit. "according to") "truth," no **escape** from that **judgment** is possible for anyone. All are without "excuse" (Rom. 2:1) and without "escape." One may be moral and he may even judge his contemporaries as totally enmeshed in a depraved lifestyle, but yet he is judged by God because he does **the same things** (cf. v. 1).

2:4. By not exacting His divine penalty on sinful humanity immediately, God is displaying **the riches of His kindness** (*chrēstotētos*, "benevolence in action," also used of God in 11:22; Eph. 2:7; Titus 3:4), **tolerance, and patience** (cf. Acts 14:16; 17:30; Rom. 3:25). God's purpose is to lead people **toward repentance**—a return to Him—through His kindness. (This word for "kindness" is *chrēstos*, a synonym of *chrēstotētos*, also trans. "kindness," used earlier in the verse.) Both words mean "what is suitable or fitting to a need." *Chrēstos* is used of God in Luke 6:35 and 1 Peter 2:3 and of people in Ephesians 4:32. Not realizing (lit., "being ignorant of") God's purpose, people showed contempt for (*kataphroneis*, "you thought down on") God's attributes and actions (cf. "suppress the truth," Rom. 1:18). People knew of God's Being through natural revelation (1:19-21, 28), but did not know the purpose of His kindness.

2. IMPARTIALITY (2:5-11)

2:5-6. Why are people ignorant of God's intention to be kind? (v. 4) And why do they despise it? It is because of their stubbornness (lit., "hardness"; *sklērotēta*, whence the Eng. "sclerosis") and their unrepentant heart(s). So God's wrath against people's sins is being stored up like a great reservoir until the day when it will all be poured forth in His righteous judgment. On that day God will give to each person according to what He has done (quotation of Ps. 62:12 and Prov. 24:12). God's judging will be based on the standard of truth (Rom. 2:2) and it will be impartial (v. 11).

2:7-11. God will bestow eternal life on those who by persistence in doing good seek (pres. tense, "keep on seeking") glory, honor, and immortality. On the other hand wrath and anger will be the portion of the self-seeking . . . who reject (lit., "keep on disobeying") the truth and follow (pres. tense, "keep on obeying") evil (*adikia*, "unrighteousness"; cf. 1:18). Each one who does ("keeps on producing") evil will receive trouble and distress, whereas each one who does ("keeps on working") good will have glory, honor (cf. "glory and honor" in 2:7), and peace. This just recompense by God is without regard to ethnic background or any other consideration except what each person has done.

A person's habitual conduct, whether good or evil, reveals the condition of his heart. Eternal life is not rewarded for good living; that would contradict many other Scriptures which clearly state that salvation is not by works, but is all of God's grace to those who believe (e.g., Rom. 6:23; 10:9-10; 11:6; Eph. 2:8-9; Titus

3:5). A person's doing good *shows* that his heart is regenerate. Such a person, redeemed by God, has eternal life. Conversely a person who continually does evil and rejects the truth *shows* that he is unregenerate, and therefore will be an object of God's wrath.

The statement first for the Jew, then for the Gentile (lit. "Greek") does not imply special consideration for Jews. Instead, in the light of the divine standard of impartiality (God does not show favoritism), it emphasizes that the entire human race is dealt with by God.

The phrase "the day of God's . . . judgment" (Rom. 2:5) taken by itself may seem to lend support to the idea of a single general judgment of all humanity. However, the Scriptures do not support such a concept. This phrase must be interpreted in conjunction with passages which clearly indicate that several judgments of different groups occur at different times (cf. judgment of Israel at Christ's Second Advent, Ezek. 20:32-38; the judgment of Gentiles at Christ's Second Advent, Matt. 25:31-46; the great white throne judgment, Rev. 20:11-15). The focus of this passage is on the *fact* that God will judge all peoples, not on the details of who will be judged when.

3. JESUS CHRIST (2:12-16)

2:12. God's impartiality in judgment is also seen in the fact that He will deal with people in accordance with the dispensation in which they live. "The Law was given through Moses" (John 1:17), which marks the beginning of the dispensation of Law. The Law was provided for God's Chosen People Israel, and the Gentiles were considered outside the Law. Therefore Paul declared, All who (lit., "as many as") sin apart from the Law (lit., "without Law") will also perish apart from the Law. Gentiles who sin will perish, but the Law of Moses will not be used as a standard of judgment against them. On the other hand the Jews who sin under (lit., "in the sphere of") the Law will be judged by the Law. The Gentiles are not excused from God's judgment, but they will not be judged according to the standard (the Mosaic Law) that was not given to them.

2:13. Reading the Mosaic Law was a regular part of each synagogue service, so that Jews were those who hear the Law.

However, being recognized as **righteous** was not the automatic concomitant of being a Jew and hearing the Law. Those **who will be declared righteous** (a forensic action usually trans. "justified," e.g., 3:24; see comments on 1:17 on "justify") are **those who obey the Law** (lit., "the doers of the Law"). James made the same point (James 1:22-25). Again (cf. comments on Rom. 2:7-10) God does not give eternal life or justification to those who perform good works, but to those who believe (trust) in Him and whose conduct reveals their regenerate hearts.

2:14-15. The Jews looked down on the **Gentiles** partly because they did **not have the** revelation of God's will in the Mosaic **Law.** But, as Paul pointed out, there are moral Gentiles who **do by nature things required by the Law.** Such persons show that the Law is not to be found only on tablets of stone and included in the writings of Moses; it is also inscribed in their hearts and is reflected in their actions, consciences, and thoughts. The Law given to Israel is in reality only a specific statement of God's moral and spiritual requirements for everyone. Moral Gentiles by their actions **show that the requirements** (lit., "the work") **of the Law are written on their hearts.** This is confirmed by **their consciences,** the faculty within human beings that evaluates their actions, along with .their thoughts that either accuse or excuse them of sin. This is why Paul called such Gentiles **a law for themselves** (v. 14).

Conscience is an important part of human nature, but it is not an absolutely trustworthy indicator of what is right. One's conscience can be "good" (Acts 23:1; 1 Tim. 1:5, 19) and "clear" (Acts 24:16; 1 Tim. 3:9; 2 Tim. 1:3; Heb. 13:18), but it can also be "guilty" (Heb. 10:22), "corrupted" (Titus 1:15), "weak" (1 Cor. 8:7, 10, 12), and "seared" (1 Tim. 4:2). All people need to trust the Lord Jesus Christ so that "the blood of Christ" might "cleanse [their] consciences" (Heb. 9:14).

2:16. The Greek text of this verse begins with the phrase "in the day." The words **this will take place** are not in the Greek but are supplied to tie this verse back to the main idea of this section (vv. 5-13), namely, God's righteous judgment (v. 5). Verses 14-15 are actually a parenthetic idea (as indicated in the NIV).

This was brought to mind by verse 13 and the Jewish prejudice against the Gentiles. The certainty of divine judgment is emphasized by the words **God will judge** (lit., "God judges"). The Agent of divine judgment is **Jesus Christ** (cf. John 5:22, 27; Acts 17:31). This judgment will deal with **men's secrets** (lit., "the hidden things of men") and will reveal those things and prove God's judgment right (cf. 1 Cor. 4:5). Paul's **gospel** is not the standard of God's judgment. The idea is that the righteous judgment of God is an essential ingredient of the gospel Paul preached and a reason for trusting Jesus' finished redemption.

In this section (2:1-16) God is seen as the Creator-Sovereign of the universe conducting the moral government of His human creatures. God's absolute standards are known. God punishes the wicked and rewards the righteous impartially according to their works, which reveal their hearts. Since no human being—Jesus Christ excepted—can be declared righteous (justified) by God on the basis of his own merit, every human is condemned by God. At this point in Paul's argument the way a person can secure a righteous standing before God has not yet been presented. Here the emphasis is on the justice of God's judgment, leading to the conclusion that nobody on his own can be declared righteous by God.

C. Condemnation against unfaithful Jews (2:17-3:8)

1. CONDEMNATION BECAUSE OF THEIR HYPOCRISY (2:17-24)

2:17-20. Paul undoubtedly had the Jews as well as moral Gentiles in mind in the group he addressed as "you who pass judgment on someone else" (v. 1). But there he did not refer to them by name as he did here—**if you call yourself a Jew** (lit., "if you are named a Jew"). In Greek this is a first-class conditional sentence in which the conditional statement is assumed to be true. Paul was addressing individuals who were truly called Jews and who, in fact, gloried in that name. This fact is followed by a list of eight other moral and religious details in which the Jews gloried in their sense of superiority to the Gentiles, all of these included as part of the "if" clause (vv. 17-21a).

The verbs used in this list are all in the present tense or have the force of the present, which emphasizes the habitual nature of the action: (1) The Jews **rely on the Law;** they put their confidence in the fact that God gave it to them. (2) The Jews **brag about** their **relationship to God** (lit., "boast in God"; cf. v. 23), which means they glory in their covenantal ties with God. As a result of these two things the Jews (3) **know His will** (they have an awareness of God's desires and plan) and they (4) **approve of** (*dokimazeis*, "to test and approve what passes the test") **what is superior** (*diapheronta*, "the things that differ and as a result excel"; the same Gr. word in Phil. 1:10 is trans. "what is best"). They have a concern for spiritually superior standards. These abilities of Jews exist because they (5) **are instructed** (lit., "are being instructed") **by the Law.** Their catechetical lessons as youths and the regular reading of the Law in the synagogues provided this continuing instruction.

Though the next verb (in Rom. 2:19) continues the first-class conditional structure begun in verse 17, it also marks a transition of thought. It is the perfect tense of a verb which means "to seek to persuade," in which tense it has the meaning "to believe." (6) Many Jews were **convinced** and as a result believed certain things about themselves in relationship to Gentiles. Paul listed four of these: **a guide for the blind, a light for those who are in the dark, an instructor** (*paideutēn,* "one who disciplines, a trainer") **of the foolish,** and **a teacher of infants.** (7) This belief by Jews rested in their having **in the Law the** embodiment (*morphōsin,* "outline, semblance"; used elsewhere in the NT only in 2 Tim. 3:5) **of knowledge and truth** (the Gr. has the definite article "the" with both nouns: "the knowledge and the truth").

2:21-24. Without doubt as Paul enumerated this list of moral and religious distinctives, he got repeated affirmative responses from his Jewish readers. The Jews gloried in their special spiritual position, which contrasted with the Gentiles. The apostle then summed up all these distinctives in the clause, (8) **You, then, who teach others.** Then Paul asked the question, **Do you not teach yourself?** This question is followed by a series of questions on specific prohibitions in the Law—against **stealing,** committing **adultery,** hating **idols**—each of which a Jew ("you" throughout Rom. 2:17-27 is sing., not pl.) was guilty of doing after telling others not to do those things. Paul indicted such a Jew for hypocrisy: **You who brag about** ("are boasting in"; cf. v. 17) **the Law, do you dishonor God by breaking the Law?** An honest Jew would have to respond to Paul's questions by admitting his guilt and his hypocrisy. Paul did not condemn this hypocrisy of the Jews on his own authority; he quoted their own Scriptures (the close of Isa. 52:5, in the LXX). Their hypocrisy dishonored God; also it caused **Gentiles** to blaspheme God. "Why should we honor God," Gentiles may have reasoned, "when His Chosen People do not follow Him?"

2. CONDEMNATION BECAUSE OF THEIR TRUST IN RITES (2:25-29)

The Jews trusted not only in the Law of Moses, as the preceding paragraph shows (vv. 17-24), but also in circumcision as the sign of their special covenantal relationship with God. But Paul argued that trust in the rite itself was meaningless and was a basis for God's judgment.

2:25-27. Circumcision has value if you observe ("are practicing") **the Law.** Conversely, **if you break the Law** (and they did), **you have become as though you had not been circumcised.** In the Greek this second part of verse 25 is interesting: "If you are a lawbreaker, your circumcision has become a foreskin." In other words a Jewish lawbreaker is just like a Gentile lawbreaker; the Jews' rite of circumcision counts for nothing.

The opposite is also true. **If those who are not circumcised** (lit., "if the foreskin," a word used by Jews as a slang expression for a Gentile; cf. the comments on v. 25) **keep** (*phyllasē,* "guard" and therefore "keep" or "observe"; cf. 1 Tim. 5:21) **the Law's requirements** (and apparently some Gentiles did), **will they not be regarded as though they were circumcised?** Paul concluded that a Gentile who **obeys** ("fulfills") **the Law** judges a Jew who, despite his having **the written code and circumcision,** is **a lawbreaker.** A Gentile who obeys what the Law requires, even though he does not know the Law (Rom. 2:14) is in God's sight similar to a circumcised Jew. This thought would be revolutionary for Jews who considered themselves far superior to Gentiles (cf. vv. 17-21).

2:28-29. These verses form the conclusion to the entire section that begins with verse 17. Being a true or geuine Jew is not a matter of **outward** or external things (such as wearing phylacteries, paying tithes, or being circumcised). Genuine **circumcision** is not the physical rite itself. Rather, a genuine Jew **is one inwardly** and true **circumcision is . . . of the heart** and **by the Spirit.** The NIV has rendered the Greek words "in spirit" as "by the Spirit," as though they refer to the Holy Spirit. However, it is better to understand this verse as saying that circumcision of heart fulfills "the spirit" of God's Law instead of mere outward conformity to the Law. Some Jews followed the Law's regulation outwardly, but their hearts were not right with God (Isa. 29:13). A circumcised heart is one that is "separated" from the world and dedicated to God. The true Jew receives his **praise . . . not from men** (as did the Pharisees) **but from God,** who sees people's inward natures (cf. Matt. 6:4, 6) and discerns their hearts (cf. Heb. 4:12).

3. CONDEMNATION BECAUSE OF THEIR
   UNBELIEF (3:1-8)

3:1-2. A characteristic mark of Paul's style, particularly in this letter to the Romans, is to ask and answer an obvious question his discussion has raised in his readers' minds. The natural response to the preceding material (2:17-29) is, **What advantage** (*perrison,* "overplus"), **then, is there in being a Jew?** Expressed in other words the question is, **What value** (*ōpheleia,* "advantage") **is there in circumcision?** The first question pertains to Paul's words in 2:17-24, and the second question to his words in 2:25-29. Paul's response is immediate and direct: **Much in every way!** He was not saying that being a Jew or being circumcised had *no* gains.

By the phrase **First of all** Paul suggested that he was going to list a number of items, though actually he stated only one. He did this same thing elsewhere (1:8; 1 Cor. 11:18). In this case the item he stated is the most important and in a sense includes any others that could have been mentioned. The Jews

have been entrusted (the Gr. past tense could be rendered "were entrusted") **with the very words** (*logia,* pl. of *logos,* "word" or "statement") **of God.** This can refer to the entire Old Testament but here it probably means just the promises and commands of God. Yet, though in that privileged position, the Jews were unable to live up to God's standards.

3:3-4. The fact that the chief benefit of being a Jew was being "entrusted with the very words of God" raised another question. **What if some did not have faith?** This verb "did not have faith" also means "be unfaithful." This is preferred since the same verb is rendered "entrusted" in verse 2. It is true that some Jews did not believe the promises of God, but also some Jews were unfaithful to their trust. **Will their lack of faith** (this noun can also mean "unfaithfulness," which is preferred here) **nullify God's faithfulness?** To that possibility Paul responded, **Not at all** (*mē genoito,* "Let it not be," a frequent exclamation by Paul; cf. vv. 6, 31; 6:1, 15; 7:7, 13; 11:1, 11). Though some Jews did not believe or were unfaithful (evidenced by their sinful conduct mentioned in 2:21-23, 25), God remains faithful to His Word (cf. Deut. 7:9; 1 Cor. 1:9; Heb. 10:23; 11:11; 1 Peter 4:19). This concept of God's faithfulness in spite of Israel's unbelief is developed more fully in Romans 9-11.

Paul continued, **Let God be true and every man a liar.** This means, "Let God keep on being true even though every man becomes a liar." This idea is taken from Psalm 116:11. As still further support, Paul quoted Psalm 51:4.

3:5-6. The apostle then pursued his argument with additional questions. The first is, **What shall we say** to the idea that the Jews' **unrighteousness** served to accentuate **God's righteousness?** Could they conclude that God's **wrath** on Jews is therefore **unjust?** Paul immediately interjected, **I am using a human argument,** and responded with the answer, **Certainly not!** (*mē genoito,* the same response as in v. 4; cf. v. 31) **If that were** the case, that **God** were unfair in judging unfaithful Jews, then He would be barred from judging **the world.** And of course, that could not be. So, since God will judge the world (cf. 2:5) He will not be unfair in extending His wrath on guilty Jews (cf. 2:11).

3:7-8. A second question is this: If someone's lack of truth enhances God's **truthfulness,** how can God in fairness condemn (lit., "judge") him **as a sinner?** In other words, since sin seemingly benefits God, how could He turn around and judge sinners for their sin? Paul raised these two questions, which are examples of unsaved people's casuistry, because some opponents were falsely accusing him of advancing them and proclaiming, **Let us do evil** (lit., "the evil things") **that good** (lit., "the good things") **may result.** The apostle did not reply to these slanders. He assigned such persons to God and simply observed, **Their condemnation** (*krima,* "judgment") **is deserved.** Later, however, he did discuss a similar question (6:1). To suggest, as did these two questions (3:5, 7), that God is unfair in condemning sin is to blaspheme the very nature of God. Such persons who question God's condemning are therefore themselves condemned!

D. Condemnation against all human beings (3:9-20)

In this section Paul concluded not only his indictment of the Jews but also the first section of his discussion that God's righteousness is revealed in condemnation against the sinful human race.

1. ALL ARE UNDER SIN (3:9-18)

3:9. Paul asked, **What shall we conclude then?** and, **Are we any better?** The exact meaning of this Greek verb *proechometha* (used only here in the NT) is difficult to determine. It seems best to take the question as coming from Jewish readers to whom Paul has just been writing and to translate it, "Are we preferred?" Both the material preceding and Paul's answer **(Not at all!)** support this solution. "Not at all" is literally "not by any means." This is not Paul's characteristic *mē genoito,* used in verses 3, 6, 31, and elsewhere. Jews have advantages over Gentiles (2:17-20a; 3:1-2), but God does not give them preferential treatment.

As evidence that the Jews have no preferred position, Paul stated that he had previously accused both **Jews and Gentiles** as **all under sin,** that is, they stand under sin's power and control and under the condemnation that results from it (cf. 1:18; 2:5). The order of accusation was

first Gentiles (1:18–2:16) and then Jews (chap. 2). This order is reversed here because the Jews were most recently discussed.

3:10-12. To validate his accusation that everybody is "under sin" Paul quoted in verses 10-18 from six Old Testament passages. Romans 3:10-12, taken from Psalm 14:1-3, makes the point that all people without exception are not **righteous** (cf. Rom. 1:18, 29-31), do not understand **God** (cf. 1:18b, 28) nor seek (lit., "seek out") Him, **have turned away** from Him (cf. 2:5; Isa. 53:5), are **worthless** (from *achreioō,* "become useless," used only here in the NT), and do not do **good** (*chrēstotēta,* "kindness," or "benevolence in action"; cf. 2 Cor. 6:6; Gal. 5:22; and comments on Rom. 2:4). Apart from the indwelling Holy Spirit people cannot exhibit this fruit of the Spirit (Gal. 5:22). They have no inner spiritual capacity whereby they can normally and automatically exercise genuine kindness toward others. Instead sin causes them to be selfish and self-centered.

These seven condemnatory phrases end with the words **not even one,** which are also in Romans 3:10. This repetition stresses that not a single exception in the human race (except, of course, the Son of God) can be found.

Though Paul did not quote Psalm 14:2, "The Lord looks down from heaven on the sons of men," that verse is significant, for what follows in that psalm is God's indictment of humanity.

3:13-18. These verses describe the vileness and wickedness of various parts of the human body, indicating figuratively that every part contributes to a person's condemnation. In sequence these quotations are taken from Psalm 5:9 (Rom. 3:13a); Psalm 140:3 (Rom. 3:13b); Psalm 10:7 (Rom. 3:14); Isaiah 59:7-8 (Rom. 3:15-17); and Psalm 36:1 (Rom. 3:18). They pertain to three actions: talking **(throats . . . tongues . . . lips . . . mouths;** vv. 13-14), conduct **(feet;** vv. 15-17) and seeing **(eyes;** v. 18). Their speech is corrupt **(open graves;** cf. James 3:6), dishonest **(deceit;** cf. Ps. 36:3), damaging **(poison;** cf. James 3:8), and blasphemous **(cursing and bitterness;** cf. James 3:9-10). From talking of sin, they commit sin, even to the point of quickly murdering (cf. Prov. 1:11-12, 15-16). As a result they and others are destroyed materially and spiritually, are miserable, and **know** no inner **peace** (cf. Isa. 57:21). All this is summarized in Paul's words, **There is no fear of God before their** eyes. Fearing God (i.e., reverencing Him by worship, trust, obedience, and service) is the essence of a godly person (cf. Job 28:28; Prov. 1:7; 9:10; Ecc. 12:13). So for a Jew not to fear God was the height of sin and folly. In these verses (Rom. 3:10-18) Paul left no basis whatsoever for Jewish readers to say that his point that Jews are sinners contradicts the Old Testament!

2. ALL ARE CONSCIOUS OF SIN (3:19-20)

3:19-20. Paul concluded his discussion with a final statement to the Jews concerning the purpose and ministry of **the Law.** He included himself with his Jewish readers when he said, **Now we know.** The principle is obvious: the Law's pronouncements are **to those who are under the Law.** The Law was not a special talisman that the Jews could obey or ignore as they wished; they were "under" it and accountable to God (cf. Jews and Gentiles being "under sin," v. 9). The Law's ministry was **so that every mouth may be silenced** (lit., "stopped"), **and the whole world held accountable** (lit., "become answerable") **to God.** No one can argue in his own defense that he is not under sin. The Law points up God's standards and illustrates people's inability to live up to them.

Finally, **the Law** is not a way for a person to **be declared righteous** (justified) **in His sight** (cf. 3:28). That was not its purpose (Acts 13:39; Gal. 2:16; 3:11). Instead, **the Law** was given so that **through** it **we become conscious** (lit., "through the Law is full knowledge") **of sin** (cf. Rom. 5:20; 7:7-13). The Mosaic Law is an instrument not of justification but of condemnation.

III. God's Righteousness Revealed in Justification (3:21-5:21)

In God's condemnation of the human race His own personal infinite righteousness was revealed along with the fact that not a single human being—the Lord Jesus Christ excepted—has ever or will ever be able to meet that standard and be accepted by God on his own merit. Now in this second major section of Romans Paul discussed God's "provided righteousness" for people through

Jesus in justification. Justification is a forensic declaration of righteousness as a result of God's imputing to believers Christ's righteousness, provided by God's grace and appropriated through faith.

A. Provided righteousness explained (3:21-31)

3:21. By the words **but now** Paul introduced a sharp contrast with what preceded. He had just affirmed, "No one will be declared righteous in His [God's] sight by observing the Law" (v. 20). This is now followed by the statement, **Apart from Law** (in the Gr. this phrase is in the emphatic first position) **a righteousness from God . . . has been made known** (i.e., made plain). This in essence repeats the words of 1:17a. But Paul added the fact that **the Law and the Prophets testify** to this fact. What Paul was introducing about God's righteousness was not foreign to the Old Testament. "The Law and the Prophets" was often used of the entire Old Testament (see references at Matt. 5:17), the Law referring to the first five books and the Prophets, the other books. In Romans 4 Paul illustrated this truth from the Law (Abraham: Gen. 15:6; Rom. 4:1-3, 9-23) and from the Prophets (David: Ps. 32:1-2; Rom. 4:4-8).

3:22. The first part of this verse is not a new sentence in the Greek; it is an appositional clause, and could be rendered, "a righteousness from God **through faith.**" These words reminded Paul again of the Jewish insistence on their special position before God. As a result he added, **There is no difference** (cf. 10:12), introduced in the Greek by the word "for" to tie it to what precedes. Any prior privilege the Jews had is gone in this Age when God is offering a righteous standing before Him to all sinful people on the basis of faith in Christ alone. Since all are "under sin" (3:9), salvation is available "to all" on an equal basis.

3:23. Paul explained that "no difference" existed among human beings because **all have sinned.** The Greek is literally, "all sinned" (*pantes hēmarton*). The same two Greek words are used in 5:12 (cf. comments on that verse). Since the entire human race was plunged into sin with Adam, all (whether Jews or Gentiles) are sinners. It is impossible to say there is a "difference," that the Jews' privileges (2:12-21; 3:1) exclude them from God's condemnation.

Not only did all sin, but also all **fall short.** This single Greek verb is in the present tense, stressing continuing action. It can be translated "keep on falling short." The simple fact is that as a sinner not a single human being by his own efforts is able to measure up to **the glory of God.** God's glory is His splendor, the outward manifestation of His attributes. God desires that humans share that splendor, that they become like Him, that is, Christlike (cf. "glory" in 5:2; 2 Cor. 3:18; Col. 1:27; 2 Thes. 2:14). Yet their sin keeps them from sharing it.

3:24. In view of man's sin God has stepped in with His provided righteousness, because all who believe **are justified** (the pres. tense may be trans. "are being declared righteous," i.e., each person as he believes is justified). "Justify" (*dikaioō*) is a legal term, meaning "declare righteous" (not "make righteous"; cf. Deut. 25:1). See comments on Romans 1:17 on Paul's frequent use of this verb and its related noun "righteousness."

God's justification of those who believe is provided **freely** (*dōrean*, "as a free gift," i.e., without charge) **by His grace.** God justifies by the instrument of His grace, His unmerited favor. Grace too is a favorite word of Paul's, used by him in Romans 24 times (in the Gr.). But God would not declare a person righteous without an objective basis, without dealing with his sin. That basis is **the redemption that came by Christ Jesus.** The Greek word for "redemption" is *apolytrōsis*, from *lytron,* "a ransom payment." *Apolytrōsis* is used 10 times in the New Testament (Luke 21:28; Rom. 3:24; 8:23; 1 Cor. 1:30; Eph. 1:7, 14; 4:30; Col. 1:14; Heb. 9:15). (See the chart, "New Testament Words for Redemption" at Mark 10:45.) The death of Christ on the cross of Calvary was the price of payment for human sin which secured release from the bondage of Satan and sin for every person who trusts God's promise of forgiveness and salvation.

3:25a. God presented Him, Christ, **as a Sacrifice of atonement.** The Greek word for "Sacrifice of atonement" is *hilastērion,* rendered "propitiation" in the KJV and the NASB. This noun is used elsewhere in the New Testament only in Hebrews 9:5 for the mercy seat (NIV, "the place of atonement") of the tabernacle's ark of the covenant. There a goat's blood was sprinkled on the Day of Atonement to cover (atone) Israel's sins (Lev. 16:15), and satisfy God for another year. Jesus' death is the final sacrifice which completely satisfied God's demands against sinful people, thus averting His wrath from those who believe. (The verb *hilaskomai,* "to satisfy by a sacrifice, to propitiate," is used in Luke 18:13 ["have mercy"] and Heb. 2:17 ["make atonement"]. And the related noun, *hilasmos,* "propitiation," appears in 1 John 2:2; 4:10.)

Christ, God's propitiatory Sacrifice for sin, was "presented" (lit., "set forth"), in contrast with the tabernacle's mercy seat which was hidden from view. This work of Christ is **through faith in His blood** (cf. Rom. 5:9). It is appropriated by faith (cf. 3:22). By the death of Jesus and the shedding of His blood the penalty for sin has been paid and God has been satisfied or propitiated. The phrase "in (or by) His blood" probably should go with "a sacrifice of atonement," not with "through faith." A believer places His faith in Christ, not in His blood as such.

3:25b-26. God's purpose in Christ's death was **to demonstrate His justice** (i.e., God's own judicial righteousness, *dikaiosynēs;* cf. comments on 1:17) **because in His forbearance** (*anochē,* "holding back, delay") **He had left the sins committed beforehand unpunished** (cf. Acts 17:30). Why did God not always punish sins in the past? Does this mean He is not righteous after all? Previously Paul said God was forbearing because He wanted to lead people to repent (Rom. 2:4). Here God is said to be forbearing because He anticipated His provision for sins in the death of Jesus Christ. Such forbearance was an evidence of His grace (cf. Acts 14:16; 17:30), not of His injustice.

Paul was so insistent that God's righteousness be recognized that (Rom. 3:26) he repeated (from v. 25) the words **to demonstrate His justice** (*dikaiosynēs,* "righteousness"). God's purpose in the redemptive and propitiatory death of Jesus Christ was so that He could be seen to be **just** (*dikaion,* "righteous") **and the One who justifies** (*dikaiounta,* "the One who declares righteous") **the man who has faith in Jesus.** God's divine dilemma was how to satisfy His own righteousness and its demands against sinful people, and at the same time how to demonstrate His grace, love, and mercy to restore rebellious, alienated creatures to Himself. The solution was the sacrifice of Jesus Christ, God's incarnate Son, and the acceptance by faith of that provision by individual sinners. Christ's death vindicated God's own righteousness (He is just because sin was "paid for") and enables God to declare every believing sinner righteous.

3:27-28. After explaining God's provided righteousness for sinners, Paul considered five questions (in Gr.) which he anticipated his readers might ask. Two are in verse 27, two in verse 29, and the other in verse 31. The first is, **Where, then is boasting?** How can Jews have any boasting in their special position? (2:17-20, 23) Paul's response was abrupt: **It is excluded** ("completely shut out").

Since justification is by grace (3:24) through faith (vv. 22, 25-26), boasting because of one's accomplishments (works) is ruled out. This prompted a second question: **On what principle?** ("Law" here in the Gr. means "principle.") **On that of observing the Law?** (lit., "through works") Paul's response was, **No** (lit., "not at all," an intensive form), **but on that of faith.** Doing works (i.e., observing the Law) is no basis for boasting for the Law cannot justify. It was not given for that purpose (cf. v. 20). The apostle then summarized, **For we maintain** (the verb *logizometha*, "to reckon," here has the idea of coming to a settled conclusion) **that a man is justified** ("declared righteous") **by faith** (cf. vv. 22, 25-27) **apart from observing the Law** (lit., "apart from works of Law").

3:29-30. The next two questions cover the same issue of Jewish distinctiveness from a different angle. Because the Gentiles worshiped false gods through idols, the Jews concluded that Yahweh, the true and living God (Jer. 10:10), was **the God of Jews only.** That was true in the sense that the Jews were the only people who acknowledged and worshiped Yahweh (except for a few proselyte Gentiles who joined with Judaism). But in reality Yahweh, as the Creator and Sovereign of all people, is the God of all people. Before God called Abraham and his descendants in the nation Israel to be

His Chosen People (Deut. 7:6) God dealt equally with all people. And even after God's choice of Israel to be His special people, God made it plain (e.g., in the Book of Jonah) that He is **the God of** everyone, **Gentiles** as well as Jews. And now since there is "no difference" among people for all are sinners (Rom. 3:23) and since the basis for salvation has been provided in the sacrificial death of Jesus Christ, God deals with everyone on the same basis. Thus **there is only one God** (or "God is one"). Paul no doubt had in mind here the "Shema" of Israel: "Hear, O Israel: The LORD [*Yahweh*] our God [*'Ĕlōhîm*], the LORD [*Yahweh*] is One" (Deut. 6:4). This one God over both Jews and Gentiles **will justify** all who come to Him regardless of background (**circumcised** or **uncircumcised**) on the **same** human condition of **faith.**

3:31. The final question is, **Do we, then, nullify the Law by this faith?** Paul responded in his characteristic expletive, **Not at all!** (*mē genoito,* "Let it not be"; cf. comments on v. 4) and then explained, **Rather, we uphold the Law.** The purpose of the Mosaic Law is fulfilled and its place in God's total plan is confirmed when it leads an individual to faith in Jesus Christ (cf. v. 20; Gal. 3:23-25). Paul repeatedly affirmed that faith, not works of the Law, is the way of salvation. He wrote the word "faith" eight times in Romans 3:22-31! (See vv. 22, 25-28, 30 [twice], and 31.)

B. Provided righteousness illustrated (chap. 4)

The Apostle Paul had presented his case that God declares people righteous on the principle of faith instead of works. If his position is true, he should be able to illustrate it from the past. This he did with Abraham, the patriarch of Israel (cf. John 8:39), and David as well (cf. comments on "the Law and the Prophets," Rom. 3:21).

1. BY FAITH NOT WORKS (4:1-8)

4:1. Paul introduced his illustration of Abraham with the first of six occurrences of the question, **What then shall we say?** (6:1; 7:7; 8:31; 9:14, 30) He referred to **Abraham** as **our forefather.** ("Forefather" is used only here in the NT.) Undoubtedly this was to distinguish Abraham's physical ancestry from his spiritual fatherhood, mentioned later in 4:11-12, 16. What had this patriarch **discovered in this matter?** What lesson could Paul's readers learn from the biblical record of Abraham's experience?

4:2-3. The Rabbis taught that **Abraham** had a surplus of merit from his works that was available to his descendants. Paul built on that idea and agreed that, assuming that **Abraham was justified by works, he had something to boast about** (cf. boasting or bragging in 2:17, 23; 3:27). **But,** Paul insisted, his boasting could only be before other people, **not before God.** If a person could establish his finite righteousness by works—though that was impossible—he could never boast of it in God's presence. Paul then turned to an authority his readers would acknowledge and asked, **What does the Scripture say?** He quoted Genesis 15:6, which states that Abraham's faith in God and His promise **was credited to him as righteousness.** Because he believed, God imputed righteousness to his account ("credited," *elogisthē,* from *logizomai,* is an accounting term). Paul had quoted this verse before (Gal. 3:6).

4:4-5. The apostle then discussed the significance of this Scripture quotation. He pointed out that a worker's **wages are** what are owed him because he earned them, and are **not** graciously given **to him as a gift.** Conversely, a person **who** is not working but is believing on (these participles are in the pres. tense) **God who justifies the wicked** (*asebē,* "the ungodly, impious"; cf. 5:6), **his faith is credited as righteousness** (cf. 4:3). Abraham was the latter kind of person as the Scripture stated. He was justified not because he worked for it but because he trusted God.

4:6-8. This fact about Abraham was also true of **David,** whose description of God's gracious dealing with him Paul quoted from Psalm 32:1-2. A person, like David, **to whom God credits righteousness apart from works,** is blessed. Such a person's sins **are forgiven** and **covered.** And instead of his **sin** credited (*logisētai*) to his account, God credits (*logizetai;* cf. Rom. 4:3) righteousness to **him.**

2. BY FAITH NOT RITES (4:9-12)

4:9-10. Paul again raised the question of the Jews' special position (cf.

2:17-21a; 3:1-2). The way the question is worded in the Greek suggests the answer, that **this blessedness** is **for the uncircumcised** (Gentiles) as well as **for the circumcised** (Jews). But in response Paul turned again to the example of Abraham. He repeated the authoritative scriptural declaration that Abraham was declared righteous on the basis of his **faith.** Then Paul asked whether **Abraham's** justification occurred **before** or **after he was circumcised.** Answering his own question, Paul stated, **It was not after, but before!** (The Gr. has lit., "not in circumcision, but in uncircumcision.") Abraham's age when he was declared righteous (Gen. 15:6) is not stated. But later when Hagar bore him Ishmael, he was 86 (Gen. 16:16). After that, God instructed Abraham to perform the rite of circumcision on all his male descendants as a sign of God's covenant with him; this was done when Abraham was 99 (Gen. 17:24). Therefore the circumcision of Abraham followed his justification by faith by more than 13 years.

4:11-12. Therefore, Paul argued, **the sign of circumcision** was **a seal of** Abraham's being declared righteous because of his **faith** which he received **while he was still uncircumcised** (lit.,"in uncircumcision"). Circumcision, as a "sign" or "seal," was an outward token of the justification Abraham had already received. God's purpose was that Abraham be **the father of all who believe** and are thereby justified. This included both the uncircumcised (Gentiles) and the **circumcised** (Jews). Jews must do more than be **circumcised** to be right with God. They must also **walk in the footsteps of . . . faith,** like **Abraham** (cf. 2:28-29). Obviously, then, the rite of circumcision, which many Jews rely on for salvation, contributes in no way to one's status before God. It gives them no special standing before Him because they must be declared righteous on the basis of faith in God.

3. BY FAITH NOT THE LAW (4:13-17)

4:13. The Jews also considered the Mosaic Law, a special revelation of God's standards for human conduct, as the basis for their special standing before God. Therefore Paul turned next to it, declaring, **It was not through Law** ("not" is emphasized by its position at the beginning of the Gr. sentence) that Abraham and his offspring (lit., "seed") received the promise that he would be heir of the world.

God's promise in Genesis 12:1-3 preceded the giving of the Law by several centuries (cf. Gal. 3:17). Being "heir of the world" probably refers to "all peoples on earth" (Gen. 12:3), "all nations" (Gen. 18:18), and "all nations on earth" (Gen. 22:18), for through Abraham and his descendants all the world is blessed. He is thus their "father" and they are his heirs. These promises of blessing are given to those to whom God has imputed righteousness, and this, Paul added once again, is by faith. Believers of all ages are "Abraham's seed," for they enjoy the same spiritual blessing (justification) which he enjoyed (Gal. 3:29). (However, God has not abrogated His promises to Abraham about his physical, believing descendants, the regenerate nation Israel, inheriting the land [Gen. 15:18-21; 22:17]. These promises still stand; they will be fulfilled in the Millennium.)

4:14-15. As Paul explained, if Jews could become heirs by obeying the Law, then faith has no value (kekenōtai, "it has been made empty"; cf. the noun kenos, "empty, without content," in 1 Cor. 15:10, 58). Also the promise is worthless (katērgētai, "has been made invalid"). The reason this would be true is that Law brings wrath (lit., "the Law keeps on producing wrath") as a consequence of disobedience. No one can keep the Law fully; therefore God, in wrath against sin, judges those who disobey.

Paul then stated a related general principle: And where there is no law, there is no transgression. A person may still be sinning in his action, but if there is no command prohibiting it his action does not have the character of a transgression, an overstepping of a prohibition (cf. Rom. 5:13).

4:16. Paul then drew his conclusion. Therefore. "On account of this") the promise comes by (ek, "out of") faith so that it may be by (kata, "according to the standard of") grace. Responding in faith to God's promise is not meritorious, since the promise springs from His grace, His disposition of favor toward those who deserve His wrath. The human exercise of faith is simply the prerequisite response of trust in God and His promise. Since

faith and grace go together, and since the promise is by grace, the promise can be received only by faith, not by the Law.

Another reason the promise is by faith is so that it **may be guaranteed to all Abraham's offspring, not only** the Jews **(those . . . of the Law) but** to all who exercise **faith** in God. If the promise were fulfilled for those who keep the Law, then no Gentiles (or Jews either) could be saved! But this cannot be, because **Abraham . . . is the father of us all,** that is, all who believe (cf. "our" in v. 1; also cf. Gal. 3:29).

4:17. Paul then supported his conclusion in verse 16 with scriptural authority, quoting God's covenantal promise from Genesis 17:5. The fact that believers in this Church Age are identified with Abraham and God's covenant with him does not mean that the physical and temporal promises to Abraham and his physical descendants are either spiritualized or abrogated. It simply means that God's covenant and Abraham's response of faith to it have spiritual dimensions as well as physical and temporal aspects (cf. comments on Rom. 4:13). The quotation is in effect a parenthesis. Therefore the latter part of verse 17 connects with the close of verse 16: "He is the father of us all . . ." **in the sight of God.** (The words He is our **father** are not in the Gr., but are added in the NIV for clarification.) **God . . . gives life to the dead and calls things that are not** (lit., "the nonexisting things") **as though they were** (lit., "as existing").

Identifying God in this way obviously refers to God's promise in Genesis 17 following the statement quoted above that Abraham and Sarah would have a son of promise when Abraham was 100 and Sarah was 90 (Gen. 17:17, 19; 18:10; 21:5; cf. Rom. 4:19). That he would be the ancestor of many nations seemed impossible in his and Sarah's childless old age.

4. BY FAITH IN GOD'S PROMISE (4:18-25)

4:18. Though humanly there was no hope of ever having a child, the old patriarch believed God's Word. **Against all hope, Abraham in hope believed.** God honored his faith, and he **became the father** (ancestor) **of many nations.** This was in accord with God's promise, **So shall your offspring be** (a quotation of Gen. 15:5).

4:19. Verses 19-21 restate in specific details the first part of verse 18 about Abraham's hope. Abraham **without weakening in his faith . . . faced the fact** (lit., "considered carefully") **that his body was as good as dead** (some Gr. mss. add the word "already"), a reference to the patriarch's advanced age (Gen. 17:17; 21:5). Abraham also considered carefully **that Sarah's womb was also dead.** She was unable to conceive a child, as had been demonstrated through their life together (cf. Gen. 16:1-2; 18:11) and as was certainly true for her at age 90 (Gen. 17:17).

4:20-21. In spite of the humanly impossible situation, Abraham **did not waver through** (lit., "by") **unbelief.** "Waver" (*diekrithē*) means "to be divided" (sometimes trans. "doubt," as in James 1:6). The patriarch **was strengthened in his faith** (lit., "was empowered [*enedynamōthē,* from *endynamoō*] by means of faith"). God, responding to Abraham's faith, empowered him and Sarah physically to generate the child of promise. Also he **gave glory to God,** that is, he praised God by exalting or exclaiming His attributes. Abraham was **fully persuaded that God had power** (*dynatos,* "spiritual ability") **to do what He had promised.** What confidence in God this spiritual forefather possessed! He "in hope believed" (Rom. 4:18); he was not weak in faith despite insuperable odds (v. 19); he was not divided in his thinking by unbelief (v. 20a); he was empowered by faith (v. 20b); and he was fully persuaded God has the ability to do what He had said (v. 21).

4:22. Paul concluded his illustration about Abraham by saying, This is why (*dio kai,* "wherefore also") **it was credited to him as righteousness.** Abraham's response of faith to God and God's promise to him was the human requirement for God's justifying Abraham, for God's declaring that Abraham stood righteous before Him. No wonder God credited such faith with righteousness!

4:23-24. Verses 23-25 apply the truth about justification and its illustration in Abraham to the apostle's readers—from the believers in Rome who first read this letter to people today. The divine declaration of Abraham's justification was **written not for him alone, but also for us, to whom God will credit**

righteousness. Such an act of justification, however, is not for everyone. It is **for us who believe in Him who raised Jesus our Lord from the dead** (lit., "out from dead ones"; cf. 6:4; 8:11). Repeatedly in this chapter Paul referred to Abraham and other believers having righteousness credited to them because of their faith (4:3, 5-6, 9-11, 23-24).

4:25. Mentioning the Lord Jesus led Paul to state again the Savior's central place in God's program of providing righteousness for sinful people by grace through faith. Both Christ's death and His resurrection are essential to that work of justification. **He was delivered over** (by God the Father; cf. 8:32) **to death for our sins** (lit., "on account of or because of" [*dia* with the accusative] "our trespasses" [*paraptōmata,* "false steps"; cf. 5:15, 17, 20; Eph. 2:1]). Though not a direct quotation, these words in substance are taken from Isaiah 53:12 (cf. Isa. 53:4-6). Also He **was raised to life for** ("on account of" or "because of" [*dia* with the accusative]) **our justification.** Christ's death as God's sacrificial Lamb (cf. John 1:29) was to pay the redemptive price for the sins of all people (Rom. 3:24) so that God might be free to forgive those who respond by faith to that provision. Christ's resurrection was the proof (or demonstration and vindication) of God's acceptance of Jesus' sacrifice (cf. 1:4). Thus because He lives, God can credit His provided righteousness to the account of every person who responds by faith to that offer.

In chapter 4, Paul presented several irrefutable reasons why justification is by faith: (1) Since justification is a gift, it cannot be earned by works (vv. 1-8). (2) Since Abraham was justified before he was circumcised, circumcision has no relationship to justification (vv. 9-12). (3) Since Abraham was justified centuries before the Law, justification is not based on the Law (vv. 13-17). (4) Abraham was justified because of his faith in God, not because of his works (vv. 18-25).

C. *Provided righteousness enjoyed (5:1-11)*

5:1. The apostle now turned to a presentation of the experiential results (suggested by the connective *oun,* trans. **therefore)** of the believers' justification—

121

God's declaring them righteous—on the basis of faith (cf. 3:21–4:25). The participial clause since we have been justified (cf. 5:9) through faith describes antecedent action to the main clause, we have peace (echomen) with God. Some of the important Greek manuscripts read, "Let us have peace (echōmen) with God." This seems to be the preferred reading. If so, then the sense is, "Let us keep on having (in the sense of enjoying) peace with God." Peace has been made by God through our Lord Jesus Christ (cf. Eph. 2:14a), which fact is demonstrated by God's justification. A believer is not responsible for having peace in the sense of making it but in the sense of enjoying it.

5:2. The Lord Jesus, besides being the Agent of the believer's enjoyment of peace with God, is also the One through whom we have gained access (prosagōgēn, "privilege of approach" to a person of high rank; used elsewhere only in Eph. 2:18; 3:12) by faith into this grace in which we now stand. Though the phrase "by faith" is not supported by the best Greek manuscripts, it is the human means of the access. Believers in Christ stand in the sphere of God's grace (cf. "grace" in Rom. 3:24) because Christ has brought them to this position. He is their means of access.

In the Greek text the sentence, And we rejoice in the hope of the glory of God, is coordinate to the clause, "We have peace" (5:1). Like that clause, this one too may be translated, "Let us keep on rejoicing." Because of Christ, Christians eagerly anticipate the time when they will share Christ's glory, in contrast with their falling short of it now (3:23). In that sense He is "the hope of glory" (Col. 1:27; cf. Rom. 8:17-30; 2 Cor. 4:17; Col. 3:4; 2 Thes. 2:14; Heb. 2:10; 1 Peter 5:1, 10). Certainly such a prospect is cause for joy and even boasting! (Kauchōmetha, "rejoice," is lit., "boast" or "exult," here in a pure sense; this Gr. word is also used in Rom. 5:3, 11 where it is trans. "rejoice.")

5:3-4. Believers can enjoy the peace with God that has been achieved and the glorious future in God's presence that awaits them. But how should they react to the experiences of life that are often adverse and difficult? They are to rejoice in their sufferings. The word "rejoice" is kauchōmetha, the same word in verse 2. "Sufferings" is thlipsesin, "afflictions, distresses, pressures." James wrote along the same line: "Consider it pure joy, my brothers, whenever you face trials of many kinds" (James 1:2). This is more than mere Stoic endurance of troubles, even though endurance or steadfastness is the first result in a chain-reaction outgrowth from distress. This is spiritual glorying in afflictions because of having come to know (from oida, "to know by intuition or perception") that the end product of this chain reaction (that begins with distress) is hope. Suffering brings about perseverance (hypomonēn, "steadfastness," the ability to remain under difficulties without giving in; cf. Rom. 15:5-6; James 1:3-4). Only a believer who has faced distress can develop steadfastness. That in turn develops character (dokimēn ["proof"] has here the idea of "proven character"), which in turn results in hope. As believers suffer, they develop steadfastness; that quality deepens their character; and a deepened, tested character results in hope (i.e., confidence) that God will see them through.

5:5. A believer's hope, since it is centered in God and His promises, does not disappoint him. "Disappoint" means "put to shame because of disappointment" in unfulfilled promises. This affirmation concerning hope in God is a reflection of Psalm 25:3, 20-21 (cf. Ps. 22:5; Rom. 9:33; 1 Peter 2:6). The reason this hope (resulting finally from affliction) does not disappoint is that God has poured out His love into our hearts. God's love, so abundant in believer's hearts (cf. 1 John 4:8, 16), encourages them on in their hope. And this love is poured out by (better, "through," dia with the genitive) the Holy Spirit, whom He has given us. The Holy Spirit is the divine Agent who expresses to a believer the love of God, that is, God's love for him. The reality of God's love in a believer's heart gives the assurance, even the guarantee, that the believer's hope in God and His promise of glory is not misplaced and will not fail. This ministry of the Holy Spirit is related to His presence in believers as the seal of God (Eph. 4:30) and as the earnest or down payment of their inheritance in glory

(2 Cor. 1:21-22; Eph. 1:13-14). Later Paul wrote that the Holy Spirit Himself has been poured out in believers (Titus 3:6). Each believer has the Spirit of Christ (Rom. 8:9) in the sense that He is indwelt by the Holy Spirit (cf. 1 John 3:24; 4:13).

5:6-8. Having mentioned the pouring out of God's love, Paul now described the character of God's love, which explains why its pouring out assures believers of hope. God demonstrated His love by the death of His Son, Jesus **Christ.** This demonstration was first, **at just the right time** (cf. Gal. 4:4). Second, it was **when we were still powerless** (asthenōn, "without strength, feeble"; cf. John 5:5). Third, it was **for** (hyper) **the ungodly** (asebōn, "impious"; cf. Rom. 4:5). Clearly Christ's death was a substitutionary death, a death in place of others. The Greek preposition hyper often means "on behalf of," but occasionally it means "in place of," its meaning here. This is clear from the statement in 5:7, which also has hyper. A person willing to **die for a righteous man** or **for a good man** obviously is offering himself as a substitute so that the righteous or good man can continue to live. This is the highest expression of human love and devotion. However, God's love contrasts with human love in both nature and degree, because **God demonstrates** ("keeps on showing") **His own love for us in this: While we were still sinners, Christ died for us** (hyper, "in our place"). Though a few people might possibly be willing to die to save the lives of good people, though that is rare, Christ went well beyond that. He died in the place of the powerless ("feeble," v. 6), the ungodly (v. 6; 4:5), sinners (5:8), and even His enemies! (v. 10).

5:9-11. The participle translated **have . . . been justified** ("declared righteous") ties these verses to the argument at the beginning of the chapter (cf. v. 1). The immediate connection, however, is with what preceded (vv. 6-8). God gave proof of His love by having Christ die in the place of humans "while we were still sinners." Because of the sinner's response by faith (v. 1) to Christ's sacrifice on the cross, God has declared him righteous. Certainly that now-declared-righteous person will not be forsaken by God's love, which has been poured out effusively in his heart. Since

the divine dilemma of justification (3:26) has been solved on the basis of Jesus' shed **blood** (cf. 3:25), certainly Jesus Christ will see that justified sinners will **be saved from God's wrath.** Believers will never be condemned to hell (John 5:24; Rom. 8:1) nor will they be the objects of God's coming Tribulation wrath (1 Thes. 1:10; 5:9).

Here this same truth is repeated in different words (Rom. 5:10). Reconciliation, the third great achievement of Jesus' sacrificial death on Calvary, is presented (also v. 11). This great triumvirate—redemption (3:24; 1 Cor. 1:30; Gal. 3:13; Eph. 1:7); propitiation (Rom. 3:25 [NIV: "sacrifice of atonement"]; 1 John 2:2; 4:10 [NIV: "atoning sacrifice"]); reconciliation (Rom. 5:10-11; 2 Cor. 5:18-20; Col. 1:22)—is totally the work of God, accomplished through the death of Jesus Christ. Redemption pertains to sin (Rom. 3:24), propitiation (or satisfaction) pertains to God (3:25), and reconciliation is for people (cf. **we were reconciled**). Reconciliation is the removal of enmity that stands between people and God (cf. "enemies" in 5:10; Col. 1:21). Reconciliation is the basis of restored fellowship between people and God (cf. 2 Cor. 5:20-21).

If (Rom. 5:10) may be rendered "since"; it assumes that the reconciliation **through the death of His Son** is true. In addition, reconciliation was done **when we were God's enemies** (lit., "being enemies"). Since reconciliation was accomplished by Jesus' death, certainly **His life** is able to insure the complete and final salvation of believers. "His life" is His present life (not His life on earth) in which He intercedes (Heb. 7:25) for believers. He died for His enemies; surely He will save those, His former enemies, who are now fellowshiping in Him. Because Christians, God's reconciled ones, share in Christ's life, they will **be saved.** Not only is future salvation assured, **but we also rejoice in God** ("but also boasting [kauchōmenoi] in God") here and now. This is what Paul already exhorted believers to do (Rom. 5:1-3). The assurance and guarantee of it all is the fact that **through . . . Christ . . . we have now received reconciliation** (lit., "the reconciliation"). Since God has reconciled godless enemies to Himself, they should enjoy that peace with Him.

D. Provided righteousness contrasted (5:12-21)

5:12. Paul had now finished his description of how God has revealed and applied to humans His provided righteousness on the basis of the sacrificial death of Jesus Christ received by faith. One thing remains to be done—to present the contrastive parallelism between the work of Jesus Christ (and its results in justification and reconciliation) and the work of another man, Adam (and its results in sin and death). Paul began by saying, **Therefore** (lit., "because of this"; cf. 4:16), and started his comparison, **just as;** but he became concerned by other matters and did not return to the comparison until 5:15. Paul explained that **sin** (in Gr., "the sin") **entered** (*eisēlthen*, "entered into") **the world through one man; and,** in accord with God's warning (cf. Gen. 2:16-17), **death** (in Gr., "the death") **through sin.** God's penalty for sin was both spiritual and physical death (cf. Rom. 6:23; 7:13), and Adam and Eve and their descendants experienced both. But physical death, being an outward, visible experience, is in view in 5:12-21. Paul concluded, **And in this way death** ("the death") **came to all men.** "Came" is *diēlthen*, literally "passed or went through" or "spread through." *Eisēlthen*, "entered into" (the first clause in the verse) means that sin went in the world's front door (by means of Adam's sin); and *diēlthen*, "went through," means that death penetrated the entire human race, like a vapor permeating all of a house's rooms. The reason death spread to all, Paul explained, is that **all sinned.**

The Greek past (aorist) tense occurs in all three verbs in this verse. So the entire human race is viewed as having sinned in the one act of Adam's sin (cf. "all have sinned," also the Gr. past tense, in 3:23). Two ways of explaining this participation of the human race in the sin of Adam have been presented by theologians—the "federal headship" of Adam over the race and the "natural or seminal headship" of Adam. (Others say that people merely imitated Adam, that he gave the human race a bad example. But that does not do justice to 5:12.)

The federal headship view considers Adam, the first man, as the *representative* of the human race that generated from him. As the representative of all humans, Adam's act of sin was considered by God to be the act of all people and his penalty of death was judicially made the penalty of everybody.

The natural headship view, on the other hand, recognizes that the entire human race was seminally and *physically* in Adam, the first man. As a result God considered all people as participating in the act of sin which Adam committed and as receiving the penalty he received. Even adherents of the federal headship view must admit that Adam is the natural head of the human race physically; the issue is the relationship spiritually. Biblical evidence supports the natural headship of Adam. When presenting the superiority of Melchizedek's priesthood to Aaron's, the author of Hebrews argued that Levi, the head of the priestly tribe, "who collects the 10th, paid the 10th through Abraham, because when Melchizedek met Abraham, Levi was still in the body of his ancestor" (Heb. 7:9-10).

5:13. Though **sin** entered human experience through the act of Adam's sin (in which the entire human race participated seminally), sin expressed itself repeatedly in people's actions (cf. Gen. 6:5-7, 11-13) from the point of its entrance "until" (not **before,** as the NIV has it) **the Law was given.** However, as Paul had already said, "Where there is no Law there is no transgression" (Rom. 4:15). This does not mean that **sin** does not exist unless there is a Law. It means that sin does not have the character of being a transgression apart from **Law** and therefore **sin is not taken into account** (lit., "imputed, reckoned") as such.

5:14. The fact that sin did exist during the period from Adam to the Law is proved by the fact that **death reigned from the time of Adam to the time of Moses** (lit., "from Adam until Moses"). And death also reigned over people who had not broken **a command as did Adam** (cf. "death reigned," v. 17, and "sin reigned in death," v. 21). Adam had disobeyed a specific command of God (Gen. 2:17) and committed a transgression, something that his descendants did not do when they sinned till other specific commands from God were received. But yet all Adam's descendants had sinned with Adam (Rom. 5:12), and therefore death did reign (cf. Gen. 5:5, 8, 11, 14, 17, 20, 27, 31). Since death was present, that proved all had sinned in Adam (cf. comments on Rom. 5:12).

The mention of Adam by name (cf. "one man," v. 12) brought Paul back to the point of referring to him, who was a pattern of the One to come. A parallelism exists between Adam and Jesus Christ as heads of groups of human beings (cf. 1 Cor. 15:45-49), but the parallelism is more contrastive than comparative.

5:15. The details of the parallelism between Adam and Christ (begun by Paul in v. 12 with the words "just as") are given in verses 15-17. The apostle made clear the contrastive nature of the parallelism by stating, **But the gift** (charisma, "grace-gift") **is not like the trespass.** What Christ "gives" contrasts with what Adam did, his "trespass" (paraptōma, "false step"; also mentioned in 4:25; 5:16-18, 20). The point of the first contrasting parallel is the degree—**how much more.** The trespass of the one man brought physical death to **the many,** in this case the entire human race to date with two exceptions—Enoch and Elijah. By contrast, **God's grace—and the gift** (viz., righteousness, as stated in v. 17; cf. v. 16) **that came by the grace of the one Man, Jesus Christ**—abounded **to the many!** If this latter "many" is identical with the first (the many who died, which is possible, but is not required by the text) and constitutes the entire human race, then "God's grace and the gift" by means of "grace" abound in the sense of reaching and being available to all people, but not necessarily being appropriated by all.

5:16. Here Paul presented a second contrasting parallelism; this one is different in kind. He began by emphasizing the contrast: **Again, the gift of God is not like the result of the one man's sin.** Literally, the Greek is, "Also not as through the one who sinned is the gift." Obviously here a noun paralleling "the gift" is missing in the text. Some suggest "the judgment" from what follows; others the transgression, or the death, or the condemnation. It seems best to leave it indefinite as does the Greek text and to translate it by "the result" (as does the NIV) of that which happened.

Paul continued, **The judgment followed** ("was out of") **one sin** (lit., "one," i.e., Adam) **and brought condemnation.** God passed judgment (krima) on Adam and he (and the entire human race) received condemnation (katakrima, "punishment"; katakrima occurs elsewhere only in v. 18 and 8:1). **But,** by contrast, **the gift** (charisma, "grace-gift," i.e., righteousness, 5:17; cf. v. 15) **followed** ("was out of") **many trespasses and brought justification** (dikaiōma, "a declaration of righteousness," also used in 1:32, 2:26; 5:18; 8:4). God's grace, as Paul stated repeatedly, beginning in 3:24, is the basis of a person's being justified, declared righteous. And this was in the face of "many trespasses" (paraptōmatōn; cf. 5:15, 17-18, 20). One man (Adam) trespassed (v. 15) God's command, and everyone since has repeatedly overstepped God's instructions.

5:17. The third contrasting parallelism (cf. vv. 15-16) combines the two preceding ones and involves both a difference in degree (**how much more;** cf. v. 15) and a difference in kind ("death" and "life"; cf. v. 16). The first-class condition in the first part of the verse assumes the statement to be true, **if** (since) **death reigned** (cf. v. 20) **through that one man.** This fact is confirmed by verses 12 and 14. Death is a tyrant, ruling over people and bringing every person under its fear and into its grip (cf. Heb. 2:15).

As a result it also is true that **those who receive God's abundant provision of grace and of the gift** (cf. Rom. 5:15) **of righteousness reign in life through the one Man, Jesus Christ.** The Lord Jesus is the Agent of all of God's provision for people. Whereas death reigns like a tyrant over all, believers in Christ, who receive God's grace, reign in life. In the one case people are dying victims under a ruthless ruler; in the other they themselves become the rulers (cf. Rev. 1:6) whose kingdom is one of life! The fact that it is "those who receive" God's grace and gift emphasizes that the provision made for all in Christ's sacrificial death and offered to all by God must be appropriated by an individual by faith to become effective (cf. "received" in John 1:12).

5:18-19. In these verses Paul concludes his basic parallelism between

Adam and Jesus Christ begun in verse 12 and the contrasts between them in verses 15-17. Paul reduced the contrast to the briefest possible statement. **Consequently** (lit., "so then"), **just as the result of one trespass** (*paraptōmatos,* "false step"; cf. vv. 15-17, 20) **was condemnation** (*katakrima,* "punishment"; cf. v. 16) **for all men, so also the result of one act of righteousness was justification that brings life for all men.** The "one righteous act" (lit. Gr.) was Christ's death on the cross. One trespass (Adam's sin) is contrasted with one righteous act (Christ's sacrifice). The result of Adam's sin (everyone under God's condemnation) is contrasted with the result of Christ's work (justification offered to all). One brought death; the other brings life. Once again the "all men" in the first half of the sentence includes the entire human race (cf. "all men" in v. 12, and "the many" in the first half of v. 15). This implies the same dimensions for the "all men" in the second half of the verse (cf. "many" in the second halves of vv. 16, 19). The provision in the one righteous act, therefore, is potential and it comes to the entire human race as the offer and opportunity which are applied only to "those who receive" (v. 17).

The same conclusion is stated in different words in verse 19, where Adam's act is called **disobedience** and the sacrificial death of Jesus Christ is called **obedience.** As a result **the many** (cf. first halves of vv. 15, 18) **were made** (lit., "stand constituted as") **sinners** (cf. 11:32). In the second half of 5:19 **the many** means "those who receive" (v. 17; cf. "many" in the second half of v. 16). They are not simply declared righteous (the verb *dikaioō* is not used here), but they **will be made righteous** in the process of sanctification, culminating in glorification in God's presence. The word "made" (from *kathistēmi*) means "stand constituted as," the same verb used in the first half of verse 19 in the words "were made sinners."

5:20-21. A remaining question in this discussion is, Where does the Mosaic Law fit into all this and why? Paul explained, **The Law was added so that the trespass** (*paraptōma,* cf. vv. 15-19) **might increase** ("abound"). The word "added" should be rendered "came in beside," for it translates the verb *pareisēl-*

then. Two similar verbs, *eisēlthen* and *diēlthen,* were used in verse 12. Galatians 2:4 is the only other place in the New Testament that uses the Greek verb for "came in beside."

Is the statement in Romans 5:20a a purpose or a result clause? The coming of the Mosaic Law (clearly meant here in light of vv. 13-14) did *result* in the abounding of "the trespass" (the consequence of any law), but (also in the light of vv. 13-14 and 4:15) the Mosaic Law came in "so that" (*purpose*) abounding sin might be recognized as abounding trespass.

The result was that **where sin increased** (lit., "abounded"; cf. 5:20) **grace increased all the more** ("overflowed superlatively"; cf. "overflow" in v. 15). What a contrast! No matter how great human sin becomes, God's grace overflows beyond it and abundantly exceeds it. No wonder Paul wrote that God's grace "is sufficient" (2 Cor. 12:9). God's goal (*hina,* **so,** introduces a purpose clause) is that His **grace might reign through righteousness** (the righteousness of Christ provided for people) **to bring eternal life through Jesus Christ our Lord.** Once again Paul spoke of reigning in connection with life. In verse 17 those who received God's gift "reign in life" through Christ. Here God's grace is personified as reigning and bringing eternal life.

By the time the Apostle Paul had reached this point he had not only described how God's provided righteousness is revealed in justification but he also was anticipating how it is to be revealed through regeneration and sanctification.

IV. God's Righteousness Revealed in Sanctification (chaps. 6–8)

God's provided righteousness involves more than declaring believers righteous on the basis of faith. In Romans the first clue to this fact is in 5:5: "God has poured out His love into our hearts by the Holy Spirit, whom He has given us." The presence of the Holy Spirit within believers and God's reproduction of an attribute of His (His love) in believers speak of their new natures and their new lives. This new kind of life, with the sanctifying ministry of the Holy Spirit, is now discussed at length by Paul in chapters 6–8.

Contrasts between Adam and Christ in Romans 5:15–21

	One Man (Adam)	One Man (Christ)
v. 15	*One* man's *trespass* → *many* died	*One* Man's grace → *gift* of grace (righteousness) to *many*
v. 16	*One* (Adam) → judgment and condemnation	*Many trespasses* → gift → justification
v. 17	Through *one* man's *trespass* → death reigned	Through *one* Man Jesus Christ → believers reign in life
v. 18	*One trespass* → condemnation for *all* men	*One* act of righteousness → justification offered to *all* men
v. 19	Disobedience of *one* → *many* constituted sinners	Obedience of *One* → *many* constituted righteous
v. 21	Sin reigned in death	Grace reigns to bring eternal life

→ = led to or results in

A. Ground of sanctification (6:1-4)

6:1-2. The questions that open this section demand reflection. A review of God's provision by grace through Jesus Christ should elicit praise to God. But the teaching on God's justification of sinful people (3:21–5:21) and the statement of 5:20 in particular might lead some to suggest what Paul expressed: **Shall we go on sinning so that grace may increase?** Some may have reasoned that since grace increases "all the more" when sin abounds, then believers ought to sin more so they could experience more grace! The apostle voiced this idea only to reject it vehemently: **By no means!** (*mē genoito;* cf. comments on 3:4) In no way is the abundance of God's grace designed to encourage sin.

Then Paul explained why such a thought cannot be entertained. The fact is, Christians **died to sin** (cf. 6:7, 11). The Greek aorist (past) tense for "died" suggests a specific point when the action occurred, at salvation. Death, whether physical or spiritual, means separation, not extinction (cf. vv. 6-7, 14). Death to sin is separation from sin's power, not the extinction of sin. Being dead to sin means being "set free from sin" (vv. 18, 22). That being true, Paul asked, **How can they live in it any longer?** Obviously believers cannot *live* in sin if they *died* to it.

6:3-4. Paul explained in more detail the spiritual basis for his abrupt declaration, "We died to sin" (v. 2). Whether the Roman Christians knew it or not, the fact is **that all of us who were baptized into Christ Jesus were baptized into His death.** The question here is whether Paul had in mind Spirit baptism (1 Cor. 12:13) or water baptism. Some object to taking Romans 6:3 as Spirit baptism because that verse speaks of being "baptized into Christ" whereas 1 Corinthians 12:13 speaks of Spirit baptism placing the believer into Christ's *body.* Of course, both are true: the believer is "baptized" (placed into) Christ and also into the body of Christ, and both are done by the Holy Spirit.

Others take Romans 6:3 to refer to water baptism, but the problem with that is that it seems to suggest that baptism saves. However, the New Testament consistently denies baptismal regeneration, presenting water baptism as a public attestation to an accomplished spiritual work (cf., e.g., Acts 10:44-48; 16:29-33). The spiritual reality Paul spoke of is that by faith believers are "baptized (placed) into Christ" and thereby are united and identified with Him. This spiritual reality is then graphically witnessed to and pictured by believers' baptism in water. The one baptism (by water) is the visible picture of the spiritual truth of the other baptism (identification with Christ; cf. Gal. 3:27, "baptized into Christ . . . clothed with Christ").

This is supported by the statement, **We were therefore buried with Him through baptism into death.** Christ's burial shows that He actually died (cf. 1 Cor. 15:3-4). Christians' "burial" with Christ shows that they in fact died with Him to their former sinful ways of living. The purpose of their identification with Christ in His death and burial is **that just as Christ was raised from the dead** (lit., "out from dead ones"; cf. Rom. 4:24; 8:11) **through the glory** (a synonym for God's power; cf. Eph. 1:19; Col. 2:12) **of the Father, we too may live a new life** (lit., "so also in newness of life we should walk about"). The Greek word "newness" (*kainotēti*) speaks of life that has a new or fresh quality. The resurrection of Jesus was not just a resuscitation; it was a new form of life. In the same way the spiritual lives of believers in Jesus have a new, fresh quality. Also, a believer's identification with Jesus Christ in His resurrection, besides being the start of new spiritual life now, is also the guarantee of physical resurrection.

This work of God at salvation in identifying a believer with Christ's death, burial, and resurrection—thus separating him from sin's power and giving him a new quality of life—is the basis of the Holy Spirit's continuing work in sanctification.

B. Attitudes for sanctification (6:5-23)

Sanctification begins with regeneration, the implanting of spiritual life in a believer. From that starting point sanctification is God's progressively separating a believer from sin to Himself and transforming his total life experience toward holiness and purity. The process of sanctification for a believer never ends while he is on earth in his mortal body. It is consummated in glorification when that believer through death and resurrection or through the Rapture stands in the presence of God "conformed to the likeness of His Son" (8:29). A believer's identification with Jesus Christ by faith is both the ground and the goal of sanctification. The process of translating that identification into the daily experience of progressive sanctification, however, demands three attitudes of mind and action on a believer's part. These Paul discussed in 6:5-23.

1. RECKON (6:5-11)

The first attitude for sanctification demanded of believers is to "count" (pres. imper., "keep on counting") themselves dead to sin but alive to God in Christ Jesus (v. 11). Being able to reckon something as true, however, depends on knowing and believing certain things. These things to know and believe are stated in verses 5-10.

6:5-7. The first clause should be translated, "Since (not **if**) **we have become united** in the likeness of **His death**," because the statement is assumed to be true and is true. It affirms the certainty of the second clause of the sentence, which promises that believers are **united with** Christ **in** the likeness of **His resurrection.** As a result **we know** (*ginōskontes* suggests experimental or reflective knowing, not intuitive knowledge as in *eidotes* in v. 9) **that our old self was crucified with Him.** Literally, the last portion of this sentence is, "our old man was crucified together," obviously with Christ. A believer's "old man" is the person as he was spiritually before he trusted Christ, when he was still under sin (3:9), powerless and ungodly (5:6), a sinner (5:8), and an enemy of God (5:10). ("Old self" or "old man" does not refer to the sin nature as such. The Bible does not teach that the sin nature was eradicated at salvation or is ever eradicated in this life.)

The "old man" was "crucified" with Christ (cf. "baptized into His death," 6:3; and "united with Him in His death," v. 5) **so that the body of sin might be rendered powerless.** The phrase "the body of sin" does not mean that a human body is sinful in itself. It means that one's physical body is controlled or ruled by sin (cf. comments on "body of death" in 7:24). This was the condition of each believer before his conversion. But now at salvation the power of controlling sin is broken; it is "rendered powerless" or ineffective (*katargēthē*; trans. "nullify" in 1 Cor. 1:28).

The next clause (Rom. 6:6b-7) in effect explains the first clause (v. 6a). In his unregenerate state a believer was enslaved **to sin.** But his "old man" was crucified (identified) with Christ, and that is the basis for deliverance from enslavement to sin. **Anyone who has died has been freed from sin.** The words "has been freed" are a loose rendering of *dedikaiōtai*, literally, "has been justified or declared righteous." The perfect tense of this verb describes a past action with a continuing effect or force. Sin no longer has the legal right to force its mastery and control on a believer, for he has died with Christ.

6:8-11. These verses state much the same truth as verses 5-7 and in the same format, beginning with **if** ("since"). Those who by faith receive Jesus Christ and are identified with Him have **died with Christ** (cf. vv. 3, 5). Because this is true, **we believe** (pres. tense, "we keep on believing") **that we will also live with Him.** The sharing of the resurrection life of Christ begins at the moment of regeneration, but it will continue as a believer shares eternity with the Lord. Again as a result **we know** (*eidotes,* "intuitive knowledge," perceiving a self-evident truth [cf. v. 15], not *ginōskontes,* "experimental or reflective knowledge" as in v. 6) that Christ's resurrection was a removal from the sphere of physical death to an unending spiritual form of life. Having experienced physical death once and having been removed from its realm by resurrection life, Jesus **cannot die again** (lit., "dies no more"). In resurrection Jesus Christ was victorious over death (Acts 2:24) and **death no longer has mastery** (*kyrieuei,* "rules as lord"; cf. Rom. 6:14) **over Him** as it does over all other human beings (John 10:17-18).

Paul summarized this discussion by stating that Jesus in His physical **death . . . died to sin** (i.e., in reference to sin) **once for all** (*ephapax;* cf. Heb. 7:27; 9:12; 10:10). This stands in opposition to the doctrine and practice of the so-called perpetual sacrifice of Christ in the Roman Catholic Mass. Contrariwise, **the life He lives, He lives** (pres. tense, "keeps on living") **to God.** Resurrection life is eternal in quality and everlasting in duration. Furthermore, God is its Source and also its Goal. What is true of Jesus Christ in reality and experience, believers

who are identified with Him by faith are commanded to reckon true for themselves. They are to **count** themselves **dead to** (in reference to) **sin but alive to God.** Since they are dead to its power (Rom. 6:2), they ought to recognize that fact and not continue in sin. Instead they are to realize they have new life **in Christ;** they share His resurrection life (cf. Eph. 2:5-6; Col. 2:12-13).

2. YIELD (6:12-14)

6:12. The attitude of mind that a believer has died to sin must be translated into action in his experience. Paul commanded, **Therefore do not let sin reign** (pres. imper., "do not let sin continue to reign") as it did before salvation. The present imperative negative can also be translated, "Stop letting sin reign." When sin reigns in people's lives and bodies, they **obey its evil desires.** Sin enslaves (v. 6), making a person subject to his own desires. *Epithymia* refers to "longings" or "desires," which may be either good or evil, depending on how the word is used. Here, in the case of sin, the desires are evil. **In your mortal body** means that sin manifests itself through one's physical actions in this body. The Greek here stresses that the body is mortal or dying. Perhaps this suggests the foolishness of giving in to the desires of a body that is transitory and decaying. To give in to a dying master is strange indeed.

6:13. Actually this verse repeats the command of verse 12 in more specific terms. **Do not offer** (lit., "do not continue to present," or "stop presenting") **the parts of your body** (lit., "your members"; cf. v. 19) **to sin, as instruments** (*hopla,* frequently in military context, "weapons" or "armor"; cf. 13:12; 2 Cor. 6:7; 10:4) **of wickedness** (*adikias,* "unrighteousness" in contrasting parallelism with righteousness, later in Rom. 6:13). On the contrary, in sharp contrast, Paul commanded, **offer** (aorist imper., "present once and for all"; also used in v. 19) **yourselves to God, as those who have been brought from death to life** (lit., "as if being alive out from dead ones"; cf. John 5:24) **and offer the parts of your body** (lit., "and your members") **to Him as instruments** (*hopla*) **of righteousness** (*dikaiosynēs*). A related passage is Paul's exhortation, "Offer your bodies as living sacrifices . . . to God"

(Rom. 12:1). Because they were once dead in sin (cf. Eph. 2:1) but have been given new life (Rom. 6:11) believers ought to live for God. Their bodies should be used not for sin (v. 12) or unrighteousness (v. 13) but for promoting righteousness (cf. "bodies" and "body"; 7:5, 23; 1 Cor. 6:15).

6:14. God's design is that **sin shall not be your master** (*kyrieusei*; "shall not rule as lord"; cf. v. 9). The reason this should not happen is that **you are not under Law, but under grace.** Paul had already explained that "the Law was added so that the trespass might increase" (5:20), and elsewhere he declared, "The power of sin is the Law" (1 Cor. 15:56). If believers were still under the Law, it would be impossible to keep sin from exercising mastery. But since believers are "under grace," this can be done by following Paul's instructions.

3. SERVE (6:15-23)

6:15-16. The mention that believers are "under grace" (v. 14) raised another aberrant idea that the apostle refuted. The question is, **Shall we sin because we are . . . under grace** instead of the Law? The Greek aorist (past) tense here may have the sense of committing an act of sin now and then, in contrast to living a life of sin as stated in verse 1. Paul's response was the same as before (v. 2): **By no means!** (*mē genoito*; cf. comments on 3:4) Again he proceeded to explain why that idea cannot be accepted. He asked, **Don't you know** ("perceive intuitively" a self-evident truth; cf. 6:9) that in effect there is no middle ground between being a slave **to sin** and a slave **to obedience** to God. As the Lord Jesus said, "No one can serve two masters. . . . You cannot serve both God and money" (Matt. 6:24; Luke 16:13). Paul also pointed out that being a slave to sin **leads to death** (cf. Rom. 6:21, 23). This is not physical death only or even spiritual death only, but death in general as the natural consequence and inevitable concomitant of sin (cf. Gen. 2:17). On the other hand being a slave to obedience (to God and His gospel obviously) **leads to righteousness** (again righteousness in the general sense as equivalent to eternal life or glorification). Death is the normal consequence of sin (which is disobeying God); righteousness

is the normal consequence of obeying God and living for Him.

6:17-18. This discussion reminded the Apostle Paul of what the grace of God had already accomplished in his readers' lives and he burst forth in praise. Before they responded to the gospel they had been **slaves to sin,** but they **wholeheartedly** (lit., "out from hearts," thus inwardly and genuinely, not merely externally) **obeyed** (cf. "obedience" in 1 Peter 1:2) **the form of teaching to which** they **were entrusted.** Hearing the teaching of God's Word, they committed themselves to those truths. That commitment was evidenced by their response to the gospel and their being baptized. The result was that they **have been set free from sin and have become slaves** (past tense in Gr.) **to righteousness** (cf. Rom. 6:22). This is positional and must be manifested in daily experience, but it demonstrates again that there is no middle ground. Christians are not to give in to sin because they are dead to it and no longer slaves of it. It is totally contrary to God's plan for slaves of righteousness to become enslaved to sin!

6:19. To talk of being "enslaved" to righteousness and to God is not correct in one sense, Paul wrote, because God does not hold His children in bondage. But the word "slavery" appropriately describes an unregenerate person's relationship to sin and to Satan. So Paul used "slavery" for contrasting the relationship of the believer as well. Before developing this idea further, the apostle in effect apologized for its use—I **put this in human terms** (lit., "I am speaking in human fashion")—**because you are weak in your natural selves** (lit., "your flesh"). Apparently Paul felt that his readers' spiritual perception was feeble so he used this terminology from human experience. Then he basically repeated the ideas of verses 16-17. Unsaved Romans had offered their bodies **to impurity and to ever-increasing wickedness** (lit., "lawlessness"; cf. 1:24-27; 6:13). They had voluntarily become enslaved! But Paul exhorted believers now to offer themselves as slaves **to righteousness leading to holiness** (perfect holiness, as the end of the process [cf. v. 22]) in contrast with their former impurity.

6:20-23. Paul once again stated that slavery **to sin** and to **righteousness** are mutually exclusive (cf. vv. 13, 16). But he went on to indicate the superiority of being enslaved to righteousness and God. The **benefit** (this Gr. word is usually trans. "fruit") of enslavement to sin was that it produced things that a believer is **now ashamed of.** But even worse, "the end of **those things** is **death**" (lit. trans.). Responding to the gospel by faith and accepting Jesus Christ completely reverses things for an individual. He is now . . . **set free from sin** (cf. v. 18) and has been enslaved to God with the result that he has **the benefit** of **holiness** (cf. v. 19), the subject of chapters 6–8. The sinful life gives no benefit (6:21), but salvation gives the benefit of a holy, clean life (v. 22). Whereas the "end" (*telos*) or result of sin is death (v. 21), the "end" of salvation **is eternal life.** Paul then summarized these contrasts. **The wages** (the Gr. word *opsōnia* originally meant a soldier's pay) **of sin is death** (eternal death here, in contrast with "eternal life" in v. 23b). This death is eternal separation from God in hell, in which unbelievers suffer conscious torment forever (Luke 16:24-25). This is the wages they have earned and deserve because of their sin (cf. Rom. 5:12; 7:13). By contrast, **the gift** (*charisma*, "grace-gift") **of God is eternal life** (cf. John 3:16, 36). Eternal life is a gift that cannot be earned (cf. Eph. 2:8-9; Titus 3:5).

Three times in this chapter Paul wrote that sin results in death (Rom. 6:16, 21, 23). But believers have been set free from sin (vv. 18, 22) and are no longer slaves to it (vv. 6, 20) but are "slaves to righteousness" (vv. 16, 18-19; cf. v. 13). Because they are alive to God (v. 11) and have eternal life (v. 23) they should present themselves to Him (vv. 13, 19) and live accordingly, not letting sin master them (vv. 6, 11-14, 22).

C. Conflict in sanctification (chap. 7)

It is one thing for a believer to understand that his identification with Jesus Christ means that he has died to sin (6:2) and to count or reckon that to be true (6:11). But it is something else for him to deal with the sin nature that remains within and its efforts to express itself in his thoughts and actions. This is the internal conflict in the area of sanctification that every believer faces.

1. THE BELIEVER AND THE LAW (7:1-6)

7:1-3. Verses 1-6 relate to 6:14, the intervening verses (6:15-23) being a digression raised by the question in 6:15. The statement that a believer identified with Jesus Christ in His death is no-longer "under Law" (6:14) should not have surprised Paul's readers because they were **men who know the Law.** This statement should not be restricted to Jewish believers in the church at Rome because Gentiles also knew the principle **that the Law has authority** (*kyrieuei,* "rules as lord"; cf. 6:9, 14) **over a man only as long as he lives.** This is a self-evident truth, which Paul then illustrated by marriage. **A married woman** (lit., "the under-a-man woman") **is bound** (perf. tense, "has been bound and stands bound") **to her husband as long as he is alive. But if her husband dies** (in Gr., a third-class condition indicating a real possibility) **she is released** (perf. tense, "has been and stands discharged") **from the law of marriage** (lit., "from the law of the man"). She is bound to him by marriage as her husband while he lives, and obviously his death frees her from that marriage.

Then Paul continued the illustration, pointing out that if **a wife marries** (lit., "if she comes to") **another man while her husband is still alive she is called** (future tense, "shall be publicly known as") **an adulteress.** Conversely, on the death of her **husband** she is free from that marriage (cf. 7:2). So she **is not an adulteress if she marries** (lit., **"even though** she comes to") **another man.** A widow who marries again is not guilty of adultery.

7:4-6. In these verses Paul applied his illustration of marriage to a believer and the Law. He said, **You also died** (lit., "you were put to death," as was true of Jesus) **to the Law.** Just as a believer "died to sin" (6:2) and so is "set free from sin" (6:18, 22), so he also died to the Law and is separated and set free from it (6:14; cf. Gal. 2:19). As a wife is no longer married to her husband when he dies, so a Christian is no longer under the Law. This separation was **through the body of Christ,** that is, because of Christ's death on the cross.

As a result Christians **belong to another, to Him who was raised from the** dead (cf. Rom. 6:4, 9). This One of course is the Lord Jesus Christ. In a sense believers are united to Him as His bride (Eph. 5:25). God's purpose in all this is in order that we might bear fruit to God (cf. Rom. 6:22; Gal. 5:22-23; Phil. 1:11). Only a person who is spiritually alive can bear spiritual fruit, that is, holy living (cf. John 15:4-5). A person who is married to Christ can bear spiritual progeny. Paul moved from the second person plural (you) to the first person plural (we), including himself along with his readers.

The apostle continued, For when we were controlled by the sinful nature (lit., "For when we were in the flesh"; *sarx* often means sin nature; cf. Rom. 7:18, 25) the sinful passions aroused by the Law were at work in our bodies. This describes a believer before he was saved (cf. 6:19). The Law by its prohibitions aroused sinful passions, as explained in 7:7-13. In that sense unsaved Gentiles were "under" the Law. Consequently their progeny was not "fruit to God" (v. 4) but fruit for death. Sin, Paul repeatedly affirmed, leads to death (5:15, 17, 21; 6:16, 21, 23; 7:10-11, 13; 8:2, 6, 10, 13).

But now, being identified with Christ, believers are dead to the Law. Like a widow released from marital obligations, so believers are released from the Law and its arousal to sin. The purpose of this release "from the Law" is so that they may serve (a better rendering is "be slaves"; cf. "slave[s]" in 6:6, 16 [thrice], 17-18, 20, 22) in the new way of the Spirit, and not in the old way of the written code. The word "Spirit" may be "spirit" (lowercase "s") to contrast with the written document, the Law. The thought then is that believers do not live by the "oldness" of the Law but by the "newness" of a regenerated spirit. Or "Spirit" may refer to the Holy Spirit, the Source of new life. (Cf. comments on "the Spirit" and "the letter," 2 Cor. 3:6.)

2. THE LAW AND SIN (7:7-13)

The involvement of the Mosaic Law in the discussion of a believer's identification with Christ and death to sin raises a question about the Law's relationship to sin.

7:7-8. Is the Law sin? Paul's response again was a vehement denial. Certainly not! (*mē genoito*; cf. comments on 3:4) The Law arouses sin (7:5) but that does not mean the Law itself is sin. In fact, Paul said later, the Law is holy (v. 12) and spiritual (v. 14). Paul went on to explain that the Law made sin known (cf. 3:19-20). Then to be specific, he mentioned coveting. The Law's prohibition, Do not covet (Ex. 20:17; Deut. 5:21), makes people want to covet all the more. Paul knew sin as a principle and specifically, covetousness as an expression of it, and that knowledge came through the Law. Paul described how it worked. The indwelling principle of sin, seizing the opportunity (lit., "taking a start point" [*aphormēn*, a base for military operations or for an expedition]) afforded by the commandment (cf. Rom. 7:11), produced in me every kind of covetous desire. The Law is not the cause of the act of sin; the principle or nature of sin within an individual is. But the Law's specific commandments stimulate the sin principle into acts that violate the commandments and give those acts the character of transgression (4:15; cf. 3:20; 5:13b, 20a). As Paul concluded, Apart from Law, sin is dead. This does not mean that sin has no existence without the Law (cf. 5:13), but that without the Law sin is less active, for the Law arouses "sinful passions" (7:5).

It is significant that, beginning with verse 7 and continuing through this chapter, the Apostle Paul turned to the first person singular, presenting his personal experience. Up to this point he had used the third person, the second person, and even the first person plural. But now he described his own experience, allowing the Holy Spirit to apply the truth to his readers.

7:9-12. Some generalize the words, Once I was alive apart from Law, to refer to the experience of mankind in the period between the Fall and the giving of the Mosaic Law. But there is no basis for this. Evidently the apostle was speaking of his personal experience as a child and perhaps even a youth prior to his awareness and understanding of the full impact of God's commandments. The clause, but when the commandment came, does not speak of the giving of the Mosaic Law, but the dawning of the significance of the commandment ("Do not covet") on Paul's mind and heart before his conversion. The result was that the principle of sin within made its presence and power known (it **sprang to life**) in his violations of the **commandment**. As a result Paul **died** spiritually (cf. 6:23a) under the sentence of judgment by the Law he had broken. The commandment not to covet was given to help people see how to live, but it actually produced **death** because of the sin in human hearts.

Repeating from 7:8 his description of sin's relationship to the commandment, Paul declared that **sin . . . deceived me.** Apart from the Law, the principle of sin was dormant and inactive; but using the commandments of the Law, it demonstrated its controlling force over one's actions. So this sin deceived him (*exēpatē-sen*, "led [him] astray"; cf. 2 Cor. 11:3; 1 Tim. 2:14) and **put** him **to death** (lit., "killed" him), not physically but spiritually. Sin is like a personal enemy within (cf. Gen. 4:7). **The Law**, instead of being sin (Rom. 7:7), **is holy, and the commandment** not to covet (which, as a part of the Law, represents the whole) **is holy, righteous, and good.**

7:13. Paul then considered still another possible misunderstanding in his effort to clarify the relationship of sin and the Law. Taking the last-mentioned quality of the commandment ("good"), he asked, **Did that which is good, then, become death to me?** Once again his immediate response was a vehement denial (**By no means!** *mē genoito*; cf. comments on 3:4), followed by an explanation. The principle of **sin**, not the Law, becomes **death** to an individual (5:12). But **sin uses the commandment**, the **good** thing, as an agent or instrument to keep on producing **death in** a person and thereby **sin** is seen as **utterly** (lit., "exceedingly") **sinful.** The internal principle or nature of sin uses the specific commandments of the Law of God—in part and in the whole; a "holy, righteous, and good" thing in itself—to manifest its true nature as opposed to God and to demonstrate its power within individuals.

3. THE BELIEVER AND SIN (7:14-25)

7:14. Understanding the conflict in personal sanctification involves seeing the relationship between a believer and his indwelling sin. In verse 14 Paul made a transition from the previous subject (vv. 7-13) to the next one. The statement, **The Law is spiritual** (cf. v. 12), is not only the

conclusion of Paul's previous argument but also an accepted fact among people. The Law comes from God who is Spirit (John 4:24) and expresses God's will for human living. Paul, using himself as the example, said the problem is that **I am unspiritual** (*sarkinos*, "fleshy, made of flesh"). In addition he was **sold as a slave** (perf. tense, "had been sold and remained in that state") **to sin** (lit. "under the sin"; cf. "under sin" in Rom. 3:9).

In relating his personal experience in 7:14-25 Paul consistently used the present tense whereas he had used the imperfect and aorist tenses. Obviously he was describing his present conflict as a Christian with indwelling sin and its continuing efforts to control his daily life. The clause, "sold under sin" (KJV), describes an unregenerate person; but sin also resides in a believer, who is still subject to sin's penalty of physical death. As a result, indwelling sin continues to seek to claim what it considers its property even after one has become a Christian.

7:15-17. At the start Paul confessed, **I do not understand what I do** (lit., "what I am producing I do not know"). He was like a little boy whose honest answer to why he did something wrong is, "I don't know." A person's actions are at the dictate of someone or something besides himself that he really does not understand and cannot explain. Paul continued to present this quandary he faced: **For what I want to do I do not do** (lit., "For what I am wishing, that I am not doing," *prassō*) and conversely, **What I hate I do** (lit., "What I am hating that I am doing," *poiō*). No difference of emphasis can be put on this verse on the two Greek verbs translated "do" (even though such difference is significant elsewhere), because the occurrence of those two verbs is reversed in verse 19. This statement can be made by an unregenerate person in his highest moral and ethical moments, but it can also be said by a regenerate person. There is no reason to conclude that Paul was not describing his experience as a believer at that time. Paul said, **I agree that the Law is good.** Here the Greek word for "good" is *kalos*, "beautiful, noble, excellent," whereas in verse 12 it is *agathē*, "useful, upright." Because of this evidence, Paul concluded, **It is no longer I myself who do it** (lit., "no longer am I myself producing it"; cf. v. 15) **but it is sin living in me** (lit., "but the dwelling-in-me sin"). This does not mean Paul was avoiding personal responsibility for his actions; he was speaking of the conflict between his desires and the sin within him.

7:18-20. Paul's experience convinced him that "the Law is good" (v. 16). But he also concluded, **I know that nothing good lives in me.** Then he hastened to explain that by the phrase "in me" he meant **in my sinful nature** (*sarki*, "flesh"; cf. vv. 5, 25). This is not literal physical or material flesh, but the principle of sin that expresses itself through one's mind and body.

As support for this conclusion Paul explained, **For I have the desire to do what is good** ("For to wish is present with me" [or "is lying beside me"]), **but I cannot carry it out** (lit., "but to produce the good is not"). Paul then repeated in slightly different words the statement of verse 15b, and then in verse 20 he repeated in effect his statement in verse 17. Paul recognized that even as a believer he had an indwelling principle of sin that once owned him as a slave and that still expressed itself through him to do things he did **not want to do** and not to do things he desired to do. This is a problem common to all believers.

7:21-23. Paul was a person who tried to learn from his experiences, so now he concluded, **I find this law at work.** This is not the Mosaic Law, of course, but a principle drawn from experience. Also in 8:2 "law" (*nomos*) means principle. This law or principle is the reality of ever-present **evil** in an individual whenever he wants **to do good.** Paul held fast to the fact that, as he said, **In my inner being I delight in God's Law** (cf. 7:25). "In my inner being" is literally, "according to the inner man." (The "inner man" is used in the Gr. NT also in 2 Cor. 4:16 and Eph. 3:16.) Delight in God's Law was the psalmist's response, stated repeatedly in Psalm 119 (e.g., vv. 16, 24, 47; cf. Ps. 1:2). Because of regeneration, a believer has a new nature or capacity for loving spiritual truths. Yet, recognizing the facts of experience, Paul said he saw **another law** or principle **at work within** him. This is the principle of sin. Paul called it "sin living in me" (Rom. 7:17, 20), "evil" **right**

there **with me** (v. 21), and "the sinful nature" (vv. 5, 18, 25).

This principle is continually doing two things: **waging war against the law of** the believer's **mind and making** him a **prisoner of the law of sin at work within** his **members.** The indwelling principle of sin is constantly mounting a military campaign against the new nature, trying to gain victory and control (cf. "slave" in vv. 14, 25 and "slaves" in 6:17, 19-20), of a believer and his actions. The new nature is called "the law" of the "mind" (*noos*; cf. 7:25) because it has the capacity for perceiving and making moral judgments. Further, despite a believer's identification with Jesus Christ's death and resurrection and his efforts to have Christ-honoring attitudes and actions, he cannot in his own power resist his indwelling sin nature. In and of himself he repeatedly experiences defeat and frustration.

7:24-25. Paul expressed that frustration in his exclamation, **What a wretched man I am!** Significantly Paul's description of himself is part of John's picture of the church of Laodicea—"wretched" (Rev. 3:17). The apostle then asked, **Who will rescue me from this body of death?** Paul recognized that as long as he was in his mortal body he would face the conflict with the indwelling sin principle and would have defeat in his own strength. Here he wrote of the "body of death"; in Romans 6:6 he wrote of the "body of sin." These mean that sin works through one's human body (cf. 6:6, 12-13, 19; 7:5, 23), bringing death (6:16, 21, 23; 7:10-11, 13; 8:10). Paul's answer to this question was triumphant and immediate: **Thanks be to God—through Jesus Christ our Lord!** Paul in this answer was looking to the final triumph of Jesus Christ for His people. Just as believers are identified with Him in His death and resurrection by faith here and now, so they will join their resurrected and exalted Lord for all eternity in new bodies, free forever from the presence of sin (8:23; Phil. 3:20-21). Meanwhile, in this life, Paul concluded, **I myself in my mind** (*noi*; cf. *noos* in Rom. 7:23) **am a slave** (lit., "am serving as a slave") **to God's Law, but in the sinful nature** (*sarki*, "flesh"; cf. vv. 5, 18, where *sarki*, from *sarx*, is also trans. "sinful nature") **a slave to the law of sin** (cf. "slave to sin," v. 14). While awaiting freedom from the presence of sin, believers still face conflicts between their regenerated minds (or new natures or capacities) and their sin natures or capacities.

D. Power for sanctification (8:1-17)

8:1. The question naturally arises, Must a believer spend his whole life on earth frustrated by ongoing defeats to indwelling sin? (7:21-25) Is there no power provided to achieve victory? The answer to the first question is no and to the second, yes. In chapter 8, Paul described the ministry of the indwelling Holy Spirit of God who is the source of divine power for sanctification and the secret for spiritual victory in daily living. But first Paul reminded his readers that **therefore**—since deliverance is "through Jesus Christ our Lord" (7:25)—**no condemnation** (katakrima, "punishment") awaits **those who are in Christ Jesus,** as a result of their faith and identification with Him (cf. 6:13; John 5:24). They are justified, declared righteous, and therefore stand in His grace (Rom. 5:2) and not under His wrath (1:18), and possess eternal life (5:17-18, 21). Christ is the sphere of safety for all who are identified with Him by faith. In the better Greek manuscripts, 8:1 ends here. The words "who do not live according to the sinful nature but according to the Spirit" were probably transcribed from verse 4.

8:2. The word **because** (gar, "for"), connects **through** (lit., "in") **Christ Jesus** in this verse with the identical phrase "in Christ Jesus" in verse 1. (In the Gr. word order of the sentence in v. 2, "in Christ Jesus" follows **the law of the Spirit of life.**) If 7:7-25 is Paul's testimony of his struggle as a believer with indwelling sin, then "the Spirit of life" is the Holy Spirit of God, not the spirit of the new nature each believer receives. The Holy Spirit is the Member of the Godhead who regenerates every believing individual (Titus 3:5) and bestows new life (John 3:5-8), the resurrection life of Christ (Rom. 6:4, 8, 11). Romans 8:2 has the second mention of the Holy Spirit since 5:5, but He is mentioned 18 more times through 8:27. This law ("principle"; cf. 7:23) **set me free** (the Gr. aorist tense suggests a once-for-all act of freedom at salvation) **from the law of sin and death.** That principle is called the principle "of sin and death"

because sin, as Paul said repeatedly, produces death (5:15, 17, 21; 6:16, 21, 23; 7:10-11, 13; 8:6, 10, 13). As the principle of sin it contrasts with the Spirit; as the principle that brings death it also contrasts with the Spirit who gives life. For the pronoun translated **me** some Greek manuscripts read "us" and others "you" (sing.). The difference is incidental; the truth stated applies to every believer.

8:3-4. Having stated the fact of freedom, Paul then explained how it is achieved. He declared again the impossibility of attaining freedom over sin through the (Mosaic) Law. It **was powerless to** free from sin. Not that the Law was weak in itself (as many translations suggest), for it was good (7:12). But because of **sinful** human **nature,** the Law could not deliver from sin. The words "sinful nature" translate sarx (lit., "flesh"), which can mean either human sinful corruption or human weakness (cf. 7:5, 18, 25; 8:4-5, 8-9, 12-13).

God accomplished deliverance over sin, however, **by sending His own Son in the likeness of sinful man** (lit., "likeness of flesh of sin"). Jesus was sent not in sinful flesh but in the likeness of it. His human nature was protected and preserved from the indwelling principle of sin that has plagued all other human beings since Adam (cf. Luke 1:35). He was also sent, literally "concerning or for sin" (peri harmartias, not as the NIV has it, **to be a sin offering).** In other words He came to do something about sin. What He did was to condemn it; by His death on the cross, **He condemned sin** (katekrinen, "passed a judicial sentence on it"; cf. katakrima, "punishment," Rom. 8:1) so that those in Christ are not condemned. The goal of this was so **that the righteous requirements of the Law**—a life of holiness (Lev. 11:44-45; 19:2; 20:7)—could **be fully met** as believers do **not live according to the sinful nature but according to the Spirit.** The provision of deliverance from the power of sin is through the death of Jesus Christ, but experiencing it in one's daily conduct comes through the controlling power of the Holy Spirit.

8:5-8. In these verses Paul answered the implied question, What does it mean to **live according to the sinful nature** and according to the Spirit? He explained that the former means having **their minds set on** (*phronousin*, pres. tense, "keep on being mindful of or aspiring for") **what that nature desires**. An unbeliever cares only for his sinful interests and has no regard for God. The exact opposite is true of **those who live** according to **the Spirit**. They aspire for or **have their minds set on what the Spirit desires.** The sinful nature and the indwelling Spirit are in conflict (Gal. 5:17).

But what difference does it make whether a person is mindful of the flesh or of the Spirit? Again Paul explained. **The mind** (*phronēma*, "mind-set, aspirations"; cf. Rom. 8:6b-7) **of sinful man** (*tēs sarkos*, "of the flesh") **is death,** that is, it is equivalent to death, or it leads to death in all its forms (physical and spiritual). On the other hand **the mind** (*phronēma*, "mind-set, aspirations") **controlled by the Spirit** (lit., "of the Spirit") **is life** (eternal resurrection life) **and peace** immediately (5:1) and ultimately. In 8:7-8 Paul focused only on **the sinful mind** (*phronēma tēs sarkos*, "mind-set, aspirations of the sin nature"; cf. v. 6) to explain why he said (v. 6) that it ends up in death: (1) It **is hostile to God** (cf. 5:10); (2) **it does not submit** (pres. tense, "is not submitting") **to God's Law;** and (3) **it** cannot **do so.** The result is that **those controlled by the sinful nature cannot** (pres. tense, "are not able to") **please God.** The unsaved lead lives that are totally void of spiritual life and ability. A believer, then, who gives in to his sin nature is acting like the unsaved (cf. 1 Cor. 3:3).

8:9-11. After speaking objectively about the two types of persons, Paul now addressed his readers directly. **You, however, are controlled not by the sinful nature but by the Spirit** (lit., "But you are not in the flesh but in the Spirit"), **if** (*eiper*, "if, as is the fact"; cf. v. 17) **the Spirit of God lives** (pres. tense, "is dwelling") **in you** (cf. v. 11). The indwelling Holy Spirit gives a believer a totally different life (2 Cor. 5:17). The opposite, however, is also true: **If anyone does not have the Spirit of Christ, he does not belong to Christ** (lit., "this one is not of Him"). Since only the Holy Spirit gives spiritual life, a person cannot be related to Christ apart from the Spirit.

The interchange of the titles "Spirit of God" and "Spirit of Christ" argues for the deity of Jesus Christ. This statement also makes it clear that the indwelling presence of the Holy Spirit is the identifying mark of a believer in Jesus Christ (cf. 1 John 3:24; 4:13). Another significant fact is that Romans 8:10 equates the indwelling presence of Christ (**Christ is in you**) with the indwelling presence of the Holy Spirit (vv. 9, 11). This adds further support to the biblical doctrine of the Trinity. Verse 10, like verses 9b and 11, is a conditional statement in which in Greek the condition is assumed to be true; **if** can be understood as "since" or "because." As a result of Christ's indwelling presence, **your body is dead** (or, "subject to death"; cf. 7:24) **because of sin, yet your spirit is alive because of righteousness.** Because of God's imputed righteousness, a believer is alive spiritually. The eternal, spiritual life of God is implanted by the indwelling Holy Spirit and Jesus Christ here and now, even though a believer's body is mortal.

Then Paul wrote about an even better promise (8:11). Since God **raised Jesus from the dead** (lit., "out from dead ones"; cf. 4:24; 6:4), God promises believers in whom His **Spirit . . . is living** (cf. 8:9) that He **will also give life to** their **mortal bodies through His Spirit.** In other words, God promises spiritual resurrection life now (6:4, 8, 11) for each believer's mortal body and physical resurrection in the future for that mortal body (6:5; 1 Cor. 6:14; 15:42, 53; 2 Cor. 4:14).

8:12-14. Paul drew a conclusion and made an application from his previous discussion. **Therefore . . . we have an obligation.** Each believer's responsibility is a positive one—to live each day in the control and power of the Holy Spirit. But first Paul expressed this truth negatively—**not to the sinful nature, to live according to it.** Each Christian is to refuse to follow the inclinations and desires of his sin nature. He is to deny the efforts of that nature to impose its lifestyle on him (cf. Titus 2:12). The reason is that a **sinful** manner of life results in death. This does not suggest that a believer who sins will face eternal death in hell; instead, it means he will not enjoy his spiritual life. He will seem like an unsaved person (1 Cor. 3:1-4) and will be unable to enjoy the indwelling presence of the Spirit. **You**

will die is literally, "you are about to die," or "you are at the point of dying." On the other hand, **if by the Spirit you put to death** (pres. tense, "are putting to death") **the misdeeds of the body, you will live.** A few Greek manuscripts have "flesh" instead of "body." But the body is the vehicle by which one's sin-nature expresses itself (cf. Rom. 6:6, 13). Only by the Holy Spirit's power can a believer put to death the sins of his former life (cf. Eph. 4:22-31; Col. 3:5-9). This is what Paul referred to when he said "count yourselves dead to sin" (Rom. 6:11).

Paul then continued his explanation. **Those who are led** (pres. tense, "are being led") **by the Spirit of God are sons of God.** Many Bible students see no difference between the word translated "sons" in 8:14 and the word translated "children" in verse 16. However, in verse 16 the Holy Spirit's indwelling presence attests *the believer's birth relationship to God* (tekna, "children," is lit., "born ones"). But in verse 14 the Holy Spirit's control and direction attests *the believer's privileges in God's family* as a "son" (huios means a child mature enough to take on adult family privileges and responsibilities). A son in God's family is led by God's Spirit.

8:15-17. In contrast with the control of sin, which enslaves to the point of **fear,** believers have **received the Spirit of sonship.** The word translated "sonship" (huiothesias) means "placing as a son" and is frequently translated "adoption" (as in, e.g., v. 23). Believers are adopted sons (Gal. 4:5; Eph. 1:5), not slaves (Gal. 4:7); so they need not be enslaved to sin or in fear. In New Testament times adopted sons enjoyed the same privileges as natural-born sons. So, instead of cowering in slave-like fear, Christians can approach God in an intimate way calling Him *Abba,* **Father.** "Abba" is a Greek and English transliteration of the Aramaic word for father (used elsewhere in the NT only in Mark 14:36; Gal. 4:6). Besides being adopted into God's family as sons, believers also are His children (tekna, "born ones") by the new birth (John 1:12; 1 John 3:1-2). And **the Holy Spirit,** who gives believers life, **testifies with** (not to) their **spirit**(s) of the fact of the new birth.

In many families children inherit their parents' estates; each child is an heir and the children together are co-heirs.

Similarly, since Christians **are God's children,** they **are** His **heirs** (cf. Gal. 4:7), **and** they are **co-heirs with Christ.** They are recipients of all spiritual blessings (Eph. 1:3) now, and in the future they will share with the Lord Jesus in all the riches of God's kingdom (John 17:24; 1 Cor. 3:21-23). Sharing with Jesus Christ, however, involves more than anticipating the glories of heaven. For Jesus Christ it involved suffering and abuse and crucifixion; therefore being co-heirs with Christ requires that believers **share in His sufferings** (cf. John 15:20; Col. 1:24; 2 Tim. 3:12; 1 Peter 4:12). In fact believers do share in His sufferings; **if indeed** translates *eiper,* which means "if, as is the fact" (cf. Rom. 8:9). Then after the suffering they will **share in His glory** (2 Tim. 2:12; 1 Peter 4:13; 5:10).

E. Goal of sanctification (8:18-27)

8:18. In one sense this verse is the conclusion of the preceding paragraph in which believers are assured of being heirs of Christ's coming glory. However, Paul reminded his readers that sharing in the glory of Christ in the future required sharing "in His sufferings" in this life. But after careful figuring (*Logizomai,* **I consider**) Paul concluded **that our present sufferings are** far outweighed by **the glory that will be revealed in** (as well as to and through) **us.** This future glory is so great that present sufferings are insignificant by comparison. Also the glory is forever, whereas the suffering is temporary and light (2 Cor. 4:17). Certainly this truth can help believers endure afflictions. Romans 8:18 also serves as a topic sentence for the following discussion on the relationship between believers and the whole Creation, both in their afflictions and in their future glory.

8:19-21. The interrelationship of man with the physical creation of which he is a part and in which he lives was established in God's sentence of judgment on Adam after the Fall (Gen. 3:17-19). In Romans 8:19-21 Paul demonstrated that this relationship has a future aspect in connection with God's program of salvation for people. He declared, **The Creation waits in eager expectation** (lit., "for the strained expectation [apokaradokia is used only one other time in the NT, in Phil. 1:20] of the Creation keeps on eagerly awaiting") **for the sons of God to**

be revealed. The verb for "eagerly waits" (*apekdechomai*) is used seven times in the New Testament, each time to refer to Christ's return (Rom. 8:19, 23, 25; 1 Cor. 1:7; Gal. 5:5; Phil. 3:20; Heb. 9:28). The revealing of the sons of God will occur when Christ returns for His own. They will share His glory (Rom. 8:18; Col. 1:27; 3:4; Heb. 2:10), and will be transformed (Rom. 8:23). All of nature (inanimate and animate) is personified as waiting eagerly for that time.

The reason for this eager anticipation is stated in verse 20. **For the Creation was subjected to frustration.** The Greek word *mataiotēti* ("futility, frailty, purposelessness"; cf. Eph. 4:17; 2 Peter 2:18) describes the change and "decay" (cf. Rom. 8:21) that prevails in all created things. This was not a voluntary subjection because the created world as such had no choice. Instead it was a decree of God, the sovereign Creator, **who subjected it.** (This probably refers to God, not, as some have suggested, to Adam.) And yet it was **in hope,** that is, in anticipation of a coming day when the "frustration" would be removed (cf. vv. 24-25). God judged the totality of His Creation along with people for their sin (Gen. 3:14, 17-19).

When God's program of salvation for people is completed and **the children of God** together experience their **glorious freedom** from sin, Satan, and physical decay, then the **Creation itself will be liberated from its bondage to decay.** God had cursed the physical Creation as a part of His judgment on people for sin because of their position and authority over the Creation as God's representatives (Gen. 1:26-30; 2:8, 15). Similarly, since God's program of salvation for people is one of a new Creation (2 Cor. 5:17; Gal. 6:15), the physical world also will be re-created (Rev. 21:5). This will take place in two stages. First will be the renovation of the present cosmos in conjunction with the return to earth of the Lord Jesus and the establishment of the messianic kingdom on earth (Isa. 11:5-9; 35:1-2, 5-7; 65:20, 25; Amos 9:13). The second stage will be creation of "a new heaven and a new earth" (Rev. 21:1; cf. 2 Peter 3:7-13).

8:22-23. In one sense verse 22 is an appropriate conclusion to the preceding paragraph, summing up the present cursed state of the physical creation. Paul said, **We know** (*oidamen,* continuing state of knowledge that grows out of perception) that the whole Creation has been groaning as in the pains of childbirth (lit., "keeps on groaning together and keeps on travailing together") **right up to the present time.** The emphasis on "together" in these verbs does not include believers in Christ, who are specifically mentioned in verse 23, but involves the various parts of the natural Creation. At the same time verse 22 introduces this new paragraph, which sets forth the hope of future deliverance from suffering under the curse of sin.

Paul had begun this section by referring to the believers' "present sufferings" (v. 18), a subject to which he returned in verse 23. Believers are described as the ones having **the first-fruits of the Spirit.** This is an appositional use of the genitive and means that the Holy Spirit *is* "the firstfruits" (*aparchēn*) of God's work of salvation and re-creation in believers. Elsewhere the Holy Spirit is called "a deposit (down payment or earnest) guaranteeing our inheritance" (Eph. 1:14; cf. 2 Cor. 1:22), a similar idea. A farmer's "firstfruits" were the initial harvesting of his first-ripened crops. This first installment was a foretaste and promise that more harvest was to come. Similarly God the Holy Spirit, indwelling believers, is a foretaste that they will enjoy many more blessings, including living in God's presence forever.

Because of "present sufferings" (Rom. 8:18) believers, like the Creation, **groan inwardly** (cf. v. 22; 2 Cor. 5:2) as they **wait eagerly** (from *apekdechomai,* the same word used of the Creation in Rom. 8:19 and of the manifestation of hope in v. 25) **for** their **adoption as sons,** which is identified as **the redemption of** their **bodies.** The word "adoption" (*huiothesian,* "placing as a son"; trans. "sonship" in v. 15) describes a believer's legal relationship to God as a result of God's grace received by faith. (Regeneration, however, describes a believer's relationship to God as a result of the new birth.) Israel had received adoption by God (9:4), a reality undoubtedly growing out of her covenantal ties with God (Deut. 7:6-9). In one sense each believer has already received the adoption because he has "received the Spirit of sonship" (lit., "adoption," Rom. 8:15) and is a son of God (Gal. 4:6-7). At the same time, as Romans 8:23 states, believers still anticipate their adoption in its completeness, which is said to be "the redemption" (apolytrōsin; etymologically the Gr. word describes a release or deliverance or manumission achieved by a ransom payment [lytron]; cf. comments on 3:24) of their bodies. This is called the revelation of the sons of God (8:19) and "the glorious freedom of the children of God" (v. 21). It will occur at the Rapture of the church when believers will be raised and transformed with glorious bodies (1 Cor. 15:42-54; 2 Cor. 5:1-5; Phil. 3:20-21; 1 Thes. 4:13-18). Paul called that day "the day of redemption" (Eph. 4:30).

8:24-25. God has promised that a believer's body will finally be delivered from sin and its effects by the work of His Son. Those who respond by faith to that promise have **hope,** a confident expectation of that bodily redemption (cf. Gal. 5:5). This is the final step of salvation and it was in that anticipation that **we were saved.** The redemption of the body (Rom. 8:23) obviously has not yet occurred **(Who hopes for what he already has?),** but it is hoped for and eagerly anticipated **(wait** is from apekdechomai; cf. vv. 19, 23) with steadfast endurance **(patiently** is lit., "through endurance") in present sufferings (v. 18).

8:26-27. These verses point out that believers are not left to their own resources in their sufferings (v. 18) and groaning (v. 23). **The Spirit helps** (pres. tense, "keeps on helping") **us in** (the Gr. here does not have the words rendered "us in") **our weakness.** It is not that the Spirit helps in those occasional times when Christians are weak; their state is one of weakness and the Spirit continually helps them. The Greek word for weakness (astheneia) may include physical, emotional, and spiritual disability (cf. comments on James 5:14) evidenced by inward "groaning" (Rom. 8:23). "Helps" translates synantilambanetai, a rich word that pictures someone helping another carry a heavy load. (It is used elsewhere in the NT only in Luke 10:40.)

One evidence of their weakness is the fact that believers **do not know what they ought to pray** (lit., "what we should pray as it is necessary"). In their weakness both the content and the manner of proper prayer eludes them, **but the Spirit Himself** comes to their rescue and **intercedes** (pres. tense, "keeps on interceding") **for us with groans that words cannot express.** Natural Creation groans (Rom. 8:22) and believers groan (v. 23), and so does the Holy Spirit. This has nothing to do with praying in tongues, as some suggest. The groaning is done by the Holy Spirit, not believers, and is not stated in words. The help the Spirit gives (v. 26) is His interceding. "Intercedes" translates hyperentynchanei, which occurs only here in the New Testament; it means "approaches or appeals to someone." The One **who searches our hearts** is God (1 Sam. 16:7; Heb. 4:13), and He **knows** (oiden, "knows perceptively or intuitively") **the mind of the Spirit, because the Spirit intercedes** (entynchanei; cf. Rom. 8:26) **for the saints in accordance with God's will.** Even though the Spirit's words are not expressed, the Father knows what the Spirit is thinking. This is an interesting statement about the Father's omniscience and the intimacy within the Trinity. The Lord Jesus continually intercedes for believers in God's presence (v. 34; Heb. 7:25) and the Holy Spirit also intercedes on their behalf! Though believers are ignorant of what to pray for and how to voice those requests, the Spirit voices their requests for them.

F. Certainty of sanctification (8:28-39)

This section on the doctrine of a believer's sanctification (vv. 28-39) logically follows the discussion of its goal or end (vv. 18-27). To discuss the goal of sanctification—a believer's hope, which he awaits eagerly and steadfastly—is pointless unless realizing that goal is certain. God provided that certainty and confirms the believer's hope, since sanctification from its beginning in regeneration to its completion in glorification is ultimately God's work, which believers appropriate by faith (cf. Phil. 1:6).

8:28. Believers, Paul began, know of sanctification's certainty, and that knowledge is gained by spiritual perception. Christians **know** intuitively (oidamen)—though they may not always fully understand and sense it experientially—**that in**

all things God works for the good of those who love Him (lit., "to the ones who love God He works all things together unto good"). The things themselves may not be good, but God harmonizes them together for believers' ultimate good, because His goal is to bring them to perfection in His presence (cf. Eph. 1:4; 5:27; Col. 1:22; Jude 24). Even adversities and afflictions contribute to that end. The active voice present tense of the verb *synergei* ("He works together") emphasizes that this is a continuing activity of God. And His working is on behalf of "those who love Him," who are further identified as the ones **who have been called according to His purpose.** It is significant that a believer's love for God *follows* God's calling of him and is undoubtedly the product of the indwelling Holy Spirit (cf. Rom. 5:5; 1 John 4:19). The word for "purpose" is *prothesin*, God's plan (Paul used the same word in Rom. 9:11; Eph. 1:11; 3:11). "Called" means more than being invited to receive Christ; it means to be summoned to and given salvation (cf. Rom. 1:6; 8:30).

8:29-30. These verses give Paul's explanation of what it means to be one who has "been called according to His purpose" and why God keeps on working all their experiences together to their benefit (v. 28). Believers are those God **foreknew.** This does not mean simply that God foreknows *what* believers will do, but that God foreknows *them*. Nor does divine foreknowledge merely mean an awareness of or acquaintance with an individual. Instead it means a meaningful relationship with a person based on God's choice (cf. Jer. 1:4-5; Amos 3:2) in eternity before Creation. "He chose us in Him before the Creation of the world" (Eph. 1:4).

This eternal choice and foreknowledge involves more than establishing a relationship between God and believers. It also involves the goal or end of that relationship: **Those God foreknew He also predestined to be conformed to the likeness of His Son** (cf. 1 John 3:2). The entire group that is brought into relationship with God in His eternal plan by divine foreknowledge and choice is **predestined** (*proōrisen*, "predetermined"; cf. Eph. 1:5, 11). God determined beforehand the believers' destiny, namely,

conformity to the image of Jesus Christ. By all saints being made like Christ (ultimate and complete sanctification), Christ will be exalted as **the Firstborn among many brothers.** The resurrected and glorified Lord Jesus Christ will become the Head of a new race of humanity purified from all contact with sin and prepared to live eternally in His presence (cf. 1 Cor. 15:42-49). As the "Firstborn" He is in the highest position among others (cf. Col. 1:18).

Between the start and finish of God's plan are three steps: being **called** (cf. Rom. 1:6; 8:28), being **justified** (cf. 3:24, 28; 4:2; 5:1, 9), and being **glorified** (cf. 8:17; Col. 1:27; 3:4), and in the process not a single person is lost. God completes His plan without slippage. "Glorified" is in the past tense because this final step is so certain that in God's eyes it is as good as done. To be glorified is another way of saying that God's children will be "conformed" to His Son; and that is God's ultimate "purpose." No longer will they "fall short of the glory of God" (Rom. 3:23).

8:31-32. It is astounding to realize that God's plan of salvation for people is a program that reaches from eternity past to eternity future which God will carry out perfectly. Recognizing this, Paul asked and answered (in vv. 31-39) seven questions to drive home the truth that a believer's eternal salvation is completely secure in God's hands. The first question is general, **What, then, shall we say in response to this?** (cf. 4:1; 6:1; 9:14, 30) The obvious response to 8:28-30 would be to say "Hallelujah," or to stand in open-mouthed amazement.

This leads to a series of six more specific questions. The first is, **If God is for us, who can be against us?** Obviously, Satan and his demonic hosts are against believers (cf. Eph. 6:11-13; 1 Peter 5:8), but they cannot ultimately prevail and triumph over believers. God is the self-existent One and the sovereign Creator and, since He is for believers, no one can oppose believers successfully. He is for believers to the extent that **He . . . did not spare His own Son, but gave Him up for us all.** The word "spare" (*epheisato*, from *pheidomai*) is the same word used in the Septuagint in Genesis 22:12 where the NIV translates it "withheld." God said to Abraham, "You have not withheld your son." Then God directed Abraham to spare Isaac and to offer a ram as a substitute (Gen. 22:2-14), whereas God offered His own Son as the Sacrifice for sin (John 1:29). In view of this supreme act of God's grace, **How will He not also, along with Him, graciously give us all things?** Since God gave the greatest Sacrifice of all, His own Son, He will certainly not hesitate to give believers all other things pertaining to and leading to their ultimate sanctification (cf. 2 Peter 1:3).

8:33-34. The next two questions Paul raised and answered are forensic or legal in nature. **Who will bring any charge** (*enkalesei*, "make a formal accusation in court; press charges"; cf. Acts 19:40; 23:29; 26:2) **against those whom God has chosen?** Satan is identified as "the accuser" of God's people (Rev. 12:10; cf. Zech. 3:1). His accusations are valid, because they are based on the believer's sinfulness and defilement. But Satan's accusations will be thrown out of court, because **it is God who justifies.** The Judge Himself declares the accused person righteous on the basis of his faith in Jesus Christ (Rom. 3:24; 5:1). As a result all accusations are dismissed and no one can bring an accusation that will stand.

The related question is, **Who is He that condemns?** The Greek participle *ho katakrinōn* can have a future sense, "will condemn," which seems preferable here. (Cf. *katakrima*, "condemnation, punishment" in 8:1.) Jesus Christ is God's appointed Judge (John 5:22, 27; Acts 17:31), so Paul answered this question by stating, **Christ Jesus.** But Jesus is the very One whom the believer has trusted for salvation. Furthermore, He is the One **who died**—more than that (lit., "but more") **who was raised to life**—who **is at the right hand of God** (cf. Luke 22:69; Acts 2:33; 5:31; Eph. 1:20; Col. 3:1; Heb. 1:3, 13; 8:1; 10:12; 12:2; 1 Peter 3:22) **and is also interceding for us.** The Lord Jesus Christ is indeed the Judge, but He is also the One with whom each believer is identified by faith. As a result he is a believer's Sacrifice for sin (cf. Rom. 5:8; 8:32), his new life (a believer shares in Christ's resurrection life; 6:4, 8, 11; Eph. 2:5-6; Col. 2:13), his Intercessor (cf. Heb. 7:25; also the Holy Spirit intercedes, Rom.

8:26-27) and his Defense (1 John 2:1). Certainly the Judge will not condemn His own who are in Him by faith! (cf. Rom. 8:1)

8:35-37. Paul's final questions are in verse 35: **Who shall separate us from the love of Christ?** The context (vv. 37, 39) shows that "the love of Christ" is His love for believers (not their love for Him; cf. 5:5). The apostle suggested seven things a believer might experience (Paul experienced all of them; 2 Cor. 11:23-28) that some might think could come between a believer and Christ's love—**trouble** (*thlipsis*, "pressure or distress"; mentioned frequently by Paul in 2 Cor.) **or hardship** (*stenochōria*, lit., "narrowness," i.e., being pressed in, hemmed in, crowded) **or persecution or famine or nakedness or danger or sword.** These things—stated in increasing intensity—do not separate Christians from Christ; instead they are part of the "all things" (Rom. 8:28) God uses to bring them to conformity to His Son. Then Paul quoted Psalm 44:22 to remind his readers that in this life the people of God must face much affliction (cf. John 16:33) including even martyrdom for some. In the early days of the church one or more Christians were martyred every day, or faced the possibility of it. Their persecutors valued Christians' lives as nothing more than animals to be butchered.

In all these adversities (cf. "all things" in Rom. 8:28 and "all things" in v. 32 with **all these things** in v. 37), rather than being separated from Christ's love, believers are **more than conquerors** (pres. tense, *hypernikōmen*, "keep on being conquerors to a greater degree" or "keep on winning a glorious victory") **through Him who loved us.** Jesus Christ and His love for believers enable them to triumph (cf. 2 Cor. 2:14).

8:38-39. Paul then ended his discussion on believers' safety in Jesus Christ and the certainty of their sanctification with a positive declaration—**For I am convinced** (perf. tense, "I stand convinced"; cf. 15:14) **that** nothing can **separate** believers **from the love of God** (God's love for them, not their love for God; cf. v. 35). Paul's list of 10 items begins with death, where the list of 7 items in verse 35 ended. These elements in God's universe include the extremes of existence: (1) **death** and (2) **life** (in either

141

death [2 Cor. 5:8-9] or life, believers are in God's presence); the extremes of created spiritual armies: (3) **angels** and (4) **demons** (angels would not and demons could not undo God's relationship with His redeemed ones); the extremes in time: (5) **the present** and (6) **the future** (nothing known now, e.g., the hardships listed in Rom. 8:35, or in the unknown time to come); spiritual enemies: (7) **powers** (perhaps Satan and his demons; cf. Eph. 6:12; or possibly human governments); the extremes in space: (8) **height** and (9) **depth** (nothing overhead or underneath can suddenly come swooping down or up to sever believers from God's love); and (10) everything in the entire created realm. Absolutely nothing in His **Creation** can thwart His purpose for believers **in Christ**. What a climactic way to affirm the certainty of believers' salvation!

V. God's Righteousness Revealed in Sovereign Choice (chaps. 9–11)

Since God is the self-existent Being who is the Creator of everything that exists outside Himself, He is sovereign and can therefore use and dispose of His Creation as He wishes. This sovereignty reveals not only His personal righteousness but also His provided righteousness.

A. God's sovereign choice enunciated (9:1-29)

Paul here discussed God's sovereign choice because of a practical problem. The Jews gloried in the fact that as Israelites they were God's Chosen People (Deut. 7:6; cf. Rom. 2:17-20a; 3:1-2). But now in God's program of salvation in the church, Jewish involvement was decreasing while Gentile participation was becoming dominant. Had God, then, abandoned the Jewish people? This is ultimately explained by God's sovereign choice, a principle which has always been in operation even within the Chosen People of Israel and between Israel and other nations. Now this principle operates in God's purposes for Israel and the church and in His dealings with Jews and Gentiles within the church.

1. ISRAEL'S PRIVILEGES (9:1-5)

9:1-5. By repetition in positive and negative terms (internally attested by the witness of his own **conscience** [cf. comments on 2:15] in the presence of **the Holy Spirit**) Paul affirmed his deep **anguish of heart** over the rejection of the gospel by the vast majority of Jews. His desire for their salvation was so strong that he was at the point of wishing (imperf. tense, **I could wish**) that he **were cursed and cut off from Christ for** his kinsmen, the Israelites.

Paul then listed seven spiritual privileges which belonged to the people of Israel as God's chosen nation: **the adoption as sons** (cf. Ex. 4:22), **the divine glory** (cf. Ex. 16:10; 24:17; 40:34; 1 Kings 8:11), **the covenants** (Gen. 15:18; 2 Sam. 7:12-16; Jer. 31:31-34), **the receiving of the Law** (Deut. 5:1-22), **the temple worship** (latreia, "sacred service," which may also include service in the tabernacle), **and the promises** (esp. of the coming Messiah). Also the Israelites were in the line of promise from its beginning in **the patriarchs** (cf. Matt. 1:1-16; Rom. 1:3) to its fulfillment in the Messiah, **who is God over all, forever praised! Amen.** This is a clear affirmation of the deity of Messiah. Some take these words as a separate sentence (see NIV marg.), but the NIV text seems preferable.

2. THE CHOICE ILLUSTRATED (9:6-18)

a. Isaac over Ishmael (9:6-9)

9:6-9. The failure of the Jews to respond to the gospel of Christ did not mean **God's Word had failed**. Instead this rejection was simply the current example of the principle of God's sovereign choice established in the Old Testament. Paul reminded his readers of a truth he had presented earlier: **For not all who are descended from Israel are Israel,** that is, spiritual Israel (cf. 2:28-29).

Then Paul gave three Old Testament illustrations of God's sovereignty (Isaac and Ishmael, 9:7b-9; Jacob and Esau, vv. 10-13; and Pharaoh, vv. 14-18). The first two show that God made a sovereign choice among the physical descendants of Abraham in establishing the spiritual line of promise. Ishmael, born to Hagar (Gen. 16)—and the six sons of Keturah as well (Gen. 25:1-4)—were Abraham's **descendants** (sperma), but they were not counted as **Abraham's children** (tekna, "born ones") in the line of promise. Instead, as God told Abraham (Gen. 21:12), **It is** through Isaac that your offspring will be reckoned (lit., "in Isaac seed [*sperma*] will be called to you"). Paul repeated the principle for emphasis in different words: It is not the natural children (lit., "the born ones of the flesh") who are God's children (*tekna*, "born ones of God"), but it is the children (*tekna*) of the promise who are regarded as Abraham's offspring (*sperma*). To be a physical descendant of Abraham is not enough; one must be chosen by God (cf. "chosen" in Rom. 8:33) and must believe in Him (4:3, 22-24). God's assurance that the promise would come through Isaac, not Ishmael, was given to Abraham: At the appointed time I will return, and Sarah will have a son (a somewhat free quotation of Gen. 18:10 from the LXX).

b. Jacob over Esau (9:10-13)

9:10-13. The second Old Testament illustration of God's sovereign choice is drawn from the second generation of Jewish ancestry. Apparently God purposed to establish this principle clearly at the beginning of His relationship with His Chosen People. This illustration emphasizes God's sovereignty even more than the first since it involves God's choice of one twin over another. (In the case of Abraham's sons, God chose the child of one woman over the child of another woman.) In addition, in the case of Rebecca's children God's choice was indicated before the twins were born or had done anything good or bad. This demonstrated that God's sovereign choice was not by works, even foreseen works, but by Him who calls (cf. "called" in 1:6; 8:28, 30). God's plan (8:28; 9:11), and not man's works (4:2-6), is the basis of His election. Rebecca was informed, The older will serve the younger (cf. Gen. 25:23), a divine choice confirmed by God's declaration, Jacob I loved, but Esau I hated (cf. Mal. 1:2-3). Esau, the older, did not actually serve Jacob, his younger twin; but Esau's descendants, the Edomites, did (cf. 1 Sam. 14:47; 2 Sam. 8:14; 1 Kings 11:15-16; 22:47; 2 Kings 14:7). God's "love" for Jacob was revealed in His choice of Jacob and God's "hatred" for Esau was seen in His rejecting Esau for the line of promise. Hatred in this sense is not absolute but relative to a higher choice (cf. Matt. 6:24; Luke 14:26; John 12:25).

c. Pharaoh (9:14-18)

9:14-18. With the words, What then shall we say? (cf. 4:1; 6:1; 8:31) Paul introduced the question undoubtedly in his readers' minds, Is God unjust in choosing Isaac over Ishmael, and Jacob over Esau? The Greek negative particle (*mē*) with a question implies a negative response. Paul responded in his usual emphatic way, Not at all! (*mē genoito*; cf. comments on 3:4) The issue in such matters is not justice but sovereign decision, as God's word to Moses (Ex. 33:19) quoted by Paul indicates. As the sovereign God, He has the right to show mercy to whomever He chooses. In fact, He is not under obligation to extend mercy to *anyone*. Therefore experiencing His mercy does not . . . depend on man's desire (lit., "the one willing") or effort (lit., "the one running"). No one deserves or can earn His mercy.

The Apostle Paul then presented his third illustration, the Egyptian Pharaoh of the Exodus. To him God said through Moses, I raised you up (i.e., brought you onto the scene of history) to display My power in you and that My name might be proclaimed in all the earth (cf. Ex. 9:16). God's power (cf. Rom. 9:22) was demonstrated as He freed the Israelites from under Pharaoh's hand. And other nations heard about it and were awed (Ex. 15:14-16; Josh. 2:10-11; 9:9; 1 Sam. 4:8). It is significant that Paul introduced this quotation with the words, For the Scripture says, for he equated the words of God with the words of Scripture. Paul concluded, God has mercy on whom He wants to have mercy (cf. Rom. 9:15) and He hardens whom He wants to harden ("make stubborn"; cf. Ex. 4:21; 7:3; 9:12; 10:27; 14:4, 8; cf. 14:17). Because of God's choice, Pharaoh then hardened his own heart (Ex. 7:13-14, 22; 8:15, 19, 32; 9:7, 34-35). All this shows that God chooses and works sovereignly, but not arbitrarily. Yet Pharaoh was responsible for his actions.

3. THE CHOICE EXPLAINED (9:19-29)

9:19-21. Once again Paul anticipated the questioning response of his readers: Then why does God still blame us? (The Gr. word trans. "then" probably goes with the preceding statement rather than this question, though this also makes good sense.) **For who resists** (perf. tense, "has taken and continues to take a stand against") **His will?** (*boulēmati*, "deliberate purpose") These questions are still raised by those who reject the biblical doctrine of God's sovereignty. If God makes the choices, how can He hold man responsible? Who can go against what He does?

In response Paul reaffirmed the reality of God's sovereignty and the effrontery of such questions. **But who are you, O man, to talk back to God?** (cf. Isa. 45:9) Man, the created one, has no right to question God, the Creator. Paul then quoted a clause from Isaiah 29:16: **Shall what is formed say to Him who formed it, Why did You make me like this?** Drawing an analogy between the sovereign Creator and a potter, Paul asked, **Does not the potter have the right to make out of the same lump of clay some pottery for noble purposes** (lit., "one vessel [pot or vase] unto honor") **and some for common use?** (lit., "unto dishonor") Obviously a potter from the same pile takes some clay to form a finely shaped and decorated vase and takes other clay to make a cooking pot (cf. Jer. 18:4-6). And the clay has no right to complain! The sovereign Creator has the same authority over His creatures, especially in light of man's origin from dust (Gen. 2:7).

9:22-26. Having stated that God is like a potter, Paul now applied this illustration to God's sovereign purpose for different people. He stated the two alternatives as conditional clauses (**What if. . . ?**) and left unstated the obvious common conclusion: Does not God have that right? The one alternative is that **God . . . bore with great patience** (cf. 2 Peter 3:9) **the objects** (lit., "vessels"; cf. Rom. **9**:21) **of His wrath—prepared for destruction** (*apōleian*, "ruin"). The perfect participle "prepared" describes past action with a continuing result or state. "Prepared" may be reflexive ("prepared themselves"), but it seems preferable to take it as passive ("were prepared"). The thought is that they have been and are in a state of readiness or ripeness to receive God's wrath. The objects of God's wrath are the unsaved (1:18), who will suffer eternal judgment (John 3:36). God has patiently endured their antagonism to Him (cf. Acts 14:16; Rom. 3:25), but their judgment is coming. Those who oppose

Him and refuse to turn to Him (Matt. 23:37) are then "prepared" by Him for condemnation. They are "storing up [God's] wrath" against themselves (Rom. 2:5). In hell they will experience **His wrath,** and **His power** will be made known (cf. 9:17). God does not delight in wrath, and He did not choose some people to go to hell. **Choosing** (v. 22) should be rendered "willing." Some are prepared by God for eternal judgment not because He delights to do so, but because of their sin. In view of their sin, which makes them "ripe" for destruction, God is willing to exhibit His wrath, and He will do so at the proper time.

The other alternative relates to God's dealings with **the objects** (lit., "vessels"; cf. v. 21) **of His mercy.** God chose them as such in order **to make the riches of His glory known** and **He prepared them in advance for glory** (cf. 8:29-31; Col. 1:27; 3:4). The verb "He prepared in advance" (Rom. 9:23) is *proētoimasen,* "He made ready beforehand," which God does by bestowing salvation. (The word "prepared" in v. 22 is *katērtismena,* "are made or prepared or ripened.")

Up to this point Paul had been speaking conditionally and objectively, but in verse 24 he was more direct—**even us**—because he and his readers were some of the vessels of mercy sovereignly chosen by God. God **not only** chose them **but He also called** them, including **Jews** and **Gentiles.** The point is that God's sovereign choice was manifested not only in the Jews' ancestry (in Isaac and Jacob, vv. 6-13), but also in Paul's generation and today. To back up his conclusion and particularly the part about Gentiles, Paul quoted two verses from **Hosea** (2:23; 1:10). God directed Hosea to give his children symbolic names—one son Lo-Ammi (**not my people**) and the daughter Lo-Ruhamah (**not . . . loved**). These represented God's abandonment of the Northern Kingdom of Israel to the Assyrian Captivity and Exile (Hosea 1:2-9).

God was not permanently casting away the people of Israel, however. In the verses quoted by Paul God promised to restore them as His beloved and as His **people.** By ethnic heritage the Gentiles were **not** God's **people,** so Paul was led by the Spirit of God to apply these verses to Gentiles—and Jews also—who were sovereignly chosen by God and **called** to be His people in Christ. The quotation of Hosea 2:23 is rather free with the order of the clauses reversed to fit the application to Gentiles. Paul was applying these verses from Hosea to the Gentiles, not reinterpreting them. He was not saying that Israel of the Old Testament is part of the church.

9:27-29. Here Paul quoted Old Testament verses to support the fact that God in His sovereign choice and calling always includes a Jewish segment, though it is a minority. The passages quoted (Isa. 10:22-23 and 1:9, both from the LXX) make it clear that in God's judgment on rebellious Israel He by sovereign choice preserves and saves a **remnant.** Those promises were fulfilled in the Captivity and Exile of both Israel and Judah and in the destruction of Jerusalem in A.D. 70 and will also be fulfilled in the national end-time deliverance of Israel (Rom. 11:26-27). Even today the same principle is true. Jews who become members of the church, the body of Christ, are what Paul later called "a remnant chosen by grace" (11:5), which included himself (11:1).

B. God's sovereign choice applied (9:30–10:21)

1. ISRAEL'S STUMBLING (9:30–10:4)

9:30-33. Once again Paul asked his familiar rhetorical question, **What then shall we say?** (cf. 4:1; 6:1; 8:31; 9:14) preparatory to his summation of this situation. His identification of **the Gentiles** (lit., "the nations") as the ones who **have obtained . . . a righteousness that is by** (*ek*, "out from") **faith** is interesting. As Paul stated later, the church included Jewish as well as Gentile believers (11:1-5), but by the time of Paul's third missionary journey the increasing rejection of the gospel by the Jews and the predominance of Gentiles in the church led the apostle to speak of "the Gentiles" as antithetical to **Israel.** The latter **pursued** ("kept on pursuing") **a Law of righteousness, but has not attained it.** "A Law of righteousness" refers to the Mosaic Law (cf. 7:7, 12, 14). To seek to attain righteousness by observing the Law requires that it be kept perfectly (cf. James 2:10). Why did Israel not attain it? **Because they pursued it not by** (*ek*, "out from") **faith but as if it were by** (*ek*, "out from") **works.** The Israelites did not

admit their inability to keep the Law perfectly and turn by faith to God for forgiveness. Instead a few of them kept trying to keep the Law by their own efforts. Consequently **they stumbled** (cf. Rom. 11:11) **over the "stumbling Stone."** The Lord Jesus Christ, "the stumbling Stone" (cf. 1 Peter 2:4-8), did not conform to the Jews' expectations, so they rejected Him instead of responding to Him by faith. To show that God anticipated this, Paul quoted from Isaiah 8:14 and 28:16 (cf. Rom. 10:11), combining the two statements to indicate the two contrasting reactions by **men** to the **Stone** that God placed **in Zion** (cf. "Zion" in 11:26).

10:1-4. Having stated the fact of Israel's stumbling in the preceding verses, Paul now explained the reason for that stumbling. But first, in words reminiscent of the opening verses of chapter 9, the apostle expressed his deep personal spiritual burden for the salvation of the people of Israel. Perhaps with his own experience in mind (cf. Acts 26:11; Gal. 1:13-14; Phil. 3:4-6) Paul affirmed, **For I can testify** (pres. tense, "I testify, bear witness") **about them that they are zealous for God.** Israel was called "the God-intoxicated people." Paul had to acknowledge, however, that **their zeal is not based on** (lit., "according to") **knowledge** (*epignōsin*, "intensive, full knowledge"). The Jews obviously had knowledge of God but not full knowledge. Otherwise they would not have stumbled over Christ by seeking to gain righteousness on the basis of works.

Paul continued his explanation of Israel's failure and their misguided zeal. **Since they did not know** (the participle *agnoountes* means "being ignorant," here in the sense of not understanding) **the righteousness that comes from God.** The NIV implies that the people of Israel did not understand the God-provided righteousness expounded in this letter to the Christians in Rome (cf. Rom. 1:17). That may be true, even though they should have known from their own Scriptures (cf. Gen. 15:6; Ps. 32:1-2). But here preferably the righteousness in view is the righteousness God requires for people to be accepted by Him, which is God's own infinite righteousness. The Jews did not really understand God's own infinite righteousness, which is why they were continuing to seek **to establish their own** (cf. Isa. 64:6). Little wonder then that **they did not submit to** ("place themselves under") **God's righteousness,** that is, the righteousness God provides through Christ by faith. The Greek in Romans 10:4 includes the coordinating particle *gar,* "for" (not trans. in the NIV). It introduces a statement that is crucial to Paul's explanation of Israel's stumbling— **Christ is the end of the Law so that there may be righteousness for everyone who believes.** The word translated "end" *(telos)* stands in the emphatic first position in the Greek sentence. It means that Christ is the designed end (termination) or Purpose-Goal of the Law (cf. Gal. 3:24), the Object to which the Law pointed.

The Law did not and could not of itself provide righteousness before God for individuals (cf. Rom. 3:20; 7:7). But Christ fulfilled the Law (Matt. 5:17-18) by keeping it perfectly during His sinless life (cf. John 8:46) and then gave His life in payment for the penalty of sin and the broken Law (cf. Eph. 2:15; Col. 2:13-14). The Law then pointed to Him as the Source of the God-provided righteousness it could not supply (Gal. 3:24). A godly Jew who trusted Yahweh and followed the Levitical system, including the sin offering and the trespass offering, would most likely be inclined to respond to Christ by faith and would receive God's righteousness (i.e., be justified; Acts 13:39; Rom. 3:24; 4:3, 5). He then could meet the requirements of the Law by the indwelling Holy Spirit (8:4). Conversely, a Jew who sought by works to establish his own righteousness would not recognize Christ as "the end of the Law" and would stumble over Him.

2. GOD'S GRACIOUS OFFER (10:5-15)

10:5-8. In presenting God's gracious offer of salvation in Christ and the provision of righteousness by faith, Paul first stated the contrast of the by-works approach to achieving righteousness. He wrote, **Moses describes** (lit., "writes") **the righteousness that is by the Law.** Then Paul quoted Leviticus 18:5, **The man who does these things will live by them.** If a Jew were to receive righteousness by keeping the demands of the Law, that would be human achievement; it would not be from God. However, a Jew would need to keep the entire Law perfectly all his life—an impossible task (James 2:10). But then Paul also quoted Moses in support of his righteousness-by-faith position centered in Christ as "the end of the Law" and the means by which righteousness is available for everyone who believes. It does not seem appropriate that Paul was merely borrowing Moses' words and applying them to something foreign in Moses' thought. This suggests, then, that **righteousness . . . by faith** is not a new concept, but had been proclaimed to Israel by Moses.

The material Paul quoted in Romans 10:6-8 is taken somewhat freely from Deuteronomy 30:12-14 with clauses quoted here and there. The material in Deuteronomy was part of Moses' charge to the generation of Israel about to enter the land of Canaan. This exhortation was the conclusion of Moses' prophetic description of God's dealing with Israel. Blessing was promised for faith and obedience, and chastisement would result from rejection and disobedience. If Israel forsook God, Moses said, she would face worldwide dispersion and affliction. When the people then finally do turn to God in faith, He will restore them to blessing, prosperity, and prominence among the nations (Deut. 30:1-10). The point of Moses' exhortation (Deut. 30:11) is that the generation to whom he was speaking had the message (it was very **near you** and **in your mouth,** Deut. 30:14) and could respond by faith (**in your heart,** Deut. 30:14) and walk with God in obedience. Since the Israelites in Moses' day had the message, they did not need to ask that it be brought down from heaven or that someone "cross the sea to get it" (Deut. 30:13). Instead, **the word** (Moses' instructions) was "near" them (Deut. 30:14).

In effect, Paul indicated that the same truth applied to his generation, with the added fact that Christ had come in the flesh (John 1:14) and had been resurrected. Therefore there was no need for anyone to ask **to bring Christ down** (in His Incarnation) or **to bring Christ up from the dead;** He had already come and had been resurrected. The message of righteousness by faith in Paul's day was "near" his readers (available to them) and this was "the word" (*rhēma,* "saying") **of faith** he was **proclaiming** (*rhēma,* "the spoken word" is also used in Eph. 5:26;

6:17; 1 Peter 1:25). Thus the gospel, "the word of faith," is available and accessible.

10:9-13. In these verses Paul stated the content of that message concerning faith. Confessing **with the mouth that Jesus is Lord** is mentioned first to conform to the order of the quotation from Deuteronomy 30:14 in Romans 10:8. The confession is an acknowledgement that God has been incarnated in Jesus (cf. v. 6), that Jesus Christ is God. Also essential is **heart**-faith **that God raised Him from the dead** (cf. v. 7). The result is salvation. The true order is given in verse 10: **For it is with your heart that you believe and are justified** (lit., "it is believed unto righteousness"), **and it is with your mouth that you confess and are saved** (lit., "it is confessed unto salvation"). Yet these are not two separate steps to salvation. They are chronologically together. Salvation comes through acknowledging to God that Christ is God and believing in Him.

Paul then (v. 11) supported his position by requoting part of Isaiah 28:16 (cf. Rom. 9:33), adding the Greek word translated **everyone.** God responds with the gift of provided righteousness to each individual who believes. Then Paul reminded his readers of God's impartiality, as he did when discussing human sinfulness (3:22). Just as all who sin will be judged, so all who believe will be saved and **richly** blessed. This conclusion also is supported by a quotation from Joel 2:32: **Everyone who calls on the name of the Lord will be saved.** To **call on** the Lord means to pray in faith for salvation. (On the significance of the "name," see comments on Acts 3:16.)

10:14-15. After proclaiming God's gracious offer in Christ, Paul confronted the natural questions that arise, each additional question building on the key verb from the preceding question. God's promise of salvation to "everyone who calls" on Him (v. 13) begins the process. **How, then, can they call on the One they have not believed in?** Previously, to call on the Lord was equated with trusting Him or believing in Him (cf. vv. 11 and 13), but here it follows the believing. When one believes in Christ, he "calls" on Him. Believing, in turn, is based on hearing, and hearing is based on **someone preaching . . . and how can they preach unless they are sent?** (Since the Gr. word

kēryssō, "preach," means "to be a herald, to announce," it is not limited to proclamation from a pulpit.) Carrying God's gracious offer involves human beings whom God has brought to Himself and then uses as His heralds. They share God's message of salvation because He will save everyone who calls on His name. Paul quoted from Isaiah 52:7 concerning the eagerness of the bearers of **good news.** Those who bear it have **beautiful . . . feet,** that is, their message is welcome. In Isaiah 52:7 the messenger announced to Judah that God had ended their Exile in Babylon (cf. Isa. 40:9-11). But Paul applied Isaiah 52:7 to the Jews of his day to whom the gospel was being given.

3. ISRAEL'S REJECTION (10:16-21)

10:16-18. Paul had made it clear that God's gracious offer of righteousness by faith was given to all, Jews and Gentiles alike (cf. v. 12). His focus in this chapter, however, has been on the people of Israel and their response to that offer (cf. v. 1). Therefore when he wrote, **But not all the Israelites** (the Gr. text simply says "all") **accepted the good news,** he obviously had in mind the Jews' failure to respond. ("Accepted" translates *hypēkousan,* a compound of the verb "to hear." It means "to hear with a positive response," and so "to obey, to submit to.") This is borne out by Paul's confirming quotation of Isaiah 53:1: **Lord, who has believed our message?** This failure of the Jews to respond to the good news was true in Jesus' days on earth (John 12:37-41) and in Paul's day as well. However, the indefinite "all" of the Greek text (Rom. 10:16) is appropriate, because the response to the gospel among the Gentiles was also far less than total. Paul explained, **Consequently, faith comes from hearing the message** (lit., "is out from hearing"; cf. v. 14) **and the message is heard through the word of Christ** (lit., "and the hearing is through the saying [*rhēmatos;* cf. v. 17] concerning Christ"). The Greek word *akoē* ("hearing") can mean the thing heard (the message; v. 16) or the act or sense of hearing (v. 17).

Someone, however, might insist that the Jews were not given adequate opportunity to hear the message. So, Paul said, **But I ask** ("say"), **Did they not hear?** He then quoted Psalm 19:4, concerning God's general revelation in the cosmic heavens (cf. Rom. 1:18-20). However, that psalm also discusses God's special revelation in the Old Testament (Ps. 19:7-11). Paul's obvious answer to his question is that Israel had ample opportunity by both general and special revelation to respond to God. Certainly she heard.

10:19-21. With these verses the argument takes a turn. The apostle anticipated another objection. Someone might argue, "Yes, Israel heard but she did not understand that God purposed to offer righteousness by faith to all mankind, including Gentiles." So Paul wrote, **Again I ask** (lit., "But I say"), **did Israel not understand?** (egnō, "know") His answer this time was from two Old Testament quotations, one as early as **Moses** (Deut. 32:21) **and** the second by **Isaiah** (Isa. 65:1). Both Old Testament leaders wrote about God's turning to the Gentiles, whom the Jews thought had **no understanding** (asynetō, "senseless"; cf. Rom. 1:21, 31). And yet **concerning Israel,** God has been gracious in spite of her disobedience (a quotation of Isa. 65:2). Israel's continuing rebellious and unbelieving disobedience was judged by God's turning to the Gentiles (Rom. 10:20; cf. Acts 8:1-8, 10). At the same time God has not withheld salvation from Jews. He has **held out His hands,** imploring them to return to Him.

C. God's sovereign choice fulfilled (chap. 11)

To this point in this major section of Romans (chaps. 9–11) God's personal righteousness and His provided righteousness for people has been displayed primarily in Israel's rejecting Christ and rebelling against God, and in God's choosing and turning to Gentiles in grace. These themes continue in this chapter, but God's sovereign choice also involves His restoring Israel and His being magnified thereby.

1. IN ELECTION OF GRACE (11:1-10)

11:1-6. Paul's transition from chapter 10 is seen in the repetition of his rhetorical clause "I ask" (10:18-19). **I ask then** is literally, "Therefore, I say." The apostle's question is, **Did God reject His people?** In Greek the question is asked to elicit a negative reply: "God did not reject His people, did He?" This is reinforced by Paul's characteristic negative ejaculation, **By no means!** (mē genoito; cf. comments on 3:4) Then Paul presented himself as his first proof. He had responded by faith to Jesus Christ and had received God's provided righteousness, and yet he was **an Israelite** (cf. Phil. 3:5) and of **the tribe of Benjamin.** Though small, Benjamin was a significant tribe (Saul, Israel's first king, was from Benjamin). If God could save Paul (Acts 9; 22; 26), He certainly could save other Jews (1 Tim. 1:15-16). Then he positively declared, **God did not reject His people** (quoted from 1 Sam. 12:22; Ps. 94:14), **whom He foreknew** (proegnō, "had a meaningful relationship with"; cf. Amos 3:2; and cf. comments on Rom. 8:29). God had chosen Israel as His covenant people from eternity past and entered into a relationship with them that will never be destroyed (cf. Jer. 31:37).

Paul's second proof that God has not rejected His people was taken from Israel's history during Elijah's ministry. The prophet was deeply depressed, having fled for his life from Jezebel. Paul said, **Elijah . . . appealed to** (entynchanei, "petitioned"; trans. "intercedes" in Rom. 8:27 and "is . . . interceding" in 8:34) **God against Israel.** Paul then quoted part of the prophet's complaint (1 Kings 19:10, 14), reversing the order of the details quoted and concluding with Elijah's lament, **I am the only one left, and they are trying to kill me.** Elijah considered himself the only believing person left in Israel. Paul asked, **And what was God's answer** (lit., "the divine response") **to him?** God was not limited to one fearful, depressed prophet; He had **reserved for** Himself a godly remnant in Israel that numbered **7,000** (1 Kings 19:18). The preservation of the faithful remnant was a work of God.

After the historical illustration Paul drew a conclusion for his day: **So too, at the present time there is a remnant chosen by grace** (lit., "a remnant according to the election of grace has come to be"). Paul was only one of many in his generation elected to faith from the people of Israel. In every generation of the church "a remnant chosen by grace" has been called from among the Jews. Paul added that this choice is totally **by**

God's **grace** (cf. Eph. 2:8-9) and he emphasized the antithesis between **grace** and **works** (cf. Rom. 4:4-5; 9:30-32).

11:7-10. Paul then discussed what "a remnant chosen by grace" out of **Israel** meant for the people as a whole. The situation was ironic. The Jews zealously sought to be accepted by God on the basis of works and the righteousness of the Law (cf. 10:2-3). However, they were not accepted by God; only **the elect** were, because of God's sovereign choice by grace. **The others were hardened** (cf. 11:25). What it means to be hardened is seen from Paul's explanatory and supporting quotations. The first is taken from both Deuteronomy 29:3-4 and Isaiah 29:10, and indicates that hardening involves spiritual drowsiness (**stupor** is the rendering of *katanyxeōs*, "a numbness resulting from a sting"), blindness, and deafness (cf. Isa. 6:9-10). The second quotation (in Rom. 11:9-10) is of Psalm 69:22-23, which predicts that the very things which should have been the source of nourishment and blessing to Israel (**table** means their blessings from the hand of God, which should have led them to Christ; cf. Gal. 3:24) became the occasion for their rejection of God (**a snare and a trap, a stumbling block;** cf. Rom. 9:32-33) and God's judgment (**retribution**) on them. Because they refused to receive God's truth (cf. Isa. 6:9-10; John 5:40) **their backs** will **be bent** under the weight of guilt and punishment **forever.**

2. IN GENTILES (11:11-24)

11:11-12. Paul asked still another question he anticipated from his readers. **Did they stumble** (cf. 9:32) **so as to fall beyond recovery?** Literally, the Greek says simply, "Did they stumble so that they fell?" But the tense of the verb "fell" and its contrast with the verb translated "stumble" imply the idea of falling beyond recovery. Once again the question in Greek was worded to elicit a negative answer, and for the 10th and last time in Romans, Paul responded, **Not at all!** (*mē genoito*; cf. 3:4, 6, 31; 6:2, 15; 7:7, 13; 9:14; 11:1) "They" refers to "the others" (v. 7), the majority of the people of Israel, excluding the "remnant chosen by grace" (v. 5).

Israel experienced not a permanent fall, but a stumbling. It served at least two divine purposes: (a) to offer **salvation . . . to the Gentiles,** and (b) to **make Israel envious** (lit., "to the provoking of them to jealousy"; cf. Deut. 32:21). Twice already in his ministry Paul had turned away from unbelieving Jews to the Gentiles (Acts 13:46; 18:6), and he would do so at least once more in Rome (Acts 28:25-28). In so doing he was fulfilling these purposes of God. But Paul was convinced that Israel's **transgression** (*paraptōma*, "false step," which seems to fit with "stumble"; cf. *paraptōma*, trans. "trespass" in Rom. 5:17-18, 20) was temporary. So he looked beyond its immediate results (**riches for the world and . . . riches for the Gentiles**) to the possibility of its removal (**how much greater riches will their fullness bring!**). "World" here means mankind, not the physical world (cf. "world" in 11:15). Certainly the world has been enriched spiritually because of so many Gentiles coming to Christ (cf. comments on "reconciliation" in v. 15). But even greater riches will be enjoyed by Gentiles after the conversion of Israel at the Lord's return (cf. v. 26). Israel's "fullness" suggests a large-scale conversion (cf. "full number [lit., 'fullness'] of the Gentiles," v. 25).

11:13-15. Paul then singled out a part of the Christian community at Rome, saying, **I am talking to you Gentiles.** Though writing, Paul used terms referring to oral communication, a fact with implications for the inspiration of the Scriptures. Paul then affirmed his special position as **the apostle to the Gentiles** (cf. Acts 9:15; Gal. 1:16; 2:7-8; Eph. 3:8), and declared, **I make much of** (lit., "I glorify" or "I magnify") **my ministry.** Part of Paul's purpose for magnifying his service to the Gentiles was to provoke to jealousy his fellow Jews (Rom. 11:11), resulting in the salvation **of some of them** (cf. 9:1-4; 10:1). Any such Jews won to Christ would be part of the "remnant chosen by grace." Then Paul reminded his Gentiles readers that Israel's **rejection** meant **the reconciliation of the world** in the purpose of God. Because Israel rejected Christ, the gospel was taken to these Gentiles. In Scripture reconciliation is a work of God in the death of Christ which does not *actually* restore an individual to fellowship with God but provides the basis for him to be restored to fellowship (cf. 2 Cor. 5:18-20). This statement serves to explain the meaning of the phrases "riches for the world" and "riches for the Gentiles" in Romans 11:12. (When a person comes to Christ by faith God's work of reconciliation is appropriated to him and he then has fellowship with God and the spiritual enmity is removed.)

Because Paul was convinced that Israel's stumbling is temporary, he asked, **What will their acceptance be but life from the dead?** (lit., "out from dead ones") This question explains the clause, "How much greater riches will their fullness bring" (v. 12). Israel's "acceptance" of Christ is related to "the first resurrection" (Rev. 20:4-6), the resurrection of life (John 5:29, KJV). The first resurrection includes dead and living saints at the Rapture (1 Thes. 4:13-18), martyred Great Tribulation saints raised at Christ's return (Rev. 20:4, 5b), and believing Old Testament saints (Dan. 12:1-2). The second resurrection will include all the wicked dead to be judged at the great white throne judgment (Rev. 20:5a, 12-13). The teaching that there will be one general resurrection of all humanity at one time fails to take these distinctions into account.

11:16. Paul was convinced that Israel's stumbling is temporary rather than permanent and that the nation will be restored as God's people. With two illustrations Paul showed why he believed this. His first illustration was taken from God's instructions to Israel to take "a cake from the first of [their] ground meal and present it as an offering" (Num. 15:20) after they entered the land of Canaan and reaped their first wheat harvest. This offering was to be repeated each year at their harvests. The cake made from the first ground meal of the wheat harvest was sanctified or made holy by being offered to God. As Paul explained, **If the part of the dough offered as firstfruits** (lit., "If the first-fruits") **is holy, then the whole batch is holy** (lit., "the lump is also"). Paul's second illustration was that of a tree: **If the root is holy, so are the branches.**

In both illustrations the principle is the same: what is considered first contributes its character to what is related to it. With a tree, the root obviously comes first and contributes the nature of that type of tree to the branches that come later. With the cake presented to the Lord, the flour for the cake is taken from the ground meal, but that cake is formed and baked first and presented as a firstfruit. Since it is set apart to the Lord first, it sanctifies the whole harvest. The firstfruits and the root represent the patriarchs of Israel or Abraham personally, and the lump and the branches represent the people of Israel. As a result Israel is set apart (holy) to God, and her "stumbling" (rejection of Christ) must therefore be temporary.

11:17-21. In the apostolic generation God put aside as a whole the people of Israel, an action Paul described as one in which **some of the branches have been broken off.** The apostle then spoke directly to Gentile Christians: **And you** (sing.), **though a wild olive shoot, have been grafted in among the others and now share in the nourishing sap from the olive root** (lit., "have become a co-partner of the root of the fatness of the olive"). To be so blessed by God and His grace, however, is no reason to **boast,** which Paul warned against. Since they were like "a wild olive shoot" grafted to a regular cultivated olive tree, they were indebted to Israel, not Israel to them. "Salvation is from the Jews" (John 4:22).

Normally a branch of a cultivated olive tree is grafted into a wild olive tree, the opposite of what Paul spoke of here. But he knew that grafting the wild into the cultivated was not the norm (though it was done), for later he said it was "contrary to nature" (Rom. 11:24).

To reinforce his warning Paul declared, **You do not support the root, but the root supports you.** The root of the tree is the source of life and nourishment to all the branches, and Abraham is "the father of all who believe" (4:11-12, 16-17). So Gentile believers are linked to Abraham; in one sense they owe their salvation to him, not vice versa.

The apostle anticipated the rebuttal a Gentile believer might make: **Branches were broken off so that I could be grafted in.** Though that was not the real reason the branches were broken off, Paul accepted the statement for the sake of argument. Then he pointed out that the real reason the branches were broken off was Israel's **unbelief** and that any Gentile as a grafted-in branch stands (cf. 5:2) **by faith.** Therefore Paul warned Gentile

Christians individually again, **Do not be arrogant** (lit., "Do not think high" of yourself; cf. 12:16) **but be afraid,** have a proper fear of God.

Paul reminded them, **For if God did not spare the natural branches,** Israel, **He will not spare you either.** In Greek this is a first-class condition in which the conditional statement beginning with "if" is assumed to be true. As clearly stated in the previous verses, this speaks of Israel's "fall" (11:11), "loss" (v. 12), and "rejection" (v. 15), for "the branches have been broken off" (v. 17) "because of unbelief" (v. 20). This section (vv. 11-21) explains the righteousness of God's sovereign choice. If God is righteous in temporarily putting aside Israel as a whole for unbelief, He certainly could put aside the Gentiles for boasting and haughtiness.

11:22-24. In these verses Paul summarized his whole discussion of God's sovereign choice in temporarily putting Israel aside corporately and proclaiming righteousness by faith to all mankind. **Consider** (*ide*, "see, behold") **therefore the kindness** (*chrēstotēta*, "benevolence in action"; also used of God in 2:4; Eph. 2:7; Titus 3:4) **and sternness of God.** "Sternness" translates *apotomian*, used only here in the New Testament (cf. the adverb *apotomōs* in 2 Cor. 13:10 ["be harsh"] and Titus 1:13 ["sharply"]). God's sovereign choice involved severity toward the Jews **who** stumbled **(fell;** cf. Rom. 11:11) in unbelief and were hardened (v. 25), but that same decision displayed the goodness of God toward individual Gentiles. God's continuing His goodness to the Gentiles depends on their continuing **in His kindness.** If Gentiles do not continue in God's kindness, they **also will be cut off.** This does not suggest that a Christian can lose his salvation; it refers to Gentiles as a whole (suggested by the sing. **you**) turning from the gospel much as Israel as a nation had done.

Conversely for the people of Israel, **if they do not persist** (lit., "continue") **in unbelief, they will be grafted in, for God is able to graft them in again.** At issue is not God's ability but God's decision. God sovereignly chose to put Israel aside corporately because of unbelief and to extend righteousness by faith to everyone. This demonstrates His decision to graft Gentiles into the spiritual stock of Abraham (cf. 4:12, 16-17; Gal. 3:14).

Obviously, therefore, **if** the unbelief which caused Israel's rejection by God is removed, God is able and will graft the people of Israel **(the natural branches)** back into the spiritual stock to which they belong **(their own olive tree).** After all, as Paul wrote earlier, "Everyone who calls on the name of the Lord will be saved" (Rom. 10:13).

The "olive tree" is not the church; it is the spiritual stock of Abraham. Believing Gentiles are included in that sphere of blessing so that in the Church Age both Jews and Gentiles are in Christ's body (Eph. 2:11-22; 3:6). Yet someday Israel as a whole will turn to Christ (as Paul discussed in Rom. 11:25-27). This passage does not teach that the national promises to Israel have been abrogated and are now being fulfilled by the church. This idea, taught by amillenarians, is foreign to Paul's point, for he said Israel's fall is temporary. While believing Gentiles share in the blessings of the Abrahamic Covenant (Gen. 12:3b) as Abraham's spiritual children (Gal. 3:8-9), they do not permanently replace Israel as the heirs of God's promises (Gen. 12:2-3; 15:18-21; 17:19-21; 22:15-18).

3. IN ISRAEL'S SALVATION (11:25-32)

11:25-27. Israel's corporate stumbling, which is temporary, not permanent, is called a **mystery.** In Scripture a mystery is not a truth difficult to understand, but a truth previously unrevealed (and therefore unknown) which is now revealed and publicly proclaimed (cf. Eph. 3:9; Col. 1:26; at Matt. 13:10-16, see the chart that lists NT mysteries). Paul wanted to make sure his Gentile readers knew about the mystery concerning Israel in God's sovereign choice. God's purpose was **so that you may not be conceited** (lit., "wise in yourselves"). God's sovereign plan to put Israel aside temporarily in order to show grace to Gentiles is no basis for conceit on the part of the Gentiles; it is designed to display further the glory of God.

God purposed that some from all nations should by faith receive the righteousness provided by grace. In order to achieve this goal Israel's relationship as God's Chosen People was rescinded for a time and **Israel** is now experiencing a **hardening in part until the full number** (*plērōma*, "fullness") **of the Gentiles has come in.** There is a fullness for Israel (Rom. 11:12) and a fullness for the Gentiles. God is now "taking from the Gentiles a people for Himself" (Acts 15:14).

In Romans 11:25 are two specific facts about Israel's hardening (cf. vv. 7-8): (a) it is partial, "in part" (because throughout this time "there is a remnant chosen by grace," v. 5), and (b) it is temporary (because it will end when God's sovereignly chosen number of Gentiles has been saved).

"Hardening" is *pōrōsis* ("hardening, dulling"); it differs from the verb *sklērynei* ("hardens") used of Pharaoh (9:18) and the noun *sklērotēta* ("stubbornness," lit., "hardening," 2:5). The first noun (*pōrōsis*) refers to dullness, the second suggests stubbornness.

After "the fullness of the Gentiles" (11:25, KJV) the partial hardening of Israel will be removed and **all Israel will be saved,** that is, "delivered" (in the OT "saved" often means "delivered") from the terrible Tribulation by the Messiah, **the Deliverer.** To confirm this, Paul quoted from Isaiah 59:20-21 and 27:9. The statement, "All Israel will be saved" does not mean that every Jew living at Christ's return will be regenerated. Many of them will not be saved, as seen by the fact that the judgment of Israel, to follow soon after the Lord's return, will include the removal of Jewish rebels (Ezek. 20:34-38). Following this judgment God will then remove **godlessness** and **sins** from the nation as He establishes His New Covenant with regenerate Israel (cf. Jer. 31:33-34).

11:28-29. Here Paul summarized God's dealings with Israel and with the Gentiles. In order for God to bring **the gospel** to Gentiles He had to deal with Israel corporately as **enemies.** But in relation to God's choice **(election)** of Abraham and His covenant with him and **the patriarchs,** Israel is beloved. Because God chose Abraham, Isaac, and Jacob (cf. 9:6-13), He loves the nation and will carry through on His promises. This is another reason Israel's hardening must be temporary (cf. 11:15, 22-25) and she must finally be saved corporately: God chose her. And **God's gifts and His call are irrevocable** (lit., "for not repented of are the grace-gifts and the calling of God"). He does not revoke what He has given or whom He has chosen ("call" means election and salvation; cf. 1:6; 8:30).

11:30-32. The Gentiles to whom Paul wrote **were at one time disobedient to God,** but in this Age of Grace Gentiles **(you) have now received mercy.** When Adam disobeyed (5:19) all were constituted sinners because all humanity sinned in Adam (5:12). (Cf. "disobedient" in Eph. 2:2; 5:6; and "disobedience" in Heb. 4:6, 11.) Israel **(they)** is **now** corporately **disobedient** to God so **that** when **God's mercy to** the Gentiles **(you)** reaches its full number (Rom. 11:25), Israel will again **receive mercy** (cf. vv. 26-27). God's ultimate purpose is to **have mercy on . . . all.** To do so justly **God has bound** (*synekleisen,* "enclosed, shut in on all sides") **all men over to disobedience.** "All have sinned and fall short of the glory of God" (3:23). "Jews and Gentiles alike are all under sin" (3:9), so that "there is no difference" (3:22). When the Gentiles rejected God and disobeyed Him (1:17-21), God chose Abraham and his descendants as His special people. Now the disobedience of the Jews enables God to show mercy to the Gentiles. Then, when that purpose is achieved, He will again show mercy to Israel corporately.

4. TO GOD'S GLORY AND PRAISE (11:33-36)

11:33-36. As Paul ended his discussion on the revelation of God's righteousness in His sovereign choice, he burst forth in a doxology of praise to God. He exclaimed, **Oh, the depth of the riches of the wisdom and knowledge of God!** The plan of God for the salvation of all people demonstrates God's infinite knowledge and His ability to use it wisely. God has revealed some of **His judgments and His paths** ("ways") so that people may know them, but it is humanly impossible to exhaust them. **Beyond tracing out** translates the one word *anexichniastoi,* which means "incapable of being traced by footprints." In Ephesians 3:8, its only other use in the New Testament, it is rendered "unsearchable" and refers to the riches of Christ.

The apostle then quoted Isaiah 40:13, which shows that **God** is the sole Designer of His wise plan. No one knows His **mind** or gives Him advice. This is followed by a free quotation from Job

41:11, which testifies to God's sole responsibility for His acts. **God** is indeed the Sovereign of all things, the One to whom all creatures are accountable and whom all should glorify. He is under no obligation to **repay** anyone, for no one **has ever given** Him anything. Paul concluded, **For from Him and through Him and to Him are all things.** God is the first Cause, the effective Cause, and the final Cause of everything. His deep ways are beyond man's discovering (Rom. 11:33); beyond man's knowing (v. 34a), beyond man's counseling (v. 34b), and beyond man's giving (v. 35). "All things" come from Him and by means of Him (John 1:3; Col. 1:16a; Rev. 4:11) and are for Him and His glory (Col. 1:16b). Therefore, **To Him be the glory forever! Amen** (cf. Rom. 15:6; 16:27; 1 Peter 4:11; Rev. 5:12-13). God is the only proper One to magnify (1 Cor. 1:31). The all-sovereign God deserves the praise of all His creatures.

VI. God's Righteousness Revealed in Transformed Living (12:1–15:13)

Paul divided several of his letters into two major sections, a doctrinal portion and a practical one. He followed that pattern in this epistle too, though the doctrinal part is more than twice as long as the practical. (In both Eph. and Col. the doctrinal and the practical sections are about equal in length.)

A. The basic consecration (12:1-2)

12:1-2. The start of this practical section is indicated by Paul's exhortation **I urge** (the first word of v. 1 in the Gr. text). **Therefore** also shows a transition (cf. "therefore" in 3:20; 5:1; 8:1). The basis of Paul's exhortation is **God's mercy** (oiktirmōn, rendered "compassion" in 2 Cor. 1:3; Phil. 2:1; Col. 3:12, and "mercy" in Heb. 10:28). God's compassion has been described in detail in the first 11 chapters of Romans. The content of Paul's urging is **to offer your bodies** (cf. Rom. 6:13) **as living sacrifices.** A Christian's body is the temple of the Holy Spirit (1 Cor. 6:19-20). In the KJV "offer" is translated "present" (Rom. 12:1) and "yield" (6:13, 16, 19). The word "bodies," mindful of the Old Testament sacrifices, represents the totality of one's life and

activities, of which his body is the vehicle of expression. In contrast with Old Testament sacrifices this is a "living" sacrifice. Such an offering is **holy** (set apart) **and pleasing** (cf. "pleasing" in 12:2) **to God.** Furthermore, it is **spiritual** (logikēn; cf. 1 Peter 2:2) **worship** (latreian). Latreian refers to any ministry performed for God, such as that of the priests and the Levites. Christians are believer-priests, identified with the great High Priest, the Lord Jesus Christ (cf. Heb. 7:23-28; 1 Peter 2:5, 9; Rev. 1:6). A believer's offering of his total life as a sacrifice to God is therefore sacred service. In the light of Paul's closely reasoned and finely argued exposition of the mercies of God (Rom. 1–11), such an offering is obviously a desirable response for believers.

Paul then stated general implications of a believer's offering his life to God as a sacrifice. Such an offering represents a complete change in lifestyle, involving both a negative and a positive aspect. First, Paul commanded, **Do not conform** (lit., "Do not be conformed"; this Gr. word occurs elsewhere in the NT only in 1 Peter 1:14) **any longer to the pattern of this world** (aiōni, "Age"). Living according to the lifestyle of "the present evil Age" (Gal. 1:4; cf. Eph. 1:21) must now be put aside. Then Paul commanded, **But be transformed** (pres. passive imper., "keep on being transformed") **by the renewing of your mind.** The Greek verb translated "transformed" (metamorphousthe) is seen in the English word "metamorphosis," a total change from inside out (cf. 2 Cor. 3:18). The key to this change is the "mind" (noos), the control center of one's attitudes, thoughts, feelings, and actions (cf. Eph. 4:22-23). As one's mind keeps on being made new by the spiritual input of God's Word, prayer, and Christian fellowship, his lifestyle keeps on being transformed.

Paul added, **Then you will be able to test and approve** (dokimazein, "prove by testing" [1 Peter 1:7, "proved genuine"], i.e., ascertain) **what God's will is— His good, pleasing** (cf. Rom. 12:1), **and perfect will.** These three qualities are not attributes of God's will as the NIV and some other translations imply. Rather, Paul said that God's will itself is what is good, well-pleasing (to Him), and perfect. "Good," for example, is not an adjective

(God's "good" will) but a noun (God's will is what is good—good, i.e., for each believer).

As a Christian is transformed in his mind and is made more like Christ, he comes to approve and desire God's will, not his own will for his life. Then he discovers that God's will is what is good for him, and that it pleases God, and is complete in every way. It is all he needs. But only by being renewed spiritually can a believer ascertain, do, and enjoy the will of God.

B. In Christian ministry (12:3-8)

12:3-5. A believer's consecration to God and his transformed lifestyle is demonstrated in his exercising his spiritual gifts in the body of Christ. As an apostle of Christ (**by the grace given me;** cf. 1:5; 15:15-16) he warned his readers individually (**every one of you**), **Do not think of yourself more highly** (hyperphronein, "think higher") **than you ought.** An inflated view of oneself is out of place in the Christian life. Then Paul encouraged them, **But rather think** (phronein) **of yourself with sober judgment** (sōphronein, "sound thinking"), **in accordance with the measure of faith God has given you.** God has given each believer some faith by which to serve Him. By his involved word play on various forms of the verb phroneō, "to think," Paul emphasized that human pride is wrong (cf. 3:27; 11:18, 20) partly because all natural abilities and spiritual gifts are from God. As a result every Christian should have a proper sense of humility and an awareness of his need to be involved with other members of Christ's body. As Paul explained, a parallelism exists between a believer's physical **body** which has parts with differing functions and the community of believers **in Christ** as a spiritual **body** (cf. 1 Cor. 12:12-27; Eph. 4:11-12, 15-16). The point is that **each member** functions to serve the body, not the body to serve the members. The diversity of the **many** accompanies the unity of the body. Therefore it is important to think soundly about oneself and to evaluate properly God's gifts and their uses.

12:6-8. Paul then applied what he had just said (vv. 3-5) to the exercise of God-given abilities for spiritual service (vv. 6-8). He built on the principle, **We**

have different gifts (cf. v. 4, "not all have the same function"; cf. 1 Cor. 12:4). The grace-gifts (charismata) are **according to God's grace** (charis). He listed seven gifts, none of which—with the possible exception of **prophesying**—is a sign gift. The Greek text is much more abrupt than any English translation; **let him** is supplied for smoother English. One's "prophesying" is to be done **in proportion to his faith;** a better translation would be "in agreement to the (not 'his') faith." That is, prophesying—communicating God's message, to strengthen, encourage, and comfort (1 Cor. 14:3)—is to be in right relationship to the body of truth already revealed (cf. "faith" as doctrine in Gal. 1:23; Jude 3, 20). The other six gifts mentioned here are **serving . . . teaching . . . encouraging . . . contributing . . . leadership,** and **showing mercy.** Contributing to people's **needs** is to be done with generosity (en haplotēti), not skimpily (cf. 2 Cor. 8:2; 9:11, 13). Managing, leading, or administering (proistamenos, lit., "standing before"; cf. proistamenous, "who are over," 1 Thes. 5:12) is to be done **diligently** (en spoudē, "in eagerness, earnestness"), not lazily or halfheartedly. And bestowing mercy is to be done **cheerfully** (en hilarotēti, "in gladness"), not with sadness. Three of these seven gifts are mentioned in 1 Corinthians 12:28 (prophets, teachers, administration); two (prophets and pastor-teachers) are included in Ephesians 4:11; and two (administering and serving) are listed in 1 Peter 4:10-11. Whatever one's gift, he should exercise it faithfully as a stewardship from God.

C. In social relationships (12:9-21)

This section consists of a lengthy series of short exhortations or commands. The statements relate to a Christian's relationships to other people, both saved and unsaved.

12:9-10. Paul began these specific exhortations with the key ingredient for success: **Love must be sincere.** This is God's love, which has been ministered to believers by the Holy Spirit (5:5) and must be ministered by them to others in the Holy Spirit's power. "Sincere" translates anypokritos (lit., "without hypocrisy"), also used of love (2 Cor. 6:6; 1 Peter 1:22), of faith (1 Tim. 1:5; 2 Tim. 1:5), and of wisdom (James 3:17).

This first command is followed by a pair of related basic commands—**Hate what is evil; cling to what is good.** Many Bible students consider these two clauses as explanatory of the sincerity of love, translating the verse, "Let love be unfeigned, abhorring the evil and cleaving to the good." Hating various forms of sin is frequently mentioned in Scripture (Pss. 97:10; 119:104, 128, 163; Prov. 8:13; 13:5; 28:16; Heb. 1:9; Rev. 2:6). Turning from evil is to accompany adhering to the good (cf. 1 Peter 3:11).

Divine love is to be exercised with other believers. The Greek adjective *philostorgoi*, translated **devoted,** suggests family affection. As in Romans 12:9, the second clause in verse 10 can be understood as explaining the first command. Verse 10 may be translated, "With **brotherly love** have family affection for **one another,** in honor giving place to **one another**" (cf. Phil. 2:3, "consider others better than yourselves").

12:11-12. Paul then provided a series of exhortations concerning a believer's personal attitudes, attitudes that will make him more attractive to others. In verse 11 the key thought is the last clause—**serving** (*douleuontes; diakonian* in v. 7 is trans. "serving") **the Lord**—and the first two clauses explain how a believer is to serve as the Lord's "slave" (*doulos;* cf. 1:1): **never . . . lacking** ("not shrinking, not hesitating, not being lazy") **in zeal** (*en spoudē*, "diligence," rendered "diligently" in 12:8), and being fervent in spirit. **Keep your spiritual fervor** is literally, "being fervent, or boiling (*zeontes*, used only here and in Acts 18:25 of Apollos) in the spirit" (either the Holy Spirit or one's inner" life). These two commands also balance each other as negative and positive commands (cf. Rom. 12:9). As believers serve God as His slaves they should be enthusiastic and diligent.

The three exhortations in verse 12 can be understood either as independent items or as additional descriptions of how believers should serve the Lord. They are to be **joyful in hope,** because their hope in Christ is the basis of their rejoicing (5:2-5; 1 Peter 1:6-9). **In affliction** (*thlipsei*, "distress, trouble, pressure"; cf. Rom. 8:35) believers are to be **patient** (*hypomenontes*, "being steadfast, having endurance"; cf. 5:3). Also Christians should continue **in prayer** to God for wisdom,

guidance, and strength (cf. 1 Thes. 5:17). Being **faithful,** NIV's translation of *proskarterountes*, should be rendered "persisting in" or "devoted to" (cf. Acts 1:14; 2:42; Col. 4:2).

12:13. Returning to Christians' responsibilities to other believers, Paul exhorted them, **Share with God's people who are in need** (lit., "sharing [*koinōnountes*, 'having in common'] the needs of the saints"). This characterized the Jerusalem church (Acts 2:44-45; 4:32, 34-37). This concern also motivated the church in Antioch (Acts 11:27-30) and the Apostle Paul (1 Cor. 16:1-4; 2 Cor. 8–9; Rom. 15:25-27) to give to the church in Jerusalem. In the same vein the apostle commanded, **Practice hospitality** (lit., "pursuing friendliness to strangers"). Both ministries, meeting needs and being hospitable, involve helping others.

12:14-16. Paul's exhortations in this section relate to a believer's reactions to the actions and emotions of others, whether Christians or not. The hatred displayed in persecution usually evokes response in kind, but Paul commanded, **Bless those who persecute you; bless and do not curse** (cf. Matt. 5:44). Perhaps Paul thought of Stephen (Acts 7:59-60) and of Jesus Christ (Luke 23:34). They both modeled these words and responded to persecution even to death by praying for God's forgiveness of their persecutors.

Christians should be able to empathize with others, both believers and unbelievers. Paul commanded, **Rejoice with those who rejoice; mourn with those who mourn.** Related to this is the next command, **Live in harmony with one another** (lit., "having the same attitude toward one another"; cf. Rom. 15:5; Phil. 2:2; 1 Peter 3:8). Being in harmony with other Christians is basic to being able to empathize with them. This idea is then presented in negative and positive details: **Do not be proud** (lit., "not thinking highly" of yourself; cf. Rom. 11:20; 12:3) and **be willing to associate with people of low position** (cf. James 2:1-9). These orders are summarized in the command, **Do not be conceited** (lit., "Do not become wise concerning themselves"; cf. Prov. 3:7; Rom. 11:25), an attitude that makes empathy impossible.

12:17-18. The exhortations in verses 17-21 relate primarily to believers' relationships with unbelievers, speaking as they do of those who do evil toward believers (v. 17) and are the "enemy" of believers (v. 20). The Old Testament principle of justice was "eye for eye" (Ex. 21:24), but Paul commanded, **Do not repay anyone evil for evil** (cf. 1 Peter 3:9). On the positive side Christians are **to do what is right** (*kala*, "beautiful," used here in the ethical sense of good, noble, and honorable). Paul then commanded believers, **Live at peace with everyone** (cf. "live in harmony with one another," Rom. 12:16). But recognizing that limits exist, Paul included the words, **If it is possible, as far as it depends on you.** Harmony with others may not always be achievable, but believers should not be responsible for that lack of peace (cf. Matt. 5:9).

12:19-21. Referring again to the negative (cf. v. 17a) Paul then exhorted his readers **not to take revenge** after they are misused. Instead they should **leave room for God's wrath** (lit., "for the wrath"), because God has promised to avenge His people: **It is Mine to avenge, I will repay** (Deut. 32:35; cf. Heb. 10:30). David's refusal to kill Saul on two occasions when it seemed that God had delivered Saul into David's hands is a classic biblical example of this principle. In light of God's promise to execute vengeance, a Christian should therefore **feed** his **enemy** and quench his thirst—in short, respond to his evil with Christian love. Heaping **burning coals on his head**, along with the first part of Romans 12:20, is a quotation from Proverbs 25:21-22. The coals on the head may refer to a ritual in Egypt in which a person showed his repentance by carrying a pan of burning charcoal on his head. Helping rather than cursing an enemy may cause him to be ashamed and penitent. As Paul summarized, **Do not be overcome by evil,** giving in to the temptation to retaliate, **but overcome evil with good** (cf. Matt. 5:44, "love your enemies"). Again positive and negative commands are put together (cf. Rom. 12:9, 11, 16-20).

D. In relation to authority (13:1-7)

13:1-3. Rome was the imperial capital, the seat of the empire's civil government. As residents in Rome, Paul's initial readers were aware of both the glory and the shame of that city in the days of Nero, who reigned from A.D. 54 to 68. But they were also citizens of Christ's kingdom (Phil. 3:20; Col. 1:13). Appropriately, therefore, Paul discussed a Christian's relationship to his government and civil rulers. Both in its length and specific details this discussion is the key New Testament passage on the subject (cf. 1 Tim. 2:1-4; Titus 3:1; 1 Peter 2:13-17).

The apostle's basic exhortation is, **Everyone must submit himself to the governing authorities** (lit., "higher authorities"). The basic reason for such submission is that those authorities are **established** by **God** (cf. Dan. 4:17, 25, 34-35). An individual **who rebels against the authority,** therefore, **is rebelling against** (lit., "has taken a stand against") **what God has instituted** (lit., "the ordinance of God"). Such persons are thus actually rebelling against God, and bring civil and/or divine **judgment on themselves.** Those who obey and **do right** need have no fear of authorities; in fact, civil leaders **commend** those who do good.

13:4-5. Furthermore, a civil leader **is God's servant,** a concept often forgotten today. By commending those who do right (v. 3), a civil leader himself does **good** (v. 4). But on the other hand he bears arms **(the sword)** as **God's servant** (the second time in this verse Paul referred to the ruler this way; cf. v. 6), as **an agent of wrath.** Governmental force, properly used, helps prevent tyranny and executes justice; it brings **punishment on the wrongdoer.** A Christian has two reasons to be submissive to civil authorities—to avoid **possible punishment** (lit., "the wrath") and to heed his **conscience,** which prods him to obey God's ordinances.

13:6-7. A Christian's responsibility to civil authorities involves more than obedience (vv. 1, 5). It also includes support by paying **taxes** (cf. Matt. 22:21). This is because the leaders, as **God's servants** (cf. Rom. 13:4), are supposed to **give their full time to governing** and need support through taxes from citizens, Christians included. So a Christian ought to **give everyone what** he owes **him** (lit., "repay everyone his dues"), whether substance **(taxes** and **revenue)** or **respect** and **honor.**

E. In light of the future (13:8-14)

13:8-10. Discussion of believers' obligations to civil authorities evidently triggered Paul's thinking concerning believers' debts to others. He commanded, **Let no debt remain outstanding** (lit., "Do not keep on owing anyone anything") **except the continuing debt to love one another** (lit., "except loving one another"). This is not a prohibition against a proper use of credit; it is an underscoring of a Christian's obligation to express divine love in all interpersonal relationships. A Christian should never fall short, and so be "in debt," in loving others (John 13:34-35; 1 Cor. 16:14; Eph. 5:2; Col. 3:14; 1 John 3:14, 23; 4:7, 11, 21).

The importance of continually showing love is seen in the explanation, **For he who loves his fellow man** (lit., "the other one") **has fulfilled the Law** (cf. Matt. 22:39; Mark 12:31). Love, not mere external conformity to rules, is the essence of the Law (cf. Gal. 5:14).

Paul then quoted various specific commands from the social section of the Ten Commandments. These prohibitions—**not to commit adultery . . . murder . . . steal** and **covet**—are the 7th, 6th, 8th, and 10th commandments, in that order (Ex. 20:13-15, 17). Paul summed up that entire section of the Law by quoting Leviticus 19:18. The Jewish Rabbis and the Lord Jesus summarized the social section of the Law in the same words (cf. Matt. 22:39). Paul then expressed this principle in other words, **Love does no harm** (lit., "Love does not keep on working evil") **to its neighbor,** and then he repeated (cf. Rom. 13:8) his basic assertion that **love** fulfills **the** Mosaic **Law.** Only in Christ can a person meet this or any of the other requirements of the Law (8:4).

13:11. Expressing divine love is a Christian's constant responsibility, but it is especially crucial in **understanding the present time** (lit., "knowing the season"). Paul was not referring to time in general but to the end-time and to the imminent return of the Lord Jesus. It is a time, therefore, for spiritual vigilance and industriousness: **wake up from your** (some mss. have "our," which conforms to the context) **slumber** (cf. Eph. 5:14; 1 Peter 5:8). This need for alertness is **because our salvation** (ultimate or final salvation realized at the return of the Savior; cf. Rom. 8:23; Heb. 9:28; 1 Peter 1:5) **is nearer now than when we first believed** (cf. James 5:8). Each passing day in the faith brings final salvation and deliverance closer.

13:12. Paul considered the time of Christ's return and the consummation of salvation for believers (v. 11) as the start of a new **day.** The present time, while Christ is absent (John 14:2-3; Acts 1:11) and Satan is at work (2 Cor. 4:4; Eph. 2:2), is described as **the night** (cf. 2 Peter 1:19). Since "the day" **is almost here,** Paul urged his readers to **put aside the deeds of darkness and put on the armor of light.** Christians are soldiers in a conflict who need to be alert and equipped for battle (Eph. 6:10-17; 1 Thes. 5:8). Upright, Christ-honoring living is often referred to as being in the light (John 12:36; Eph. 5:8, 14; Col. 1:12; 1 Thes. 5:5; 1 John 1:7; 2:10).

13:13-14. In verse 13 Paul repeated his exhortation of verse 12, changing the figure from warfare to lifestyle. He charged, **Let us behave decently, as in the daytime** (lit., "day"). Crime, violence, and wickedness are associated with darkness and the night (John 1:5; 3:19-20; 8:12; 12:35, 46; Eph. 5:8, 11; 6:12; 1 Thes. 5:7; 1 Peter 2:9; 1 John 1:5-6; 2:9, 11). Perhaps this contrast was suggested to Paul by his phrase "deeds of darkness" (Rom. 13:12). At any rate the activities and attitudes he listed—**orgies and drunkenness . . . sexual immorality and debauchery . . . dissension and jealousy** (cf. Gal. 5:19-21)—are certainly "deeds of darkness." It is interesting that Paul linked jealousy with immorality. Such actions and attitudes have no place in a Christian's life. He belongs to "the light"; these deeds and thoughts belong to the darkness.

A Christian's lifestyle must be pure and holy, especially in view of Christ's approaching return (cf. Rom. 13:11-12; 1 John 3:3). The secret to living chaste lives is for Christians to **clothe** themselves **with the Lord Jesus Christ** (cf. "put on," Eph. 4:24; Col. 3:10). At salvation they were "clothed with Christ" (Gal. 3:27), so they should conduct themselves accordingly. Also the secret includes **not** thinking **about how to gratify the desires of the sinful nature** (lit., "and do not make forethought [*pronoian*] for the flesh [*sarkos;* cf. Rom.

8:3-5, 8-9, 12-13] for lusts"). For a Christian to plan out specific ways to gratify his sinful nature is wrong and out of bounds.

F. In dealing with other Christians (14:1–15:13)

Paul had discussed various aspects of a Christian's responsibilities in interpersonal relationships (12:9-21; 13:8-10), but relationships with other believers loom large and involve special problems that require discussion. Harmonious relationships within the family of God are important.

1. WITHOUT JUDGING (14:1-12)

Christians are at different levels of spiritual maturity. They also have diverse backgrounds that color their attitudes and practices. The first lesson to learn in living harmoniously with other Christians, therefore, is to stop judging others.

14:1-4. The focus in these verses is on **him whose faith is weak** (lit., "the one being weak in faith"), which appears in the emphatic first position in the sentence. Paul commanded believers to **accept** (pres. middle imper., "keep on taking to yourselves"; cf. 15:7) such a person, **without passing judgment on disputable matters** (lit., "but not unto quarrels about opinions"). A believer with certain scruples is not to be welcomed into the fellowship with the intent of changing his views or opinions by quarreling with him about them.

One area of differing scruples pertains to food, in particular the eating of meat. **One man's faith allows him to eat everything, but another man, whose faith is weak, eats only vegetables** (lit., "but the one being weak eats vegetables"). The reason some Christians then were vegetarians is not stated. Since the issue is related to their Christian faith, it could be to insure against eating meat offered to idols (cf. 1 Cor. 8; 10:23-30). The reason for a believer's scruple is not the point, however; its existence alongside a differing opinion was Paul's concern.

In such a situation neither believer should judge the other. **Look down on** (*exoutheneitō*; also used in Rom. 14:10) should be translated "despise" or "reject with contempt" (cf. "treat . . . with

contempt," Gal. 4:14; 1 Thes. 5:20). The reason a "strong" Christian (cf. Rom. 15:1) should not despise a "weak" one, and the reason that a weak Christian should **not condemn** (*krinetō*) the strong one is that **God has accepted** (same verb as in 14:1) both of them. (Another reason for not downgrading others is given later in v. 10.) As a believer, he is a servant of God and he is accountable to God, his Judge. Any Christian tempted to judge another believer must face Paul's question, **Who are you to judge** (lit., "the one judging") **someone else's servant?** (*Oiketēn*, "domestic servant," is not the usual word *doulos*, "slave.") The present participle, "the one judging," suggests that Paul sensed some judging of others was occurring among the Christians at Rome. But such criticizing is wrong because a domestic servant should be evaluated by his . . . **master,** not by fellow believers. Therefore, Paul concluded, **And he will stand** (lit., "he shall be made to stand"), **for the Lord is able to make him stand.** Even if a believer despises the scruples of another Christian, God can defend the second person.

14:5-8. A second area of differing opinions was the significance of special days. **One man considers one day more sacred than another; another man considers every day alike** (cf. Col. 2:16). Which position a person held meant nothing to the apostle. His concern was that **each one should be fully convinced in his own mind** (cf. Rom. 14:14, 22), examining his heart to be sure he is doing what he feels the Lord would have him do. And he should hold his opinion **to the Lord.** This is true for any issue where an honest difference of opinion among Christians exists, whether in keeping or not keeping **special** days or eating or abstaining from **meat,** or in other matters not prohibited by Scripture. All belongs **to the Lord** and is sanctioned by Him (1 Cor. 10:25-27; 1 Tim. 4:3-5). A believer's individual accountability to the Lord in every area and experience of life is paramount. Each Christian in both life and death is seen by the Lord, and is accountable to Him, not to other Christians. **So whether we live or die, we belong to the Lord.**

14:9-12. In these verses Paul stated the theological basis for his exhortation for Christians to desist from and to resist judging one another. One of the reasons for the Lord Jesus' redemptive death and resurrection is to be **the Lord of both the dead and the living.** Since Jesus is the Lord, Christians should not **judge** (*krineis*) **or . . . look down on** (*exoutheneis,* "despise" or "reject with contempt"; cf. v. 3) one another, their brothers, in such matters. One Christian is not above another as his judge; all are equally under Christ, the Judge.

As Lord, Jesus will one day review and evaluate the ministry of His servants at His **judgment seat** (*bēma;* see comments on 2 Cor. 5:10). Paul affirmed the certainty of this event by quoting Isaiah 49:18 and 45:23, pertaining to everyone standing **before** Christ and confessing Him as Lord (cf. Phil. 2:10-11). At that event **each** believer **will give an account** (lit., "a word") **of himself to God.** Since Paul was writing to the Christians in Rome (Rom. 1:7) and included himself with them in the first personal plural pronoun and verb ("*we* will all stand," 14:10), "God's judgment seat" is only for believers in the Lord. What is here called *God's* judgment seat is the judgment seat of Christ in 2 Corinthians 5:10. Because God judges through His Son (John 5:22, 27), this judgment seat can be said to belong to both the Father and the Son. The issue of the believer's eternal destiny will not be at stake; that was settled by his faith in Christ (cf. Rom. 8:1). Each believer's life of service will be under review in which some loss will be experienced (cf. 1 Cor. 3:12-15), but he will be rewarded for what endures (cf. 1 Cor. 4:4-5). This judgment of believers climactically demonstrates God's lordship.

2. WITHOUT HINDERING (14:13-23)

Paul's warning against judging relates to Christians' attitudes and actions toward the convictions of other believers (vv. 1-12). The other side of the coin is evaluating the impact of one's own convictions and actions on other Christians. In this section Paul warned against causing other Christians to stumble (hindering their spiritual growth) by asserting that one is free to live in accord with convictions not shared by other believers.

14:13-14. Paul's opening sentence is both the final charge on the previous subject and the introduction to the new one: **Therefore, let us stop passing judgment on** (*krinōmen,* "condemning") **one another** (pres. tense subjunctive, "no longer let us keep on judging or condemning one another"). **Instead** a Christian should judge *himself* and his actions so that he does not place a **stumbling block** (*proskomma,* lit., "something a person trips over"; cf. 1 Cor. 8:9 and comments on Rom. 14:20-21) **or obstacle** (*skandalon,* lit., "trap, snare," and hence "anything that leads another to sin"; cf. 16:17) **in** his **brother's way** (lit., "to the brother").

Returning to the subject of food (14:2-3, 6), Paul expressed his own conviction (cf. v. 5) as a Christian **that no food** (lit., "nothing") **is unclean** (*koinon,* "common") in itself (cf. Acts 10:15; Rom. 14:20; 1 Cor. 8:8). The problem, however, is that not all Christians—especially some from a Jewish heritage—shared Paul's conviction. Therefore Paul properly concluded, **But if anyone regards** (lit., "but to the one reckoning") **something as unclean** ("common"), **then for him it is unclean** (cf. Titus 1:15). But if someone persisted in holding that conviction, he could bring harm to others. That is the point Paul made next (Rom. 14:15-18).

14:15-18. How should a Christian whose convictions allow him to eat everything respond to one with scruples against certain foods? In Christian love he ought to forgo his liberty in Christ to avoid being a spiritual hindrance to his spiritual **brother.** If he persists in exercising his liberty so that his brother **is distressed** (*lypeitai,* "grieved, hurt"), Paul concluded, then the Christian exercising his liberty is **no longer acting** (lit., "walking") **in love.** Such persistence could cause the spiritual destruction of a **brother for whom Christ died. Destroy** renders the word *apollye,* which often means eternal ruin. Here it may mean temporal ruin; a Christian forced to act contrary to his scruples, even though more strict than necessary, even may find himself ruined by his wounded conscience (cf. 1 Cor. 8:10-12). Persisting in one's freedom could also result in his Christian liberty (**what you consider good**) being blasphemed (**spoken of as evil,** *blasphēmeisthō*).

Such things should not happen. After all, food is not that important an

ROMANS

issue (1 Cor. 8:8); it is **not** the sum and substance of **the kingdom of God. But . . . righteousness** (upright living), **peace** (cf. Rom. 12:16, 18; 14:19) **and joy in** (the sphere of) **the Holy Spirit** (cf. 15:13) are essentials of Christian fellowship and harmony. A concerned believer insists on right conduct, harmony, and joy rather than forcing his own lifestyle on others. As a result the Christian **who serves** (pres. participle, *douleuōn*, "who keeps on serving as a slave") **Christ in this way**—in Christian love, pursuing righteousness, peace, and joy in the Holy Spirit—**is pleasing** (cf. 12:1; 15:1; Heb. 13:21) **to God and approved by men** (in contrast with being evil spoken of, Rom. 14:16).

14:19-21. Continuing his emphasis on not hindering another Christian's spiritual life, Paul urged his readers, **Let us therefore make every effort** (lit., "Let us keep on pursuing") **to do what leads to peace** (lit., "the things of peace"; cf. v. 17) **and to mutual edification** (lit., "and the things of building up one another"; cf. 15:2; 1 Thes. 5:11). To Paul **food** and one's personal convictions about it were not so important as the spiritual health of a fellow Christian and **the work of God.** Therefore **it is wrong** to insist on one's personal freedom in Christ concerning food **(all food is clean;** cf. Rom. 14:14, "no food is unclean") and drink if it **causes someone else to stumble** (*proskommatos,* "a stumbling block"; cf. vv. 13, 21). **Meat or drink** or **anything else** should be put aside if it causes a **brother to fall** (*proskoptei,* "stumble"; cf. *proskomma,* in vv. 13, 20). At times one's Christian liberty must be relinquished for the sake of others. As Paul wrote to the Corinthians, "Everything is permissible—but not everything is constructive" (1 Cor. 10:23). And "be careful . . . that the exercise of your freedom does not become a stumbling block to the weak" (1 Cor. 8:9).

14:22-23. Concerning personal convictions in areas where different views exist, Paul concluded, **So whatever you believe about these things** (lit., "The faith that you have," or "Do you have faith?") **keep between yourself and God.** A Christian must not insist on influencing a believer with tighter scruples to change his ways. It should be something "in his own mind" (v. 5), for he lives "to the Lord" (v. 8). Paul considered a Christian like himself who had a clear conscience

on such matters **blessed** (lit., "happy"). On the other hand, a Christian **who has doubts is condemned** (perf. pass. verb, "stands condemned") **if he eats.** If a Christian eats food or does anything when he has doubts in his own mind as to whether it is right or wrong before God (one who is "weak" in faith, vv. 1-2), his action does **not** spring **from** (*ek,* "out of") his **faith** or trust in God and is therefore wrong. As Paul generalized, **Everything that does not come from** (*ek,* "out of") **faith is sin.** The principle is, "When in doubt, don't." The "strong" Christian (15:1) is wrong if he causes a weak brother to sin (by doing something while doubting, 14:20), and a weak brother (vv. 1-2) who goes against what he doubts also sins (v. 23).

3. AS IMITATORS OF CHRIST (15:1-13)

Paul had written that Christians should not despise or condemn others (14:1-12) nor should they hinder the conduct of other Christians (14:13-23). Now he gave a third principle to observe when a believer is dealing with fellow Christians: he is to follow the example of the Lord Jesus Christ. Jesus was supremely the Person who ministered on behalf of others, not for Himself. It is fitting, therefore, that those who take His name should imitate Him.

15:1-4. Paul summarized the previous discussion (chap. 14) by saying, **We who are strong** (obviously in convictions and conscience) **ought** (pres. tense, emphasizing continuing obligation; its first position in the sentence underscores its importance) **to bear with the failings** (lit., "infirmities, weaknesses") **of the weak** (lit., "nonstrong"). The strong ought not despise the weak; they ought to bear with them. Also the strong should **not** seek **to please** themselves. This last clause is the key; a Christian should not be self-centered, but should be concerned about the spiritual welfare of others. Pleasing others, however, is not the end in itself, but is **for** their **good, to build** them **up** (lit., "unto edification"; cf. "edification" in 14:19). This is the example the Lord Jesus Christ left. **Even He did not please Himself.** He came "to do the will" of the Father who sent Him (John 4:34) and to please Him (John 5:30; 8:29). To support this statement Paul quoted a part of a verse from a messianic psalm (Ps. 69:9).

160

Christ was insulted by others because of His associations with God the Father.

Then Paul stated a significant principle concerning the purpose and ministry of the Scriptures: **For everything that was written in the past was written to teach us** (lit., "for our instruction"). **The Scriptures** serve to give believers **endurance** (hypomonēs, "steadfastness in the face of adversities") and **encouragement** so that they **might have hope** (pres. tense, "keep on having hope"; cf. Rom. 5:3-5). As Christians learn from the *past* (what is written in the OT about others who did not please themselves) they are motivated to endure and be comforted in the *present*, looking ahead in hope (confidence) to the *future*.

15:5-6. The steadfast **endurance and encouragement** a Christian receives from the Scriptures (v. 4) come ultimately from **God** (v. 5), the Author of the Scriptures. Paul prayed that God would give his readers **a spirit of unity** (lit., "to think the same"; 12:16, "live in harmony," has the same Gr. construction) as they **follow Christ Jesus** (lit., "according to Christ Jesus"). The ultimate purpose of this unity was **that with one heart and mouth** (a unity of inward feeling and outward expression) they would **glorify** (pres. tense, "keep on glorifying") **the God and Father of our Lord Jesus Christ** (2 Cor. 1:3; Eph. 1:3; 1 Peter 1:3 have the same wording about God). This is the final purpose of Christians individually and of the church corporately (cf. Rom. 15:7; 1 Cor. 6:20; 2 Thes. 1:12).

15:7. Since the goal of interpersonal relationships among Christians is a unified glorying of God, Paul concluded his commands with **Accept one another** (pres. imper., "keep on accepting or receiving one another"). Significantly this is the same command Paul gave the strong Christians when he opened this entire discussion (14:1). The Model of acceptance for Christians, however, is the Lord Jesus, who **accepted** us. The Lord received believers when they were not only "powerless" (5:6, lit., "weak") but also "ungodly" (5:6), "sinners" (5:8), and "enemies" (5:10). Certainly Christians can receive others who differ with them on nonessential matters. Jesus **Christ** received them so that they can **bring praise to God** (lit., "unto glory of God"), which

is the purpose of Christian unity (15:6).

15:8-12. Having pointed to the Lord Jesus as the Model for Christians, Paul proceeded to discuss Jesus' ministry and its objectives: **Christ** became **a servant** (the word "deacon" comes from this Gr. noun *diakonon*) **of the Jews** (lit., "to the circumcision"). Jesus was born a Jew as God's Messiah for Israel. God had two objectives to accomplish through Jesus' ministry. The first was **to confirm the promises made to the patriarchs** (cf. 9:4-5). God's second objective in Christ's ministry was **so that** (lit., "and that," because the following clause is coordinate with the preceding one) **the Gentiles may glorify God** (cf. 15:6) **for His mercy.** God had made covenants only with Israel (9:4), not with the Gentiles (cf. Eph. 2:12), so God had no covenantal promises to confirm with the Gentiles. Any spiritual blessings that come to the Gentiles spring solely from the mercy of God. Nevertheless God eternally purposed to bless the Gentiles spiritually through the Lord Jesus as their Messiah and through His covenants with Israel (e.g., Gen. 12:3; cf. John 4:22).

God's two purposes in the ministry of Christ are being achieved now while Israel nationally has been set aside (cf. Rom. 11:1-31) and the church is being formed of both Jews and **Gentiles** (Eph. 2:14-22). And it will be achieved in the future when Israel is restored to her place as head of the nations and becomes a means of blessing to everyone (cf. Deut. 30:1-10).

To demonstrate the validity of his statement concerning the ministry of Christ and its purposes, particularly the one relating to Gentiles, the Apostle Paul quoted four Old Testament passages, introducing the series with the formula, **As it is written** (perf. tense, "it stands written"). Significantly these quotations are taken from all three divisions of the Old Testament—"the Law of Moses, the Prophets, and the Psalms" (Luke 24:44)—and from three great Jewish heroes: Moses, David, and Isaiah. The first quotation (Rom. 15:9) is from David's song of deliverance (2 Sam. 22:50; Ps. 18:49); the second (Rom. 15:10), from Moses' valedictory song to the people of Israel (Deut. 32:43); the third (Rom. 15:11), from both the shortest and the middle chapter of the Bible (Ps. 117:1); and the fourth (Rom. 15:12), from Isaiah's messianic prophecy (Isa. 11:10).

A progression of thought can be traced through the four quotations. In the first, David praised God **among the Gentiles** (Rom. 15:9); in the second, Moses exhorted the Gentiles, **Rejoice . . . with His people** (v. 10); in the third the psalmist commanded the Gentiles to **praise the Lord** (v. 11; cf. v. 7); and in the fourth, Isaiah predicted that **the Gentiles will live under the rule of the Root of Jesse** (the Messiah) and they **will hope in Him** (v. 12). The Old Testament never presented the Gentiles as "heirs together with Israel, members together . . . in the promise in Christ Jesus" (Eph. 3:6), but it certainly did see them as receiving blessing from God's fulfilling His covenantal promises to His people Israel.

15:13. Several times Paul's words sound as if he were ending this epistle (vv. 13, 33; 16:20, 25-27). This verse (15:13) is in effect a benedictory prayer. The description of God as **the God of hope** relates to hope mentioned in the preceding verses and to the promises of God recorded in the Scripture which give hope (v. 4). Paul desired God to fill his readers **with all joy and peace** (cf. 14:17). Joy relates to the delight of anticipation in seeing one's hopes fulfilled. Peace results from the assurance that God will fulfill those hopes (cf. 5:1; Phil. 4:7). These are experienced as believers **trust in Him** (cf. Heb. 11:1). As a result believers **overflow with hope by the power of the Holy Spirit** (cf. Rom. 15:19). The achievement of all God's purposes for the spiritual welfare of His children comes from the power given by the Spirit of God. What a fitting closing reminder to the apostle's discussion of Christian living.

VII. Concluding Remarks (15:14–16:27)

Though all Paul's letters have closing remarks, he devoted more space to them in Romans than in any other epistle. This was due at least in part to the fact that he had never visited the city and its churches and to his desire to establish personal relationships with his readers. Another factor undoubtedly was his plan to visit Rome in the future.

A. Personal plans (15:14-33)

In writing to a group of people whom he had never met as a group, Paul showed admirable restraint in avoiding personal references to himself. Only once did he use himself as an example (7:7-25), and his other personal remarks are few (1:8-16; 9:1-3; 10:1-2; 11:1). Now as he closed his letter he felt led to discuss his philosophy of ministry and his plans in light of it.

15:14-16. Paul had demonstrated in this letter and elsewhere his ability to be straightforward, even almost blunt, and forceful. Yet he also had a deep concern for the feelings of others and an ability to use effective principles of interpersonal relations. This is seen in his statement, **I myself am convinced** (perf. tense, "I stand convinced"; cf. 8:38), **my brothers, that you yourselves are full of goodness, complete in knowledge** (perf. tense, "having been filled with all knowledge," not in the absolute sense, but in the sense that they had an understanding of the full scope of Christian truth), **and competent** (lit., "being able") **to instruct** (nouthetein, "to counsel, admonish"; cf. Col. 1:28; 3:16) **one another.** Paul did not have a low opinion of the Roman Christians; on the contrary he considered them spiritually informed and spiritually mature. Why then did he write on such basic Christian themes? Paul explained, **I have written** (past tense, "I wrote") **you quite boldly on some points** (lit., "in some measure") **as if to remind you of them again.** This was what Peter did as well (2 Peter 1:12; 3:1-2).

Paul was qualified to remind his readers of those points **because** he had his special position as a result of God's **grace** (cf. Rom. 1:5). He was **a minister** (leitourgon, a "public servant") **to the Gentiles.** This ministry was carried out as a **priestly duty** (the Gr. verb hierourgounta means "to work in sacred things") and involved his **proclaiming the gospel of God** (cf. 1:2-4). Because of his sharing the good news with **Gentiles** (11:13; Gal. 1:16; 2:2, 7-9; Eph. 3:8; Col. 1:27; 2 Tim. 4:17) they became **an offering acceptable** (the words **to God** are not in the text but are obviously understood), **sanctified** (perf. tense, "having been sanctified" or "having been set apart") **by the Holy Spirit** (cf. 1 Peter 1:2). Like a priest, Paul introduced Gentiles to God, and then presented them like an offering to the Lord. God's willingness to accept Gentiles, set apart by the work of the Holy Spirit, shows His plan in the Church Age is to unite Jews and Gentiles in one body (Eph. 3:6).

15:17-19. As a result of his special ministry by God's grace to the Gentiles, Paul affirmed, **Therefore I glory** (lit., "I have boasting") **in Christ Jesus in my service to God** (lit., "in the things relating to God"). This was no boasting in mere human achievements, as Paul explained: **I will not venture to speak of anything except what Christ has accomplished through me in leading the Gentiles to obey God** (lit., "unto the obedience of the Gentiles"). "Obedience" is a synonym for coming to Christ (cf. 1:5; 1 Peter 1:2; cf. "obey" in Rom. 16:26) for God "commands all men everywhere to repent" (Acts 17:30).

Paul recognized that all credit goes to Christ. And yet Paul was involved; God worked **by what** he had **said and done.** The apostle had been used by God to perform **signs** (*sēmeiōn*, miracles that signify theological truths) **and miracles** (*teratōn*, miracles that produce wonder). Luke referred to a miracle God performed through Paul at Cyprus (Acts 13:11, making Elymas blind), "signs and wonders" at Iconium (Acts 14:3; cf. Acts 15:12) and miracles at Lystra (Acts 14:8-10, 19-20), Ephesus (Acts 19:11-12), Troas (Acts 20:9-12), and Malta (Acts 28:1-8). Signs, wonders, and miracles authenticated the work of the apostles (2 Cor. 12:12; Heb. 2:3-4). And all this, Paul said, was **through the power of the Spirit** (cf. Rom. 15:13). Anything Paul achieved that was worthy of praise had God's grace as its source, Jesus Christ as its motivation and goal, and the Holy Spirit as its energy.

The result was that Paul preached the gospel **from Jerusalem all the way around to Illyricum.** Literally, this reads, "from Jerusalem and in a circle (i.e., Jerusalem and its environs) even to Illyricum." "The gospel of God" (v. 16) is here called **the gospel of Christ.** The New Testament records several of Paul's visits to Jerusalem after his conversion (Acts 9:26-28 [cf. Gal. 1:17-19]; Acts 11:27-30; 15:2 [cf. Gal. 2:1]; Acts 18:22). In

the last reference Jerusalem is not named, but the words "he went up and greeted the church" obviously refers to the church at Jerusalem. Paul's visit to Illyricum is not mentioned elsewhere in the New Testament. This area, also known as Dalmatia, corresponds approximately to modern-day Yugoslavia. It is west and north of Greece (see the location on the map between Acts and Rom.). At one time Titus went to Dalmatia (2 Tim. 4:10). A logical suggestion is that Paul went into Illyricum from Macedonia while waiting for a response to 2 Corinthians before going on to Corinth (Acts 20:1-3; 2 Cor. 13:1-2, 10). This visit was fresh in his mind since Corinth was the city where he wrote Romans (see the *Introduction* to Rom.).

15:20-22. Reference to the geographical extent of his ministry (v. 19) led Paul to declare something of his philosophy of outreach: **It has always been my ambition to preach the gospel where Christ was not known** (lit., "named"). Paul purposed to be a true pioneer evangelist, opening virgin territory to the good news of God's grace in Jesus Christ. This was **so that he would not be building on someone else's foundation** (cf. 1 Cor. 3:10). Paul then expressed his ministry goal in a quotation of the second half of Isaiah 52:15 and explained, **This is why I have often been hindered** (imperf. tense, "I was being hindered many times") **from coming to you.** Up to this time Paul had always found new areas for ministry in Asia Minor and the Grecian Peninsula so that he had not yet felt free to look beyond to Rome and Spain.

15:23-24. Perhaps his visit to Illyricum convinced Paul that no more virgin territory for the gospel lay in Asia Minor and the Grecian Peninsula. This does not mean that he had visited every center, but the gospel had been introduced and local churches had been established that could complete the work (cf. Acts 19:8-10). At any rate Paul concluded, **There is no more place for me to work in these regions** (lit., "having no more place in these regions"). Coupled with this was his **longing for many years to see** the Roman Christians. At the beginning of this epistle he had expressed this desire to visit them (Rom. 1:10-11, 13). Paul continued, **I plan to do so** (this clause does not occur in the Gr. text, but the idea is implied) when (the indefiniteness of the Gr. clause requires "whenever") I go to Spain (cf. 15:28). Spain was then a Roman colony where many Jews lived; it was the western limit of the empire. He hoped to visit them while passing through. Apparently he did not plan a long stay in Rome. They could then assist him on his journey there (lit., "and by you to be sent forward there"); that is, they would encourage him on to Spain. Paul would proceed to Spain only after he had enjoyed (lit., "I am filled full with," "I am satisfied with") their company for a while. Paul paid the Roman believers the sincere compliment that their fellowship would refresh and satisfy him spiritually (cf. 1:13). He also wanted to impart a spiritual gift to them, thereby strengthening them (1:11) and to have some spiritual harvest among them (1:13), that is, to be able to help them grow in Christ.

15:25-27. Paul balanced his tentative plans for the future with the business immediately at hand. I am on my way to Jerusalem in the service of the saints there (lit., "ministering [diakonōn] to the saints"). Paul's visit to Jerusalem was to deliver the voluntary offering from churches for the poor among the saints in Jerusalem (cf. Acts 24:17; 1 Cor. 16:1-4; 2 Cor. 8:13-14; 9:12-13; Gal. 2:10). The churches of Asia Minor contributed to the offering also, but Paul mentioned only Macedonia and Achaia, the areas closest to Rome and those on his mind for obvious reasons. (See the location of these two portions of Greece on the map between Acts and Rom.)

The voluntary nature of the contribution (koinōnian, "fellowship") is stressed by the repetition of the verb, were pleased (cf. Rom. 15:26-27; 2 Cor. 8:10-12). At the same time Paul recognized the churches had an obligation: Indeed they owe it to them (lit., "and they are debtors to them"). This sense of moral obligation had undoubtedly prompted Paul to suggest the offering. Since the Gentiles have shared in the Jews' spiritual blessings (lit., "in their spiritual things"; cf. Rom. 11:11-12, 17-18; 15:12; Gal. 3:14; Eph. 3:6), Gentile Christians certainly ought to share with (leitourgēsai, "to minister to, serve"; cf. leitourgon in Rom. 15:16) the Jews their

material blessings (lit., "in fleshly things"; cf. Gal. 6:6).

15:28-29. Again Paul said that after going to Jerusalem he would go to Spain and visit the Romans on the way (cf. v. 24). Paul got to Rome, but not when or in the manner he anticipated! (Acts 27-28) Whether he ever got to Spain no one knows for sure. Christians should plan ahead, but they should also be flexible. Paul, not boastfully but simply confident of God's provision, promised that his visit would be a spiritual blessing to the Roman Christians: I will come in the full measure of the blessing of Christ, that is, with Christ's blessing to share with them (cf. Rom. 1:11-13).

15:30-33. The Apostle Paul recognized his need for intercessory prayer support from his readers and asked for it again and again (Eph. 6:19-20; Col. 4:3-4; 1 Thes. 5:25; 2 Thes. 3:1-2; Phile. 22). Here he entreated the Romans by our Lord Jesus Christ and by the love of the Spirit to join him in his struggle through prayer. "The love of the Spirit" is probably the love given by the Spirit (cf. Rom. 5:5), not love for the Spirit. Recognizing that divine love, they would be motivated to pray. A Christian's intercession is a means of sharing in the ministry of others.

Paul's specific request was that he would be rescued from the unbelievers (lit., "the disobedient") in Judea and that his service (diakonia) in Jerusalem would be acceptable to the saints. Paul was aware of the problems that lay before him in Jerusalem (Acts 20:23), and he was deeply concerned that the offering from the Gentile Christians be delivered and distributed properly. If these objectives were accomplished, according to Paul, he could then by God's will go to them with joy and . . . be refreshed with them. The word rendered "refreshed" suggests that Paul would be able to rest or relax with them in the knowledge of a job well done. Paul closed this section with a brief benediction: The God of peace (cf. Rom. 16:20; also cf. "the God of hope," 15:13) be with you all. Amen. This is the third benediction in this chapter (cf. vv. 5, 13).

B. Personal greetings (16:1-16)

The capital city of Rome was a magnet that drew people from all over the empire. In addition Paul's travels to many of the major population centers—Jerusalem, Syrian Antioch, Philippi, Athens, Corinth, Ephesus—brought him into contact with the mobile segment of Roman society. These factors help explain the presence of Paul's many friends in Rome, but his knowledge of their whereabouts remains a tribute to his deep concern for people.

16:1-2. Phoebe (which means "bright, radiant") was Paul's emissary to deliver this letter, so he wrote officially, **I commend to you our sister Phoebe.** The relationship mentioned is spiritual, not familial. Phoebe was **a servant of the church in Cenchrea,** a seaport a few miles east of Corinth (cf. Acts 18:18; and see the map between Acts and Rom.). The word *diakonon,* "servant," is used for the office of deacon (Phil. 1:1; 1 Tim. 3:8, 10, 12) as well as used generally (Rom. 15:8; 1 Cor. 3:5). Use of the word with the phrase "of the church" strongly suggests some recognized position, a fact appropriate for a person serving as Paul's emissary. Paul not only officially commended her (cf. 2 Cor. 3:1), but also asked the Roman Christians **to receive her in the Lord in a way worthy of the saints and to give her any help** (lit., "and to stand by her in whatsoever matter") **she may need from you.** Paul explained, **for she has been a great help** (*prostatis,* "a protectress, succorer") **to many people, including me.** So they should help her since she had helped others.

16:3-5. This list of greetings (vv. 3-16) that Paul wanted conveyed to friends in Rome is the longest in any of his epistles. He mentioned 26 people by name, and referred to many others (vv. 5, 10-11, 13-15). Several women are included in the list: Priscilla (v. 3), Mary (v. 6), Tryphena and Tryphosa (v. 12), Persis (v. 12), Rufus' mother (v. 13), and Nereus' sister (v. 15). Two others are possibly women—Junias (v. 7) and Julia (v. 15).

Paul first met **Priscilla and Aquila** when he arrived in Corinth on his second missionary journey (Acts 18:2) and worked with them at their trade of tentmaking. They had come to Corinth from Rome because of Claudius' decree that all Jews must leave Rome. They accompanied Paul when he left Corinth

(Acts 18:18), but stayed in Ephesus when the party stopped briefly (Acts 18:19). There they ministered to Apollos (Acts 18:26) and undoubtedly to Paul during his stay in Ephesus on his third journey, because they sent greetings to the Corinthian Christians (1 Cor. 16:19). Shortly after that, they must have moved back to Rome and still later returned to Ephesus (2 Tim. 4:19).

Paul paid them great praise, calling them **my fellow workers in Christ Jesus** and revealing that **they risked their lives for me** (lit., "they lay down their own neck for my soul"). In what way they risked their lives is not known. **All the** Gentile **churches,** Paul added, were **grateful to them.** Paul also sent greetings to **the church that** met **at their house.** The Christians in Rome apparently worshiped in numerous homes such as Priscilla and Aquila's. This couple had had a house church in Ephesus (1 Cor. 16:19) and probably wherever they lived. Other churches in homes are mentioned in Colossians 4:15 and Philemon 2.

Epenetus, to whom greetings were sent, is mentioned only here, but is called by Paul **my dear friend** (lit., "the one loved by me"; cf. Stachys, v. 9). He **was the first convert** (lit., "the firstfruits") **to Christ in the province of Asia.** Paul reached Asia, the western portion of modern-day Turkey, on his third missionary journey (Acts 19:10), after having been prevented from going there on his second journey (Acts 16:6).

16:6-7. Mary is identified simply as one **who worked very hard** ("toiled much"; cf. v. 12). Some Greek manuscripts read Mariam, the Hebrew form, which probably identifies this woman as a Jew.

Andronicus and Junias, greeted together, may have been husband and wife; Junias can be either masculine or feminine. Paul called them **my relatives,** which probably refers to a tribal, not a family kinship (cf. 9:3). He also mentioned four other "relatives" (16:11, 21). He said Andronicus and Junias had **been in prison with** him (lit., "my fellow prisoners"); when or where this occurred is not mentioned (cf. 2 Cor. 11:23). Paul commended them as **outstanding** (*episē-moi,* lit., "having a mark [*sēma*] on them," therefore "illustrious, notable, outstand-

Paul's Concluding Benedictions in His Epistles

Romans 16:20b	"The *grace of our Lord Jesus* be with you."
1 Corinthians 16:23	"The *grace of the Lord Jesus* be with you."
2 Corinthians 13:14	"May *the grace of the Lord Jesus Christ,* and the love of God, and the fellowship of the Holy Spirit be with you all."
Galatians 6:18	"The *grace of our Lord Jesus Christ* be with your spirit, brothers. Amen."
Ephesians 6:24	"*Grace* to all who love *our Lord Jesus Christ* with an undying love."
Philippians 4:23	"The *grace of the Lord Jesus Christ* be with your spirit."
Colossians 4:18	"*Grace* be with you."
1 Thessalonians 5:28	"The *grace of our Lord Jesus Christ* be with you."
2 Thessalonians 3:18	"The *grace of our Lord Jesus Christ* be with you all."
1 Timothy 6:21b	"*Grace* be with you."
2 Timothy 4:22	"The Lord be with your spirit. *Grace* be with you."
Titus 3:15b	"*Grace* be with you all."
Philemon 25	"The *grace of our Lord Jesus Christ* be with your spirit."

ing") **among the apostles.** The word "apostles" is probably used here in the broader, general sense in which Barnabas, Silas, and others were called apostles (Acts 14:14; 1 Thes. 2:7). Or it could mean the apostles in the limited sense, referring to the reputation this pair had among the Twelve. Paul added, **They were** (perf. tense, "they came to be and still are") **in Christ before I was.** So they had been believers for about 25 years.

16:8-11. Ampliatus was one Paul loved **in the Lord.** This was high praise from the apostle. **Urbanus** was called **our fellow worker in Christ,** and **Stachys** was addressed as **my dear friend** (lit., "the one loved by me"; cf. Epenetus, v. 5). Paul said **Apelles** was **tested and approved** (*ton dokimon,* "the one approved through testing"; cf. the same word trans. "approved," 14:18; the related infinitive *dokimazein* is trans. "to test and approve," 12:2). Without naming other individuals Paul sent greetings to **those who belong to the household of Aristobulus,** perhaps a grandson of Herod the Great. (See the chart on the Herods at Luke 1:5.) A household may have included family members and servants. (However, the Gr.

simply has "those out of, belonging to Aristobulus"; cf. Rom. 16:11).

Herodion was greeted as **my relative,** but once again the relationship was probably tribal and not familial (cf. vv. 7, 21). The name may identify this person as belonging to Herod's family. Once again without naming individuals Paul sent greetings to **those in the household of Narcissus** (lit., "those out of, belonging to Narcissus"; cf. v. 10). But Paul restricted his greetings to the ones **who are in the Lord,** which probably indicated Narcissus' family was divided spiritually.

16:12-13. Paul sent greetings jointly to **Tryphena and Tryphosa,** identifying them as **those women who work hard** ("toil") **in the Lord.** Some believe they were sisters, possibly even twins. Then **Persis,** addressed as **my dear friend** (lit., "the one loved"), was **another woman who has worked very hard** ("toiled much") **in the Lord.** Interestingly four women were said to have "worked hard" (cf. Mary, v. 6).

Whether **Rufus** is the same person mentioned in Mark 15:21 or not is uncertain. If so, then he, as a son of Simon of Cyrene, was a North African.

Paul said Rufus was **chosen in the Lord,** a statement true of every believer (cf. Eph. 1:4). Consequently the word translated "chosen" may mean "eminent," since it was given to Rufus as a statement of distinction. The greeting included Rufus' **mother who,** Paul said, had also **been a mother to** him. Paul obviously did not say she was his actual mother, but he had been the recipient of her motherly care.

16:14-16. The next five names mentioned together (v. 14) evidently had something in common, perhaps as leaders of another house church. This may be indicated by the reference to **the brothers with them.** They are all common names, particularly among slaves.

Julia may have been the wife of **Philologus.** Two other husband-wife teams were Priscilla and Aquila (v. 3) and (possibly) Andronicus and Junias (v. 7). **Nereus and his sister** were then greeted, though the sister's name is not given. And finally, greetings were sent to **Olympas and all the saints with** him. This group may have been the leaders of another house church (cf. v. 14).

Of all these individuals only Priscilla and Aquila are mentioned elsewhere in the New Testament for certain; yet Paul knew them all individually and sent personal greetings to them and their associates. Paul cannot properly be charged with not being "a people person." He closed this section with the command, **Greet one another with a holy kiss,** the mode of salutation similar to the handshake today (cf. comments on 1 Cor. 16:20; also cf. 2 Cor. 13:12; 1 Thes. 5:26; 1 Peter 5:14) and with a general word of salutation, **All the churches of Christ send greetings** (lit., "greet you").

C. Final words (16:17-27)

16:17-20. Paul could not resist giving a final word of warning that they **watch out for** spiritual enemies: **those who** are divisive and seek to hinder the Lord's work (who **put obstacles** [*skandala,* "traps, snares"; cf. 14:13] **in your way that are contrary to the teaching you have learned**). Believers are to **keep away** (pres. imper., "keep on turning away") **from** such false teachers, who were **not serving** (*douleuousin,* "serving as slaves"; cf. 14:18) **Christ,** but were slaves to their

own appetites (lit., "bellies"; cf. Phil. 3:19). They were selfish gluttons. The problem, however, was that **by smooth talk and flattery they** deceived **the minds** (lit., "hearts") **of naive people** (*akakōn,* "innocent, unsuspecting").

Paul hastened to assure the Romans that he did not consider *them* naive. Their **obedience** (to Christ; cf. Rom. 1:5; 15:18; 1 Peter 1:2) was well known and Paul was glad for them. But he was concerned that they **be wise about what is good, and innocent about what is evil** (*kakon*). The word for "innocent" is *akeraious,* "unmixed, simple, pure." In Greek it was used of wine that was not diluted and of metal that was not weakened in any way. The word is used in the New Testament in only two other places: Matthew 10:16 ("innocent") and Philippians 2:15 ("pure"). Christians should be innocent about evil, not following the ways of the world (Rom. 12:2).

To conclude this warning Paul added the promise, **The God of peace** (cf. 15:33; Heb. 13:20) **will soon crush Satan under your feet** (cf. Gen. 3:15). The false teachers (Rom. 16:17-18) were under Satan's influence, but he will be destroyed and God will establish peace (Rev. 20:1-6). Then Paul gave another benediction (cf. Rom. 15:13, 33) about God's **grace.** (See the chart, "Paul's Concluding Benedictions in His Epistles.")

16:21-24. These few verses contain personal **greetings** from some of Paul's associates: first, **Timothy, my fellow worker,** and then **Lucius, Jason, and Sosipater, my relatives.** Once again these men were not members of Paul's family, but fellow countrymen (cf. vv. 7, 10). These may be the men of the same names mentioned elsewhere (Acts 13:1; 17:5-9; 20:4; cf. 2 Cor. 9:4).

Then **Tertius,** who was Paul's stenographer for this epistle, sent greetings. So did **Gaius,** Paul's host in Corinth, who apparently had a church meeting in his home. This Gaius was probably not the same Gaius who was from Macedonia and traveled with Paul (Acts 19:29) nor the Gaius who was from Derbe (Acts 20:4). The Gaius mentioned here in Romans was probably Paul's convert whom he baptized (1 Cor. 1:14). **Erastus sent greetings.** He was **the city's** director of public works (lit., "the city's steward," a high position in Corinth). Paul called **Quartus** our **brother,** undoubtedly meaning a spiritual brother, not a physical one. Romans 16:24 (NIV marg.), which repeats the benediction in verse 20b, is not found in a number of the major Greek manuscripts and is not considered genuine.

16:25-27. The apostle finally came to his closing benediction. This letter to the Romans is Paul's longest and most complete statement of the message he proclaimed, what he here called **my gospel** (cf. 2:16; 2 Tim. 2:8) **and the proclamation of** (i.e., concerning) **Jesus Christ.** The truth of this message is the means of spiritual life and stability, as Paul expressed his praise to God **who is able to establish you** (cf. 1 Peter 5:10).

Paul said that aspects of this message (e.g., Rom. 11:25; 1 Cor. 15:51; Eph. 5:32) and in a sense the total message (cf. Eph. 3:3-9; Col. 1:26-27) are **the mystery hidden for long ages past, but now revealed and made known.** The message of the gospel of Christ was "hidden" in the Old Testament, but is revealed in the New. In **the prophetic writings** (of the OT; cf. Rom. 1:2), given **by the command of the eternal God** (1 Tim. 1:17), Christ was referred to (Luke 24:44-45), but even the prophets themselves were not fully aware of all they wrote (1 Peter 1:10-12). **But now** in the Church Age their writings are understood.

The goal of this "revelation of the mystery" (Rom. 16:25) is **that** people of **all nations might believe and obey** Christ (cf. 1:5; 15:18; 1 Peter 1:2). Paul's concern for the geographical spread of the gospel is evident here (cf. Matt. 28:19), appropriate in view of his writing to the believers at the empire's capital city.

Paul then identified specifically the object of his benediction: **To the only wise God.** In the Greek this phrase is followed immediately by the words **through Jesus Christ.** This indicates that the wisdom of God is displayed supremely through Christ (cf. Col. 2:3). According to the Greek text the benediction then ends, **be glory forever! Amen** (cf. Rom. 11:36). God the Father ultimately is the One to be praised and to whom glory belongs (cf. 1 Cor. 15:24-28).

BIBLIOGRAPHY

Barnhouse, Donald Grey. *Exposition of Bible Doctrines Taking the Epistle to the Romans as a Point of Departure.* Reprint (10 vols. in 4). Grand Rapids: Wm. B. Eerdmans Publishing Co., 1952-64.

Barrett, C.K. *A Commentary on the Epistle to the Romans.* Harper's New Testament Commentaries. New York: Harper & Row Publishers, 1957.

Best, Ernest. *The Letter of Paul to the Romans.* Cambridge: Cambridge University Press, 1967.

Black, Matthew. *Romans.* New Century Bible. London: Marshall, Morgan & Scott, 1973.

Bruce, F.F. *The Epistle to the Romans: An Introduction and Commentary.* The Tyndale New Testament Commentaries. Grand Rapids: Wm. B. Eerdmans Publishing Co., 1963.

Cranfield, C.E.B. *A Critical and Exegetical Commentary on the Epistle to the Romans.* The International Critical Commentary. 6th ed. 2 vols. Edinburgh: T. & T. Clark, 1975, 1979.

Godet, Frederic Louis. *Commentary on Romans.* 1883. Reprint. Grand Rapids: Kregel Publications, 1977.

Harrison, Everett F. "Romans." In *The Expositor's Bible Commentary,* vol. 10. Grand Rapids: Wm. B. Eerdmans Publishing Co., 1976.

Hendriksen, William. *Exposition of Paul's Epistle to the Romans.* New Testament Commentary. 2 vols. Grand Rapids: Baker Book House, 1980, 1981.

Hodge, Charles. *Commentary on the Epistle to the Romans.* 1886. Reprint. Grand Rapids: Wm. B. Eerdmans Publishing House, 1950.

Hunter, Archibald MacBride. *The Epistle to the Romans: Introduction and Commentary.* London: SCM Press, 1955.

Ironside, H.A. *Lectures on the Epistle to the Romans.* Neptune, N.J.: Loizeaux Bros., 1928.

Johnson, Alan F. *Romans: The Freedom Letter.* Everyman's Bible Commentary. 2 vols. Chicago: Moody Press, 1976.

Moule, H.C.G. *The Epistle of St. Paul to the Romans.* 1892. Reprint. Minneapolis: Klock & Klock Christian Publishers, 1982.

Murray, John. *The Epistle to the Romans.* 2 vols. Grand Rapids: Wm. B. Eerdmans Publishing Co., 1959, 1965.

Sandlay, William, and Headlam, Arthur C. *A Critical and Exegetical Commentary on the Epistle to the Romans.* The International Critical Commentary. 5th ed. Edinburgh: T. & T. Clark, 1955.

Stifler, James M. *The Epistle to the Romans.* Chicago: Moody Press, 1960.

Thomas, W.H. Griffith. *Romans: A Devotional Commentary.* 3 vols. London: Religious Tract Society, n.d. Reprint (3 vols. in 1). Grand Rapids: Wm. B. Eerdmans Publishing Co., 1946.

Vaughan, Curtis, and Corley, Bruce. *Romans: A Study Guide Commentary.* Grand Rapids: Zondervan Publishing House, 1976.

Wiersbe, Warren W. *Be Right.* Wheaton, Ill.: Scripture Press Publications, Victor Books, 1976.

1 CORINTHIANS

David K. Lowery

INTRODUCTION

According to Greek legend, Sisyphus was a king of Corinth. For defying the gods with his insolent wit he was sentenced to the eternal drudgery of pushing a huge stone up a hill. When he would reach the summit, the stone would roll back to the bottom and force resumption of the task. Camus, a 20th-century philosopher, found in this legend of the Corinthian king a picture of modern man's condition, the purposeless absurdity of life.

If Camus had read the two biblical letters sent to the Corinthians, he would have gotten a different picture, one with a message of purpose and hope for misdirected people. The attitude of these Corinthians, like their legendary king, smacked of proud self-centeredness. But instead of dealing with a capricious Zeus, these first-century Corinthians interacted with the gracious and loving God and His messenger, the Apostle Paul.

Author and Readers. That Paul is this letter's author there is little doubt. Even the most imaginative critics find no objection on this point. The apostle came to Corinth (Acts 18:1-18) on his second missionary journey (probably in the spring of A.D. 51 as the proconsulship of Gallio likely began later that year, in July). There Paul met Aquila and Priscilla who had left Rome in A.D. 49, when Claudius issued an edict ordering the expulsion of Jews from that city. The couple ran a tent-making business, a trade also practiced by Paul. Since no mention is made of their conversions, they were probably Christians when Paul met them. With a kinship along spiritual, ethnic, and vocational lines, Paul was naturally attracted to them.

According to his custom Paul attended the synagogue and took part in its services, seeking to persuade his hearers that Jesus is the Messiah. When the synagogue was closed to Paul, he went next door to the house of a synagogue listener who heard and believed, a Gentile named Titius Justus (Acts 18:7). He was one of many people in Corinth who belonged to the Lord.

From a human point of view Paul probably had reason to wonder if many saints would be found in Corinth. The ancient city had a reputation for vulgar materialism. In the earliest Greek literature it was linked with wealth (Homer *Iliad* 2. 569-70) and immorality. When Plato referred to a prostitute, he used the expression "Corinthian girl" (*Republic* 404d). The playwright Philetaerus (*Athenaeus* 13. 559a) titled a burlesque play *Ho Korinthiastēs*, which may be translated "The Lecher." And Aristophanes coined the verb *korinthiazomai* to refer to fornication (*Fragment* 354). According to Strabo (*Geography* 8. 6-20) much of the wealth and vice in Corinth centered around the temple of Aphrodite and its thousand temple prostitutes. For this reason a proverb warned, "Not for every man is the voyage to Corinth."

For a hundred years after 146 B.C. no one cared to make the voyage to Corinth. The city was destroyed because of its revolt against Rome. Only a few columns in the temple of Apollo survived the razing. All its citizenry was killed or sold into slavery.

But this favorable location did not go unused for long, as Julius Caesar refounded the city as a Roman colony in 46 B.C. In 27 B.C. it became the governmental seat for Achaia, from which seat Gallio as proconsul would allow Paul's proclamation of the gospel. It was onto this new stage, which nonetheless preserved the vices of the old, that Paul stepped in A.D. 51.

Contacts and Correspondence. The nature and number of Paul's contacts and correspondence with the Corinthians after his first visit in A.D. 51 is subject to considerable debate. A defense for the scheme of events to be presented may be found in several of the works cited in the *Bibliography.*

1. The length of Paul's stay on this first tour of ministry was one and one-half years, after which he sailed in the fall of A.D. 52 to Ephesus enroute to Jerusalem. Priscilla and Aquila accompanied Paul to Ephesus where they remained to meet and instruct the gifted Alexandrian Apollos whom they subsequently sent on to Corinth for ministry there (Acts 18:18-28).

2. While Apollos was ministering in Corinth (Acts 19:1), Paul returned to Ephesus on his third missionary journey in the fall of A.D. 53 for a period of about two and one-half years (Acts 19). It was probably during the early part of Paul's ministry in Ephesus that he wrote the letter mentioned in 1 Corinthians 5:9, a letter misunderstood by the Corinthians (5:10-11) and later lost.

3. Paul learned of this misunderstanding and of further problems in the church at Corinth from the household of Chloe (1:11). Then an official delegation—Stephanas, Fortunatus, and Achaicus (16:17)—brought Paul specific questions on issues dividing the church. First Corinthians was written, probably in A.D. 54 or 55, to address these matters.

4. But apparently this did not resolve the problems in the church. It is possible that Timothy was the bearer of this news (4:17; 16:10). Paul then decided to revisit the church which he called in 2 Corinthians 1:15 and 2:1 the "painful" visit (cf. 2 Cor. 13:1, which speaks of a third visit, the last leg of Paul's third missionary journey), because of the action of the man referred to in 2 Corinthians 2:5 and 7:2.

5. After his second visit and return to Ephesus, Paul sent a letter borne by Titus, which it grieved him deeply to write (2 Cor. 2:4) apparently because of its disciplinary nature (2 Cor. 7:8-9).

6. After the silversmiths' riot Paul left Ephesus bound for Troas to meet Titus. Because Paul could not find him there, he anxiously pushed on to Macedonia, apparently with grave concern about Titus' safety (2 Cor. 2:12-13; 7:5). There he met Titus who brought good news about the general well-being of the Corinthian church but bad news about a group opposed to Paul.

7. From Macedonia Paul wrote 2 Corinthians and followed it up with his third visit during the winter of A.D. 56-57 (Acts 20:1-4).

Purpose and Nature of the Letter. If Ephesians is a letter concerned with the universal church, 1 Corinthians is pointedly concerned with the local church. If anyone thinks his church has more than its share of riffraff and woe, he need only turn to this letter (and its companion, 2 Cor.) to put his problems in perspective. First Corinthians provides a glimpse of life inside one first-century church, and far from saintly it was. Yet that is the reason Paul wrote this letter—to make positional sanctification practical. The spirit of the world seemed more influential in the Corinthian church than the Spirit of God, despite the splendidly evident gifts given by the Spirit. Paul wanted to change that. He directed his message along three lines:

1. The first six chapters were an attempt to correct the contentions in the church brought to his attention by Chloe's servants (1:11) and to bring about unity in perspective and practice.

2. Beginning in chapter 7, Paul addressed himself to certain questions (introduced by the phrase *peri de,* "now concerning") about marital issues (7:1, 25), liberty and responsibility (8:1), spiritual gifts and church order (12:1), money for impoverished saints in Jerusalem (16:1), and the availability of Apollos (16:12).

3. In chapter 15 he reaffirmed and defended the doctrine of the Resurrection, which some denied. It is possible that Paul saw this as a fundamental ill affecting all the preceding discussion, so he placed it at the climax of his letter.

Standing above all the issues with which this letter deals is the very existence of a church in Corinth, a testimony to the power of God and the gospel.

OUTLINE

I. Introduction (1:1-9)
   A. Salutation and description of the writer and readers (1:1-3)

COMMENTARY

I. Introduction (1:1-9)

The introductions to Paul's letters are frequently seedbeds for issues expanded on later; his prefatory words in 1 Corinthians are no exception. He touched on his calling to be an apostle, the Corinthians' calling to be saints, and the unity which is theirs in Christ.

A. Salutation and description of the writer and readers (1:1-3)

1:1. The legitimacy of Paul's apostleship and its denial by some is hinted at in this letter (chap. 9), but receives explicit defense in 2 Corinthians. In the first words in 1 Corinthians **Paul** affirmed his appointment to this position **by the will of God** to represent not his own interests but those **of Christ.**

Sosthenes was probably Paul's amenuensis and may have been the synagogue ruler publicly thrashed by the Jews (Acts 18:17). If so, he illustrates how God can turn the worst circumstances to a believer's ultimate advantage.

1:2. The church belongs to **God,** not man. Had the Corinthians recognized this, their problem of division might not have existed. Those who compose the church have been **sanctified,** set apart by God as His possession. The burden of Paul's letter was that the Corinthians' practice might more nearly approximate their position. **Christ Jesus** as **Lord** was to be obeyed. Herein was unity for Christians not only in Corinth but **everywhere.**

1:3. Grace was what brought them together and what they needed to display mutually so that relational **peace** would be maintained. These qualities, especially needed in the Corinthian church, were produced by God in those dependent on Him.

B. Thanksgiving for the effects of God's grace (1:4-9)

Thanksgiving for a church so rife with problems may seem a bit strange. If Paul's only resources had been his own, the prospects of reforming a group like the Corinthians would have been dim indeed. But God was at work and that, for Paul, was a matter of thanksgiving.

1:4. However prone the Corinthians may have been to self-exaltation, it was because of God's **grace** alone that they were members of the body which existed **in Christ Jesus.**

1:5. It was only because they were a part of His body that they had been so **enriched** with the **speaking** and **knowledge** gifts such as tongues, prophecy, discernment of spirits, and/or interpretation (12:4-11). These gifts were not given to be abused as the Corinthians had done, but to be used for the good of all the church.

1:6. The presence of these gifts also bore **testimony** to the effectiveness of Paul's message **about Christ.** Though it might have been feebly delivered (2:1-5), God securely implanted His Word.

1:7-8. Because it was God's work, Paul had no question about the outcome. Because the Corinthian believers were justified by God's grace, they would stand before Him **blameless** (*anenklētous*, "free from accusation"; cf. Col. 1:22) when **Christ** returns. Thus they could **eagerly wait** (*apekdechomenous*; used seven times in the NT of the return of Christ: Rom. 8:19, 23, 25; 1 Cor. 1:7; Gal. 5:5; Phil. 3:20; Heb. 9:28) for Him.

1:9. This was so because God . . . is **faithful** and He had **called** the Corinthians **into fellowship with His Son Jesus Christ.** But one cannot enjoy fellowship with Christ while being at odds with other members of His body (Matt. 5:23-24). So it is on this note that Paul made his transition from what God had done in the past and will do in the future to what the Corinthians needed to do in the present, namely, mend their divisions.

II. Divisions in the Church (1:10–4:21)

Dissension in their church was the first problem openly addressed by Paul.

A. The reality of division (1:10-17)

1:10. Paul appealed to **brothers,** not to adversaries, in the most authoritative fashion, **in the name of** the Lord **Jesus Christ.** This is the 10th reference to Christ in the first 10 verses, leaving no doubt as to the One Paul believed should be the source and focus of Corinthian unity. His appeal was for harmony, not the elimination of diversity. He desired a unity of all the parts, like a quilt of various colors and patterns blended together in a harmonious whole.

1:11-12. Instead of this unity, however, the fabric was coming apart at the seams, or so **Chloe's** servants said. While the divisions were certainly real, it is possible, on the basis of Paul's remark in 4:6, that he made adaptations with regard to party heads so that the names cited— **Paul, Apollos, Cephas**—were illustrative, in order to avoid worsening an already deplorable situation.

1:13. The three questions in this verse were rhetorical and expected a definite no. The universal body of **Christ** is not **divided,** and neither should its local expression be. No man won salvation for the Corinthians, nor did any of them owe their allegiance to anybody except Christ.

1:14-17. Paul's imitation of Christ apparently touched every aspect of his ministry. According to John 4:2, Jesus did not **baptize,** but left it to His disciples. This was usually Paul's practice too. Could Paul then have believed baptism was necessary for salvation? Such is impossible (cf. 1 Cor. 4:15; 9:1, 22; 15:1-2). Not that baptism is pointless. It was commanded by Christ (Matt. 28:19) and practiced by the early church (Acts 2:41), which makes it, with the Lord's Supper, an ordinance of the church. But it is what an ordinance gives testimony to, not what it effects, that is more important.

Paul's primary charge was **to preach the gospel** (9:16) **not with words of human wisdom.** Brilliantly persuasive eloquence may win a person's mind but not his heart, whereas the unadorned words of the gospel, though seemingly foolish by human standards, are made effective by the Spirit of God (2:4-5).

B. *The causes of division (1:18–4:5)*

From a human point of view, the message of the gospel, at the heart of which was the suffering and dying Savior, seemed foolishly contradictory. No less so was the principle that he who would be greatest must be the servant of all (Matt. 23:11-12). But this was precisely what Paul meant to affirm in his analysis of the causes of division in Corinth.

1. A MISUNDERSTANDING OF THE MESSAGE (1:18–3:4)

Fundamentally the Corinthians needed a renewal of their minds (Rom. 12:2). They were trying to live their Christian lives on the basis of unsanctified common sense which has self-preservation as its ultimate goal. This kind of life is self-seeking, self-serving, and ultimately self-destructive (Luke 9:24-25).

1:18. It was that very point which Paul wanted to drive home to the Corinthians. **The message of the Cross** cuts to the heart of self-centeredness. Paul saw it as central to salvation which he understood to be a process begun by justification, advanced by sanctification, and climaxed in glorification. Paul spoke most pointedly in this verse and in the letter as a whole to the second of these phases, progressive sanctification. "The message of the Cross" is the message of self-renunciation, of obedience to God which may lead as it did in Jesus' case to humiliation and death, but which ultimately leads not to self-destruction but to preservation (Mark 8:34-35) and exaltation (2 Tim. 2:12; Rev. 22:5). That was the recurring theme in these verses (1 Cor. 1:17-18, 23-24; 2:2, 8), an idea **those who are perishing** consider **foolishness** (cf. Luke 9:23-25).

1:19. As he often did, Paul illustrated his point by an example of Israel who, following humanly wise counsel, formed an alliance with Egypt as a defense against Assyria, when in fact only the miraculous intervention of God was able to save them (cf. Isa. 29:14; 2 Kings 18:17–19:37).

1:20-21. It was the same with all human wisdom, whether of the esteemed Jewish **scholar** or Greek **philosopher.** The

brilliance of man cannot appreciate the plan of God (Isa. 55:8-9). It is not self-confident erudition but self-effacing faith that allows one to enter the narrow way.

1:22-25. It was not on man's terms and initiative but on God's that man found what he needed, **the power of God and the wisdom of God.** In the preaching of **Christ crucified** God **called** people by opening their eyes of faith to believe the gospel.

1:26-31. Were not the situation so grievous, one could almost imagine a smile of incredulity on Paul's face as he wrote these words and urged the Corinthians to survey their own congregation. From a human viewpoint wisdom, influence, and high breeding were apparently in short supply. If God had chosen on the basis of such criteria, He would have passed them by. But when God called, he turned the world's standards upside down and usually chose the ordinary rather than the outstanding in order **that no one may boast before Him** (v. 29) but only in the Lord. For **Christ** alone personified the **wisdom from God** (v. 30) and in Him the Corinthians experienced **righteousness,** that is, justification (Rom. 4:24-25), **holiness,** that is, sanctification (2 Thes. 2:13-15), and **redemption,** that is, glorification (Rom. 8:23; Eph. 4:30). In the wisdom of God the plan of salvation was accomplished by a crucified Christ hidden from the wise and learned but revealed to simple believers (cf. Matt. 11:25-26).

2:1-5. On this note, Paul made his transition to a third point in his illustration of the futility of human **wisdom,** compared with the power and wisdom of **God.** That was seen also in the manner of his ministry which he described as characterized by **weakness and fear and with much trembling** (v. 3). Some see in this a Paul chastened by his encounter with the Athenian philosophers and therefore temporarily shaken and unsure. But that was probably not so. The phrases simply describe a spirit of dependence and subjection to God's authority (cf. Eph. 6:5; Phil. 2:12), which marked his ministry. It was also true that his manner of preaching was unimpressive from a human point of view (2 Cor. 10:10). Paul readily admitted this and even used it as a point in his argument. His preaching was not marked by **eloquence** or **persuasive**

words such as characterized the sophists, the traveling teachers of that day, but was instead the unembellished message of a crucified Christ as the only means of salvation. Faith, then, was induced by a demonstration of the Spirit's power and was not a product of human ingenuity or rhetorical flourish. Paul wanted to be sure their faith would not rest on men's wisdom, but on God's power.

2:6. In Paul's disclaimer about his own brilliance he did not mean that God puts a premium on ignorance and rejects wisdom of any sort. There was a wisdom taught by the Spirit which Paul wanted his readers to grasp firmly. Some of his readers had done so (no doubt Paul hoped that someday all would do so). He referred to them as the mature, probably including the individuals mentioned in 16:15-18. They are the same people he described as spiritual people (2:13, 15). The reason the rulers of this age (cf. 1:20) did not understand this wisdom was because they lacked the Spirit (2:14), and thus were coming to nothing.

2:7. The message which Paul proclaimed was God's secret wisdom, known only by God's revelation (Matt. 11:25). At the heart of this wisdom is the plan of salvation intended for our glory, determined before time began (Eph. 1:4).

2:8. As did John in his Gospel (John 17:1), Paul linked glory with the crucified Lord, an utter paradox to both Jews and Gentiles (1 Cor. 1:23) who nonetheless unwittingly (Luke 23:34) took part in that central act of God's plan of salvation.

2:9-10. The blessings of salvation were prepared by the Father, carried out by the Son, and applied by the Spirit (Eph. 1:3-14) to all believers who as a result love God (1 John 4:19). The only way the Corinthians could know this was by the Spirit, who knows and reveals these deep things of God about salvation.

2:11. Paul illustrated this by pointing out that nobody can fully fathom the thoughts of anyone else. How much more necessary, then, is the work of the Spirit if the thoughts of God are to be known.

2:12. It was for that purpose, in part, that the Spirit who is from God came (John 16:13), not just to some Christians but to all (1 Cor. 12:13).

2:13. It was this message of salvation which Paul proclaimed and now ex-pounded further. It did not originate in man but in God and was taught by the Spirit. Paul then expressed these spiritual truths which were a message of wisdom (cf. v. 6). The Greek word *pneumatikois* may be neuter gender and so translated spiritual words as in the NIV ("expressing spiritual truths in spiritual words"). Or it may be masculine gender and translated "spiritual men" ("interpreting spiritual truths to spiritual men," as in the NIV margin). Both senses are possible, but Paul's primary point in this passage was not how the message of wisdom was received but who received it, as suggested by the context: Paul spoke the message of wisdom to "the mature" (v. 6). Thus verse 13 parallels verse 6 and forms a kind of bracket, in keeping with well-written Greek style.

2:14. Since only spiritual people are able to receive spiritual truths, it follows that the man without the Spirit, an unregenerate person, would not and could not receive the message of wisdom regardless of his intellectual abilities or accomplishments (1:20). Like a deaf critic of Bach or a blind critic of Raphael is the unregenerate critic of God's Word.

2:15-16. On the other hand a person possessing the Spirit and guided by Him is able to evaluate and apply all things the Spirit reveals (v. 10).

The spiritual man can be judged only by God (4:3-5), not by unregenerate people (2:15) or by worldly Christians (3:1-3). To have the mind of Christ is to be obedient to God's revelation (Phil. 2:5-8), as were the spiritual people in the Corinthian church.

3:1-4. However, this was not true of all at Corinth. When Paul came and preached Christ to them, they believed. By faith they were justified and granted peace with God (Rom. 5:1-2). No doubt Paul taught them all the blessings that came to them as Christians, what Paul called milk. At that time their way of thinking and living was only beginning to be transformed (Rom. 12:2). They were still greatly influenced by worldly thinking and behavior—they were infants in Christ.

But "the message of the Cross" (1 Cor. 1:18) concerned more than justification. It also concerned sanctification. It called for a renewal of attitude and action in response to God's revelation. It called for righteousness in thought and deed (Heb. 5:11-14). And this part of the message of "Christ . . . crucified" (1 Cor. 2:2), this **solid food** (3:2), the Corinthians had spurned. As a result they were **still worldly** (v. 3). Instead of mature behavior characterized by humility and concern for others—obedience to God—the Corinthians were infantile, self-centered, and therefore divisive (v. 4; cf. 1:12). They wanted lives of exaltation (4:8) without lives of humiliation (4:9-13) because they did not understand that "Christ . . . crucified" was a message concerned not only with justification but also with sanctification (cf. Phil. 2:1-8). This misunderstanding was at the root of their disunity.(cf. 1 Cor. 1:10; 3:4), which error Paul wanted to correct.

2. A MISUNDERSTANDING OF THE MINISTRY (3:5-4:5)

A second and related cause of division in their church concerned the ministry. The Corinthians had focused on men when in fact God alone was the source of blessing (3:5-9) and ministers were only servants accountable to Him (3:10-17). Since that was so, a minister needed to beware of cultivating the praise of men—as certain leaders in the Corinthian church apparently were doing (3:18-23), and needed instead to seek by faithful service to gain the praise of God (4:1-5).

3:5-9. Apollos and **Paul** were given their ministries by Christ (Eph. 4:11). They were the *means*, not the *cause*, whereby the Corinthians believed (cf. 1 Cor. 2:4-5). God alone produced results. **God made** the seed **grow** (3:6). Therefore God alone should get the credit (v. 7). As servants, Paul and Apollos were not competing against each other but were complementing each other's ministries (v. 8). Their purpose was to bring the church to maturity, to Christlikeness (Eph. 4:12-13). In accord with their faithfulness to that task would come their reward (cf. 1 Cor. 4:2-5). For though a minister served the church he was basically responsible to God. Paul and Apollos were fellow workers who belonged to God and worked for Him in His **field,** the church (3:9).

3:10-17. Paul then shifted metaphors for the church from a field to a **building.** Paul used in various ways the metaphor

of Christians individually and collectively as a building in which God dwells, a **temple.** Jesus had referred to His physical body as a temple (John 2:19-22). In another letter Paul applied the same imagery to Christ's spiritual body, the universal church (Eph. 2:21). Paul also called the body of each individual Christian a temple (1 Cor. 6:19). In this passage, however, it was the local church which he described as a building of God, a temple in which God's Spirit lives (3:16).

Paul now further developed the theme of a minister's accountability for his labor (v. 8). Though it was true that every Christian in the Corinthian church was given at least one gift, or ability to minister in some way to other church members (12:11), it was primarily the leading ministers Paul was concerned about, who functioned in a capacity like that of Apollos and himself (cf. 3:5, 21-22).

3:10. Not every minister, however, labored to the same effect in this building process. Paul had **laid a foundation** in Corinth with the message of the Cross. Apollos too had labored beneficially in Corinth (Acts 18:27-28). Apparently so also had Peter, whom Paul here called "Cephas" (1 Cor. 1:12; 3:22). But as Paul wrote, **someone else** was ministering in Corinth, and Paul's words to him and others like him were a warning.

3:11. Jesus Christ alone was the **foundation,** the basis of salvation (Acts 4:12). But others had come to Corinth and preached a different gospel (2 Cor. 11:4). Perhaps such a one was present in Corinth when Paul wrote this letter.

3:12. In verses 12-17 Paul described three kinds of builders or ministers: the expert (v. 14; cf. v. 10), the unwise (v. 15), and the destructive (v. 17).

The materials used in the building may be interpreted in at least four ways: (a) The **gold, silver, costly stones** refer to the enduring quality of the builder's work; and the **wood, hay, or straw** suggest work that is temporary and valueless. This view is supported by "work" (v. 13) and "what he has built" (v. 14). (b) The three expensive materials suggest sound doctrine which the builder "builds" into people's lives, and the three valueless materials are false doctrines. (c) The first three materials refer to the worker's worthy motives, and the other three point to his unworthy motives (cf. 4:5). (d) The "gold, silver, costly stones" refer to believers who constitute the church (this is supported by similar uses of the metaphor in Eph. 2:22; 2 Tim. 2:20; and 1 Peter 2:5), and the "wood, hay, or straw" represent unregenerate people present in the church (*chorton*, rendered "hay" in 1 Cor. 3:12, is used of unbelievers in James 1:10, where the NIV renders it "wild flower").

3:13. The **day** of judgment is when Christ will judge the quality of His servants' **work** (2 Cor. 5:10). It is not a question of salvation which is a gift (Rom. 6:23), or a matter of individual deeds (Eph. 2:8-9), but of service which is judged on the basis of quality not quantity. Considerable apparent success can be had by dint of human effort and wisdom (cf. 1 Cor. 2:4), but unless it is empowered by God in accordance with His plan it cannot last (Ps. 127:1).

3:14-15. The image of fire associated with the coming of Christ is used elsewhere in the New Testament (2 Thes. 1:7; Rev. 18:8). What the **reward** for the expert builder consists of was not detailed, though praise (1 Cor. 4:5) is certainly a part. The inept builder will see the **loss** of his labor, but **he himself will be saved**, like a burning stick snatched from a fire (Amos 4:11; Jude 23). Before such judgment the various materials may coexist and appear indistinguishable (cf. Matt. 13:30).

3:16-17. However, a local church (**you** here is pl.) might come to the point where its structure is so weak that it collapses entirely or exists in name only, that is, it is destroyed. Paul did not want this to happen in Corinth (2 Cor. 11:3, 13). If it did, the false minister would be paid back in kind by God Himself (an application of the OT *lex talionis* [Gen. 9:6; cf. 2 Cor. 11:15]). The destroyer would be destroyed (Matt. 13:41-42). The words **Don't you know** (1 Cor. 3:16) are the first of 10 occurrences of the clause in this letter (cf. 5:6; 6:2-3, 9, 15-16, 19; 9:13, 24; each time it introduces an indisputable statement).

3:18-23. Since this was so, Paul gave a pointed warning to ministers (vv. 18-20) and to the congregation in Corinth (vv. 21-23). Ministers could avoid self-deception by evaluating their ministries

and realizing that **the wisdom of this world** reflects the mind of Satan (Eph. 2:2) and **is foolishness in God's sight** (1 Cor. 3:19). Paul supported this fact by quoting from Job 5:13 and Psalm 94:11. The members needed to see that the practice of **boasting** (1 Cor. 3:21) **about** ministers was similarly a self-centered spirit. Instead, they should boast in **God** (cf. 1:31) to whom they belonged (3:23; cf. 1:2, 15:28) and who was the source of their every blessing (cf. 1:30).

4:1. It follows then that all who minister for Christ are responsible to Him. The word translated **servants** (*hypēretas*) differs from that used in 3:5 (*diakonoi*) and stresses subordination and responsibility to a superior. The **secret things of God** refers to God's wisdom, the message of the Cross known only by the Spirit's revelation (2:7-10).

4:2. Paul was concerned that he and ministers like him proclaim this message faithfully in the interests of their Master.

4:3-4. He was not deflected from this ministry because the worldly wise rejected it. From a human point of view he was not competent to **judge** even his own motives, much less the quality of his service. How then could others decide these matters?

4:5. Therefore premature judgment, whether it led to the exaltation of some ministers (3:21) or to the humiliation of others (4:10), was wrong. Only at the divine bar would all the facts be known and even there grace will be displayed— **each** faithful minister **will receive . . . praise.**

C. The cure of division (4:6-21)

Paul concluded his address to the problem of division in the church by putting his finger unambiguously on their problem: pride (v. 6). He then suggested a practical cure—imitation of him (v. 16).

4:6. Throughout this discussion Paul avoided singling out guilty persons by name. Instead he applied the problem cases to **Apollos** and himself (and Peter and Christ; cf. 1:12; 3:4-6, 22-33). Now Paul and Apollos would serve as curative examples of men under authority who did **not go beyond what** was **written.** They obeyed the Word of God, not their own inclinations or worldly opinions. From the example of their lives Paul hoped the Corinthians would **learn** the lesson of humility. (The verb "learn" is *mathēte*, and the related noun *mathētēs* is translated "disciple," or "one who practices what he is taught.") This was a difficult lesson, for the Greeks believed humility was a despicable trait of a slave, a sign of weakness, not a characteristic of great men (Plato *Laws* 6. 774c).

4:7. But humility is the only acceptable posture of a person in relation to the God who gives a wide variety of gifts (v. 7a) on the basis of grace (v. 7b) and therefore alone is deserving of praise (v. 7c; cf. 1:4-9). Paul underscored these truths in this series of rhetorical questions.

4:8. The posture of humility should be taken by all Christians. Paul set forth the pattern of Christ's life to the Philippians (Phil. 2:5-11). It was marked first by humiliation and then crowned by exaltation. The Corinthians had apparently dispensed with the first half. They wanted their exaltation immediately—no more sickness, no more suffering, no more pain. This is no more possible today than it was when Paul wrote to these self-deluded Corinthians, but nonetheless many follow in their train.

The Corinthians thought they had all they wanted (1 Cor. 4:8a), but they should have been hungering and thirsting for the practical righteousness they so desperately needed (Matt. 5:6). They thought of themselves as **kings** in need of nothing when in fact they were as needy as the foolish king in the children's tale of the emperor's new clothes, who blithely paraded nakedly before his subjects (cf. Rev. 3:17-18).

4:9-13. Paul was no fool. He did not like suffering. He wished they were right. But they weren't. The apostles followed the path of Christ's humiliation. As He marched a parade route to His death, so did they (cf. 2 Cor. 2:14). As Christ had suffered deprivation and defamation, so did His servants, and in His Spirit they endured and responded with grace (Luke 23:34). The apostles lived out the message of the Cross. But the Corinthians were complacent and secure with their "theology of the palace" (cf. Amos 6:1-7).

4:14-17. Prompted by love, Paul issued a warning. His purpose in writing the biting irony of the preceding verses was **not** simply **to shame** the Corinthians. But if it did not shame them, they were

calloused indeed. His goal was to bring about a change of heart and manner of life in them. His motivation was love like that of a **father** for his **children.** Many ministers might address, advise, and instruct the Corinthians, but only one had planted the seed that brought them life. More than any guardian (Gal. 3:24) Paul had their interests at heart. For that reason he urged them to **imitate** him (1 Cor. 4:16; cf. vv. 9-13). He had one spiritual child who did just that, namely, **Timothy** (Phil. 2:20). Timothy could **remind** them by precept and example of Paul's **way of life in Christ Jesus,** which was in turn an imitation of their Lord.

4:18-21. Paul anticipated that not all would be moved by his appeal. **Some,** probably the unnamed party leaders (v. 5) or guardians (v. 15), were **arrogant,** which was the cause of the Corinthians' division problem. They might not be swayed by exhortation. They required action. And that, Paul knew, he was capable of meting out in the power of the Spirit (Acts 13:9-11). When he had preached to the Corinthians, he had not depended on his own ability but on the **power** of the Spirit (1 Cor. 2:4-5). He would rely on this same power for discipline (2 Cor. 10:4-6). This was the authority of God's rule (cf. Acts 5:3-11). Though Paul loved the Corinthians he knew that a loving father did not shy away from discipline (cf. Heb. 12:7). If it were needed, he would wield **a whip** (*rabdos,* a "rod"). From the Greco-Roman point of view this "rod" was a symbol of discipline executed by one in authority. Paul himself had been punished by rods more than once (Acts 16:22-23; 2 Cor. 11:25). But he preferred a visit characterized by **love and . . . a gentle spirit.**

III. Disorders in the Church (chaps. 5–6)

In the spirit of love but with the need for their discipline in mind, Paul turned in his letter to deal with certain disorders in the church, including their failures to discipline an immoral brother (chap. 5), to resolve personal disputes in a godly manner (6:1-11), and to maintain sexual purity (6:12-20).

A. Failure to discipline a sinner (chap. 5)

Pride is the opposite of love because it produces self-concern, while love responds to the needs of others. Corinthian pride had produced not only disunity but also indifference and an unwillingness to exercise discipline within the church.

5:1. The issue concerned a Corinthian Christian who was carrying on an incestuous affair with his stepmother, a relationship prohibited both in the Old Testament (Lev. 18:8; Deut. 22:22) and in Roman law (Cicero *Cluentes* 6. 15 and Gaius *Institutis* 1. 63). The fact that Paul said nothing about disciplining the woman suggests that she was not a Christian.

5:2. The shameful situation did not seem to faze the Corinthians in the least. If anything, the affair may have even bloated their arrogant spirits. The godly response would have been **grief** for this brother (cf. 12:26; Gal. 6:1-2), leading to discipline which would exclude him from intimacy with the congregation until he would repent (cf. Matt. 18:15-17).

5:3-5. In view of the Corinthian indifference to the matter, Paul was compelled to act. By the authority vested in him as an apostle, he **passed judgment on** the offender which he asked the church to enact at their next meeting. Here was an example of the power he had earlier referred to (4:20-21). What the exercise of this power accomplished is not certain. The translation of the Greek word *sarkos* by **the sinful nature** suggests the idea that the man's fleshly appetites were to be annulled. However, several factors suggest a different discipline, namely corporeal affliction—with *sarkos* understood as "body" (as in the NIV margin). (The result, of course, is the same—the man's purification.) First, the latter is the usual meaning of the term when it is juxtaposed with **spirit**, which signifies the whole man in his inner and external being. Second, the word translated **destroyed** (*olethron*) is a strong term, the noun form of which (*olethreutou*) occurs elsewhere in this letter (10:10) where it is translated "the destroying angel" who killed men. Third, Paul also spoke in this letter about a discipline which leads to death (11:30) with the same end in view—the ultimate preservation of the person (11:32; cf. 1 Tim. 1:20; 1 John 5:16).

So it seems probable that Paul intended this man should be excluded from the fellowship of the congregation, thus physically expressing his exclusion from God's protection which he formerly enjoyed (cf. Job 1:12) and thrusting him out into the arena of the world (1 John 5:19) where Satan would bring about his death. It thus became a painful example of the price of self-centered indifference and a powerful reminder of the demand for holiness in God's temple (1 Cor. 3:17; 6:19).

5:6. There was, of course, no excuse for the Corinthians' pathetic behavior. Paul reminded them of a truth they already knew but were failing to practice—**a little yeast** soon permeates **the whole batch of dough.** A small sickness can eventually kill a body. The need for church discipline is based on the same principle.

5:7-8. As the literal **yeast** was removed from the house during **the Festival** of Unleavened Bread (Ex. 12:15-20; 13:1-10), so that which it illustrated, sin, was to be removed from the house of God, the local church, during its "Festival of Unleavened Bread," a continual observance for a Christian who has found in Christ's death on the cross the once-for-all sacrifice of the **Passover Lamb** (cf. John 1:29; Heb. 10:10, 14). This was nowhere more true than in the celebration which commemorated that sacrificial act, the Lord's Supper, the quintessential act of fellowship for Christians. Probably Paul meant to exclude the unrepentant Christian from this meal in particular.

5:9-10. In an earlier **letter** Paul had given direction on this subject but the Corinthians had applied it only to those outside the church. Paul showed the absurdity of such a view by noting that such compliance would necessitate **leaving this world.** Paul was certainly no advocate of monasticism (or its separatistic kind in Protestantism).

5:11. What he called for was disciplinary action for **anyone** associated with the church, whether **a brother** or one in name only, who took part in the church while continuing a life of sin. The discipline demanded for such a one was exclusion from fellowship with other members. Certainly the prohibition extended to an exclusion from eating the communal meal, the Lord's Supper. Other social contact might also have been excluded. It was unlikely, however, that the sanctioned individual was barred from all congregational meetings, for the church's ministry might lead to his conviction and repentance (14:24-25).

5:12-13. It was not Paul's **business** to judge **those outside the church** (cf., e.g., his silence about the woman in 5:1); still less was it the business of the Corinthians. But discipline *within* the church was their responsibility.

Those in the world **God will judge** (cf. Acts 17:31). But those within the Christian community who continue in sin with an unrepentant spirit, the church should discipline by expulsion.

B. Failure to resolve personal disputes (6:1-11)

The topic of judgment continued as Paul shifted to another disorder afflicting the Corinthian church. The same laxity in dealing with the immoral brother was found in cases of personal disputes between members which the church refused to adjudicate. It was yet another manifestation of the divisive spirit which racked the congregation.

With the introductory phrase "Do you not know," Paul pointed toward certain truths which should have prevented the problem in the first place. The phrase recurs six times in this chapter alone. (Outside this letter this construction appears only three other times in the NT.) Paul had used it before (3:16; 5:6) and would subsequently use it again (9:13, 24) to the same effect. The implication that they should have known these things must have painfully hit home to a church enamored with its own wisdom and knowledge.

6:1. Paul's chagrin about this issue was great, not only because it further divided the church, but also because it hindered the work of God among the non-Christians in Corinth (cf. 10:32). Those related by faith needed to settle their disputes like brothers, not adversaries (cf. Gen. 13:7-9).

6:2. The first of six **do you not know** phrases in this chapter (cf. vv. 3, 9, 15-16, 19) concerned the role of saints in judging (cf. John 5:22; Rev. 3:21). Paul had probably taught this doctrine in Corinth in the course of his founding the church there, since he cited it as an indisputable proposition.

6:3. Since they were going to judge supernatural beings (the fallen **angels,** 2 Peter 2:4; Jude 6), surely they should handle mundane matters satisfactorily.

6:4. The form of the Greek word (*kāthizete,* **appoint**) may be a statement (indicative) or a command (imper.). The NIV has taken it as a command, making the difficult phrase **men of little account** refer to those in the church not too highly esteemed for their "wisdom"; but Paul considered them more than adequate for the task.

"Appoint" may be indicative (and therefore a question; see alternate trans. in marg.) which seems more likely in view of verse 5. If so, the participle translated "men of little account" would be better rendered "men who have no standing" **in the church,** that is, non-Christians. The sad refrain of verse 1 to which Paul would refer yet a third time in verse 6 was thus heard again.

6:5-6. No doubt the statement in verse 5 reddened some of the **wise** Corinthians' faces. Certainly a part of Paul's concern in this issue was the harmful effect such legal wrangling would have on the cause of the gospel in Corinth (9:23). Such lawsuits certainly did not glorify God (10:31-33).

6:7-8. Because their greed dishonored God, Paul concluded that the important issue was lost before the case had begun. He therefore said that mundane loss was preferable to the spiritual loss which the **lawsuits** produced. As it was, the Corinthian lawsuits seemed not to have been so much a matter of redressing wrong or seeing justice served as a means for personal gratification at the expense of fellow believers. This was "body life" at its worst!

6:9-10. Paul's third reminder (**Do you not know . . .** cf. vv. 2-3) was probably meant to complement the thought of verse 4, but it also illustrated the gap which existed between the Corinthians' future position and their present practice. **The wicked** would have no share in God's future **kingdom** because they were not related to Christ, the Heir (cf. Mark 12:7). The wicked would one day be judged by the saints (1 Cor. 6:2) on the basis of their works (Rev. 20:13) which would condemn them. Yet the saints were acting no differently.

The word *adikoi* ("the wicked") in 1 Corinthians 6:9 was used in verse 1, there translated "the ungodly." The verb form *adikeite* ("do wrong") however, was used in verse 8 to describe the Corinthians' behavior. Their future role should have radically affected their practice in the present (cf. 1 John 3:3). If they thought otherwise, Paul warned, they were **deceived** (cf. 1 Cor. 5:11; Rev. 21:7-8; 22:14-15).

The list of offenders was similar to that noted earlier (1 Cor. 5:10-11), which no doubt corresponded to problems in Corinth and in other large cities of the day (cf. Eph. 5:3-6). Homosexuality and male prostitution, for example, were especially characteristic of Greco-Roman society. Plato lauded homosexual love in *The Symposium* (181B). Nero, emperor at the time Paul wrote this letter, was about to marry the boy Sporus (Suetonius *Lives of the Caesars* 6. 28), an incident bizarre only in its formality, since 14 of the first 15 Roman emperors were homosexual or bisexual.

6:11. Some (but not all) the Corinthian Christians had been guilty of the sins listed in verses 9-10, **but** God had intervened. They **were washed . . . by the Spirit** (cf. Titus 3:5), **sanctified** in the Son (cf. 1 Cor. 1:2), and **justified** before God (cf. Rom. 8:33). This fact of justification was an appropriate thought for those judicially carping Corinthians.

C. *Failure to practice sexual purity (6:12-20)*

The theme of legality continued as Paul turned to another problem troubling the Corinthian assembly. This problem was the issue of freedom from the Old Testament Law in the area of sexual relationships. Paul addressed this issue in the manner of a dialogue, the diatribe style, familiar to his readers. This also enabled him to prepare them for both his subject matter and his approach in the rest of the letter, which concerned answers to questions and objections they had raised.

The issue of the limits of liberty (v. 12) was developed later by Paul in chapters 8–10. To a degree this subject also colored the discussion on public worship in chapters 11–14. The question of a Christian's relationship to food (6:13) was taken up in chapter 8. The resurrec-

tion of Christ (6:14) was expounded in chapter 15. The church as the body of Christ (6:15) was enlarged on in chapter 12. The sanctity of sex (6:16), about which Paul quoted Genesis 2:24 on the divine establishment of marriage, occupied his attention in chapter 7.

6:12. The words, **Everything is permissible for me,** had apparently become a slogan to cloak the immorality of some in Corinth. The statement was true but it required qualification. Paul qualified liberty with the principle of love applied to both neighbor and self (cf. Mark 12:31). Liberty which was not **beneficial** but detrimental to someone else was not loving (1 Cor. 8:1; 10:23) and was to be avoided. So too, liberty which became slavery (**I will not be mastered by anything**) was not love but hatred of self.

6:13-14. Food for the stomach and the stomach for food was another slogan by which some Corinthians sought to justify their immorality. They reasoned that "food" was both pleasurable and necessary. When their stomachs signaled hunger, food was taken to satisfy them. So too, they argued, sex was pleasurable and necessary. When their bodies signaled sexual desire, they needed to be satisfied. But Paul drew a sharp line between the stomach and the **body.** The body (*sōma*) in this context (cf. 2 Cor. 12:3) meant more than the physical frame; it referred to the whole person, composed of flesh (the material) and spirit (the immaterial; cf. 2 Cor. 2:13 with 7:5). The "body," therefore, was not perishable but eternal (1 Cor. 6:14), and it was **not meant for sexual immorality** (*porneia*) but for union with the Lord (vv. 15-17), which is reciprocal (cf. Eph. 1:23). The eternality of the body, the future destiny of the individual, was made certain by Christ's resurrection (1 Cor. 6:14; cf. 15:20).

6:15-17. So too the work of the Spirit (cf. 12:13) has affected Christians' present destiny and joined them to Christ (6:15). Could a Christian practice immorality without grieving Christ? (cf. 12:26) **Never!**

The union of two people involves more than physical contact. It is also a union of personalities which, however transient, alters both of them (6:16). Paul quoted Genesis 2:24 (**The two will** become one flesh) not to affirm that a man and a prostitute are married but to indicate the gravity of the sin (cf. Eph. 5:31-32).

A Christian's union with Christ likewise affects both him and the Savior, and one cannot act without affecting the other.

6:18. Corinthian Christians, when faced with immorality, should respond as did Joseph (Gen. 39:12)—they should run. **Flee from sexual immorality.** Immorality was a unique sin but not the most serious (cf. Matt. 12:32). It was, however, an offense against the sinner and those with whom he was related.

It is possible that the statement **All other sins a man commits are outside his body** (the word "other" is a translator's addition and is not represented by any word in the Gr. text) should be taken as a third slogan (cf. 1 Cor. 6:12-13) bandied about by some in Corinth. If so, then Paul's rejoinder (**he who sins sexually sins against his own body**) is a straightforward denial. The Greek construction is similar to that in verse 13.

6:19-20. Among those grieved was the **Holy Spirit** who indwells every Christian (**who is in you;** cf. 12:13; 1 John 3:24). Also God the Father is grieved, for He seeks **honor** (Matt. 5:16), not shame, from those who are **bought at a price** (cf. 1 Cor. 7:23), that price being "the precious blood of Christ" (1 Peter 1:19).

IV. Difficulties in the Church (chaps. 7:1-16:12)

The note on which Paul concluded chapter 6, "honor God with your body," could well serve as the guiding principle for this fourth section in which he answered questions put to him by the Corinthians on the topics of marriage (chap. 7), personal liberty (8:1–11:1), church order (11:2–14:40) and doctrine (chap. 15).

A. Counsel concerning marriage (chap. 7)

1. MARRIAGE AND CELIBACY (7:1-9)

Paul had spoken in chapter 6 on the dangers of sexuality outside of marriage. Then he turned to the duty of sexuality within marriage. Probably abandonment of marital duties on the part of some in Corinth had contributed to the immorality he had just described.

7:1. The phrase **not to marry** may be an overtranslation of the Greek phrase "not to touch a woman." Paul probably intended it as a euphemism for sexual intercourse (cf. Gen. 20:6; Prov. 6:29). This too may have been a slogan for some in Corinth (cf. 1 Cor. 6:12-13) who argued that even those who were married should abstain from sexual intercourse. All that Paul said, however, was that celibacy was a **good** state and not to be depreciated.

7:2. However, marriage with sexual intercourse was much more common. For an individual to try to maintain a celibate state apart from the enablement of God (cf. v. 7) would lead to **immorality.** For that reason Paul encouraged people to marry.

7:3-4. Paul stressed the equality and reciprocity of the husband and wife's sexual relationship by emphasizing the responsibilities of each to satisfy the other.

7:5. Some in Corinth were trying to practice celibacy within marriage. Apparently this refraining from sex within marriage was a unilateral decision of one partner, not a mutually agreed-on decision (vv. 3-4). Such a practice sometimes led to immorality on the part of the other mate (v. 5b; cf. v. 2). Paul commanded that they stop this sort of thing unless three conditions were met: (a) The abstention from sexual intercourse was to be a matter of **mutual consent** on the part of both husband and wife. (b) They were to agree beforehand on a **time** period at the end of which normal intercourse would be resumed. (c) This refraining was to enable them to **devote** themselves **to prayer** in a concentrated way.

7:6. Paul presented this possibility for temporary abstention from sexual intercourse in marriage **as a concession** if the preceding stipulations were met. He did not want his advice construed as a **command.** The suggestion that Paul was referring to marriage itself as a "concession" is unlikely in view of Genesis 1:28, the first command to mankind in the Bible, and in view of Paul's Jewish background where marriage was obligatory for all men except the sexually impotent (Mishnah *Niddah* 5. 9).

7:7. Paul, however, did not want any stigma to be attached to the single state, so he affirmed, as he had done earlier

(v. 1), that celibacy was good. Paul, in fact, thought it to be an excellent state, and wished that everyone could see the benefits of celibacy from his point of view. He realized, however, that marriage or remaining single was more than a matter of weighing alternative benefits; each was a **gift from God**. It is God who enables each Christian to be married or single (cf. Matt. 19:12).

7:8-9. What Paul wrote in verses 1-2 he now pointedly applied to those in Corinth who were sexually experienced (cf. "virgins," v. 25). **The unmarried** included divorced persons of both sexes as well as widowers, with **widows** mentioned separately (cf. vv. 39-40). For these Paul affirmed the suitability of remaining single, if they had the appropriate enablement from God (v. 7). Paul, no armchair theologian, anticipated the practical question of how a person can know whether he or she is able to remain celibate. Paul gave his judgment; if one lacks sexual **control**, he does not have the gift of celibacy, and should **marry**.

2. MARRIAGE AND DIVORCE (7:10-24)

Paul's advice to married Christians is summed up in verse 24 after he addressed, in turn, individual Christians married to one another (vv. 10-11), Christians married to non-Christians (vv. 12-16), and other external physical and vocational states for Christians (vv. 17-23).

7:10-11. Paul's direction to Christians married to one another was like that of Jesus Himself (Mark 10:2-12): as a rule, no divorce (cf. Matt. 5:32). The difference in language between **separate** (*chōristhē-nai*) on the part of the **wife** (1 Cor. 7:10) and **divorce** (*aphienai*) on the part of the **husband** (v. 11) was probably due to stylistic variation as the word translated "separate" (*chōrizō*) was commonly used in the vernacular as a term for divorce (William F. Arndt and F. Wilbur Gingrich, *A Greek-English Lexicon of the New Testament,* 4th ed. Chicago: University of Chicago Press, 1957, p. 899). When problems occurred in a Christian marriage, the resolution was to be sought in reconciliation (cf. Eph. 4:32), not in divorce.

7:12-13. The rest referred to Christians who were married to non-

Christians. Jesus, in the course of His ministry, never had addressed this issue (cf. vv. 10, 25). But Paul, with no less authority (cf. v. 25) did. Some divorces may have been initiated because of the command of Ezra to the Israelites in Jerusalem after the Exile (Ezra 10:11) to divorce themselves from pagan spouses. Paul affirmed that the same principle should operate in a believer-unbeliever marriage as in a marriage of two Christians: as a rule, no divorce. A Christian husband **must not divorce** (*aphietō*) an unbelieving **wife**, and a Christian wife **must not divorce** (*aphietō*) a non-Christian **husband**.

7:14. Divorce was to be avoided because the Christian spouse was a channel of God's grace in the marriage. Within the "one flesh" relationship the blessing of God which came to the Christian affected the family as a whole (cf. Jacob in Laban's household [Gen. 30:27] and Joseph in Potiphar's [Gen. 39:5]; also cf. Rom. 11:16). It is in this sense that **the unbelieving** spouse was **sanctified** and the children were **holy**.

7:15. However, there were exceptions to the rule of no divorce. If **the unbeliever** insisted on a divorce, he was not to be denied (the word trans. **leaves** is *chōrizetai*, the verb used in v. 10). Should this occur, the Christian was **not bound** to maintain the marriage but was free to marry again (cf. v. 39). Paul did not say, as he did in verse 11, that the Christian in this case should "remain unmarried." (However, some Bible students say that not being "bound" means the Christian is not obligated to prevent the divorce, but that it does not give freedom for remarriage.)

The second part of this verse in which Paul affirmed that **God** had **called** Christians **to live in peace** could be understood as a separate sentence. The same conjunction (*de,* **but**) which introduced the exception at the beginning of this verse was repeated by Paul, probably to indicate another shift in thought and a return to the main point in this section, namely, the importance for the Christian spouse of preserving the marriage union and living "in peace" with the non-Christian. (For a similar digression in a discourse on the general rule of no divorce, see Matt. 19:9.) Paul's point was that a Christian should strive to preserve the union and to keep the peace, but with the understanding that marriage is a mutual not a unilateral relationship.

7:16. Paul then stated a second (cf. v. 14) and crucial reason why a Christian should stay married to a non-Christian. God might use the Christian mate as a channel of blessing (cf. v. 14), leading ultimately to the point where the unbelieving spouse would believe the message of the Cross and experience salvation (cf. 1 Peter 3:1-2).

7:17. The general principle which Paul affirmed in dealing with decisions affecting a Christian's marital status was again stated three times (vv. 17, 20, 24; cf. also v. 26): in brief, "stay put." The call to conversion radically altered an individual's spiritual relationship but need effect no changes at all in physical relationships that were not immoral.

7:18-19. The external operation of **circumcision** or the obliteration of the same (cf. [apocryphal] 1 Maccabees 1:15-16) was a matter of little importance compared with **keeping God's commands,** which for Paul meant being controlled by the Spirit (cf. Rom. 2:25-29).

7:20-23. Likewise, a Christian's vocational **situation** is a matter of little consequence (if status can be changed, well and good; if not, it is not a matter for worry). What matters is that every Christian should realize he is **Christ's slave** and needs to render obedience to Him. Every vocation then becomes Christian service performed for the Master (cf. Eph. 6:5-8).

7:24. The fact that **God** had **called** each one to a vocation and sought from each one faithful service in that calling elevated and sanctified both the work and the worker. A Christian could then "live in peace" (v. 15) in his calling and carry it out as one **responsible to God.**

3. MARRIAGE AND MINISTRY (7:25-38)

The basic principle Paul had been setting forth (viz., to continue in one's present position) was then applied to those who had never married. Apparently this was in response to a question put to him. Paul urged them to remain single, for three reasons: (a) an impending time of distress for Christians (vv. 26-28), (b) the imminent return of Christ (vv. 29-31), and (c) the opportunity for undistracted service for Christ (vv. 32-35).

7:25. Virgins here were sexually inexperienced people who had never married. Jesus had never specifically addressed the propriety of marriage per se (cf. Matt. 19:10-12, 29) but Paul gave his **judgment** on the issue which they could take as **trustworthy** counsel. (He of course was writing under the inspiration of the Holy Spirit and hence his "judgment" was as authoritative as Christ's words; cf. 1 Cor. 7:40.)

7:26-28. The present crisis may have referred to persecution then being suffered by the Corinthians (cf. John 16:33; 2 Tim. 3:12; 1 Peter 4:12) or to an experience of suffering which Paul anticipated would shortly befall them (in which case the words could be trans. "impending crisis"). In view of his silence in the letter about any present suffering on their part the latter point of view (and trans.) is preferred. (Cf. 1 Cor. 4:8 which intimates a perceived state of well-being or even positive euphoria.) Still, when persecution came, as Paul felt it surely would, its onslaught could be handled more ably by single than by married persons. However fearsome the thought of martyrdom (cf. 13:3) might be to a single person, it was doubly so to a married person responsible for a spouse and children. With these conditions in view marriage would not be wrong (**if you do marry, you have not sinned**), but it would be inexpedient.

7:29-31. The second reason Paul felt the single state was advantageous was the potential it offered for detachment from temporal situations. The phrase **the time is short** referred to the Lord's return (cf. Rom. 13:11), but it was also a summary philosophy of life for Paul who lived not for the temporary but for the eternal (cf. 2 Cor. 4:18). This detachment from temporal matters should characterize all Christians but it was more complex for the married (cf. Mark 13:12) for whom, nonetheless, devotion to their Lord should occupy first place in life (Luke 14:26). Paul certainly was not recommending abandoning marital duties (cf. 1 Cor. 7:3-5).

Instead he was calling for a commitment to eternal matters and a corresponding detachment from the institutions, values, and substance of **this world** which was **passing away** (v. 31). Such a commitment was more easily made and enacted by a single person.

7:32-35. Paul's third reason was a development of the second. The single state has potentially fewer encumbrances and distractions than the married state, so it more easily facilitates a spirit of **undivided devotion to the Lord.** In the Sermon on the Mount, Jesus warned His followers against letting concern for the material aspects of this life distract them from devotion to God (Matt. 6:25-34). The poor widow (Mark 12:44) gave all her material sustenance to God as an act of singular devotion. A **married** man or woman with a needful concern for the well-being of his family would have been less likely to do that. The situation illustrates Paul's point that the single life with its greater simplicity in obligations allows a potentially greater commitment of time, resources, and self **to the Lord** than would be possible for a married person dutifully carrying out the marital and familial obligations attached to that state.

7:36-38. The interpretation and translation of this passage is difficult, as the alternate marginal translation indicates. The issue revolves around whether the indefinite pronoun **anyone** (v. 36) refers to a father or to a prospective bridegroom. The NIV translators, following most modern commentators, have adopted the latter point of view but have included the traditional interpretation in the margin. The strength of the bridegroom view lies in the fact that it permits a consistent subject for the verbs used throughout the passage, a strength which the NIV translators forfeited by making the **virgin** the subject of the phrase **getting along in years.** This decision was possibly prompted by the need to explain why the bridegroom might be thought to act improperly (i.e., his delay in consummating the marriage may, with her advancing age, adversely affect her chance of ever getting **married**). The bridegroom view, however, faces a lexical difficulty in the meaning of two verbs (*gameō* and *gamizō*) for marriage. In order to sustain the bridegroom view it is necessary to understand the terms as virtual synonyms, meaning "to marry." But *gamizō* usually means "give in marriage," and *gameō* means simply "marry," as these words do in the other

New Testament passages where they occur together (Matt. 24:38; Mark 12:25). This distinction in meaning continued to be recognized even in the second century (Apollonius Dyscolus *Syntax* 3. 153). So it seems that the marginal reading is to be preferred.

Paul, then, gave advice to a father who in the first-century culture exercised great decision-making authority in matters affecting his family. A father may have decided that his daughter should not marry, possibly due to reasons similar to those Paul had mentioned in 1 Corinthians 7:25-34. But in coming to this decision, the father had not reckoned with the fact that his daughter might not be able to remain single. She might not possess the gift of celibacy (v. 7). If so, Paul recommended that the father should not feel obligated to hold to his previous commitment but instead let his daughter marry. However, the father should feel free to follow through on his conviction to keep his daughter single (v. 37) if three conditions were met: (a) He had a **settled** and firm conviction about the propriety of her celibacy. (b) He was in a position where he was free to exercise his authority, that is, he was not a slave in which case the master could determine the daughter's destiny. (c) He was **under no compulsion** from evidence which suggested that his daughter was not able to remain single but required marriage instead. If these conditions were met, then the father did well **not to give her in marriage.**

4. REMARRIAGE AND WIDOWS (7:39-40)

7:39-40. Paul's earlier counsel to widows (vv. 8-9) was to remain single. In that previous context, however, he acknowledged the fact that not all were equipped to do so. The only constraint Paul placed on a widow who sought remarriage was the obligation to marry another Christian (**he must belong to the Lord**)—an obligation which though previously unstated, he no doubt meant to apply to all who sought marriage partners. That point alone, however, affected a widow's options. Within that condition she might choose whom she wanted and find with that husband great happiness, though Paul added that in his **judgment** she would be **happier** if she remained single. This advice was not only from Paul's heart but also guided by the **Spirit of God,** who equipped both single and married Christians (v. 7) for their respective roles.

B. Counsel concerning Christian liberty (chaps. 8–14)

Paul's reply to the Corinthians' question concerning the propriety of eating the meat of an animal offered in a pagan sacrifice touched off an extensive response, probably because he sensed that this particular issue was another manifestation of the Corinthians' self-centeredness, which produced other similar problems in the church.

Two words which seemed to epitomize the Corinthians' point of view were "freedom" (*eleutheros,* 9:1, 19; *eleutheria,* 10:29) and "rights" (*exousia,* 8:9; 9:4-6, 12, 18). Paul used and qualified these words in these chapters by stressing the importance of a love for others which sought their "good" (*sympherō, -os,* 10:24, 33; 12:7; cf. 6:12) by "strengthening" or "building" them up (*oikodomeō, -ia,* 8:1, 10; 10:23; 14:3-5, 12, 17, 26). These two themes, "me first" or "you first," and Paul's development of them as they affected believers in relation to pagan worship and Christian worship, unified these chapters. Secondarily Paul showed that the former attitude ultimately brought God's disapproval (*adokimos,* 9:27) and His discipline (10:5-10; 11:30-32).

1. CHRISTIAN LIBERTY IN RELATION TO PAGAN WORSHIP (8:1-11:1)

Ordinarily the Greeks and Romans burned the less desirable portions of an animal in the course of their sacrifices and retained the choicer parts for personal consumption at banquets celebrating the sacrifices. If a sacrifice were made in connection with a state function, the meat which remained was frequently sold in the marketplace. The Corinthians' questions apparently concerned (a) the acceptability of buying and eating meat from one of these sacrificial animals; (b) the acceptability of eating this meat as an invited guest in a friend's home; (c) the acceptability of attending one of these pagan sacrifices and enjoying the meal of celebration which followed in the temple precincts. Paul spoke to each of these issues.

a. The principle of brotherly love (chap. 8)

Paul struck right to the heart of the matter in these preliminary verses by stating a basic principle: love is superior to knowledge (cf. chap. 13).

8:1. Much as he had begun his reply on marital questions, Paul may have quoted a Corinthian sentiment (**we all possess knowledge**) with which he basically agreed but which required qualification. **Knowledge** was essential in correctly responding to their questions but those who thought they had it did not, as Paul would show.

8:2-3. In the first place, knowledge about God was always partial (13:12). In the second place, true knowledge led to **God** and a love for Him which Paul knew must issue in love for others (cf. 1 John 4:20-21).

8:4. With the principle stated it now remained to be applied to the particular instance in question. The statements which follow the two **thats** (**an idol is nothing at all** and **there is no God but One**) may well have been Corinthian affirmations with which Paul could wholeheartedly agree. An "idol" indeed was "nothing" (Ps. 115:4-8), for there is only one God (Deut. 4:35, 39). Hence **eating food sacrificed to idols** was, in itself, inconsequential.

8:5-6. The pantheon of the Greeks and Romans, not to mention the **gods** and **lords** of the mystery religions, were indeed numerous, but one God alone is real (Deut. 10:17). The **Father** is the source of all (Gen. 1:1) and the One for whom the Corinthians should live (1 Cor. 10:31). The **Lord Jesus Christ** was the agent of Creation (Col. 1:16) and the One **through whom** the Corinthians lived (1 Cor. 12:27; Eph. 1:23).

8:7-8. If all Corinthian Christians could have agreed that an idol was nothing and that there was only one God (v. 4), then they might have eaten the idol meat with impunity. However, such was not the case. All, in fact, did *not* possess knowledge. The **conscience** of some Christians was not strengthened on this point by the truth. They were still ignorant and had not come to the point where they could accept eating this kind of meat as a matter of indifference. For them it was wrong, and so to eat it was sin (cf. Rom. 14:23). Paul denied the validity of their scruples, but in the advice which followed he suggested that the solution would be found in love, not in knowledge.

8:9. When knowledge uninformed by love dictated one's behavior, Paul warned that spiritual harm would result. The **exercise of . . . freedom** by the knowledgeable could in certain circumstances become an obstacle, **a stumbling block** in the **weak** Christian's walk with God (cf. v. 13).

8:10. As an illustration Paul posed a situation in which a **weak** Christian saw a knowledgeable brother enjoying a meal **in an idol's temple** and was by this example encouraged to join in, even though he could not do so with the clear conscience before God that the knowledgeable Christian enjoyed.

8:11. As a consequence the conscience of this **weak** believer was seared (cf. 1 Tim. 4:2), and his capacity to distinguish right from wrong was lost (cf. Titus 1:15) leading to his spiritual ruin and physical death (cf. 1 Cor. 10:9-10; Rom. 14:15). *Apollytai,* rendered **is destroyed,** often refers to physical death (e.g., Matt. 2:13; Acts 5:37). The selflessness of **Christ** was an example for the knowledgeable. If Christ loved **this brother** so that he was willing to give up His exalted rights and even His life (Phil. 2:6, 8), surely the strong could give up his right to eat such meat.

8:12. To be arrogantly indifferent to the need of weaker Christians results in **sin** not only against them (for **you . . . wound their weak conscience;** cf. v. 7) but also **against Christ** of whose body they are members (12:26-27; cf. 1:30; Matt. 25:40, 45). Paul experienced this point acutely on the Damascus Road (Acts 9:4-5).

8:13. In summary Paul stressed the priority of brotherly love. He did not demand that the knowledgeable relinquish their right, but he illustrated how he would apply the principle to himself. Paul did not want any **brother to fall** (cf. v. 9) but to be "built up" (cf. v. 1), and knowledge governed by love accomplished that.

As a final note to this chapter it should be understood that Paul did not say that a knowledgeable Christian must abandon his freedom to the ignorant prejudice of a "spiritual" bigot. The "weak brother" (v. 11) was one who followed the example of another Christian, not one who carped and coerced that knowledgeable Christian into a particular behavioral pattern. Also it was unlikely that Paul saw this weak brother as permanently shackling the freedom of the knowledgeable Christian. The "weak brother" was no omnipresent phantom but an individual who was to be taught so that he too could enjoy his freedom (Gal. 5:1).

b. The regulation of privilege (9:1–10:13)

(1) The positive example of Paul (chap. 9). Paul ended his warning about exercising freedom if it had detrimental effects on a brother with a statement expressing his willingness to be a vegetarian if it would keep a brother from faltering in his faith (8:13). He then illustrated how he practiced what he preached in this matter of rights when applied to food and drink. It seemed that the rumblings of doubt about his apostleship, which would later call forth an extended defense (esp. 2 Cor. 10–13), had already started. Paul neatly illustrated the principle expressed in 1 Corinthians 8 by relating it to the issue which seems to have been a bone of contention concerning his apostleship. That issue was his steadfast refusal to derive material support from those to whom he was ministering, so no one could say he was motivated by money (cf. 2 Cor. 2:17).

9:1-2. Paul affirmed that his position as **an apostle** was like that of the knowledgeable Christian in this matter of freedom and rights. The four questions in these verses were rhetorical and expected an affirmative reply, though some among the Corinthians may have denied one or all of them. The third and fourth questions seem directly related to apostolic authority, but apparently Paul believed that the fourth one was more significant than the third. In the course of an extended defense of his **apostleship** in 2 Corinthians he never mentioned seeing the **Lord** (cf. Acts 1:21) but he returned repeatedly to the theme of this verse (1 Cor. 9:2) that the Corinthians themselves were his vindication (2 Cor. 3:1-3; 5:12; 7:14-16; 8:24).

9:3. Paul's **defense** looked forward (to vv. 4-23) and not back (to vv. 1-2, which guaranteed a right he had willingly forfeited). Paul's defense, then, was an explanation of why he refused to be maintained at the church's expense even though he had a right to such support (vv. 1-2). This served also as a positive example of his counsel to the knowledgeable brother who was concerned about his rights (chap. 8).

9:4-6. The word **right** in these verses is the same word (*exousia*) translated "freedom" in 8:9. It links the chapters, though Paul's subject here was not sacrificial meat but ordinary **food.** To bring out the meaning of these rhetorical questions the phrase "at the expense of the church" could be added to verses 4-5 (cf. Matt. 10:10-11). Paul was not alone in refusing this right but had an ally in **Barnabas.** Commitment to this practice may have marked their first missionary journey together (Acts 13:1–14:28) and apparently continued to characterize their separate ministries.

9:7. Paul saw the right of maintenance as a principle which extended beyond the apostles to others in the church; he illustrated the point along six different lines. The first was custom. The **soldier,** farmer, and shepherd are all supported by their work.

9:8-10. Second, the Old Testament itself substantiated the principle of just remuneration. Paul's illustration and interpretation has perplexed many commentators. Why did Paul, after referring to the practice of not muzzling a grain-treading ox, then ask, **Is it about oxen that God is concerned?** Was he changing the sense of the Old Testament passage? Not among the perplexed was Luther who tried to cut this Gordian knot by observing that since oxen cannot read, Paul's point in the passage was transparent. Problems nonetheless remain for less exuberant interpreters. The solution is probably found in the context of Deuteronomy 25:4 which Paul quoted. That chapter contains instructions not about animal husbandry but human relationships. Not muzzling an ox, therefore, was probably a proverbial expression concerning just remuneration, properly understood and interpreted as such by Paul. A modern parallel would be the adage, "You can't teach an old dog new tricks," which is commonly applied in contexts other than canine obedience.

9:11. Paul's third illustration grew out of verse 10 and his discussion of Deuteronomy 25:4, but it concerned a basic principle of community reciprocity: beneficial service should be rewarded. If Paul had been used to bring **spiritual** riches to the Corinthians (1 Cor. 1:5), **material** recompense was surely not **too** much to expect.

9:12. A fourth line of appeal was made to the precedent of other Christian leaders. Paul had earlier alluded to the ministry of Peter (Cephas) (v. 5). Though unattested, it is probable that Peter ministered in Corinth (cf. 1:12; 3:22; 15:5) and was supported during that time by the church. The same was probably also true of Apollos (1:12; 3:4-6, 22; 4:6; 16:12). If the church supported them, their founding father Paul was surely no less deserving.

Yet Paul did not exercise **this right** (cf. 8:9) because he did not want to **hinder** the response of anyone to **the gospel.** Had he been materially recompensed for his ministry, some might have presumed he was simply another itinerant educator motivated by profits (cf. 2 Cor. 2:17) and would have refused him a hearing. To avoid being a "stumbling block" (1 Cor. 8:9) to any, Paul relinquished his right to receive **support from** those to whom he ministered.

9:13. Paul had temporarily interrupted his catalog of illustrations on the right of recompense to underscore the rationale behind his own refusal to exercise that right, despite its general practice by other worthy servants of Christ (v. 5). He then offered a fifth example in support of the right of remuneration by citing the practice of the priesthood. Old Testament priests were remunerated for their service (Num. 18:8-32), and so were the pagan priests with whom the Corinthians were probably more familiar (cf. 1 Cor. 8:10).

9:14. In the sixth place Paul appealed to the weightiest point of all, the instruction of Jesus that those who give out **the gospel** should derive support from it (Luke 10:7).

9:15. With this catalog of arguments completed Paul had convincingly established his **rights** in relation to the Corinthian church. However, he underscored once again (cf. v. 12) his refusal to exercise those rights. He expressed one reason in verse 12, a desire to avoid any hint of mercenary motivation in his ministry. A second and related reason was now stated: the opportunity to affirm the integrity of his commitment to the ministry (cf. 2 Cor. 11:9-12). This was Paul's **boast:** he ministered willingly and freely from his heart (cf. 2 Cor. 2:17).

9:16. Of course Paul's "call" to the ministry was unique. Others have responded voluntarily to the call to follow Christ (Mark 3:13; John 1:37-39), but Paul was flattened by it (Acts 22:6-10). Like Jonah, Paul was **compelled to preach** (cf. 1 Cor. 1:17), and like that prophet, **woe** to him if he shirked his task.

9:17. The condition, **if I preach voluntarily,** was not true of Paul as he had just said, so he had no claim to any special recompense since he was **simply discharging the trust committed to** him (cf. Luke 17:10).

9:18. Did he then not have any **reward?** Yes; two, in fact. First, he had his boast (v. 15) that he offered the gospel **free of charge,** and no one could deny that (cf. 2 Cor. 11:9-10). Second, he had the opportunity to see the gospel at work among those to whom he preached (1 Cor. 9:19, 23), and these results, the believers themselves, were his reward (cf. 2 Cor. 7:3-4). The word translated "reward" (*misthos*) may also refer to a wage. Paul had shunned material recompense, but he was not without a reward or return for his labor. He had the joy of reaping. To widen that harvest he would gladly give up certain **rights,** among them the right to material support, in order to enjoy both the integrity of his boast about his ministry and the results of his ministry (cf. John 4:36).

9:19. Paul had not shackled the exercise of his rights in the area of food and drink alone (as he had intimated the knowledgeable Christians should do, 8:9-13), but he had applied it to numerous facets of his ministry so that **though** he was **free** (*eleutheros;* cf. 8:9; 9:1) he voluntarily became a **slave** (cf. Phil. 2:6-7) for the good of others (1 Cor. 10:33) whom he wanted **to win** (9:22).

9:20. Though Paul was primarily an apostle to the Gentiles (Gal. 2:8), he never lost his concern for the salvation of his own people (Rom. 9:3). He made it his custom to seek out the synagogue in each town he entered (Acts 17:2) in order **to win the Jews** (Rom. 1:16). No verse points out more starkly Paul's own consciousness of what he was, both before and after meeting Christ. Before, he was the Jew's **Jew,** faultless with regard to legalistic righteousness (Phil. 3:6). Afterward, he was a new man (2 Cor. 5:17; Gal. 2:20), who had found in Christ the righteousness he had sought (Rom. 10:4; 1 Cor. 1:30). He was still a Hebrew (2 Cor. 11:22; Phil 3:5), but he was no longer a Jew living according to the Law (**I . . . am not under the law**). Still, he was willing to subject himself to the scruples of the Jews (e.g., Acts 21:23-36) in order to gain a hearing for the gospel and **to win** them to Christ. Yet he never compromised the essence of the gospel at the heart of which was salvation by faith, not works (Gal. 2:16; Eph. 2:8-9) and freedom from legalism (Gal. 2:4-5).

9:21. In contrast to the Jews, "those under the Law" (v. 20), **those not having the Law** were the Gentiles. Among Gentiles, Paul was willing to abandon past scruples of a morally indifferent sort, such as eating meat offered sacrificially to a pagan god (10:27; cf. Acts 15:29), in order **to win** Gentiles to Christ. But though Paul was a forceful advocate of liberty (Gal. 5:1), he did not suggest he was an advocate of libertinism (cf. 1 Cor. 6:12-20). He was still under authority, but not to the Old Testament Law. He was responsible to God (cf. 3:9) and Christ (cf. 4:1) and was enabled by the Spirit to fulfill the law of love (Rom. 13:8-10; Gal. 5:13-25), the opposite of lawlessness (cf. Matt. 24:12 where lawlessness drives out love). **Christ's law** (Gal. 6:2) was to love God and man (Mark 12:30-31), which law Paul obeyed (1 Cor. 10:31-33).

9:22. In his references to Jews and Gentiles in the preceding verses, Paul explained his voluntary restraint of freedom in order to reach unbelievers with the gospel. Some suggest that **the weak** in this verse refers to Jews and Gentiles together in a state of unbelief and so was intended to summarize Paul's previously stated convictions (cf. Rom. 5:6 where "the weak" are also called "the ungodly"). It is more likely, however, that Paul was referring explicitly to the weak Corinthians described in 1 Corinthians

8:9-11 (cf. Jew, Greeks, and the church of God in 10:32). His concern to win them was not in the preliminary sense of justification as in the case of unbelieving Jews and Gentiles (9:20-21) but to win the Corinthians in terms of sanctification and maturity in Christ (cf. Matt. 18:15)—and so to save them for God's ongoing work in their lives (cf. 1 Cor. 5:5; 8:11). Paul's condescension to the scruples and customs of all men (cf. "everyone" in 9:19) found application on a momentary case-by-case basis since it would be impossible to satisfy simultaneously the penchants of both Jews and Gentiles alike.

9:23. Paul voluntarily did this in order to gain the widest possible hearing for **the gospel** and so to **share in its blessings** as God's fellow worker (3:9), reaping the joyful harvest of many won to Christ (cf. John 4:36).

9:24-25. Paul's commitment to this course of ministry did not come easily. It required personal discipline (**strict training**) like that of an athlete who strove for supremacy in his field (cf. 15:10). To that end Paul willingly gave up certain privileges which might otherwise be his to enjoy so that he could win **the prize.** The prize for Paul was not the temporary **crown** (*stephanon*) bestowed by men (in the biennial games near Corinth the "crown" was a pine wreath) but the eternal **crown** bestowed by Christ (3:13-14; 2 Cor. 5:10). Paul's crown would be the consummation of the reward (1 Cor. 9:18) he partially enjoyed, the opportunity to glory before Christ in those he had been able to win (2 Cor. 1:14; Phil. 2:16; 1 Thes. 2:19).

9:26-27. Paul's dictum of becoming "all things to all men" (v. 22) could have been construed as the aimless capitulation of an unprincipled man. But it was just the opposite! Every move made in the course of his race was calculated to further his pursuit of the prize (cf. Phil. 3:13-14). Every blow struck was meant to land squarely on his opponent and send him reeling from the contest (cf. Eph. 6:12; James 4:7). To achieve this, Paul would not let his body master him (cf. 1 Cor. 6:12); sometimes he denied even its demand for rightful privileges and pleasures (8:9) for a greater good (10:33). Paul was competing well himself and had called many to join him (the word

preached is *kēryxas*, the noun form of which signified a herald who summoned contestants to a race), but that did not guarantee him a victorious finish. He held out the possibility that even he could be **disqualified for the prize.** The single Greek word translated by that phrase (*adokimos*) literally means "unapproved." In other contexts it was applied to the unsaved (e.g., Rom. 1:28; Titus 1:16). Here Paul was not addressing the issue of salvation, nor for that matter was even the prize specifically in mind. Rather, he seemed concerned with continuance in the race. Like the brother who had indulged in immorality (1 Cor. 5:1-5), Paul's life could be cut short by the disciplinary disapproval of God. God had disciplined in the past (10:6-10), was disciplining in the present (11:30-32), and would discipline in the immediate future (5:5). Paul was concerned that some might not be able to say with him one day, "I have fought the good fight, I have finished the race" (2 Tim. 4:7), but would find themselves cut off in the midst of the contest by the disciplinary action of God.

(2) The negative example of Israel (10:1-13). **10:1.** So that the Corinthians might not think God's discipline would be an unlikely eventuality for a people so blessed as they (1:5), Paul cited the illustration of another group of people who were greatly blessed by God but yet experienced His severe discipline. Israel of old was reckless and unrestrained after her physical and spiritual freedom from tyranny in Egypt. As a result God meted out severe discipline by cutting short the lives of many Israelites. They were all in the "race" (9:24), but almost all were disqualified (9:27) in spite of their advantages.

Five advantages were enjoyed by Israel. First, **all** the liberated Israelites enjoyed the supernatural guidance (Ex. 13:21) and protection (Ex. 14:19-20) of the pillar of **cloud** in their Exodus from Egypt. The Corinthians had similarly experienced God's guidance (cf. Luke 1:79) and protection (cf. 1 Peter 1:5). Second, **all** Israelites **passed through the sea** and experienced a miraculous deliverance from those who sought to take their lives (Ex. 14:21-28). So too had the Corinthians experienced a miraculous deliverance—salvation (cf. Heb. 2:14-15; Gal. 1:4).

191

10:2. Third, the Israelites **were all baptized into Moses,** that is, united with their spiritual head, God's servant, who became the object of their trust (Ex. 14:31; cf. John 5:45). The Corinthians had been baptized into the body of Christ (1 Cor. 12:13) of which He is the Head (Eph. 1:22) and in whom they trusted (Matt. 12:21; Eph. 1:12).

10:3. As a fourth privilege, the Israelites **all** enjoyed **spiritual food,** the supernatural bread from heaven (Ex. 16:4, 15). The Corinthians too had eaten bread from heaven (cf. John 6:31-34).

10:4. As a fifth advantage, Paul listed the **spiritual drink** enjoyed by Israel in the desert (Ex. 17:6). According to Paul, **Christ** was the source of this supernatural water. Since the incident of the rock which produced water marked the beginning of Israel's wilderness wanderings (Ex. 17:1-7) and happened again near the ending of their wanderings (Num. 20:1-13), Paul concluded that Christ **accompanied them.** Christ too was the source of supernatural water for the Corinthians (cf. John 4:10-14).

It is possible that these five blessings were intended by Paul to reflect the two ordinances of baptism (1 Cor. 10:1-2) and the Lord's Supper (vv. 3-4) which the Corinthians may have thought communicated a magical protection like similar rites in some of the mystery religions. The Corinthians did seem to have a distorted view and practice of both of these ordinances (cf. 11:17-34; 15:29) which required correction.

10:5. The presence of supernatural privileges in the lives of Old Testament Israelites did not produce automatic success. On the contrary, in spite of their special advantages, **most of them** (in fact, all but two members of one generation, Joshua and Caleb) experienced God's discipline, were disqualified, and died in **the desert** (Num. 14:29). In light of this, Paul's avowed need for personal self-discipline (1 Cor. 9:27) was genuine since even Moses was disqualified for the prize (Num. 20:12).

10:6. Since this was so, the Corinthians' complacency in matters of self-discipline and their corresponding penchant for self-indulgence required immediate remedial action. Christian freedom was not meant to lead to self-indulgence

but to selfless service (cf. Gal. 5:13), as the behavior of past Israelites illustrated.

Paralleling the fivefold blessings enjoyed by Israel in their newfound freedom from Egypt, Paul proceeded to recount a fivefold failure experienced by Israel during this time. He began with the Israelites' craving for the pleasures of Egypt, summarized in their plaintive cry, "Give us meat to eat!" (Num. 11:4-34, esp. v. 13) God gave them what they wanted but while the meat was still between their teeth, He struck them with a plague. The Israelites named the cemetery for those who were killed "Kibroth Hattaavah" ("graves of craving"; Num. 11:34). The application to the Corinthian situation was obvious (cf. 1 Cor. 8:13).

10:7. Second, many in Israel failed by participating in idolatry (Ex. 32:1-6) and paid for it with their lives (Ex. 32:28, 35). Apparently some Corinthians were interested in more than meat in the pagan temples (1 Cor. 8:10; 10:14). For those who thought they as Christians could take part in idolatry with impunity, Paul intended, with illustrations like this, to knock out the false props which supported their behavior (v. 12) before God intervened and took their lives.

10:8. A third failure among the privileged Israelites was in the area of **sexual immorality.** In the Israelites' case the immorality was associated with idolatry (Num. 25:1-2), which also characterized much pagan worship in the first century. But the Corinthians indulged in immorality in contexts other than idolatry, as the instances of rebuke in 1 Corinthians 5:1 and 6:18 illustrate. As God had brought death to the immoral among the Israelites (Num. 25:4-9), He could do in Corinth (e.g., 1 Cor. 5:5), a sobering thought for the libertines who said, "Everything is permissible" (6:12; 10:23).

A possible solution to the apparent discrepancy in the death count found in Numbers 25:9 (24,000) and Paul's figure of **23,000** may reside in the phrase **one day.** Moses and most of Israel were mourning the death of those who had been executed by the judges (Num. 25:5) or killed by an ongoing plague. Meanwhile Phineas was dispatching an Israelite man and Moabite woman in their last act of immorality (Num. 25:6-8), which brought to completion God's discipline of the immoral Israelites and ended the death toll by plague at 24,000, a number probably intended as a summary figure. Another explanation of the 24,000 in Numbers (contra. Paul's 23,000) is that the former included the leaders (cf. Num. 25:4), whereas the latter did not.

10:9. The Israelites' fourth failure was the presuming of some to question the plan and purpose of God on their trek to Canaan. As a result they **were killed by snakes** (Num. 21:4-6). Did the Corinthians think that they knew better than God the path that would bring them to heaven? (cf. 1 Cor. 1:18–3:20)

10:10. Israel's fifth failure, which God disciplined with death, occurred when they spoke rebelliously against God's appointed leaders, Moses and Aaron (Num. 16:41-49). Was Paul facing a similar situation as an outgrowth of the Corinthians' party spirit? (cf. 1 Cor. 1:11; 4:18-19) It is possible that each of these failures found expression in the Corinthian issue of eating food sacrificed to idols.

10:11. God's dealings with Israel were more than a matter of historical curiosity for Paul. They were **examples** (cf. v. 6) and **warnings** for the Corinthians that the God with whom they had to deal, who was bringing His interaction with people to a close in this **fulfillment of the ages,** was the same God who disciplined the Israelites with death and would do so again (cf. 11:30).

10:12. If the Corinthians believed their **standing** in Christ and corresponding freedom could be exercised in sin with impunity, they were wrong, possibly dead wrong.

10:13. After kicking out the props of false security, Paul pointed toward the One on whom the Corinthians could rely. The temptations that **seized** the Corinthians were like those people had always faced. They could be met and endured by depending on **God,** who is **faithful.** Part of the Corinthian problem, of course, was that some in the face of temptation were not looking for **a way out** by endurance, but a way in for indulgence.

c. The application to idolatry (10:14-11:1)

10:14-15. The **therefore** (*dioper*) introduced Paul's application of Christian freedom to eating food sacrificed to idols. He gave advice in three areas: (a) meat in the pagan temple (vv. 14-22; cf. 8:10); (b) meat in the marketplace (10:25-26); (c) meat in the home (vv. 27-30). His advice on the first count was uncomplicated— **flee from idolatry** (cf. 6:18, "flee from sexual immorality"). He believed that the rhetorical questions which followed would lead **sensible people** like the Corinthians (cf. 4:10) to agree.

10:16-17. Paul's point in these verses about the Lord's Supper was like that made earlier (5:6-8). The collective worship of Christians at the Lord's Supper expressed the unity among the members and their **participation** (*koinō- nia,* "fellowship") **in the blood of Christ** and **in the body of Christ.** The **one loaf** of bread, of which **all partake,** pictured their unity as members of the **one body** of Christ.

10:18. Likewise in the worship of **Israel,** the participants identified with what was sacrificed and with each other.

10:19-21. The same was true of pagan worship. It was true that **an idol** was nothing (8:4; cf. Ps. 115:4-7), but the ultimate reality behind pagan religion was demonic. Pagan **sacrifices** were **offered to demons, not to God.** Through his minions "the god of this age" blinded unbelievers and kept them from the truth (2 Cor. 4:4). There could be no union for good between Christ and Belial (2 Cor. 6:15). So those who were the temple of God (1 Cor. 3:16; 6:19) should shun the temple of idols (cf. 2 Cor. 6:14-18). No magical contamination was conveyed, but the corrupt character of the participants would be harmful for believers (1 Cor. 15:33). Being **participants with demons** was unthinkable for those who are participants with Christ (10:21; cf. v. 16).

10:22. Most importantly such behavior displeased God (cf. Deut. 32:21). Did the "strong" Corinthians (1 Cor. 8:7-10) require the same discipline as Israel? (10:7; Ex. 32:28, 35)

10:23-24. The principle of freedom (**everything is permissible;** cf. 6:12) was to be regulated by love for others. Activities that are not **beneficial** or **constructive** or that do not promote **the good of others** (cf. 10:33) should be avoided.

10:25-26. For a Christian who bought meat at a market with the intent of eating it at home, Paul recommended that selections be made without reservation. No one could contaminate what God had made clean (cf. Acts 10:15) since **everything** belongs to Him (Ps. 24:1).

10:27-30. For a Christian who accepted an invitation to another's home Paul recommended eating from all the fare without scrupulous reservation. But if another Christian guest piped up (cf. 8:7-13) that the food had been part of a pagan **sacrifice,** the knowledgeable Christian should defer to the uninformed scruples of the weaker brother. To exercise his rightful freedom to eat might cause the brother with the scrupulous **conscience** to follow that example and cause him to sin (cf. Rom. 14:14-23).

A knowledgeable Christian did not need to alter his convictions to accord with the conscience of a weaker brother (1 Cor. 10:29b), but he did need to alter his behavior when in the weaker brother's presence. Otherwise the weak brother might act against his conscience and harm himself (cf. 8:11), which would bring denunciation on the strong brother. What the knowledgeable Christian could enjoy privately **with thankfulness** became in the presence of the weaker brother a contemptible act eliciting condemnation (**why am I denounced** [*blasphēmoumai*] **because of something I thank God for?** cf. 8:12; Rom. 14:16, 22). An echo of 1 Corinthians 8:13 concluded the matter.

10:31-11:1. The principle which summarized Paul's response to the question of eating food offered as a pagan sacrifice was an application of the command to love God and neighbors. Christian behavior should be **for the glory of God.** Also it should build up the church of God by leading some to new birth (v. 33b) and others to maturity in the process of salvation (justification, sanctification, glorification; cf. 1:30). Christians should avoid behavior that would cause others—whether Jews (cf. 9:20), **Greeks** (cf. 9:21), **or the church of God . . . to stumble** (lit., "fall"; cf. 10:12). (Interestingly this reference to Jews separate from the church shows that the NT church did not replace the Jewish nation. This argues strongly for premillennialism.)

The One who perfectly exemplified love for God and others was Christ (cf. Rom. 15:3; Phil. 2:5-8). Displaying the same spirit in his ministry, Paul urged the Corinthians to **follow** his **example** in this matter of food from a pagan sacrifice. They should allow their freedom to be regulated by love.

2. CHRISTIAN LIBERTY IN RELATION TO CHRISTIAN WORSHIP (11:2–14:40)

The theme of personal freedom exercised without regard for the needs of others or the glory of God (which characterized the issue about eating food sacrificed to idols [8:1–11:1]) seems no less a part of this section which deals with practices affecting the assembly of the church. Here too Paul responded to the Corinthians' spirit of self-indulgence by stressing the principle of glorifying God and building up each other in the church.

a. The state of women in worship (11:2-16)

Paul began (11:2-16) and ended (14:34-35) his discussion of Christian freedom as it pertained to worship with remarks directed primarily at the behavior of women in the Corinthian church. Some have questioned whether his comments in this section refer to the actual meeting of the church or to extrachurch occasions in which a woman might pray or prophesy. The fact that Paul appealed to church practice elsewhere as a feature of his argument in this section (11:16) suggests that he was discussing church meetings. Modern distinctions between meetings of the church for worship and other meetings of Christians seem based more on expediency than biblical evidence.

11:2. The Corinthians had expressed to Paul, either in their letter or via their spokesmen (cf. 1:11; 16:17), that they remained devoted to Paul and to the **teachings,** the central doctrines of the faith, which he had communicated to them (cf. 11:23; 15:1, 3). For this Paul commended them: **I praise you.**

11:3. Paul no doubt appreciated the Corinthians' goodwill toward him. But more importantly, he wanted to see behavior in keeping with a Christian's calling. As a prelude to his exhortation, Paul characteristically laid down a theological basis. In this instance it concerned headship. The word **head** (*kephalē*) seems to express two things:

subordination and origination. The former reflects the more usual Old Testament usage (e.g., Jud. 10:18), the latter that of Greek vernacular (e.g., Herodotus *History* 4. 91). The former is primary in this passage, but the latter may also be found (1 Cor. 11:8). The subordination of Christ to God is noted elsewhere in the letter (3:23; 15:28). His subordination to the Father is also true in His work as the "agent" of Creation (8:6; cf. Col. 1:15-20).

11:4. When a man prayed aloud publicly or exercised the gift of **prophecy** by declaring a revelation from God (cf. 12:10), he was to have his physical **head** uncovered so that he would not dishonor himself and his spiritual **head**, Christ (v. 3).

The alternate translation in the NIV margin, which interprets the man's covering as long hair, is largely based on the view that verse 15 equated the covering with long hair. It is unlikely, however, that this was the point of verse 4 (cf. comments on v. 15).

11:5-6. It cannot be unequivocally asserted but the preponderance of evidence points toward the public head covering of women as a universal custom in the first century in both Jewish culture ([apocryphal] 3 Maccabees 4:6; Mishnah, *Ketuboth* 7. 6; Babylonian Talmud, *Ketuboth* 72a-b) and Greco-Roman culture (Plutarch *Moralia* 3. 232c; 4. 267b; Apuleius *The Golden Ass* 11. 10). The nature of the covering varied considerably (Ovid *The Art of Love* 3:135-65), but it was commonly a portion of the outer garment drawn up over the head like a hood.

It seems that the Corinthian slogan, "everything is permissible," had been applied to meetings of the church as well, and the Corinthian women had expressed that principle by throwing off their distinguishing dress. More importantly they seem to have rejected the concept of subordination within the church (and perhaps in society) and with it any cultural symbol (e.g., a head-covering) which might have been attached to it. According to Paul, for a woman to throw off the covering was an act not of liberation but of degradation. She might as well shave **her head,** a sign of disgrace (Aristophanes *Thesmophoriazysae* 837). In

doing so, she **dishonors** herself and **her** spiritual **head,** the man.

11:7-9. The **man,** on the other hand, was not to have **his head** covered because he was **the image and glory of God.** Paul based this conclusion on Genesis 1:26-27. A woman's (a wife's) **glory** and image was derived from (1 Cor. 11:8) and complementary to (v. 9) that of the man (her husband). Man, then, was God's authoritative representative who found in woman a divinely made ally in fulfilling this role (Gen. 2:18-24). In this sense she as a wife is **the glory of man,** her husband. If a married woman abandoned this complementary role, she also abandoned her glory, and for Paul an uncovered woman's head gave symbolic expression to that spirit.

11:10. Paul offered a third reason (the first reason was the divine order— God, Christ, man, woman, vv. 3-6; the second reason was Creation, vv. 7-9) why womanly insubordination in the church should not exist. **Angels** were spectators of the church (4:9; Eph. 3:10; 1 Tim. 5:21; cf. Ps. 103:20-21). For a woman to exercise her freedom to participate in the church without the head covering, the **sign of** her **authority** (*exousia;* a liberating term; cf. 1 Cor. 7:37; 8:9; 9:4-6, 12, 18), would be to bring the wisdom of God (Eph. 3:10) into disrepute.

Other (but less acceptable) explanations have been suggested for the words **because of the** "angels": (a) evil angels lusted after the women in the Corinthian congregation; (b) angels are messengers, that is, pastors; (c) good angels learn from women; (d) good angels are an example of subordination; (e) good angels would be tempted by a woman's insubordination.

11:11-12. Men and women together in mutual interdependence, complementing each other, bring glory to God (cf. 10:31). Neither should be **independent** or think themselves superior to the other. Woman's subordination does not mean inferiority. Man is not superior in being to woman. Eve came from Adam, and each man born in the world comes from a woman's womb (11:12). **God** created them both for each other (Gen. 1:27; 2:18).

11:13-15. Paul had based his previous reasoning for maintaining the **head**

covering as a woman's expression of her subordination on arguments rooted in special revelation. Now he turned to natural revelation (cf. Rom. 1:20) for a fourth argument in support of his recommendation. Mankind instinctively distinguished between the sexes in various ways, one of which was length of hair. Exceptions to this general practice were due either to necessity (e.g., Apuleius *The Golden Ass* 7. 6, "to escape in disguise") or perversity (Diogenes *Laertius, Lives* 6. 65). No abstract length of hair was in mind so much as male and female differentiation. The Spartans, for example, favored shoulder-length hair for men (cf. Lucian *The Runaways* 27) which they tied up for battle (Herodotus *History* 7. 208-9), and no one thought them effeminate.

Long hair was a woman's **glory** because it gave visible expression to the differentiation of the sexes. This was Paul's point in noting that long hair was given **to her as a covering.** Natural revelation confirmed the propriety of women wearing the physical covering (cf. Cicero *On Duties* 1. 28. 100). She has a natural covering, and should follow the custom of wearing a physical covering in a public meeting.

Some Bible students, however, say that the Greek *anti*, rendered "as" (i.e., "for" or "in anticipation of") should be translated in its more normal sense of "instead of." According to that view, a woman's hair was given instead of a physical covering, for it in itself *is* a covering. In this view women should pray with long hair, not short hair. This view, however, does not explain the woman's act of covering or uncovering her head, mentioned in 1 Corinthians 11:5-6.

11:16. Paul's fifth argument for maintaining the status quo on head-coverings came from universal church **practice.** Paul was not trying to foist a new behavioral pattern on the Corinthians but simply to hold the line against self-indulgent individual excess in the name of freedom. As in the case of food offered to idols (8:1–11:1), Paul dealt with the immediate issue but also put his finger on the root of the problem, the Corinthian pursuit of self-interest which was unwilling to subordinate itself to the needs of others (cf. 10:24) or the glory of God (10:31). Throwing off the head

covering was an act of insubordination which discredited God.

Whether women today in church services should wear hats depends on whether the custom of head coverings in the first century is to be understood as a practice also intended for the present day. Many Bible students see that for today the principle of subordination (not the command to wear hats) is the key point in this passage. The intent of the custom of women wearing hats today, for fashion, seems far different from the purpose of the custom in the first century.

b. The state of Christians at the Lord's Supper (11:17-34)

At Jesus' institution of the Lord's Supper with His disciples (Matt. 26:26-29; Mark 14:22-25; Luke 22:15-20) the bread and cup were part of a meal, with the bread probably broken near the beginning (cf. "when He had given thanks," 1 Cor. 11:24) and the cup taken at the end (cf. "after supper," v. 25). By the time Paul wrote, the Lord's Supper was celebrated in two stages which consolidated the partaking of the bread and cup at the end of a communal meal. The worship with the bread and cup came to be called the "Eucharist" (*Didache* 9:1; Ignatius *Letter to the Philadelphians* 4), from the Greek word for "thanksgiving" (*eucharisteō*). The communal meal was called the *Agapē* (Jude 12; Pliny *Letters* 10. 96. 7), a Greek word for "love."

What bothered Paul about the Corinthian celebration was that the *Agapē* meal had become an occasion not marked by love for fellow Christians but one of self-centered indulgence. In the subsequent development of the church the celebrations came to be divided (Ignatius *Letter to the Smyrneans* 8; 1-2; and [apocryphal] Acts of John 84), possibly on the mistaken assumption that Paul had advised the Corinthians to do that (cf. 1 Cor. 11:22, 34).

11:17. As in the preceding discussion on womanly excesses in worship, Paul had no commendation (but cf. v. 2) for the Corinthians when it came to their practice of the Lord's Supper. In fact an experience meant to build up the church was actually having the opposite effect: **your meetings do more harm than good.**

11:18-19. The church was divided at a celebration which was meant to express unity (cf. 10:17). If these **divisions** (*schismata*; 1:10; 12:25) were related to those noted earlier (1:10–4:21), then one factor contributing to those divisions is evident here, namely, economic differences in the church (11:21).

Paul did not want to believe the report about their divisions (v. 18b), but he knew that sin was inevitable (cf. Luke 17:1) and would not pass unnoticed by God. **God's approval** (*dokimoi*) resumed a point Paul had discussed earlier (1 Cor. 9:27–10:10), where he used in 9:27 the contrasting word "disqualified" (*adokimos*).

In the whole nation of Israel, freed from bondage in Egypt and bound for the Promised Land of Canaan, only two of that vast company gained God's approval and entered the land (cf. 10:5). Many in the Corinthian assembly did not have this approval, which His discipline on them demonstrated (cf. 11:30-32). If the Corinthians thought the ordinances of the Lord's Supper and baptism somehow communicated magical protection to the participants (cf. 10:12; 15:24), Paul's excoriation must have been doubly painful since their behavior at this rite was directly linked to their chastisement (11:30-32)—the very thing they sought to avoid.

11:20-21. The Lord's Supper should have been the remembrance of a preeminently selfless act, Christ's death on behalf of others. Instead the Corinthians had turned the memorial of selflessness into an experience of selfishness and had made a rite of unity a riotous disunity. While **one** brother went **hungry** because he lacked the means to eat well, **another** brother drank to excess.

11:22. If the Corinthians wanted private parties they could have them in their **homes.** The meeting of the church was no place for a sectarian spirit of any sort, especially since the Lord's Supper was intended to commemorate just the opposite spirit. To act in a spirit of selfish disregard for the needs of a brother was to **despise the church of God,** composed not of lifeless stones but of living people who could be grievously hurt. Did the Corinthians somehow think their libertarian acts were a matter for **praise?** (cf. 5:1-2) Just the opposite!

11:23-24. Paul proceeded to remind the Corinthians of what they knew but had denied by their actions. Whether this teaching came to Paul directly (by a vision; cf. Gal. 1:12) or indirectly (by men; 1 Cor. 15:1), it came with the Lord's authority. The bread represented the incarnate body of Christ unselfishly assumed (Phil. 2:6-7) and unselfishly given on the cross for the benefit of others (2 Cor. 8:9; Phil. 2:8), that kept needing to be remembered (cf. 1 Cor. 4:8-13).

11:25. The wine was a poignant reminder of Christ's **blood,** without the shedding of which there could be no forgiveness from sin (Heb. 9:22) and through which cleansing and a **new** relationship (**covenant**) with God was made (Heb. 9:14-15). The word "covenant" referred to a relationship in which one party established terms which the other party accepted or rejected. The focus of the Old Covenant was the written Word (Ex. 24:1-8). The focus of the New Covenant is the Living Word (John 1:14-18). Christ intended the **cup** to be a representational (cf. John 10:9; 1 Cor. 10:4) reminder of Him: **do this . . . in remembrance of Me.**

11:26. The Lord's Supper was a visible sermon that proclaimed "the message of the Cross" (1:18, 23; 2:2, 8), that is, the reality of **the Lord's death,** and also the certainty of His return (**until He comes**) (cf. John 14:1-4). Though there apparently was no prescribed schedule for the observance of the Lord's Supper (cf. Ignatius *Letter to the Ephesians* 13:1), **whenever** it was celebrated its message of humiliation and subsequent exaltation (Phil. 2:6-11) went forth. This was a needed reminder to all saints, especially those in Corinth (cf. 1 Cor. 4:8-13).

11:27-29. The Corinthians' despicable behavior at the communal meal was not without result, which Paul proceeded to point out. Nowadays when this passage is read before participation in the Lord's Supper, it is usually intended to produce soul-searching introspection and silent confession to Christ so that no one will sin against the spiritual presence of the Lord by irreverent observance. Paul's application was probably more concrete. No doubt his experience on the Damascus Road (Acts 9:4-5) contributed to this, for the body of Christ is the church, which consists of individual believers (cf.

1 CORINTHIANS

1 Cor. 12:12, 27). His body, the church, is also pictured by the bread of Communion (5:7; 10:16-17). Thus to sin against another believer is to sin against Christ (8:12). Those **guilty of sinning against the body and blood of the Lord** were those who despised a poorer member by utter disregard for his need (11:21-22). These came to the remembrance of Christ's work of unity and reconciliation (cf. Eph. 2:15-16) with a trail of deeds that had produced disunity and alienation! If these would **examine** (*dokimazetō,* "test to approve," 1 Cor. 11:28) themselves, they would see that they lacked God's approval (*dokimoi,* v. 19) in this behavior. They should seek out the wronged brother and ask his forgiveness. Only then could a true spirit of worship flourish (cf. Matt. 5:23-24 and *Didache* 14. 1-3). Coming to the Lord's Supper without that sin confessed brought **judgment** on the guilty participants. Only by recognizing (*diakrinōn,* "properly judging") the unity of **the body of the Lord**—and acting accordingly—could they avoid bringing "judgment" (*krima*) on themselves.

11:30-32. What that **judgment** entailed was then explained by Paul. In brief, it was sickness and death (cf. 10:1-11). The solution was self-examination (*diekrinomen,* 11:31; cf. vv. 28-29; 5:1-5; 10:12), self-discipline (9:27), and promoting of unity. The alternative was God's judging (*krinomenoi,* 11:32), which was a discipline that they were then experiencing. This was not a loss of salvation, but of life (cf. 5:5).

11:33-34. If the believers were self-disciplined, they should **wait** in the *Agapē* meal till all arrived. This also may have implied sharing the meal with others (cf. v. 22). If the demands of hunger were too great for some, they should satisfy those pangs **at home** before coming to the assembly. The Lord's Supper was a time not for self-indulgence but for mutual edification (v. 26). If the former prevailed, God would continue to discipline severely. Other matters—apparently less serious aberrations related to the Lord's Supper—Paul would attend to when he returned to Corinth (16:5-9).

c. The state of spiritual gifts (chaps. 12-14)

Related to the subject of irregularities in the worship of the Corinthian church, was a question on the nature of spiritual gifts and their exercise in the public assembly. This subject should also be considered under the broader rubric of Christian freedom which Paul had been qualifying and regulating by the principle of love (starting with 8:1). The need for such regulation was certainly evident. A self-indulgent spirit, which debauched the principle of freedom in other areas, found similar expression in the area of spiritual gifts, and produced selfishness and disunity (12:7, 25; 14:4) and apparent chaos in the assembly (14:23, 33, 40).

Paul dealt with the problem by describing the nature and purpose of gifts (12:1-30), the superiority of love (12:31-13:13), and the regulating of the exercise of gifts by love (chap. 14). As in other areas, so in using gifts in the church, believers should promote the glory of God and the good of others instead of self-satisfaction.

(1) Unity and diversity of gifts (12:1-31a). **12:1-3.** Before Paul began his discussion of **spiritual gifts** he thought it necessary to confront, at the outset, any in the Corinthian assembly who might contradict his message (cf. 14:37). It is probably in this regard that 12:3 is to be understood. Many explanations of the verse have been offered (though most commentators "handle" the problem by ignoring it).

Paul apparently believed that some of the Corinthians' problems were due not entirely to their worldly attitudes (3:3) but also to the presence of false teachers who preyed on their spiritual immaturity and exacerbated the problems. The pagan background out of which many had come (and some were still coming; cf. 8:10; 10:14, 20-21) did not help them ascertain the presence of false prophets. When they **were pagans,** they had been **influenced and led astray to dumb idols** (12:2). Certainly lifeless idols are totally helpless in such matters! (In the Corinthians' vaunted wisdom they showed themselves to be unusually gullible [cf. 2 Cor. 11:1-21, esp. 19-20].)

Paul therefore laid down a simple test related to the person of Christ. The false teachers obviously claimed that their visions, revelations, and messages (cf. 2 Cor. 12:1) were from God, but they apparently denied the humanity of Christ, as expressed by the words **Jesus be**

198

cursed. This may have been a factor in the Corinthians' aversion to Paul's "message of the Cross" (1 Cor. 1:10–4:13). It may be surprising today to realize that the earliest Christological heresy (Docetism) denied Jesus' humanity, not His deity. John had to deal with the same problem years later (1 John 4:1-3).

Also Jesus who had suffered was now the Jesus who reigns as Lord, whom Paul represented (1 Cor. 1:1) and who was to be obeyed. Only believers, speaking by the Holy Spirit, acknowledge that Jesus is Lord. Nonbelievers—including false teachers—deny His sovereign lordship. Thus anyone who tries to controvert Jesus' authority and His Word will suffer the consequences (14:38; 16:22).

12:4-6. Paul had referred to God, Jesus, and the Holy Spirit in verse 3. Now in reverse order he stressed the unity of the Godhead in relation to the different spiritual gifts. The Holy Spirit gives a diversity of gifts (cf. "Spirit" in vv. 7-9, 11) so that individuals can serve the Lord and His body, the church, in various ways (cf. vv. 7, 27), all empowered by God and exercised under His aegis (cf. vv. 18, 24). Though there are different kinds (dia-ireseis) of gifts . . . service, and working, the same Spirit . . . the same Lord (Christ), and the same God are involved in all of them.

12:7-10. The gifts had a unity in source (vv. 4-6), and they also had a unity in purpose. They were given, not for personal enrichment (cf. 14:4; 1 Peter 4:10), but for the common good of the body of Christ, the building up of others (1 Cor. 10:24; 14:12). Paul listed some of the gifts here. Others, along with some of these, are given in Romans 12:6-8; 1 Corinthians 12:28-31; Ephesians 4:11; 1 Peter 4:10-11.

The list here includes nine gifts. (1) Wisdom refers to insight into doctrinal truth. Paul exercised and expressed this gift in this letter (e.g., 2:6). (2) Knowledge refers to the ability to apply doctrinal truth to life. Paul also exercised and expressed this gift in this letter (e.g., 12:1-3; 11:3). (Cf. the recurrence of the phrase "Do you not know" in 3:16; 5:6; 6:2-3, 9, 15-16, 19; 9:13, 24; also cf. 8:1-3, 10-11.) (3) Faith as a spiritual gift is probably an unusual measure of trust in God beyond that exercised by most

Christians (e.g., 13:2). (4) Healing is the ability to restore health (e.g., Acts 3:7; 19:12) and also to hold off death itself temporarily (Acts 9:40; 20:9-10). (5) Miraculous powers may refer to exorcising demons (Acts 19:12) or inducing physical disability (Acts 13:11) or even death (Acts 5:5, 9). (6) Prophecy is the ability, like that of the Old Testament prophets, to declare a message of God for His people (1 Cor. 14:3). (7) Ability to distinguish between spirits is the gift to differentiate the Word of God proclaimed by a true prophet from that of a satanic deceiver (cf. 2 Cor. 11:14-15; 1 John 4:1). If the Corinthians possessed this gift (cf. 1 Cor. 1:7), it was not being put to good use (cf. 12:1-3). (8) Tongues refers to the ability to speak an unlearned, living language (e.g., Acts 2:11). (9) Interpretation was the ability to translate an unlearned, known language expressed in the assembly (1 Cor. 14:27).

With the possible exception of faith, all these gifts seem to have been confirmatory and foundational gifts for the establishment of the church (cf. Heb. 2:4; Eph. 2:20) and were therefore temporary.

12:11. The gifts were not meant to be selected by individuals or personally solicited by them, but were instead given by the . . . Spirit . . . as He determined. "The Spirit" is referred to six times in verses 7-11.

12:12. This verse forms an excellent three-part summary of the rest of the chapter. (a) The human body is a unit (cf. v. 13 on the unity of the body of Christ). (b) The human body has many parts, with a necessary diversity in its members (cf. vv. 14-20). (c) The parts of the human body work together as one, with a dependent mutuality as each part fulfills an important function (cf. vv. 21-26). Likewise the body of Christ has a diversity of parts functioning together (vv. 27-30).

12:13. The One who gave the diverse gifts, the Spirit, was also the medium in which, by which, and with which (possible translations of the Gr. preposition en; cf. Matt. 3:11) that unity exists. The baptism of the Spirit is experienced by all who believe, at the moment of salvation (cf. Rom. 8:9). In that baptism, believers, regardless of nationality (whether Jews or Greeks) or station of life (**slave or free**), are identified with Christ (**baptized . . . into one body**) and are indwelt by the Spirit (**given the one Spirit to drink;** cf. John 4:14; 7:38-39).

12:14-20. Different parts are needed if a body is to exist (v. 19). So too, no believer should think of himself or his gift as inferior and so desire another member's gift. The gifts were not haphazardly distributed (cf. v. 11) but carefully **arranged** according to the perfect will of God (v. 18).

12:21-26. In the diversity of the bodily parts there was a corresponding mutual dependence. A person with a seemingly greater gift should not imagine that he could function alone since a bodily member cut off from the natural body would cease to exist. More importantly, one thought to possess a lesser gift should in fact be accorded greater attention by the other members of the body (cf. 14:1-5) just as in the natural body special deference in attention to dress is paid to those parts of the body deemed less presentable (12:22-24). Possibly Paul was reaching back in thought beyond the immediate discussion of gifts when he referred to **weaker** members (v. 22; cf. 8:7-13) and **less honorable** ones (12:23; cf. 11:22) who also required special care and consideration. This too was part of God's plan (**God . . . combined the members**), that members of the spiritual body would demonstrate a mutual concern for the well-being of others (12:25b-26; 10:24, 33) so that rivalry would cease (**so that there should be no division in the body;** 1:10; 11:18) and genuine unity would exist (12:26).

12:27-31a. The unifying member in the spiritual **body is Christ.** As the Head (Eph. 1:22; cf. 1 Cor. 11:3) He possesses the body and sovereignly expresses His will. His command is that love should prevail among the members (John 15:12). This was the force which would maintain unity within the diversity and to this subject Paul would shortly move (1 Cor. 12:31b-13:13).

For a third time (cf. 12:18, 24, 28), however, Paul stressed the fact that God, not man, assigned the gifts. As he discussed another sample of gifts (some repeated from vv. 7-10 and some new), it was the members, the people so gifted, to

whom he referred. Since the gifts included in the two lists in this chapter contain novelty and redundancy (which is the case elsewhere in passages detailing gifts, e.g., Rom. 12:6-8; Eph. 4:11; 1 Peter 4:10-11—the gift of teaching being the only gift which appears in each list), probably no complete catalog existed.

The fact that Paul assigned ordinal numbers (**first . . . second . . . third**) to the first three gifts suggests that these may have been relegated to a lesser role by the Corinthians (cf. 1 Cor. 12:21-24). Those three kinds of gifted members—**apostles . . . prophets . . . teachers**—probably were rated lower than those who had the more spectacular gift of tongues. But the first three gifts may have been **greater** (v. 31) because of their extensive value to the whole body of Christ. This may be why he listed them first and then said that the church should **eagerly desire** (v. 31) the exercise of those **gifts** in the assembly (cf. 14:1-5). Gifted apostles, prophets, and teachers characteristically ministered to a *whole* church, and so would engender unity and mutual edification. The gift of **tongues,** on the other hand, suited the Corinthian penchant for self-expression and the pursuit of personal freedom. This self-centeredness also afflicted the church in other areas (e.g., eating sacrificial foods, women in worship, celebration of the Lord's Supper). Love for others was an essential need in the Corinthian church, and to that fundamental attribute Paul then turned to pay eloquent tribute.

(2) Superiority of love to all gifts (12:31b-13:13). **12:31b.** Though Paul greatly valued spiritual gifts, he valued even more a quality of life which the Spirit produced. Spiritual gifts were variously apportioned to individuals in the church so that no single gift was possessed by every member (cf. vv. 19-30). On the other hand the Holy Spirit sought to produce the fruit of the Spirit in every Christian (Gal. 5:22-23), chief among which was love. This was more important than the gifts, and when displayed it would help correct the Corinthian aberrations which surrounded their possession and use of God's gifts (cf. 1 Cor. 14:1).

The **way** Paul referred to was a manner of life preeminently characterized by love (cf. John 15:9-17). Jesus and John the Baptist followed this way of righteousness (Matt. 3:15; 21:32) by obediently practicing the will of God and exhorting their followers to do the same (Matt. 5:6, 10, 20; 6:33). This same manner of life and consequent conduct Paul called the way of love (1 Cor. 14:1; cf. Rom. 13:8-10), which he followed and exhorted the Corinthians to do the same (1 Cor. 14:1; cf. 11:1).

13:1. Some have suggested that this "hymn to love" (chap. 13) was composed by Paul on a previous occasion (under the Spirit's inspiration, of course) and inserted in the letter at this point (under the Spirit's direction) because of its telling appropriateness. This may be so, for the balance in form and substance reflects Paul at his best (but cf. 1:25-29, a passage which exhibits superb parallelism). Still, these verses so directly touch the many issues raised in this letter that if they were previously composed, the Corinthians and their problems were never far removed from Paul's mind as he wrote.

Eloquence was greatly admired in the first century and the Corinthians were no exception, though they found little of it in Paul (cf. 2:1, 4; 2 Cor. 10:10). This may explain in part their fascination with tongues. Paul's application of this and the following conditional clauses (1 Cor. 13:2-3) to himself was forceful since he could claim exceptional experiences, particularly in regard to the languages of **men** (14:18) **and of angels** (cf. 2 Cor. 12:4). But the statement was probably meant to include every imaginable mode of speech. It was a statement of hyperbole concerning exalted eloquence, which if void of love might be momentarily electrifying like a clash of **gong** or **cymbal** but then vanished just as quickly. Love on the other hand produces eternal effects (cf. v. 13).

13:2. Even **the gift of prophecy** (cf. 12:10) which Paul championed as a great gift for the Corinthian church (14:1) or the gifts of wisdom, **knowledge,** and **faith** (cf. 12:8-9) were nothing compared with **love.** Paul was not depreciating those gifts but was appreciating love by showing it to be incomparable.

13:3. Even self-sacrifice can be self-centered (cf. Matt. 6:2), and the ultimate sacrifice, here depicted as self-immolation (cf. Dan. 3:17-18; [apocryphal] 2 Macca-

bees 7:5; Strabo *Geography* 15. 1. 73) is ultimately futile without **love.**

13:4. Paul shifted from the first person to the third person and replaced himself with a personification of love. Some have seen in verses 4-6 the fruit of the Spirit (Gal. 5:22-23); others have seen here a description of Christ Himself. As different sides of the same coin, both are applicable and provided a solution to the many Corinthian problems. Love, defined by 14 predications (half of them negative, half positive) constituted the "way." **Love,** Paul wrote, **is patient . . . kind . . . does not envy** or **boast, and is not proud.**

Patience (*makrothymia*) is the capacity to be wronged and not retaliate. The Corinthian church had many members who had been wronged (e.g., in lawsuits [1 Cor. 6:8] and the poor at communal meals [11:21-22]). The response of love to these wrongs would be a display of kindness and goodness. Envy and boasting seemed to abound as two poles of the same problem (e.g., divisions [1:10; 3:3, 21]; gifts [12:14-25]). The Corinthians had no monopoly on pride though they seemed to. The verb *physioō* occurs only seven times in the New Testament, six of which are found in this letter (cf. 4:6, 18-19; 5:2; 8:1).

13:5. Paul then gave four negative descriptions of love: **It is not rude** nor **self-seeking** nor **easily angered, and it keeps no record of wrongs.** Rudeness found expression in the problem of women in worship (11:2-16), the disorders at the Lord's Supper (11:17-22), and the general organization of worship (14:26-33). Self-satisfaction was a pervasive disorder particularly manifested in the eating of food sacrificed to idols (8:9; 10:23-24). People who are not easily angered usually do not start lawsuits (as in 6:1-11). Love does not record wrongs, though there was ample opportunity for doing so in Corinth (e.g., 6:8; 7:5; 8:11).

13:6. Love does not delight in evil (e.g., incest [5:1-2, 8]), **but rejoices** in **truth** (5:8).

13:7. Love **always protects** (cf. 8:13), **trusts** (cf. 15:11), **hopes** (cf. 9:10, 23), and **perseveres** (*hypomenei*, "remains steadfast in the face of unpleasant circumstances"; cf. 9:19-22).

13:8. Following this elaboration of the preeminence (vv. 1-3) and perfections

(vv. 4-7) of love, Paul concluded with a discussion of its permanence (vv. 8-13). **Love never fails,** in the sense it will never come to an end. Positively stated, it is eternal. This is not true of the spiritual gifts. Some of the gifts were foundational (e.g., **prophecies** and **knowledge;** cf. Eph. 2:20) and confirmatory (e.g., **tongues;** cf. 2 Cor. 12:12; Heb. 2:4). Every gift is linked in some way to building up the church to maturity—some (prophecy, knowledge, tongues) functioning in the early years of the Church Age and others continuing on till the church is perfected. When that perfection is achieved, the gifts will have served their purposes and will be rendered obsolete. But this will not happen to love.

13:9-10. As Paul explained it, the gift of knowledge (v. 8), essential as it was, was not exhaustive. The ability to **prophesy,** however crucial for the church's life, was of limited scope. The gifts were temporary blessings in an **imperfect** age. One day they would give way to **perfection,** toward which all the gifts pointed.

What Paul meant when he referred to the coming of perfection is the subject of considerable debate. One suggestion is that perfection described the completion of the New Testament. But verse 12 makes that interpretation unlikely. A few have suggested that this state of perfection will not be reached until the new heavens and new earth are established. Another point of view understands perfection to describe the state of the church when God's program for it is consummated at the coming of Christ. There is much to commend this view, including the natural accord it enjoys with the illustration of growth and maturity which Paul used in the following verses.

13:11. Paul elsewhere described the purpose of gifts by an illustration employing the imagery of growth and maturity. According to Ephesians 4:11-16, the gifts were to be used to bring the church from a state of infancy to adulthood. The word translated "mature" in that passage (Eph. 4:13) is the word translated "perfection" (*teleion*) in 1 Corinthians 13:10. In the Ephesians passage, maturity is defined as "attaining to the whole measure of the fullness of Christ." Such a state will obviously not exist until Christ's second coming.

It would appear that the same perspective was developed in this passage to the Corinthians. Paul applied the illustration to himself (cf. vv. 1-3). The threefold talking, thinking, and reasoning were probably meant to balance the thrice-mentioned gifts (v. 8). With the coming of adulthood, such gifts become passé. Paul's use of the word **became** (*gegona,* a perf. tense verb, probably proleptic; cf. Rom. 13:8; 1 Cor. 14:23) was of course to be understood in the context of the illustration. It does not indicate that he personally or the church collectively had yet arrived at that point (cf. Phil. 3:12). It would not, on the other hand, necessarily rule out a gradual obsolescence of certain gifts as the church progressed toward maturity.

13:12. A city like Corinth, famous for its bronze mirrors, would have particularly appreciated Paul's final illustration. The perfection and imperfection mentioned in verse 10 were deftly likened to the contrasting images obtained by the indirect **reflection** of one's face viewed in a bronze mirror and the same face when viewed directly. Such, Paul said, was the contrast between the imperfect time in which he then wrote and the perfect time which awaited him and the church when the partial reflection of the present would give way to the splendor of perfect vision. Then Paul would **see** God (cf. 15:28; 1 John 3:2) as God now saw Paul. Then partial knowledge (cf. 1 Cor. 8:1-3) would be displaced by the perfect knowledge of God.

13:13. Paul completed his three-paneled portrait of love (vv. 1-3, 4-7, 8-13) with a final triad: **faith, hope, and love.** Much discussion has focused on whether faith and hope were portrayed by Paul as being (with love) eternal. The solution is probably found in verse 7. Faith is an expression of love (the word "trusts," *pisteuei,* v. 7, is the verb form of the noun "faith," *pistis*), as is hope (cf. Gal. 5:5-6). Faith and hope, as manifestations of love, will endure eternally. So too everyone who follows the way of love (1 Cor. 14:1) finds "the most excellent way" (12:31b), because every individual characterized by love carries that mark eternally. The spiritual gifts will one day cease to exist, but love will endure forever.

(3) Priority of prophecy to tongues (14:1-25). Chapter 13 is one of the most sublime digressions in any letter in any language. But it was nonetheless a deviation from the central theme of gifts and their use by the church which Paul began in chapter 12 and then concluded in chapter 14. Paul had intimated in chapter 12 that the Corinthians were perverting the purpose of gifts from a unifying influence on the church to one fostering fragmentation and discord (esp. 12:21-25). A contributing factor to their factious spirit was the Corinthian pursuit of individual freedom and personal enhancement at the expense of other members of the body whose needs may have been trampled or ignored along the way. Manifestations of this self-centeredness affected each of the problem issues taken up since chapter 8.

The focal problem in the matter of the use and abuse of gifts seemed to be the Corinthian fascination with tongues, a gift which apparently lent itself most readily to perversion from something intended "for the common good" (12:7) to something employed for personal enhancement (14:4). Paul's corrective was not to stifle the use of gifts (14:39; cf. 1 Thes. 5:19-20) but to urge that their use be regulated by love. The gifts of the Spirit should be controlled by the fruit of the Spirit, chief among which was love (Gal. 5:22). This would lead to exercising the gifts so they would benefit the church body as a whole (14:5) and also honor God (14:25, 33, 40). By way of illustration and correction, Paul compared and contrasted the Corinthians' preoccupation with tongues with their apparent disinterest in prophecy.

14:1. That chapter 13 was something of a digression, however sublime, may be seen by the way Paul wove together the two strands which concluded chapter 12 (v. 31) and which began chapter 14 (v. 1). He did this in a chiasmus, a common literary style that connected a series of related words, phrases, or ideas by reversing their order of discussion in the second instance, for example, a^1, b^1, b^2, a^2. As a final note to his discussion on the unity and diversity of the gifts, Paul had exhorted the Corinthians to desire (a^1) exercising the gifts which were of greatest benefit to the church as a whole (cf.

12:31). He then affirmed (b^1) that, however splendid and profitable the gifts were, there was a greater way of life (chap. 13). Chapter 14 picked up on this note as Paul urged (b^2) his readers to make this **way of love** (14:1) the definitive characteristic of their own course of life (cf. John 13:34-35). This in turn would lead them to "desire (a^2) the greater gifts," among which was **prophecy** (cf. 1 Cor. 12:31).

14:2. What Paul meant by speaking **in a tongue** is a matter of considerable debate. One common view is to see Paul's use of the word "tongue" (_glōssa_) against the background of first-century pagan religions and thus define it as ecstatic speech similar to that expressed by the sibylla, or female prophetesses. The Cumaen sibyl (cf. Virgil _Aeneid_ 6. 77-102) was the most famous of the 10 female prophetesses claimed by various regions. Others see the tongues-speaking in 1 Corinthians as ecstatic speech similar to that of Pythia, the female oracle at Delphi (Plutarch _Moralia_ 5. 409e) or similar to the maenads of Dionysus in their ecstatic frenzy (Ovid _Metamorphoses_ 3. 534, 710-30; cf. Euripides _Bacchae_). That the Corinthians may have thought of this gift as analogous to the pagan ecstatics is certainly possible, but to suggest that Paul used the term with reference to this pagan background is hardly enlightened scholarship. In fact the seedbed for most of Paul's theological concepts and the usual source of his terms was the Old Testament. This is evident by Paul's use of _glōssa_ outside of these three Corinthian chapters. He used the word 21 times in 1 Corinthians 12–14 but only 3 other times in his other letters. Each of Paul's other uses was either in a quotation from the Old Testament (Ps. 5:9 in Rom. 3:13; Isa. 45:23 in Rom. 14:11) or in an allusion to it (Isa. 45:23 in Phil. 2:11). In all three instances he used the word "tongue" as a figure of speech for the statement or confession made. Whether good (Rom. 14:11; Phil. 2:11) or bad (Rom. 3:13) the statement was clearly intelligible.

The same may be said of the meaning of the word _glōssa_ elsewhere in the New Testament. Whether it was used literally of the physical organ (e.g., Mark 7:33; James 3:5; Rev. 16:10) or figuratively of human languages (e.g., Acts 2:11; Rev.

1 CORINTHIANS

5:9; 7:9; 10:11; 11:9; 13:7; 14:6; 17:15), it nowhere referred to ecstatic speech. If it is reasonable to interpret the unknown with the help of the known, the obscure by the clear, then the burden of proof rests with those who find in this term a meaning other than human language. The context of this verse is the assembled congregation in Corinth (1 Cor. 11:2–14:40, esp. 14:4-5) in which utterance in a tongue was given without the benefit of interpretation (cf. vv. 13, 19). Apparently no native speaker of the tongue was present in the assembly (cf. vv. 10-11), and no one was given supernatural enablement to interpret it. The utterances therefore were **mysteries,** truths requiring a supernatural disclosure which God had not provided the Corinthians in this particular instance. As a result, the expression of tongues became an exercise in futility for the assembly as a whole, with only the speaker deriving some benefit (v. 4) in **his spirit** (cf. v. 14), the sentient aspect of his being (*pneuma;* cf. Matt. 5:3; Acts 17:16; 2 Cor. 2:13).

14:3. One with the gift of prophecy (cf. 12:10), on the other hand, spoke in the tongue of his listeners, in this case Greek, and edified them by proclaiming God's Word in such a way that it gave them **strengthening,** (*oikodomēn,* "edification"), **encouragement,** (*paraklēsin*), **and comfort** (*paramythian,* "consolation," used only here in the NT).

14:4. A person with the gift of tongues (cf. 12:10) who spoke without the benefit of the gift of interpretation (cf. 12:10) could edify **himself** but not others in **the church.** The edification resulted from the fact that the user of a gift experienced the confirmation that he was the individual object of God's grace (cf. 12:18, 28) and able to offer praise to God (14:16). Though he himself would not comprehend the content of that praise, his feelings and emotions would be enlivened, leading to a general exhilaration and euphoria. This was not a bad thing. Paul certainly was no advocate of cold, dispassionate worship. The gifts were not given for personal enrichment, however, but for the benefit of others (12:7; cf. 10:24; 1 Peter 4:10). Personal edification and exhilaration were often natural by-products of the legitimate exercise of one's gift, but they were not the main reasons for its exercise.

14:5. Paul had no intention of depreciating the gift of **tongues;** he was simply interested in appreciating the gift of prophecy. There was nothing wrong with the gift of tongues; in fact Paul thought it would be good if everyone had the gift. Of course he had said the same thing about celibacy (7:7), but in neither instance did he expect universal compliance with his statement. Since both were gifts from God, neither should be despised. In a church gathering, however, the gift of prophecy and its exercise was greatly to be preferred to uninterpreted tongues simply because the former built up others. As already stated, the tongues gift was confirmatory and thus temporary (see comments on 13:8). Thus those instructions, specifically directed to the Corinthians' misuse of tongues, are not directives for the use of tongues today (cf. comments on 14:21-22).

14:6. Two illustrations (in v. 6 and vv. 7-9) made this plain. In the first, Paul used himself with a possible glance back to his initial ministry in Corinth. He could have **come** proclaiming his message in the tongue of a language which they did not know (cf. v. 18), but it would have produced only disinterest at best (v. 11) or at worst, derision (v. 23). As it was, he brought them a **revelation** from God (cf. 2:10) by his ministry of **prophecy** (12:29), or he brought them a word of **knowledge** (cf. 2:12) by his ministry of **instruction** (12:29; cf. 14:26) which they would understand and to which they could respond (cf. vv. 24-25).

14:7-9. The same was true in a musical **tune** or a **call** to **battle.** To be profitable for others the notes of a **flute** or **harp** or **trumpet** needed to be **clear** and **intelligible;** otherwise they amounted to no more than the venting of air with consequences which, besides being annoying (v. 7), might be devastating (v. 8).

14:10-12. Human communication operated on the same principles as instrumental communication. The word **languages** in verse 10 is *phōnōn,* the plural of the same word *phōnēn,* rendered "sounds" of the harp (v. 7) and "call" of the trumpet (v. 8). Human sounds, apart from a shared understanding of their meanings, were worthless. So was the Corinthian preoccupation with uninterpreted tongues. That was why Paul did

204

not discourage their interest in **spiritual gifts** but did encourage them to pursue those gifts that benefited all in **the church** (v. 12; cf. 12:31; 14:1).

14:13. Interpreted tongues, like prophecy, could benefit the assembly (cf. Acts 19:6). Therefore the gift of interpretation should be requested of God. If no one was present who was able to interpret, the tongues-speaker was to keep silent (1 Cor. 14:28).

14:14-15. It was also true that however beneficial the gift of tongues might be to its recipient (cf. v. 4), when coupled with the gift of interpretation it had much more value because it involved not only the feeling aspects of a person, but his mental faculties as well.

14:16-17. If it were true that one who possessed the gift of tongues would find his worship enhanced by the possession and use of the gift of interpretation (v. 15), it was certainly true that anyone listening to him who did not have the same gift could not empathize with the tongues-speaker. At least another person with the gift of tongues could identify with the exhilaration experienced in the exercise of the gift. However, a Christian with a different gift required intelligible communication if he were to gain any benefit from what was said and so have a basis for affirming his agreement by saying an **Amen.** But such comprehension did not exist if the tongue were not interpreted and so the brother was **not edified.**

14:18-19. Paul's concern to harness the enthusiasm for the gift of **tongues** in Corinth was not motivated by sour grapes. When it came to the gift of tongues, he could outtalk them **all.** But Paul was not primarily interested in self-fulfillment. Instead he was concerned with ministering to **others** and thereby glorifying God (cf. 10:31-33). For that reason he did not use his gift of tongues with the assembled **church** but he did exercise his gift of prophecy (14:6). That, in fact, was in accord with God's purpose. Where then did tongues fit into God's purpose? Paul discussed that next.

14:20. The Corinthian infatuation with tongues was for Paul another manifestation of their immaturity and worldliness (cf. 3:1-3). This he hoped would change, especially in regard to an enhanced appraisal of prophecy and a recognition of the importance of this gift for the assembled church. His final words, contrasting prophecy and tongues (14:21-25), were intended to conclude the exhortation begun in verse 1.

14:21-22. This summary argument in verses 21-25 began with the citation of a portion of Isaiah's prophecy against Israel (Isa. 28:11-12). Because Israel refused to **listen** to God's message proclaimed by His prophets, Isaiah predicted that another message would come. This one would be delivered in a foreign tongue unintelligible to the Israelites, yet unambiguous (cf. 2 Kings 17:23). The foreign tongue symbolized God's rejection (cf. Deut. 28:49; Isa. 33:19), His disciplinary response to Israel's stiff-necked rebellion against Him (cf. 2 Kings 17:14; Acts 7:51). Foreigners instead of Israel became the temporary servants of God (cf. Isa. 5:26; Hab. 1:6; Matt. 21:43; Rom. 10:19-21), and their foreign tongue was a punitive **sign** to Israel of what had taken place.

That seems to be the significance which Paul attached to tongues. As such, the primary arena for its exercise was **not** the company of **believers but . . . unbelievers** (cf. Matt. 13:10-15, on parables). Uninterpreted **tongues** had their place but not in the church where **prophecy** benefited **believers** (1 Cor. 14:3).

14:23-25. Tongues were of benefit in an assembly of believers only if they were interpreted. But this seems not to have been the Corinthians' practice. Instead they apparently poured forth their gift of tongues in unrestrained fashion. As a result believers with some other gifts were nonplussed by the behavior of the tongues-speakers (v. 16). Furthermore, newcomers (*idiōtai,* those who attended but were not believers) and other **unbelievers** (*apistoi*) who were aware of but as yet unconvinced by the gospel message (unlike those of vv. 21-22 who had forthrightly rejected it) would find their behavior positively ridiculous. **Will they not say that you are out of your mind?** This, Paul suggested, would certainly not advance the cause of Christ in Corinth. But prophecy was desirable because it would not only benefit believers (v. 3) but would also expose unbelievers not to a

1 CORINTHIANS

scene of chaos but to one of conviction
(cf. John 16:8) and judgment (1 Cor.
2:15)—which would lead to personal
disclosure (**the secrets of his heart will be
laid bare**) and the **worship of God**.

(4) Propriety in the use of gifts
(14:26-40). In this section Paul drew to a
conclusion his discussion of gifts (chaps.
12-14). He also concluded the whole
section dealing with Christian liberty in
relation to worship (11:2–14:40). What is
most striking to a modern reader is the
apparent lack of any fixed order of
service and the absence of any reference
to particular individuals being responsible for specific ministries. The whole
church seemed to exercise their gifts by
spontaneously ministering to one another.

14:26. As he had done throughout
the letter, Paul addressed the Christian
community in Corinth as **brothers**, a
general term including both sexes (e.g.,
1:10; cf. 1 Peter 5:9). When the church
met, anyone was free to participate by
contributing **a hymn, or a word of
instruction** (cf. 1 Cor. 14:6; probably a
lesson based on the OT), **a revelation**
from one gifted in prophecy (cf. vv. 6,
29-32), or a word from one gifted in **a
tongue** followed by **an interpretation** of
what was said. The controlling principle
in this free participation was the rule of
love. All that was said and done was to
have as its goal the need of **strengthening**
(*pros oikodomēn*, "edifying") others (cf. vv.
4-5).

14:27-28. Though there was no
established order for a service, it was to
be conducted in an orderly way (v. 40).
The services were to have balanced
participation on the parts of gifted
members. Those gifted with **a tongue**
who wanted to contribute to a service
could do so but only **two or three** at any
one service and then only if individuals
gifted in interpretation were present who
could translate the language. If **no
interpreter** were present, the tongues-
speaker was to **keep quiet**. Though his
gift was without benefit to the church if
uninterpreted, it did have some other
benefits (cf. vv. 4, 14-15, 22).

14:29. The directions for those
exercising the gift of prophecy did not
differ from those for tongues. **Two or
three prophets** could **speak** at each

service and what they **said** was to be
carefully considered. Since they would
speak in Greek **the others** in the congregation would understand and evaluate
their messages. (Or perhaps "the others"
referred to those with the gift to distinguish between spirits.) The words **weigh
carefully** translate the verb *diakrinetōsan*,
related to the noun *diakriseis* in 12:10,
which speaks of distinguishing "between
spirits." It was their responsibility to
ascertain if the message delivered was
indeed from God (cf. 1 John 4:1).

14:30. A prophet might have received **a revelation**, probably in a vision
or dream, sometime prior to the meeting
of the church at which he subsequently
related it. However, a prophet might also
experience a revelation during the
service. If such occurred, a prophet in the
midst of speaking should draw his
message to a close to let the other gifted
member speak. Whatever the Corinthian
services were, they were not dull.

14:31. The principle which regulated
the exercise of tongues applied similarly
to prophets. What was said was to benefit
everyone by way of instruction or
encouragement in the Christian life (cf.
v. 3).

14:32-33a. Paul apparently did not
believe the **prophets** were any more
restrained than their fellow members
gifted in tongues. So he gave the prophets
an instruction that was similar to what he
gave the tongues-speakers (v. 28). **The
spirits** referred to a prophet's spiritual
gift, which did not **control** the gifted
member, but he controlled it (cf. v. 30). If
two or three prophets spoke in a particular service, others gifted and with
something to say could do so on another
occasion. The church was not a forum for
personal pontification or self-glorification;
it was a place where people were to be
built up and God was to be honored (cf.
10:31-33). The service and those who
took part in it should reflect the character
of God. He is a **God . . . of peace**, not
disorder, and His Spirit worked to
produce the same fruit (Gal. 5:22) in
believers' lives.

14:33b-36. Some of the verses in this
section (vv. 34-35) were felt by some
early copyists to be out of place at this
point in the letter and so were transposed
to the end of the chapter. A more drastic

approach taken by some recent commentators is to regard these verses as spurious and unworthy of comment. Though the exact meaning of these verses is difficult to determine, neither expedient has much to commend it. In fact it seems that the guiding thread which prompted these comments by Paul about women was the same theme developed in the preceding verses addressed to those gifted in tongues and prophecy. The church members needed to exercise self-control on occasion, a self-control expressed by silence (vv. 28, 30, 34) in order that the assembly might be characterized by peace.

Apparently certain women in the Corinthian assembly needed to hear this refrain. More than uncovered heads were amiss in regard to their participation in worship services (11:2-16), and Paul was not about to dodge the problem.

Whether the admonition for silence was directed to all women (cf. 11:2-16) or only to those who were married may be debated. The word translated **women** (*gynaikes*) was used to refer to women generally (as in all 11 occurrences in 11:3-15), or to unmarried women (e.g., 7:34), or to married women (e.g., 5:1; 9:5; and all 14 occurrences in chap. 7 except once in 7:34). The context alone aided the readers in distinguishing between the alternative meanings.

Two indications strongly suggest that married women were in view in this passage. The first is the word **submission** (*hypotassesthōsan*, v. 34). When it occurs elsewhere in the New Testament with specific reference to a woman, it always refers to a married woman who was to be subject to her husband (Eph. 5:22; Col. 3:18; Titus 2:5; 1 Peter 3:1, 5).

The second indication is the phrase **their own husbands** (1 Cor. 14:35), whom the inquisitive women were to consult if they had questions. This would obviously be a difficult assignment for single women (e.g., 7:34) or those with unbelieving husbands (e.g., 7:13).

First Timothy 2:11-15, which enjoins women to be quiet in worship, is frequently cited as a parallel to this passage. But there too, married women were probably in view, as verse 15 would not apply to an unmarried woman. Also, when Eve is named in the Old Testament,

it is as Adam's wife (Gen. 3:20; cf. 2 Cor. 11:2-3, the only other NT passage besides 1 Tim. 2:13-14 that names Eve), and her submission is rooted in that relationship (Gen. 3:16, the text Paul probably referred to in 1 Cor. 14:34). In addition, the noun *hēsychia* in 1 Timothy 2:11-12 means "quietness, absence of disorder," whereas the verb *sigaō* in 1 Corinthians 14:28, 34 means "remain silent." (See comments on 1 Tim. 2:11-14 and 2 Thes. 3:12).

Paul then wanted silence on the parts of married women whose husbands were present in the assembly, but he permitted the participation of other women when properly adorned (1 Cor. 11:2-16). Such silence would express their subordinate (but not inferior) relationship to their husbands. This contrasts with a disturbance caused by their talking to their husbands during the service.

The Corinthian believers were not to think of themselves as exclusive, independent interpreters or recipients of **the Word of God** (14:36). They, like those in **all the congregations** (v. 33b), were to submit to God's truth by conforming to this standard of conduct.

14:37-40. These verses were Paul's conclusion not only to the immediately preceding directives (vv. 33b-36) but also to all his discussion about Corinthian irregularities in worship and the needed correctives (11:2-14:36). He expected some opposition (cf. 11:16; 14:36), but warned that those who opposed him did so at their own peril (cf. 4:18-21). Anyone who **ignores** the Lord's commands would find **himself . . . ignored** by Him at the last day (cf. 3:17; Gen. 9:6; Matt. 10:32-33), because his actions would show that he never knew the Lord (cf. 1 Cor. 8:3; Matt. 7:22-23; 1 John 4:6).

The conclusion was that the Corinthians should give special attention to the gifts which were most beneficial to the church as a whole (12:31; 14:1) without denigrating the other gifts. They should see that their services were conducted in a **fitting** (cf. 11:2-16; 14:34-36) **and orderly** (cf. 11:17-34; 14:26-33) **way.**

C. Counsel concerning the Resurrection (chap. 15)

Some have suggested that Paul reserved this chapter on the Resurrection till last because he thought that a firm belief in it would help solve many of the Corinthians' problems. Certainly if the message of Christ crucified were foolishness to the Greek mind (1:23), the corollary doctrine of the Resurrection was no less so (cf. Acts 17:31-32). The implicit denial of the Resurrection on the part of some may be seen in the Corinthian conviction that the present era represented the consummation of God's material blessings (1 Cor. 4:8; cf. 6:2) and sexual immorality was a matter of no lasting consequence (5:1; cf. 6:9, 13-14).

Like the problems previously discussed (1:10–6:20), the denial of the Resurrection by some in the church was a matter apparently reported to Paul (15:12) and not something the Corinthians themselves had included among their questions in their letter to him (cf. 7:25; 8:1; 12:1; 16:1, 12). As in his response to the Thessalonian confusion on the Resurrection (1 Thes. 4:13-18), Paul began with a fundamental affirmation of the faith (cf. 1 Cor. 15:3-4; 1 Thes. 4:14) and expanded on it.

1. THE CERTAINTY OF BODILY RESURRECTION (15:1-34)

a. Historical argument (15:1-11)

15:1-2. The **gospel** Paul had **preached** in Corinth (2:1-2) had not changed; but he feared that just as there had been declension in the church concerning the message of Christ crucified and its implication for believers, the same was happening with regard to the message of Christ resurrected. As the former message was an essential element in the Corinthians' experience of ongoing salvation (the pres. tense of the verb **saved** focuses on sanctification), so was the latter. To reject bodily resurrection eviscerated "the gospel" and made faith **vain** (*eikē*, "without cause" or "without success"; cf. vv. 14, 17) because it had an unworthy object (cf. 15:13, 17). Believing the gospel includes holding **firmly** to belief in Christ's resurrection. Unless one holds firmly, his belief is "in vain"; cf. Matt. 13:18-22).

15:3-5. Paul included himself in the company of all believers when he spoke of receiving the truth of Christ's death and His resurrection on behalf of sinful people. These verses, the heart of the gospel, were an early Christian confession

which Paul described **as of first importance**. It was really a twofold confession: **Christ died for our sins** and **He was raised**. The reality of this was verified by the Scriptures (e.g., Ps. 16:10; Isa. 53:8-10) and by historical evidence verified by time in the grave and out of it, in the presence of the living. The fact **that He was buried** verified His death, and the fact **that He appeared** to others verified His resurrection. **Peter,** the first male witness, was soon joined by the remaining disciples who composed the Lord's immediate circle.

15:6. Later a much larger company of believers witnessed His resurrection. The **500 . . . brothers** may have formed the audience who received the commission recorded in Matthew 28:18-20 (cf. Acts 1:3-8). Since **most of** those were **still living** when Paul wrote 1 Corinthians, they could be consulted.

15:7-8. Some have debunked this Resurrection appearance as simply the pious vision of believers seeing with the eyes of faith. But Paul could have cited the testimony of two for whom that was not true, **James,** the half brother of Jesus, and himself. Like Paul, James probably came to faith (cf. John 7:5 with Acts 1:14) because of an appearance of the resurrected Christ (Acts 9:3-6; 22:6-11). Paul considered himself **abnormally born** because he lacked the "gestation" period of having been with Christ during His earthly ministry (cf. Acts 1:21-22). It seems that **the apostles** were a body wider than the previously mentioned Twelve (cf. comments on Eph. 4:11), but were all distinguished by having seen the resurrected Christ (1 Cor. 9:1) which made Paul the last of their company.

15:9. Because he was the last, like a runt, untimely born, Paul could call himself **the least of the apostles.** He felt less deserving of the office because he had been an opponent of the **church** (cf. Acts 22:4; 1 Tim. 1:15-16) which he now served (2 Cor. 4:5).

15:10. He realized, however, that his past was simply a backdrop on which to display **the grace of God** (cf. 1:3), the grace to which Paul had been so responsive. Indeed Paul was without peer in his devotion (cf. 9:19-29). The history of the church confirms that his devotion **was not without effect** (*kenē*, "empty"; cf. 15:14). He had **worked harder** than any of the other apostles, as he traveled more, suffered more opposition, wrote more New Testament epistles, and founded more churches. Yet Paul knew and ministered with the recognition that it was not his power but God's (2:4-5) which produced results (3:6).

15:11. In the final analysis it was not the messenger but the message which was important (cf. 1:18-4:5), and in that regard the apostolic message was that the crucified Christ became the resurrected Christ, which message Paul did **preach** and the Corinthians **believed.**

b. Logical argument (15:12-19)

15:12. Paul then turned to consider the claim of some that no one **dead** could experience bodily **resurrection.** He pressed that tenet to its logical consequences within the framework of the Christian faith.

15:13. To deny a bodily resurrection in principle was to deny the **resurrection of Christ.** Presumably some in Corinth had done this, and Paul wanted to warn them and others of the serious consequences which would result from such disbelief.

15:14. Not the least of those consequences was the fact that a denial of the Resurrection tore the heart out of the gospel message and left it lifeless. If that were so, the Corinthians' **faith,** however vital, would be **useless** (*kenē,* "empty"; cf. vv. 2, 10, 17) since its object would be a dead man.

15:15-16. Second, the apostles of the church would turn out to be crass charlatans since their message uniformly affirmed the truth of Christ's resurrection (cf. v. 11).

15:17. Third, the Corinthians' salvation would be only a state of mind with no correspondence to reality. Their **faith** would be **futile** (*mataia,* "without results"; cf. *kenē,* "empty," in vv. 10, 14, *eikē,* "without cause" or "without success," v. 2). The Resurrection was God's validation that the redemption paid by Christ on the cross was accepted (Rom. 4:25). Without the Resurrection there could be no certainty of atonement and the Corinthians would remain in a state of alienation and sin.

15:18. Fourth, if Christ were not raised, the loved ones among the Corinthian believers who had died entered not

bliss but perdition. The pagan concept of a liberated spirit was a lie. Without the Resurrection the sting of death would remain, with lasting painfulness (cf. vv. 54-56).

15:19. Fifth, if there were no Resurrection, the pagans would be right. The "foolishness of the Cross" (1:18) would be just that, and men such as Paul and the apostles who had suffered for the gospel (4:9-13) could only be **pitied.** Those who lived for the pleasure of the moment would be right and the sacrifices of Christians would only be cruel, self-inflicted jokes (cf. 15:32).

c. Theological argument (15:20-28)

15:20. Paul had explored the logical negations which followed from a denial of the bodily resurrection of Christ (vv. 12-19). He then considered the theological tenet that the destiny of Christians was bound up in the destiny of Christ, and he set forth the positive consequences of this union. Speculation had given way to affirmation: **Christ has indeed been raised from the dead.** And He is the **firstfruits,** an Old Testament word (e.g., Ex. 23:16, 19) here used in the sense of a preliminary installment of what will be both an example and a guarantee of more to come (cf. Rom. 8:23).

15:21-22. Death came to all those related to Adam by natural birth because of the disobedience of one **man.** As the father of mankind Adam in his sin brought death to everybody (cf. Gen. 3:17-19; Rom. 5:12). But because of the obedience (Phil. 2:8) of another **Man** (1 Tim. 2:5) **resurrection** will come to **all** those related to Him by spiritual birth. Paul would later expand this grand truth in his letter to the Romans (Rom. 5:12-19). Those who are a part of the body of Christ (1 Cor. 12:27) will one day follow the lead of their Head (Col. 1:18), but will not do so immediately.

15:23. There will be a sequence in the unfolding of the final events. Paul was not concerned to detail all future resurrections since he was addressing the church and was primarily interested here in fixing their place in the scheme of things. As he had earlier affirmed (v. 20), Christ was their sample and surety.

As He promised (John 14:2-3) Christ will return for those who compose the church and the dead in Christ will be raised (1 Thes. 4:16). No time frame was indicated in this sequence but a period of almost 2,000 years has now elapsed.

15:24. Following the resurrection of the church, another period intervenes until **the end** when Christ will deliver His **kingdom to God the Father** (cf. Matt. 13:41-43). Some interpreters dispute that an interval of any sort was hinted at by Paul and find instead the coming of Christ and the consummation of all things as virtually simultaneous events. As in the preceding verse, no time frame was specified and the chronological sequences set forth may indeed be almost momentary (1 Cor. 15:5) but then again they may be prolonged (cf. v. 23). If about 2,000 years can elapse between the first and second phases in this selected presentation of events, a lapse of half that time, that is, a millennium, between the second and third phases should cause no consternation.

15:25-26. Death as a personification of Christ's ultimate opponent (cf. v. 55; Heb. 2:14) will be nullified. It is not human bodies which will **be destroyed,** as some in Corinth were saying, but the destroyer of bodies, death itself.

15:27-28. The reprise of these verses is found in verse 57. It is by the power of God that the incarnate **Christ** victoriously mediates His authority (cf. Phil. 3:21). This work of **the Son** will find ultimate completion in the glory of the Father (cf. John 17:4-5). That too is the ultimate goal of the church (cf. 1 Cor. 10:31; Eph. 1:6, 12, 14). When God is **all in all** (cf. Rom. 11:36), the new creation will be consummated and the resurrected Christ and His church will share in that experience (cf. Rev. 22:1).

d. Experiential argument (15:29-34)

In this fourth collection of arguments against those who deny the Resurrection, Paul drew on Corinthian practice (v. 29) and also on his own way of life (vv. 30-32).

15:29. Up to 200 explanations have been given of this verse! Most of these interpretations are inane, prompted by a desire to conform this verse to an orthodox doctrine of baptism. It is clear from the context, however, that Paul distinguished his own practice and teaching from that described here. He merely held up the teaching of being **baptized for the dead** as a practice of some who denied the Resurrection.

How the false teachers came to this view may never be known, but just across the Saronic Gulf, north of Corinth, lay Eleusis, the center of an ancient mystery religion lauded by Homer (*Hymn to Demeter* 478-79) and widely popular (cf. Cicero, himself an initiate, in *De Legibus* 2. 14. 36). Part of the rites of initiation into this pagan religion were washings of purification in the sea without which no one could hope to experience bliss in the life hereafter (cf. Pindar *Fragment* 212; Sophocles *Fragment* 753). A vicarious participation in the mysteries was not unknown either (cf. Orphica *Fragment* 245). Given the Corinthian propensity for distortion in matters of church practice (11:2-14:40), it was likely that some in Corinth (possibly influenced by the Eleusinian mystery) were propounding a false view of baptism which Paul took up and used as an argument against those who denied the Resurrection. No interpretation of this text is entirely satisfactory, but this view has as its chief strength the natural reading of the Greek verse, an asset singularly lacking in other explanations. Also it is noteworthy that Paul referred to **those** (not "we") who are "baptized for the dead."

15:30-32. In contrast to the practice of those cited in verse 29, Paul now mentioned his own lifestyle as a forceful statement of his conviction about the certainty of the Resurrection. Some of the Corinthians may have accused Paul of duplicity (cf. 2 Cor. 1:12-14; 2:17; 6:8), but no one thought him a fool even though he affirmed that he would be one if he ministered without certainty of the Resurrection. Many times his life was imperiled (**I die every day;** cf. 2 Cor. 6:4-5; 11:23-28). At least once he thought he would die (2 Cor. 1:8-9), probably referred to here as his fight with **wild beasts** at **Ephesus.** Though this was probably not an arena experience, it was like it in that Paul saw no hope of deliverance. Why face that if this life were all there is? The Epicureans (and less philosophical men before them; cf. Isa. 22:13) would be right—pursue pleasure and avoid pain (cf. Epicurus *Letter to Menoeceus* 128). But Paul knew there was more, and his life testified to that fact (cf. 1 Cor. 9:24-27; 2 Cor. 4:16-18).

15:33-34. Paul's concluding advice with reference to those who continued to deny the Resurrection was like his former counsel concerning immoral people in the church (chap. 5)—don't associate with them. Previously he had compared immorality in the church to yeast in bread (5:6). Here he quoted the pagan writer Menander (*Thais* 218) to the same effect: **Bad company corrupts good character.** False teachers should be avoided (cf. 2 Cor. 6:14-7:1) because though they claimed great knowledge they were in fact **ignorant of God** (cf. 1 Cor. 8:2). Were the wise Corinthians this easily deceived? (cf. 2 Cor. 11:3)

2. ANSWERS TO CERTAIN QUESTIONS (15:35-58)

In the preceding section (vv. 1-34) Paul had taken up the question implicit in verse 12, why believe in the Resurrection? He answered it with arguments rooted in history, logic, theology, and experience. He then addressed two other questions: How is the resurrection achieved? What is the nature of a resurrected body?

a. Answers about the resurrection of the dead (15:35-49)

15:35-37. One objection to belief in anyone's resurrection might be its incomprehensibility. This was the point of the questions **How are the dead raised? With what kind of body will they come?** Paul did not consider these sorts of questions a wise person would ask, as is obvious from his response, **How foolish!** (lit., "how senseless or thoughtless") to his imaginary interlocutor. Belief in the Resurrection was like belief in seedtime and harvest. Neither could be completely understood but both were real. As a plant which sprouted from a seed was directly linked to it but remarkably different from it, so too was the relationship of a natural and a resurrected body.

15:38-41. The variety in Creation reflects the will of the Maker (Gen. 1:1-26). The differences in the animate creation (**men . . . animals . . . birds . . . fish**) and inanimate creation (**sun . . . moon . . . stars**) give expression to the splendor of God and bring Him praise (cf. Ps. 148:13). The differences in splendor

between the **earthly bodies** and the **heavenly bodies** suggested to Paul the differences between a natural and a spiritual body (cf. Dan. 12:3 where resurrected saints were compared to stars; also Matt. 13:43).

15:42-44a. An earthly **natural body** is fallen and so is temporal, imperfect, and weak. A heavenly **spiritual body** will be eternal, perfect, and powerful (cf. 2 Cor. 5:1-4). Like a seed sown in the earth and the plant which proceeds from it, there is continuity but a gloriously evident difference.

15:44b-49. Discussion of the contrast between Adam and Christ (mentioned earlier in v. 22) is resumed here. Adam exemplified the earthly (v. 40) natural body (the word trans. **being,** v. 45, *psychē,* is related to *psychikos,* which is trans. **natural** in v. 44). **Adam** gave his nature to all who followed him (the man without the Spirit is the natural [*psychikos*] man; cf. 2:14). **The last Adam,** Christ, exemplifies the heavenly **spiritual** body (15:22) which those who belong to Him (v. 23; cf. 2:15) will likewise assume at His coming from heaven (cf. Phil. 3:20-21). The full harvest will be like the firstfruits (1 Cor. 15:23; cf. Col. 1:18). First the seed must die; then the spiritual body will emerge.

b. Answers about the Rapture of the living (15:50-58)

15:50. What about those who are *not* dead at Christ's coming? Paul now turned to answer that unexpressed question. With all that had preceded about the need for the natural body to give way to the spiritual, it followed that **flesh and blood,** the natural body, could not enter the eternal state (cf. vv. 24-28).

15:51-52. Paul had revealed the same truth to the Thessalonians (1 Thes. 4:15-17). The Rapture of the church was a **mystery** (*mystērion*) in that it had not been known in the Old Testament but now was revealed. (Cf. other "mysteries"— now revealed truths—in Matt. 13:11; Luke 8:10; Rom. 11:25; 16:25; 1 Cor. 4:1; Eph. 1:9; 3:3-4, 9; 5:32; Col. 1:26-27; 2:2; 4:3; 2 Thes. 2:7; 1 Tim. 3:9, 16; Rev. 1:20; 10:7; 17:5.) The dead in Christ will first be raised, and then the living will be instantaneously transformed. The **trumpet,** as in the Old Testament, signaled the appearance of God (cf. Ex. 19:16). It is the last blast for the church because this appearance shall never end (cf. 1 Cor. 13:12). (There is no basis for posttribulationists equating this trumpet with the seventh trumpet in Rev. 11:15-19. The trumpets in Rev. pertain to judgments during the Tribulation, whereas the trumpet in 1 Cor. 15:52 is related to the church.)

15:53-54. Like the dead (vv. 42-43), the living will exchange the temporal and imperfect for the eternal and perfect (cf. 13:10). For those who belong to Christ, death's power will be removed.

15:55. As in the allusion to Isaiah 25:8 (1 Cor. 15:54), Paul again recalled an Old Testament passage which prophesied the cessation of death (Hosea 13:14). (The recollections were adapted by Paul and do not correspond exactly to any of the extant Gr. or Heb. texts.) The apparent victories of Satan, in the Garden of Eden (Gen. 3:13) and on Golgotha (Mark 15:22-24) were reversed on the cross (Col. 2:15; Heb. 2:14-15) and vindicated in the resurrection of Christ. From the vantage point of the certain resurrection of the saints, Paul voiced his taunt against death and Satan.

15:56-57. As the word **victory** which ended verse 54 led Paul into the exaltation in verse 55, so the word **sting** which ended verse 55 led him into this brief digression in verses 56-57. Like other theological nuggets in this chapter (vv. 21-22), these verses were later given expanded discussion in Paul's letter to the Romans (Rom. 7:7-13). **Death** came as a result of man's rebellion and disobedience against the command of God (Gen. 3:17-19). The **Law,** which epitomized the command of God, was thus the mirror against which human rebellion and disobedience was starkly portrayed. Like the first Adam, all who followed him rebelled (cf. 1 Cor. 2:14). But through the obedience of the last Adam, **our Lord Jesus Christ** (15:45; cf. Rom. 5:19; Phil. 2:8-11), came "victory" and life (1 Cor. 15:22; cf. 2:15-16).

15:58. Paul's doctrinal declarations led to practical directives and this chapter's conclusion was no exception. The Corinthians were urged to **stand firm** in the apostles' teaching (v. 2), unmoved by the denials of false teachers (cf. Eph. 4:14). This certainty, especially concerning the Resurrection, provided an impetus to faithful service (cf. 1 Cor. 3:8; Gal. 6:9) since labor **in the** resurrected **Lord is not** futile (*kenos,* "empty"; cf. 1 Cor. 15:10, 14, 17, 30-32).

D. *Counsel concerning the collection for the poor (16:1-4)*

The flow of the previous chapter, from a prolonged discourse on doctrinal matters to a concluding exhortation on practical diligence, moved smoothly to a discussion of a practical expression of that faith—care for the needs of others and in particular, the needy in Jerusalem.

16:1. At this appropriate juncture, Paul took up the Corinthian inquiry (cf. 7:1) concerning a proposed **collection for God's people** (cf. 1:2) in Jerusalem (15:3). The Corinthians had apparently heard about the collection through members of **the Galatian churches,** the oldest of all the Pauline-planted churches (Acts 13:14–14:23) in Derbe, Lystra, Iconium, and Pisidian Antioch. Paul's instruction to them was repeated to the Corinthians.

16:2. Paul never used the word "tithe" when he discussed giving, even though he gave more attention to giving than any other New Testament writer. Giving should be a systematic, weekly practice on Sunday when the church meets together. Giving was also to be proportionate—**in keeping with** one's **income** (cf. Acts 11:29). The income of some would permit them to give a greater proportion, while others, due to their few resources and other constraints on them, would be limited to lesser contributions. What was important was that giving be a unified ministry with **each one** participating, regardless of his income. Then when it came time to deliver the contributions to the saints in Jerusalem, no last-minute **collections** would need **to be made,** and the gift could be sent off gladly, not grudgingly (2 Cor. 9:5)—as would be true if it were wrung out by emotional appeals or personal pressure.

16:3-4. Paul's practice in money matters was scrupulously aboveboard. Not only did he avoid solicitation for himself (cf. 9:12, 15), but also when he acted to meet the needs of others he avoided direct involvement in handling the **gift.** He preferred instead that individuals from the various contributing congregations elect representatives to bear their gift (cf. 2 Cor. 8:19-21) whom he might then **accompany** to the presentation.

E. Counsel concerning future visits (16:5-12)

The mention of his planned arrival in connection with the collection sparked another brief digression on the subject of future visits.

16:5. It was Paul's plan to leave Ephesus, his place of ministry at that time (v. 8), and journey **through Macedonia,** the region north of Corinth where the churches of Philippi, Thessalonica, and presumably Berea (cf. Acts 20:4, a delegate from Berea accompanied Paul) flourished. They too were planning to make a contribution to the needy in Jerusalem (cf. 2 Cor. 8:1-4).

16:6-7. On that journey (cf. Acts 19:21) Paul hoped to be able to **spend** some time with the Corinthians, possibly as long as **the winter** since travel by sea in that season was ill-advised (cf. Acts 27:9-44). This, in fact, he eventually did (see the *Introduction*) but not on the schedule here set forth. This change of plans became a source of trouble for him with the Corinthians later (cf. 2 Cor. 1:15–2:1). What Paul meant by the words **you can help me on my journey** is clarified later (1 Cor. 16:11). He desired that his departure be marked by "peace," which would be in keeping with the Lord's will (cf. James 4:15).

16:8-9. For the time being, Paul intended to **stay on at Ephesus** in ministry, where the opportunities and the opposition were both great. One or the other of these situations may have arisen while he was writing this letter (cf. 4:19). It says something about Paul's perception of his ministry that the presence of opposition was a sign to him of the viability of his labor and reason for pressing on, not running away (cf. Acts 19:30-31). Those who opposed him in Corinth (1 Cor. 4:18-21) probably took note of this.

16:10-11. In the meantime Paul intended to send his beloved assistant **Timothy** to Corinth. The younger man sometimes traveled in Paul's place (cf. Phil. 2:19-24). That Timothy might have cause **to fear while** ministering in Corinth confirms, as this letter indicates, that working with the Corinthian church was

no picnic. However, it probably says more about the character of Timothy, a man devoted to Christ (Phil. 2:19-21) but lacking Paul's robust boldness (cf. 1 Tim. 4:12; 2 Tim. 1:7-8; 2:1).

The identity of **the brothers** accompanying Timothy is not clear. It appears that Timothy went out from Ephesus with Erastus (Acts 19:22). They may have been joined by some of the men who later composed Paul's traveling party for delivering the collection (Acts 20:4).

16:12. The last of the Corinthian questions (cf. 7:10) concerned **Apollos.** They apparently inquired about the possibility of a return visit from him. Paul said he had **strongly urged** Apollos to do this but that the gifted Alexandrian had decided to stay on in Ephesus with Paul, and not join Timothy and Erastus in their trip (Acts 19:22). Earlier in the letter, Paul had described himself and Apollos as fellow workers under God (1 Cor. 3:9). This verse bears eloquent tribute to the fact that Paul conducted himself not as a master but as a partner with others who labored in ministry.

V. Conclusion (16:13-24)

A. Exhortation on appropriate conduct and commendation (16:13-18)

16:13-14. Paul began the conclusion with a pointed exhortation along a fivefold line. The command, **Be on your guard** (*grēgoreite*) might be rendered "be diligent" in carrying out the will of God (cf. 15:58, "give yourselves fully to the work of the Lord"). In view of the Corinthians' susceptibility to false teachers (cf. 2 Cor. 11:3) the exhortation to **stand firm in the faith** was a timely reminder (cf. 1 Cor. 15:1, 58). So too were the closing exhortations (similar to the Gr. text of several Pss., e.g., 27:14; 31:24) to **be men of courage** and **be strong,** that is, marked by maturity (cf. 1 Cor. 14:20) and not infants easily swept aside (cf. Eph. 4:14). That sort of diligence and commitment is required if **everything** is to be done **in love** (cf. 1 Cor. 12:31b–14:1).

16:15-16. Achaia was the Roman province extending over central and southern Greece of which Corinth was the capital. Those in **the household of Stephanas** were among the first converts in the region (cf. Acts 17:34, for some in Athens believed), and they were among those who assumed responsibility for the general welfare of the church. Sometimes Paul appointed elders (Acts 14:23) but in this instance members of Stephanas' household voluntarily took on the responsibility (cf. 1 Tim. 3:1). Paul recognized their position as ordained by God and urged others to **submit to** them. As an aside, it may be said that this text argues strongly against the view that infants were in view when a household was referred to. It is difficult to see how infants could be of **service to the saints.** One primary qualification for church leadership was a willingness to serve (cf. Matt. 23:11; Luke 22:26). To those who labored with this spirit, submission on the part of others in the church was due.

16:17-18. By their very presence, three men from the Corinthian church—**Stephanas, Fortunatus, and Achaicus**—were able to refresh and encourage Paul despite the fact that they probably also brought confirmation of the bad news earlier reported by Chloe's people (1:11). These men were the probable bearers of the letter to which Paul had responded (7:1 et al.).

B. Salutation, imprecation, and benediction (16:19-24)

16:19. The churches . . . of Asia, perhaps those indicated in Revelation 2–3, joined with Paul in sending **greetings** to their sister church in Corinth (cf. 1 Cor. 1:2). **Aquila and Priscilla** were tentmakers whom Paul met in Corinth and with whom he lived. They had followed Paul to Ephesus and remained there in ministry, making their house available as a meeting place (cf. Rom. 16:3-5). They would, of course, know and be known by many in the Corinthian church.

16:20. All the brothers may refer to those from the Corinthian church in Ephesus at the time of writing (1:11; 16:17), or to believers in Ephesus who met in a house(s) other than that of Aquila and Priscilla, or simply to the collective community of Christians in the province of Asia.

The **holy kiss** (cf. 2 Cor. 13:12; Rom. 16:16; 1 Thes. 5:25; 1 Peter 5:14) was primarily a symbolic expression of the love, forgiveness, and unity which should exist among Christians. As such, it became associated with the celebration of the Lord's Supper as a prelude to its

observance (cf. Justin *Apology* 1. 65. 2). It was a mark of the familial bond which united believers. There is no indication that it was restricted to one's own sex in the New Testament era (cf. Luke 7:37, 45). The suggestion to separate the sexes for the exchange of the kiss arose in the late second century due to concern about criticism from non-Christians and the danger of erotic abuse (cf. Athenagorus *Supplication* 32; Clement of Alexandria *Pedagogue* 3. 81. 2-4). By the third century it seems that the sexes were separated (*Apostolic Constitutions* 2. 57. 17), and by the fourth century the clergy and laity were also kept apart (*Apostolic Constitutions* 8. 11. 9). Such, however, was apparently not the case in the New Testament church where love for one another was openly expressed.

16:21. At this point Paul stopped dictating the letter (cf. Rom. 16:22; Gal. 6:11) and wrote the final words himself.

16:22. Paul's personal note began with a passionate warning probably aimed at false teachers (cf. 12:3) whom he believed to be already present in the congregation (cf. 2 Cor. 11:3-4). The verb **love** (*philei*) is related to the noun *philēmati* for "kiss" (1 Cor. 16:20). It expresses adoration and devotion, qualities absent in false brethren. Paul invoked God's wrath on these false teachers (cf. Gal. 1:8-9) and in the same breath appealed to Christ to return (cf. Matt. 7:21-23; Rev. 22:20). **Come, O Lord!** renders the Greek words *marana tha* ("Maranatha"), which transliterate the Aramaic "Lord, come."

16:23-24. To the congregation of Christians in Corinth, Paul invoked what they sorely needed, the continued **grace of the Lord Jesus** (cf. 1:4). He assured them of what they hardly deserved, his fervent though unrequited (cf. 2 Cor. 6:11-13; 12:15) **love** (*agapē*). He embraced the disunited lot of them (cf. 1 Cor. 1:10) as their spiritual father **in Christ Jesus** (4:15).

BIBLIOGRAPHY

Deluz, Gaston. *A Companion to First Corinthians*. Edited and translated by Grace E. Watt. London: Darton, Longman and Todd, 1963.

Godet, Frederic Louis. *Commentary on First Corinthians.* Edinburgh: T. & T. Clark, 1889. Reprint (2 vols. in 1). Grand Rapids: Kregel Publications, 1977.

Gromacki, Robert G. *Called to Be Saints: An Exposition of 1 Corinthians.* Grand Rapids: Baker Book House, 1977.

Grosheide, F.W. *Commentary on the First Epistle to the Corinthians.* The New International Commentary on the New Testament. Grand Rapids: Wm. B. Eerdmans Publishing Co., 1953.

Hodge, Charles. *An Exposition of the First Epistle to the Corinthians.* Reprint. Grand Rapids: Wm. B. Eerdmans Publishing Co., 1974.

Ironside, Henry Allen. *Addresses on the First Epistle to the Corinthians.* New York: Loizeaux Brothers, 1938.

Johnson, S. Lewis, Jr. "1 Corinthians." In *The Wycliffe Bible Commentary.* Chicago: Moody Press, 1962.

Lenski, R.C.H. *The Interpretation of St. Paul's First and Second Epistles to the Corinthians.* Minneapolis: Augsburg Publishing House, 1963.

Mare, W. Harold. "1 Corinthians." In *The Expositor's Bible Commentary,* vol. 10. Grand Rapids: Wm. B. Eerdmans Publishing Co., 1976.

Morris, Leon. *The First Epistle of Paul to the Corinthians.* Tyndale New Testament Commentaries. Grand Rapids: Wm. B. Eerdmans Publishing Co., 1958.

Parry, R. St. John. *The First Epistle of Paul the Apostle to the Corinthians.* Cambridge: At the University Press, 1916.

Redpath, Alan. *The Royal Route to Heaven.* Westwood, N.J.: Fleming H. Revell Co., 1960.

Robertson, Archibald, and Plummer, Alfred. *The First Epistle of St. Paul to the Corinthians.* The International Critical Commentary. Edinburgh: T. & T. Clark, 1914.

2 CORINTHIANS

David K. Lowery

INTRODUCTION

Few portions of the New Testament pose as many problems for translators and interpreters as does 2 Corinthians. Few, therefore, are the preachers who undertake a systematic exposition of its contents. For those undaunted by its demands, however, an intimate picture of a pastor's heart may be found as the Apostle Paul shepherded the wayward Corinthians and revealed a love which comes only from God.

Author and Readers. Apart from certain portions of the letter which are sometimes mentioned as non-Pauline interpolations (e.g., 6:14–7:1) most agree that 2 Corinthians came not from the hand of a pseudonymous writer but from the heart of the Apostle Paul. It was sent to a church which he had founded (Acts 18:1-17) on his second missionary journey. He worked there for one and one-half years. Like its winter seas, Corinth was a tempestuous city. (See its location on the map between Acts and Rom.) But what apprehension Paul may have felt was at least partially allayed by a vision in the night (Acts 18:9-10) in which the Lord assured him not only of his personal safety but also revealed that many in this city were appointed to faith. There was ample reason to doubt both affirmations. Not many months before, Paul had been beaten and jailed in Philippi and subsequently had been hounded out of Thessalonica and Berea by irate Jews. A sizable community of Jews resided in Corinth. Nor would Corinth have seemed a likely field in which the seed of the gospel could find fertile soil. True, new Corinth was not the same city once pilloried by Athenian playwrights and philosophers as the home of lechers, harlots, and fornicators (see *Introduction* to 1 Cor.) but its refounding by Rome in 46 B.C. did little to upgrade its moral climate. When Paul wrote the Romans and described the degraded course of rebellious mankind (Rom. 1:21-32), he did so from Corinth where he likely saw the sad portrayal that he wrote about.

Unhappily, the church in Corinth was not immune to this debauchery and came in for correction in Paul's first letter to them (e.g., 1 Cor. 5–6). But it was not only in sexual matters that the Corinthians were still children of their age. They were also easily impressed by external qualities such as eloquence and superior human wisdom (1 Cor. 2) and spectacular gifts such as tongues (1 Cor. 12–14). They walked by sight rather than by faith (cf. 2 Cor. 5:7), a fact Paul sought to amend by his correspondence and visits.

Contacts and Correspondence. The nature and number of Paul's contacts and correspondence with the Corinthians is a matter not easily agreed on. The controversy concerns how many letters Paul dispatched to Corinth (opinions range from three to five), and how many times (two or three) and when he visited them. A discussion of the alternative reconstructions may be found in the more extensive commentaries noted in the *Bibliography* (e.g., Barrett, Hughes). While not affecting the understanding of 1 Corinthians, the accepted scheme of Paul's visits and letters to Corinth does shape the interpretation of 2 Corinthians. In the following comments on the text, the view is taken that four letters were sent and three visits made.

1. Paul first came to Corinth in the spring of A.D. 51 and ministered there for one and one-half years. He sailed in the fall of A.D. 52 with Priscilla and Aquila to Ephesus where they remained while Paul continued on to Jerusalem. At Ephesus, Priscilla and Aquila met Apollos whom they instructed and subsequently sent to Corinth for a period of ministry (Acts 18:18-28).

2. While Apollos ministered in Corinth (Acts 19:1) in the fall of A.D. 53 Paul returned to Ephesus on his third missionary journey. Paul remained there for two and one-half years, establishing it as a center for evangelizing the surrounding provinces as well (Acts 19). The letter mentioned in 1 Corinthians 5:9 (a letter misunderstood by the Corinthians [1 Cor. 5:9-11] and now lost) was probably written during the early stages of this Ephesian ministry.

3. Paul learned of the misunderstanding and of additional problems in the Corinthian church from members of the household of Chloe (1 Cor. 1:11). He then received an official delegation in the form of Stephanas, Fortunatus, and Achaicus (1 Cor. 16:17), who brought corroborating news and specific questions on issues dividing the church. First Corinthians, Paul's second letter to the church, was written to address these matters.

4. But apparently the problems in the church were still not resolved. It is possible that Timothy (cf. 1 Cor. 4:17; 16:10) was the bearer of this news. Paul then decided to pay the church a second visit, sailing directly from Ephesus to Corinth. This, it seems, was the "painful visit" referred to in 2 Corinthians 2:1, apparently because of the action of the man mentioned in 2:5 and 7:12 and the failure of the Corinthians to support Paul.

5. After this visit and Paul's return to Ephesus he sent a third letter to the Corinthians (now lost, like the first) borne by Titus. It grieved Paul deeply to write this (2 Cor. 2:3-4) because of its stark disciplinary nature (7:8-9). After a riot provoked by silversmiths (Acts 19:23-41) Paul left Ephesus in the spring of A.D. 56, bound for Macedonia (Acts 20:1) with a preliminary stop in Troas where he hoped to rendezvous with Titus (2 Cor. 2:13) and receive news about the situation in Corinth. Because he could not find Titus there, he anxiously pushed on to Macedonia, apparently with grave concern about Titus' safety (7:5-6). There he met Titus, who brought good news about the general well-being of the Corinthian church but bad news about a group opposed to Paul.

6. From Macedonia Paul wrote a fourth letter, 2 Corinthians.

7. Paul then made his third visit to Corinth during the winter of A.D. 56-57 (Acts 20:2-3).

These steps, in summary, are: (1) First visit to Corinth. (2) First letter to Corinth (now lost). (3) Second letter to Corinth (1 Cor.). (4) Second visit to Corinth (a "painful visit," 2 Cor. 2:1). (5) Third letter to Corinth (now lost). (6) Fourth letter to Corinth (2 Cor.). (7) Third visit to Corinth.

The two lost letters were obviously not intended by God to be part of the biblical canon.

Purpose and Nature of the Letter. No letter of Paul's is more personal and intimate in nature than 2 Corinthians. In it he bared his soul and professed his abiding love for the Corinthians despite the apparent fickleness of their affection for him.

What concerned Paul preeminently was the presence of false teachers, claiming to be apostles, who had entered the church. They promoted their own ideas and at the same time sought to discredit both the person and message of the apostle. Second Corinthians was written to defend the authenticity of both his apostleship and his message. This was not carried out in a self-protecting spirit but because Paul knew that acceptance of his ministry and message were intimately bound with the Corinthian church's own spiritual well-being.

Who were these opponents of Paul? This is a widely debated issue. One view sees these men as Hellenistic Jews (i.e., Jews whose first language was Gr. either from Palestine, like Stephen, or from the diaspora, like Timothy). Though they claimed to be followers of Christ, they promoted themselves as men in the line of Moses.

A second view is that those claiming to be apostles of Christ were Jews of a Gnostic or Docetic stripe who rejected the earthly sufferings of Jesus in His humiliation and promoted the glory of Jesus in His exaltation as the norm of life in this world. These false teachers were already present when Paul wrote 1 Corinthians (cf. 4:8-21; 12:3), but later they became more vocal in their opposition to Paul and his theology.

A third view is that these opponents were Palestinian Jews claiming to be apostles of Christ. Some who hold this position also feel these opponents were ostensibly concerned to bolster the position of the Jerusalem apostles, James, Peter, and John. They elevated the Law and promoted allegiance to themselves as interpreters of it.

Probably an unequivocal portrait of these opponents will never exist, but there is no disputing the havoc they wreaked in the Corinthian church and the heartaches they brought Paul. Though it is only in the final chapters of 2 Corinthians that Paul challenged them frontally, their influence pervades the entire letter in its threefold development.

1. The first seven chapters are largely a discussion of Paul's ministry as it specifically affected his relationship with the Corinthians and then generally as it reflected the paradoxes that mark the ministry of a servant of Christ. The accusation, no doubt broached by Paul's opponents, that his ministry and message were as suspect as his travel plans, he pointedly rebutted.

2. Chapters 8 and 9 concern the collection for the poor in Jerusalem. The Corinthians had initially welcomed the opportunity to participate but were failing to carry through on their commitment, possibly because Paul's opponents had intimated that he was profiting from their contributions.

3. The final four chapters include (a) a defense of his apostleship and (b) a denunciation of those who opposed him and Christ. Above all else, Paul's identification with Christ marks this letter. His affirmation to the Galatians, "I no longer live, but Christ lives in me" (Gal. 2:20), is graphically portrayed in 2 Corinthians 10–13.

Unity. All of Paul's letters have sections which digress or are discontinuous, but in no letter is this tendency so evident as in 2 Corinthians. The circumstances under which it was composed likely contributed to this but that has not satisfied the numerous advocates who find interpolations rife in 2 Corinthians. Five proposed interpolations may be noted.

1. Second Corinthians 2:14–7:4 is considered by some a separate letter that disrupts the otherwise smooth connection between 2:13 and 7:5.

2. Within the larger unit just noted, 6:14–7:1 is frequently held to be an extraneous section breaking the former bond of 6:13–7:2. According to some, this passage is the previous "letter" mentioned in 1 Corinthians 5:9.

3. Second Corinthians 8 is held by some to be an interpolated portion of a different letter because 9:1 begins as if no comment on the collection preceded it while the transition into that subject in chapter 8 is felt to be unduly abrupt.

4. Some believe chapters 10–13 are a separate letter either preceding 1–9 and forming the "severe letter" or following it by some lapse in time and so forming a fifth and final letter in the Corinthian correspondence.

5. Second Corinthians 11:32–33 seem to be an awkward intrusion in the flow of thought from 11:31–12:1 and is thought to be interpolated by a subsequent reviser of the letter.

While the sections noted are problematic, the proposed resolutions and the resulting truncated letter are even more so. No explanation of how the fragmented lot emerged to form canonical 2 Corinthians has found even minimal acceptance. That, coupled with the fact that not a shred of manuscript evidence exists to support any interpolation, produces a burden no theory can reasonably bear. Thus 2 Corinthians has a cohesive (though digressive) unity.

OUTLINE

COMMENTARY

I. Introduction (1:1-11)

Poised in Macedonia, about to travel to Corinth for a third visit, Paul prepared for his coming by sending this letter. The name of the writer and its recipients followed by a greeting conforms to the usual style of letter writing in the first century (cf. Acts 23:26).

A. Salutation and description of writer and readers (1:1-2)

1:1. Though Paul's description of himself as an apostle was not unusual, in no letter was it more controversial than this one. A defense of the fact that he was **an apostle of Christ Jesus** occupied the heart of this letter. Unlike the false apostles who opposed him in Corinth, **Paul** was sent by Christ Jesus (Acts 9:15). Not a station of his own choosing, apostleship was pressed on him by God (Acts 22:14).

One of Paul's much-loved associates in the ministry was **Timothy.** He is also mentioned in the opening verses of other epistles: Philippians, Colossians, 1 and 2 Thessalonians, Philemon. Timothy joined him near the beginning of the second journey (Acts 16:1-3) and proved to be an invaluable colleague (cf. Phil. 2:19-22). Timothy also had experience ministering at Corinth (Acts 18:5; cf. 1 Cor. 16:10-11; 2 Cor. 1:19), so his association with Paul in the greeting was more than a formality. Though Timothy was a protégé of Paul, the apostle considered him a **brother** (as also in Col. and Phile.).

While there was room for concern about the immediate destiny of **the church of God in Corinth** (cf. 2 Cor. 11:3), Paul was confident that those who composed it belonged to God (cf. Acts 18:10) and no power could wrest them from Him (Rom. 8:38-39). This was true not only of the Corinthians, of course, but also of all Christians living in the region surrounding the capital of **Achaia.** They too were **saints,** set apart by God for service to Him, but they were not immune to the controversy in Corinth or its consequences.

1:2. Grace refers to the love of God in action with **peace** its result. Both aspects were displayed in Jesus' ministry (John 1:14; 14:27). Paul hoped that this salutation would find expression in the Corinthians' lives as he shepherded them. (See the chart, "Paul's Introductions to His Epistles" at Rom. 1:1-7.)

B. Thanksgiving for God's comfort (1:3-11)

One of the many paradoxes of the Christian life is that the grace of God is most keenly experienced not in the best but in what seem to be the worst of times. However much a Christian longs for exaltation (cf. 1 Cor. 4:8), it is often in humiliation that he finds grace (cf. 2 Cor. 12:9). That theme pervades this letter and finds poignant expression in Paul's thanksgiving.

1:3-4. Troubles (*thlipsei*, "pressures, distresses") are mentioned nine times by Paul in this letter (vv. 4 [twice], 8; 2:4; 4:17; 6:4; 7:4; 8:2, 13; sometimes the word is trans. "troubles," other times "hardships"). Paul also used the corresponding verb *thlibō* three times in this epistle ("distressed," 1:6; "hard-pressed," 4:8; "harassed," 7:5). Troubles are experienced by all Christians. And the Apostle Paul probably endured more pressures than nearly all his readers. Troubles, Paul said, help Christians shift their perspective from the external and temporal to the internal and eternal (cf. 1:9; 4:17-18).

The source of **all comfort** in the midst of troubles is **God** Himself, to whom Paul gave three titles: the **Father of our Lord Jesus Christ** (cf. identical wording in Eph. 1:3; 1 Peter 1:3), **the Father** (i.e., the Originator) **of compassion, and the God of all comfort.** This same God had sustained Paul through his suffering (2 Cor. 1:8-9) and delivered him from it (v. 10). "Compassion" translates the Greek *oiktirmōn*, used only four other times in the New Testament (rendered "mercy" in Rom. 12:1 and Heb. 10:28, and "compassion" in Phil. 2:1 and Col. 3:12). Just as spiritual gifts are not intended solely for the recipients' benefit but are to be used in turn for the service of others (cf. 1 Peter 4:10), so comfort **received from God** enables believers to **comfort** others. The comfort of God is channeled through people (cf. Acts 9:10-19; 2 Cor. 7:6) and by means of prayer (1:11). (Paul used a form of "comfort" five times in the Gr. [four are trans. in the NIV] in vv. 3-4, and five more times in vv. 5-7!)

1:5-7. The sufferings Paul experienced were a consequence of his relationship to **Christ** (cf. Matt. 5:11; Col. 1:24). As Paul continued to preach the gospel, he suffered at the hands of men (e.g., 2 Cor. 11:23-26) and from privations which were a part of his task (11:27). But Paul's sufferings for Christ were accompanied by a **comfort** that overflowed.

In referring to **the sufferings of Christ** (1:5), **sufferings we suffer** (v. 6), and **our sufferings** (v. 7), the apostle probably had in mind either the suffering he experienced in Asia which he referred to next (v. 8) or the pain brought to him by the problems of the Corinthian church (cf. 11:28-29). Both kinds may be in mind, but if it was primarily the latter to which he referred (cf. 7:5) then the Corinthians' own suffering was similar. Paul's severe letter (7:8) produced in them a profound sorrow as they understood how their reprehensible behavior had grieved Paul (7:9). It had certainly **distressed** him to write it (2:4) but he did it out of love for them, for their **comfort and salvation** (cf. 7:10). The aspect of salvation suggested here is their advance in sanctification, which in fact this letter produced (cf. 7:11). The Corinthians' response brought comfort to both themselves and Paul (7:13) and reaffirmed Paul's **hope** (1:7) that God indeed had His hand on their lives (cf. Heb. 12:7-8). In addition, the Corinthians' comfort produced in them **patient endurance** (*hypomonē*, steadfastness in the face of unpleasant circumstances; cf. 2 Cor. 6:4; Rom. 5:3; Col. 1:11; James 1:3).

1:8-11. The **hope** in **God** which

sustained Paul in his relationship with the Corinthians was also effective in his own life. An experience in Asia (see map between Acts and Rom.) had brought him to the end of himself. Apparently the Corinthians had some knowledge of this hardship, possibly communicated to them by Titus, but they did not appreciate its severity. Rather than gloss over his feeling of despair and helplessness in this situation Paul underscored it forcefully to illustrate how powerless both he and the Corinthians were apart from God and to stress how important is prayer as a means of effecting God's gracious intervention and aid.

Just what **the hardships** were is debated. Commentators in the 19th century and earlier held that the phrase **in the province of Asia** referred to Ephesus. Paul's experience was linked with that mentioned in 1 Corinthians 15:32, in which he mentioned fighting with wild beasts, a possible allusion to the contention instigated by Demetrius and his fellow silversmiths (Acts 19:23-41). However, no mention is made in that account of any harm coming to Paul. Twentieth-century opinion seems more disposed to locating this experience somewhere in the outlying region of the province of Asia (in the western end of what is today Turkey). One such suggested area is the Lycus Valley, where Paul may have experienced a beating by the Jews (cf. 2 Cor. 11:24), which nearly killed him. Or perhaps he contracted a drastic illness with similar devastating results. All such views are merely conjectures. Being unable to be specific in identifying this experience permits believers today to apply this to themselves, especially when they find themselves in desperate circumstances where deliverance seems impossible.

Paul believed he would die. He was **under** such **great pressure** (*thlipseōs*; cf. 1:4) **far beyond** his human **ability to endure, so that** he **despaired even of life** and **felt the sentence of death** (cf. 4:10-12, 16; 11:23-25). Certainly the Christian life was for him no bed of roses! Some suggest that this experience irrevocably altered Paul's perspective on his own destiny. Before this he expressed the hope that he might be numbered among those who would be alive at the coming of Christ (cf. 1 Cor. 15:51-52; 1 Thes.

4:15-17). Now his focus was on the resurrection (cf. Phil. 3:10-11).

What was sure was Paul's trust that God would **deliver** him from the **peril** of death (cf. 2 Cor. 4:8-14) until his course was run (2 Tim. 4:7), and his task completed. Then later God, he knew, would **deliver** him from **the dead** (cf. 1 Cor. 15:55; 2 Cor. 4:14). Paul had a firm hope in the Corinthians (1:7) and also in the Lord (v. 10). **The prayers** (v. 11) of the Corinthians were part of this deliverance, a means ordained by God to fulfill His will among people.

II. Apostolic Ministry (1:12–7:16)

One reason Paul wrote this letter was to answer insinuations raised in Corinth about the authenticity of his apostleship, the propriety of his conduct, and the sincerity of his commitment to those Christians. Later (in chaps. 10–13) Paul gave a defense of the genuineness of his apostleship. Questions about the propriety of his conduct, especially as it concerned "the collection," are addressed in chapters 8 and 9. The burden of these preceding chapters (1:12–7:16) is an emotional affirmation by Paul of his sincere commitment to the ministry in general and to the Corinthians in particular.

A. Changed plans defended (1:12–2:11)

Who raised the questions in the Corinthians' minds about Paul's supposed lack of commitment to the church in Corinth or his alleged insincerity? No one knows for sure. But a reasonable conclusion is that they were broached by false apostles (11:4, 13) who hoped to discredit their chief rival. Though Paul reserved his open confrontation with these opponents for the conclusion of his letter, a polemic pervades even these early chapters.

1:12. Paul met questions concerning his motives head-on. He could affirm with confidence—**this is our boast**—that the moral sensibilities of his **conscience** (cf. 4:2; 5:11), intensified by his knowledge of God's Word, were without censure regarding his conduct, **especially in** his **relations with** the Corinthians (cf. 1 Cor. 4:3-4). He said three things about his conduct. (1) It was with a singleness of heart. Instead of **holiness** (*hagiotēti*) Paul probably wrote "simplicity in the sense of

singlemindedness" (*haplotēti*; cf. 2 Cor. 11:3). These two Greek words could easily have been confused by a manuscript copyist. (2) His conduct was in **sincerity** (cf. 1 Cor. 5:8; 2 Cor. 2:17) of purpose that could stand the closest scrutiny. (3) His conduct was **not** in keeping with **worldly** (*sarkikē*, lit., "fleshly," i.e., human) **wisdom,** for that is ultimately self-serving. Instead it was **according to God's grace,** that is, he was guided by a love for others and sought what was in their best interests.

1:13-14. Paul's letters were like his conduct: simple, sincere, not in manmade wisdom but in God's grace. Paul had no hidden meanings or ulterior motives in his correspondence with the Corinthians. He was aboveboard and straightforward in person; and he was the same way in his letters. He felt the Corinthians must acknowledge this to a degree (**in part**). And he hoped that this provisional assent would one day grow into their wholehearted acceptance and endorsement (**understand fully**). That in fact was how Paul viewed them. He was confident of the genuineness of their conversions (cf. 1 Cor. 9:1-2). And he felt they would eventually come to vindicate him and even **boast of** (*kauchēma*, "exult over") him **in the day of the Lord Jesus** (cf. Phil. 2:16), that is, at the judgment seat of Christ (cf. 2 Cor. 5:10-11).

1:15-16. In this spirit of confidence in his relationship with the Corinthians, Paul had proposed a journey from Ephesus that would have permitted him **to visit** them **twice.** This was apparently a change in the plans he had stated earlier (1 Cor. 16:5-7). At that time he hoped to go to Corinth by way of Macedonia and spend the winter with them, a course of action he eventually followed (cf. Acts 20:1-3). The change included the opportunity for two visits: first from Ephesus to Corinth and then on **to Macedonia;** then a second stop as he retraced his route. The two visits were meant to express Paul's affection for them. He wanted to see them as often as possible.

1:17. But Paul changed his mind about this itinerary (cf. 2:1), and his opponents said his vacillating was a sign of a fundamental unreliability, affecting not only where he went but what he said. Paul fervently denied this. He did not make **plans in a worldly** (i.e., self-serving; cf. "worldly" in 1:12) **manner** altering them for reasons of self-interest. Nor did he talk out of both sides of his mouth to further his own ends. He would explain the reason for his change in plans (1:23–2:2), but for the moment he was more concerned with the accusation that his message was equivocal or unreliable.

1:18-20. The source of stability for Paul in his ministry was God Himself, who **is faithful,** and the **message** Paul preached was no less certain than God. Since Paul did not vacillate in his message **(Yes and No,** v. 18), he did not vacillate in his plans either **(Yes, yes and No, no,** v. 17). At the heart of that message was the person of **Jesus Christ who** completely affirms all God's **promises** to people. The only proper response to God's message is **Amen** (lit., "let it be so"). It was this response of obedience to God that brought Paul **and Silas and Timothy** to Corinth in the first place and caused them to exalt Christ among the Corinthians in the synagogue (Acts 18:5). In Christ the promises to Abraham and David are fulfilled (Rom. 1:3; 11:5; Gal. 3:16) and the Law was brought to an end (Rom. 10:4), a truth apparently contested by Paul's opponents (cf. 2 Cor. 3). Nevertheless this message proclaimed by Paul and his associates resulted in the Corinthians' salvation and in turn brought **glory** to God.

1:21-22. Those who speak the "Amen" in response to the gospel message experience firmness and security **in Christ.** At the moment of belief **God** anoints each believer with the Holy Spirit so that like Christ (*Christos* means "the Anointed One"), he may glorify God by his life (cf. Matt. 5:16). John wrote that believers receive this anointing from God (1 John 2:20, 27). It is a pouring out of the Holy Spirit on the believer, reminiscent of the anointing of priests with oil.

A further consequence of the Spirit's presence is the **seal of ownership** (cf. Eph. 1:13-14) which also is accomplished at the moment of faith. A seal on a document in New Testament times identified it and indicated its owner, who would "protect" it. So too, in salvation, the Holy Spirit, like a seal, confirms that Christians are identified with Christ and are God's property, protected by Him (cf. 1 Cor. 6:19-20). It was probably this thought that caused Paul to describe

himself as a slave of Christ (Rom. 1:1; Phil. 1:1).

A third work of the Spirit at salvation is His confirmation that what God has begun He will complete. Present redemption is only a foretaste of what eternity holds (cf. Rom. 8:23), and the presence of **His Spirit in our hearts** (cf. Rom. 5:5; 2 Cor. 5:5) is like **a deposit, guaranteeing what is to come.** These last seven words are a translation of one Greek word *arrabōna*, a down payment which obligates the payer to make further payments. The same Greek word is used again in 5:5 and Ephesians 1:14 (cf. "the firstfruits of the Spirit," Rom. 8:23).

1:23-24. Paul had earlier begun to explain his change of plans (v. 15). There he had mentioned his "message" (v. 18) in connection with his own integrity, which led to his digression in verses 19-22. He now returned to explain his altered plans.

He understood that his changed plans had caused a problem in Corinth. This is evident from the strength of his declaration, **I call God as my witness** (cf. Rom. 1:9; Phil. 1:8; 1 Thes. 2:5, 10). With a solemn oath (with God as the Judge) Paul staked his life on the truthfulness of his explanation which followed. It was out of consideration for the Corinthians, a desire to avoid disciplinary action **(to spare you)** that Paul had deferred his visit. Even though he had great authority as an apostle (2 Cor. 10:2-8; cf. 1 Cor. 5:4-5; 1 Tim. 1:20) Paul was reluctant to wield it. He did not **lord it over** their **faith,** that is, domineeringly take advantage of the fact that they came to faith in Christ through him. Dictatorial means can produce compliance but not the obedience that comes from faith which he sought. Authoritarian domination is often the manner of false apostles and the kingdom they serve (cf. 2 Cor. 11:13-15), but it was not the way of Christ (Luke 22:25-27) nor of those who stand in His stead (1 Peter 5:3). Paul assured the Corinthians, **We work with you** (lit., "we are fellow workers"; cf. 1 Cor. 3:9); he did not work against them or over them.

2:1-2. A servant of Christ is no stranger to pain and suffering (Matt. 5:10-12; John 15:18-20; 1 Peter 2:21). Paul had his share (cf. 2 Cor. 1:4-10; 11:16-32) which he did not shirk. But he was no fool. If he could avoid it and still accomplish his work he would do so. This belief led to his change of plans with the Corinthians.

When his first **painful visit** occurred is an unsettled issue. It could have taken place after his founding visit but before the writing of 1 Corinthians, as many suggest. It is odd, however, if that was so, that no mention or intimation of such a visit is found in that letter. More likely, he went to Corinth from Ephesus after writing 1 Corinthians. His "painful visit" may be linked to the projected double visit previously mentioned (2 Cor. 1:15-16) and may thus refer to the first part of those unconsummated plans. During that visit some painful event transpired which **grieved** the Corinthians and Paul (see comments on 2:5). To spare further grief for both of them Paul deferred his visit.

2:3-4. He decided instead to write a letter, a daring venture in view of the Corinthians' propensity for misunderstanding (cf. 1 Cor. 5:9-10). If his "painful visit" (2 Cor. 2:1) had occurred before he wrote 1 Corinthians, the letter here referred to (**I wrote as I did**) would be that letter. But if, as seems more likely, the "painful visit" occurred after he **wrote** 1 Corinthians, the letter Paul referred to followed 1 Corinthians and is now lost (not having been intended by God as a part of the inspired Scriptures). (See point 5 under "Contacts and Correspondence" in the *Introduction.*)

What that letter contained can only be conjectured from the comments which follow in 2 Corinthians 2:5-11 and 7:5-12. What is clear was Paul's depth of feelings for the Corinthians and the level of his own discomfort experienced in writing the letter (**great distress** [*thlipseōs;* "troubles or pressures"; cf. 1:4] **and anguish of heart and with many tears**) and in his waiting for news from Titus concerning its reception (cf. 7:5-8).

2:5. The event that made his visit painful (v. 1) and prompted the severe letter seems to have centered around the action of a certain man at Corinth. Whether he was a member of the Corinthian church or someone visiting them is not clear. Paul did, however, regard him as a Christian.

What this individual did to cause grief is uncertain. In the past many writers identified him with the incestuous

man whom Paul had judged (1 Cor. 5). Relatively few now hold this view because of the severity of that judgment (cf. 1 Cor. 5:5) when compared with this situation, and the unlikelihood that 1 Corinthians is the letter referred to in 2 Corinthians 2:3-4.

Paul's diffidence in this verse sug-. gests the more likely alternative that his authority as an apostle was affronted or challenged at some point in the course of his painful visit (v. 1). The Corinthians apparently failed to make the connection between a challenge to Paul's authority and their own spiritual well-being. They had regarded this as a personal problem requiring no action on their parts, a view which Paul had dispelled in his letter and which they now realized.

2:6. Their response had been to discipline the offender. **Punishment** may be too strong a translation of the Greek word *epitimia.* Perhaps "censure" is better. This discipline, whatever it was, was made **by** the church "as a whole" (*hē hypo tōn pleionōn*) rather than the **majority** (cf. 7:11).

2:7-8. Paul had reason to believe that their pendulum might swing too far (cf. 7:11). They were no longer dispassionate spectators of the wrongdoer, and might become impassioned prosecutors. In that case he would **be overwhelmed by excessive sorrow** (lit., "grief"). The offender was apparently penitent so Paul urged the church **to forgive and comfort him** (for in fact it was they who had been wronged, 2:10) and extend "comfort" to him. As a church they were to affirm their **love for** this fellow Christian and admit him to their fellowship (cf. 1 Cor. 5:11). (**Reaffirm** may be too strong for the word *kyrōsai;* it occurs elsewhere in the NT only in Gal. 3:15 where it is trans. "has been duly established.")

2:9-11. Paul's concern in this matter was not simply personal vindication or primarily that an erring brother be brought in line but that the Corinthian congregation could demonstrate the strength of their commitment to Paul (cf. 7:2). Their love and devotion to him would be affirmed by their being **obedient** to his directives (cf. John 15:14).

The expression of their solidarity with him was mutual. As one with him, they could **forgive** this offender who had wronged them by wronging Paul. Like their own sorrow for this wrong (2 Cor. 7:8) repentance resulted (cf. 7:9) so that Paul could offer forgiveness. Otherwise, **Satan might** use a bitterness of spirit to vitiate Paul's or the Corinthians' ministry. It was important that fellowship between Paul, the Corinthians, and the repentant offender be restored so that the incident **not** become an occasion for Satan to drive a wedge between the church and Paul. This was one of Satan's **schemes** (cf. 11:13-14) which Paul had worked so strenuously to thwart.

In sum, his plans had changed. But that was out of concern for the well-being of the Corinthian church. In place of a personal visit Paul had sent Titus with a letter and accomplished his purpose. But he did not know that until he met Titus in Macedonia. The interim was not an easy time for Paul as 2:12-16 indicate.

B. Glorious ministry described (2:12–7:16)

The interim period between Paul's dispatch of Titus with the letter (2:4; 7:6-7) and his return to report on the state of affairs in the Corinthian church was a turbulent time for Paul. He apparently sensed in an acute way his own helplessness and weakness and came to appreciate afresh how utterly dependent he was on God to accomplish anything of lasting value in his ministry. That theme pervades this section. A ministry is glorious because God is in it.

1. TRIUMPHANT IN CHRIST (2:12–3:6)

2:12-13. Paul had planned to rendezvous with **Titus** at **Troas** (see map between Acts and Rom.) and be apprised of the Corinthian situation. Before proceeding to Greece Paul had hoped to minister in Troas, a favored Roman colony. **The Lord had opened a door** (cf. 1 Cor. 16:9; Col. 4:3) for him, that is, had given him a favorable opportunity **to preach the gospel of Christ.**

But those hopes were dashed when Titus failed to appear. In addition to his apprehension about the church in Corinth, Paul was now also concerned about Titus' safety. For all Paul knew Titus might have been carrying with him a portion of the proposed Corinthian collection (cf. 2 Cor. 8:6) and fallen prey to bandits. Why else had he failed to meet Paul in Troas? Thus Paul **had no**

peace of mind (*anesin tō pneumati*, lit., "relief in spirit"; *anesin* is also used in 7:5 and 8:13).

Despairing at his own inability to concentrate on the great potential for ministry in Troas (cf. 7:5-6) Paul **said good-by to** the church there and pushed **on to Macedonia.** The door would remain open for him and on his return (cf. Acts 20:5-11) God used him mightily in their midst, but for the moment Paul departed, unable to rise to the occasion, no doubt feeling like a beaten man (cf. 2 Cor. 4:9).

2:14. At this juncture Paul broke off his narrative to the Corinthians, not to resume it until 7:5. (Cf. "Macedonia" in 2:13 and 7:5.) But this transition is fitting. The defeated Paul drew attention from himself to the triumphant **Christ** in whose train, by the grace of God, he found himself.

Paul's words in 2:14 are based on a Roman **triumphal procession,** the victory parade awarded a conquering general in which enemy prisoners were forced to march. Through Christ, **God** the Victor had vanquished His enemies (cf. Rom. 5:10; Col. 2:15) and Paul, Christ's captive, was now marching in His parade! Paul, who had been "taken captive" by Christ (in Phile. 23 "fellow prisoner" is lit. "fellow captive"; cf. 1 Cor. 4:9), was now led in triumph. This "triumph in defeat," by a slave who was free, was the paradox of the ministry which Paul subsequently amplified (e.g., in 2 Cor. 4:7-12; 6:9-10).

In a Roman triumph processional incense was burned. Paul compared this to **the knowledge of** Christ, which like a **fragrance** was diffused **everywhere** throughout the world via the preaching of the gospel.

2:15-16. The gospel produces paradoxical results. As a bearer of this message Paul was identified with it so that he could refer to himself as **the aroma of Christ.** In the Septuagint the term "aroma" (*euōdia*) was used of Old Testament sacrifices (Gen. 8:21; Ex. 29:18; Lev. 1:9; Num. 15:3). Paul's life was a sacrificial offering (Rom. 12:1), well-pleasing to God. The course of his life in proclaiming God's message while at the same time suffering rejection and attack by many was an extension of Jesus' life as the Servant of God (cf. Col. 1:24).

The heart of the gospel is that

225

through Jesus' death people may receive life and resurrection (1 Cor. 15). To those who rejected the gospel and disbelieved the message of Christ crucified and raised Paul was like the stench of death in their nostrils (Acts 17:32). They continued on the path to destruction. But to those who believe, their salvation leads on to glorification (cf. 2 Cor. 4:17; Rom. 8:18, 30). For them the gospel is like **the fragrance of life.**

This twofold consequence of Paul's ministry staggered him. **Who is equal to such a task?** He answered this question later (2 Cor. 3:5-6). For the moment, however, he recalled the work of the false apostles. They thought themselves more than adequate but it was because their message and motivation differed so radically from Paul's. To that point he needed to respond.

2:17. In Paul's day there was apparently no lack of false apostles (cf. 2 Peter 2:1). According to Paul, the ministry of the **many** false apostles was a matter of self-interest. **Unlike** them, he had ministered in Corinth without charge (cf. 2 Cor. 11:7-12; 12:14), though in principle he had no problem accepting material remuneration for spiritual labor (1 Cor. 9). What characterized the false apostles were their messages and their motives. Like dishonest merchants they selfishly hawked their wares. Paul said they **peddle** God's Word. This word *kapēleuontes,* "to hawk, peddle," is used only here. Paul may have had in mind Isaiah's description of Jerusalem's unscrupulous Israelites who "diluted" their wine with water to increase their profits (Isa. 1:22; cf. Lucian's description [*Hermotimus* 59] of similarly unscrupulous philosophers). So too these false apostles adulterated **the Word of God for profit.** They served themselves, not **God** whom Paul represented. They were "greedy for money" (1 Peter 5:2), an evidence of their falsehood. But Paul ministered **with sincerity** (cf. 2 Cor. 1:12).

3:1-3. Aware of the tactics of his opponents, Paul realized that his swipe at the false apostles and defense of his own ministry might be turned against him. His first question in verse 1 (**Are we beginning to commend ourselves again?**) suggests that this had happened before (cf. 1 Cor. 9).

Related to this, some might suppose

Paul had to commend himself because he could find no one else to do so. His opponents obviously carried **letters of recommendation,** a common practice in the first century (cf. Oxyrhynchus papyri 1. 32). Paul himself followed this practice at various times on behalf of those who served with him (Rom. 16:1-2; 2 Cor. 8:22-24). Paul, however, had reason to doubt the authenticity of their letters (4:2). Unlike those false letters, apparently unavailable to public scrutiny, Paul's letter of commendation could be examined **by everybody.** His "letter" was the Corinthians themselves! And they were **a letter . . . written** by **the Spirit of the living God** dispatched by **Christ** Himself. The false apostles' commendation was human; Paul's was divine (cf. 1 Cor. 2:1-5).

When Paul spoke of that **letter written on our hearts,** "hearts" probably included Timothy and Titus. **On tablets of human hearts** alluded to the nature of the New Covenant (Jer. 31:33). In contrast with the Old Covenant inscribed in stone (Ex. 24:12), the New Covenant is inscribed on human hearts (Ezek. 11:19; 36:26). As the New is far superior to the Old, so was Paul's commendation compared with that of the false apostles.

3:4-6. Paul's **confidence** was founded not on human resources but on divine ones. He was confident in the Corinthians because the Holy **Spirit** had worked in them. Their faith rested on God's power (1 Cor. 2:1-5). Likewise his own sufficiency and **competence** in the ministry was derived wholly **from God** (cf. 1 Tim. 1:12).

Paul's emphasis on the **New Covenant** implies that his opponents were ministers of the Old Covenant. The Mosaic Covenant was a written revelation of the righteousness God asked of Israel (e.g., Ex. 19–23). It was accepted with an oath of obedience and a blood sacrifice (Ex. 24). When Israel proved unable and unwilling to remain faithful to that covenant, God graciously intervened and promised a New Covenant (Jer. 31:31-34; 32:40), new (*kainēs*) both in time and in quality. It was inaugurated by Christ in His sacrifice on the cross (Luke 22:20), and is entered into by faith (Phil. 3:9) and lived out in dependence on the Spirit (Rom. 7:6; 8:4). (However, the physical and national aspects of the New Covenant which pertain to Israel have not been appropriated to the church. Those are yet to be fulfilled in the Millennium. The church today shares in the soteriological aspects of that covenant, established by Christ's blood for all believers [cf. Heb. 8:7-13].)

Reliance on human rather than divine authority in letters of commendation was shortsighted and dangerous (2 Cor. 3:1-3). Even more so was the attempt to fulfill God's righteousness apart from divine enablement. Those who did so found that **the letter kills** (cf. Rom. 7:10-11). But those who trust in Christ find that **the Spirit gives life** (cf. Rom. 8:2).

2. GLORY FROM THE SPIRIT (3:7-18)

In the preceding portion of this letter (2:12–3:6) Paul had begun an explanation and a defense of his ministry. Prompted by the inference that his credentials were inadequate Paul cited the internal attestation of the Spirit as superior to any external human commendation. In so doing he intimated that those challenging him proclaimed an adulterated message based on the Old Covenant, acceptance of which could only lead to death.

To underscore the superiority of the New Covenant to that of the Old, particularly as it was proclaimed by his opponents, Paul discussed Exodus 34:29-35. His point was to show that the Old Covenant, because it came from God, was glorious. But because its fulfillment was based on human initiative, it ultimately was transitory and "fading" (katargeō, 2 Cor. 3:7, 11, 13), needing to be replaced by the New Covenant and the Spirit's ministry which is eternal (Heb. 9:14). To illustrate this, Paul contrasted the fading radiance of God's glory on the face of Moses (2 Cor. 3:7) with the ever-increasing radiance of Christians (v. 18).

3:7. The Old Covenant **ministry** of Moses **brought death** to people. It was not the fault of Moses or the Law, which was "holy, righteous, and good" (Rom. 7:12; cf. 1 Tim. 1:8). It was the fault of human sin (Rom. 7:10-11). Still even this ministry of death had a **glory,** though transitory and **fading** (cf. 2 Cor. 3:11, 13), which was visually illustrated by the Old Covenant's intended obsolescence.

When Moses came down from Mount Sinai with the tablets of the Ten Commandments, his face was so radiant

that the people were afraid to approach him (Ex. 34:29-30). The Old Testament, however, does not mention the fading of this radiance. On the contrary, a part of Jewish tradition maintained that Moses carried the glory of that encounter to his grave (Targum Onkelos; Deut. 34:7). It seems unlikely, however, that Paul would have put forth a novel interpretation which might be easily rejected, especially a view central to his argument, when he had exercised such care thus far in developing this letter.

3:8-11. On this point, the fading of Moses' **glory,** Paul proceeded to argue for the superiority of the New Covenant. The ministry of the Old Covenant, by means of the commandments, condemned **men** (cf. Rom. 7:11). The **ministry of** the New, by means of **the Spirit,** leads men to faith in Christ and the imputation of His **righteousness** (Rom. 3:21-22; 4:24). Like a candle before the sun the Old Covenant paled and passed away (Gal. 3:19-25) before the grandeur of the New, which is eternal (Heb. 13:20). If the Old is **glorious,** how **much more glorious** is the New!

3:12. Because the New Covenant is eternal its recipients had the certain **hope** of acceptance by God. This permitted Paul to be **bold** and candid in speech and action.

3:13. In contrast was the ministry of **Moses** who veiled **his face** as he addressed Israel so that they could not see **the radiance** (produced by those meetings with God) **fading away.** Why did he do this? Did Moses believe that the rebellious Israelites would be less inclined to obey God if they witnessed a diminishing of this awesome radiance? Or did Moses consider them unworthy recipients of this display of God's glory and so veiled his face as a commentary on the hardness of their hearts? Perhaps it was the latter.

3:14-16. Whatever was Moses' reason for using the **veil,** his action proved to be prophetic. Not only was ancient Israel unwilling or unable to comprehend (**their minds were made dull**) the transitory and preparatory nature of **the Old Covenant,** but the dullness remained with subsequent generations. The Jews of Paul's day (**to this day**) failed to perceive that the Old Covenant was a preliminary message, not the final word of God's revelation. Though the cloth that veiled

Moses' glory and the Old Covenant was gone, Paul said a perceptible spiritual veil remains and has not been removed (cf. 4:3-4; Rom. 11:7-8, 25).

The veil of unbelief that covers their hearts can be taken away only in Christ (2 Cor. 3:14), that is, whenever anyone turns to the Lord. Moses removed his physical veil in the presence of the Lord. So for any Jew—or anyone—who turns in faith to Christ the Lord his spiritual veil is removed. The Lord who mediated the Old Covenant is the same Lord who established the New.

3:17. In the Old Covenant when Moses entered the Lord's presence he removed his veil (Ex. 34:34). In the New Covenant it is the Spirit who removes the veil. The Holy Spirit is the personal "Agent" of Christ; He is the Spirit of the Lord (cf. Rom. 8:9). The Two are One in purpose (John 15:26; 16:6-15) and in result (Rom. 8:15; Gal. 5:1). Paul's words the Lord is the Spirit (2 Cor. 3:17; cf. v. 18) do not confuse these two Persons of the Godhead. Instead, they affirm the Holy Spirit's deity.

A major result of the New Covenant is freedom. Elsewhere Paul compared those under the Old Covenant to children of slavery and those under the New to children of freedom (Gal. 4:24-31). This freedom is possible because Christ has redeemed from the penalty of the Law those who believe so that they become children of God (Gal. 4:5-7). This freedom as children is confirmed by the Spirit, who enables Christians to call God Father (Rom. 8:15; Gal. 4:6).

3:18. The glory evident in Moses' face was a diminishing radiance (vv. 7, 13). By contrast, in the faces of Christians is God's ever-increasing glory (cf. 4:6). ("Ever-increasing glory" is the NIV's rendering of the Gr. phrase, "from glory into glory," i.e., from one stage of glory to another.) Christians' glory, like that of Moses, is a reflection of the Lord's glory. But unlike Moses' transitory glory a believer's glory is eternal. This is because of God's abiding presence through the Holy Spirit (4:17). This glory is the experience of salvation available in the New Covenant and mediated by the Spirit who leads Christians from justification through sanctification to glorification. As believers manifest the fruit of the Spirit (Gal. 5:22-23), they are progres-

sively being transformed (the same word Paul used in Rom. 12:2) into His likeness. Christlikeness is the goal of the Christian walk (Eph. 4:23-24; Col. 3:10). No wonder Paul said the New is far superior to the Old!

3. POWER FROM GOD (4:1-15)

The New Covenant ministry is glorious because of the certain triumph of Christ (2:14) and the transforming work of the Spirit (3:18), but it is not without its hardships. Physically, the demands of Paul's ministry sometimes seemed too much for him to bear (cf. 1:8; 11:23-27). No less excruciating were the spiritual demands (cf. 7:5; 11:28-29) brought on by those he served (e.g., 2:4) and those he opposed (e.g., 2:5). He reflected on these experiences in this passage and pointed to what sustained him, namely, the power of God (4:7).

4:1. The ministry (*diakonia*, "service"; also used in 5:18; 6:3; 8:4; 9:1; 12-13; 11:8) of the New Covenant was given to Paul in spite of his past (cf. 1 Cor. 15:9-10; 1 Tim. 1:13) because of God's grace and compassion on him. That same mercy sustained Paul through the many painful episodes that marked his ministry (cf. 2 Cor. 1:3-11) and enabled him to overcome feelings of despair (cf. 7:6). Thus he could write, we do not lose heart (4:1, 16). "Give up" in Luke 18:1 is the same verb translated "lose heart." Though discouraged at times, the great apostle never quit.

4:2. One source of discouragement was the disquieting state of affairs in Corinth. This was caused by the activity of false apostles in the church and the passivity of the Christians. In the face of sharp accusations Paul found it necessary to defend himself before people who should have trusted him implicitly. Already he had adroitly parried the attacks of his accusers several times in the letter (e.g., 1:17; 2:17; 3:1), but he felt forced to do so again (e.g., 6:3; 7:3; 10-13). Some accused him of using the gospel deceitfully to serve his own ends (deception translates the Gr. *panourgia*, "trickery, cunning"; in 11:3 this word is used of Satan). Perhaps Paul had the collection in mind (12:16-18; cf. 2:17). In response he pointed to the openness (we have renounced secret and shameful ways . . . setting forth the truth plainly)

and boldness (cf. 3:12) which characterized his proclamation of the gospel.
Unlike his opponents, he did not **distort**
("falsify") **the Word of God**. Thus he
could **commend** himself (cf. 6:4) before
others and God (cf. **conscience** in 1:12;
5:11).

4:3-4. Of course many people,
particularly Jews (3:14-15), did not accept
the **gospel**. To them it was **veiled**. But
Paul would not change it to make it more
palatable, as his opponents had done
(11:4). The gospel was rejected by people
who were unable and unwilling to accept
it (cf. 1 Cor. 1:18; 2:14). They disbelieved
and were abetted in their unbelief by
Satan, **the god of this Age** (cf. Eph. 2:2)
who, though defeated by Christ (Heb.
2:14), continues his hold over the present
world (1 Peter 5:8; 1 John 5:19). His
blinding of peoples' **minds** makes it
impossible for them to **see the light of
the gospel**.

The gospel, then, is not obscure. In
fact, it points to **Christ** who, as **the image
of God** (cf. Col. 1:15), revealed God the
Father by His words and actions (cf. John
1:18; 14:9).

4:5. Christ was the Focus of Paul's
message and the Object of his concern.
Contrary to what Paul's accusers suggested (v. 2), he labored to advance the
cause of Christ (**for Jesus' sake**) and not
his own interests. **Jesus** was the crucified
Christ and the resurrected **Lord**. Since
Paul served Christ, he also served the
church, Christ's body (Eph. 1:22-23).
While serving the Corinthians, however
unworthy they were, Paul was serving his
Lord (cf. Matt. 25:40).

4:6. The reason Paul served the
church and openly proclaimed the gospel
was because of God's work in his life.
Much as in creating the world God acted
to bring **light . . . out of darkness** (Gen.
1:2-4), so in spiritual creation He brings
light to **the hearts** of those in darkness
(cf. Luke 1:78-79; Acts 26:18). This had
been Paul's experience on the Damascus
Road, when "a light from heaven flashed
around him" (Acts 9:3). Confronted with
the risen Lord, he became a new creation
(cf. 2 Cor. 5:17). **The light** in believers'
lives is **the knowledge of** God's salvation,
a **glory** issuing from and seen **in the face
of Christ** and reflected by Paul (cf. 3:18).
When people were in the darkness of sin,
they had no knowledge of God, no

experience of His life and salvation (Eph.
4:18).

4:7. The message of salvation and
the results it produces are glorious and
divine. By contrast the bearer of the
message is a mere mortal person. The
contrast is like a great **treasure** contained
in common **jars of clay**. A deepening
sense of his own unworthiness, compared
with the grandeur of his message,
characterized Paul's life (cf. Eph. 3:7-9).
God intended this sharp contrast so that
no one would question the source of the
gospel and its **all-surpassing power.**
Salvation is the work of **God** not men (cf.
1 Cor. 2:5; 3:7).

4:8-9. In his earlier letter Paul had
compared himself and his fellow apostles
to "men condemned to die in the arena"
(1 Cor. 4:9). The metaphors employed
here evoked the same imagery to describe
the demands of the ministry, contrasting
human helplessness on one hand with
divine enablement on the other. The
contrasts include physical (cf. 2 Cor.
1:8-9; 6:5, 9) as well as psychological
affliction (cf. 6:4, 8; 7:5-6). **Hard-pressed**
is the participle *thlibomenoi*, related to
thlipsis ("trouble, pressure, hardship"; cf.
1:4). Interestingly the words **perplexed**
and **in despair** render two similar Greek
words: *aporoumenoi* ("despairing") and
exaporoumenoi ("totally despairing").
Without God's intervention these troubles would have broken Paul (cf. 1:8-10).

4:10-11. The paradoxes in verses 8-9
dramatically contrast the weakness which
marked the humiliation of Jesus' earthly
life and the power associated with His
heavenly exaltation (13:4). In 1 Corinthians Paul had said the content of his
message is "Christ crucified" (1 Cor.
1:23). In this letter he referred to his own
life as a demonstration of this humiliation, a constant reminder that through
human weakness the power of God is
seen to greatest effect (2 Cor. 12:9-10). In
his own **body** he carried **around . . . the
death of Jesus,** that is, he suffered
intensely for Jesus and bore physical scars
resulting from wounds inflicted by
beatings and a stoning because of his
testimony **for Jesus' sake** (cf. 1 Cor. 4:11;
2 Cor. 6:5, 9; 11:23-25; Gal. 6:17). He was
always being given over to death, that is,
he constantly faced death (cf. 2 Cor. 1:9).
Paul noticed that God usually chose weak
people to serve Him (cf. 1 Cor. 1:26-29).

He subsequently argued for the genuineness of his apostleship on the basis of his sufferings (2 Cor. 11:23-24) and his weakness (11:30; 12:5).

However, **the life of Jesus** was also **revealed in** Paul's **body**, that is, it was evident that he was alive spiritually (cf. 4:16). By means of these experiences his transformation into Christlikeness advanced (3:18).

4:12. But though Paul saw suffering as paradoxically beneficial for himself (Phil. 3:10), he was ultimately motivated by the example of his Lord who gave His life on behalf of others (Mark 10:45; cf. Phil. 2:5-8). Paul believed his own sufferings were a means through which God could minister to the Corinthians (2 Cor. 1:5-6; cf. Eph. 3:10; 2 Tim. 2:10). As Christ had brought life to others through His suffering and death, so Paul's suffering (with **death . . . at work in** him [cf. 2 Cor. 4:10-11]) was a means of causing spiritual **life** to be **at work in** others (Col. 1:24).

4:13-14. What enabled Paul to endure in the face of this suffering? His quotation of Psalm 116:10 gives the answer. The psalmist referred to "the anguish of the grave" (116:3), but he affirmed his confidence that God would deliver him "from death" (116:8). That same confidence was Paul's, so with the psalmist he could declare **I believed.** The second part of the quotation, **Therefore I have spoken,** is from the psalmist's words about his own suffering: "Therefore I said, 'I am greatly afflicted.' " Paul did not quote these last words from Psalm 116:10. But he probably expected his readers to understand that he had in mind his own disclosure of suffering in the preceding verses (2 Cor. 4:8-12) and throughout this letter.

Paul could speak of his suffering and death because he was confident that God would deliver him (cf. 1:9-10). This confidence was founded on the resurrection of Christ, the Firstfruit and Guarantee of resurrection for all who place their faith for salvation in Him (1 Cor. 15:12-19; 1 Thes. 4:14).

4:15. All this suffering that Paul experienced was for the **benefit** of Christians like the Corinthians (cf. v. 12). And yet Paul had said he suffered "for Jesus' sake " (v. 11). This illustrates how he identified the church with Christ.

Paul's ministry to the church, Christ's body (Eph. 1:22-23), was also a ministry to Christ (cf. Matt. 25:40).

The grace of God, His unmerited goodness and kindness, was extended to **more and more people** through the gospel Paul preached. Those who heard and responded in belief received salvation and gave thanks to God (cf. Eph. 1:6, 12, 14). As more came to the Savior, it caused **thanksgiving to overflow** (or increase). This verse underscores the selflessness of Paul's ministry. It was for the benefit of others and **to the glory of God** (cf. Mark 12:33), not for himself (cf. 2 Cor. 2:5).

4. ETERNAL PERSPECTIVE (4:16–5:10)

Paul well knew what it was to suffer in ministering for Christ. His distress at not finding Titus in Troas had been a part of that suffering. Remembrance of that painful experience (2:12-13) and God's provision of comfort (7:5-6) touched off this intervening meditation (in 2:12–7:4) on the greatness of the New Covenant ministry. The ministry triumphed in Christ (2:12–3:6), was glorious because of the ministry of the Spirit (3:7-18), and received its power from God (4:1-15). Now Paul turned to another aspect of this ministry, its eternal perspective.

4:16. Paul was not immune to discouragement in his ministry (1:8). In fact, Titus' failure to meet him in Troas disturbed him deeply (2:13; 7:5-6). It was just one of many experiences (e.g., 4:8-9; 11:23-29) which wore him down and reminded him of his mortality (4:11). But God had given him "this ministry" (v. 1) and God—the triumphant Son (2:14), the glorious Spirit (3:18), and the powerful Father (4:7)—was at work in it. God was also the assurance of his resurrection (4:14). Because of all this Paul did **not lose heart** (i.e., "give up"; cf. v. 1; Luke 18:1).

True, his earthly mortality was increasingly evident; **outwardly** he was **wasting away** (cf. 2 Cor. 1:8-9; 4:8-12). But his heavenly destiny was also increasingly evident (vv. 17-18). While physically he grew weaker, spiritually he experienced the renewing (cf. Rom. 12:2; Col. 3:10) work of the Holy Spirit **day by day.** He was becoming increasingly like Christ (2 Cor. 3:18), a prelude to what will be (cf. Rom. 8:23; 1 John 3:2).

4:17-18. Part of the means used by God in this transforming, renewing process is suffering (cf. 1 Peter 4:1, 13-14). Paul compared the sufferings he had experienced, severe as they were (2 Cor. 11:23-29), to **light and momentary troubles** (*thlipseōs*, "pressures, hardships"; cf. 1:4). They were nothing in view of the **eternal glory** that would be his when he would be in Jesus' "presence" (4:14) and would be like Him (1 Cor. 15:49; Phil 3:21; 1 John 3:2). This is amazing: all of his heavy, continuous burdens were, he said, "light" (the Gr. *elaphron* means "light in weight, easy to bear"; used in the NT only twice: here and in Matt. 11:30) and "momentary" (the Gr. *parautika* means "brief, for the slight moment, on the spot"). Though, as he wrote in 2 Corinthians 1:8, his hardships were "far beyond" (*hyperbolēn*) his ability to endure, he said his coming **glory . . . far outweighs them all** (*hyperbolēn eis hyperbolēn* is lit., "extraordinary unto the extraordinary").

This eternal perspective and hope in things to come sustained Paul in the midst of the temporary sufferings that marked his ministry. As he elsewhere reminded the Corinthians, the world and its present sufferings are passing away (1 Cor. 7:31). **What is seen** (the material) **is temporary, but what is unseen** (the spiritual) **is eternal.** The temporal will be replaced by a "glory that will never fade away" (1 Peter 5:4), an "eternal glory in Christ" (1 Peter 5:10). Therefore, Paul said, believers should look not on what is seen but, ironically, on what cannot be seen. What the inner man "sees" surpasses what physical eyes see.

5:1. Few chapter divisions are more unfortunate than this one since what follows (5:1-10) details the thought expressed in 4:16-18. Failure to appreciate this fact unduly complicates these already difficult verses by removing their contextual constraints.

Paul had referred to his mortal "body" (4:10-11) as "wasting away" (4:16). Now he compared his body to a worn-out **earthly** (*epigeios*, "on the earth") **tent** (*skēnous*) soon to be **destroyed.** In Christ's incarnate body He "lived (*eskēnōsen*, lit., 'tabernacled or tented') among us (John 1:14). This is why the eternal perspective (2 Cor. 4:17) should be maintained (the second Gr. word in 5:1 is

gar ["for"; trans. **now** in the NIV], introducing the reason for what preceded). An earthly body is temporary; a heavenly body is **eternal.**

The reference to the heavenly body as **a building from God, an eternal house in heaven, not built by human hands** is reminiscent of Jesus' description of His own resurrection body as a temple "not made by man" (lit., "not made by hand"; Mark 14:58). Second Corinthians 5:1 briefly summarizes what Paul had earlier written to the Corinthians about the nature of the resurrection body (1 Cor. 15:34-54). The confident assertion, **we know,** was based on the argument set forth in 1 Corinthians 15.

5:2-4. Paul had written about fixing his eyes "not on what is seen but on what is unseen" (4:18). These verses express the same sentiment. Paul's present life was "wasting away" (4:16) and he faced "death" (4:11-12). Using a figure of speech (metonymy of the effect [groaning] substituted for the cause [suffering]), Paul twice said **we groan** (5:2, 4; cf. Rom. 8:22-23). But someday, when **our heavenly dwelling** (2 Cor. 5:2, 4) is received, all such groaning and being **burdened** will give place to laughter and exultation (cf. Luke 6:21; 1 Cor. 15:51-55). **What is mortal** will **be swallowed up by life** in immortal, imperishable spiritual bodies in heaven (Phil. 3:21). For Paul his present mortal life was like nakedness, marked by humiliation and privation. Who would want to focus on this abject state in view of the eternal glory that awaited him? (2 Cor. 4:17-18)

A number of commentators and theologians have seen in these verses reference to an "intermediate state," a period between death and resurrection. This view takes one of two forms: (a) Dead (though conscious) believers are without a body while awaiting their resurrection bodies, or (b) dead (though conscious) believers receive an "intermediate body" that somehow differs from their forthcoming resurrected bodies. (According to either of these intermediate-state views, Paul was suggesting that he hoped to live till the return of Christ so that he would not experience an "intermediate state.") These views, however, seem unwarranted. Paul had only two conditions in view since 4:16, the temporal and the eternal. The introduction of a third is therefore unlikely. It seems clear from 5:4 that being **in this tent** (cf. 2 Peter 1:13), and **unclothed** describe mortality while being **clothed** and possessing a **heavenly dwelling** depict immortality, without specifying any intervening stages.

5:5. This present condition of fading mortality, however disquieting it may be, is not without design. As Paul had just written, ordinary mortals, like common jars of clay, are the means through which God displays, by contrast, His own all-surpassing power (4:7).

Equally encouraging is the realization that in the life of each Christian God has begun the transforming process that will one day culminate in possessing a heavenly body and perfect Christlikeness. The surety of that consummation is the Holy **Spirit**, whose presence and transforming work (3:18) forms the beginning and is guaranteeing the completion of God's gracious salvation (Rom. 8:23; Eph. 4:30). (On the words **as a deposit, guaranteeing what is to come,** see comments on the word *arrabōna* in 2 Cor. 1:22.)

5:6-8. With this perspective Paul could be **confident** (5:6, 8; cf. 7:16) and encouraged (cf. 4:1, 16), even in his period of mortality. These verses (5:6-8) recapitulate the theme first discussed in 4:16-18. To be **at home in the body** means to dwell in "the earthly tent" (5:1), to be outwardly "wasting away" (4:16), to be in a state of mortality **away from the** immediate presence of the **Lord** (cf. 1 Cor. 13:12).

What sustained Paul was the realization that this was a temporary and transitory state (2 Cor. 4:18). He focused not on present but on future conditions, not on the seen but the unseen. To live this way is to **live by faith, not by sight.** It is to live in light of ultimate rather than immediate realities (cf. Rom. 8:24-25), to be obedient to God's commands despite the hardships that obedience produces (e.g., 2 Cor. 11:23-29). Such was Paul's life. If the choice were his, he would have seized the opportunity to depart this pilgrimage life and take up residence (be **at home**) **with the Lord** (Phil. 1:21-23). But the constraints of his commission caused him to press on (cf. Phil. 1:24; Eph. 3:1-13).

5:9-10. Motivating Paul in this perseverance was his **goal to please** his Lord (cf. Gal. 1:10; Col. 1:10), a desire in effect during his earthly sojourn (**at home in the body**), which would be undiminished in heaven (**away from it**) (cf. 2 Cor. 5:6).

Contributing to this goal was Paul's knowledge that he would one day be evaluated by his Master. He wanted to please Him and to hear from Him, "Well done, My good servant!" (Luke 19:17) In his previous letter Paul had mentioned this judgment (1 Cor. 3:12-15) with particular reference to Christian teachers (1 Cor. 4:1-5). Now he affirmed that **all** Christians will be evaluated at **the judgment seat of Christ** (cf. Rom. 14:12), which will follow the Rapture of the church. Believers will be recompensed **for the things** they have **done** in their earthly lives (**while in the body**). Their **good** deeds will evoke one response (cf. 1 Cor. 4:5; Eph. 6:8) and the **bad** (*phaulon*, "worthless") will evoke another (1 Cor. 3:15; Col. 3:25). Salvation is not the issue here. One's eternal destiny will not be determined at the judgment seat of Christ. Salvation is by faith (Eph. 2:8-9), but deeds issuing from that faith (1 Thes. 1:3) will be evaluated.

This perspective on a day of judgment and the prospect of eternity had a salutary effect on Paul. It enabled him to persevere in the face of hardship (2 Cor. 4:7-12). And it motivated him to be faithful in discharging his ministry (5:11; cf. 1 Cor. 4:2-4).

5. MESSAGE OF RECONCILIATION (5:11-6:2)

The description of the ministry sustained by Paul touched on the work of Christ (2:12-3:6), the work of the Spirit (3:7-18), and the work of the Father (4:1-15). He also spoke of the eternal viewpoint required for the ministry to be carried out effectively (4:16-5:10). He now turned to the heart of that ministry, the message.

5:11-12. Though Paul knew that his salvation and eternal destiny were obtained by faith in Christ (Eph. 2:8-9), the thought of one day standing before his Savior (2 Cor. 5:10) awed him. It was the contemplation of that moment that moved Paul **to fear the Lord** and impelled him on in His service (cf. Matt. 10:28). The purpose of his ministry was to persuade men to "be reconciled to God" (2 Cor. 5:20).

The personal defense which follows (vv. 11-12) indicates that Paul met opposition in carrying out that commission. Understandably, a Christian's message is intimately bound up with his life and ministry (1 Thes. 1:5); the two are hardly separable. Since this is so, Paul had to justify and defend his conduct in order to win a hearing for his message. He followed the tactic used earlier in the letter, affirming before God the sincerity of his motives (cf. 2 Cor. 1:12, 23) and calling on the Corinthians to confirm this by their own experiences with him (cf. 1:14; 4:2).

The apostle, unlike his opponents, put no stock in external credentials or associations (3:1-2; cf. 5:16a). It was not the externality of the Law but the internality of the Spirit that authenticated his ministry (3:3; cf. Rom. 2:28-29). Nor was he concerned simply about his own reputation among the Corinthians (cf. 1 Cor. 3:21; Gal. 1:10; 1 Thes. 2:6). What did concern him was the reception of his message. He needed to be regarded as a servant of Christ so that his message would be regarded as the message of God (cf. 1 Cor. 4:1). If they took pride ("exulted") in him, the messenger, then they could answer his and their opponents, who looked on the outward appearance (what is seen) rather than what one is like inwardly (in the heart; cf. 1 Sam. 16:7).

5:13. To affirm his sincerity, Paul was willing to be thought a fool (cf. 11:16-17, 21). Who but one out of his mind ("insane"; cf. 11:23; Mark 3:21) would show such disregard for himself? (cf. 1 Cor. 4:9-13) Would a sane person willingly face a riotous mob intent on destroying him? (Acts 19:30; 21:35-40) Who would be crazy enough to walk back into a city in which he had just been stoned and dragged out? (Acts 14:19-20) Only a person who was utterly devoted to God would show so little regard for himself. Such a man was Paul.

Yet the Corinthians also knew well the prosaic, "sane" side of Paul the teacher (Acts 18:11) and loving father (1 Cor. 4:14-16). Whether they considered him insane or not, his ministry was selfless: It is for you. In his own way Paul had expressed the summation of the Law,

loving God with all his heart, soul, and mind, and loving his neighbor as himself (Mark 12:26-31).

5:14-15. Why would Paul live that way? (v. 13) Because Christ had lived that way (cf. Mark 3:21). Though possessing divine prerogatives, He willingly became incarnate and followed the path of obedience to the cross (Phil. 2:6-8), dying for all (not just the elect, as some suggest; cf. 1 Tim. 2:6; Heb. 2:9; 1 John 2:2). By faith Paul was identified with Jesus in His death and resurrection (Rom. 6:3-4; Gal. 2:20). And Paul lived with the same selfless abandon the Lord had. Christ's love, which had converted him, now compelled him (cf. 1 John 3:16).

Later in discussing "the ministry of reconciliation" (2 Cor. 5:18-19), Paul developed the historical and objective implications of Christ's atonement. His concern in those verses was the subjective application of the Savior's objective work. All those who by faith entered into the benefits of Christ's sacrifice (and now live spiritually) should respond by living selflessly and being involved in that ministry of reconciliation. They should no longer live for themselves but for Him. Paul was certainly doing this; therefore the Corinthians should exult in him (v. 12).

5:16. As a result of his conversion Paul no longer evaluated people on the basis of externals. He implied that his opponents, and to a certain extent those influenced by them, did (v. 12).

At one time this had been true of Paul also. He had opposed Christ and His followers (Acts 22:4-5; 1 Cor. 15:9) because he had regarded Christ (lit., "knew Christ") from a worldly (lit., "according to flesh"; cf. 2 Cor. 1:12) point of view. He had information about Jesus, but this was not the same as believing in Him. Mere information about Jesus cannot transform a person from self-centeredness to selflessness (5:15). Only conversion could effect that, as it had done for Paul (Acts 9:1-20).

5:17. No one was more able to reflect on that transformation than Paul who switched from a persecutor of Christ to a proclaimer of Christ (Acts 9:5, 20-22). He was in Christ (a phrase Paul used repeatedly in his epistles to speak of a believer's spiritual relationship to Christ) because he believed the message of the gospel and was identified by faith with Christ (2 Cor. 5:14-15; cf. Rom. 6:3-4; Gal. 2:20; 6:14). To be in Christ is to be a **new creation** (cf. Gal. 6:15). This new creation is brought about by the Holy Spirit, the Agent of regeneration (Titus 3:5) and the Giver of divine birth (John 3:3, 6-8). God's new creative work, begun in each one who believes in Christ, will one day be consummated on a universal scale (Rev. 21:4-5). The **old** life of slavery to self and sin **has gone** (2 Cor. 5:16; cf. Rom. 6:6-14; Eph. 4:22; Col. 3:9). The **new** life of devotion to Christ means that one has new attitudes and actions (cf. 2 Cor. 5:14-15; Rom. 6:4; Eph. 4:23–5:2).

5:18-19. Like the first Creation (of the universe), the new creation is initiated by God: **All this is from God** (cf. 4:6; 1 John 4:10). Also, like the first Creation, the new creation becomes a reality **through** the work of **Christ** (cf. Col. 1:16). Christ's death on the cross makes possible human reconciliation to **God** (Rom. 5:10-11). Reconciliation involves removing rebellious and sinful man's enmity toward God (Rom. 5:10). This is one of the many marvelous accomplishments of the Godhead on behalf of a person the moment he believes in Christ for salvation from sin. Because Christ bore mankind's sin on the cross (1 Peter 2:24), He made peace possible (Eph. 2:11-19). No longer need people be the objects of God's wrath (Rom. 5:9). By trusting themselves to the **reconciling** work of **Christ** alone, people pass from God's wrath to God's blessing (Acts 16:30-31; Rom. 8:1) and from spiritual death to spiritual life (John 5:24; Eph. 2:1, 5). Then **men's sins** are no longer counted, that is, imputed or reckoned, **against them,** for Christ has taken them on Himself (2 Cor. 5:21; 1 Peter 2:24; 3:18). This is the treasure of the gospel which Paul proclaimed (2 Cor. 4:7), **the message of reconciliation** (5:19) delivered in **the ministry** (cf. 4:1) **of reconciliation** (5:18).

5:20. Few verses more precisely summarize Paul's ministry and message (cf. Acts 26:16-18). As Christ had preached peace to all men (Eph. 2:17) on the basis of what He would accomplish (Eph. 2:16), Paul continued that proclamation in His stead. The immediate representative of God's message of reconciliation was Paul, whose ministry is shared by all who are "in Christ" (2 Cor. 5:17, 19). All believers should serve Christ as His **ambassadors.** Paul's appeal was not a perfunctory pronouncement but an impassioned plea ("we try to persuade men" [v. 11]) addressed to the world **on Christ's behalf: Be reconciled to God** (cf. 1 Tim. 2:3-4).

5:21. Paul now summarized the basis of this message. The Cross epitomized the love of God (John 3:16) and of Christ (John 15:13; Rom. 5:8). The Savior was sinless: He **had no sin.** He was "without sin" (Heb. 4:15), and "in Him is no sin" (1 John 3:5). He took on Himself the sin of the world (John 1:29; 1 Peter 2:24; 1 John 2:2). **God made Him . . . to be sin for us** (cf. Isa. 53:4-6, 10). The sins of the world were placed on Him so that, in turn, His **righteousness** could be given those who trust Him (Rom. 5:17) and are thus **in Him.** That gift of righteousness is obtainable only by faith (Rom. 3:22; 6:23; Eph. 2:8-9; Phil. 3:9).

6:1. How could the Corinthians possibly **receive God's grace in vain?** One sure way was to disbelieve the message Paul had expressed in 5:21. False apostles in Corinth preached a message different from Paul's gospel (11:4). If they were Judaizers (cf. 3:7-11; 11:22), they probably denied Paul's message that the righteousness of God was obtained only by faith. To believe a truncated gospel meant to believe "in vain" (cf. 1 Cor. 15:2). Paul had reason to believe that some in Corinth had done just that (2 Cor. 11:2-3). "Vain" translates *kenon* ("empty, without content, without result, useless"; cf. 1 Cor. 15:14, 58; Gal. 2:2; Phil. 2:16; 1 Thes. 3:5).

6:2. Paul's quotation from Isaiah 49:8 was a rebuttal to Judaizers who wanted to impose the Mosaic Law as a means of obtaining righteousness. In Isaiah God announced that salvation would be universally offered not only to stubborn Israel but also to the Gentiles (Isa. 49:6). The quotation underscored the fact that **salvation** is **God's** initiative: **in . . . My favor I heard you, and . . . I helped you.** Jesus inaugurated this message of God's grace in His ministry (Luke 4:18-21) and Paul communicated it. **The day of salvation** is the present Age of Grace. Paul urged the Corinthians not to spurn that grace by turning to Judaistic legalism (cf. 2 Cor. 3:12-16; Gal. 3:1-6).

To do so would be "to receive God's grace in vain" (2 Cor. 6:1).

6. MARKS OF THE MINISTRY (6:3-10)

In 5:11-14 Paul began a defense of his ministry which led in turn to an explanation of his message (5:15-21). Now he returned to the topic of his ministry and its problems (6:3-10).

Paul had stressed that the commendation (5:12) the Corinthians should have been looking for in their ministers was not external letters (3:1), self-recommendations (10:18), or religious credentials (11:22) but the internal testimony of the Spirit (cf. Rom. 2:28-29). Now he suggested that there *are* some external credentials that mark a minister of God but they are hardly the sort the Corinthians would think of or his opponents would like to match. Paul's authenticating marks of the ministry were his sufferings as a servant and the sustaining enablement of God to carry on (cf. 2 Cor. 4:8-10). These were valid credentials for "the servants of God" (6:4; cf. 11:16–12:10; 1 Cor. 4:9-13; Gal. 6:17).

6:3. Paul was concerned more about defending his **ministry** (*diakonia,* "service"; cf. 4:1) than defending himself. To that end he scrupulously avoided behavior that would vitiate his ministry as Christ's ambassador (5:20) and God's fellow worker (6:1). Of course Paul knew that the message of the Cross would offend many (2:16; 1 Cor. 1:18). And he knew that many considered him a fool (cf. 2 Cor. 11:16). But he did not want to offend by self-serving conduct that would bring disrepute to God or spiritual ruin to a fellow Christian. (**Stumbling block** is from the Gr. *proskopēn;* in 1 Cor. 8:9 "stumbling block" translates *proskomma,* a synonym of the word in 2 Cor. 6:3).

6:4-5. As **servants** (*diakonoi;* cf. "service" [*diakonia*] in v. 3) **of God** Paul and his associates faced various trials without regard for themselves. But with God's help they had **great endurance** (*hypomonē,* "steadfastness," also used in 1:6; cf. 4:7-9). This was the sort of commendation the Corinthians should have required for authenticating their ministers (cf. 3:1; 5:12). Paul listed nine trials, in three sets of three each (6:4-5). Then he mentioned nine inner qualities (vv. 6-7), followed by nine pairs of paradoxes (vv. 8-10). In 11:22-27 his

groupings are mostly fours. First he mentioned general difficulties: **troubles** (*thlipsesin;* cf. 1:4), **hardships, and distresses** (lit., "narrow spaces," i.e., circumstances that hem in; in Rom. 8:35 this word is rendered "hardship"). Then the apostle listed three specific kinds of persecution he endured in his ministry: **beatings** (cf. 1 Cor. 4:11; 2 Cor. 6:9; 11:23-24; Gal. 6:17), **imprisonments, and riots.** He experienced all three of these in Philippi (Acts 16:19-23). The third group describes impositions he accepted as part of the demands of ministry. He was not averse to **hard work** (1 Cor. 4:12; Acts 18:3-4) nor a stranger to **sleepless nights** (2 Cor. 11:27) or to **hunger** (1 Cor. 4:11; 2 Cor. 11:27).

6:6. Paul balanced his nine kinds of trials (in three triads) with nine internal qualities. The first eight are given in four couplets. **Purity** referred to practical righteousness, and **understanding** was a practical knowledge which displayed sensitivity in dealing with others. **Patience** (*makrothymia,* lit., "long temper") is the ability to bear up under the oversights and wrongs afflicted by others without retaliating (cf. Gal. 5:22; Eph. 4:2; Col. 1:11; 3:12; 2 Tim. 4:2; James 5:10). **And kindness** (*chrēstotēti;* cf. Gal. 5:22; Col. 3:12) is love in action.

In the Holy Spirit may be a metonymy, a figure of speech in which the cause stands for the effects. If so, then the Holy Spirit represents that which He causes, namely, spiritual fruit (Gal. 5:22-23) or control by the Spirit (Eph. 5:18). Or possibly the phrase (*en pneumati hagiō*) should be translated "in a spirit of holiness" to describe Paul's dedicated attitude. He hoped his **sincere** (*anypokritō,* lit., "without hypocrisy"; cf. "sincere [*anypokritou*] faith" in 1 Tim. 1:5) **love** (cf. Rom. 12:9) would be evident to his readers and would evoke in them a similar response (2 Cor. 6:12-13).

6:7. The apostle's ministry advanced because of his spiritual resources. **In truthful speech** he proclaimed the gospel (4:2) and relied on **the power of God** in the person of the Spirit to produce results (10:4; cf. 1 Cor. 2:4-5). Relying on God, Paul was completely equipped **with weapons of righteousness** to cope with the attacks of the adversary from any quarter (**right** or **left**) and to send him fleeing (cf. 2 Cor. 10:3-6; Eph. 6:11-18; James 4:7).

6:8. In nine pairs of paradoxes (vv. 8-10) Paul spoke of conflicting responses to his ministry (vv. 8-9a), of his own responses to opposition (vv. 9b-10a), and of the results of his labors (v. 10b, c). Some who believed welcomed Paul like Christ Himself (Gal. 4:14) but more often he faced insults and **dishonor** (1 Cor. 4:10; 1 Thes 2:2). He was maligned by outsiders (1 Cor. 4:13) and also by some within the church (Rom. 3:8), who gave him a **bad report.** He and his associates were **genuine** apostles, yet some **regarded** them **as impostors.** So he found it necessary to defend his ministry against the calumnies of opponents (1 Cor. 9:1-2; 2 Cor. 10:7).

6:9. Paul said he was **unknown** perhaps in the sense of people not acknowledging him or his ministry. But he was **known** by God (2 Tim. 2:19). Though he was **dying** (cf. 2 Cor. 1:8-9; 4:10-11; 11:23), **yet** he lived (cf. 1:10; 4:16), and though **beaten** (6:5; 11:23-25) he was **not killed.** He endured (6:4) these agonies because God sustained him (cf. 4:7-9).

6:10. Such a life would seem to lead naturally to sorrow. Yet because of his trust in God Paul was **always rejoicing** (cf. Acts 16:23-25; Phil. 4:4). Being **poor** and bereft of even basic material necessities (cf. 1 Cor. 4:11), Paul could nonetheless dispense spiritual values, **making many rich** (cf. Eph. 3:8). Though materially he had **nothing,** yet he was **possessing everything** by way of spiritual blessings (1 Cor. 3:21-23; Eph. 1:3).

7. ANTICIPATED RESPONSE (6:11-7:16)

In this section Paul pulled together the strands of the discussion about his ministry to the Corinthian church. He had defended his changed plans out of deference and love for them (1:12-2:11). He then turned to a description of his apostolic ministry in which he contrasted his own impotence with the omnipotence of God (2:12-6:10). Not an exercise in self-indulgence, Paul's point was to produce some changes in the Corinthian church: he sought not only an acceptance of his ministry and message but also a rejection of the influence of his opponents, the false apostles. This was not Paul's final word on this subject (cf.

chaps. 10-13) but it was a forceful beginning.

6:11-13. Whatever failings Paul may have had, dissimulation was not one of them. Candor in speech and an unrestrained affirmation of **affection** (*splanchnois;* cf. 7:15; Phil. 1:8; 2:1; Col. 3:12; Phile. 7, 12, 20; 1 John 3:17) had marked his letter to this point (e.g., 2 Cor. 2:3-4). And he wanted the Corinthians to reciprocate. The depth of his feelings is noted by his calling them **Corinthians.** Only rarely did he name his readers in the midst of a letter. When, for example, he was greatly exercised about the declension in the Galatian churches, he sharply rebuked them by name (Gal. 3:1). On the other hand when he recalled the Philippian church's faithful support of him in the early days of his ministry and in his prison experience, he called them by name (Phil. 4:15). Blending frustration and affection, Paul similarly hailed the Corinthians and called for them to respond with unrestrained love (**my children—open wide your hearts;** cf. 2 Cor. 7:2-3).

6:14-15. What hampered the Corinthians' open, loving response, which Paul called for? (v. 13) Answer: rival suitors vied for their affections and allegiance. Though verses 14-15 are often applied to various sorts of alliances (e.g., mixed marriages, improper business associations), Paul's primary association was probably ecclesiastical. The rival suitors were possibly pagan idolaters (cf. 1 Cor. 10:14) or more likely false apostles (cf. 2 Cor. 11:2-4). In censure or affection Paul was equally candid (cf. 6:11).

The solution to the dilemma was for the Corinthians to separate from the false apostles. Whatever may have been their own and others' estimation of their spiritual status, Paul considered the false apostles to be **unbelievers** (cf. 11:13-15) from whom the Corinthians needed to separate. But Paul did not say that Christians should have no contacts whatever with unbelievers. Earlier he argued the absurdity of such a position (1 Cor. 5:9-10). But religious unbelievers might lead believers astray from "sincere and pure devotion to Christ" (2 Cor. 11:3), and the fact concerned Paul greatly. A **believer** can be rightly **yoked** only with **Christ** (Matt. 11:29-30).

To illustrate, Paul asked five rhetorical questions (2 Cor. 6:14-16), posing antitheses that reflect the wide chasm between the kingdom of Christ and the kingdom of Satan (cf. Col. 1:13). **Belial** (the Gr. *Beliar* is a spelling variation) transliterates an Old Testament word that means "worthless person." In Greek it came to mean "a lawless person." It was then used of Satan, the most worthless and lawless of all.

6:16. Paul's fifth rhetorical question provided a transition to his citing several Old Testament verses. Their cumulative effect bolstered Paul's exhortation (v. 14a). The church is **the temple of God** (cf. 1 Cor. 3:16) where the Spirit of God and Christ dwells (cf. Matt. 28:19-20; Eph. 2:22). The promise of **God to live** among His people was ultimately fulfilled in Christ (Matt. 1:23).

6:17. Enjoying God's presence requires personal holiness. Paul cited a portion of Isaiah 52:11 and Ezekiel 20:41, passages that speak of Israel's redemption. God's people are redeemed from pagan bondage (**come out from them and be separate**) in order to be clean before God (**touch no unclean thing**) and thus enjoy fellowship with Him (**I will receive you**). In Galatians Paul spoke of the bondage of those who are under the obligation of the Law (Gal. 3:13-14; 4:5; cf. 2 Cor. 3:7-9). Paul wrote to Titus that redemption implied two things: (a) deliverance "from all wickedness" and (b) a purified people who are "His very own, eager to do what is good" (Titus 2:14). Personal purity makes it possible to serve God and be received by Him.

6:18. A redeemed people are brought into a special relationship with God the **Father** as His **sons and daughters** (cf. Isa. 43:6). Those who identify with Christ by faith in Him may call God "Father" (Eph. 2:18; Gal. 4:5-6). From these sons and daughters God wants obedience (Deut. 32:19-21) as He did from David, His people's chief representative, and from David's lineage (2 Sam. 7:14; cf. Ps. 89:30-34).

7:1. **These promises** refer to God's assurances of His presence (6:16) and fellowship (6:17b-18) to those who obey Him. This obedience requires purification (**let us purify ourselves**), which here implies separation (*katharisōmen*; cf. Matt. 8:3; Deut. 19:13) **from everything that contaminates body and spirit** and from

every person who pollutes the truth (cf. 2 Cor. 2:17; 4:2). "Body and spirit" refers to the whole person in his external and internal aspects (cf. 7:5). In an attitude of **reverence for God** (cf. 5:11) which produces obedience, sanctification (**holiness**) can be perfected, that is, completed or matured. This is a maturing, growing holiness, an increased Christlikeness (3:18), a progressive sanctification (not sinless perfection).

7:2. Having given a warning about the rival suitors for the Corinthians' affections (6:14–7:1), Paul resumed his appeal for mutual love, mentioned in 6:11-13. The accusations made about him were unfounded. He could offer disclaimers (e.g., 2:17; 4:2; 6:3), but the Corinthians' conviction of his integrity was his best rejoinder. Unhappily, however, this was yet lacking.

7:3-4. Paul did not blame the Corinthians for their vacillation. His rivals were impressive (11:3-5), much more so than he (10:7-12), at least in externals. The Corinthians' vacillation had not produced disaffection in Paul. On the contrary his love was unabated (cf. 6:13; 7:1) and his **confidence** in them was unimpaired. He had **pride** ("exulting") and **joy** (cf. v. 7) in them **in all** his **troubles** (*thlipsei*, lit., "trouble" [sing.]; cf. 1:4). No doubt this was primarily due to his confidence that God was at work in them (1 Cor. 1:4-9) but also partially due to the news Titus had brought him when the two finally met in Macedonia (2 Cor. 7:5-7).

7:5-7. Paul's frame of mind and **body** before Titus' arrival was far from placid (cf. 2:13). He **had no rest** (*anesin*, "relief"; also used in 2:13; 8:13). The great apostle, which he was not hesitant to admit (cf. 2:4; 6:10). He candidly admitted that his **conflicts . . . fears** and depression (**downcast**) were brought on by apparent opposition or persecution in **Macedonia,** by anxiety about Titus' well-being, by his reception by the Corinthians, and by their response to his letter.

However, the ample **comfort** of God (cf. 1:3-7) more than met his needs through **the coming of Titus** and the good news he brought. Titus had been well received by the Corinthians. They did love Paul and longed for him and were concerned for him. And they were remorseful (they had **deep sorrow**) at

237

their failure to support him during his "painful visit" (2:1). They had responded positively to his severe letter (2:4).

7:8-9. Paul's harsh **letter** (see point 5 under "Contacts and Correspondence" in the *Introduction*) had **hurt** them. It had hurt Paul too. He had not relished his role as a disciplinarian, and in fact he apparently had wished he had not sent it with Titus. Yet because of the results his **regret** was mollified. In **sorrow** the Corinthians acknowledged their failure and redressed the wrong (cf. 2:6).

7:10-11. They had exemplified **repentance,** a change of mind involving action in accord with God's will. As such it was a **godly sorrow** (like Peter's remorse after his denial of Christ). This was not a **worldly sorrow** which **brings death** (like Judas' "sorrow" after he betrayed the Lord; Matt. 27:3-5). The Corinthians' genuine **sorrow . . . produced** several things: (a) an **earnestness** or concerted effort to make amends, (b) an **eagerness to** vindicate themselves, (c) **indignation** against Paul's opponent (2 Cor. 2:5-11), (d) **alarm** at their own passivity and its injurious effects (2:1-4), (e) **longing** and **concern** for Paul (cf. 7:7), and (f) **readiness to see justice done** (2:6).

In all this they **proved** they were **innocent** by virtue of their repentance. They had sinned not so much by doing wrong but by failing to do right (cf. James 4:17) and of this they had repented (2 Cor. 7:10).

7:12. Paul's primary motive in writing the letter (2:3-4) was to benefit the Corinthians. Uppermost in his mind was their well-being which Paul realized was bound up with their acceptance of his message and of him as an apostle. Paul **wrote** that he was **not** concerned about disciplining the offending brother and ameliorating the situation of **the injured party.** But this was apparently a Semitic way of saying that they were not his *primary* concern (Luke 14:26 gives another example of exclusivism as a way of stating priorities). It is doubtful that "the injured party" refers to the incident in 1 Corinthians 5:1 because no offended party was mentioned there. (In fact, the injured party in the incest incident may have been deceased.) Possibly Paul was the injured party (cf. 2 Cor. 2:5), but if so it was a curiously oblique self-designation (cf. Mark 14:51; John 13:23).

7:13-16. The Corinthians' positive response to Paul and his letter had been a great **encouragement** to him (cf. v. 4). Added to this was Titus' elation at the reception he received. Despite Paul's affirmed confidence in the Corinthians, **Titus** might have been understandably hesitant to undertake this mission (cf. 1 Cor. 16:10-11). But any trepidation **Titus** may have felt proved groundless. Actually the Corinthians responded to him with deference, **receiving him with fear and trembling.** They zealously sought to carry out Paul's directives (2 Cor. 7:7, 11). As a result Titus had great **affection** (*splanchna,* "inner emotion"; cf. 6:12; Phil. 1:8; 2:1; Col. 3:12; Phile. 7, 12, 20; 1 John 3:17) **for** the Corinthians. Paul knew this was God's doing (2 Cor. 7:6), but like a good pastor he commended the Corinthians and expressed his **confidence** (5:6, 8) in them after their positive response. He could only hope that the subjects he was about to discuss (in chaps. 8-9 and 10-13) would meet with the same spirit.

III. Gracious Giving (chaps. 8-9)

Having explained his changed plans (1:12-2:11) and having described the nature and orientation of his ministry (2:12-7:16), Paul now turned to the subject of gracious giving. This was no abstract topic; it concerned the collection for the poor in Jerusalem which Paul had been organizing for several years (cf. Gal. 2:10; Rom. 15:25-28). The Corinthians, hearing about "the collection," asked Paul what part they might have in it (cf. 1 Cor. 16:1). Paul instructed them concerning these arrangements (1 Cor. 16:2-3). Good intentions had not been translated into fruition, however, so Paul asked Titus to look into the matter (2 Cor. 8:6).

What factors interrupted the Corinthians' good intentions? No one knows. But one likely possibility was the presence of the false apostles who received support from the church and may have diverted to themselves some of the monies intended for that collection (cf. 2:17; 11:20). As a result, Paul's refusal to accept support was a sore point with the Corinthians (cf. 11:7-12; 12:13-18).

Titus had found the Corinthians in need of an encouraging word which Paul delivered in chapters 8-9 of this letter. This—in conjunction with Titus' work and that of unnamed assistants (8:23; cf. Acts 20:1-4), climaxed by Paul's visit (Acts 20:3)—brought the collection in Corinth to a successful conclusion (cf. Rom. 15:26; Acts 24:17).

A. *Examples of liberality (8:1-9)*

Whenever possible, Paul preferred to motivate and instruct by deed as well as by words. He did not hesitate to urge the Corinthians and others to imitate his manner of life (cf. 1 Cor. 4:16; 11:1a; 1 Thes. 1:6; 2 Thes. 3:7-9). But he was also quick to point to other worthy examples, including Timothy (1 Cor. 4:17; Phil. 2:19-20), Epaphroditus (Phil. 2:18), and of course, Christ (Phil. 2:5; 1 Cor. 11:1b; 1 Thes. 1:6) and God the Father (Eph. 5:1). Paul gave the Corinthians two examples of liberality: the Macedonian churches and Christ.

8:1-2. The Macedonian churches— those in Philippi, Thessalonica, and Berea—had initially experienced **the grace** of God in the person of Paul and his proclamation of the gospel (Eph. 3:2-12) during his second missionary journey. In Philippi (Acts 16:12-40), Thessalonica (Acts 17:1-9), and Berea (Acts 17:10-15), the apostle preached the gospel and founded churches. The believers in these places suffered because of their faith (Phil. 1:29-30; 1 Thes. 1:6), but they remained steadfast (Phil. 1:5; 1 Thes. 1:7). They even contributed at that early juncture to Paul's material support (Phil. 4:15).

While their material welfare apparently deteriorated (cf. Phil. 4:10), their spiritual well-being increased commensurately. Paul attributed this to the grace of God, His unmerited favor. They had ample reason to be sorrowful (**severe trial** is lit., "in much testing of troubles" [*thilpseōs*; cf. 2 Cor. 1:4]), but they rejoiced. Though in **extreme poverty,** they could make others **rich.** Though they had nothing, they possessed everything that really matters (6:10). Like Paul, the Macedonian churches had learned that God's grace is sufficient to take their weaknesses and through them to display God's power (4:7-12; 12:9; Phil. 4:13).

8:3-5. The Macedonians were eager channels of **God's** blessing because they lived in accordance with His **will** (v. 5). Their actions revealed their love and devotion to God and others (cf. Mark 12:28-31; Phil. 2:3-8, 20-21; 1 Thes. 4:9-10). **Entirely on their own** initiative the Macedonians became involved in the collection. Paul, perhaps thinking they too were suitable candidates for aid, hesitated to approach them about the need in Jerusalem. However, like the poor widow Jesus commended (Mark 12:41-44), they were undeterred by their own penury and gave selflessly, trusting God to meet their needs (Phil. 4:19). One could wish that today more churches were like the Macedonians who **pleaded . . . for the privilege of sharing.**

8:6-7. In the light of this effusion of God's grace on the Macedonians (vv. 1-5), could the Corinthians, who had benefited so richly from God's grace (excelling **in faith, in speech, in knowledge, in complete earnestness, and . . . love;** cf. 1 Cor. 1:4-7), do any less? Paul thought not, so he dispatched **Titus** to administer the Corinthians' portion of the collection, to give them opportunity to **excel in this grace of giving.** ("Grace of giving" [2 Cor. 8:7] and **act of grace** [v. 6] both translate the one Gr. word "grace." Giving is the essence of grace!) Titus had gained experience in the collection and distribution of charitable monies elsewhere (cf. Acts 11:29-30; Gal. 2:1). But it is unknown when he became involved with the Corinthian collection.

In writing to the Romans Paul had mentioned the gift (God-given spiritual ability) of "contributing to the needs of others" (Rom. 12:8). The right use of this divine gift was to *give* generously. Paul himself had certainly given unsparingly to the Corinthians, and they in turn had professed their affection for him (2 Cor. 8:11). Paul wanted them to excel in their "giving" because giving expresses love (1 John 3:11, 16-18).

8:8-9. Paul, ever sensitive to the charge that he dominated the churches he founded (cf. 1:24), preferred that their motivation not stem from external commands (e.g., 8:7b). He wanted them to be motivated by their internal devotion (**the sincerity of your love**) to him and more importantly to the **Lord.** Could the Corinthians face being compared with the Macedonians in this regard? Or could they face being compared with their Lord, who is supremely worthy of emulation?

Few statements surpass verse 9 as a pithy summary of the gospel (cf. 5:21).

From the splendor of heaven **Christ** came to the squalor of earth. The Incarnation was an incomprehensible renunciation of spiritual and material glory. The One who **was rich,** who had everything, **became poor,** making Himself nothing (Phil. 2:7). He assumed mankind's debt of sin and paid for it with His life (Phil. 2:8). The Corinthians had directly benefited from His generosity (**your** and **you** are emphatic). He became what they were (poor) so that they could become what He was and is (rich). Therefore was a material offering to Him (cf. Matt. 25:34-40) too much to ask? (1 Cor. 9:11)

B. Advice and arrangements for the collection (8:10–9:5)

Concluding that the Corinthians would not refuse his appeal, Paul offered a brief rationale for the collection and an explanation of how it should be handled.

8:10-12. Paul's **advice** (cf. v. 8) was, **finish** what you have begun (cf. v. 6). Best wishes—**desire** and **eager willingness**—are no substitute for good deeds (cf. James 2:15-16). An individual's giving should be commensurate with his **means . . . according to what one has;** cf. 1 Cor. 16:2). By that standard the Macedonian gift, like the poor widow's offering (Mark 12:41-44), might in one sense be easy to equal but in another sense be hard to exceed.

8:13-15. A guiding principle for material exchange among churches is **equality.** Paul was not wanting some church to have relief (*anesis;* cf. 2:13; 7:5) while the Corinthians were **hard pressed** (*thlipsis;* cf. 1:4). That would be like robbing Peter to pay Paul!

Paul no doubt approved of the Jerusalem church's early efforts in meeting each others' needs by having everything in common (Acts 2:44). This expressed their mutual concern for all members of the body of Christ (cf. 1 Cor. 12:25). This principle was modeled after a divine pattern. When God gave food to the Israelites in the wilderness He did so equally according to their needs (Ex. 16:16-18). The church should not do less.

8:16-17. Like Timothy (Phil. 2:19-20), **Titus** was genuinely concerned about the welfare of those he served. In a self-centered world, such a **concern** was a distinguishing feature valued by Paul in his associates. No dictator (cf. vv. 8, 23),

Paul had asked Titus to lend his assistance to a project which it seems Titus had eagerly (**with much enthusiasm**) and independently (**on his own initiative**) determined to do.

8:18-21. To accompany Titus was an unnamed, highly respected (**praised by all the churches**) representative probably from the Macedonian churches. He would take their **gift** to its destination in Jerusalem. Paul's motivation in organizing this collection was **to honor the Lord** (cf. Matt. 25:40; Gal. 2:10). To that end he scrupulously worked to avoid bringing any disrepute on His name through charges of mismanagement or avarice (2 Cor. 8:20; cf. 12:17-18).

8:22-24. In addition to the previously mentioned brother (v. 18) and **Titus,** Paul's **partner and fellow worker,** a third member (anonymously called **our brother**) was appointed to join the collection party. He was apparently an appointee of the Macedonian churches. He was **zealous,** and he and the other unnamed brother (v. 18) were **an honor to Christ.** His presence served both to help buffer Paul from accusations of personally profiting from the collection and also to spur the Corinthians on toward completing their project. By their giving, the Corinthians could demonstrate (cf. 9:13) their **love** (cf. 8:8).

9:1-2. The Corinthians' need to complete what they had eagerly begun (8:6, 10) concerned Paul. He had not found it necessary **to write** about the need to give aid to Jerusalem Christians. The Corinthians had agreed enthusiastically (8:11) to be involved in **this service** (*diakonias*) **to the saints** (cf. 8:4; 9:12-13). They were eager **to help** (cf. 8:4), a fact that Paul had relayed **to the Macedonians** the year before, which in turn had spurred the Macedonians on (**stirred . . . them to action**). The difference between the Macedonians and the Corinthians, however, lay in their diligence in seeing the project through to completion. Slow starters, the Macedonians finished quickly. But the Corinthians, willing in spirit, needed help in disciplining the flesh (cf. Matt. 26:41; Rom. 6:19).

9:3-4. Therefore Paul was sending Titus and **the two brothers** mentioned in 8:18-24 to aid in arranging the details for the Corinthians' consummation of the collection. Paul had boasted (cf. 9:2)

about the Corinthians' enthusiasm to contribute (8:10-11) and hoped that the promising clouds would indeed produce rain (cf. Hosea 6:3-4; Jude 12). If the Corinthian promise to give went unfulfilled, both Paul and the Corinthians themselves **would be ashamed** in the presence of the less able but more noble **Macedonians** who might accompany him on his third visit (2 Cor. 13:1).

9:5. To circumvent that possibility Paul had arranged for Titus **and the brothers** (8:23) to help the Corinthians get their financial house in order. The two "brothers" with Titus may possibly have been the Macedonians Jason of Thessalonica (Acts 17:5) and Sopater of Berea (Acts 20:4; cf. Rom. 16:21). Then when Paul arrived, no collections would have to be made (1 Cor. 16:2) under pressure which might resemble exploitation (cf. 2 Cor. 7:2; 9:7; 12:17-18). Such motivation is unworthy of Christ's servants. Instead, giving should be a willing response to God's grace, **not** something done **grudgingly.** Paul now turned to that subject.

C. Reward of generosity (9:6-15)

In the grace of God Christians are rewarded in three ways for their generosity: (1) the givers are enriched (vv. 6-10); (2) the receivers' needs are met (vv. 11-12); and (3) God, the Source of all blessing, is praised (vv. 13-15).

9:6-7. Why should the Corinthians give generously? (v. 5) Paul gave two reasons. (1) A principle holds true in both the natural and the spiritual spheres: the size of a harvest corresponds to the scope of the sowing (cf. Prov. 11:24-26). A man may enjoy all his grain by eating it, or he may "lose" some of it by sowing it and later reaping a bountiful harvest. A spiritual harvest, of course, may differ in kind from the seed sown. Material seed may reap a spiritual harvest (2 Cor. 9:9; cf. 1 Cor. 9:11). (2) Another reason for giving generously is that God loves generosity. God prizes not the size of the gift (cf. Acts 11:29; 1 Cor. 16:2), but the giver's sincerity (**not reluctantly**), spontaneity (not **under compulsion**), and joyful willingness (**a cheerful giver**).

9:8. Ultimately Christians can dispense only what they have received, whether material (Acts 14:17) or spiritual (Rom. 5:17). The good work is done through God's enabling (cf. Phil. 1:6).

Regardless of how desperate one's circumstances, a person who wants to give can do so in dependence on God (cf. Phil. 4:11-13; e.g., the widow of Zarephath, 1 Kings 17:9-16; and the Macedonians, 2 Cor. 8:1-3). Once again Paul sounded the note that man's inability, by contrast, showcases God's work (4:7). This verse is full of words indicating inclusiveness in God's enabling: **all grace . . . in all things at all times, having all that you need . . . in every good work.** In the words "all things," "all times," and "all . . . you need," the Greek heaps three words one after the other: *panti pantote pasan.* **God** is indeed sufficient! His *"every"* grace *abounds* so that believers can **abound** "in *every* good work."

9:9-10. The abounding grace mentioned in verse 8 refers to more than provision for one's needs of the moment. Charity reaps an eternal reward (cf. Prov. 19:17; Matt. 25:40). A person who "fears the Lord" (Ps. 112:1) and **gives gifts to the poor** (from Ps. 112:9, which Paul quoted) will be vindicated on the last day (cf. Matt. 6:1). Practical **righteousness endures forever** not only through the deeds but in the doer as he is progressively transformed into Christlikeness (2 Cor. 3:18). Ultimately a believer's reward is the culmination of the process (Phil. 3:14, 21). The One who supplies what is needed is God alone (Phil. 2:13). God (**who supplies seed . . . and bread**) enlarges **the harvest** (rewards or blessings) that results from righteous, generous living. The riches of **righteousness** are inestimable (cf. 6:10).

9:11-13. The more one gives to others, the more he is enriched, and thus he **can be generous on every occasion.** Such a generous spirit toward others results in more and more people giving **thanksgiving to God.**

One expression of this generosity was the contribution to the Jerusalem saints, administered by Paul. **Not only** would **this service** (vv. 12-13; cf. 8:4; 9:1) meet the pressing **needs** of Jerusalem Christians **but** it would **also** overflow in **many expressions of thanks to God** and bring **praise** to God. The Corinthian participation in this charitable gesture would demonstrate the reality of their **confession** and the vitality of their spiritual lives.

9:14-15. Because the Corinthians

sent material aid, they reaped the intercessory **prayers** of the Jerusalem Christians who in praising **God** invoked His blessings on their Corinthian brethren. This spirit of selflessness is a consequence of God's **surpassing grace** (cf. "grace" in 8:1, 9; 9:8) supremely expressed in the ministry of the Lord Jesus Christ (8:9). This section on giving concludes (9:15) where it began (8:1), with the grace of God. **Thanks** in 9:15 is the word *charis* ("grace, favor"). Believers are to bestow "favor" on **God** because of His favors bestowed on them. **His** greatest **gift** (*dōrea*) is eternal salvation, spiritual riches, through His rich Son who became poor (8:9). Such a gift is **indescribable** (*anekdiēgētō*, "unable to recount or tell fully," used only here in the NT). Those who have benefited from such a spiritual gift (stemming from God's grace) should not hesitate to benefit others with material gifts. The Corinthians finished this work and sent a gift to Jerusalem (Rom. 15:26).

IV. Affirmative Action (10:1–13:10)

Paul had no easy transition to the subject he reserved for last. Because of this, these final four chapters have sometimes been thought to be from a different letter, possibly written earlier (see "Unity" in the *Introduction*) or a fifth letter, dispatched after chapters 1–9 were written and delivered. But transitions to difficult subjects are notoriously awkward and are usually put off to the end of a conversation or letter. Though Paul had been indirectly polemical in the preceding portions (e.g., 2:17; 3:1, 7-18; 4:2-4; 5:12, 16; 6:14), he saved for now the direct confrontation which he could not avoid. The false apostles needed to be challenged openly and the Corinthians' affections needed to be won over to a singular devotion to Christ and His apostle.

A. Appeal for obedience (10:1-6)

The remarks about the collection (chaps. 8–9) amounted to a mild appeal and call to action. In chapter 10 Paul's subject matter and the intensity of his appeal were amplified. Paul believed that the danger of people defecting from him and his gospel were decidedly real. By appealing for obedience, he tested the

confidence that Titus said the Corinthians had in him (7:16).

10:1-2. Paul was loath to take stern action, but the situation demanded it. His model for this was **Christ.** Christ's **meekness** (cf. Matt. 11:29) was a strength of spirit that enabled Him to accept calmly the wrongs done against Himself (e.g., Matt. 27:12-14), but to act with a powerful vengeance on behalf of others (e.g., John 2:15-16). Meekness epitomizes the strength that comes from loving others rather than self.

Gentleness (*epieikeias,* "graciousness," occurring in the NT only here and in Acts 24:4) is the active corollary to this meek disposition. This was the attitude in which Paul ministered, a spirit which could easily be construed as weakness and timidity by the world's **standards.** His opponents, the false apostles (2 Cor. 11:13), acknowledged his "bark." In a letter (cf. 1 Cor. 4:19) and through a delegate like Titus, Paul appeared **bold.** But his "bite," they said, lacked teeth, at least by worldly standards.

10:3-5. The weapons of the world are learning, personal influence, impressive credentials (1 Cor. 1:26), rhetorical polish (1 Cor. 2:1), and the like. These things Paul had discounted and discarded (Phil. 3:4-8). He did **not wage war as the world does** or use their weapons.

The **weapons** Paul used were the proclaimed Word of God and prayer (Eph. 6:17-18), weapons with **divine power.** In dependence on God (1 Cor. 2:4-5) these weapons, frail by worldly standards, are able **to demolish** the **arguments and every pretension** of the gospel's foes. Neither the god of this Age (2 Cor. 4:4) nor his henchmen (11:15) could oppose **the knowledge** (or power) **of God** on which Paul relied. No **thought** (*noēma;* cf. 2:11), including those of his opponents, is beyond the reach of the One who "catches the wise in their craftiness" and "knows that the thoughts of the wise are futile" (1 Cor. 3:19-20; cf. Job 5:13; Ps. 94:11).

The object of Paul's warfare was to **make** people **obedient.** Paul was not interested in making them subject to himself or any other man after the manner of the world (cf. 2 Cor. 1:24; 11:20; Luke 22:25).

10:6. His approach to this particular confrontation in Corinth was twofold.

First, it was necessary that the Corinthian church express their subjection to Christ by demonstrating loyalty to His representative Paul (5:20; cf. 7:15). In this way their **obedience** would be **complete.** Second, when Paul was sure they had repudiated his opponents (cf. 6:14-18), he could then deal directly with the false apostles, knowing that the church supported him. He was ready **to punish** their acts **of disobedience** to Christ. The word "punish" (*ekdikēsai*) could more forcefully be translated "avenge" (cf. 1 Cor. 3:17). In other contexts it describes the wrath of God directed against the enemies of His people (Num. 31:2; Deut. 32:43; Rev. 19:2).

B. *False apostles confronted (10:7–11:15)*

Though Paul had parried the accusations of his opponents at previous points in the letter (3:1, 7-18; 4:2-4; 5:12, 16; 6:14), they had not been the direct focal point of his address. Now they were. Who these opponents were can only be answered tentatively. Apparently they were Jews (11:22) but where they came from is not known. They believed themselves apostles of Christ (10:7; 11:23), a claim Paul rejected (11:13). They brought letters of recommendation (3:1), indulged in self-commendation (10:18), and identified themselves with certain so-called "super-apostles" (cf. 11:5).

These false apostles may have been sent out by those who at the Jerusalem Council had urged the circumcision of Gentiles and obedience to the Law of Moses (Acts 15:5). Of course this appeal was largely unheeded by the apostles and elders (Acts 15:23-29). The false apostles claimed to bear a message of righteousness (2 Cor. 11:14) which Paul called a false gospel (11:4). They may have proclaimed a legalistic righteousness based on external conformity to Mosaic legislation (3:7-15). Ultimately they were self-serving, seeking monetary gains from the Corinthians (2:17) and possibly also indulging in sensuality (12:21). Legalism and self-centeredness are two sides of the same coin (Matt. 6:2, 15-16; 23:5-7) with self-indulgence the ultimate result (Matt. 23:25; cf. Phil. 3:2).

10:7-8. A major factor contributing to the Corinthians' dilemma concerning apostolic authority was their superficiality and shallowness. They looked **only on the surface of things.** They were oriented to externalities and worldly wisdom (cf. 1 Cor. 3:1). As a result the false apostles found them fair game. In order to retrieve this indiscriminate church Paul would have to engage in what he found personally repugnant—self-commendation. His goal was not self-enhancement but restoration of the Corinthians. To that end he wielded his **authority** as an apostle of Christ. And he did so **freely** and without being **ashamed of it.** He tore down the "strongholds," "arguments," and every "pretension" of his opponents (2 Cor. 10:4-5) but he built up believers.

10:9-11. Paul anticipated that his previously written words about his apostolic authority (v. 8) or his **letters** might **frighten** the Corinthians. He also anticipated that his words (vv. 4-6) might raise smirks on the lips of the false apostles and a depreciatory remark about his bite not equaling his bark. He did not deny that his public presence was superficially **unimpressive** (cf. v. 1). He was not a polished speaker (11:6) by design as much as by default (cf. 1 Cor. 2:1-5). If the false apostles equated his rhetorical skills with the power granted him by God as an apostle, they would do so at their peril. True, his letters contained awesome commands about handing men over to Satan for the destruction of their flesh (1 Cor. 5:5; cf. Acts 13:11; 1 Tim. 1:20). But his subsequent action would show that he did what he said.

10:12. Paul's opponents (and any who sided with them) could be censured on several counts. The first was the inadequate standard by which they evaluated themselves. The false apostles compared themselves not with the divine standard exemplified by Christ but with other men, using human standards. In doing so, Paul said, no matter how much they vaunted their human wisdom they showed **themselves** to be **not wise,** but fools (cf. 1 Cor. 1:20).

10:13-14. The false apostles were censured on a second count. Even if Paul granted for the moment the legitimacy of their apostleship it was he, not they, who had been designated the apostle to the Gentiles (cf. Gal. 2:8). God had authenticated Paul's commission by producing fruit in Corinth—**we did get as far as you with the gospel of Christ** (cf. 1 Cor. 3:6).

The false apostles had grossly overstepped their bounds. They had gone **beyond proper limits** (cf. 2 Cor. 10:15) but Paul had **not**.

10:15-16. Paul's third censure concerned the claims of the false apostles. They had overstepped their bounds but they had also exaggerated their accomplishments. The church in Corinth was a result of Paul's ministry not theirs. Unlike his opponents he did not **boast about work already done . . . by others**. The Corinthians may have had many so-called guardians but they had only one "father," Paul (1 Cor. 4:15). He was the one they should imitate (1 Cor. 4:16). As their **faith** grew and they matured, he could then **expand** his **area of activity** by evangelizing other Gentiles **in the regions beyond** them, even as far away as Spain (Rom. 15:23-24). They could take part in this work by prayer (Eph. 6:19-20) and financial support (cf. 1 Cor. 16:6; Phil. 4:15-17). But first they needed to get their own house in order (2 Cor. 10:6).

10:17-11:1. To **boast** in men is ultimately self-impoverishing (cf. 1 Cor. 3:21). However legitimate and necessary the censuring of his opponents was, along with validating his own work, Paul ultimately believed that both were exercises in **foolishness**. Paul had reminded the Corinthians of this in an earlier letter (1 Cor. 1:31) quoting from Jeremiah 9:24, as he did here. Why did the Corinthians continue to be enamored of men, simply a form of self-adulation, when in fact their spiritual vitality was entirely due to the grace of God? (1 Cor. 1:30; 3:7) Paul certainly had not sought the commendation of the Corinthians nor was he seeking to commend **himself**. He knew he would one day stand before the judgment seat of Christ (2 Cor. 5:10). There only the Master's approval (Luke 19:17) will matter. Self-commendation and the praise of men (cf. Matt. 6:2, 6, 16) will count for nothing (Rom. 2:29; 1 Cor. 4:5). Let the Corinthians make no mistake about it: Paul's rebutting his opponents and reviewing his own labor was not for his own benefit. He subjected himself to this "folly" because he loved them and they needed it (2 Cor. 12:11). Such was his love for them that he would willingly be made a fool if by so doing he could rescue them.

11:2-4. While they may have thought otherwise, they were in peril. The tragedy of Eden was ominously close to reenactment. As **Christ** was elsewhere compared with Adam (Rom. 5:14; 1 Cor. 15:21-22, 45), Paul here compared the church in Corinth to **Eve**. Instead of resisting (cf. James 4:7; 1 Peter 5:9) the devil's inducement to disobedience Eve listened and succumbed (Gen. 3:1-6). The serpent enticed her by his **cunning** (*panourgia*, "trickery"; cf. 2 Cor. 4:2). The devil's representatives in Corinth (11:13-15) were also seductive. They should have been spurned (cf. 6:14-15) but instead were tolerated (11:4). Worse still, if the church like Eve obeyed the lie they would be guilty of disobedience to God and disloyalty to Christ, whom they were singlemindedly to love and obey. (**Sincere** renders the Gr. noun *haplotētos*, "simplicity in the sense of singlemindedness"; cf. 1:12).

In Paul's metaphor the church was a **virgin** betrothed **to Christ** at conversion. As the servant of God's grace he acted as their spiritual father (1 Cor. 4:15). Until the marriage was consummated at Christ's coming, exclusive **devotion to Christ** should prevail (cf. Eph. 5:25-27). The Corinthians, however, were periously close to forsaking that devotion and the spirit of liberty in which it flourished. They were dangerously open to **a different gospel** and **a different spirit** (i.e., bondage to Law; 2 Cor. 3:7-18; cf. Gal. 4:17-5:1).

11:5-6. The Corinthians vacillated in their devotion to the Lord because of the threefold appeal of the false apostles. First, these false teachers apparently associated themselves and their mission with the original apostles. The designation **"super-apostles"** was used by the false apostles of themselves, or was Paul's ironical portrayal of their adulation of the Twelve (or of Peter, James, and John; Gal. 2:9). The false apostles hoped to derive authority by claiming to be associated with the Twelve. Without demeaning the Twelve, Paul affirmed his own status as an apostle of similar rank: **I am not in the least inferior** (cf. 2 Cor. 12:11). His basis for this claim would follow shortly (11:22–12:10).

Second, the false apostles appealed to the Corinthians' desires for superiority in rhetorical excellence. Paul admitted he was not an accomplished rhetorician, a

trained speaker (cf. 10:10). (However, if he were, he was choosing not to use his rhetorical abilities; cf. 1 Cor. 2:1-5). His apostleship was not a matter of show but of substance. *What* Paul said was more important than *how* he said it. The Corinthians could not deny the content of his message and its transforming consequences (cf. 1 Cor. 4:15; 9:1-2).

11:7-9. A third way the false apostles appealed to the Corinthians was in their method of supporting themselves. When Jesus sent out disciples on missionary tours, He directed them to derive shelter and sustenance from those to whom they ministered (Luke 9:3-4; 10:4-7). This apparently became the usual practice for Christian missionaries (1 Cor. 9:4-6; cf. *Didache* 11:4-6), and it was followed by the false apostles in Corinth. However, Paul and those associated with him (e.g., Barnabas, 1 Cor. 9:6) differed by supporting themselves as best they could without ministerial remuneration (cf. 1 Cor. 4:12; 1 Thes. 2:9; 2 Thes. 3:8). Occasionally Paul accepted unsolicited support from **churches** to whom he had ministered (e.g., the Philippian church in **Macedonia;** Phil. 4:15-16). But he did so uneasily (cf. Phil. 4:10-13), calling it "robbery" (2 Cor. 11:8) to take from poor people. He did not want to be **a burden to** them.

11:10-12. Paul had various reasons for adhering to this general practice (e.g., 1 Cor. 9:17-18; 2 Thes. 3:9-10). His main reason may have been his desire to emulate Christ who became poor even as He enriched others (2 Cor. 8:9). An immediate reason in Corinth for maintaining this practice was that it barred the false apostles from any claim of equality to Paul in apostolic ministry (11:12), and so was anathema to them. However, it was not too well received even by the beneficiaries, the Corinthians. They thought that Paul's hesitation to accept remuneration from them showed that he did **not** love them. Paul, nonetheless, stood his **ground.**

11:13-15. Though Paul had been mild in his remarks about the "super-apostles" (v. 5), here he gave the **false apostles** a withering denunciation. They were only shams, claiming to be ambassadors of Christ when in fact they were emissaries (**servants,** *diakonoi*) of **Satan.** Like Satan's masquerade **as an angel of** **light,** they were **masquerading** (*metaschēmatizomenoi*, "changing the outward form") **as apostles** and **servants of righteousness.** Like whitewashed tombs they may have looked righteous but inside there was only death and decay (cf. Matt. 23:27-28), prefiguring **their** doom (**end;** cf. 1 Cor. 3:17).

Who were these false apostles? Numerous suggestions have been made, ranging from Hellenistic charismatics to Palestinian Gnostics (see J.J. Gunther, *St. Paul's Opponents and Their Background.* Leiden: E.J. Brill, 1973). Several factors suggest, however, that they were Palestinian Jews, members of the Jerusalem church who were false brothers (cf. Gal. 2:4) in Paul's estimation. They carried commendatory letters from the church (2 Cor. 3:1), possibly under the auspices of the Jerusalem Council, to survey compliance with the Jerusalem decree (Acts 15:20-21). That there were self-appointed delegations to enforce Mosaic ordinances before this is certain (Acts 15:24), and it is possible that the false apostles in Corinth were mavericks of this sort. Paul did not contest their appeal to the authority of the "super-apostles." But he did refute the value of such an appeal and the notion that apostolic authority was a matter of human association rather than divine accreditation.

C. Apostolic credentials (11:16–12:10)

Like most people, the Corinthians were slow to absorb the truth that divine standards differ radically from those of the world. Paul had tried to make this clear in his former letter concerning the message of the Cross: the wisdom of God is foolishness to the world (1 Cor. 1:18-25). If, however, the Corinthians persisted in looking at things from the world's point of view, he would accommodate himself to their perspective. But he would still try to lead them to realize that divine accreditation should be seen not against the backdrop of human greatness but human weakness. The marks of an apostle were the marks of Christ, including weakness and suffering (2 Cor. 13:4; cf. Isa. 53:3-4; Mark 9:12). In this passage (2 Cor. 11:16–12:10) Paul recounted his frailties and with poignant irony said, in essence, "These are the credentials of an apostle" (cf. 1 Cor. 4:9-13).

11:16-18. Following the advice of

Proverbs 26:5, Paul again answered the foolish Corinthians according to their folly. He had previously asked them to "put up with" a bit of foolishness (2 Cor. 11:1); he now resumed this approach. He did so not by choice but by necessity because they had tolerated and welcomed the false apostles. The Corinthians received those false teachers because of the latter's external qualifications and self-aggrandizement. This is like valuing a gem on the basis of its size rather than its quality. Paul's challenge to the believers was a "contest of folly," entered into in order to win the Corinthians. The word fool (vv. 16-17, 19, 21; 12:6, 11) is from the adjective *aphrōn,* meaning "ignorant," not *mōros,* which means "stupid." In 2 Corinthians Paul frequently spoke of boasting, not in a haughty way but in an effort to affirm his claim as an apostle. In his boasting he was not talking as the Lord would, as the Lord never defended Himself in this way, but Paul chose to, though reluctantly.

11:19-21a. The irony in these verses borders on sarcasm. Its sting is tempered only by Paul's motive which was to correct this wayward church. The Corinthians, thinking themselves wise . . . put up with fools—a naive, foolish thing to do! Though Paul may have been accused of "lording it over" the Corinthians (1:24), the false apostles were the ones they should fear. In the name of Christ they would exploit and enslave the Corinthians to gratify themselves. (Here the Gr. word for exploits means "devour," like a parasite. This differs from the word rendered "exploit" in 7:2 and 12:17-18.) Jesus accused the legalistic Pharisees of the same rapacious practice (Mark 12:40). Paul said he had been too weak for that. He had presented himself to the Corinthians as their servant and Christ as their only Lord (2 Cor. 4:5).

11:21b-22. Paul was now ready to begin comparing the external qualifications apparently believed by the Corinthians and the false apostles to be matters of great importance. It is usually believed that the questions asked and answered by Paul describe himself and the false apostles. It is possible, however, that Paul is comparing himself with the so-called "super-apostles" (v. 5), the Twelve, to whom the false apostles appealed as their source of authority and with whom they

identified. If so, this would strengthen the comparison (noted in v. 5 and 12:11), would accord well with what Paul had previously written about himself and the Twelve (1 Cor. 15:10), and would eliminate the awkwardness of 2 Corinthians 11:23 as applied to the false apostles immediately after what Paul had written in verse 13. So, while these questions may describe the false apostles who claimed to be the proxy of the Twelve, they may also be understood as Paul's comparison of himself with the Twelve and his superiority, from a human point of view, to them.

The designation **Hebrews** may be an ancestral description but in this context (with **Israelites**) it may also be a linguistic distinction. The term is used elsewhere in the New Testament only twice (Acts 6:1; Phil. 3:5). In Acts 6:1 it clearly distinguished the Semitic-speaking Jews from those whose primary or exclusive language was Greek. Though Paul was born in Tarsus, he was apparently reared in a Semitic-speaking home of Jewish parentage whose orientation was to the homeland of Palestine.

As one of the Israelites Paul traced his lineage through the tribe of Benjamin (Phil. 3:5). As one of **Abraham's descendants** he was circumcised on the eighth day (Phil. 3:5; cf. Gen. 17:9-14); more importantly, Paul was Abraham's descendant by faith (cf. Rom. 4:16). From a human viewpoint Paul's credentials were impeccable (cf. Phil. 3:4-6).

11:23. If Paul were comparing himself with the false apostles rather than the Twelve in these verses (cf. comments on vv. 21b-22) then the phrase **servants of Christ** describes their designation of themselves, previously repudiated by Paul (v. 13) but here adopted for the sake of argument. The thrust of his argument was on quantifiable "service," an absurd measurement in itself (in 1 Cor. 3:13 Paul stressed quality in God's evaluation of Christian service). Paul noted the absurdity of this comparison himself (**I am out of my mind;** cf. 2 Cor. 5:13), but the Corinthian preoccupation with comparisons had forced him to it.

In intensity and scope of ministry no apostle or even group of apostles (cf. 1 Cor. 15:10) could match Paul's record of service. What is remarkable about Paul's catalog of achievements is his focus not on what might be called the triumphs of his ministerial experience but on its defeats. He left unmentioned the times when he seemed to be riding a surge of divine power such as at Ephesus (e.g., Acts 19:11) and chronicled instead the experiences in which he seemed to be dashed helpless to the ground. Like his Lord, who displayed the glory of God in His passion and death (John 13:31), Paul boasted in his sufferings and weaknesses (cf. Gal. 6:14).

The details concerning his ministry which Paul disclosed in this verse reveal how fragmentary is his biographical information in the Book of Acts. The writing of this letter coincided with the events mentioned by Luke in Acts 20:2. At this point in Luke's narrative he mentioned only one imprisonment (in Philippi), one beating (also in Philippi; Acts 16:22), and one brush with **death** (the stoning in Lystra; Acts 14:19). Yet in 2 Corinthians Paul referred to numerous incidents of this kind. Perhaps they occurred before his formal missionary journeys (Acts 13–20), or maybe Luke did not find it necessary to record them.

11:24. This verse makes it clear that Paul's statement in Romans 9:3—wishing himself cursed if by so doing Israel could be saved—was no empty declaration. **Five times** Paul **received** the synagogue's punishment (of 39 **lashes** each) in the course of ministering to fellow **Jews.** Death could occur under the 39 lashes because according to the Mishnah the person delivering the scourging was not liable for a victim's death (Makkoth 3.14).

11:25-26. The apostle to the Gentiles **was beaten** by fellow Jews. Also the Romans inflicted their punishment on Paul by beating him **with rods,** though they did so illegally since he was a Roman citizen (Acts 16:37). The acclaimed Roman peace was not much protection for Paul either. Roman law and order in Lystra did little to stop the mob that **stoned** Paul and left him for dead (Acts 14:19). Nor were the Roman highways and seaways placid avenues of travel. In addition to shipwreck (cf. Acts 27:27-44, though future to Paul's writing 2 Cor.) and river crossings with the consequential threat of death from drowning or exposure, Paul's itinerant ministry (he was **constantly on the move**) exposed him to countless dangers. He needed to be wary of professional **bandits** (cf. Luke 10:30),

and attacks by Jews (his **own country-men**) and **Gentiles** alike (e.g., Acts 14:19; 16:19). He faced dangers everywhere—**in the city . . . in the country . . . at sea** (cf. **open sea,** v. 25). Even within the churches, such as Corinth, he faced the danger of attack instigated by or at the hands of **false brothers.**

11:27. In addition to living with dangers Paul willingly endured numerous privations in discharging his apostolic ministry. His decision to refuse remuneration for his ministry (cf. vv. 7-9) was not made lightly. Working night and day (cf. 1 Thes. 2:9) so as not to burden anyone for the necessities of life (2 Thes. 3:8), Paul still often found himself with insufficient **food,** drink, and clothing to meet even his minimal needs. He experienced sleepless nights, **hunger . . . thirst, and cold.**

Earlier in 2 Corinthians Paul had referred to being persecuted (2 Cor. 4:9), at the point of death (4:10-12), facing "beatings, imprisonments, and riots," and experiencing "hard work, sleepless nights, and hunger" (6:5). Here (11:23-27) his list of sufferings is far more complete.

11:28-29. It is difficult to comprehend the pain Paul must have felt from these physical afflictions and deprivations. But the spiritual struggles of his ministry were an even greater burden.

These verses climax the catalog of his ministerial suffering. **Concern for** others, not for himself, weighed heavily on him. In 1 Corinthians (12:25) Paul had written at length about the church as a body composed of various members knit together by a mutual concern for each other. Here he revealed the daily burden of the concern he experienced not just for the well-being of the Corinthian church, which would have taxed the noblest spirit, but concern for the well-being of **all the churches** established through his ministry.

In 1 Corinthians 12 he noted that in a spiritual body "if one part suffers every part suffers with it" (1 Cor. 12:26). Here he revealed how that sentiment found expression in his own life. He identified with the weak whether physically (cf. Phil. 2:26) or, more likely, spiritually (1 Cor. 9:22), in their pitiable state (cf. 1 Cor. 8:12; Rom. 14:15). **Who is weak, and I do not feel weak?** If anyone was led into sin, Paul so identified with the sinner that he too felt the consequences of the act. **Who is led into sin, and I do not inwardly burn?** David compared his state of sin under God's hand to "the heat of summer" (Ps. 32:4), a likely inspiration for the equally vivid inner "burning" Paul felt at the knowledge of a brother led astray.

11:30. Paul had taken the standards of the Corinthians and false apostles and turned them upside down. His catalog of sufferings could hardly have been what they expected to read. He boasted not in his power but in his **weakness.** (In chaps. 11–13, Paul spoke frequently of being "weak" [11:21, 29; 12:10; 13:4, 9] and of having "weakness[es]" [11:30; 12:5, 9-10; 13:4].) Yet to Paul this was "boasting," not a contrived or ironical account. Paul's **boast** was that his life was like that of Christ. As Jesus had been "a Man of sorrows and familiar with suffering" (Isa. 53:3), so had Paul (2 Cor. 11:23-27). As Jesus "took up our infirmities and carried our sorrows" (Isa. 53:4) so, in a different sense, had Paul (2 Cor. 11:28-29). Paul's **boast** was that he was like the suffering Servant. It was certainly a grand claim though hardly perceived as such by false apostles and worldly Corinthian believers (1 Cor. 3:3).

11:31. Any one of the severe sufferings Paul had described in the preceding verses might kill an average person. But Paul—one man—endured them all.

Paul was aware that his reliability was suspect among the Corinthians (cf. 1:12-18). For that reason he asserted his veracity: **I am not lying** (cf. 1:18; 11:11). His vow of truthfulness applied not only to the preceding sufferings but also to the following description of his incident in Damascus (11:32-33) and the account of his visionary experience (12:1-6).

11:32-33. Paul mentioned this escape from **Damascus,** an event which occurred early in his life as a Christian (cf. Acts 9:19-25), as a typical or quintessential experience in his work as an apostle. It epitomized the transformation that had taken place in his relationship with God, and sharply contrasted his state with that of the false apostles. Like them, he carried commendatory letters from Jerusalem to Damascus (Acts 9:2), but when he was en route God struck him down and he encountered the risen Christ. He had left for Damascus with great human authority and zeal (Acts 9:1); he departed abjectly conscious of his own weakness. He was hunted by Jew and Gentile alike (Acts 14:5), but delivered by God through the agency of fellow Christians. His exit (by being **lowered in,** of all things, **a basket**), not his entrance, typified the apostolic life (cf. 1 Cor. 4:9-12). How different were the false apostles, who were like the unconverted Saul!

12:1. A second line of comparison the Corinthians insisted on (cf. v. 11) concerned **visions and revelations.** Like Paul's external credentials (11:22-23) he believed this parading of credentials was an exercise in futility (**there is nothing to be gained**) for building up the church (10:8). He did it, however, in the hope that it would silence his critics and enable him to minister freely. He also neatly turned his readers' attention from these irrelevant credentials to those that were an apostle's authentic marks. What distinguished "servants of Christ" (11:23) was their likeness to the suffering Servant (Isa. 53). If one had exalted "visions and revelations" (2 Cor. 12:1), he should have a corresponding appreciation of his own weakness and humility (vv. 9-10).

12:2-4. Paul's indirect reference to himself as **a man in Christ** showed that he regarded this great experience not as a consequence of inherent worthiness or spiritual excellence but because he was "in Christ." As such it anticipated what everyone in Christ will one day experience, the presence of Christ in heaven.

This event occurred **14 years** earlier, sometime in the years A.D. 42–44 before Paul's missionary journeys reported in Acts. Paul was raptured (**caught up** is from the same verb *harpazō* used in 1 Thes. 4:17 of saints at the Rapture) **to the third heaven,** the dwelling place of Christ and the saints, which Jesus called **paradise** (Luke 23:43; cf. Rev. 2:7). Temporal and spatial sensations were absent (**whether** he was **in the body or apart from the body** he did **not know**). What he heard he was forbidden to communicate, possibly because it applied to him alone (cf. Acts 9:16). The experience, however, no doubt contributed to Paul's conviction that "our light and momentary troubles are achieving for us an eternal glory that far outweighs them all" (2 Cor. 4:17).

12:5-6. Paul boasted about **a man** (cf. "a man in Christ," v. 2, and "this man," v. 3) because his accent was on Christ, not himself. The Corinthian preoccupation with the external and the spectacular was regrettable to Paul (cf. 1 Cor. 14:20). He could boast of these things truthfully (2 Cor. 12:6; cf. 1 Cor. 14:18; Phil. 3:4), by which he implied that the claims of other men in Corinth were suspect. But what mattered to Paul was not his achievements but God's work through him and the gospel that he preached.

12:7-9. So that Paul would not forget this, God gave him a constant reminder of his weakness. Countless explanations concerning the nature of his **thorn in the flesh** have been offered. They range from incessant temptation, dogged opponents, chronic maladies (such as ophthalmia, malaria, migraine headaches, and epilepsy), to a disability in speech. No one can say for sure what his was, but it probably was a physical affliction (for the work of **Satan** in this, cf. 1 Cor. 5:5; 10:10). It is understandable that Paul would consider this thorn a hindrance to wider or more effective ministry (cf. Gal. 4:14-16) and that he would repeatedly petition God for its removal (2 Cor. 12:8). But he learned from this experience the lesson that pervades this letter: divine power (**My power,** v. 8; **Christ's power,** v. 9) is best displayed against the backdrop of human **weaknesses** (cf. 4:7) so that God alone is praised (10:17). Rather than removing the problem God gave him **grace** in it. This grace is sufficient (*arkei,* i.e., adequate in the sense of providing contentment). (The Gr. words trans. **to keep me from becoming conceited** occur in 12:7 twice, at the beginning and end of the verse. The NIV translates only the first one.)

12:10. God's grace transformed Paul's perspective. Experiences in his ministry he would naturally abhor, he could welcome supernaturally because the evidence of Christ's power in the midst of them brought glory to Him, not Paul. When Paul came to the end of himself, Christ alone was seen. **When he was weak, then** Christ, by His strength, could make Paul spiritually **strong.** ("Power," *dynamis,* in v. 9, is the word "strength," thus matching "strong," *dynatos,* in v. 10).

D. Recommended response (12:11-13:10)

Paul hoped, when he visited the Corinthians, to see two responses to his letter: (1) repentance (involving obedience to God) for wrong, and (2) an affirmation of loyalty to himself and his associates as authentic servants of Christ.

12:11. The boasting was over. Paul had played the part demanded of him by the Corinthians—the **fool.** Instead of coming to his defense against the innuendos and calumnies of the false apostles, the Corinthians remained passive spectators, forcing Paul to offer his own defense. Paul knew that he was more than equal to stand comparison with even the greatest of the Twelve (cf. 11:5), as shown by the catalog of credentials he had just given. But it was a foolish endeavor because these credentials were ultimately not his but God's. He was **nothing.** As he had written the Corinthians before, "I worked harder than all of them—yet not I, but the grace of God that was with me" (1 Cor. 15:10).

12:12. The supernatural acts accomplished through God's grace should have sufficed to quiet all suspicion about Paul's apostleship. **Signs** (*sēmeiois,* miracles with emphasis on their significance; e.g., Jesus' seven "signs" in John); **wonders** (*terasin,* unusual events that engender awe); **miracles** (*dynamesin,* wonderworks resulting from supernatural power)—all these are the evidences **that mark an apostle** (cf. Acts 2:22, 43; Heb. 2:4). Though no miraculous signs or wonders done in Corinth were recorded in the Acts account of Paul's ministry in that city, such miracles certainly occurred (they **were done among you**). Paul also performed miracles before and after the Corinthian ministry. A demon was cast out of the servant girl in Philippi (Acts 16:18), and Paul's ministry in Ephesus was marked by numerous miracles (Acts 19:11). Of course the greatest miracle was a church in Corinth planted by Paul but given life by God (1 Cor. 3:6). Remarkable too was his **great perseverance,** again a result of the empowerment of God (Acts 18:9-11). All these evidences pointed to Paul as a true apostle and to his opponents as "false apostles" (2 Cor. 11:13).

12:13-15. In only one sense was Paul

different from other true apostles: he was self-supporting and took no remuneration from the Corinthians. And he would not change his way, for he refused to be a **burden to** them (vv. 13-14, 16). His imminent **third** visit would be no different (cf. 13:1; and see point 7 under "Contacts and Correspondence" in the *Introduction*). Like a father with his spiritual **children** Paul wanted to care for the church without cost to them. While he refused remuneration for different reasons (cf. 11:10; 1 Cor. 9:17) not the least among them was his **love** for the Corinthians. And he would gladly have received the same "coinage" from them (cf. 2 Cor. 6:11-13).

12:16-18. Paul could live with the fact that the Corinthians' recompense of love would be less than his investment of love in them. But he found it intolerable that they charged him and his associates with underhanded self-gratification (when just the opposite was true). Apparently the false apostles suggested that Paul's unwillingness to accept support from the church was simply a cloak to disguise his love of money and the designs he had on the collection. **Titus** was obviously implicated in this, as was one of the two brothers who accompanied him at Paul's recommendation (cf. 8:22). Paul asked the obvious question: What evidence could be mustered to lend the slightest credence to this allegation? Was there any hint of misconduct in the behavior of **Titus** or **our brother?** Were not Paul's actions equally impeccable? Had either of them ever exploited (cf. 2:11; 7:2) the Corinthians? Paul hoped that the absence of evidence would silence his critics (though the history of his relationship with the Corinthian church hardly boded well for such a result).

12:19-21. The motive behind the apologetic which Paul wove through this letter was not self-preservation. Paul's Judge was **God**, not any human court (1 Cor. 4:3-4; 2 Cor. 5:10). On the contrary, he had undertaken this difficult letter out of concern for the Corinthians (**for your strengthening**) in the hope of rectifying the disorders in the church before punishment became necessary (13:2). Like a father with his children, any punishment which he was compelled to administer would grieve him as well

(12:21). It was for just this reason he had canceled his previously projected third visit (1:23-2:4). They had responded well to his earlier letter (7:8-13) but the entrance of the false apostles threatened to revive their former divisiveness.

The eight sins Paul mentioned (12:20) are all explainable in the context of church division, as are the three sins of verse 21 in the climate of lax morality which disunity produces. (See comments on these three in Gal. 5:19.) While the legalistic bent of the false apostles might be thought to quash the sins of the flesh listed in 2 Corinthians 12:21, the sad truth is that legalism and immorality are frequent bedfellows (cf. Phil. 3:3, 19; John 8:3-7).

13:1-3. Paul's second **visit to** Corinth (2:1) had been a humbling experience (12:21), not only because of the offense against him (cf. 2:5-11) but because many in the church were living contrary to the will of God (12:21). Paul had warned them about the consequences of sin then and he did so again in this letter. Following Jesus' application of Deuteronomy 19:15 to errant brethren (Matt. 18:16), Paul promised discipline for the unrepentant. The proof of his apostolic authority which they wanted would be given but in terms they would be wise to avoid (cf. 1 Cor. 5:5). Though Paul was weak, **Christ** whom he served was **not** (cf. 2 Cor. 10:4).

13:4. The paradox of Christ was the paradox of Paul. With **God's power** at His disposal (Matt. 26:53) Christ nonetheless followed the course of **weakness** to the cross. In the Resurrection the magnitude of that untapped power was displayed (Eph. 1:19-21). This side of the grave Paul like Jesus followed the path of "weakness" but as in Jesus' life, a glimmer of **God's power** showed through (e.g., Matt. 4:23; 2 Cor. 12:12). Paul wanted this power to be used for constructive rather than punitive purposes (cf. 13:10; 10:2-6), power that would enable him **to serve** them.

13:5-7. Throughout the letter Paul subjected himself and his ministry to scrutiny. Now he handed the lens to the Corinthians, with the challenge that they consider their own conduct (**yourselves** is in the emphatic position in Gr.). Paul's question is usually construed with regard to positional justification: were they

Christians or not? But it more likely concerned practical sanctification: did they *demonstrate* that they were in the faith (cf. 1 Cor. 16:13) and that Christ was in them by their obeying His will? To stand the test was to do what was right. To fail was to be disobedient and therefore subject to God's discipline. The words fail(ed) the test (2 Cor. 13:5-6) and failed (v. 7) render the Greek word *adokimoi* ("disapproved"; cf. *adokimos* in 1 Cor. 9:27).

Whatever doubts the Corinthians may have had about Paul's conduct (e.g., 2 Cor. 1:17, 2:17; 7:2) he believed that a sober evaluation would lead them to vindicate him. He hoped they would not be disapproved by God; and he hoped they would see that *he* was not disapproved by God. Still it was their reputation or standing, not his, that concerned him.

13:8-10. For himself, Paul knew he was powerless against the truth, the will of God. His experience on the Damascus Road had taught him that (Acts 9:1-6). Like Jesus his Lord, he was willing to spend and be spent on behalf of others (cf. 2 Cor. 8:9; 12:15). In his weakness he was made strong (12:8, 10) and so were they (13:9). He was concerned about the Corinthians' welfare (cf. Phil. 2:20-21). Perfection (*katartisin*) may be translated "restoration." This noun occurs only here in the New Testament but is kin to the verb *katartizesthe* translated "aim for perfection" in 2 Corinthians 13:11 and elsewhere used for repairing nets (Matt. 4:21).

As a conclusion to this warning (2 Cor. 12:20-21; 13:5-7), this prayer for restoration of their ways was certainly fitting. Then Paul could be spared the pain of disciplining those he loved (cf. 2:2) and instead he could work with them for their joy (1:24) and for building them up (13:10).

V. Conclusion (13:11-14)

Did the Corinthians respond positively to Paul's warning? Yes. Paul had conditioned the expansion of his ministry in other areas on the problems in Corinth being resolved (10:15-16). He followed the writing of this letter with a visit of three months during which time he wrote the letter to the Romans. In that letter he wrote "Now . . . there is no more place for me to work in these regions" (Rom. 15:23). His appeal had been heeded. The Corinthians were now obedient.

A. Appropriate conduct (13:11-12)

13:11-12. Paul's final appeal was a call for unity: Aim for perfection (i.e., "be restored or complete"; see comments on "perfection" in v. 9), listen to my appeal, be of one mind (cf. Phil. 2:2), live in peace. This unity could be realized only as they depended on God who supplies love (cf. 2 Cor. 13:14) and peace. Such unity was expressed by a holy kiss (cf. Rom. 16:16; 1 Cor. 16:20 [see comments there]; 1 Thes. 5:26; 1 Peter 5:14).

B. Salutations and benediction (13:13-14)

13:13-14. The saints of Macedonia, with whom Paul was staying at the time he wrote 2 Corinthians (see the *Introduction*), sent their unified greetings. In closing, Paul invoked the blessing of the Triune God so that the grace manifested by Christ, the love expressed by God the Father (cf. "the God of love," v. 11), and the fellowship created by the Holy Spirit might be experienced in Corinth.

BIBLIOGRAPHY

Barrett, C.K. *The Second Epistle to the Corinthians.* Harper's New Testament Commentaries. New York: Harper & Row, 1973.

Bruce, F.F. *1 and 2 Corinthians.* London: Oliphants, 1971.

Gromacki, Robert G. *Stand Firm in the Faith: An Exposition of II Corinthians.* Grand Rapids: Baker Book House, 1978.

Hanson, Richard P.C. *2 Corinthians.* London: SCM Press, 1954.

Héring, Jean. *The Second Epistle of Saint Paul to the Corinthians.* London: Epworth Press, 1967.

Hodge, Charles. *An Exposition of the Second Epistle to the Corinthians.* Reprint. Grand Rapids: Baker Book House, 1980.

Hughes, Philip Edgcumbe. *Paul's Second Epistle to the Corinthians.* The New International Commentary on the New Testament. Grand Rapids: Wm. B. Eerdmans Publishing Co., 1962.

Kent, Homer. *A Heart Opened Wide: Studies in II Corinthians*. Grand Rapids: Baker Book House, 1982.

Moule, H.C.G. *The Second Epistle to the Corinthians*. Fort Washington, Pa.: Christian Literature Crusade, 1976.

Plummer, Alfred. *A Critical and Exegetical Commentary on the Second Epistle of St. Paul to the Corinthians*. The International Critical Commentary. Edinburgh: T. & T. Clark, 1915.

Schelke, Karl. *The Second Epistle to the Corinthians*. New York: Herder & Herder, 1969.

Tasker, R.V.G. *The Second Epistle of Paul to the Corinthians: An Introduction and Commentary*. The Tyndale New Testament Commentaries. Grand Rapids: Wm. B. Eerdmans Publishing Co., 1958.

Thrall, Margaret E. *The First and Second Letters of Paul to the Corinthians*. London: Cambridge Press, 1965.

GALATIANS

Donald K. Campbell

INTRODUCTION

Importance of the Epistle. Galatians, though one of Paul's shorter epistles, is highly esteemed as one of his greatest and most influential. Since both Romans and Galatians teach the doctrine of justification by faith, the former has been considered by some to be an expansion of Galatians and the latter has been called "a short Romans."

Like 2 Corinthians the Epistle of Galatians eloquently defends Paul's apostolic authority and contains in summary form what the apostle taught. In particular it contains a clear statement of justification by faith and builds on that foundation a defense of Christian liberty against any form of legalism.

In the early church, as the separation between Judaism and Christianity was taking place, the letter to the Galatians no doubt helped clarify that cleavage. Centuries later it played such a key role in the Reformation that it was called "the cornerstone of the Protestant Reformation." This was because its emphasis on salvation by grace through faith alone was the major theme of the preaching of the Reformers. Luther was especially attached to Galatians and referred to it as his wife. He lectured on the book extensively and his *Commentary on Galatians* was widely read by the common people.

The profound influence of this small epistle continues. It is indeed the "Magna Charta of Christian Liberty," proclaiming to modern generations that salvation from the penalty and power of sin comes not by works but by grace through faith in God's provision.

Authorship. The Pauline authorship of Galatians has, except for a few radical critics, been generally acknowledged. Even when the higher critics of 19th-century Germany were denying apostolic authorship of book after book, the Tübingen school regarded Galatians as Pauline. The reasons for this are based on the clear testimony of both internal and external evidence. Importantly, the author of the letter calls himself Paul both in the salutation (1:1) and later in the body of the letter (5:2). Most of chapters 1 and 2 are autobiographical and harmonize consistently with the events of Paul's life recorded in Acts. The theology of Galatians is the theology of Paul as taught in his other writings such as Romans.

The external evidence for Pauline authorship of Galatians is also convincing. In the second and third centuries Galatians was attributed to Paul and quoted by Irenaeus, Clement of Alexandria, and Origen. Even the heretics of that time, including Marcion, assumed it was written by Paul.

It must be concluded that no real doubt existed in the early church nor should any exist today as to the Pauline authorship of Galatians.

Original Readers. The Epistle of Galatians was addressed "to the churches in Galatia" (1:2). Where was "Galatia," and who were the "Galatians"? (cf. 3:1) This question is complicated by the fact that Galatia had two meanings when this epistle was written. First, it referred to the area in Asia Minor where the Gauls had settled after migrating from western Europe through Italy and Greece. The territory was limited to the north central and east central areas of Asia Minor and its principal cities were Ancyra, Pessinus, and Tavium. But in 25 B.C. this kingdom was converted to a Roman province, and territory was added to the south, including the cities of Antioch, Iconium, Lystra, and Derbe.

A debate has raged for centuries over whether Paul wrote his Galatian letter to

Christians living in northern or southern Galatia. The North Galatian theory held that Paul visited the geographical district of Galatia in the north and established churches there. This church-planting ministry would have taken place on Paul's second missionary journey after he left the southern Galatian region and before he came to Troas (cf. Acts 16:6-8). A second visit to the northern territory is apparently described in Acts 18:23.

The South Galatian theory was advanced by Sir William Ramsay. In this view the churches addressed in the epistle were those of Derbe, Lystra, Iconium, and (Pisidian) Antioch, cities Paul visited initially on his first missionary journey (cf. Acts 13–14). Thus while there is no account in Scripture of churches having been established in North Galatia, even on the second missionary journey, churches were established in South Galatia, according to Acts.

Other arguments which tend to favor the South Galatia theory are that the main roads from Paul's hometown of Tarsus pass directly through the cities of South, not North Galatia; the Judaizers were not likely to bypass the southern cities for the northern cities; a large Jewish element which could be addressed by the Judaizers lived in the southern cities; representatives of South Galatia accompanied the offering for the poor in Jerusalem but none were from North Galatia (cf. Acts 20:4); Barnabas who is mentioned but not introduced (cf. Gal. 2:1, 9, 13) would not have been known by the believers in the northern cities since he traveled with Paul only on the first journey. For these and other reasons many New Testament scholars now favor the view that Paul wrote the Galatian letter to Christians in the cities of South Galatia.

Time and Place of Writing. Those who identify the recipients of Galatians as the believers in the southern cities of Galatia generally consider that the epistle was written from Antioch of Syria in about A.D. 48 just before the Jerusalem Council (Acts 15). While some chronological problems remain with this view, it is perhaps the best of the available options. After the first missionary journey Paul and Barnabas returned to Antioch. Peter came down from Jerusalem to visit them, fellowshiped with them, and then with-drew from the Gentile Christians only to be publicly rebuked by Paul for his inconsistent behavior. Meanwhile, Judaizing false teachers had infiltrated the churches in Galatia, denying Paul's authority as an apostle and teaching that circumcision was necessary for salvation. Reacting quickly and vigorously to Peter's actions and the threatened lapse of the Galatians into legalism, Paul wrote this strong letter prior to attending the Jerusalem Council.

Purpose of the Epistle. The Judaizers in Galatia both discredited Paul and proclaimed a false gospel. It was necessary that Paul vindicate his apostleship and message, a task he undertook in the first two chapters. In this autobiographical section Paul demonstrated convincingly that his apostleship and his message came by revelation from the risen Christ. In chapters 3 and 4 Paul contended for the true doctrine of grace, that is, for justification by faith alone. Finally, to show that Christian liberty does not mean license the apostle, in chapters 5 and 6, taught that a Christian should live by the power of the Holy Spirit and that when he does he manifests in his life not the works of the flesh but the fruit of the Spirit.

Galatians was written to remedy a desperate situation, to call early Christians back from the Mosaic Law to grace, from legalism to faith. It is an emphatic statement of salvation by faith apart from works and is as relevant today as when it was originally penned.

OUTLINE

I. Introduction (1:1-10)
   A. The salutation (1:1-5)
   B. The denunciation (1:6-10)
II. Personal: A Defense of Paul's Authority (1:11–2:21)
   A. He was independent of the apostles (1:11-24)
      1. Thesis: Paul's gospel was a revelation (1:11-12)
      2. Events before Paul's conversion (1:13-14)
      3. Events at Paul's conversion (1:15-16a)
      4. Events after Paul's conversion (1:16b-24)

COMMENTARY

I. Introduction (1:1-10)

A. The salutation (1:1-5)

1:1. The opening of the Galatian epistle is both typical and atypical. Though the salutation includes the usual identification of author and recipient together with a customary greeting, the usual expression of thanksgiving and praise for believers is totally absent. Further, there is an abruptness about the opening words which plunges the reader immediately into one of Paul's major concerns, namely, that his apostolic credentials had been challenged. Though not one of the original Twelve, **Paul** claimed equality with them as **an apostle.** The word *apostolos* connotes authority and refers to a person who has a right to speak for God as His representative or delegate.

Paul's apostleship did not originate with men (it was **not from men**), that is, he was not appointed an apostle by any official body such as the leaders in Jerusalem or Antioch. Neither did his apostleship originate with any one man, however important (**nor by man**) not even Ananias, who assisted Paul in Damascus (cf. Acts 9:10-17), nor Barnabas, who played a strategic role in opening doors of ministry for Paul in both Jerusalem and Antioch (cf. Acts 9:27; 11:25-26). Rather, Paul made the bold claim that his call was of heavenly origin, from God the Father and the risen Lord Jesus Christ. This is the only direct mention of the resurrection of Christ in the epistle. It emphasizes the importance of that event to Paul's apostleship, for he was not called during the earthly ministry of the Lord but by the resurrected Christ.

1:2. Joining with Paul in the sending, though not the writing, of this letter were all the brothers with him. These were the apostle's fellow workers, perhaps Barnabas as well as the prophets and teachers with whom Paul ministered in Antioch (cf. Acts 13:1). Mentioning these colaborers emphasized the fact that the teachings of this epistle were not peculiar to Paul but were held in common with others.

The recipients of the letter were the churches in Galatia. (See map before Rom.) This was then a circular letter probably directed to the churches founded during the first missionary journey of Paul and located in Derbe, Lystra, Iconium, and (Pisidian) Antioch.

1:3. The traditional Greek and Hebrew forms of greeting, grace and peace, were always used by Paul in his salutations to express the hope that the believing readers might be sustained by daily portions of these blessings. "Grace and peace" find their source in God our Father and the Lord Jesus Christ. (See the chart, "Paul's Introductions to His Epistles" at Rom. 1:1-7.)

1:4-5. Paul concluded his salutation with a magnificent statement regarding the work of Christ on the cross and its delivering power, another major emphasis of this epistle. Christ gave Himself for our sins (cf. 1 Tim. 2:6; Titus 2:14; 1 Peter 3:18). His death was voluntary and final. It satisfied God's righteous demands against sinners, reconciled people to God, and provided for human redemption. One purpose of Christ's death is to rescue us from the present evil age. The gospel is an emancipating message. It delivers believing sinners from the power of the present world system through the power of the indwelling Christ just as certainly as it delivers them from eternal judgment to come. Was Paul hinting that the Old Testament Law, so strongly promoted by the Galatian legalizers, would be impotent to accomplish such great things?

In His redemptive work Christ accomplished the will of . . . God (Gal. 1:4c; cf. Heb. 10:7-10). Further, in that obedience the Savior brought glory to God (Gal. 1:5; cf. John 17:1). Redeemed saints will in addition give glory to God forever because of the redeeming work of Jesus Christ.

Thus Paul had already drawn the lines of battle by touching on two vital concerns. He had affirmed his own apostleship and had declared that the basis of man's salvation lies solely in the work of Christ and not in any human works.

B. The denunciation (1:6-10)

Conspicuous by its absence is Paul's usual expression of thanksgiving to God for his readers. Instead he vented his astonishment and anger over the Galatians' defection. When compared with the opening of 1 Corinthians this is even more striking, for despite the Corinthians' deep moral defection Paul nonetheless expressed commendation. But here in the face of theological departure he did not express thanks, thus emphasizing the more serious nature of doctrinal apostasy.

1:6-7. Paul's astonishment was over an almost inconceivable turn of events—the Galatian believers were in the process of turning away (deserting, *metatithesthe*, as in a military desertion) from the truth. Part of the apostle's amazement was because it was happening so quickly after his last visit to them, or so soon after the false teachers began their insidious work. The departure was not simply from a system of theology but from God Himself, the One who had called them by the grace of Christ (the dominant theme of the epistle). In exchange they were embracing a different gospel, one that was false. Paul insisted that a gospel of legalism which adds work to faith is not the same kind of gospel that he preached and by which they were saved. It was actually an attempt to pervert the gospel of Christ. And Paul was aware of the fact that at the very time he was writing this epistle the false teachers were at work troubling or throwing the Galatians into confusion (cf. Acts 15:24; 20:29-30).

1:8. To emphasize the fact that the true gospel of the grace of God cannot be changed, Paul first stated a hypothetical case. If he (a divinely called apostle) or an angel (a heavenly messenger) were to alter the gospel message—a highly improbable situation—then let him be accursed or eternally condemned (*anathema*).

1:9. In this verse Paul seemed to repeat himself, but he actually advanced his thought. Paul and Barnabas had given a warning of judgment when they had preached to the Galatians. Now Paul repeated it. A zealous champion of the purity of the gospel of grace, Paul said it again: If anybody were preaching a different gospel (which the false teachers were), he would come under God's eternal judgment. It is not difficult to understand why Paul reacted so strongly, because the Judaizers were impugning the Cross; for if works were necessary for salvation, then the work of Christ was not sufficient (cf. 2:21). Furthermore a great deal is at stake for lost people. When the gospel message is corrupted, the way of salvation is confused and people are in danger of being eternally lost.

1:10. Apparently the Judaizers had charged Paul with teaching freedom from the Law in order to curry the Gentiles' favor. But the tone of this letter, specifically the harsh language Paul had just used, was hardly calculated to win the approval of men. Men-pleasers simply do not hurl *anathemas* against those who proclaim false gospels. Indeed, if the apostle had wanted to please men, he would have remained a zealous Pharisee and promoter of the Law rather than becoming a servant of Christ. Elsewhere Paul affirmed his purpose to please God, not men (cf. 6:12; 1 Thes. 2:4).

II. Personal: A Defense of Paul's Authority (1:11–2:21)

Paul then took up in more detail the challenge to his authority as an apostle. Was he a self-appointed impostor? Arguing autobiographically, Paul declared that (a) he was an apostle before he met the other apostles; (b) when he did meet them he was received as an equal; (c) and he even found it necessary to rebuke Peter, the reputed chief apostle.

A. He was independent of the apostles (1:11-24)

1. THESIS: PAUL'S GOSPEL WAS A REVELATION (1:11-12)

1:11-12. First, Paul certified that the gospel did not originate with man. Manmade religions emphasize human merit and the necessity of human works for salvation. Paul's message did not. Second, the apostle declared that he did not receive the gospel from any human source. Though he heard Stephen preach and had personal contacts with Ananias and Barnabas, he was not indebted to them for his knowledge of spiritual truth. Third, Paul affirmed he did not receive the gospel he preached by means of some course of instruction. Even though that was the way the Galatians received the gospel (as Paul had instructed them), the apostle on the other hand received it by revelation from Jesus Christ. This was the highest authority. How then could the Galatians question his authority and message? And how did they dare deviate from this divinely revealed truth?

2. EVENTS BEFORE PAUL'S CONVERSION (1:13-14)

1:13-14. By appealing to his personal history Paul established beyond any doubt that he did not learn his gospel from men. Beginning with his preconversion life, he showed that his only relationship to the church was that of a fanatic persecutor of it. Standing before Herod Agrippa II, Paul summarized his frenzied oppression of Christians (cf. Acts 26:9-11). Coupled with this was the fact that he was also zealous to advance as a Pharisee in Judaism. He felt driven to excel over other Jews his own age. He loved the Law and was zealous for the traditions of his fathers. He no doubt spent much time studying the Law of Moses and the accompanying Rabbinical traditions. Thus who could accuse Paul of not being acquainted with the teachings of Judaism when he knew them better than the Judaizers?

3. EVENTS AT PAUL'S CONVERSION (1:15-16A)

1:15-16a. The contrast with the preceding (vv. 13-14) is striking and is occasioned by God's intervention in the life of Saul of Tarsus: But . . . God. Nowhere is this intervention more graphically described than in Acts 9. Here Paul simply enumerated three things God did for him. First, God set him apart from

birth. Paul knew that God had providentially set him apart from birth and that all his life to this point was a preparation for his ministry as a proclaimer of the gospel of God's grace. Second, God **called** Paul **by His grace.** This is a reference to the time of Paul's salvation. He responded to God's efficacious call and received Jesus Christ as Savior. In Romans (8:30) Paul gave the sequence of God's work in salvation: "Those He predestined, He also called; those He called, He also justified; those He justified, He also glorified." Third, God **was pleased to reveal His Son in** Paul. Blinded as he had been to the deity of Jesus Christ and thinking that the Nazarene was a fraud, God gave Paul an outward vision of Christ on the Damascus Road and later an inner revelation concerning the full significance of the person and work of the Savior. The purpose of this revelation was that Paul **might preach Him among the Gentiles.** The Book of Acts gives full account of Paul's ministry to the non-Jewish world on his missionary journeys. He became known as the apostle to the Gentiles (cf. Acts 9:15; 13:46-47; 26:20; Rom. 11:13; 15:16; Eph. 3:8; 1 Tim. 2:7). Thus Paul emphasized that both his conversion and his commission owed nothing to man but were of God. How else could such a transformation—from persecutor to preacher—be explained?

4. EVENTS AFTER PAUL'S CONVERSION (1:16B-24)

1:16b-17. Paul had emphasized that he did not receive his message from men before or at the time of his conversion. Now he affirmed that he was free from human influences afterward as well. Though Paul met other Christians after his conversion he did not **consult** them on doctrine. If he had been uncertain about the gospel, he could readily have gone **to Jerusalem** for a seminar with the **apostles,** but he did not. Rather he **went immediately into Arabia.** It is doubtful that he went there to evangelize but rather to be away from men and alone with the Lord for personal study, meditation, and to receive further revelation. This zealous student of the Law now pondered the meaning of his conversion and looked for the things concerning Christ in the Old Testament (cf. Luke 24:27). The product of these days in Arabia was the Christian theology that Paul explained in his epistle to the Romans.

The point of Paul's declaration is clear. He formed his theology not by consulting with others, but independently as he sought God's guidance.

1:18-20. Paul then reinforced his previous argument by asserting that he waited **three years** after his conversion to go **to Jerusalem,** time that was spent in Arabia and Damascus (v. 17). Would he have waited that long if he had needed theological instruction from the disciples? When he did go, it was **to get acquainted with Peter,** that is, it was a personal visit lasting only **15 days.** Paul then left because of a plot against his life (cf. Acts 9:29). Meanwhile Paul had had a meaningful time coming to know the noted apostle, but there is no suggestion that Peter gave him theological instruction or apostolic endorsement for his ministry. Of the rest of the apostles Paul met only **James, the Lord's brother,** a leader in the church in Jerusalem (cf. Acts 12:17). To stress the truth of what he had just said— no doubt in the face of a Judaizer's charge that he had misrepresented his relationship to the apostles—Paul put himself on oath, calling God to be his witness that he was telling the truth.

1:21-22. After his abbreviated visit in Jerusalem Paul worked for an extended time in **Syria and Cilicia,** which is why he **was personally unknown to the churches of Judea** (cf. Acts 9:30; 11:25). He was not commissioned for this ministry by the apostles, and because of the distance between him and Jerusalem he could not have been under their authority or subject to their oversight.

1:23-24. The churches in Judea by this time had almost forgotten Paul. The only **report** they had recently **heard** was that this one who had once **persecuted** the church was **now preaching the faith he once tried to destroy.** This would of course include the doctrine of justification by faith apart from circumcision or works. And in the face of this report the Judean believers **praised God because of** Paul. This was a telling blow to the false teachers. The Jewish Christians in Judea rejoiced in the same gospel the Judaizers sought to undermine.

B. He was recognized by the apostles (2:1-10)

While chapter 2 continues Paul's defense of his apostolic authority and the gospel he preached, he focused not on the source of his message but on its content. Further, whereas in chapter 1 he emphasized his independence from the other apostles, he now demonstrated that there was a basic unity between himself and them.

2:1. Much debate has centered on the question of the identification of this trip which Paul took to **Jerusalem** with **Barnabas,** a Jewish believer, and **Titus,** a Gentile believer. The Book of Acts mentions five Jerusalem visits made by Paul after his conversion: (1) the visit after he left Damascus (Acts 9:26-30; Gal. 1:18-20); (2) the famine visit (Acts 11:27-30); (3) the visit to attend the Jerusalem Council (Acts 15:1-30); (4) the visit at the end of the second missionary journey (Acts 18:22); (5) the final visit which resulted in Paul's Caesarean imprisonment (Acts 21:15–23:35). Scholars are divided primarily over whether Galatians 2:1 refers to the famine visit or to the Jerusalem Council visit. But in the context in which he is listing all contacts with human authorities, why would Paul omit reference to his second trip to Jerusalem? And if the reference is to the Council of Acts 15, why did not the apostle allude to its decrees? It seems this passage has the famine visit in view.

2:2. Paul went to Jerusalem on his second visit **in response to a revelation.** That is, he went because God directed him to, not because the Jerusalem leaders had summoned him or called him "on the carpet" for preaching to **the Gentiles.** The reference may well be to Agabus' prophecy of a famine which prompted Paul and Barnabas to go to Jerusalem on a relief mission (cf. Acts 11:27-30). Paul seized this opportunity to consult with the other apostles **privately** concerning the message he was preaching to the Gentiles. This does not mean Paul sought their approval of its truth and accuracy, for he had received the gospel from God by revelation. Rather, he wanted them to consider its relationship to the gospel they were proclaiming. But if the Jerusalem leaders insisted on circumcision and other requirements of the Law for Gentile

converts, Paul's labor (**running**) among the Gentiles was **in vain.** It was not that the apostle had any doubts or misgivings about the gospel he had preached for 14 years (Gal. 2:1), but that he feared that his past and present ministry might be hindered or rendered of no effect by the Judaizers.

2:3-5. It now becomes apparent why Paul brought **Titus** along on this Jerusalem trip. He was a test case. Would the Jerusalem apostles force the rite of circumcision on a Gentile believer? Paul knew that both Jews and Gentiles are accepted by God through faith in Jesus Christ without any distinction and that the church should do the same. The apostle declared that this truth was affirmed in Jerusalem because Titus was **not . . . compelled to be circumcised, even though he was a Greek.** But this victory did not come easily. Pressure to have Titus circumcised was brought to bear by certain **false brothers** (cf. 2 Peter 2:1). No doubt these were Judaizers, whose chief slogan is found in Acts 15:1: "Unless you are circumcised according to the custom taught by Moses, you cannot be saved." These "false brothers" ("sham Christians," NEB) were like spies or fifth-column agents who penetrated to search out weak areas of enemy positions. In this case they **infiltrated** (*pareisēlthon*; lit., "sneaked in alongside," used only here and in Rom. 5:20) the **ranks,** that is, they intruded without invitation into the apostles' private conference. Their goals were twofold: first, **to spy on** (*kataskopēsai*, used only here in the NT) **the freedom we have in Christ.** With hostile intent they purposed to observe the apostles' freedom from the Mosaic Law and from the legalism it engenders. Second, they intended to **make** Christians **slaves.** They wanted to bring believers back into bondage, to enslave them to the Law's rules and ceremonies. Specifically they strongly insisted that Titus be circumcised. But Paul stood absolutely firm because **the truth of the gospel** was at stake for the Galatians, and the entire Christian church. To impose circumcision on Titus would be to deny that salvation was by faith alone and to affirm that in addition to faith there must be obedience to the Law for acceptance before God. Thus the basic issue of the gospel was involved and Paul would not deviate or yield for a moment.

2:6. Having completed his discussion of Titus, Paul resumed the narrative relating to his conference with the apostles in Jerusalem and declared that they **added nothing to** his **message.** They did not correct or modify Paul's message but recognized its divine source and affirmed its truth and completeness. But why did the apostle speak in what appears to be a derogatory manner about some of the Jerusalem leaders? In verse 2 he referred to them as "those who seemed to be leaders"; in verse 6 he described them as **those who seemed to be important;** and in verse 9 he finally named "James, Peter, and John" as "those reputed to be pillars." In view of the fact that Paul's purpose in this passage was to emphasize his unity with the apostles, it seems best to explain these allusions as stemming from the fact that the Judaizers, in order to disparage Paul, had made much of the Jerusalem leaders. While there may be irony in Paul's expressions, he declared that he was not awed by the past or present stations of James, Peter, and John. Indeed they endorsed Paul's message and received him as an equal.

2:7-9. Further, **James, Peter, and John** recognized that Paul had been divinely commissioned to preach **the gospel to the Gentiles, just as Peter had to the Jews.** Thus Paul jolted the Judaists by declaring that the leaders in Jerusalem approved of his mission to the Gentiles.

It should be noted that Peter and Paul did not preach two gospels, as might be inferred from the KJV rendering, "the gospel of the uncircumcision" and "the gospel of the circumcision." There was one gospel though it was preached by different apostles to two distinct groups of people. The reason the apostles concluded that Paul's commission was equal to Peter's was the fact that God gave success to both as they preached. This was sealed by James, Peter, and John in their extending to Paul **and Barnabas the right hand of fellowship.** This was a sign of agreement and trust and an indication to all present that they endorsed the division of labor whereby the Jerusalem apostles were appointed to evangelize the Jews and Paul was entrusted to carry the gospel **to the Gentiles.**

2:10. The only request from the leaders in Jerusalem was that Paul **remember the poor** which he affirmed he **was eager to do.** It had been concern for the poor which brought Paul to Jerusalem in order to bring them financial relief (cf. Acts 11:29-30). It was the same concern which motivated him on his third missionary journey to raise large welfare offerings for needy Christians in Jerusalem (cf. 1 Cor. 16:1-3). Such offerings would alleviate human suffering, but they would also demonstrate genuine concern on the part of Gentile Christians for Jewish Christians. This in turn would help promote unity and love among believers and help prevent the kinds of misunderstandings which were undermining the Galatian churches.

C. He rebuked the reputed chief of the apostles (2:11-21)

In this final historical incident Paul related how he found it necessary to oppose even Peter, the reputed chief of the apostles, for conduct which threatened to compromise the gospel. The contrast with the previous section is dramatic.

2:11. When Paul visited Jerusalem, Peter (and others) gave him "the right hand of fellowship"; but when **Peter** visited **Antioch,** Paul **opposed him to his face.** The time of Peter's trip to Antioch is not known. There is no reference to it in the Book of Acts, but perhaps the visit occurred soon after Paul, Barnabas, and Titus returned to Antioch from Jerusalem. At any rate Peter's conduct in Antioch produced a tense face-to-face confrontation between two Christian leaders. Paul felt compelled to rebuke and condemn Peter for his actions, thus defending the gospel and demonstrating again his own independence and equality as an apostle.

2:12. On arrival at Antioch, Peter found Jewish and Gentile Christians fellowshiping together at mealtimes without regard to Jewish dietary laws. Because of the vision Peter had received at the house of Simon the tanner (Acts 10:9-15, 28), he felt free **to eat with the Gentiles,** and did so on a regular basis. While it lasted, this was a beautiful demonstration of the unity of Jew and Gentile in Christ. **But** a breach occurred when some arrived from Jerusalem who were shocked at Peter's conduct. These emissaries **came from James** and belonged **to the circumcision** party, but it is doubtful that they had James' endorsement. Nonetheless Peter was influenced by their presence and slowly but surely **began to draw back and separate himself from the Gentiles.** The verb tenses (imperf.) indicate a gradual withdrawal, perhaps from one joint meal a day, and then two; or it may be that he began a meal with Gentiles but finished it with only Jewish Christians. By such actions Peter in effect was teaching that there were two bodies of Christ, Jewish and Gentile. And that was heresy. But why did Peter create this breach? Not because of any change in theology, but simply out of fear. Once, after preaching to Gentile Cornelius, Peter courageously defended himself before the Jerusalem leaders (cf. Acts 11:18); but this time he capitulated to some Jewish friends.

2:13. Like falling dominoes the defection of Peter brought the defection of **the other Jews** and finally **even Barnabas.** The pressure must have been great for Barnabas to succumb because he was from Cyprus, a Gentile center, and was involved in a missionary program with Paul to reach Gentiles with the gospel. All of them—Peter, the other Jewish Christians, and Barnabas—were guilty of **hypocrisy** because while confessing and teaching that they were one in Christ with Gentiles, they were denying this truth by their conduct.

2:14. The response of Paul was electric. What Peter had initiated created a public scandal and therefore deserved a public rebuke. Further, the defectors **were not acting** according to **the truth of the gospel,** that is, they were denying by their actions the truth that on the basis of Jesus Christ's death and resurrection Jews and Gentiles who believe are accepted equally by God. Paul therefore asked Peter before them all, "If you, who are a Jew, do not live like a Jew but like a Gentile, why on earth do you try to make Gentiles live like Jews?" (PH) It was a stinging rebuke. Peter's response is not recorded. He stood condemned. He was acting contrary to his own convictions, was betraying Christian liberty, and was casting a slur on fellow believers. Such behavior needed this severe reprimand.

2:15. But how far did the rebuke extend? Considerable discussion has centered on the question as to whether Paul's direct remarks to Peter were limited to verse 14 or whether, as in the NIV, they continued to the end of the chapter. While it is impossible to determine, it would seem that Paul uttered more than one sentence in reproving Peter. The remaining verses of the chapter develop, then, the inconsistency between Peter's behavior and his beliefs. At the same time they form a superb transition and introduction to chapters 3 and 4 in which Paul defended the key doctrine of justification by faith.

Paul's argument was addressed to those who were **Jews by birth,** including Peter and himself, who in spite of their superior advantages were saved by faith. Why then bind the Law on **Gentile sinners** (said in irony because of Peter's actions), who likewise were saved by faith in Christ?

2:16. In this verse, one of the most important in the epistle, the word *justified* occurs for the first time. It is a legal term, borrowed from the law courts and means "to declare righteous." Its opposite is "to condemn." But since people are condemned sinners and God is holy, how can people be justified? In answer, the apostle made a general declaration that negatively **man is not justified by observing the Law,** but positively, justification is **by faith in Jesus Christ.** This is a strong affirmation of Paul, Peter, and the rest—introduced by **We . . . know.** It is followed by a statement in which Paul explained that he had put this doctrine to the test and validated it in his own experience (v. 16b). Finally, in verse 16c the apostle reaffirmed that justification is by faith and not by works (cf. Gen. 15:6).

2:17-18. Paul's opponents argued, however, that since justification by faith eliminated the Law, it encouraged sinful living. A person could believe in Christ for salvation and then do as he pleased, having no need to do good works. Paul hotly denied the charge, especially noting that this made **Christ** the promoter of **sin.** On the contrary, if a believer would return to the Law after trusting Christ alone for salvation, that Law would only demonstrate that he was a sinner, **a lawbreaker.** Though Paul used the first person here, he clearly had in mind Peter, who by his act of withdrawing from

GALATIANS

Gentile fellowship was returning to the Law.

2:19-20. Paul then distinguished himself from Peter, contrasting what he did with the Law with what Peter did with the Law. Paul described the transformation in a person who has come to God by faith in Christ in terms of a death and a resurrection. The concept is repeated in both verses and the reference in both cases is to a believer's union with Christ in His death and resurrection. First, Paul stated that **through the Law he died to the Law.** The Law demanded death for those who broke it, but Christ paid that death penalty for all sinners. Thus the Law killed Him and those joined to Him by faith, freeing them to be joined to another, to **live for God** (cf. Rom. 7:4).

In Galatians 2:20 Paul enlarged on the meaning of verse 19. He "died to the Law" because he was **crucified with Christ;** he was able "to live for God" because **Christ** lived in him. Basic to an understanding of this verse is the meaning of union with Christ. This doctrine is based on such passages as Romans 6:1-6 and 1 Corinthians 12:13, which explain that believers have been baptized by the Holy Spirit into Christ and into the church, the body of all true believers. Having been thus united to Christ, believers share in His death, burial, and resurrection. Paul could therefore write, **I have been** "crucified with Christ" (lit., "I have been and am now crucified with Christ"). This brought death to the Law. It also brought a change in regard to one's self: **and I no longer live.** The self-righteous, self-centered Saul died. Further, death with Christ ended Paul's enthronement of self; he yielded the throne of his life to Another, to Christ. But it was not in his own strength that Paul was able to live the Christian life; the living Christ Himself took up His abode in Paul's heart: **Christ lives in me.** Yet Christ does not operate automatically in a believer's life; it is a matter of living the new life **by faith in the Son of God.** It is then faith and not works or legal obedience that releases divine power to live a Christian life. This faith, stated Paul, builds on the sacrifice of Christ **who loved us and gave Himself for us.** In essence Paul affirmed, "If He loved me enough to give Himself for me, then He loves me enough to live out His life in me."

2:21. Summing up his case against Peter, Paul declared, **I do not set aside the grace of God.** The clear implication is that Peter and the others who followed him were setting aside God's grace. The essence of grace is for God to give people what they have not worked for (cf. Rom. 4:4). To insist on justification or sanctification by works is to nullify the grace of God. Further, such insistence on legal obedience also means **Christ died for nothing.** If righteousness comes by keeping the Law, the Cross was a futile gesture, the biggest mistake in the universe.

III. Doctrinal: A Defense of Justification by Faith (chaps. 3-4)

In the first two chapters of the epistle Paul established the divine origin of his apostleship and his message. Then he turned to the Galatians who were being urged to add works to faith, to keep the Mosaic Law in addition to placing faith in Christ as the grounds of acceptance before God. The Galatian Christians would receive, the Judaizers thought, a more complete salvation and a greater sanctification if they would obey the Law. But, Paul argued, to supplement the work of Christ is to supplant it. There can only be one way of salvation, and that is by faith in Christ alone.

A. Vindication of the doctrine (chap. 3)

1. BY THE EXPERIENCE OF THE GALATIANS (3:1-5)

3:1. Paul's tone was direct and severe as he remonstrated, **You foolish Galatians!** To embrace a doctrine which declared the death of Christ unnecessary was irrational (cf. 2:21). It would almost appear they had been **bewitched,** cast under some evil spell by a malign influence. For this they were, however, without excuse because the Savior had been **clearly portrayed** (*proegraphē*; lit., "to write for public reading" as with the posting of a public announcement) **as crucified** before them. Paul had vividly and graphically proclaimed the crucified Christ to the Galatians; yet their eyes had been diverted from the Cross to the Law. They were without excuse.

262

In order to demonstrate convincingly that faith alone is God's method of dealing, the apostle asked four questions.

3:2. (1) *How did you receive the Holy Spirit?* This rhetorical question pointed to the time of their conversions, when they received the Holy Spirit (cf. 4:6). Thus Paul did not question their salvation but challenged them to consider whether they were saved and received the Spirit by faith or on the basis of works. It was of course by faith, when they heard Paul preach the gospel. As an essentially Gentile church they did not possess the Mosaic Law anyway.

3:3. (2) *How will you be sanctified?* Presupposing the answer that the Galatians became Christians by faith, Paul asked if they were **so foolish** as to think they could begin the Christian life in one way (by faith) and move on to spiritual maturity in another (by works). This was what the Judaizers promoted (cf. 4:10; 5:2; 6:13), but the means of justification and sanctification were (and are) the same. There was no provision under the Law for the Holy Spirit to do a work of sanctification. The Galatian believers probably thought that keeping the old Law would aid them in their spiritual lives, but it would not.

3:4. (3) *Did you suffer in vain?* The third question looked back on the persecution the apostles and new believers experienced in the region of Galatia. As Paul and Barnabas retraced their steps at the end of the first missionary journey, they warned the Galatian converts that they would suffer as Christians (Acts 14:21-22). Persecution evidently soon followed, and Paul reminded them that if they turned from grace to Law they would brand their former position in error and would then have **suffered so much for nothing.** But the apostle was unwilling to believe that this was so.

3:5. (4) *On what basis did God perform miracles?* That **miracles** were performed among the Galatians by divine power was recorded in the Book of Acts (14:3, 8-11). It was clear, furthermore, that these supernatural works were not the result of the works of **the Law** but from the hearing that leads to faith. The Galatians did not know the Law, and Paul's message was that of justification by faith.

2. BY THE EXAMPLE OF ABRAHAM (3:6-9)

3:6. The Judaizers claimed to have the Old Testament on their side, especially looking to Moses as their teacher. But Paul went centuries farther back and said, **Consider Abraham.** How was he, the father of Jewish people, justified? The answer was simple and direct. Noting Genesis 15:6, Paul declared, **He believed God, and it was credited to him as righteousness.** Abraham's faith in God's ability to perform what He promised was accepted by God as righteousness and so the patriarch was justified—before he was circumcised (cf. Gen. 17:24). How then could the Judaizers insist that circumcision was essential to being accepted by God?

3:7-8. Striking a tremendous blow at the Judaizers, Paul linked the past with the present and declared that just as **Abraham** was saved **by faith** so were those who now claimed to be his **children** (*huioi;* lit., "sons"). Abraham and his spiritual descendants, both Jews and Gentiles, have all been declared righteous by faith. Moreover, this conclusion is in harmony with **the Scripture** which states that **all nations will be blessed through** Abraham (cf. Gen. 12:3). Thus the justification of uncircumcised Gentiles was anticipated in the universal aspect of the Abrahamic Covenant when God **announced the gospel** (lit., "the good news") . . . **to Abraham.** It should not be overlooked that Paul referred to Scripture speaking as though God were speaking, so it can rightly be affirmed that what the Bible says, God says. This and similar verses (e.g., John 10:35b; 2 Tim. 3:16; 2 Peter 1:20-21) provide important support for believing in the absolute and total inspiration and authority of Scripture.

3:9. The apostle concluded this phase of his argument by stating that though provision was made for "all nations" (v. 8), only **those who have faith** receive the blessing of justification. Thus Paul drew a distinction between God's provision and human appropriation.

3. BY THE EFFECT OF THE LAW (3:10-12)

Having established the fact that justification is by faith from the experiences of the Galatians and of Abraham, Paul then showed the illogic of reliance on the Law.

3:10-11. Contrary to what the Judaizers taught, the Law could not justify; it could only condemn. Paul quoted Deuteronomy 27:26 to show that the Law demanded perfection and that a curse was attached to failure to keep any part of it. The breaking of only one command even once brings a person under the curse; and since everybody fails at some point, all are under the curse. The proposition that a person can gain divine acceptance by human effort is therefore totally destroyed. Quoting the Old Testament again, Paul showed that even during the dispensation of Law legal obedience was not the basis for a justified standing before God . . . because, as the Prophet Habakkuk wrote, The righteous will live by faith (Hab. 2:4).

3:12. But perhaps faith and the Law could be combined; perhaps both are needed. Quoting again from the Old Testament Paul proved this to be scripturally impossible. Law and faith are mutually exclusive. The basic principle of the Law is found in Leviticus 18:5: The man who does these things will live by them. Only perfect performance could win divine approval under the Law, but since that was not achievable the Law could only condemn a person (cf. James 2:10) and cause him to cast himself on God in faith.

4. BY THE WORK OF CHRIST (3:13-14)

3:13. The positive side of Paul's argument emphasized that there is hope for all who have broken the Law and are therefore under its curse. That hope is not in man but in Christ who redeemed us from the curse of the Law. But how did Christ redeem (*exēgorasen*, lit., "buy out of slavery"; cf. 4:5; see chart "New Testament Words for Redemption" at Mark 10:45) man? The answer is by becoming a curse for us. This is a strong declaration of substitutionary redemption whereby Christ took the penalty of all guilty lawbreakers on Himself. Thus the "curse of the Law" was transferred from sinners to Christ, the sinless One (cf. 1 Peter 3:18), and He delivered people from it. The confirming quotation from Deuteronomy 21:23 refers to the fact that in Old Testament times criminals were executed (normally by stoning) and then displayed on a stake or post to show God's divine rejection. When Christ was

crucified, it was evidence He had come under the curse of God. The manner of His death was a great obstacle to faith for Jews until they realized the curse He bore was for them (cf. Isa. 53).

3:14. Two purposes for Christ's redemptive work are given, each introduced by the Greek conjunction *hina*, "in order that" (cf. 4:5): (1) Gentiles might receive the blessing given to Abraham; as already stated (3:8) this is a reference not to personal or national blessings but to the promised blessing of justification apart from works of the Law, available to all who believe; (2) all who thus believe might receive the promise of the Spirit, that is, the Holy Spirit, who was promised (cf. v. 2). Again the apostle emphasized that salvation and sanctification come by faith, not by works.

5. BY THE PERMANENCE OF FAITH (3:15-18)

3:15-16. Even if Paul's opponents admitted that Abraham was justified by faith, those Judaizers might have argued that the Law, coming at a later time, entirely changed the basis for achieving salvation. To refute this, Paul declared that just as a properly executed Roman covenant (or will) cannot arbitrarily be set aside or changed (probably reference to ancient Gr. law), so the promises of God are immutable. Further, the promises . . . spoken to Abraham and to his seed were not fulfilled before the giving of the Law. Rather, they found fulfillment in Christ and are in effect forever. The blessing of justification by faith is therefore permanent and could not be changed by the Law. The stress on seed (cf. Gen. 12:7; 13:15; 24:7), not seeds, was made simply to remind the readers that the faithful in Israel had always recognized that blessing would ultimately come through a single individual, the Messiah (cf. Gal. 3:19). And Matthew declared Christ to be *the* Son of Abraham and the true Heir to the First Covenant's promises (Matt. 1:1).

3:17-18. Finally, Paul applied the principle of the permanence of faith by affirming that a covenant made so long before could not possibly be altered by a later giving of the Law. The Law was given 430 years after the promise. When did that lengthy period of time begin? Some have suggested it began with Abraham, in which case the 430 years included the Israelites' time of about 200 years in Canaan and about 200 years in Egypt. The Septuagint supports this view, but this conflicts with the clear statement in Exodus 12:40 that the Egyptian sojourn was 430 years. Another suggestion is that the period began with the confirming of the Abrahamic Covenant with Jacob (Gen. 35:9-12).

A third and perhaps best view is that the period began with the final confirmation of the covenant to Jacob (given in Gen. 46:1-4). Accordingly the 430 years went from the end of one era (the Age of Promise) to the beginning of another (the Age of Law). This seems to fit best with Exodus 12:40. (Gen. 15:13 and Acts 7:6, in referring to the sojourn in Egypt as 400 years, may be using rounded figures.)

During that long interval God blessed the patriarchs on the basis of faith alone, and the coming of the Law could not change this in any way. Additionally **the Law** could not alter God's dealing with **Abraham** on the basis of **a promise** because the two are fundamentally different in nature. They do not comingle; they cannot be combined. Instead, **the inheritance** (i.e., justification by faith) was given by **God** as an unconditional gift to those who believe. Contrary to the claim of the Judaizers, obedience to the Law was not necessary to gain the inheritance. God's way of salvation has always been by grace through faith.

6. BY THE PURPOSE OF THE LAW (3:19-25)

3:19. An indignant Judaizer was sure to respond with objections to Paul's insistence that the Law could not give the Holy Spirit (vv. 1-5); could not bring justification (vv. 6-9); could not alter the permanence of faith (vv. 15-18); but does bring a curse (vv. 10-12). **What, then, was the purpose of the Law?** Why *was* a change made at Sinai? Paul answered by declaring the purpose and character of the Law. First, it was given **because of transgressions,** that is, the Law was given to be a means for checking sins. It served as a restrainer of sins by showing them to be transgressions of God's Law which would incur His wrath (cf. 1 Tim. 1:8-11). Second, the Law was temporary and served **until the Seed** (the Messiah; cf. Gal. 3:16) came, after which it was no longer needed. Third, the Law was inferior because of the manner of its

bestowal. While God made promises to Abraham directly, **the Law** was established **by a mediator.** There were in fact two mediators, the **angels** representing God, and Moses representing the people.

3:20. This verse appears to be closely related to the last part of verse 19. **A mediator** implies a covenant between two parties both of whom have responsibilities, facts true of the Mosaic Covenant. On the other hand **God is One,** that is, the "promise" (v. 19) was unilateral and was given to man directly without a mediator, God alone having responsibility for fulfilling it.

3:21-22. Another question was raised: Is there conflict between **the Law** and the **promises of God?** "Perish the thought" (*mē genoito*), declared the apostle. God gave both the Law and promises, but for different purposes. And it was not the purpose of **the Law** to give **life.** Theoretically salvation could have come by the Law if people had been capable of keeping it perfectly, but they could not (Rom. 8:3-4). The **life** promised to those who sought to obey the **Law** refers to temporal blessing on earth (Deut. 8:1).

But if the Law is not **opposed to** the promises, if there is no conflict between them, how can their harmony be demonstrated? By recognizing that while the Law could not justify or give life, it did prepare the way for the gospel. What part then did Law play in this respect? It declared **the whole world . . . a prisoner of sin.** Referring perhaps to Psalm 143:1-2 or Deuteronomy 27:26, Paul declared that the whole world is trapped and under the dominion of sin (cf. Rom. 3:9, 23). When people recognize this and give up attempts to please God by their own works, the way is prepared for them to receive the promise of salvation **through faith in Jesus Christ.**

3:23-25. Continuing to comment on the purpose of the Law, Paul used two figures of speech, likening the Law to a prison and to a child-custodian relationship. **Before this faith came** means before the advent of faith in Jesus Christ (see v. 22). Justifying faith was operative in the Old Testament but faith in the person and work of Christ did not come until He was revealed. Before that, Israel was under the protective custody of **the Law,**

God thus shielding His people from the evil heathen rites surrounding them. Further, the Law served as a "tutor" (NASB). The word *paidagōgos* is difficult to render into English since there is no exact parallel to this position in modern society. Phillips suggests "a strict governess." The pedagogue here was not a "schoolmaster" (KJV) but a slave to whom a son was committed from age six or seven to puberty. These slaves were severe disciplinarians and were charged with guarding the children from the evils of society and giving them moral training. This was like the Law's function until **Christ** came and people could **be justified by faith** in Him. It is better then to understand that the Law did not *lead us to* Christ but that it was the disciplinarian *until* Christ came. Thus the reign of Law has ended for faith in Christ has delivered believers from the protective custody of the prison and the harsh discipline of the pedagogue.

7. BY THE BELIEVER'S PRESENT POSITION
(3:26-29)

Paul's vindication of the doctrine of justification by faith reached a climax in this section as he contrasted the position of a justified sinner with what he had been under the Law. Three changes are noted.

3:26-27. First, **all** who believe in **Christ** become **sons of God.** The change in person from the first to the second (**you**) indicates that Paul turned from looking at Israel as a nation to address the Galatian believers. Under the dispensation of Law, as seen in verse 24, the Law was a discipling pedagogue, and those under its supervision were regarded as children. However, now that Christ had come, the Galatian believers were adult sons **through faith** and were no longer under a Jewish slave-guardian. Why should they seek to revert to their inferior status? The exalted position of "sons of God" is explained in verse 27 to involve a living union with Christ brought about by being **baptized into Christ.** This is the baptism of (or in) the Holy Spirit, which according to Paul (1 Cor. 12:12-13) joins all believers to Christ and unites them within the church, Christ's body. This union with Him means being **clothed with Christ.** In the Roman society when a youth came of age he was given a special

toga which admitted him to the full rights of the family and state and indicated he was a grown-up son. So the Galatian believers had laid aside the old garments of the Law and had put on Christ's robe of righteousness which grants full acceptance before God. Who would want to don again the old clothing?

3:28. Second, believers **are all one in Christ Jesus.** Since all believers became one with each other, human distinctions lose their significance. None is spiritually superior over another, that is, a believing Jew is not more privileged before God than a believing Gentile (**Greek,** in contrast to **Jew,** suggests all Gentiles; cf. Col. 3:11); a believing **slave** does not rank higher than a believing **free** person; a believing man is not superior to a believing woman. Some Jewish men prayed, "I thank God that Thou hast not made me a Gentile, a slave, or a woman." Paul cut across these distinctions and stated that they do not exist in the body of Christ so far as spiritual privilege and position are concerned. Elsewhere, while affirming the coequality of man and woman in Christ, Paul did nonetheless make it clear that there is a headship of the man over the woman (cf. 1 Cor. 11:3) and that there are distinctions in the area of spiritual service (cf. 1 Tim. 2:12).

3:29. Third, believers in Christ **are Abraham's seed.** As Paul previously stated, **Christ** is *the* Seed of Abraham (vv. 16, 19); therefore being in Christ makes a believer a part of that seed and an **heir** of **the promise** to Abraham. Any discussion of the seed of Abraham must first take into account his natural seed, the descendants of Jacob in the 12 tribes. Within this natural seed there is a believing remnant of Jews who will one day inherit the Abrahamic promises directed specifically to them (cf. Rom. 9:6, 8). But there is also the spiritual seed of Abraham who are not Jews. These are the Gentiles who believe and become Abraham's spiritual seed. They inherit the promise of justification by faith as Paul explained earlier (cf. Gal. 3:6-9). To suggest, as amillenarians do, that Gentile believers inherit the national promises given to the believing Jewish remnant—that the church thus supplants Israel or is the "new Israel"—is to read into these verses what is not there.

B. Illustration of the doctrine (chap. 4)

1. A LEGAL ILLUSTRATION (4:1-7)

4:1-2. To illustrate the spiritual immaturity of those who lived under the Mosaic Law, Paul reminded the Galatian believers of certain characteristics of an **heir** as a minor **child** (*nēpios*, "infant, young child"; in contrast with *huios*, "son," in 3:7, 26). Though by birthright **he** owned **the whole estate**, nevertheless he was kept in subservience like **a slave** in that he enjoyed no freedom and could make no decisions. In fact the heir as a child was under **guardians** (*epitropous*, different from the *paidagōgos* in 3:24-25) who watched over his person, **and trustees** who protected his estate. This was true until he came of age as a son, an age that varied in the Jewish, Grecian, and Roman societies. Under Roman law the age of maturity for a child was **set by his father** and involved a ceremonial donning of the *toga virilis* and his formal acknowledgement as son and heir.

4:3. Paul applied the illustration in order to show the contrast between the believers' former position and what they now enjoyed. Formerly, in their state of spiritual immaturity (**when we were children,** *nēpioi*), they were like slaves. The scope of that **slavery** was described as being **under the basic principles** (*stoicheia*, "elements") **of the world.** Though often interpreted as a reference to the Mosaic Law, this view does not fit the Galatians, most of whom were Gentile pagans before conversion and were never under the Law. It seems better to understand the "basic principles" to refer to the elementary stages of religious experience, whether of Jews under the Law or Gentiles in bondage to heathen religions (cf. "weak and miserable principles" in v. 9, and "basic principles of this world" in Col. 2:20) Thus all were enslaved until Christ emancipated them.

4:4. But . . . God marks the fact that divine intervention brought hope and freedom to mankind. As a human father chose the time for his child to become an adult son, so the heavenly Father chose **the time** for the coming of Christ to make provision for people's transition from bondage under Law to spiritual sonship. This "time" was when the Roman civilization had brought peace and a road system which facilitated travel; when the Grecian civilization provided a language which was adopted as the *lingua franca* of the empire; when the Jews had proclaimed monotheism and the messianic hope in the synagogues of the Mediterranean world. It was then that God **sent His Son,** the preexistent One, out of heaven and to earth on a mission. The "Son" was not only Deity; He was also humanity as the expression **born of a woman** indicates. The exclusive reference to His mother harmonizes with the doctrine of the virgin birth as taught in the Gospels (cf. Matt. 1:18). Further, Christ was **born under Law** as a Jew. He kept the Law perfectly, fulfilled it (cf. Matt. 5:17), and finally paid its curse (cf. Gal. 3:13).

4:5. The reasons "God sent His Son" are twofold (again both reasons are introduced by *hina*, "in order that"; cf. 3:14). First, He came **to redeem** (*exagorasē*) **those under Law.** This is not a redemption from the curse of the Law (as in 3:13), but from a slavery to the entire Mosaic system. The emphasis is not on the penalty of the Law as in 3:13, but on its bondage. Since Christ redeemed and set free those who were under the Law, why should Gentile converts now wish to be placed under it? Second, Christ's Incarnation and death secured for believers **the full rights of sons** ("the adoption of sons," KJV). All the enjoyments and privileges of a mature son in a family belong to those who have entered into the benefits of Christ's redemptive work.

4:6. God the Father not only "sent His Son"; He also sent **the Spirit.** Thus the full Trinity is involved in the work of salvation. The Holy Spirit is a gift of God to every believer because of sonship. No sons or daughters lack the Spirit. Further, He is present within each believer's heart to give evidence of that one's position in God's family. The Spirit moves the believer to pray to God, addressing Him as **Abba, Father** (cf. Rom. 8:15). The word "Abba" is the Aramaic word for "Father." It is the diminutive form used by small children in addressing their fathers. It is appropriate to see its similarity to the English word "Daddy." Used by Christ (cf. Mark 14:36), this familiar form indicates intimacy and trust as opposed to the formalism of legalism.

4:7. To conclude, Paul declared that the Galatians were **no longer** slaves, but

267

were sons and heirs. The plural forms in verse 6 were replaced by the singular forms in verse 7 thus making the application to the reader direct and personal. In God's family, sonship carries with it heirship (cf. Rom. 8:17).

2. A PERSONAL PLEA (4:8-20)

The apostle turned from a formal argument to a personal appeal for the Galatians not to return to a slavery similar to their former bondage in paganism.

a. An appeal not to turn to legalism (4:8-11)

4:8-9. Prior to conversion the Galatians, in their ignorance of the one true **God,** were in bondage to false **gods** such as Zeus and Hermes (cf. Acts 14:11-13). But a great change took place and they came to **know God** (salvation from the perspective of man), **or to be known by God** (salvation from God's perspective). Yet having come to know (*gnontes,* from *ginōskō,* lit., "to know intimately and on a personal level") the true God, the Galatians were **turning back.** Paul was amazed and dismayed. Did they understand that they would be going back to a state of religious slavery? Was this their desire? If so, why would they be attracted to a system that was **weak** (it could not justify or energize for godly living) **and miserable** (it could not provide an inheritance). The **principles** (*stoicheia*) of that system are "of the world," as Paul had already said in verse 3.

4:10. Under the influence of the Judaizers the Galatians had at least begun to observe the Mosaic calendar. They kept **special days** (weekly sabbaths), **and months** (new moons), **and seasons** (seasonal festivals such as Passover, Pentecost, and Tabernacles), **and years** (sabbatical and jubilee years). (Cf. Col. 2:16.) They observed these special times, thinking that they would thereby gain additional merit before God. But Paul had already made it clear that works could not be added to faith as grounds for either justification or sanctification.

4:11. Reflecting concern for the Galatians, Paul expressed the **fear** that his **efforts** (*kekopiaka,* lit., "I have labored to the point of exhaustion") would be **wasted** (*eikē,* "in vain"; cf. the same word rendered "for nothing" in 3:4, "Have you suffered so much for nothing?") if their attachment to legalistic practices continued. The apostle's words disclosed his strong antipathy toward legalistic religion.

b. An appeal to remember their relationship (4:12-16)

4:12. Intensifying his appeal, Paul challenged the Galatians, **Become like me, for I became like you,** that is, "Become free from the Law as I am, for after my conversion I became like the Gentiles, no longer living under the Law." The irony, however, was that the Galatian Gentiles were putting themselves under the Law *after* their conversions.

4:13-14. The last clause of verse 12 belongs with these and the following verses in which Paul related how he was received by the Galatians on his first visit to them (cf. Acts 13-14). At that time he labored under the handicap of **an illness** but remained until he had **preached the gospel to** them. Whatever his infirmity, the Galatians **did not treat** Paul **with contempt or scorn** as a weak messenger but rather received him as one would receive **an angel** or even **Christ Jesus Himself.**

4:15-16. They had received Paul with **joy,** congratulating themselves that the apostle had preached in their midst. Their appreciation knew no limits; they would even have made the sacrifice of their **eyes** for Paul. While some think this is an indication that Paul had a disease of the eyes (his "thorn" in his "flesh," 2 Cor. 12:7), the evidence is not conclusive. This may simply be a bold figure of speech to convey the high esteem the Galatians had had for the apostle—they would have **given** him their most precious possession.

But that had all changed. They no longer contemplated his presence among them with "joy." Rather, they now acted as though he had **become** their **enemy,** for the simple reason that he had been **telling** them **the truth.** How fickle were these Galatians! They were turning against the Lord, the gospel of grace, and the messenger who brought them the news of justification by faith.

c. An appeal to consider Paul's attitude toward them (4:17-20)

4:17-18. While Paul's attitude toward the Galatians was guileless, the legalists had improper motives. The apostle spoke the truth (cf. v. 16); the Judaizers used flattery. They wanted to alienate (*ekkleisai*, lit., "to lock out") the Galatians from Paul and his teaching so that they would be shut up instead to the false teachers and their influence. In an interesting double use of the verb "be zealous" Paul said that the Judaizers were zealous to win . . . over the Galatians so that the latter would be zealous for the Judaizers! Acknowledging that it was good for anyone to be sought after, Paul nonetheless insisted that the intention must be honorable, but in the case of the Judaizers it was not.

4:19-20. The apostle, on the other hand, had always had good motives regarding the Galatians. Addressing them tenderly as my dear children (*tekna mou*, an expression found only here in Paul's epistles), Paul compared himself to a mother in the throes of birth pangs. He had experienced this once for their salvation; he was in travail again for their deliverance from false teachers.

But a sudden change in metaphors occurred with the expression until Christ is formed in you. Paul longed for these believers to be transformed into (*morphōthē*, lit., "take on the form of"; cf. *morphē* in Phil. 2:6-7) the image of Christ. This expression describes the Christian life as a kind of reincarnation of Christ in a believer's life. This is in fact God's ideal and purpose—for Christ to live His life in and then through each believer (cf. Gal. 2:20). Yet the apostle was perplexed about the Galatians because he felt their spiritual development was being arrested. He had a deep desire to be with them so that he could speak gently, though firmly, concerning his grave concerns.

3. A BIBLICAL ILLUSTRATION (4:21-31)

In a masterful stroke the apostle turned to a scriptural illustration to conclude his theological defense of justification by faith. An Old Testament story from the life of Abraham enabled Paul to review what he had already declared about contrasts between the Mosaic Law and grace, between works and faith. It also provided an opportunity for him to verbalize the pointed charge to the Galatians that they should cast out the legalizers (cf. v. 30).

a. The historical facts (4:21-23)

4:21. The Galatians had not yet submitted to the bondage of the Law but they desired to. Paul desperately wanted to stop them and turn them back to a life under grace. As a transition to what would immediately follow, he challenged the Galatians to be aware of or to understand what the Law really said.

4:22. By turning again to Abraham (Gen., as one of the Books of Moses, was considered a part of the Law) Paul was appealing to the founder of the Jewish nation from whose physical descent the Jews traced their blessings. John the Baptist and Jesus declared that physical descent from Abraham was not enough, however, to guarantee spiritual blessing (cf. Matt. 3:9; John 8:37-44). Paul reminded his readers that Abraham had two sons (those born later are not important to his illustration), and that they should consider which of the two they were most like. One son, Isaac, was born of Sarah, the free woman; the other, Ishmael, was born of Hagar, the slave woman. According to ancient law and custom the status of a mother affected the status of her son.

4:23. A second contrast concerned the manner in which the sons were conceived. Ishmael was born in the ordinary way, that is, in the course of nature and requiring no miracle and no promise of God. Isaac, on the other hand, was born as the result of a promise. Abraham and Sarah were beyond the age of childbearing, but God miraculously fulfilled His promise in bringing life out of the deadness of Sarah's womb (cf. Rom. 4:18-21).

b. The allegorical interpretation (4:24-27)

In order to emphasize the contrast between Law and grace Paul next used the historical events above as an allegory, that is, he treated those two mothers figuratively (*allēgoroumena*). He did not in any sense deny the literal meaning of the story of Abraham, but he declared that that story, especially the matters relating to the conception of the two sons, had an additional meaning. Thus he compared the narrative to the conflict between Judaism and Christianity.

(This "allegorizing" is a far cry from the practice of "allegorical interpretation"—followed by Origen, Augustine, and many others down through the ages and into the present day—in which the historical facts are relegated to a lower, less significant level and fanciful, hidden meanings unrelated to the text, are considered vastly more important.)

4:24. First, the apostle pointed to **two covenants.** One, the Mosaic, had its origin at **Mount Sinai.** Those under this legal covenant were **slaves.** As **Hagar** brought forth a slave, so does the Law. At this point the reader is expected to understand and supply the implicit reference to the Abrahamic Covenant, a gracious system represented by Sarah which through its messianic promise brought forth children who are free.

4:25-26. Next, Paul pointed to two Jerusalems. **Hagar** also stood for the first-century **city of Jerusalem,** a city enslaved to Rome and **in slavery** to the Law. Sarah, on the other hand, corresponded to the **Jerusalem . . . above,** the **mother** of all the children of grace. This heavenly city, which one day will come to earth (cf. Rev. 21:2), is now the "city of the living God" (cf. Heb. 12:22), the home of departed believers of all ages.

4:27. The quotation from Isaiah 54:1 prophesied the changing fortunes of Israel, which Paul applied to Sarah's history. Israel before her Babylonian Captivity was likened to a woman with **a husband.** The **barren woman** was Israel in Captivity. The woman bearing **more . . . children** may have pictured Israel restored to the land after the Exile, but more particularly it portrays her millennial blessings. Paul applied this passage (he did not claim it was fulfilled) in this context to Sarah, who though previously barren, was later blessed with a child, and who would ultimately enjoy a greater progeny than Hagar.

c. The personal application (4:28-31)

In applying the truth from the biblical illustration, Paul made three comparisons.

4:28. First, Paul compared the birth of **Isaac** to that of Christians. As "Isaac" experienced a supernatural birth and was a child by means of a promise, so each believer experiences a supernatural birth (John 3:3, 5) and is a recipient of the promise of salvation (Gal. 3:9, 22, 29). As **children of promise** Christians are in a

distinct category and should not live as children of bondage.

4:29. Second, the apostle compared Ishmael's persecution of Isaac to the false teachers' opposition to believers. Abraham celebrated the weaning of Isaac with a banquet. On that occasion Ishmael mocked Isaac, laughing derisively at the younger boy, since Ishmael was the elder son and assumed he would be heir to his father's estate (cf. Gen. 21:8-9). That early animosity has been perpetuated in the two peoples which descended from the two sons of Abraham and is seen in the current Arab-Israel tensions. Paul likened the Judaizers to Ishmael as those who were born out of legalistic self-effort; he charged that they continued to persecute the true believers who were **born by the power of the Spirit.** With few exceptions Paul's persecution came from the Jews, the people in bondage to the Law.

4:30. Third, Paul compared the action of Abraham to the obligation of the Galatians. When Sarah observed Ishmael mocking Isaac, she asked Abraham to expel **the slave woman and her son** lest Ishmael become a joint heir with Isaac. And God granted Sarah's request (cf. Gen. 21:10, 12). This reminded the readers that Law observance brought no **inheritance** in the family of God, and it also charged them to excommunicate the Judaizers and those who accepted their false doctrines. A fundamental incompatibility remains between Law and grace, between a religion based on works and a religion based on faith.

4:31. In conclusion, Paul affirmed that he and the Galatian believers were **not children of the slave woman** who was driven away and was denied a share in the inheritance. Rather all believers are children **of the free woman,** "heirs of God and co-heirs with Christ" (Rom. 8:17).

IV. Practical: A Defense of Christian Liberty (5:1–6:10)

Having defended both his authority as an apostle and the doctrine of justification by faith, Paul turned to defend the life of Christian freedom. Would the apostle's teaching lead the Galatians into lawlessness or into godliness? The Christian life is described as a life apart from Law, a life apart from license, a life according to the Spirit, and a life of service.

A. A life apart from Law (5:1-12)

1. TURNING TO LAW RUINS GRACE (5:1-2)

5:1. This verse summarizes chapter 4, where the theme is bondage and freedom. It also serves to introduce chapter 5. Paul declared that Christ was the great Liberator who set believers free from bondage. The apostle then appealed to the Galatians to **stand firm** (cf. 1 Cor. 16:13; Phil. 1:27; 4:1; 1 Thes. 3:8; 2 Thes. 2:15) in that liberty, for having been delivered from **slavery** to heathenism, they were in danger of becoming entangled in slavery to the Mosaic Law.

5:2. Taking up a prime example of such entanglement, namely circumcision, Paul issued a strong warning to the Galatians who were considering submitting to that rite. If they did, and were thereby seeking righteousness by works, Paul declared that **Christ will be of no value to you at all.** It is not that the apostle condemned circumcision in itself, for he had Timothy circumcised (in Galatia) so that the young man would have a wider ministry (Acts 16:1-3). But Paul was strongly opposed to the Judaistic theology which insisted that circumcision was necessary for salvation. Anyone who was circumcised for that reason added works to faith and demonstrated that he had not exercised saving faith in Christ.

2. TURNING TO LAW MAKES MAN A DEBTOR (5:3)

5:3. In addition to the fact that turning to the Law ruins grace, it also creates an entirely new obligation: a person **is obligated to obey the whole Law.** The Law is a unit, and if a person puts himself under any part of it for justification, he is a "debtor" (κJV) to the entire code with its requirements and its curse (cf. 3:10; James 2:10).

3. TURNING TO LAW IS TO FALL AWAY FROM GRACE (5:4-6)

5:4. Turning to the Law and accepting circumcision as a meritorious work has further dire implications which the Galatians were called on to consider. Anyone seeking justification **by Law** has **been alienated** (katērgēthēte) **from Christ,** that is, such a person would not be living in a sphere where Christ was operative. The KJV has a helpful rendering, "Christ is become of no effect unto you." In addition, said Paul, they would **have fallen away from grace.** The issue here is not the possible loss of salvation, for "grace" is referred to not as salvation itself but as a method of salvation (cf. 2:21 where "a Law" route is mentioned as an unworkable way to come to Christ). If the Galatians accepted circumcision as necessary for salvation, they would be leaving the grace system for the Mosaic Law system. The same error is repeated today when a believer leaves a church that emphasizes salvation by grace through faith and joins one which teaches that salvation depends on repentance, confession, faith, baptism, and church membership.

5:5. In contrast with legalists, true believers **by faith** (not works) **eagerly await** (apekdechometha; used seven times in the NT of the return of Christ: Rom. 8:19, 23, 25; 1 Cor. 1:7; Gal. 5:5; Phil. 3:20; Heb. 9:28) the consummation of their salvation (cf. Rom. 8:18-25). Then **the righteousness for which we hope** will be fully realized (cf. 1 Peter 1:3-4, 13). At the coming of Christ believers will be completely conformed to all the requirements of God's will. The inward and forensic righteousness which began at justification will be transformed into an outward righteousness at glorification. God will then publicly acknowledge all believers' full acceptability with Him.

5:6. For those **in Christ Jesus,** the true sphere of salvation, **neither circumcision nor** the lack of it is of any significance (cf. 3:28; 6:15). What matters **is faith expressing itself through love** (cf. 5:13). Though salvation is by faith apart from works, faith that is genuine does work itself out "through love" (cf. Eph. 2:10; James 2:14-18).

4. TURNING TO LAW HINDERS THE PROGRESS OF BELIEVERS (5:7-10)

5:7. Employing a metaphor he was fond of, Paul described the Galatians' Christian experience as a **race** (cf. 1 Cor. 9:24-26; 2 Tim. 4:7). They had begun their race well, but someone had **cut in on** them, causing them to break stride and stumble. Though many false teachers were disturbing the Galatians, the singular pronoun (who) indicates the leader of the Judaizers was in view here. The result was that the believers were no longer obeying the truth, but were attempting to complete the race by legalistic self-effort rather than by faith.

5:8-10. Such false teaching as the Galatians were beginning to embrace did not originate in the God who called them (cf. 1:6). He called them by and into grace. They were now being seduced by other voices into following a false gospel. And lest someone would feel that the apostle was making too much of the problem, he quoted a proverb (5:9) to the effect that false teaching, like yeast, spreads and permeates. Its converts may have been few but the believers must be on guard lest the error affect the entire church. Paul's point may also have been that one apparently small deviation from the truth could destroy the entire system. If circumcision, for example, were made necessary for salvation, the whole grace system would fall. But Paul was optimistic about the outcome. He was confident the Galatians would share his views and that the leading false teacher, whose identity was unknown to Paul, would suffer his due judgment.

5. TURNING TO LAW REMOVES THE OFFENSE OF THE CROSS (5:11-12)

5:11. Apparently Paul was charged with still preaching circumcision. Certainly before his conversion he zealously proclaimed circumcision and the Law, and it is easy to see how the apostle's attitude could be interpreted as being in favor of circumcision. Paul countered with a simple question: How is it that he was still being persecuted by Judaizers if he preached the same message they did? If Paul were preaching circumcision, the offense (skandalon, "stumbling block"; cf. 1 Cor. 1:23) of the Cross would have ceased to exist in his ministry. But it had not because people still found the gospel message, which proclaims man's total inability to contribute anything to his salvation, offensive. Thus the Cross marked the end of the Law system and rendered circumcision and obedience to the Mosaic Law unnecessary.

5:12. Speaking out of deep concern for the gospel of the grace of God, Paul uttered a strong expression. He wished that the Judaizers, who were so enthusiastic about circumcision, would go the whole way and castrate themselves, as did the pagan priests of the cult of Cybele in Asia Minor. Perhaps the resulting physical impotence pictured Paul's desire that they also be unable to produce new converts. While circumcision had once been the sign of the covenant in Israel, it now had no more religious meaning than any other ritual of cutting and marking practiced by ancient pagans.

B. A life apart from license (5:13-15)

5:13-14. In verse 1 Paul spoke of the Christian's freedom and warned against the danger of lapsing into slavery. Here the apostle again reminded believers of their freedom in Christ and warned against its being converted into license. Specifically he charged the Galatians not to use their liberty as "a base of operation" for sin to gain a foothold. Rather than liberty being used for lust, the real goal should be love. Rather than being in bondage to the Law or to the sinful nature, the Galatians were to be in bondage to one another. ("Sinful nature" is an appropriate trans. of the Gr. sarx, used by Paul in that sense seven times in Gal. 5:13, 16-17 [thrice], 19, 24; 6:8.)

Having discouraged two forms of slavery as burdensome and terrible, he commended another form that was beneficial—a slavery of mutual love. In support, Paul quoted Leviticus 19:18 and stated that the entire Law was summarized in this single command to love their neighbors. Jesus affirmed the same truth (Matt. 22:39; Luke 10:25-28). But Paul also wanted to show that Christian love is the "fulfillment" or "the carrying out" of the Law. The apostle developed this point in Romans 13:8-10.

5:15. That such love needed to be mutually expressed in the Galatian churches is made clear here. As a result of the inroads of the false teachers the church was divided and engaged in bitter strife. The followers of the legalists and those who remained steadfast were biting and devouring each other. This was far from the biblical ideal of believers dwelling together in a loving unity, and threatened the churches with destruction, that is, the loss of their individual and corporate testimonies.

C. A life according to the Spirit (5:16-26)

1. THE PROMISE OF VICTORY OVER SIN (5:16-18)

5:16. The answer to the abuses described in the previous verse is to **live by the Spirit.** The verb *peripateite* is a present imperative and is literally translated, "keep on walking." As a believer walks through life he should depend on the indwelling Holy Spirit for guidance and power. But the Spirit does not operate automatically in a believer's heart. He waits to be depended on. When a Christian does yield to the Spirit's control, the promise is that he will not in anywise (the double negative *ou mē* is emphatic) **gratify** (*telesēte*, "complete, fulfill" in outward action) **the desires of the sinful nature.** Thus, while no believer will ever be entirely free in this life from the evil desires that stem from his fallen human nature, he need not capitulate to them, but may experience victory by the Spirit's help.

5:17. Paul next explained the need for a life that is controlled and energized by **the Spirit.** The explanation is found in the fact that each Christian has two natures, a **sinful nature** received at birth, inherited from fallen Adam, and a new nature received at regeneration when said Christian became a participant in the divine nature (cf. 2 Peter 1:4). Both natures have desires, the one for evil and the other for holiness. Thus **they are in conflict with each other,** and the result can be that they keep a believer from doing what he otherwise would. In other words the Holy Spirit blocks, when He is allowed to do so, the evil cravings of the flesh. (Some hold the view that each believer *is* a new person, still possessing the fallen human nature, but not having a new nature. Others prefer to define "nature" as capacity, the old nature being that capacity to serve sin and self and the new nature the capacity to serve God and righteousness.)

5:18. In summary, Paul emphasized that a godly life is not lived **under** the rules of the **Law** but is a life **led by the Spirit.** It was important for the Galatians to know that just as justification is not possible by works so sanctification cannot be achieved by human effort. This of course does not mean that a Christian is

totally passive in either case for the response of faith is necessary—faith in Christ to save and in the Holy Spirit to sanctify.

2. THE PERIL TO VICTORY OVER SIN (5:19-21)

Since a Christian has the same sinful nature he possessed before salvation, he may fall prey to the sins that nature produces if he does not live by means of the Spirit.

5:19. The apostle declared that the sins of the flesh **are obvious,** meaning either, as some suggest, that they are public and cannot be hidden, or better, since some are private sins, that they originate with **the sinful nature** and not with the new nature indwelt by the Holy Spirit. The listed sins are commonly seen to fall into four categories. First, three sexual sins are mentioned. **Sexual immorality** (*porneia*) is often translated "fornication." From this word comes the term "pornography." *Porneia* refers to any and all forms of illicit sexual relationships. **Impurity** (*akatharsia*) is a broad term referring to moral uncleanness in thought, word, and deed (cf. Eph. 5:3-4). **Debauchery** (*aselgeia*) connotes an open, shameless, brazen display of these evils (cf. 2 Cor. 12:21 where the same words occur; *aselgeia* is included in Rom. 13:13).

5:20. Following the sexual sins, Paul cited two religious sins. **Idolatry** involved the worship of pagan gods by bowing to idols, and because of its mention just after the listing of sexual sins it probably includes the male and female prostitution so often a part of heathen religion. **Witchcraft** is the translation of the Greek word *pharmakeia* from which the term "pharmacy" comes. In ancient times the worship of evil powers was accompanied by the use of drugs to create trances. This vice will also be prominent in the Tribulation period (cf. Rev. 9:21; 18:23).

Eight societal evils are then listed (the last one in Gal. 5:21). **Hatred** (*echthrai*) is in the plural form, denoting primarily a feeling of enmity between groups. **Discord** (*eris*) is the natural result of "hatred" and no doubt a problem in the Galatian church. **Jealousy** (*zēlos*) refers not to the godly form but to the sinful and self-centered type. (These two words, *eris* and *zelos*, are also listed in Rom. 13:13.) **Fits of rage** (*thymoi*) or outbursts of temper, often come as a final eruption of smoldering jealousy. **Selfish ambition** (*eritheiai*) is a self-aggrandizing attitude which shows itself in working to get ahead at other's expense (cf. Phil. 2:3). **Dissensions** (*dichostasiai*) and **factions** (*haireseis*) describe what happens when people quarrel over issues or personalities, causing hurtful divisions.

5:21. Envy (*phthonoi*) is an evil feeling, a wrongful desire to possess what belongs to someone else. Thus the sinful nature is seen to be responsible for the breakdown of interpersonal relationships in homes, churches, and in public society.

Two sins associated with alcohol fall in a fourth category of evils. **Drunkenness** (*methai*) refers to excessive use of strong drink by individuals, and **orgies** (*kōmoi*) probably refers to the drunken carousings commonly associated with such things as the worship of Bacchus, the god of wine. Finally, to show that this long list was only representative and not exhaustive, Paul added the words **and the like.**

The apostle then solemnly warned the Galatians, as he had done when he was in their midst, that **those who live like this,** who habitually indulge in these fleshly sins **will not inherit the** future **kingdom of God.** This does not say that a Christian loses his salvation if he lapses into a sin of the flesh, but that a person who lives continually on such a level of moral corruption gives evidence of not being a child of God.

3. THE POWER FOR VICTORY OVER SIN
(5:22-23)

5:22-23. There is a pointed contrast here. As verse 16 indicated, there is no need for a believer to display the works of the flesh. Rather, by the Spirit's power he can manifest the nine graces that are now listed. It is important to observe that **the fruit** here described is not produced by a believer, but by **the Holy Spirit** working through a Christian who is in vital union with Christ (cf. John 15:1-8). The word "fruit" is singular, indicating that these qualities constitute a unity, all of which should be found in a believer who lives under the control of the Spirit. In an ultimate sense this "fruit" is simply the life of Christ lived out in a Christian. It also points to the method whereby Christ is formed in a believer (cf. 2 Cor. 3:18; Phil. 1:21).

The first three virtues are habits of mind which find their source in God. **Love** (*agapē*) is listed first because it is the foundation of the other graces. God is love and loves the world (cf. 1 John 4:8; John 3:16). Such self-sacrificing love that sent Christ to die for sinners is the kind of love that believers who are Spirit-controlled manifest. **Joy** (*chara*) is a deep and abiding inner rejoicing which was promised to those who abide in Christ (cf. John 15:11). It does not depend on circumstances because it rests in God's sovereign control of all things (cf. Rom. 8:28). **Peace** (*eirēnē*) is again a gift of Christ (cf. John 14:27). It is an inner repose and quietness, even in the face of adverse circumstances; it defies human understanding (cf. Phil. 4:7).

The second triad reaches out to others, fortified by love, joy, and peace. **Patience** (*makrothymia*) is the quality of forbearance under provocation (cf. 2 Cor. 6:6; Col. 1:11; 3:12). It entertains no thoughts of retaliation even when wrongfully treated. **Kindness** (*chrēstotēs*) is benevolence in action such as God demonstrated toward men. Since God is kind toward sinners (cf. Rom. 2:4; Eph. 2:7) a Christian should display the same virtue (cf. 2 Cor. 6:6; Col. 3:12). **Goodness** (*agathōsynē*) may be thought of both as an uprightness of soul and as an action reaching out to others to do good even when it is not deserved.

The final three graces guide the general conduct of a believer who is led by the Spirit. **Faithfulness** (*pistis*) is the quality which renders a person trustworthy or reliable, like the faithful servant in Luke 16:10-12. **Gentleness** (*prautēs*) marks a person who is submissive to God's Word (cf. James 1:21) and who is considerate of others when discipline is needed (cf. "gently" in Gal. 6:1; 2 Tim. 2:25; "gentle" in 1 Cor. 4:21; Eph. 4:2; "gentleness" in Col. 3:12; 1 Peter 3:16). **Self-control** (*enkrateia*; this noun is used in the NT only here and in Acts 24:25; 2 Peter 1:6) denotes self-mastery and no doubt primarily relates to curbing the fleshly impulses just described. Such a quality is impossible to attain apart from the power of God's Spirit (cf. Gal. 5:16). As a final summary statement Paul affirmed that there are no prohibitions (lit., **there is** not a **law) against such** virtues. In a *litotes* (understatement) he asserted that obviously no one would make laws against people who practice such things.

4. THE PROVISION FOR VICTORY OVER SIN (5:24-26)

5:24. Paul next explained that believers (lit., "those who are of Christ Jesus") need not be responsive to **the sinful nature** because they **have crucified** it. This does not refer to self-crucifixion or self-mortification. Rather, it refers to the fact that by means of the baptism of the Holy Spirit, Christians were identified with Christ in His death and resurrection. Paul declared that this had been his experience (cf. 2:20) and that of all believers (cf. Rom. 6:1-6; Col. 2:11; 3:9). While co-crucifixion took place potentially at the cross, it becomes effective for believers when they are converted. This does not mean that their sin nature is then eradicated or even rendered inactive but that it has been judged, a fact believers should reckon to be true (cf. Rom. 6:11-12). So victory over the sinful nature's **passions and desires** has been provided by Christ in His death. Faith must continually lay hold of this truth or a believer will be tempted to try to secure victory by self-effort.

5:25-26. Again Paul reminded the Galatians that in addition to a divine judgment of the sinful nature there is a divine enablement in the person of the Holy Spirit. He made the believer alive by regeneration (cf. John 3:5-6), so each believer is exhorted to **keep in step** (*stoichōmen,* trans. "follow" in Gal. 6:16) **with the Spirit.** Step by step one's Christian walk should conform to the Spirit's direction and enablement, lest believers **become conceited, provoking and envying each other.** The latter traits would be true of a walk in the flesh (cf. 5:19-21) and may point to divisions in the Galatian churches occasioned by the Judaizing error (cf. v. 15).

D. A life of service (6:1-10)

A believer is free from the Law of Moses and possesses liberty in the Spirit, but he must fulfill the law of Christ, and this can be done in the power of the Spirit. Such a life involves sacrificial service directed toward sinning Christians, burdened Christians, the pastor-teachers, and all people.

1. TOWARD THE CHRISTIAN WHO HAS SINNED (6:1)

6:1. Paul deals with a hypothetical case of a Christian who is **caught** (*prolēmphthē*) **in a sin,** or better, is "caught by a sin." The thought is that of someone running from sin but sin, being faster, overtakes and catches him. Two passages show how the legalists responded to such (cf. John 8:3-5; Acts 21:27-29). But a Christian should **restore** (*katartizete,* a word used in secular Gr. for setting broken bones and in the NT for mending fishing nets) **him.** The task of restoration is not to be undertaken by fledglings in the faith but by those **who are spiritual,** that is, believers who walk by the Spirit (cf. Gal. 5:16), and who are mature in the faith (cf. 1 Cor. 2:15; Heb. 5:13-14). Furthermore this delicate work must be done **gently** (*prautētos;* cf. Gal. 5:22) and with the consciousness that no one is immune from falling into sin (cf. 1 Cor. 10:12).

2. TOWARD THE CHRISTIAN WHO IS BURDENED (6:2-5)

6:2. A serving Christian lends a helping hand with heavy loads (*barē;* cf. comments on v. 5). Though the principle would apply to all burdens the context has special reference to the heavy and oppressive weight of temptation and spiritual failure. While the "spiritual" do the work of restoring, all believers are to become involved by prayer and encouragement. This, wrote Paul, will fulfill (*anaplērōsete*) **the law of Christ,** that is, the principle of love (cf. 5:14; John 13:34).

6:3-4. Something must be laid aside if a believer is to be a burden-bearer and that is conceit, an attitude that breeds intolerance of error in others and causes one to think he is above failure. The remedy for self-conceit is found in verse 4—everyone is told to **test** (*dokimazetō;* cf. 1 Peter 1:7) **his own actions.** This means that rather than **comparing himself** with others he should step back and take an objective look at himself and his accomplishments. **Then he can take pride in himself** over what God has done in and through his life (cf. Rom. 12:3). The Greek word *kauchēma,* rendered "pride," means personal exultation, not sinful pride.

6:5. The Christian does in fact test himself by carrying **his own load.** This does not contradict verse 2 because the reference there is to heavy, crushing, loads (*barē*)—more than a man could carry without help. In this verse a different Greek word (*phortion*) is used to designate the pack usually carried by a marching soldier. It is the "burden" Jesus assigns to His followers (cf. Matt. 11:30). There are certain Christian responsibilities or burdens each believer must bear which cannot be shared with others. Jesus assured His disciples that such burdens were light.

3. TOWARD THE PASTOR-TEACHER (6:6-9)

6:6. One responsibility of each believer is to shoulder the financial support of the pastor-teachers in the church. Perhaps the Judaizers had influenced some of the believers to slack off in their support of the teachers, a special group who were giving their full time to this ministry and who were reimbursed for their labors (cf. 1 Cor. 9:7-14). This concept of voluntary giving to provide for the Lord's servants was revolutionary since Jews were taxed for the support of their priests and Gentiles paid fees, made vows, etc., to sustain their religions. The admonition is clear that as a teacher shares the good things of **the Word of God**, a believer is to reciprocate by sharing **all good things with his instructor.**

6:7-8. These verses elaborate on the previous exhortation. First, a solemn warning is sounded that **God cannot be mocked.** No man can snub (*myktērizetai*, lit., "turn up the nose at") God whose rule, **a man reaps what he sows,** is immutable. Each sower decides what his harvest will be. If a person **sows to please his sinful nature,** that is, if he spends his money to indulge the flesh, he **will reap** a harvest that will fade into oblivion. On the other hand if he uses his funds to support the Lord's work, or **sows to please the Spirit,** and promotes his own spiritual growth, he **will reap** a harvest that will last forever. Though a broader application of the principle is legitimate it seems clear that Paul was dealing primarily with the question of financial support of Christian workers in the Galatian churches.

6:9. But Christians may become discouraged with spiritual sowing be-

cause the harvest is often long in coming. In the face of this reality the apostle charged the Galatians **not** to **become weary** or **give up** because the **harvest** is sure. (Paul included himself as he no doubt contemplated his sometimes frustrating labors on behalf of the Galatian Christians.) The reaping will come at God's **proper time,** which may be only in part in this life and in full in the life to come at the judgment seat of Christ.

4. TOWARD ALL MEN (6:10)

6:10. Christians have a measure of responsibility **to all people** to **do good,** when the occasions arise. When Jesus fed the 5,000, both saved and unsaved participated. So the benevolence of Christians should not be restricted, except that believers are to have the priority. As in a home, family needs are met first, then those of the neighbors.

This passage then speaks clearly about Christian social responsibility, but it should be noted that it is addressed to individual believers. The church is not an agency for social work, though individual Christians are charged to minister in this way as they are able and have opportunity (cf. Rom. 12:17-21).

V. Conclusion (6:11-18)

As Paul brought the Galatian letter to a close, he again emphasized some of the great issues discussed throughout the epistle. The conclusion contains both a summary and final statement of the issues the apostle felt so strongly about.

A. Paul's autograph (6:11)

6:11. At this point Paul took the pen from his scribe and wrote the rest of the letter himself, a practice he often followed (cf. 1 Cor. 16:21; Col. 4:18; 2 Thes. 3:17). The **large letters** he used probably did not refer to the length of the epistle as some have suggested but to the size of the letters he inscribed. It may be that Paul wrote the conclusion in capital letters after the rest of the epistle was penned mostly in lowercase letters. While it has often been suggested that he did so because he was afflicted with weak eyesight, it is more likely, given the tone of the letter, that the apostle sought in this way to give a final emphatic thrust to his message.

B. Paul's adversaries (6:12-13)

6:12-13. The Judaizers who insisted that circumcision was necessary for salvation (cf. Acts 15:1), in summary, (1) were only men-pleasers (cf. Gal. 1:10) seeking **to make a good impression outwardly;** (2) were afraid of persecution (6:12b); (3) wanted to **boast** about the number of Galatians they hoped to win over to circumcision as a religious and merit-earning rite (v. 13). The legalists knew the offense of the Cross would be softened if they openly proclaimed justification by faith *and works* (i.e., circumcision) and if they could claim conversions to that position in Galatia.

C. Paul's boast (6:14-16)

6:14. The contrast is vivid as Paul declared his boasting to be **in the Cross of our Lord Jesus Christ.** For the Judaizers the Cross was an object of shame; for Paul it was the object of glorying. They gloried in the flesh; he gloried in the Savior. The "Cross" speaks of the atonement of Christ with which Paul was identified (cf. 2:20) and by which **the world** was **crucified to** Paul **and he to the world.** The world system with all its allurements, fleshly displays, and religions of human effort was cast aside by Paul. He looked at the world as if it were on a cross—and the world looked at Paul as though he were on a cross.

6:15. In view of the Cross of Christ and a believer's new position with respect to the world, no outward religious symbol or lack of it **means anything** as a way of salvation (cf. 5:6). The only thing that matters is to be a part of the **new creation** by the new birth (cf. 2 Cor. 5:17).

6:16. Peace and mercy from God are available to those who walk according to **this rule,** that is, according to the message of salvation by grace through faith alone. This blessing is pronounced on believing Galatians and on believing Jews. (The NIV errs in trans. **even to the Israel of God** rather than "and upon the Israel of God" as in the NASB.) While some believe that "Israel of God" is the church, the evidence does not support such a conclusion. First, the repetition of the preposition ("upon" or "to") indicates two groups are in view. Second, all the 65 other occurrences of the term "Israel" in the New Testament refer to Jews. It

would thus be strange for Paul to use "Israel" here to mean Gentile Christians. Third, Paul elsewhere referred to two kinds of Israelites—believing Jews and unbelieving Jews (cf. Rom. 9:6). Lest it be thought that Paul is anti-Semitic, he demonstrated by means of this benediction his deep love and concern for true Israel, that is, Jews who had come to Christ.

D. Paul's benediction (6:17-18)

6:17. Paul's calling as an apostle and the message he preached had been challenged by the Judaizers. He asked for an end to such **trouble,** and he offered as a final proof to his critics **the marks of Jesus** on his **body.** These "marks" (*stigmata*) meant signs of ownership such as were branded on slaves and cattle. Paul referred to the scars on his body, which were caused by persecution for Christ's sake (cf. 1 Cor. 4:11; 2 Cor. 4:10-11; 6:5, 9; 11:24-25), because they demonstrated he was a slave of Christ and not just a people-pleaser.

6:18. Paul's final word of benediction is noteworthy. While no greetings or personal salutations dim the solemnity of the epistle, the apostle ended as he began, expressing his heartfelt desire that **the grace of** God would be their abiding portion (cf. 1:3). And uniquely among all of Paul's epistles he ends with a reminder of his love for them, calling them **brothers.** How could the Galatians fail to respond in obedience to the persuasive and ultimately tender appeal found in this letter?

BIBLIOGRAPHY

Boice, James Montgomery. "Galatians." In *The Expositor's Bible Commentary*, vol. 10. Grand Rapids: Zondervan Publishing House, 1976.

Bruce, F.F. *The Epistle to the Galatians.* The New International Greek Testament Commentary. Grand Rapids: Wm. B. Eerdmans Publishing Co., 1982.

Burton, Ernest DeWitt. *A Critical and Exegetical Commentary on the Epistle to the Galatians.* The International Critical Commentary. Edinburgh: T. & T. Clark, 1921.

Cole, R.A. *The Epistle of Paul to the*

GALATIANS

Galatians. Tyndale New Testament Commentaries. Grand Rapids: Wm. B. Eerdmans Publishing Co., 1965.

Gromacki, Robert G. *Stand Fast in Liberty: An Exposition of Galatians.* Grand Rapids: Baker Book House, 1979.

Ironside, H.A. *Expository Messages on the Epistle to the Galatians.* New York: Loizeaux Brothers, 1941.

Lightfoot, J.B. *The Epistle of St. Paul to the Galatians.* Reprint. Grand Rapids: Zondervan Publishing House, 1957.

Luther, Martin. *A Commentary on St. Paul's Epistle to the Galatians.* Reprint. Grand Rapids: Kregel Publications, 1979.

Stott, John R.W. *The Message of Galatians.* Downers Grove, Ill.: InterVarsity Press, 1968.

Strauss, Lehman. *Devotional Studies in Galatians and Ephesians.* New York: Loizeaux Brothers, 1957.

Tenney, Merrill C. *Galatians: The Charter of Christian Liberty.* Revised. Grand Rapids: Wm. B. Eerdmans Publishing Co., 1960.

Vos, Howard F. *Galatians: A Call to Christian Liberty.* Chicago: Moody Press, 1970.

Wuest, Kenneth S. *Galatians in the Greek New Testament for the English Reader.* Grand Rapids: Wm. B. Eerdmans Publishing Co., 1944.

EPHESIANS

Harold W. Hoehner

INTRODUCTION

Authorship. Twice in this epistle Paul referred to himself by name as the author of the book (1:1; 3:1). Yet the Pauline authorship of Ephesians has been greatly disputed in recent years. Some critics think that the book reflects aspects of vocabulary, style, and doctrine that differ from Paul's writings. Though the book has a close affinity with Colossians, critics claim that Ephesians is uncharacteristic of Paul. They suggest that the book was pseudonymous, that is, it was written by someone who did not use his own name but who instead claimed to be Paul.

However, pseudonymity was not practiced by the early Christians. Also this book is regarded by many as the crown of all Paul's writings. Thus it seems strange that a disciple of Paul would be greater than Paul in theological and spiritual perception. Furthermore, Ephesians was extensively and undisputably accepted in the early church as Paul's letter. There is no strong reason for rejecting the Pauline authorship of Ephesians.

Destination. Some scholars view this epistle as encyclical, a circular letter to be distributed to several undesignated local churches in the province of Asia or some other area. This is supported by two observations: (1) the words "in Ephesus" (1:1) do not appear in three early Alexandrian Greek manuscripts, and (2) it is strange for Paul not to mention by name any of the individuals in a church where he had lived and worked for three years (Acts 20:31). However, it seems better to accept "in Ephesus" as genuine because of the wide geographical distribution of the Greek manuscripts that do include those words. Also no manuscripts of this epistle mention any other city, and none have only the word "in" followed by a

space to insert a city's name. The prescript or title "To the Ephesians" appears in all manuscripts of this epistle. Furthermore, all the letters Paul wrote to churches mention their destinations.

With regard to the absence of names of individuals in Ephesus, it may be that Paul did not want to single out certain persons in this short epistle since he knew so many people there.

Even so, the epistle may still be considered a circular letter, with Ephesus being the primary church addressed since Paul had stayed there so long and since it was the capital city of the province of Asia. This helps explain the absence of personal names of Ephesian believers. If this epistle were routed to other churches after the Ephesians read it, it may have gone to Laodicea and Colosse, for Paul in writing Colossians urged the believers there to "read the letter from Laodicea" (Col. 4:16), possibly a reference to the Ephesian epistle. (For the locations of Ephesus, Asia, Laodicea, and Colosse see the map between Acts and Rom.)

Ephesians was probably delivered by Tychicus (Eph. 6:21-22), who also took Paul's letter to the Colossians (Col. 4:7-9).

Ephesus was a leading center in the Roman Empire. Paul had spent a short time in Ephesus on his way back to Antioch from his second missionary journey (Acts 18:19-22). On his third missionary journey he stayed in Ephesus three years (Acts 20:31). Several remarkable things happened in Ephesus. Paul baptized a dozen of John the Baptist's followers (Acts 19:1-7). He had discussions in the hall of Tyrannus (19:8-10). Unusual miracles occurred (19:11-12), strange events took place (19:13-16), sorcerers were converted (19:17-20), and the city rioted over silversmith Demetrius' loss of business because of people who turned to Christ from worshiping the great Ephesian goddess Artemis

(19:23-41). On Paul's return to Jerusalem from his third missionary journey he gave a moving farewell address to the Ephesian elders at the coastal town of Miletus (20:13-35). That was his last time to see them (20:36-38), unless Paul visited Ephesus after he was in Rome (cf. 1 Tim. 1:3 with 3:14).

Place and Date. Paul was a prisoner at the time he wrote this letter (Eph. 3:1; 4:1; 6:20). Scholars differ on whether Paul wrote this letter while he was imprisoned in Caesarea (Acts 24:27) in A.D. 57–59, or in Rome (28:30) in A.D. 60–62. All things considered, the Roman imprisonment seems more likely. Along with Ephesians, the Books of Philippians, Colossians, and Philemon are thought to have been written during the same time period and hence are called the "Prison Epistles" (cf. Phil. 1:7; Col. 4:10; Phile. 9). Since Ephesians gives no hint of his release from prison, as do Philippians (1:19-26) and Philemon (v. 22), it is reasonable to think that he wrote it in the early part of his stay, or about A.D. 60. This would have been when Paul was kept under guard in rental quarters (Acts 28:30). Following his release he traveled, wrote 1 Timothy and Titus, was arrested again, wrote 2 Timothy, and was martyred in Rome.

Purpose. Though no particular problem is raised in the book, the reason for writing this epistle becomes clear when one considers the contacts the apostle had with the Ephesians. On the return from his third missionary journey Paul told the Ephesian elders at Miletus (A.D. 57) to beware of evil teachers from without and of professing believers within who would teach perverse things (Acts 20:29-30). From Revelation one can see that the Ephesian church had succeeded in keeping out the false teachers (Rev. 2:2) but had failed to maintain the vibrancy of their first love for Christ (Rev. 2:4). This is substantiated in 1 Timothy 1:5, when Paul wrote from Macedonia to Timothy at Ephesus (ca A.D. 62) that the goal of his instruction was "love which comes from a pure heart and a good conscience and a sincere faith." Thus the theme of love needed to be stressed for the saints at Ephesus.

This is in harmony with the contents of Ephesians, for the verb form of "love" (*agapaō*) is used 9 times in Ephesians, whereas Paul used it only 23 times in all his other letters. Paul used the noun (*agapē*, "love") 10 times in Ephesians compared with 65 times in his other epistles. Therefore, of the 107 times Paul used the verb or noun "love," 19 are in Ephesians. Thus more than one-sixth of his references to "love" appear in this small epistle to the Ephesians. This letter begins with love (Eph. 1:4, 6) and ends with love (6:23-24).

Also Ephesians teaches that Jewish and Gentile believers are one in Christ, which is demonstrated by their love for one another. This love can come only from God. Possibly Paul, realizing they were starting to forsake their first love, wrote this epistle to encourage them to love both God and their fellow saints.

OUTLINE

COMMENTARY

I. The Calling of the Church (chaps. 1–3)

All knowledge may be divided into two categories: pure or theoretical knowledge and applied or practical knowledge. In most of his letters Paul begins with pure or doctrinal knowledge and ends with applied or practical knowledge. In this epistle the first three chapters deal with doctrine (the calling of the church) and the last three chapters

with application (the conduct of the church).

A. Prologue (1:1-2)

1:1. **Paul** was made **an apostle of Christ Jesus** through God's **will** or decision. It was not his own choosing or plan. Thus he had God's authority behind him. As an apostle Paul was commissioned and sent by God with the gospel message.

The letter is addressed **to the saints** who resided **in Ephesus.** "Saints" (*hagiois*, "holy ones") are those set apart for God's use. They are a part of the universal church by virtue of their salvation in Christ. The words "in Ephesus" are omitted by some early manuscripts (see "Destination" under *Introduction*), but strong external and internal evidence support their inclusion. If this epistle were a circular letter, it seems that Ephesus, such a strategic city in Asia Minor, would have certainly received it first. **The faithful in Christ Jesus** further defines the "saints" and could be rendered "that is, the believers in Christ Jesus." These saints were in Christ Jesus, not in Adam or the goddess Artemis of Ephesus. While believers have geographical locations (e.g., "Ephesus"), spiritually they are positioned "in Christ" (cf. "in Christ at Colosse" in Col. 1:2). Paul used "in Christ Jesus," "in Christ," or "in Him" quite frequently. In Ephesians 1:1-14 the phrase occurs nine times! Christians have their very life in Christ.

1:2. Paul's extension of **grace** (*charis*) **and peace** is different from the normal Greek letters which had only "greetings" or "greeting" (*chairein;* e.g., the apocryphal 1 Maccabees 10:18, 25; thousands of ancient papyri letters; and Acts 15:23; 23:26; James 1:1). "Grace" expresses God's steadfast love toward man and "peace" shows the relational state as a result of that grace. Paul opened his letter to the church at Ephesus with greetings to the believers there, expressing his wish that God's grace and peace be with them. (See the chart "Paul's Introductions to His Epistles" at Rom. 1:1-7.)

B. Praise for God's planned spiritual blessings (1:3-14)

Paul now moved from his general greeting to the saints at Ephesus to an expanded discussion of the reason God is to be praised—because of the spiritual blessings He has planned for believers in Christ.

In the Greek text, 1:3-14 is one sentence, which is considered by some scholars to be the most cumbersome sentence in the Greek language! In fact, Ephesians has eight lengthy sentences (1:3-14, 15-23; 2:1-7; 3:1-13, 14-19; 4:1-7, 11-16; 6:14-20). However, it is common even today for prayers and doxologies to be lengthy.

1. THE PROVISION OF SPIRITUAL BLESSINGS (1:3)

1:3. Paul stated that God is to **be** blessed or praised. The word for **praise** is *eulogētos*, from a verb that means "to speak well of." In the New Testament it is applied only to God (Mark 14:61; Luke 1:68; Rom. 1:25; 9:5; 2 Cor. 1:3; 11:31; 1 Peter 1:3), whereas in the Septuagint it is sometimes applied to man (Gen. 26:29; Deut. 7:14; Ruth 2:20). The praise should be given **to the God and Father of our Lord Jesus Christ.** In Ephesians 1:2 God is the Father of believers; here in verse 3 God is the Father of Christ (cf. v. 17; cf. similar wording in Rom. 15:6; 2 Cor. 1:3; 1 Peter 1:3). In Ephesians 1:2 the first Person of the Trinity belongs to believers, suggested by the word "our." Here in verse 3 the pronoun "our" shows that believers belong to Christ, the second Person of the Godhead. Since He is the Son of God and believers are connected with Him, they are also related to the Father.

This God who is to be praised is the One **who has blessed us.** This is a verbal form (*ho eulogēsas*) of the adjective "praise" (*eulogētos*), at the beginning of the verse. The verb means "to speak well of, eulogize, extol"; here it means "to benefit, prosper." This word is not used in classical Greek literature. For example, Zeus is not said to have bestowed any specific act of blessing on anyone. Rather he is said to have caused good luck or good fortune. However, the verb *eulogeō* is used over 400 times in the Old Testament, indicating that God bestows benefits to His children in every Age. Mary was said to be "blessed" among women and to be bearing the "blessed" Child (Luke 1:42).

Paul's use of the past tense participle "has blessed" points to this blessing or

prospering of believers as having occurred in eternity past. With what are believers blessed? **With every spiritual blessing** (in the Gr., this phrase precedes the words "in the heavenly realms"). "Every spiritual blessing" (*eulogia*) refers to every spiritual enrichment needed for the spiritual life. Since these benefits have already been bestowed on believers, they should not ask for them but rather appropriate them by faith. Similarly Joshua was not to ask for land since God had already promised it to him (Josh. 1:3-4). But he was to enter into the enjoyment of that provision.

The manner or sphere of this enrichment is **in Christ.** The place of these "blessings" is **in the heavenly realms,** as opposed to the earthly realm of the Ephesian goddess Artemis. Thus these blessings are spiritual not material, heavenly not earthly, eternal not temporal (2 Cor. 4:18; Col. 3:1-4). Five times Paul used the phrase "in the heavenly realms": in Ephesians 1:3, 20; 2:6; 3:10; 6:12.

Ephesians 1:3 tells much about God's blessings on believers: (a) *when:* eternity past; (b) *with what:* every spiritual blessing: (c) *where:* in the heavenly realms; (d) *how:* in Christ.

2. THE BASIS OF SPIRITUAL BLESSINGS (1:4-14)

Paul continued his discussion of believers' spiritual blessings by showing that they are based on the work of the three Persons of the Trinity: the *selection* of the Father (vv. 4-6), the *sacrifice* of the Son (vv. 7-12), and the *seal* of the Spirit (vv. 13-14).

a. God's election for Himself (1:4-6)

1:4. The apostle first told when God's work of election took place: **before the Creation of the world.** The word **for** at the beginning of this verse is not as literal a translation of the Greek adverb *kathōs* as "even as" (ASV, RSV) or "just as" (NASB). "As" suggests that the *way* God blesses believers (v. 3) is through the threefold work of the Trinity. But the adverb can also have a causal sense, and may be rendered "since," "because," or "insofar as" (cf. 4:32). The idea is that spiritual blessings (1:3) for believers are *because of* or on the basis of the work of the Trinity: God blesses believers because of the Father's electing, the Son's dying, and the Spirit's sealing. Both concepts seem to be included: spiritual blessings are the work of the three Persons of the Trinity, and the work of the Trinity is the basis of all a believer's spiritual blessings.

Spiritual blessings begin with and are based on election (**He chose us**), of which God is the subject and believers are the object. Election is God's sovereign work of choosing some to believe (cf. Rom. 8:30; Eph. 1:11; 1 Thes. 1:4; 2 Thes. 2:13; Titus 1:1). Salvation is God's doing, not man's (Eph. 2:8-9). Though it is an act of grace (Rom. 11:5-6; 2 Tim. 1:9), based on His will (Eph. 1:5, 9, 11), a person is responsible to believe (v. 13). "God chose you to be saved . . . through belief in the truth" (2 Thes. 2:13).

In Him indicates the sphere (cf. "in Christ" in Eph. 1:3) of election, as He is the Head and Representative of spiritual humanity (vv. 10, 22; Col. 1:18). The time of election is in eternity past, and the purpose of election is that believers will **be holy and blameless in His sight** for eternity. What God has begun in the past will be accomplished and completed in the future. Christians are "holy" (*hagious;* cf. *hagiois,* "saints," Eph. 1:1), that is, set apart to God, which is the purpose of His electing grace. In addition, the purpose of His election is to make Christians "blameless." This word *amōmous,* "without blemish," is used eight times in the New Testament (v. 4; 5:27; Phil. 2:15; Col. 1:22; Heb. 9:14; 1 Peter 1:19; 2 Peter 3:14; Rev. 14:5). In the Septuagint it is used of sacrificial animals; only those without blemish could be offered to God.

What does the phrase **in love** modify? Some agree with the NIV that it modifies the word "predestined" (Eph. 1:5). If so, then God's love is seen in predestination. More likely, it modifies the words "to be holy and blameless in His sight" for these reasons: (1) In this context the modifying phrases always follow the action words (vv. 3-4, 6, 8-10). (2) The other five occurrences of "in love" in Ephesians (3:17; 4:2, 15-16; 5:2 ["of love"]) refer to human love rather than divine love. (3) Love fits well with holiness and blamelessness, for this would denote a balance between holiness and love. God is love and believers, because of God's electing love, should manifest love with holiness.

1:5. The cause of election is God's predestination of believers unto sonship (cf. "predestined" in v. 11). **Predestined** is from *proorisas,* "marked out beforehand." Thus the emphasis of predestination is more on the *what* than the *who* in that the believers' predetermined destiny is their being **adopted as** full-fledged **sons** of God **through Jesus Christ**, the Agent of the adoption. The concept of adoption is also found in Romans 8:15 (NIV marg.), 23; Galatians 4:4-7. In adoption a son is brought into a family and is given the same rights as a child who is born into that family.

In this context it seems that predestination logically precedes election: after God looked forward to the glorious destiny of adopting believers into His family, He looked down on sinful humanity and chose believers (cf. Rom. 8:30 where "predestined" precedes "called," which refers to His efficacious saving). All this was done **in accordance with His pleasure** (cf. Eph. 1:9) **and will** (cf. vv. 1, 9, 11), that is, He delighted to impart His spiritual benefits to His children.

1:6. The ultimate goal of God's election is that believers will be to the **praise of His glorious grace.** A similar expression of praise is also given after the description of the work of the Son (v. 12) and of the Spirit (v. 14). "His glorious grace" (undeserved favor; cf. v. 7) had been **freely given us.** The words "freely given" translate the verb *echaritōsen,* from the noun "grace" (*charis*). The verb form is used only one other time in the New Testament (Luke 1:28, where Mary is said to be "highly favored"). Literally, Ephesians 1:6a might be rendered "to the praise of His glorious grace which He 'graced' to us." Since salvation is all of God's grace, Christians certainly ought to praise Him for it! And that is why they were chosen: to give Him praise (cf. "Praise be to . . . God," v. 3). **In the One He loves** stresses the manifestation of God's love to His Son (cf. "the Son He loves," Col. 1:13). This reference to Christ also furnishes the transition to the second Person of the Trinity discussed in Ephesians 1:7-12.

God the Father loves His Son; and believers, being in the Son, are also the object of God's love.

b. God's redemption in Christ (1:7-12)

1:7. Redemption (*apolytrōsin*) denotes release or deliverance from a state of slavery (cf. Col. 1:14). The idea of release is seen in some of the other verses where this Greek word appears (Luke 21:28; Rom. 3:24; 8:23; 1 Cor. 1:30; Eph. 1:7, 14; 4:30; Col. 1:14; Heb. 9:15; 11:35). (See the chart "New Testament Words for Redemption" at Mark 10:45.) This redemption is from sin (Heb. 9:15), and thus this work of Christ delivers believers from slavery to sin. This is further defined by the **forgiveness of sins** (cf. Eph. 4:32; Col. 1:14), which is the immediate result of a believer's release from sin's hold. (The word for "sins" is *paraptōma*, lit., "false steps or transgressions," also used in Rom. 4:25; 5:16-17, 20; Eph. 2:1, 5, and elsewhere.) God could not treat sin lightly for it required the sacrifice of blood (cf. Heb. 9:22).

The means of redemption is the sacrificial substitutionary death of Christ (**through His blood**; cf. Eph. 2:13; 1 Peter 1:19), which completely satisfied God's justice (Rom. 3:24-25). This was accomplished **in accordance with the riches of God's grace** (cf. Eph. 1:6; 2:7). The cost of Christ's blood is the measure of the wealth of God's unmerited favor to every believer. It was accomplished not "out of" but "according to" (*kata*) the wealth of His grace (cf. Phil. 4:19). Six times in Ephesians Paul referred to God's riches (1:7, 18; 2:4, 7; 3:8, 16).

1:8-10. God's grace is given to enable believers to understand His will. God gives them **wisdom** (*sophia*; cf. v. 17; 3:10; Col. 1:9, 28; 2:3, 23; 3:16; 4:5), objective insight into the true nature of God's revelation, **and understanding** (*phronēsei*), the subjective apprehension of it. So believers are able to grasp something of the divine purpose of the ages and to see its relevance in the present time. This is accomplished because God **made known to us the mystery of His will** (cf. "will" in Eph. 1:1, 5, 11). "Mystery" is a previously hidden truth unveiled by God's revelation (cf. Rom. 16:25; see Matt. 13:11 for a list of "mysteries" in the NT). This mystery (unveiled truth) is God's **good pleasure** (cf. Eph. 1:5) to purpose **in Christ** to **bring all things in heaven and on earth** under His headship in the consummation of time. The words **to be put into effect when the times will have reached their fulfillment** are literally, "unto the

dispensation of the fullness of the times." The "dispensation" (*oikonomia*) is an arrangement or administration. This dispensation is the millennial kingdom when "the times" in God's purposes will be completed (fulfilled), and all things both spiritual and material will be under Christ and His rule (cf. 1 Cor. 15:27; Col. 1:20).

The words "bring all things . . . together under one Head" translate one Greek word (which occurs elsewhere in the NT only in Rom. 13:9), to speak of summing up all the commandments under love. In the Millennium everything will be restored and brought together under Christ, the **one Head**. This does not suggest that everyone will be saved; instead, sin's disorder will be removed and universal peace will be established (Isa. 2:2-4; 11:1-10).

1:11-12. As a result of the spiritual blessing of insight into the mystery of God's will (vv. 8-10) Paul discussed the Jewish believers' inclusion in Christ. The **we** in verse 11 seems to be a distinct group from the anonymous "we/us" in verses 3-10. This is supported by two facts: (1) verse 11 includes the word **also** and (2) verse 13 changes to "you also," which refers to Gentile believers. Though both Jews and Gentiles participate in God's blessings, the Jews were called first (cf. Acts 3:26; Rom. 1:16).

In Ephesians 1:11 **chosen** (*eklērō-thēmen*) is not the same word used in verse 4 (*exelexato*). The word in verse 11 (used only here in the NT) means "to cast a lot" or "to appoint or obtain by lot." In this context it is best rendered "to be chosen, appointed, or destined." Jewish believers were chosen because they were predestined. But this predestination is not a matter of whim or caprice on God's part; it is **according to the plan** (*prothesin*, "purpose"; cf. Rom. 8:28; 9:11; Eph. 3:11) of God, **who works out everything in conformity with the purpose** (*boulēn*, "counsel or deliberation") **of His will** (*thelēmatos*; cf. 1:5, 9). The combination of these words—*prothesin, boulēn, thelēma-tos*—gives a forceful emphasis of God's sovereignty for including the Jewish believers in the church, which is headed up by Christ. The purpose of God's choice of the Jewish believers is that they **might be for the praise of His glory,** which parallels verse 6. The words "for the praise of His glory" serve as a refrain used after a description of the work of each Person of the Trinity (cf. vv. 6, 14). The relative clause, **who were the first to hope in Christ,** further substantiates that verses 11-12 refer to Jewish believers as opposed to Gentile believers because the Jews did precede the Gentiles chronologically in the faith (Acts 1:8; 13:46; 28:25-28; Rom. 1:16 [see comments there]; 2:9-10).

Christ has set the sinner free from his sin and has revealed His will that all things will be headed up in Christ at the end of the ages, including the Jewish believers who first trusted in Him.

c. God's seal with the Spirit (1:13-14)

God's spiritual blessings for believers are based not only on the sovereign election of the Father (vv. 3-6) and the redemptive work of the Son (vv. 7-12), but also on the seal of the Holy Spirit.

1:13-14a. And you also refers to the Gentiles in contrast with the Jews (cf. comments on vv. 11-12). **When they heard the Word of truth** (cf. Col. 1:5; 2 Tim. 2:15; James 1:18) which is further described as **the gospel of your salvation,** and **believed,** they **were** sealed with **the promised Holy Spirit.** The KJV says that the sealing occurs "after" the hearing and believing, thus connoting a second work of grace. This is wrong, for believers are sealed at the moment they hear and believe.

The last part of verse 13 is literally, "They were sealed in Him [Christ] with the Holy Spirit of promise." The word "seal" indicates security (Matt. 27:66; Eph. 4:30), authentication and approval (John 6:27), certification of genuineness (John 3:33), and identification of ownership (2 Cor. 1:22; Rev. 7:2; 9:4). God is the One who seals, Christ is the sphere in which the **seal** is done, and the Holy Spirit is the instrument of the seal. "The promised Holy Spirit" refers to Christ's promise to His disciples that He would send the Spirit (Luke 24:49; John 14:16; 15:26; 16:13; Acts 1:5).

The Holy Spirit who seals **is a deposit guaranteeing our inheritance.** The "deposit" is more than a pledge which could be returned; it is a down payment with a guarantee of more to come (cf. "the firstfruits of the Spirit," Rom. 8:23). "A deposit guaranteeing"

translates the Greek *arrabōn* (used elsewhere in the NT only in 2 Cor. 1:22; 5:5). It guarantees believers' "inheritance" of salvation and heaven (cf. 1 Peter 1:4). (See comments on "inheritance" in Eph. 1:18.) In essence, the "deposit" of the Holy Spirit is a little bit of heaven in believers' lives with a guarantee of much more yet to come.

1:14b. The believer is sealed with the Holy Spirit **until the redemption** (*apolytrōsin;* see the chart "New Testament Words for Redemption" at Mark 10:45) **of those who are God's possession.** This redemption is not release from the guilt of sin; that was spoken of in Ephesians 1:7 and the believer is already "God's possession." Instead, this is the believer's ultimate, final release from the presence of sin (cf. Rom. 8:23b; Phil. 3:20-21). The Greek word for "possession" (*peripoiēsis*) is also used in 1 Thessalonians 5:9; 2 Thessalonians 2:14; Hebrews 10:39 (see comments there); and 1 Peter 2:9. Again the doxological refrain, **to the praise of His glory,** is repeated here as it was after the description of the work of the Father (Eph. 1:6) and of the Son (v. 12).

C. Prayer for wisdom and revelation (1:15-23)

1. COMMENDATION (1:15)

1:15. Because of **(For this reason)** the believers' acquisition of every spiritual blessing—including election, predestination, adoption, grace, redemption, forgiveness, wisdom, understanding, knowledge of the mystery of His will, the sealing of the Holy Spirit, and inheritance—Paul now prayed that his readers might know God personally and intimately. Verses 15-23 are one sentence in the Greek, as are verses 3-14.

Paul **heard** of the Ephesians' **faith** in Christ, their vertical relationship, **and** their **love for all the saints,** their horizontal relationship (cf. Col. 1:4; 2 Thes. 1:3). A proper relationship with God should lead to a proper relationship with other Christians. Interestingly Paul wrote about "love with faith" in Ephesians 6:23.

2. SUPPLICATION (1:16-23)

a. The request for wisdom and revelation (1:16-18a)

1:16. Because of the Ephesians' faith

and love, Paul continued to give **thanks for** them (cf. Rom. 1:8; 1 Cor. 1:4; Phil. 1:3; Col. 1:3; 1 Thes. 1:2; 2 Thes. 1:3) and to make requests for them (cf. Phil. 1:4; Col. 1:9; 1 Thes. 1:3).

1:17. The NIV begins a new sentence here, but this verse is actually a continuation of verse 16. Paul addressed his request to **the God of our Lord Jesus Christ** (cf. v. 3), **the glorious Father,** that is, the Father to whom all glory belongs (cf. "the God of glory" in Acts 7:2 and "the Lord of glory" in 1 Cor. 2:8). The content of Paul's request is that God **may give you the Spirit of wisdom and revelation.** Though the NIV translators interpret "Spirit" (*pneuma*) as referring to the Holy Spirit, it is better to see it as disposition or attitude because of the two genitives following it ("of wisdom and [of] revelation"; cf. "a gentle spirit" in 1 Cor. 4:21). On the other hand one cannot obtain a spirit or attitude of wisdom and revelation apart from the Holy Spirit. As Isaiah wrote, "The Spirit of the Lord will rest on Him [Messiah]— the Spirit of wisdom and of understanding, the Spirit of counsel and of power, the Spirit of knowledge and of the fear of the Lord" (Isa. 11:2). "Wisdom" (*sophia*; cf. Eph. 1:8; 3:10) gives insight into the true nature of things, and "revelation" is the unveiling of the object discussed, namely, God Himself. The purpose in having this wisdom and revelation is that **you may know Him,** God, better. The Greek is the phrase, "in knowing of Him." This knowing (*epignōsei*) refers not to abstract knowledge of God or objective facts about Him, but knowing Him personally and intimately (cf. "knowledge," *epignōseōs*, in 4:13). It includes an intimate awareness of God's character and will. Philosophy says, "Know thyself," whereas Christianity says, "Know God through Jesus Christ."

1:18a. The NEB, NASB, and NIV state another request: **I pray also that the eyes of your heart may be enlightened.** However, this is not a new sentence in Greek. It seems to be parenthetical, as in the KJV, ASV, and RSV. In other words, Paul had prayed (v. 17) that they might have true spiritual insight into God, and then he included the phrase, "having the eyes of your heart enlightened" (RSV). Paul's request for them to know God was within proper bounds because their

hearts had *been* enlightened (the Gr. perf. tense indicates past action with continuing results), as discussed in verses 3-14, especially 7-9. In the Bible the "heart" is the center of one's personality.

b. The reason for wisdom and revelation (1:18b-23)

Having prayed (vv. 16-17) that they might know God personally, Paul now gave the reason: "that you may know" three facts, which are spelled out in verses 18b-23 (the first is in v. 18b, the second in v. 18c, and the third in vv. 19-23). The word "know" (*eidenai*, v. 18) is factual knowledge—much as a general needs to know the facts about his equipment and men before he goes to battle.

1:18b. The first fact to be ascertained pertains to the past. A believer's present **hope** has its source in the past when he was **called** (cf. Rom. 1:6; 8:30; Eph. 4:1, 4; 2 Tim. 1:9) to salvation. "Hope" in Scripture is the absolute certainty of a believer's victory in God (cf. Rom. 8:23-24; Eph. 4:4; Col. 1:5; 1 Thes. 1:3; 1 Peter 3:15).

1:18c. The second fact Paul wanted his readers to know refers to the future: **the riches of His glorious inheritance in the saints.** At the time of the resurrection of believers ("saints" are those set apart by God to God; cf. v. 1) God will inherit those whom He has purchased at a great price according to the riches of His grace (v. 7). This is the second of six times in Ephesians in which Paul referred to "riches" (1:7, 18; 2:4, 7; 3:8, 16). In 1:14 Paul wrote that the Christians' "inheritance" is their final redemption from the presence of sin. Here in verse 18 he wrote about God's inheritance, the saints themselves! Because of the "glorious grace" (v. 6) of "the glorious Father" (v. 17), He will receive "His glorious inheritance" (v. 18).

1:19-23. The third fact Paul wanted believers to know pertains to the present time: **His incomparably great power for us who believe.** The word "power" (*dynamis*; cf. 3:20) means a spiritually dynamic and living force. This power of God is directed toward believers. Paul then used three additional words to describe God's power. It is according to **the working** (*energeian*, "energetic power," from which comes the Eng.

"energy") of the might (*kratous*, "power that overcomes resistance," as in Christ's miracles; this word is used only of God, never of believers) of God's inherent **strength** (*ischyos*) **which He** provides (cf. 6:10; 1 Peter 4:11). This magnificent accumulation of words for power underscores the magnitude of God's "great power" available to Christians.

Then Paul mentioned three manifestations of God's power which are seen in Christ (Eph. 1:20-23). First, this energetic power was **exerted** (*energēken*) **in Christ when God raised Him from the dead and seated Him at His right hand in the heavenly realms.** God's energetic power which resurrected and exalted Christ in the past (cf. Rom. 8:34; Eph. 2:6; Col. 3:1; Heb. 1:3; 8:1; 12:2; 1 Peter 3:22) is the same power available to believers in the present (cf. Phil. 3:10). What an amazing source of spiritual vitality, power, and strength for living the Christian life! (cf. Col. 1:11) Christ's Ascension to the right hand of God involves His being exalted **above** every order of authority (cf. Col. 1:16), human and superhuman (cf. Phil. 2:8-11), whether present (**in the present Age**) or future (**the Age to come**; cf. 1 Cor. 15:23-28). The words **rule and authority, power and dominion** may refer primarily to angelic beings (cf. Rom. 8:38; Eph. 3:10; 6:12; Col. 1:16; 2:15; Titus 3:1).

A second manifestation of God's power in Christ is seen in His placing **all things under** Christ's **feet.** Whereas Adam lost his headship over Creation when he sinned, Christ was made Head over all Creation (cf. Eph. 1:10). This will be fully realized in the future (Ps. 8:6; 1 Cor. 15:27; Heb. 2:6-8).

The third manifestation of God's power in Christ is His appointment of Christ as **Head over . . . the church.** Though the final manifestation of Christ's headship over all Creation will be in the future, He is now Head over the fellowship of believers. He is also called the church's "Head" in Ephesians 4:15; 5:23; and Colossians 1:18. Though the church is implied in Ephesians 1:10, it is specifically mentioned for the first time in Ephesians in verse 22b. The church is **His body** (v. 23; cf. 4:4, 15-16; Col. 1:18). His body, the universal church consisting of all believers, is **the fullness of Him who fills everything in every way.** The

meaning of this description of His body is difficult to determine. The verb "fills" can be taken passively, meaning that Christ, the Head of the body, *is filled by* the church. That is, as the church grows it completes Christ. However, it is better to understand the word "fills" as in the Greek middle voice: Christ, the Head of the body, *fills (for Himself)* the church with blessings. The verse could then be rendered, "which is His body, which is being filled by the One who fills all things with all things (blessings)." This interpretation is preferred for these reasons: (1) Nowhere else does the New Testament state that Christ finds fullness from the church. (2) This view fits the context well because the Persons of the Godhead are completing the actions (cf. Eph. 1:10). (3) This view correlates well with 4:10-11 which speaks of Christ giving all things ("the whole universe" is lit., "all things"), namely, gifted people to the church.

This ends Paul's prayer. After demonstrating that believers have all spiritual blessings (1:3-14), Paul prayed that believers would come to know God intimately (v. 17) in order that they might know three facts: (1) the *past* call of salvation that produced hope (v. 18), (2) the *future* inheritance that God has in His saints (v. 18), and (3) the *present* power of God that is available to believers, which (a) was manifested in the past in Christ's resurrection and Ascension, (b) will be manifested in the future in Christ's headship over Creation, and (c) is presently manifested in Christ's headship over the church.

D. New position individually (2:1-10)

In chapter 1 Paul discussed God's eternal plan in choosing those who are predestined to sonship and the fact that all believers on earth and in heaven will be brought together under Christ the Head of the church. Chapters 2–3 explain the execution of this eternal plan by showing how God makes sinners saints and then places them into the church, Christ's body. In 2:1-10 Paul discussed how sinners who deserve nothing but God's wrath can become trophies of His grace.

1. THE OLD CONDITION: DEAD TO GOD (2:1-3)

At the outset it should be noted that

the grammatical subject of this long sentence (vv. 1-7) in Greek is "God" (v. 4) and the three main verbs are "made . . . alive with" (v. 5), "raised . . . up with" (v. 6), and "seated . . . with" (v. 6). The object of each of these verbs is "us," that is, believers (vv. 5-6). Thus the main assertion in verses 1-7 is that God has made believers alive, raised them up, and seated them with Christ. All the other clauses in these verses are subordinate to this main assertion. This is not really clear in the NIV which has included three additional verbs (one in v. 1 and two in v. 3) as well as the three, already mentioned, in verses 5-6.

Verses 1-3 depict the condition of unbelievers before God transformed them.

a. The condition described (2:1)

2:1. Unregenerate persons are **dead in . . . transgressions** (cf. v. 5) **and sins** (Col. 2:13). This death is spiritual, not physical, for unsaved people are very much alive physically. Death signifies absence of communication with the living. One who is dead spiritually has no communication with God; he is separated from God. The phrase "in your transgressions and sins" shows the sphere of the death, suggesting that sin has killed people (Rom. 5:12; 7:10; Col. 2:13) and they remain in that spiritually dead state. "Transgressions" (*paraptōmasin*, "false steps"; cf. Eph. 1:7; 2:5) and "sins" (*hamartiais,* "acts of missing the mark"), though slightly different in their root meanings, are basically synonymous. Both suggest deliberate acts against God and His righteousness and thus failure to live as one should. The plural of these two nouns signifies people's repetitious involvement in sin and hence their state of unregeneration.

b. The condition delineated (2:2-3)

2:2-3. Mankind's unregenerate condition is further delineated in three ways: (1) The unregenerate follow **the ways of this world.** Unbelievers follow the lifestyles of other unbelievers; they experience the world's peer pressure. "This world" (*kosmos*) is the satanically organized system that hates and opposes all that is godly (cf. John 15:18, 23).

(2) The unsaved follow **the ruler of the kingdom of the air,** that is, Satan.

"The whole world is under the control of the evil one" (1 John 5:19), also called "the god of this Age" (2 Cor. 4:4). In the middle of the Tribulation he will be cast down to the earth, no longer to rule the world or have access to God's presence (Rev. 12:9). The unsaved are now in the clutches of this "ruler" and follow in his opposition to God.

(3) The additional description, **the spirit who is now at work in those who are disobedient,** may be a further elaboration of the distant antecedent, "ways of this world," but this seems too remote. Some (e.g., NIV) suggest that it refers to "the ruler," meaning that Satan personally works in sons of disobedience. However, it seems that "the spirit" is the same as "the kingdom (*exousias*, lit. 'authority') of the air." This is the nearest antecedent and makes sense grammatically. This "spirit" then refers to the impersonal force or atmosphere, which is controlled and directed by Satan (1 John 5:19). This spirit is presently "at work" (*energountos*) in unbelievers. "In those who are disobedient" is literally, "in the sons of disobedience." The word for sons (*huiois*) has the idea of a distinctive characteristic. "A son of disobedience" is one who is a distinctly disobedient person. The Greek word translated "disobedience" and "disobedient" is used several times in the New Testament (Rom. 11:30, 32; Eph. 2:2; 5:6; Heb. 4:6, 11). It suggests conscious and active rebellion and opposition against God.

However, the unconverted not only are under the pressure of the world system and Satan's control but they also enjoy it. **All of us also lived among them at one time** is Paul's reminder to his Gentile readers that the Jews ("all of us") also joined in this disobedience. The word "lived" (*anestraphēmen;* "conducted themselves") differs from "used to live" (*periepatēsate*) in Ephesians 2:2. The conduct of the unsaved is in the sphere of **the cravings** of their **sinful nature,** in which they follow the **desires and the thoughts** of the flesh. "Sinful nature" translates "the flesh" (*sarkos*), which is unregenerated nature. This nature can manifest itself in a respectable form as well as in disreputable pursuits. The "thoughts" (*dianoiōn,* here pl., but usually sing.) suggest that even unbelievers' reasoning processes (or calculations formed by a thinking mind) are perverted. Such false reasoning directs their wills and acts (cf. Rom. 1:21).

Like the rest, we (i.e., both Jews and Gentiles) are **by nature** (naturally and innately) the **objects** (lit. "children") **of wrath.** *Tekna,* the word for "children," suggests a close relationship to one's parents (in contrast with *huioi,* "sons," which speaks of distinctive characteristics). Unbelievers have a close relationship, not with God, but with His wrath! Disobedience and unbelief lead to the wrath of God (Rom. 1:18–2:29; John 3:36).

Ephesians 2:1-3 presents a hopeless picture of an unregenerate person who deserves nothing but God's wrath.

2. THE NEW POSITION: ALIVE IN GOD (2:4-10)

The wrath of God, however, is not the entire story. Its dark background contrasts with the glorious exhibition of God's grace toward the unregenerate. Verses 4-10 set forth the grace of God which works on some unbelievers and gives them life (vv. 4-5), raises them (v. 6a), and seats them in heavenly realms with Christ (vv. 6b-10).

a. God made them alive (2:4-5)

2:4-5. The conjunction **but** introduces God's actions toward sinners, in contrast with their plight in verses 1-3. In the Greek text **God** immediately follows "but," thus placing it in an emphatic position. "God" is the subject of the whole passage. Great differences are suggested by the words "But God"! He is described as **rich in mercy.** (Cf. the "riches" of God's grace [1:7; 2:7], of God's glorious inheritance [1:18], of Christ [3:8], and of His glory [3:16].) In the Septuagint "mercy" (*eleos*) translates the Hebrew *ḥesed* ("loyal love"). In the New Testament *eleos* means "undeserved kindness" toward sinners. Thus God, who is rich in exhibiting this undeserved kindness, acts on behalf of sinners **because of His great love for us.** The noun for "love" (*agapē*) comes from the verb *agapaō* that means "to seek the highest good in the one loved." Since sinners are spiritually dead toward God, they have nothing to commend them to God. This is why Paul described this love as being "great."

God's love has done three things: (a) **made us alive with Christ,** (b) "raised us up with Christ" (2:6), and (c) "seated us

with Him in the heavenly realms in Christ Jesus" (v. 6). An unbeliever, spiritually dead, is "made . . . alive" by God "with (in association with) Christ" (cf. Col. 2:13). The "us" includes both Jews and Gentiles (cf. "us" in Eph. 2:3-4). The only way a spiritually dead person can communicate with God is to be made alive, and that must be done by the One who is Himself alive. He is the living God, "who gives life to the dead" (Rom. 4:17).

God is fully aware of the unbelievers' state. It was clearly described in Ephesians 2:1-3 and is repeated here: **even when we were dead in transgressions** (cf. v. 1). This act of God in making the unregenerate alive is an act of grace: **it is by grace you have been saved.** Paul elaborated on this last statement, which is actually parenthetical, in verse 8. The verb "have been saved" is in the perfect tense which expresses the present permanent state as a result of a past action. Because believers have been "made alive" spiritually with Christ, they have been and are saved.

b. God raised them (2:6a)

2:6a. Besides being made alive, former unbelievers also have been **raised . . . up with Christ.** This speaks of their being positionally resurrected. Christ's post-resurrection state was new, powerful, and unique. So too Christians, in whom Christ dwells, have a new, powerful, and unique life and position. This new life, power, and position demand that believers have a new set of values, as Paul stated in his companion letter to the Colossian believers: "Since, then, you have been raised with Christ, set your heart on things above, where Christ is seated at the right hand of God. Set your minds on things above, not on earthly things" (Col. 3:1-2).

c. God seated them (2:6b-10)

2:6b. Not only has God made alive and raised with Christ many who had been unbelievers, but He has also **seated** them **with Christ in the heavenly realms** (cf. 1:3, 20; 2:6; 3:10; 6:12) **in Christ Jesus.** Believers are positioned spiritually in heaven, where Christ is. They are no longer mere earthlings; their citizenship is in heaven (Phil. 3:20). He is the exalted Son of God, and they are exalted sons and daughters of God. These actions of

God toward unbelievers are similar to what God did for Christ: "He raised Him from the dead and seated Him at His right hand in the heavenly realms" (Eph. 1:20). Whereas Christ had died physically (1:20), unbelievers were dead spiritually (2:1-3). While Christ was raised physically (1:20), unbelievers are made alive and raised with Christ spiritually (2:5-6). Christ is seated in the heavenly realms physically (in His resurrected, ascended body; 1:20), but believers are seated with Christ in the heavenly realms spiritually (2:6). This divine power that can make an unbeliever have life, be raised, and exalted with Christ is the same power that presently operates in believers.

2:7. In the future eternal state, God will **show** all His Creation **the incomparable riches of His grace.** "Show" is *endeixētai,* which means "display or demonstrate" (cf. Rom. 2:15; 9:17, 22; 2 Cor. 8:24; Titus 2:10; 3:2). This display will be seen in His redeemed ones. The "riches of His grace" has been mentioned in connection with believers' redemption which brought them forgiveness of sins (Eph. 1:7). These "riches of His grace" are **expressed in His kindness to us in Christ Jesus.** This refers to salvation. The word "kindness" (*chrēstotēti*) basically means what is "appropriate or suitable." (The word is also used in Rom. 2:4; 3:12 ["good"]; 11:22; 2 Cor. 6:6; Gal. 5:22; Col. 3:2; Titus 3:4.) The appropriate expression of God's love to those who are spiritually dead is to give them life—this is "the incomparable riches of His grace, expressed in His kindness."

2:8-9. These verses explain "the incomparable riches of His grace" (v. 7), expanding the parenthetical statement in verse 5, **It is by grace you have been saved,** and adding that the means of this salvation is **through faith.** Hence the basis is grace and the means is faith alone (cf. Rom. 3:22, 25; Gal. 2:16; 1 Peter 1:5). Faith is not a "work." It does not merit salvation; it is only the means by which one accepts God's free salvation.

Paul elaborated, **And this is not from yourselves, it is the gift of God.** Much debate has centered around the demonstrative pronoun "this" (*touto*). Though some think it refers back to "grace" and others to "faith," neither of these suggestions is really valid because the demonstrative pronoun is neuter

whereas "grace" and "faith" are feminine. Also, to refer back to either of these words specifically seems to be redundant. Rather the neuter *touto,* as is common, refers to the preceding phrase or clause. (In Eph. 1:15 and 3:1 *touto,* "this," refers back to the preceding section.) Thus it refers back to the *concept* of salvation (2:4-8a), whose basis is grace and means is faith. This salvation does not have its source in man (it is "not from yourselves"), but rather, its source is God's grace for "it is the gift of God."

Verse 9 reinforces this by showing that the means is **not by works** since its basis is grace (Rom. 3:20, 28; 4:1-5; 11:6; Gal. 2:16; 2 Tim. 1:9; Titus 3:5), and its means is faith (Rom. 4:5). Therefore since no person can bring salvation to himself by his own efforts, **no one can boast** (cf. Rom. 3:27; 1 Cor. 1:29). Their boasting can only be in the Lord (1 Cor. 1:31).

2:10. This verse, beginning with **For,** tells why this salvation is not from man or by his works. The reason is that salvation is **God's workmanship.** The word "workmanship" (*poiēma*), used only here and in Romans 1:20 (where the NIV renders it "what has been made") denotes a work of art or a masterpiece. It differs from human "works" (*ergōn*) in Ephesians 2:9. Believers are God's workmanship because they have been **created** (a work only God can do) **in Christ Jesus** (cf. "in Christ Jesus" in vv. 6-7). The purpose of this creation is that believers will **do good works.** God's workmanship is not achieved by good works, but it is to result in good works (cf. Titus 2:14; 3:8).

In the clause, **which God prepared in advance for us to do,** the word "which" refers back to the "works" in the previous clause. "For us to do" is literally "in order that we might walk in them." The purpose of these prepared-in-advance works is not "to work in them" but "to walk in them." In other words, God has prepared a path of good works for believers which He will perform in and through them as they walk by faith. This does not mean doing a work for God; instead, it is God's performing His work in and through believers (cf. Phil. 2:13). This path of good works is discussed by Paul in Ephesians 4–6.

In conclusion, 2:1-10 demonstrates that though people were spiritually dead and deserving only God's wrath, God, in

His marvelous grace, has provided salvation through faith. Believers are God's workmanship in whom and through whom He performs good works.

E. New position corporately (2:11-22)

Individuals who have received God's gracious salvation are not left alone but are brought into union with other believers. In 2:11-22 Paul developed this concept of the corporate unity of saved Jews and Gentiles in the church, Christ's body (cf. 1:22-23).

1. STATEMENT OF THE UNION (2:11-13)

a. Past disunion (2:11-12)

2:11. Having completed his discussion of believers as God's workmanship (vv. 1-10), Paul began this section with the strongest inferential particle (dio, **therefore**) to alert the Ephesians to the unenviable position of having no relationship with God. Paul commanded them to **remember that formerly,** before their conversions, they were **Gentiles by birth and called "uncircumcised"** by Jews. Jews, being circumcised physically (**in the body**) disparaged all non-Jews by calling them the "uncircumcised." This physical difference between Jews and Gentiles affected every area of their lives. A great social and spiritual boundary existed between them.

2:12. The Gentiles' lack of the external sign of circumcision also meant that they lacked five privileges that God had given the nation Israel. First, they **were separate from** (lit., "without") **Christ** not only personally (true also of many Jews) but also in that they had no national hope of the Messiah.

Second, they were **excluded from citizenship in Israel.** They did not belong to the theocratic state of Israel (cf. Rom. 9:4). The word "excluded" is apēllotriōmenoi, "alienated" or "estranged." It is used only two other times (Eph. 4:18; Col. 1:21). Though some Gentiles were admitted into Judaism as proselytes, Gentiles as a whole were excluded; they were thus alienated.

Third, they were **foreigners to the covenants of the promise** (cf. Eph. 3:6). They were deprived of direct participation in God's covenants and thus had no hope of future glory and blessing as Israel did. Israel's "covenants" include the Abrahamic (Gen. 12:1-3; 15:18-21;

17:1-8), the Palestinian (Deut. 28-30), the Davidic (2 Sam. 7:16; Ps. 89:1-4), and the New (Jer. 31:31-34; Ezek. 36:24-30). These covenants—all pointing to "the promise" of the Messiah and of blessings through Him—assured Israel of a national existence, a land, a King, and spiritual blessings.

Fourth, the Gentiles were **without hope.** Unlike Israel they had no expectation of a personal Messiah-Deliverer and the Messianic Age.

Fifth, they were **without God** (atheoi, "apart from God") **in the world.** The Gentiles were in a desperate situation. They had no meaning, hope, purpose, or direction in life.

b. Present union (2:13)

2:13. But now in Christ Jesus marks the contrast both temporally ("formerly" [v. 11] as opposed to "now") and positionally ("separate from Christ" [v. 12] as opposed to "in Christ Jesus"). The Gentiles **who once were far away** (cf. v. 17) from both God and the Jews (v. 12) **have been brought near through the blood of Christ** (cf. 1:7). They have come near to God and to the Jews by means of Christ's sacrificial death. Sin separates people from God and only Christ's atonement can remove that sin barrier.

2. EXPLANATION OF THE UNION (2:14-18)

Having stated the fact of the union of Gentiles and Jews (v. 13), Paul then explained what this involves. He discussed two things in this section: the establishment of peace between Gentile and Jewish believers, and the peace between God and the people who believe in Him.

a. Assertion of peace (2:14-16)

2:14. Christ **Himself is** the **peace** between Jewish and Gentile believers, having **made the two** groups **one and** having **destroyed the barrier, the dividing wall of hostility.** "Peace" is mentioned four times in three verses (vv. 14-15, 17 [twice]). Various interpretations have been given regarding this "dividing wall," which is mentioned only here in the New Testament. Some have thought it refers to the wall in the Jerusalem temple precincts that separated the Court of the Gentiles from the Court of the Jews. But this view is invalid because Paul makes no reference to the temple in Jerusalem and because this wall was still standing when Paul wrote this epistle. Some think it referred to the curtain in the Jerusalem temple between the holy place and the holy of holies. But that was a curtain, not a wall. Others have suggested it meant the "fence" around the Law mentioned by some Rabbis. But that referred more to the protection of the Law than to the hostility mentioned in this context. The structure of the Greek words suggests that the dividing wall describes not a physical barrier, but the spiritual enmity between Jews and Gentiles, which separated them. Since Christ destroyed this enmity (cf. v. 16), Jewish and Gentile believers should have no hostility.

2:15-16. Paul now described how and why this enmity came to an end. The animosity between believing Jews and Gentiles ceased because by Christ's death (**in His flesh** suggests His actual physical death; cf. Col. 1:22) He rendered **the Law** "inoperative" (*katargēsas*) in believers' lives. Jews and Gentiles were enemies because the former sought to keep the Law **with its commandments and regulations** (cf. Col. 2:14, 21-23), whereas Gentiles were unconcerned about them. This difference was like a barrier between them. But now that the Law is inoperative ("Christ is the end of the Law" [Rom. 10:4]), Jewish-Gentile hostility is gone. Some translations (e.g., KJV, NASB) give the idea that the Law was the enemy, but that is wrong; the Law was the cause of the enmity. Christ "destroyed" the barrier (hostility) by making the Law inoperative.

Christ had two purposes in ending the hostility. The first **purpose was to create in Himself one new man out of the two, thus making peace.** The word "new" (*kainon*) means new or fresh in character or quality rather than new in the sense of recent in time (*neos*). This "new man" (Eph. 2:15), or "new humanity," is also called "this one body" (v. 16), the church. In the church, Gentiles do not become Jews, nor do Jews become Gentiles. Instead believing Jews and Gentiles become Christians, a whole new single entity.

Christ's second purpose in destroying the enmity was **to reconcile both** Jewish and Gentile believers to Himself **in . . . one body** (cf. 3:6). This reconciliation was accomplished **through the cross, by which** Christ killed (**put to death**) the enmity between people and God. Though *He* was put to death, He in turn put to death the Jewish-Gentile **hostility.** In 2:14 the reconciliation is between Jewish and Gentile believers, and in verse 16 the reconciliation is between people and God. Reconciliation (removal of enmity) between man and God is mentioned elsewhere by Paul (Rom. 5:10; 2 Cor. 5:18-20; Col. 1:20).

b. Announcement of peace (2:17-18)

2:17-18. Verse 17 begins in Greek with "and" (untranslated in the NIV). This links verse 17 with verse 14. Not only is Christ "our peace" (v. 14), but He also **preached peace.** When did Christ do this? Certainly this refers to the preaching of peace by the apostles rather than Christ Himself because Christ preached almost entirely to Jews (Matt. 10:5-6; 15:24-27). Also the peace that was preached was on the basis of Christ's death rather than during His life on earth. **Peace** is supplied both **to those who were far away** (cf. Eph. 2:13), that is, Gentiles (who were without Christ and alienated from Israel and her covenants, v. 12) and **to those who were near,** namely, Jews (who have "the covenants of the promise," v. 12).

As a result of this message of peace both Jewish and Gentile believers **have access to** God **the Father by one Spirit** (cf. 1 Cor. 12:13). Access can mean "introduction" in the sense that Christ *is* a believer's "introduction" to the Father. But it seems better to understand that Christ *gives* believers access. The Greek word for access (*prosagōgēn*, "approach") is used elsewhere in the New Testament only in Romans 5:2 and Ephesians 3:12. As so often in this book the work of the Trinity is seen. Here believers have access to God the Father through the Holy Spirit because of Christ's death on the cross.

In four ways in 2:14-18 Paul emphasized that the two (Jew and Gentile) have been united: (1) "the two" (*ta amphotera*) are made *"one"* (v. 14), (2) *"one* new man" is created "out of the two" (v. 15), (3) "in this *one* body . . . both" (*tous amphoterous*) are reconciled (v. 16), and (4) "both" (*hoi amphoteroi*) "have access . . . by *one* Spirit" (v. 18). Nothing could be clearer than the fact that this new union replaces enmity.

3. CONSEQUENCE OF THE UNION (2:19-22)

Having stated and explained the union of Jewish and Gentile believers Paul then described the consequence of that union.

a. The fact: a new relationship (2:19)

2:19. **Consequently** (*ara oun*) **you,** that is, Gentile believers, **are no longer foreigners** (*xenoi;* cf. v. 12) **and aliens.** Believing Gentiles become **fellow citizens with God's people and members of God's household.** They become a part of the company of the redeemed of all ages beginning with Adam. However, this does not mean that the church inherits the blessings promised to Israel. There are three reasons for this: (1) In the context Paul was discussing the "one new man" (v. 15), the "one body" (v. 16). This does not mean that Gentiles are incorporated into Israel but that believing Jews and Gentiles are incorporated into one new "humanity." (2) Paul specifically stated that Gentiles are incorporated "with God's people" and are in "God's household" (v. 19); he did not use the word "Israel." If Paul meant that the church became "Israel," he would have named both groups, as he did in verse 11. (3) Paul explained that this new relationship is "built on the foundation of the apostles and prophets with Christ Jesus Himself as the chief Cornerstone" (v. 20). This began on the day of Pentecost, not in the Old Testament. True, Gentile believers become a part of the redeemed of all ages (v. 19). But their being incorporated with Jewish believers into the "one new man" distinctly began when the church came into being at Pentecost.

b. The cause: a new establishment (2:20-22)

Paul described the church as a great building, a holy temple in which God dwells. This figure of God dwelling in a temple comes from the Old Testament. Paul wrote of the building's foundation (v. 20), formation (v. 21), and function (v. 22).

2:20. Paul first described the foundation of the building. The reason Gentile believers are "fellow citizens" (v. 19) is that they are **built on the foundation of the apostles and prophets.** The "prophets" are of the New Testament era, not the Old Testament. "Prophets" follows the word "apostles" here and in 3:5 and 4:11. These men received the revelation of the mystery of the church in the present Age, which had been hidden in days past, that is, in Old Testament times (3:5).

The words "apostles and prophets" could modify "the foundation." This could mean (a) that the foundation was built by them, or (b) that the foundation came from them, or (c) that they own a foundation or, as seems best, (d) that they are the foundation. The words could be translated, "the foundation which consists of the apostles and prophets." This makes the best sense when one sees in 4:11 that the apostles and prophets were gifted men given to the church as its "foundation." Furthermore, this fits well in the present context, which states that **Christ Jesus Himself** is **the chief Cornerstone,** that is, He is part of the foundation. In ancient building practices "the chief cornerstone" was carefully placed. It was crucial because the entire building was lined up with it. The church's foundation, that is, the apostles and prophets, needed to be correctly aligned with Christ. All other believers are built on that foundation, measuring their lives with Christ.

2:21. Paul then discussed the formation of the building. **In Christ the whole building is joined together.** The ASV has "each several building" (rather than "the whole building"). But it is preferable to understand the Greek to refer to one whole superstructure, perhaps in several parts. The participle translated "is joined together" is *synarmologoumenē,* used only here and in 4:16. It denotes that the various parts of the building are skillfully fitted to each other, not haphazardly thrown together. This structure **rises to become** (lit., "continually grows [pres. tense] into") **a holy temple in the Lord.** This indicates that the church is a living and growing organism, as new believers are included in this temple's superstructure (cf. 4:15-16; 1 Peter 2:5). Both Jewish and Gentile believers are being "joined together" into this one organism labeled "a holy temple" (cf. "one new man" [Eph. 2:15] and "one body" [v. 16]). The word for temple (*naos*) always refers to the sanctuary within the physical structure in Jerusalem, not to the entire temple area with its open courts (*hieron*).

2:22. Paul now discussed the function of the temple. God places individual believers into the structure; thus it is **being built together**. The goal of this temple is **to become a dwelling in which God lives by His Spirit**. In the Old Testament God's glory was in the temple, which represented His presence with the people. In this Age God dwells in His new temple which is constructed not from inanimate materials but of living believers. The Holy Spirit indwells each individual believer (cf. John 14:17; Rom. 5:5; 8:9, 11; 1 Cor. 2:12; Gal. 3:2; 4:6; 1 John 3:24; 4:13), who is thus a "temple" (1 Cor. 6:19). But the temple in Ephesians 2:21-22 refers to the Holy Spirit's *corporate* "dwelling" (cf. 1 Cor. 3:16; 2 Cor. 6:16), His "temple" composed of *all* Jewish and Gentile believers.

"By His Spirit" is literally, "by the Spirit," as it is translated in Ephesians 3:5.

In conclusion, Paul has shown that though the Gentiles were formerly outside God's household, they are now one "new man" with Jewish believers. This new entity is like a temple that is structured on the apostles and prophets, with Christ being the chief Cornerstone; it is indwelt by God through the agency of the Holy Spirit.

F. Parenthetical expansion of the mystery (3:1-13)

Having discussed the union of Jewish and Gentile believers in the church (2:11-22), Paul was about to offer a prayer on behalf of these believers. But he stopped right in the middle of a sentence (at the end of 3:1) and digressed on the subject of the mystery of Christ. He explained this mystery and his responsibility to dispense it. Then he resumed his prayer, starting with verse 14.

1. THE INTRODUCTION (3:1)

3:1. The words **for this reason** (also used in v. 14) specifically point back to 2:11-22, which dealt with the Jewish and Gentile believers being raised to a new plane. But they also more generally refer back to all the first part of the epistle in which Paul discussed God's grace to the Gentiles. The words **I, Paul, the prisoner of Christ Jesus for the sake of you Gentiles,** refer to Paul's imprisonment in Rome because of his service for Christ (cf. 4:1; 2 Tim. 1:8; Phile. 1, 9), and more particularly because of his ministry as the

apostle to the Gentiles (2 Tim. 1:11-12). Because of his faithfulness to the stewardship God had given him among the Gentiles (Eph. 3:2) bitter Jewish opposition arose against him. This resulted in his being attacked in Jerusalem and put on trial in Caesarea and Rome.

2. THE MYSTERY (3:2-6)

a. The dispensation of God's grace (3:2)

3:2. Having broken off in the middle of a sentence in verse 1, Paul began one new long sentence that ended with verse 13 (one of eight lengthy sentences in Eph.; see comments on 1:3-14). It is a conditional sentence with 3:2 serving as its introduction (**Surely** in v. 2 is lit., "If indeed") and verse 13 as its conclusion. Paul wrote of **the administration of God's grace that was given to** him (v. 2) and concluded by asking them not to be discouraged over his imprisonment in Rome (v. 13). The details of his message and ministry are in verses 3-12. Probably the NIV used "surely" because the wording implies certainty that the Ephesians had heard of his responsibility. Now he spoke of it in greater detail. The word "administration" (*oikonomia*; cf. v. 9) has the sense of stewardship or a trust to be dispensed (in 1 Cor. 9:17 *oikonomia* is trans. "trust" and in Col. 1:25 it is rendered "commission"). Paul was to administer "God's grace" (cf. Eph. 3:7), which was given to him. He elaborated on this in verses 3-6. This grace was given to him to dispense to the Gentiles (v. 1) at Ephesus (**for you**), because he was an apostle to the Gentiles (Gal. 2:7; Eph. 3:8).

b. The revelation of the mystery (3:3-5)

3:3. That is further explains that **the mystery** is the "grace" mentioned in verse 2. That mystery (a truth hitherto unknown) is not defined till verse 6. The mystery's disclosure was given to Paul **by revelation,** which in fact he had **already written briefly** about, not in another epistle, but in this one (in 2:11-22).

3:4. The Ephesian Christians would **be able to understand** his **insight** (*synesin*; cf. Col. 1:9; 2:2) **into the mystery of Christ** (cf. Col. 1:27; 2:2) by **reading** what he had "already written." Paul's next words (Eph. 3:5-6) would further enhance their understanding of it. His "insight" was not his own discovery; it was revealed by God.

3:5. Paul then revealed the time when the mystery was disclosed. The mystery **was not made known to men in other generations as it has . . . been revealed.** This statement has caused some debate among Bible students. The problem hinges on the comparative adverb "as" (*hōs*). Some take this as restrictive (a comparison of degree), which would mean that the mystery was partially revealed in the Old Testament but is now fully revealed in the Church Age. The thought of the verse should be, God has not revealed this mystery in the past *to the extent* He has now. Others see the adverb "as" to be descriptive (a comparison of kind), which means that no revelation of this mystery was given in the Old Testament but that this mystery was revealed for the first time in the New Testament.

The second view is a better interpretation for five reasons: (1) Though the restrictive sense for "as" is more common, the descriptive sense *is* used sometimes (e.g., Peter said that the disciples were not drunk "as" the Jews thought [Acts 2:15]). (In fact, sometimes "as" could be trans. "because," e.g., the second "as" in 2 Tim. 1:3.)

(2) The context supports this view for Paul wrote that this mystery was hidden in the past (Eph. 3:9).

(3) Colossians 1:26, parallel to Ephesians 3:5, does not use the comparative adverb "as," but clearly states that the mystery was "kept hidden for ages . . . but is now" (*nun de*) made manifest to the saints.

(4) The position of the temporal adverb "now" (*nun*) agrees with Colossians 1:26 in marking the contrast between the two Ages. In the past the mystery was not known but "now" it is. This is substantiated by the same temporal adverb (*nun*) in Ephesians 3:10: "The manifold wisdom of God" (which is the mystery) is "now" to be made known to the heavenly hosts. If the heavenly hosts did not know of the mystery in the Old Testament, how would people have found out about it? Since the heavenly hosts learned of the mystery through the church (which did not exist before Pentecost) certainly people in the Old Testament did not know.

(5) "Revealed" means "to uncover or unveil" something that has previously been completely covered or hidden. Therefore it would be wrong to say the mystery was *partially* uncovered in the Old Testament.

Those who hold the first view ("as" is a comparison of degree) argue that passages such as Isaiah 2:1-4 and 61:5-6 indicate that Gentiles received God's blessings along with Israel. However, these passages speak of the Millennium, not of the concept of Gentiles and Jews being in one body, the church.

This mystery was revealed **by the Spirit** (cf. Eph. 2:22), and its recipients were **God's holy apostles and prophets** (cf. 2:20; 4:11). Some have promoted the idea that this revelation was given to Paul, but 3:5 explicitly states that it was given to the apostles and prophets and that Paul was one who was to disseminate it.

c. The constitution of the mystery (3:6)

3:6. Paul now defined the **mystery.** In three compound nouns he stated that the Gentile believers with the Jewish believers **are (a) heirs together** (i.e., "fellow heirs," 2:19, KJV) of God's riches (1:3-14), (b) are **of the same body** (cf. 2:16; *syssōma* occurs only in 3:6 in the NT), **and** (c) are **sharers together in the promise** (the messianic promise; cf. 2:12; Gal. 3:29) **in Christ Jesus.** (See comments on Eph. 2:19 and 3:5 regarding the relationship of the church and **Israel.**)

Thus the mystery is not something mysterious, but is a sacred secret hidden in Ages past but now revealed. This is made possible **through the gospel:** believing Jews and **Gentiles** are in **one** body. The mystery is not that Gentiles would be saved, for the Old Testament gave evidence of that, but rather that believing Jews and Gentiles are joined **together.** That was a revolutionary concept for Jews and Gentiles alike!

3. THE MINISTRY (3:7-12)

Having described the mystery (vv. 2-6), Paul now discussed his ministry of dispensing this mystery to the Gentiles.

a. The placement into the ministry (3:7-8a)

3:7-8a. I became a servant of this gospel (cf. "gospel" in v. 6) denotes Paul's rendering of service (cf. Col. 1:23). The word "servant" (*diakonos*) stresses not the idea of subjection (as does *doulos*, "slave") but the idea of service or serving, as one who is a waiter (John 2:5, 9). This service has its basis in **the gift of God's grace** (cf. Eph. 3:2) **given to** Paul **through the working of His power** (cf. 1:19; Col. 1:29). The Greek more clearly implies that Paul's service was initiated by "the gift of God's grace" and continues by "the working (*energeian*) of His power" (*dynameōs*). Ministering **this grace**—by God's strength, not his own—was Paul's responsibility though he considered himself **less than the least of all God's people.** ("God's people" renders *hagiōn*, "saints"; cf. Eph. 1:1, 15). This denotes Paul's deep humility in view of God's incomparably generous grace.

b. The performance of the ministry (3:8b-9)

3:8b-9. Two infinitives state Paul's functioning in this ministry. First, he was **to preach to the Gentiles the unsearchable riches of Christ.** Second, he was **to make plain to everyone the administration of this mystery.** Though Paul ministered to both Jews and Gentiles (cf. comments on Acts 9:15), he was especially designated as the apostle "to the Gentiles" (Rom. 11:13; Gal. 1:16; 2:7-8).

The Gentiles can know something of the riches of Christ's blessings (cf. "the riches of God's grace" in Eph. 1:7 and 2:7 and the richness of His mercy in 2:4). Yet Christ's fathomless spiritual wealth can never be fully comprehended (*anexichniaston*, lit., "not capable of being traced by footprints"; used only here and in Rom. 11:33). Paul was to disclose publicly *to everyone*, not just the Ephesians (cf. Eph. 3:2) this stewardship of God's sacred secret (vv. 3-4, 6). This secret had been **hidden in God** (cf. v. 5), the Creator of the universe. Even before creating **all things** God had in mind this wonderful truth as part of His eternal plan (cf. 1:4, 11).

c. The purpose of the ministry (3:10-12)

3:10-12. The purpose (*hina*) of Paul's ministry **was that . . . the manifold wisdom** (*sophia*) **of God might be made known to the rulers and authorities in the heavenly realms.** In classical Greek the adjective "manifold" (*polypoikilos*) referred to the beauty of an embroidered pattern or the variety of colors in flowers (cf. *poikilēs*, "in its various forms," in

1 Peter 4:10). The "manifold wisdom of God" does not refer to redemption as such but rather to the new relationship between believing Jews and Gentiles in one body. The medium by which this wisdom is communicated is **the church;** the recipients are the angelic hosts "in the heavenly realms" (cf. Eph. 1:3). These "rulers and authorities" refer to both good and evil angels as seen in 6:12 (cf. 1:21). As the angelic hosts witness the church, they must admit that having Jews and Gentiles in one body is evidence of God's wisdom.

This mystery—that both believing Jews and Gentiles are in one body (3:6)—was revealed to the apostles and prophets (v. 5) and was disseminated by Paul (vv. 7-9). Its **purpose** was that angelic beings might see God's variegated wisdom. This whole plan was in accord with God's **eternal** intent **which He accomplished in Christ Jesus our Lord** (v. 11). This means either that God is now carrying out His eternal purpose, or that He carried it out (accomplished it) in Christ about 2,000 years ago. The latter view is preferable because (a) "accomplished" is in the past tense not the present or perfect tense, and (b) the inclusion of believing Jews and Gentiles in one body was in fact accomplished by Christ's death.

Through faith in Christ Christians have the right of address (**freedom,** *parrēsian*, lit., "courage, boldness"; cf. Heb. 3:6; 4:16; 10:19, 35) and the right of access (**approach,** *prosagōgēn;* cf. Eph. 2:18; Rom. 5:2) to **God with . . . confidence.** Though God's eternal plan was accomplished in Christ nearly two millennia ago, believers can still address God and go to Him freely and confidently.

4. THE INJUNCTION (3:13)

3:13. This verse marks the conclusion of the sentence begun in verse 2. If the Ephesians truly understood "the administration of God's grace that was given to" Paul (v. 2), they should **not . . . be discouraged because of** his **sufferings for** them. His sufferings were for their gain and glory. If Paul had not dispensed to the Gentiles the stewardship of God's grace, then Jews would not have been hostile to him and he would not have been imprisoned. His preaching brought salvation to the Gentiles, but it incurred the wrath of many Jews on him. However, many others became members of the church, Christ's body, and this was their glory.

G. Prayer for strengthened love (3:14-21)

Having stated that positionally the Gentile and Jewish believers are "one new man" (2:15), which is the body of Christ, Paul now prayed that they may be united experientially. He desired that they might genuinely know and experience Christ's love and thus exhibit it toward each other.

1. THE APPROACH TO PRAYER (3:14-15)

3:14-15. Verses 14-19 in the Greek are another of Paul's eight long sentences in Ephesians (see comments on 1:3-14). **For this reason** is an expression that is repeated from verse 1 when Paul was about to pray. He then broke off before finishing the sentence in order to elaborate on the mystery, the body of Christ, and on his ministry of dispensing the mystery. Paul's kneeling in prayer is one of several postures for praying (standing, kneeling, lying prostrate) seen in the Scriptures. The shorter reading, **the Father,** is preferred over the longer one found in the KJV, "the Father of our Lord Jesus Christ." The expression **from whom His whole family** means that all Creation including angels and humans are one family under the fatherhood of God. But this is problematic grammatically for the Greek has no pronoun ("His") before the word "whole." This also has problems theologically. A better translation both grammatically and theologically is "from whom every family" (cf. ASV, NASB, RSV). Paul was not saying that God is the Father of all but rather that He is the Prototype of all fatherhood. "Father" is derived from God, not man. He is the first Father, the only One with "underived" fatherhood. Thus every human family **derives its name,** that is, exists as a family with a father, because of Him. It is to this Father that Paul prayed.

2. THE APPEAL IN PRAYER (3:16-19)

Though the sentence begins in verse 14 and ends in verse 19, Paul's request begins in verse 16. In this prayer he asked for only one thing.

a. Petition stated: to be strengthened in the inner man (3:16-17a)

3:16-17a. The first part of Paul's request is that God, **out of** (*kata,* lit., "according to the standard of") **His glorious riches** (cf. 1:7, 18; 2:4, 7; 3:8) might **strengthen** (*krataiōthēnai,* "be strong to overcome resistance," cf. *kratous* in 1:19 and *kratei* in 6:10) believers **with power** (*dynamis,* dynamic living power; cf. 3:20) **through** the Holy **Spirit in** their **inner being[s]** (lit., "in the inner man," i.e., believers' innermost beings). The result of this is that **through faith** Christ **may dwell in** believers' **hearts,** that is, their whole personalities. "Dwell" (*katoikēsai*) refers not to the beginning of Christ's indwelling at the moment of salvation. Instead it denotes the desire that Christ may, literally, "be at home in," that is, at the very center of or deeply rooted in, believers' lives. They are to let Christ become the dominating factor in their attitudes and conduct.

b. Purpose stated: to comprehend Christ's love and to be filled unto God's fullness (3:17b-19)

3:17b-19. Paul continued his prayer by repeating his request that Christ be the center of believers' lives. He stated this in a mixed metaphor of biological and architectural terminology: **being rooted** (like a plant) **and established** (like a building) **in love.** The participles "being rooted and established" are in the perfect tense, indicating a past action with continuing results. They could be translated "having been rooted and established." The purpose of the request is that they **may have power** (*exischysēte,* "have inherent strength"), **together with all the saints, to grasp how wide and long and high and deep is the love of Christ.** These measurements most likely describe not the thoroughness of comprehension but the immensity of the thing to be comprehended.

Interestingly once again—as in (a) 1:13-14; (b) 1:17; (c) 2:18; (d) 2:22; and (e) 3:4-5—Paul spoke of the Trinity: the Father (v. 14), the Spirit (v. 16), and the Son (v. 17).

The content of this comprehension is **to know** experientially the **love** of Christ **that** supersedes all **knowledge** (cf. Phil. 4:7). The more a Christian knows about

Christ, the more amazed he is at Christ's love for him.

The final purpose is **that you may be filled to the measure of all the fullness of God.** The KJV and RSV translations, "that you may be filled with all the fullness of God," wrongly imply that the whole fullness of God can be contained in a believer's life. But this ignores the Greek preposition *eis* which denotes a goal; this is translated accurately in the NIV: "to the measure." The fullness of the Godhead is only in Christ, and only through Him is a believer made complete (Col. 2:9-10). Though in Christ this divine fullness is ideally a believer's already, Paul prayed that it might be experientially realized in each one (cf. Eph. 4:13). Experiencing God's moral excellence and perfection causes Jewish and Gentile believers to love each other. Positionally they are one in Christ; experientially they are to love each other as one in Him.

3. THE ASCRIPTION OF PRAISE (3:20-21)

3:20-21. Paul closed this prayer with a doxology. He praised God **who is able to do** far **more than** one could **ask or imagine, according to** the standard of **His power** (*dynamin*; cf. v. 16; 1:19) **that is at work** (*energoumenēn*; cf. 1:19) **within us.** No human or angel (cf. 3:10) would ever think that Jews and Gentiles could function together in one body. But with God's power of love in each believer's life, Paul was confident that Jewish and Gentile believers can function and love one another. This is astounding and though it is not naturally possible, God is able to accomplish it. Paul therefore ascribed to God **glory** which is to be manifest **in the church,** where the miracle of love will occur, **and in Christ Jesus,** who made the union of Jewish and Gentile believers possible.

Praise to Him for this accomplishment is to continue throughout eternity (cf. Rom. 11:36; 2 Tim. 4:18). This doxology serves as a fitting conclusion not only to this prayer but also to this book's first three chapters.

II. The Conduct of the Church (chaps. 4–6)

After presenting doctrinal content in the first three chapters, Paul then gave in chapters 4–6 some practical applications of those doctrines. His repeated emphasis

on a believer's "walk" (*peripateō*) is the hallmark of this section. The NIV translates "walk" as "live."

A. Walking in unity (4:1-16)

Having explained the unity of Jewish and Gentile believers, and having prayed for that unity through mutually experiencing Christ's love, Paul now showed how they were to walk in the unity of that body. This is accomplished by gifted people given to the church by Christ so that the body of Christ might grow up in all areas.

1. THE BASIS OF UNITY (4:1-6)

a. Exhortation to unity (4:1-3)

4:1. Paul exhorted them to walk **(live a life) worthy of** their **calling.** The NIV gives the impression that this walk should be on the basis that Paul was **a prisoner for the Lord.** However, the Greek does not connote this. Rather it is, "Therefore (rather than **then**) I, the prisoner of the Lord (as already stated in 3:1), beseech you to walk worthy of your calling." Thus on the basis of what Paul wrote in chapters 1–3 he implored them to walk worthily. The word "worthy" (*axiōs*) means "equal weight"; one's calling and conduct should be in balance. "The calling" refers not only to believers' salvation (cf. Rom. 1:5-6; 1 Cor. 1:9) but also to their union in one body. Therefore a Christian's conduct concerns both his personal life and his responsibility to other believers in the church.

4:2-3. Believers' attitudes are also important. Paul listed three virtues that are to enhance a believer's walk. The first of these is humility. In Greek culture, humility was thought of as a vice, to be practiced only by slaves. But Paul stated that saints should **be completely humble** in their daily walks. This is the opposite of pride. On the other hand Christians should not promote false humility, but should recognize who they are in God's program (cf. John 3:30; Rom. 12:3). This virtue is listed first because of Paul's emphasis on unity (pride promotes disunity; humility promotes unity) and to counteract their past pride, so as to facilitate obedience to and dependence on God. Christ was the supreme example of humility (Phil. 2:6-8).

Second, a believer is to be **gentle** or "meek" (*prautētos*; cf. the adverb of this word in Gal. 6:1; 2 Tim. 2:25 and the noun in Gal. 5:23; Col. 3:12; 1 Peter 3:16). This is the opposite of self-assertion, rudeness, and harshness. It suggests having one's emotions under control. But it does not suggest weakness. It is the mean between one who is angry all the time and one who is never angry. One who is controlled by God is angry at the right time but never angry at the wrong time. Moses was known as the meekest of all men (Num. 12:3, KJV). Yet he got angry when Israel sinned against God (Ex. 32). Christ was meek and humble in heart (Matt. 11:29). Yet He became angry because some Jews were using the temple as a place for thieves (Matt. 21:12-13).

Third, believers should exhibit patience (*makrothymias*). Patience is the spirit which never gives up for it endures to the end even in times of adversity (James 5:10). It is the self-restraint which does not hastily retaliate a wrong (cf. Gal. 5:22; Col. 1:11; 3:12; 2 Tim. 4:2).

Attitudes of humility, gentleness, and patience foster unity among Christians. Having stated these three virtues, Paul then stated the manner in which they are to be carried out in one's conduct: **bearing with one another in love** and making **every effort** (the Gr. has a participle, "making every diligent effort") **to keep the unity of the Spirit through the bond of peace.** Christians are not to make unity but to keep or guard what God made in creating the "one new man" (Eph. 2:15-16). They are to keep this unity "through the bond" which consists of "peace." Concern for peace will mean that Christians will lovingly tolerate each other, even when they have differences.

b. Elements of unity (4:4-6)

4:4. Without a conjunction Paul listed the seven elements of unity centered on the three Persons of the Trinity. These provide the basis for the spirit of unity that should exist in the body of believers. **One body** refers to the universal church, all believers (1:23; 2:16; 3:6). **One Spirit** is the Holy Spirit who indwells the church (2:22). The words, **just as you were called to one hope when you were called,** indicate that all believers have a common hope regarding their future with God (cf. 1 Peter 1:3; 3:15), a confidence that began at the time

they were "called" to salvation (Eph. 1:4, 18; 2:7; 4:1).

4:5. One Lord (cf. Rom. 10:12) refers to Christ, the Head of the church (Eph. 1:22-23; Col. 1:18). **One faith** speaks, most likely, not of objective faith, that is, the body of truth believed by Christians (as in Acts 6:7; 1 Tim. 3:9; 4:1, 6; Jude 3) but subjective faith which is exercised by all Christians in Christ their Lord (cf. Col. 2:7). **One baptism** may refer to water baptism, the outward symbol of the inward reality, or it may refer to a believer's identification with Christ and His death (Rom. 6:1-11; Gal. 3:27). It seems unlikely that this refers to the latter, Spirit baptism, because it is in the triad of elements that pertain to Christ, the second Person of the Trinity. Also nothing in the broader context (Eph. 4:1-16) suggests that this is the Spirit's baptism. If it refers to water baptism, then the idea is that by this single act believers demonstrate their spiritual unity.

4:6. One God and Father of all who is over all and through all and in all refers to God the Father and His relationship to all believers. The fourfold use of "all" refers to "all believers," not "all mankind." Certainly these characteristics are not common to all people. God is the Father "of" all who believe; they are His children (John 1:12; Gal. 3:26). And He is "over" all them as their Sovereign. He lives "through" them and manifests Himself "in" them.

Two observations should be noted about this list of seven unifying elements (Eph. 4:4-6). First, the Trinity is an integral part of the list. The one body of believers is vitalized by one *Spirit,* so all believers have one hope. That body is united to its one *Lord* (Christ) by each member's one act of faith, and its identity with Him is depicted by one baptism. One *God,* the Father, is supreme over all, operative through all, and resides in all. All seven components are united in the Trinity.

Second, the order in the listing of the three Persons of the Trinity is interesting. Paul began with the Holy Spirit rather than with the Father. The reason for this is that in the preceding verses he was discussing "the unity of the Spirit" (v. 3) and in verses 7-13 he discussed the gifts of the Spirit. The same order of Trinity Members is given in 1 Corinthians 12:4-6, where Paul also discussed the gifts of the Spirit.

2. THE PRESERVATION OF UNITY (4:7-16)

After discussing the basis of unity (vv. 1-6), Paul now analyzed the means of preserving that unity (cf. "keep the unity," v. 3) of the body by means of the various gifts.

a. The distribution of the gifts (4:7-11)

4:7-8. Previously Paul discussed the unity of the entire church (vv. 1-6). Now he discussed the diversity within the church (cf. unity in 1 Cor. 12:12-13, and diversity in 1 Cor. 12:4-11, 14-20). From God **each** believer receives **grace** or enablement (cf. Eph. 3:2, 7-8) **as Christ apportioned it** (lit., "according to the measure [*metron*, also used in 4:13, 16]; of the gift of Christ," i.e., the gift He is pleased to give). Each believer is to function in Christ's body by God's enablement, proportionate to the gift (spiritual ability) bestowed on him, no more and no less. This means that a variety of gifts will be exercised, as seen in verse 11; Romans 12:4-6; and 1 Corinthians 12:4-6. Furthermore, since each believer receives "grace," clergy and laity—to use a common present-day distinction—are on the same level in exercising their gifts.

Ephesians 4:8 includes a quotation from the Old Testament, which confirms God's giving of gifts. Most think it quotes Psalm 68:18 with five minor and two major changes. The two major variations are the change from the second to the third person, and the change of direction from having received gifts from men to the giving of **gifts to men.** However, it is better to think that Paul was not quoting one particular verse of the psalm but rather that he was summarizing all of Psalm 68, which has many words similar to those in Psalm 68:18. The essence of the psalm is that a military victor has the right to give gifts to those who are identified with him. Christ, having captivated sinful people by redeeming them, is Victor and gives them as gifts to the church. Whereas Romans 12 and 1 Corinthians 12 speak of gifts given to believers, Ephesians 4:7 speaks more of gifted believers given to the church (cf. v. 11).

4:9-10. Verses 9-11 serve as a com-

mentary on two words of the quotation in verse 8, namely, **ascended** (vv. 9-10) and "gave" (v. 11). In verses 9-10 Paul commented on the words **He ascended.** These two verses are parenthetical in thought because the issue of the passage is the giving of gifts. Before Christ could ascend He had to descend. What is meant by **to the lower, earthly regions,** literally, "into the lower parts of earth"? The genitive "of" can be taken in three ways: (1) "Into the lower parts, namely, the earth" (a genitive of apposition). This would refer to Christ's incarnation, His "descent" to the earth. (2) "Into the parts lower than the earth" (a genitive of comparison). This would mean that Christ descended into hades between His death and resurrection. (3) "Into the lower parts which belong to the earth" (a genitive of possession). This would refer to Christ's death and His burial in the grave. The third view best fits the context because in His death Christ had victory over sin and redeemed those who would be given as "gifts" to the church.

Christ's ascent above **the heavens, in order to fill the whole universe** probably refers to His regal relationship with the whole world, from which position He bestows gifts as He wills because of His work on the Cross. This fits well with 1:23, which speaks of Christ imparting all the fullness of His blessings to the church and to the universe. Christ, who embodies the fullness of the Godhead (Col. 2:9), fills the universe and is Head over it (cf. Col. 1:18).

4:11. This verse is a commentary on the second part of the quotation in verse 8, namely, Christ's giving gifts to Christians. The gifts to the church are gifted people. The subject **He** is emphatic in the Greek to denote that Christ Himself gives the gifted people. Five kinds of gifted people are listed in the predicate accusative, so the NIV correctly translates, **gave some to be.** The first two, **apostles** and **prophets,** were already mentioned in 2:20 and 3:5 as the foundational gifts to the church. The apostles include the Twelve, who had the office of apostleship by virtue of being with Christ (Acts 1:21-22) and having been appointed by Him (which would include Paul; 1 Cor. 15:8-9; Gal. 1:1; 2:6-9). But "apostles" also included others who were recognized as apostles, such as James (1 Cor. 15:7; Gal.

1:19), Barnabas (Acts 14:4, 14; 1 Cor. 9:6), Andronicus and Junias (Rom. 16:7), possibly Silas and Timothy (1 Thes. 1:1; 2:7), and Apollos (1 Cor. 4:6, 9). This latter group had the gift of apostleship but not the apostolic "office" as did the Twelve and Paul. Apostles, then, were those who carried the gospel message with God's authority. "Apostle" means "one sent as an authoritative delegate."

New Testament prophets were gifts to the church to provide edification, exhortation, and comfort (1 Cor. 14:3). They probably revealed God's will to the church when the biblical canon was incomplete. Since the apostles and prophets were foundational, they did not exist after the first generation of believers.

Evangelists were those engaged in spreading the gospel, similar to present-day missionaries. Pastors and teachers are listed together because they are governed by one article ("the" occurs before "pastors" but not before "teachers") and because the word "and" (kai) differs from the other "and's" (de) in the verse. This may imply that these are two kinds of gifted people whose ministries are among settled congregations (rather than itinerant ministries like those of the apostles and evangelists). More likely, they refer to two characteristics of the same person who is pastoring believers (by comforting and guiding) while at the same time instructing them in God's ways (overseers or elders are to be able to teach; 1 Tim. 3:2; Titus 1:9).

b. The intention of the gifts (4:12-16)

The purpose of the gifted believers (vv. 7-11) is to equip other believers for the ministry so as to give them stability doctrinally and practically and thus lead them to mutual edification. Like several other passages in Ephesians (1:3-14, 15-23; 2:1-7; 3:1-13, 14-19; 4:1-7; 6:14-20), 4:11-16 is one long sentence in Greek.

4:12. The purpose of the gifted men is to prepare God's people for works of service. More literally, this purpose is "for the perfecting or equipping (katartismon; cf. the verb katartizō in Matt. 4:21, 'mending' or 'preparing' nets; in Gal. 6:1, 'restore' for proper use; cf. 2 Cor. 13:11; Heb. 13:21) of the saints unto the work of the ministry" (diakonias). Gifted people (Eph. 4:11) are to minister the Word to others so that they in turn are readied to get involved in ministering to others (cf. 2 Tim. 2:2). The goal of all this is the building up or edifying of the body of Christ (cf. Eph. 4:16). This shows that all saints and not just a few leaders should be involved in the "ministry." All saints are gifted (v. 7) to serve others spiritually.

4:13. Gifted people are to minister till all the church attains (reach translates katantēsōmen, used in Acts of travelers arriving at their destinations) the three goals, each introduced by the Greek preposition (eis, "unto"): literally, (1) "unto the unity of the faith (cf. Eph. 4:5) and full knowledge (epignōseōs; cf. 1:17) of the Son of God," (2) "unto a mature man," and (3) "unto the measure (metron; cf. 4:7, 16) of the stature of the fullness of Christ." As each believer functions in accord with the gift(s) Christ has given him (v. 7) the body as a whole enjoys unity (cf. vv. 3-6) and becomes more spiritually mature (cf. v. 15), more like Jesus Christ in all His fullness (cf. 1:23; 3:19).

4:14-16. Here Paul expressed the ultimate purpose, or perhaps better, the result (hina) of gifted people equipping saints to serve the Lord and others. Negatively, believers should not be like immature infants who are easily swayed and confused, like waves being tossed back and forth (cf. Luke 8:24; James 1:6) and blown here and there (lit., "whirled around," a violent swinging that makes one dizzy) by every gust of wind of teaching . . . by the cunning, better, "trickery" (kybeia, lit., "dice-playing") of men in their deceitful scheming (panourgia, also used in Luke 20:23; 1 Cor. 3:19; 2 Cor. 4:2; 11:3), moving toward (pros indicates goal) a system of error. False teachers cause this kind of confusion regarding the truth in order to try to bring believers into their erroneous schemes. In contrast (de, Eph. 4:15) Paul stated positively that by speaking the truth in love (lit., "truthing in love," which has the idea of maintaining truth in love in both speech and life) believers may grow up into Him with reference to all things. Christ, then, is the Source of a believer's growth and also the Aim and Goal of his growth (cf. v. 13). From the Head (cf. 1:22; 5:23; Col. 1:18) the body derives its whole capacity for growth and activity (Eph. 4:16). Each member of the body is joined (2:21) by being carefully fitted together, and each member is held or brought together by means of every supporting ligament (cf. Col. 2:19) according to the standard (*kata*, with the accusative) of the measured working (*metrō*, from *metron*) of each individual. This causes the body of Christ to grow (cf. Eph. 4:15) and build itself up (cf. v. 12) in love. The phrase "in love" occurs three times (vv. 2, 15-16), thus pointing to the way unity is maintained. Significantly the word "measure" (*metron*) is also used three times in this context (vv. 7, 13, 16). Each believer is to function in Christ's body by God's enabling grace in accord with the measure of the gift Christ bestowed on him (v. 7). When each believer accomplishes that measure, then the church grows properly (v. 16), coming ultimately to the measure of Christlikeness (v. 13). Stunted growth comes when one does not allow his or others' gifts to function.

The preservation of unity is the responsibility of God's gifted people in the church (vv. 7-16). In this unity of structure is variety of function. Paul emphasized body growth, not self-growth. Each individual contributes to this unified growth as he allows his particular gift(s) to function.

B. Walking in holiness (4:17-32)

Believers are to walk in holiness as well as unity. Paul first showed negatively how a believer should not walk; then he gave the positive aspects of Christian conduct.

1. PRESENTATION OF THE OLD MAN (4:17-19)

a. His nature (4:17-18)

4:17-18. The Ephesian believers who were Gentiles (2:1-2, 11-12) were not to walk as the Gentiles do, or as implied, as they had once walked. Gentiles walked in the futility of their thinking. The word for "futility" (*mataiotēti*; cf. Rom. 1:21) suggests being void of useful aim or goal. (This noun is used only here and in Rom. 8:20 [of Creation] and 2 Peter 2:18 [of words]. The verb *mataioō* is used in Rom. 1:21, "their thinking became futile.") Unbelieving Gentiles failed to attain the true purpose of the mind, namely, to receive God's revelation which would guide them in their conduct. Since their minds could not receive God's revelation, their understanding was darkened (Rom. 1:21; 2 Cor. 4:4), being separated (lit.,

"alienated"; cf. Eph. 2:12) from the life of (that comes from) God. Their alienation is because of their ignorance of God (cf. 1 Peter 1:14); and this is because of the hardening of their hearts, their being insensitive to God and His ways.

b. His practice (4:19)

4:19. Because of their lack of sensitivity these Gentiles gave themselves over ("abandoned themselves"; cf. Rom. 1:24, 26, 28) to sensuality (*aselgeia*, "licentiousness"; cf. Mark 7:22; Rom. 13:13; 2 Cor. 12:21; Gal. 5:19; 1 Peter 4:3; 2 Peter 2:2, 7, 18; Jude 4), a life without concern for personal standards or social sanctions. Their purpose (*eis*) was to practice every kind of impurity, with a continual lust for more (lit., "in greed"), indulging in self-gratification without regard for others. This is a horrible picture of sinful people's selfish and perverted ways.

2. PRESENTATION OF THE NEW MAN (4:20-32)

a. His position (4:20-24)

4:20-24. In contrast (*de*) with the "old man" (vv. 17-19) believers did not come to know (lit., "learn") Christ that way. Their minds are no longer darkened; their lives are no longer alienated from God; their hearts are no longer hardened and impure. Christ is the Subject (you heard of Him) and the Sphere (you were taught in Him) of a believer's learning. This teaching and learning is in accordance with the truth, because He is the Truth (John 14:6). The content of this learning is twofold: (1) A believer has put off the old self which is being corrupted by its deceitful desires (cf. Eph. 4:17-19). Self-centered lusts are deceitful because they promise joy but fail to provide it. (2) He has put on the new self which has been created to be like God in true righteousness and holiness, which is based on truth (v. 24). This truth contrasts with the deceitfulness of lustful living (cf. vv. 14-15). Believers have been made new in the attitude of their minds; they are no longer futile in their thinking, darkened in their understanding, and ignorant (vv. 18-19). These are not commands, for the construction here (and in the parallel passage in Col. 3:9-10) is not imperative. They are facts that believers have learned, as is also seen in Romans 6:2-10 and 2 Corinthians 5:17. Believers are new people in Christ, and hence they can no longer live as Gentiles live, as the next exhortations state.

b. His practice (4:25-32)

Each of the following five exhortations about a believer's conduct has three parts: (1) a negative command, (2) a positive command, and (3) the reason for the positive command.

4:25. Having **put** away **falsehood,** believers are to tell the truth (cf. v. 15). Truth is conforming one's words to reality. The reason for this exhortation is that believers **are all members of one** another in Christ's **body,** the church (cf. vv. 4, 16).

4:26-27. While believers may at times be legitimately angry (with righteous **anger** against sin; cf. John 2:13-16), they are **not** to **sin.** The way to prevent such sin is to "keep short accounts," dealing with the anger before **the sun goes down.** The reason is that **the devil** would like to intensify a Christian's righteous anger against sin, causing it to become sin itself. This then gives the devil **a foothold** (lit., "a place"), an opportunity for leading that Christian into further sin. Then anger begins to control the believer rather than the believer controlling his anger.

4:28. Christians are not to **steal,** but are to **work** in order to give to the needy. A thief takes from others for his own benefit, whereas a believer is to work, **doing something useful** (agathon, "beneficial"; cf. v. 29) **with his own hands** for the purpose of sharing **with those in need.** This is true Christian charity. Work has many benefits: it provides for a person's material needs, it gives him something useful to do (something that is beneficial to himself and others), and it enables him to help others materially.

4:29-30. Believers are **not** to speak **unwholesome** (sapros, "rotten") words (cf. 5:4), but **helpful** (agathos, "good, beneficial"; cf. 4:28) words for the purpose of edification. Good words **benefit** (lit., "give grace" or enablement to) the hearers. One's words are to be true and pure and also are to contribute to benefiting others. Besides one's conscience, **the Holy Spirit** also helps guard a believer's speech. The fact that the Holy Spirit may be grieved points to His

personality. His seal of a believer remains until **the day of redemption,** the time that a believer receives his new body (cf. 1:14; Phil. 3:20-21).

4:31-32. Believers are to **get rid of** the six vices of **bitterness, rage** (thymos, "outbursts of anger"), **anger** (orgē, "settled feeling of anger"), **brawling** (kraugē, "shouting or clamor"), **slander** (blasphēmia), and **malice** (kakia, "ill will, wickedness"). Several of these vices are also listed in Colossians 3:8. The positive commands are three: (1) **be kind** (chrēstoi, lit., "what is suitable or fitting to a need"); (2) be **compassionate** (eusplanchnoi; used elsewhere in the NT only in 1 Peter 3:8; cf. splanchnoi, "inner emotions of affection," in 2 Cor. 6:12; 7:15; Phil. 1:8; 2:1; Col. 3:12; Phile. 7, 12, 20; 1 John 3:17); (3) be **forgiving** (lit., "being gracious," charizomenoi, the participle from the verb charizomai, "to give freely" or "to give graciously as a favor"). The reason for these positive commands is that **in Christ God** is kind (Eph. 2:7), compassionate (Mark 1:41), and gracious (Rom. 8:32) to believers.

C. Walking in love (5:1-6)

In applying his doctrines, Paul now for the third time used the term for "walk" (peripateō, trans. "live" in the NIV; 4:1, 17; 5:2). This is thus the third section in his discussion on the conduct of believers. God's children are to walk (live) in unity, in holiness, and in love.

1. THE POSITIVE: TO LOVE OTHERS (5:1-2)

5:1-2. Each Christian should **be an imitator of God** because he is God's child. As a child imitates his parents, so ought a believer to imitate God (cf. Matt. 5:48; Luke 6:36).

The **and** should be translated "that is" in order to convey the idea that Ephesians 5:2 explains how a believer is to imitate God: by walking in **love.** The supreme example of this love is Christ's love for His own—He **loved us;** seen graphically in His sacrificing His life on behalf of those who would believe. He willingly **gave Himself up** (cf. v. 25; John 10:11, 15, 17-18; Gal. 1:4; Heb. 9:14). This **offering** was a fragrance pleasing (and thus acceptable) **to God** (cf. Lev. 1:17; 3:16; Isa. 53:10). (The idea of **fragrant** offerings is also spoken of in 2 Cor. 2:15-16; Phil. 4:18.) Christians can imitate

God by loving others, even to the point of death if necessary (1 John 3:16).

2. THE NEGATIVE: TO ABSTAIN FROM EVIL (5:3-6)

a. Responsibility: to abstain from evil practices (5:3-4)

5:3. The self-centered vices in conduct and speech (vv. 3-4) are the opposite of the self-sacrificing love spoken of in verses 1-2. Since these vices portray selfishness and unconcern for others, a believer should **not** have **even a hint of** these sins in his life. **Sexual immorality** (*porneia*), **any kind of impurity,** and **greed are improper for** (lit., "should not be named among") believers. **God's holy people** is literally, "saints" (*hagiois*; cf. 1:1, 15).

5:4. Improprieties in speech—**obscenity** (*aischrotēs*, "shameless talk and conduct"), **foolish talk** (*mōrologia*, lit., "stupid words"), and **coarse** jesting (*eutrapelia*, "vulgar, frivolous wit")—**are out of place** for Jesus' followers, because such vices often harm (cf. 4:29), whereas **thanksgiving** is appreciation for others and is helpful. Paul was not intimating that humor itself is sin, but that it is wrong when it is used to destroy or tear down others.

b. Reason: no inheritance for evildoers (5:5-6)

5:5-6. Paul sternly warned believers that the reason they are to abstain from evil deeds (specifically, immorality, impurity, and greed; cf. vv. 3 and 5) is that those who practice them are not a part of God's kingdom. Those who have no **inheritance in the kingdom** have not been "washed," "sanctified," and "justified" as 1 Corinthians 6:9-11 so clearly demonstrates. A **greedy person . . . is an idolater** (cf. Col. 3:5) in the sense that greed, like idols, puts things before God.

Christians should not be deceived into thinking that this warning is merely **empty words** (*kenois,* trans. "empty" means void of content), for the **disobedient,** that is, the unregenerate (cf. Eph. 2:2) are the objects of **God's wrath** (cf. Col. 3:6). God's view of sin should be taken seriously. Believers should be imitators of God, not evildoers.

D. Walking in light (5:7-14)

The reason for dividing the outline here rather than between verses 5 and 6 (or between vv. 7 and 8) is because of the resumptive inferential particle (*oun,* "therefore") that marks the beginning of each new section: 4:1, 17; 5:1, 7, 15.

1. NOT BECOMING INVOLVED WITH EVILDOERS (5:7-10)

a. Command: do not get involved (5:7)

5:7. Christians, as objects of God's love (vv. 1-2), are inconsistent if they become **partners with** those who are the objects of God's wrath, those who are not "in the kingdom" (v. 5).

b. Reason: Christians are changed persons (5:8a)

5:8a. The reason (*gar,* for) believers should not be partners with the unregenerate is that Christians are no longer part of the **darkness,** in which they used to live (cf. 4:18; John 1:5; 3:19-20) **but . . . are light in the Lord** (Matt. 5:14-16; John 3:21; 8:12; Rom. 13:12; 1 Thes. 5:4-5). They have been rescued out of darkness (Col. 1:13). Now, being "in the Lord," who is the Light (John 8:12), they too are lights.

c. Command: walk as children of light (5:8b-10)

5:8b-10. The behavior of saints should correspond with their positions. Since they are **children of light,** that is, since their very nature is spiritual light, they are to **live** accordingly (Rom. 13:12). Ephesians 5:9 parenthetically explains that **the fruit of the light**—which is **goodness, righteousness** (cf. Phil. 1:11), **and truth**—reflects God's character in a believer's life. (The KJV rendering, "fruit of the Spirit," lacks good textual support.) Sinners, those in darkness, are characterized by the opposite of this fruit: evil, wickedness, and falsehood. The thought in verse 10 expands on verse 8b in that to live as children of light one must discern **what pleases the Lord** (cf. 2 Cor. 5:9; Col. 1:10). The words **find out** translate *dokimazontes,* which is literally, "putting to the test," "approving," or "discerning" (cf. Rom. 12:2).

2. NOT BECOMING INVOLVED WITH EVILDOERS' WORKS (5:11-13)

Those who profess Christ are to walk in light by not being partners with unbelievers (vv. 7-10). Now Paul mentioned that Christians are not to be involved with unbelievers' deeds (vv. 11-13).

a. Command: do not get involved but expose (5:11)

5:11. Christians are forbidden to be "sharers together" (*symmetochoi*, v. 7; cf. *metochoi* in Heb. 1:9 ["companions"]; 3:1, 14 ["share"]; 6:4 ["shared"]) with the sons of disobedience; now they are told not to take part (*synkoinōneite*) with unbelievers' actions. Their ways are **fruitless deeds of darkness** in contrast with "the fruit of the light" (Eph. 5:9). Sins bear no "fruit"; they give no benefits to oneself or others.

Christians, by conducting themselves as "children of light," **expose** the "deeds of darkness." These deeds, however, refer here to the deeds of other believers who are not walking in the light. This is because only God can expose and convict unbelievers' deeds (1 Cor. 5:12-13). Believers, on the other hand, can expose evil deeds among other Christians within the church. This the Corinthians failed to do (1 Cor. 5).

b. Reason: their works are shameful (5:12)

5:12. The things done **in secret** are too **shameful even** to talk about. The term **the disobedient** in the NIV wrongly suggests that this refers to unbelievers. However, the Greek has "what is done *by them*," thus indicating that Paul may be referring to believers who commit "deeds of darkness."

c. Explanation: light shows the true character of works (5:13)

5:13. When **light** exposes evil deeds, they become **visible,** manifest for what they really are. Seeing them as evil, a believer then cleanses himself of them (1 John 1:5-7), realizing they are detrimental not only to him but also to other believers.

3. CONCLUSION: ENLIGHTENMENT OF CHRIST (5:14)

5:14. The introductory formula, **This is why it is said,** seems to indicate a quotation from the Old Testament, but it is difficult to identify unless it is a combination of passages (e.g., Isa. 26:19; 51:17; 52:1; 60:1). Possibly it is a quota-

tion from an early Christian hymn. A believer who has committed "deeds of darkness," is to **wake up** and **rise from the dead** since he was involved with the deeds of evildoers. Christ's shining on him speaks of His approval, an indication that he is discerning and following what is pleasing to the Lord (Eph. 5:10).

Therefore verses 7-14 deal with church discipline. Believers are to walk in the **light,** and in so doing to expose other believers of any works that are unfruitful so that they too may walk in the light and please their Lord.

E. Walking in wisdom (5:15–6:9)

For a fifth time Paul used the word "walk" (*peripateō*), translated "live" in the NIV (4:1, 17; 5:2, 8, 15). Here Paul instructed believers to be wise in their walk or conduct by being filled by the Holy Spirit.

1. ADMONITION (5:15-21)

a. Proper action: to walk wisely (5:15-16)

5:15-16. The NIV's **Be very careful, then, how you live** is literally, "Look therefore carefully how you walk." Does the adverb "carefully" (*akribōs*, lit. "accurately") modify "look"? If so the first clause in verse 15 could be translated, "Therefore look carefully how you walk." (This is behind the rendering in the ASV, NASB, and NIV.) Or does "careful" modify "walk"? If so, the idea is, "Therefore look that you walk carefully" (cf. KJV). This second alternative is preferred because better Greek manuscripts place *akribōs* closer to the Greek word "walk" and because in the New Testament the Greek imperative "look" (*blepete*) is never modified by an adverb. Believers then, are to walk (**live**) carefully, so as to be **wise** or skillful and thus please the Lord. The *manner* for this careful, precise walk is **making** the right use of **every opportunity** (cf. Col. 4:5), and the *reason* for this careful walk is that **the days are evil.** Many are walking in sin, and since the time is short believers must make full use of their time to help turn them from darkness to light. This necessitates wise conduct.

b. Proper state: to become wise (5:17-21)

5:17. Rather than being **foolish** (*aphrones*, "senseless") or "unwise" (*asophoi*, v. 15), Christians are to **under-**

stand (*syniete,* "comprehend intellectually") **what the Lord's will is.** Only after one understands what pleases God (v. 1) can he carry it out in his life.

5:18. Going from the general to the specific, Paul explained how wisdom, as an intellectual and spiritual capacity, works out in one's conduct. Verse 18 includes a negative command and a positive one. The negative is to abstain from getting **drunk on wine** with which there is incorrigibility. The word *asōtia* is translated **debauchery** (NIV, RSV), "excess" (KJV), "riot" (ASV), and "dissipation" (NASB). All these give the idea of profligate or licentious living that is wasteful. In this verse the literal sense of incorrigibility seems best, for a drunken man acts abnormally. Rather than controlling himself, the wine controls him. Conversely, the positive command is, **Be filled with the Spirit.** Thus a believer, rather than controlling himself, is controlled by the Holy Spirit. It may be more accurate to say that the Holy Spirit is the "Agent" of the filling (cf. Gal. 5:16) and Christ is the Content of the filling (Col. 3:15). Thus in this relationship, as a believer is yielded to the Lord and controlled by Him, he increasingly manifests the fruit of the Spirit (Gal. 5:22-23). The Spirit's indwelling (John 7:37-39; 14:17; Rom. 5:5; 8:9; 1 Cor. 2:12; 6:19-20; 1 John 3:24; 4:13), sealing (2 Cor. 1:22; Eph. 1:13; 4:30), and baptism (1 Cor. 12:13; Gal. 3:27) occur at the time of regeneration and thus are not commanded. However, believers *are* commanded to be filled constantly with the Holy Spirit. Each Christian has all the Spirit, but the command here is that the Spirit have all of him. The wise walk, then, is one that is characterized by the Holy Spirit's control.

5:19-21. Paul then gave four results of being filled with the Spirit. First is communication with **one another with psalms** (*psalmois,* OT psalms sung with stringed instruments such as harps), **hymns** (*hymnois,* praises composed by Christians), **and spiritual songs** (a general term). Second is communication with **the Lord** by singing and making melody (*psallontes,* singing with a stringed instrument) **in the heart.** Church music, then, should be a means of believers' ministering to each other, and singing should be a means of worshiping the

Lord. Third is thanking **God the Father** (cf. 1:2-3, 17; 3:14) continually for all things (cf. Col. 3:17; 1 Thes. 5:18). Fourth, Spirit-controlled believers are to **submit to one another,** willingly serving others and being under them rather than dominating them and exalting themselves. But basic to Christians' attitudes toward others is their **reverence for Christ.** Paul next elaborated on this subject of submission (Eph. 5:22-6:9).

2. APPLICATION (5:22-6:9)

Having admonished believers to be wise by being controlled by the Holy Spirit, Paul now applied this to specific life-relationships. It is relatively easy to exhibit a Spirit-filled life for one or two hours a week in church but it takes the work of the Holy Spirit to exhibit godliness not only on Sundays but also in everyday relationships between wives and husbands, children and parents, and slaves and masters. In each of these three relationships the first partner is commanded to be submissive or obedient (5:22; 6:1, 5). But the second partner is also to show submissiveness by his care and concern for the first partner. Both partners are to act toward one another as a service rendered to the Lord.

a. Wives and husbands (5:22-33)

5:22-24. Wives are to **submit to** their **husbands.** (The verb "submit," absent in Gr. in v. 22, is borrowed from v. 21.) **As to the Lord** does not mean that a wife is to submit to her husband in the same way she submits to the Lord, but rather that her submission to her husband *is* her service rendered "to the Lord" (cf. Col. 3:18). The reason for this submission is that **the husband is the head of the wife** (cf. 1 Cor. 11:3), and this is compared to Christ's headship over the church (Eph. 5:23; cf. 4:15; Col. 1:18). **As Christ is** the Savior **of the church, His body,** so a husband should be the protector of his wife, who is "one flesh" with him (Gen. 2:24). **As the church** is in submission **to Christ, so also** a wife **should** be to her husband. It would be foolish to think of the church being head over Christ. But submission does not mean inferiority. It means that she recognizes that her husband is the head of the home and responds to him accordingly without usurping his authority to herself.

5:25. After speaking of a wife's submission to her husband (vv. 22-24), Paul then stated the measure of the husband's love for his wife (vv. 25-32). **Husbands** are commanded, **Love your wives** (cf. v. 33) **just as Christ loved the church.** The word "love" (*agapaō*) means seeking the highest good for another person (cf. 2:4). This is an unselfish love as seen in Christ's sacrificial death in which He **gave Himself up for** the church (cf. 5:2; John 10:11, 15, 17-18; Gal. 1:4; Eph. 5:25; Heb. 9:14). A wife's submission in no way hints that a husband may lord it over his spouse, as a despot commanding a slave. The "submit-love" relationship is a beautiful mixture of harmonious partnership in marriage.

5:26-27. The purpose of Christ's death was **to make** the church **holy** (*hagiasē*, "to set apart" for Himself as His own forever; cf. Heb. 2:11; 10:10, 14; 13:12) which He did by **cleansing her by the washing with water through the Word.** This is not baptismal regeneration for that would be contrary to Paul's teaching in this book as well as all his other writings and the entire New Testament. Metaphorically, being regenerated is pictured as being cleansed by water (cf. "the washing of rebirth" in Titus 3:5). The "Word" (*rhēmati*) refers to the "preached Word" that unbelievers hear (cf. *rhēma* in Eph. 6:17; Rom. 10:8, 17; 1 Peter 1:25). The ultimate purpose of Christ's death is **to present . . . to Himself** the church as **radiant** or "in splendor" (RSV). This adjective, "glorious," in NEB, is not attributive (as in NIV's "a radiant church"). It is in the predicate position because there is an article before church (to "present the church . . . glorious," NEB).

This purpose is then described negatively (**without stain or wrinkle**—no taint of sin or spiritual decay—**or any other blemish**) and positively (**holy and blameless**). These last two adjectives (*hagia*, "set apart," and *amōmos*, "without blemish," like a spotless lamb) are stated in Ephesians 1:4 as the purpose of God's election: that Christ may present His church to Himself in all its perfection (cf. "make holy" in 5:26; also cf. *hagious* and *amōmous* in Col. 1:22). Whereas human brides prepare themselves for their husbands, Christ prepares His own bride for Himself.

5:28-30. In verses 28-32 Paul applied the truths given in verses 25-27. As the church is the extension of Christ, so is the wife an "extension" of her husband. No one hates **his own body** but takes care of it. **Feeds** (*ektrephei*; cf. "bring them up" in 6:4) **and cares for** (*thalpei*; cf. 1 Thes. 2:7) is literally, "nourishes and cherishes." Thus as Christ loves the church, **His body** (of which all believers are **members**; cf. Eph. 4:25), so should **husbands . . . love their wives as their own bodies** (5:28; cf. v. 33). Men care for their bodies even though they are imperfect and so they should care for their wives though they are imperfect.

5:31-32. Verse 31 is a free rendering of Genesis 2:24, indicating that the bond between husband and **wife** is greater than that between parent and child. The greatness of the **mystery** refers to **the two** becoming **one flesh.** But then Paul returned to mention the wonderful bond between **Christ and the church,** which illustrates the love of a husband for his wife.

5:33. This is a restatement of the responsibilities of the husband and wife toward each other: **love** by the **husband** (cf. v. 25) and **respect** by **the wife.**

b. Children and parents (6:1-4)

The Spirit-controlled life (5:18) is necessary for having a good parent-child relationship.

6:1-3. Children are to **obey** their **parents.** The phrase **in the Lord** does not mean that children are to obey parents only if their parents are believers. As Colossians 3:20 clearly denotes, a child's obedience to his parents is pleasing in the Lord's sight. The reason **for this** is that it **is right** (*dikaion*); it is a proper course to follow in society. Paul then quoted the fifth commandment (Ex. 20:12; Deut. 5:16) to support the need for children to obey parents (Eph. 6:2a, 3). The parenthetical clause states that this **is the first commandment with a promise.** But this is actually the second command with a promise (cf. Ex. 20:6). Some say Paul meant that this is the first command that children need to learn. But the first, not the fifth, of the Ten Commandments should really be learned first. More likely, Paul meant that this is "first" in the sense

EPHESIANS

of being "a primary commandment," that is, of primary importance for children and it also has a promise. The promise for those who obey their parents is that they enjoy a prosperous and long life on the earth. This states a general principle that obedience fosters self-discipline, which in turn brings stability and longevity in one's life. (Stated conversely, it is improbable that an undisciplined person will live a long life. An Israelite who persistently disobeyed his parents was not privileged to enjoy a long, stable life in the land of Israel. A clear example of this was Eli's sons Hophni and Phinehas [1 Sam. 4:11].) Though that promise was given to Israel in the Old Testament, the principle still holds true today.

6:4. Fathers are addressed because they represent the governmental head of the family on whom rests the responsibility of child discipline. Fathers are not to exasperate (*parorgizete*, "provoke to anger"; used only here and in Rom. 10:19; cf. Col. 3:21) their children by unreasonable demands, petty rules, or favoritism. Such actions cause children to become discouraged (Col. 3:21). Instead, fathers are to bring them up, that is, rear or nourish (*ektrephete*, "provide for physical and spiritual needs"; also used in Eph. 5:29) them in the training (*paideia*, "child discipline," including directing and correcting; cf. "training" in righteousness [2 Tim. 3:16] and God's "discipline" of believers [Heb. 12:8]) and instruction (*nouthesia*; cf. 1 Cor. 10:11; Titus 3:10) of the Lord. Children are to obey "in the Lord" (Eph. 6:1) and parents are to train and instruct "in the Lord." He is to be the center of their relationships and of their teaching and learning.

c. Slaves and masters (6:5-9)

Paul then discussed a third group. Whereas the first two groups were directly involved in family relationships (wives and husbands, children and parents), this group was outside the immediate family. Slavery existed in Paul's day and he did not try to overthrow it (1 Cor. 7:17-24). Apparently these were Christian slaves under Christian masters.

6:5-8. Slaves' responsibilities to their masters are outlined here. Slaves were to obey (cf. v. 1) their masters with (1) respect (cf. 5:33), (2) fear (lit., "trem-

bling"), (3) sincerity (*haplotēti*, from *haplous*, "simple, without folds"), (4) as a service rendered to Christ (just as you would obey Christ . . . like slaves of Christ, doing the will of God . . . as if you were serving the Lord), (5) consistently (not only . . . when their eye is on you, but all the time), (6) with inner motivation (of heart [6:5], and from your heart [v. 6], the latter phrase being lit., "from the soul"), and (7) wholeheartedly (*met' eunoias*, "with good will or a peaceable spirit"). The reason for such service is that the Lord will reward them. He is the One who can accurately and impartially judge their performance and motivation (cf. 1 Peter 1:17).

6:9. Masters were to treat their slaves in the same way, that is, to please the Lord in their dealings with them. Slaves owners were not to keep threatening them but to treat them justly and fairly (cf. Col. 4:1; James 5:4) because they themselves were servants, with a Master who is an example to them. This, of course, is the Lord and He is the Master over both earthly masters and slaves. He shows no partiality, regardless of one's rank (cf. Eph. 6:8).

In conclusion, only a Spirit-controlled believer (5:18) is able to fulfill the obligations given in this section (5:15–6:9). Many of these verses emphasize selflessness, which results in harmony, one evidence of the Spirit's work.

F. Standing in warfare (6:10-20)

Whereas every division of 4:1–6:9 was introduced by the Greek inferential particle *oun* (4:1, 17; 5:1, 7, 15) and the verb "walk" (*peripateō*; 4:1, 17; 5:1, 8, 15), this final division is signaled by "finally" (*tou loipou*, "the rest"). This section discusses a believer's use of God's resources to help him stand against evil powers.

1. PUTTING ON THE ARMOR (6:10-13)

a. What: to be strong in the Lord (6:10)

6:10. Paul exhorted believers to be strong in the Lord and in the might (*kratei*, "power that overcomes resistance" as used in Christ's miracles) of God's inherent strength (*ischyos*; cf. "the power [*kratous*] of His inherent strength" [*ischyos*] in 1:19). Hence believers can be strengthened not only by the person of the Lord but also by His resources (cf. Phil. 4:13).

b. How: to put on God's armor (6:11a)

6:11a. The form of the Greek imperative **put on** indicates that believers are responsible for putting on God's (not their) **full armor** (*panoplian*, also in v. 13; all the armor and weapons together were called the *hapla*; cf. 2 Cor. 6:7) with all urgency. The detailed description of the armor (given in Eph. 6:14-17) may stem from Paul's being tied to a Roman soldier while in prison awaiting trial (cf. Acts 28:16, 20).

c. Why: to stand against the devil's strategy (6:11b-13)

6:11b-12. The purpose of putting on God's armor is to be able to **stand against** the **schemes** or stratagems (*methodeias*, used in the NT only here and in 4:14) of the devil or adversary (cf. 4:27). Christians are not to attack Satan, or advance against him; they are only to "stand" or hold the territory Christ and His body, the church, have conquered. Without God's armor believers will be defeated by the "schemes" of the devil which have been effective for thousands of years.

The **struggle is not** physical (**against flesh and blood**); it is a spiritual conflict against the spiritual "Mafia." Though the ranks of satanic forces cannot be fully categorized, the first two (**rulers and authorities**) have already been mentioned in 1:21 and 3:10. Paul added **the powers of this dark world** (cf. 2:2; 4:18; 5:8) and **the spiritual forces of evil.** Their sphere of activity is **in the heavenly realms,** the fifth occurrence of this phrase, which is mentioned in the New Testament only in 1:3, 20; 2:6; 3:10; 6:12. Satan, who is in the heavens (2:2) until he will be cast out in the middle of the Tribulation (Rev. 12:9-10), is trying to rob believers of the spiritual blessings God has given them (Eph. 1:3).

6:13. Some think this verse implies that a believer, having subdued all, is able to stand in victory. It is preferable to think that this is summarizing what has been stated: that having made all the necessary preparations (with **the full armor of God;** cf. v. 11), one is then ready and **able to stand** in defense. This view fits better with the context because immediately after this verse Paul de-

scribed the armor to be put on. This would be unnatural if he were speaking (in v. 13) of standing in victory. Also, to say that verse 13 refers to standing in victory but that verses 11 and 14 refer to standing in defense is inconsistent. Too, the word **stand** in verse 13 is *antistēnai*, "to withstand or stand against" (cf. James 4:7; 1 Peter 5:9).

2. STANDING WITH THE ARMOR (6:14-16)

a. The mandate: to stand (6:14a)

6:14a. Verses 14-20 make up the eighth long sentence in this epistle. Others are 1:3-14, 15-23; 2:1-7; 3:1-13, 14-19; 4:1-7, 11-16.

The imperative **stand** denotes urgency. This is followed by four Greek participles that denote either the cause or means of standing. The participles are rendered as follows in the NIV: "buckled," "in place," "fitted," "take up" (6:14-16).

b. The method: to arm (6:14b-16)

6:14b. Before a Roman soldier put on his armor, he put a belt **around** his **waist.** This held his garments together and served as a place on which to hang his armor. **The belt of truth** refers not to the facts of the gospel but to subjective truth, a believer's integrity and faithfulness. As a soldier's belt or sash gave ease and freedom of movement, so truth gives freedom with self, others, and God.

6:14c. The breastplate of righteousness refers not to justification, obtained at conversion (Rom. 3:24; 4:5), but to the sanctifying righteousness of Christ (1 Cor. 1:30) practiced in a believer's life. As a soldier's breastplate protected his chest from an enemy's attacks, so sanctifying, righteous living (Rom. 6:13; 14:17) guards a believer's heart against the assaults of the devil (cf. Isa. 59:17; James 4:7).

6:15. This verse does not speak of the spreading of the gospel, for Christians are pictured in vv. 10-16 as standing, not advancing. Instead this refers to a believer's stability or surefootedness **from the gospel** which gives him **peace** so he can stand in the battle.

6:16. The shield in a Roman soldier's attire, made of wood, was about 2 1/2' wide and 4' long. It was overlaid with linen and leather, to absorb fiery arrows. Thus it also protected the other pieces of the armor; hence Paul used the phrase, **in addition to all this. Of faith** is a genitive of content; the shield consists of faith. The idea, then, is that a Christian's resolute faith in the Lord can stop and extinguish **all the flaming arrows of the evil one** aimed at him. (Cf. "evil one" [Satan] in John 17:15; 1 John 5:19.)

3. RECEIVING THE FINAL PIECES OF ARMOR (6:17-20)

a. The mandate: to receive (6:17)

6:17. The outline is divided here because the Greek word **take** is an imperative, rather than another participle. This parallels the imperative "stand" in verse 14. The helmet and sword are the last two pieces a soldier takes up. A helmet, being hot and uncomfortable, would be put on by a soldier only when he faced impending danger. Having one's head guarded by a helmet gives a sense of safety, so **the helmet of salvation** refers either to present safety from the devil's attacks or to a future deliverance, "the hope of salvation as a helmet" (1 Thes. 5:8).

Finally, a Roman soldier would take in hand his sword, his only offensive weapon. **Of the Spirit** refers to the source or origin of **the sword**; hence it is "the sword given by the Spirit." "The sword of the Spirit" is specified as **the Word of God.** "Word" (*rhēma;* cf. Eph. 5:26; Rom. 10:8, 17; 1 Peter 1:25) refers to the preached Word or an utterance of God occasioned by the Holy Spirit in the heart. Believers need this "sword" to combat the enemy's assault, much as Christ did three times when tempted by the devil (Matt. 4:1-11).

b. The method: to care (6:18-20)

6:18. The manner in which a soldier takes up these last two pieces of armor is suggested by two Greek participles: "praying" and "being alert." When the enemy attacks—and **on all occasions**— Christians are to **pray** continually **in the Spirit** (i.e., in the power and sphere of the Spirit; cf. Jude 20). **With all kinds of prayers and requests** suggests the thoroughness and intensity of their praying. And like reliable soldiers, they are to be **keeping alert,** literally, "in all persistence" (*en pasē proskarterēsei;* the noun is used only here in the NT). Their requests are to be **for all the saints** because of Satan's spiritual warfare against Christ

and the church. In the Greek "all" occurs four times in this verse; three are translated in the NIV and the fourth is rendered as **always** (lit., "in all times" or "every time").

6:19-20. Paul asked his readers not only to **pray** in general for all saints but **also** specifically to pray **for him that he might make known the mystery of the gospel.** Here Paul probably did not refer to witnessing or preaching the gospel of Christ. Instead he may have referred to his need to be bold (twice he said **fearlessly**) and clear regarding the "mystery of the gospel" when he would be on trial before Caesar in Rome (when and if the Jewish accusers would make charges against him). The Romans looked on the Christians as a sect of the Jews, and the Jews considered them as a heretical group. In his trial Paul needed to make clear that Christians are neither a Jewish sect nor a heretical group but a new entity, the church, the body of Christ, composed of Jewish and Gentile believers. This recalls Paul's lengthy discussion of this "mystery of the gospel" in 2:11-3:11. For this reason Paul was **an ambassador in chains** (cf. Acts 28:16, 20; Eph. 3:1; 4:1; Phil. 1:7, 13-14, 16; Col. 4:3, 18; Phile. 1, 9-10, 13).

G. Conclusion (6:21-24)

1. INFORMATION (6:21-22)

6:21-22. Apparently **Tychicus** was the bearer of this epistle. Paul considered him a **dear brother and faithful servant in the Lord.** In Colossians 4:7 Paul called him by these same titles and added that he was a "fellow servant" (*syndoulos,* "fellow slave"). Tychicus is also mentioned in Acts 20:4; 2 Timothy 4:12; and Titus 3:12. Tychicus was to inform the Ephesians of Paul's welfare—**how** he was **and what** he was **doing**—in order to **encourage** them (cf. Eph. 3:13).

2. SALUTATION (6:23)

6:23. Three spiritual qualities frequently mentioned by Paul—peace, love, and faith—are referred to in this verse. The phrase **peace to the brothers** is found nowhere else in the New Testament. This **and love with faith** (cf. 1:15) have their sources in God. Paul wanted them to continue their love for other Christians, their spiritual brothers (since they are all "members of one body," 4:25) and to combine that love with their faith in God, for which they were well known. **God the Father and the Lord Jesus Christ** is similar to Paul's wording in 1:2-3, 17; 5:20.

3. BENEDICTION (6:24)

6:24. **Grace** concludes the letter, just as it had introduced it (1:2). The words **with an undying love** are literally, "in incorruption, incorruptibility, immortality" (*en aphtharsia;* cf. Rom. 2:7; 1 Cor. 15:42, 50, 53-54; 2 Tim. 1:10). It has the idea that believers' **love** for the **Lord Jesus Christ** is to be pure, not corrupted with wrong motives or secret disloyalties. Unfortunately some Ephesian believers later did lose the fervency of their love for Christ (Rev. 2:4). Paul's benediction, though unusual (cf. the chart "Paul's Concluding Benedictions in His Epistles," at Rom. 16:17-20), was certainly fitting.

BIBLIOGRAPHY

Abbott, T.K. *A Critical and Exegetical Commentary on the Epistles to the Ephesians and to the Colossians.* The International Critical Commentary. 1897. Reprint. Edinburgh: T. & T. Clark, 1979.

Barry, Alfred. "The Epistle of Paul the Apostle to the Ephesians." In *Ellicott's Commentary on the Whole Bible.* Reprint (8 vols. in 4). Grand Rapids: Zondervan Publishing House, 1981.

Barth, Markus. *Ephesians.* 2 vols. The Anchor Bible. Garden City, N.Y.: Doubleday & Co., 1974.

Bruce, F.F. *The Epistle to the Ephesians.* Old Tappan, N.J.: Fleming H. Revell Co., 1961.

Chafer, Lewis Sperry. *The Ephesian Letter: Doctrinally Considered.* Findlay, Ohio: Dunham Publishing Co., 1935.

Ellicott, Charles J. *St. Paul's Epistle to the Ephesians.* 5th ed. London: Longmans, Green, & Co., 1884. Reprint. Minneapolis: James Family Publishing Co., 1978.

Foulkes, Francis. *The Epistle of Paul to the Ephesians: An Introduction and Commentary.* The Tyndale New Testament Commentaries. Grand Rapids: Wm. B. Eerdmans Publishing Co., 1963.

Hendriksen, William. *Exposition of Ephesians.* New Testament Commentary. Grand Rapids: Baker Book House, 1967.

Kent, Homer A., Jr. *Ephesians: The Glory of the Church.* Everyman's Bible Commentary. Chicago: Moody Press, 1971.

Mitton, C. Leslie. *Ephesians.* New Century Bible Commentary. Grand Rapids: Wm. B. Eerdmans Publishing Co., 1973.

Moule, H.C.G. *Studies in Ephesians.* Cambridge: University Press, 1893. Reprint. Grand Rapids: Kregel Publications, 1977.

Robinson, J. Armitage. *Commentary on Ephesians.* 2d ed. London: Macmillan & Co., 1904. Reprint. Grand Rapids: Kregel Publications, 1979.

Simpson, E.K., and Bruce, F.F. *Commentary on the Epistles to the Ephesians and the Colossians.* The New International Commentary on the New Testament. Grand Rapids: Wm. B. Eerdmans Publishing Co., 1957.

Vaughan, Curtis. *Ephesians: A Study Guide Commentary.* Grand Rapids: Zondervan Publishing House, 1977.

Westcott, Brooke Foss. *Saint Paul's Epistle to the Ephesians.* Reprint. Grand Rapids: Baker Book House, 1979.

Wiersbe, Warren W. *Be Rich.* Wheaton, Ill.: Scripture Presss Publications, Victor Books, 1976.

Wood, A. Skevington. "Ephesians." In *The Expositor's Bible Commentary,* vol. 11. Grand Rapids: Zondervan Publishing House, 1978.

PHILIPPIANS

Robert P. Lightner

INTRODUCTION

On his second missionary journey Paul visited Philippi. Through his ministry there several people trusted Christ as their Savior. Some of these were Lydia and her family and the Philippian jailer and his family (Acts 16:14-34).

Soon after Paul's visit a local church was established in Philippi. The church helped the apostle in different ways so this epistle was written to acknowledge their help, as well as to help them.

Philippians is personal and practical in its tone and teaching. Paul emphasized the need for believers to rejoice in Christ. "Joy" (*chara*) is used four times (Phil. 1:4, 25; 2:2; 4:1); "rejoice" (*chairō*) occurs eight times (1:18 [twice]; 2:17-18; 3:1, 4:4 [twice], 10); and "glad" occurs thrice (2:17-18, 28). (In 1:26 the word "joy" is a different Gr. word; there it is the word "glad," "boast," or "glory," [*kauchēma*], which also occurs in 2:16 and 3:3.) Paul wrote frequently in this epistle about the mind of a child of God. One's manner of life is truly a reflection of what occupies his mind.

The Theme of the Epistle. Though many exhortations and challenges are given, one major theme or emphasis pervades the book. All the teachings are expressions or ramifications of this one central truth. This theme is "living the Christian life."

The Human Author. Most scholars agree that the Apostle Paul wrote the Book of Philippians. Clearly the work purports to come from him (1:1). Reference to Timothy is also significant since he was with the apostle when Philippi was evangelized (cf. Acts 16). Also the information the writer gave about himself (Phil. 3:4-6) harmonizes perfectly with Paul's life. In addition, the writings of the early church fathers attest to Pauline authorship.

The Date of the Epistle. Paul was in bondage when he wrote Philippians. But all do not agree which imprisonment he was experiencing when he wrote the book. Most believe he was in Rome at the time; some suggest he was in Caesarea; and a few argue for Ephesus.

The Scriptures give no clear indication of any imprisonment in Ephesus. As for Caesarea, Paul was confined there for two years, but imminent martyrdom is not suggested in the account which describes this confinement (Acts 23-24). His reference to the palace guard (Phil. 1:13) as well as his concern about facing possible death (vv. 20-26) argue for his writing from Rome. The date of the writing would then be A.D. 61 or 62.

The Historic Occasion. When the Philippian believers heard about Paul's imprisonment at Rome, they sent Epaphroditus, who may have been their pastor, to minister to him. Epaphroditus personally comforted Paul, expressing to him the affection of the saints in Philippi. And he brought Paul a financial contribution from them so that his confinement would be more comfortable (4:18). Three times before—twice when Paul was at Thessalonica, and once when he was at Corinth (Phil. 4:15-16; cf. 2 Cor. 11:9)—the saints ministered to his needs. The Book of Philippians might be called a thank-you note to saints in Philippi for their generous gifts.

While Epaphroditus was in Rome, he became so ill he almost died (Phil. 2:27). After he recovered, he took Paul's letter to the Philippian Christians.

Philippi was a Roman colony (Acts 16:12). After the Battle of Philippi in 42 B.C. some Roman soldiers were ordered by Anthony to live there. Then in 30 B.C. Octavian forced some people in Italy to give up their homes and settle in Philippi and elsewhere. These Philippian residents were given special privileges including

313

the "Italic right." This meant that the colonists, in return for their displacement, were treated as if their land were part of Italian soil. So the residents were citizens of Rome, their "mother city," and enjoyed the full rights of Roman citizenship, including exemption from taxes. So Paul's words (Phil. 1:27) "conduct yourselves" (lit., "live as citizens") and "our citizenship is in heaven" (3:20) had special meaning to the Christians at Philippi.

The Purposes for the Epistle. The initial reason for writing, as indicated, seems to have been to thank the Philippians for their love gift. But Paul also took advantage of this opportunity to address some of the problems in their church. Apparently rivalry and personal ambition were present among some of the saints (2:3-4; 4:2). The Judaizers were also gaining a hearing (3:1-3). In addition, an antinomian tendency was creeping in (3:18-19).

OUTLINE

COMMENTARY

I. Encouragement for Living the Christian Life (1:1-30)

A. Paul's praise of the saints at Philippi (1:1-8)

The Apostle Paul frequently began his epistles with words of greeting, praise, and commendation. Philippians was no exception. The tender tone of the entire letter is apparent at the outset.

1. INTRODUCTION (1:1-2)

1:1. Paul was the author's Gentile name and Saul his Hebrew name. As the apostle to the Gentiles (Gal. 2:7-8) he used his Gentile name. Instead of referring to his apostleship, as he frequently did in the beginning of a book, here Paul called himself a servant of the Lord. **Timothy** had a special interest in the Philippian saints (Phil. 2:20) and was associated with Paul's imprisonment (2:19, 23). Timothy was not a coauthor of this epistle, since he is spoken of in the third person (2:19-24). Both of these men of God, who had been Roman captives, were **servants** (lit., "slaves") **of Christ Jesus.** By calling the Philippian believers saints, Paul was not saying his readers were sinless. The Greek word he used, *hagioi,* means "those set apart." The saints at Philippi were set apart for God. They were **in Christ Jesus** so far as their relationship to God was concerned, though they lived at **Philippi.**

The apostle made special mention of **the overseers and deacons,** who were included among **all the saints.** The "overseers" or bishops, were also called "elders" (Titus 1:5, 7); and they were responsible for shepherding or pastoring the flock (cf. Acts 20:17, 28). The "deacons" were those church leaders who had special service responsibilities in the assembly (cf. Acts 6).

1:2. In his greeting to the Philippians, Paul used two words descriptive of Christian graces: **grace** and **peace.** The order in which he used them is significant. Before there can be any genuine peace there must be a personal response to God's grace, His unmerited favor manifested climactically at Calvary. Both grace and peace find their source in **God our Father and the Lord Jesus Christ.**

2. PRAISE FOR THEIR CONSTANT WITNESS (1:3-6)

1:3. It must have brought great joy to the Philippians' hearts as they read how the apostle often thanked God for them. Here was a letter of commendation from one who was in Roman chains some 800 miles away. About 10 years had passed since Paul had first worked among them. But the passing of time had not diminished his love or his interest in them. Every time Paul thought of them he thanked God for them.

1:4-6. None of the believers was excluded from Paul's prayers. Coming from a prisoner, this is especially signifi-

cant. It was with **joy** that the apostle also besought God on their behalf. Paul's hardships made him better, not bitter. They always do one or the other to a child of God.

The Philippian saints and Paul were partners in the things of Christ. This was true because they shared with him in his need. They gave of themselves to Paul and in turn to the cause of Christ for which he labored. But not only did they share with him in his need as a prisoner. They had also fellowshiped with them **from the first day** they trusted Christ. This brought great joy to the apostle's heart.

Great confidence gripped the apostle as he thought and prayed for the Philippians. The perfect tense of the Greek word translated **being confident** indicates that Paul had come to a settled conviction earlier and that he still was confident it was true. What was he so confident and sure of? It was that God would most certainly continue on to **completion** the **good work** He had begun in them. That good work was their salvation. It may also have included their fellowship and sharing of their bounties with Paul.

Paul had no doubt that God would continue in the Philippians what He had begun to do in them. God would work in them **until the day of Christ Jesus.** In 2:16 Paul called this "the day of Christ." Though Paul did not know when that day would occur—when all believers would be caught up to meet the Lord in the air—he did know that God would continue the work He had begun in His own children.

3. PRAISE FOR THEIR CONCERN FOR THE GOSPEL (1:7)

1:7. The first part of this verse is a sort of apology or defense for the way Paul felt about the Philippians, as expressed in verses 3-6.

The Greek allows for the phrase **since I have you in my heart** to read "since you have me in your heart." Certainly both Paul and the Philippians were in each others' hearts. However, in view of the specific reference to himself (v. 7) it seems better to accept the NIV rendering. His affection for the saints is also stated in 1:8 and 4:16.

It did not matter whether Paul was under arrest (**in chains;** cf. "chains" in 1:13-14, 17) or free; his friends at Philippi shared with him in what God was doing through him. That work concerned primarily the spread of the gospel. It was because of their partnership with him that he could propagate God's grace. Paul praised them for their concern that this good news be spread abroad.

4. PRAISE SHOWN BY HIS LOVE FOR THEM (1:8)

1:8. Paul called on God to witness to his feelings toward the Philippians. Paul was aware—as were his readers—that they could not know his heart. But God knew it perfectly. The **affection** Paul had for his readers was no mere human interest or attraction. It originated with the Lord Jesus Christ Himself. Christ's love had so overwhelmed Paul that His affection was Paul's very own. The fact that Paul told this to the Philippians demonstrates the reality and intensity of his praise for them.

B. Paul's prayer for the saints at Philippi (1:9-11)

1. PRAYER FOR LOVE (1:9-10)

The apostle assured the saints that he prayed regularly for them (v. 3). Now here (v. 9) he reported what it was he prayed for.

1:9. It was Paul's **prayer** that the Philippians' love for other believers would **abound,** run over as a cup or a river overflows. But that love should be more than sentimental; it should be knowledgeable and discerning. Having genuine spiritual **knowledge** (*epignōsis*) of God and **depth of insight** into His ways enables Christians to love God and others more. (This Gr. word for "insight" [*aisthēsis*] occurs only here in the NT.)

1:10. Paul stated two purposes for his prayer. The first is a near purpose: **to discern what is best;** and the second is a remote one: to **be pure and blameless until the day of Christ.** The idea of testing is clearly in view in the Greek word *dokimazō,* translated "discern." The testing is with a view to approving. The word was used in testing metals and coins, to determine whether they met the specified standards.

"Pure" is the translation of a Greek word used only here and in 2 Peter 3:1. It is *eilikrineis,* which comes from the words for "sun" and "to judge," thus indicating purity that is tested by the light of the

sun. Paul wanted his readers to be rightly related to God and in fellowship with Him. Paul also was concerned that their relationships with others be what God would have them to be. The word *aproskopoi,* translated "blameless," also appears in 1 Corinthians 10:32 where the same writer urged, "Do not cause anyone to stumble." Paul's desire for his friends at Philippi ought to be the concern of all believers—to be morally pure, not causing others to stumble.

2. PRAYER FOR THE FRUIT OF RIGHTEOUSNESS (1:11)

1:11. Paul also prayed that the believers in the church at Philippi would be **filled with the fruit of righteousness.** A righteous stand before God, resulting from being clothed in Christ's righteousness, ought to produce fruit for God. Such inner qualities, partially described in Galatians 5:22-23, will be evident to others. The fruit of the Spirit comes **through Jesus Christ,** for it is really His life lived out through believers. Such fruit magnifies God, not self. So a life that exhibits such traits is to be **the glory and praise of God.**

C. Paul's presentation of himself to the saints (1:12-30)

The apostle faced opposition from those outside the church and misrepresentation from some within. But this did not dissuade or distract him from fulfilling God's call. Through it all, Christ was being preached, which brought him great delight. So his bonds, instead of hindering his outreach, resulted in a greater spreading of the gospel of Christ. Paul's friends back in Philippi were apparently quite concerned about him, thinking he was discouraged and that God's plan had gone awry. Not so, the apostle responded.

1. STALWART TESTIMONY (1:12-18)

1:12-14. From his own experiences Paul wanted the believers at Philippi to learn an important truth: there are no accidents with God. Instead of Paul's ministry being curtailed because of his bondage, it was being advanced.

The advance came partly because **the whole palace guard,** as well as others, were hearing about Christ (vv. 12-13). The "palace guard" (*praitōriō*) likely refers to the praetorian guard, made up of

Roman soldiers. Though Paul resided in his own rented facility (Acts 28:30), he was guarded by these soldiers all the time. The custom was for a prisoner to be chained at the wrist to a soldier.

All in Rome who came in contact with Paul heard about Christ. It was well known that he was not under guard for being a lawbreaker. Instead he was **in chains for Christ** (Phil. 1:13). In an effort to silence the truth, the authorities had incarcerated the one who spoke it, but their plan did not work.

Paul's incarceration had another effect: it encouraged those who had been reluctant about speaking for Christ (v. 14). Large numbers of believers became bold for Christ when they saw how God was spreading the gospel through Paul. The positive response Paul received in the face of opposition caused others to speak **more courageously and fearlessly** for Christ. Paul's confinement was doing what his circumstances outside of prison could never do.

1:15-18. The people who were emboldened to speak God's Word were of two kinds. Some preached Christ **out of envy and rivalry,** but others preached Him **out of good will** (v. 15). Those who preached out of good will did so **in love** (v. 16), knowing that Paul was in chains because of his **defense of the gospel.** The word "defense" is the Greek *apologia,* also used in verse 7.

The group that preached Christ out of envy and rivalry (v. 15) had **selfish ambition** (v. 17) as their motive. They purposely wanted to **stir up trouble** for Paul while he was in bondage. They were probably not Judaizers, as some suppose, because Paul said they were preaching Christ, though insincerely. The Judaizers believed that keeping the Old Testament Law was a means of salvation. Paul had sternly rebuked them as preachers of "a different gospel" (Gal. 1:6). However, since he did not accuse these in Philippi of presenting "another gospel," it seems that they were believers who for some unknown reason did not love the apostle or appreciate his work. Though they were doctrinally sound, they promoted themselves.

What rejoiced Paul's heart was that Christ was being preached, even though it was from wrong motives by some (Phil. 1:18). Since the content of the preaching

was the same for both groups, the apostle could rejoice. He did not **rejoice** because there was a faction among members of Christ's body, for this brought him grief. Instead, it was the preaching of Christ that brought him joy.

2. SETTLED CONVICTIONS (1:19-26)

1:19. As a man of convictions, Paul shared his assurance that his fetters would eventually result in his **deliverance.** The Greek word translated "deliverance" here was used in different ways in the New Testament. It often meant spiritual deliverance—salvation, being born again. Here (v. 19) Paul used the word to refer to either the final stage of his salvation (cf. Rom. 5:9) or future vindication in a Roman court. It seems unlikely that he had his release in mind since in the next two sentences he wrote of the real possibility of his near death.

The bases on which the apostle's assurance rested were the **prayers** of the saints and the **help given by the Spirit of Jesus Christ** (Phil. 1:19). He knew he could count on the Philippians' prayers, and also on the Holy Spirit's ministry (cf. Rom. 8:26-27). "Help" (*epichorēgias*) carries the meaning of "support," much as a ligament provides support in a physical body. (This Gr. word is used in the NT only here and in Eph. 4:16.)

1:20. Paul was not sure whether he would experience release or martyrdom for his faith. He was certain of one thing though, that he wanted Christ to be **exalted** in his **body** either way (cf. "in the body," vv. 22, 24). This was Paul's expectation and hope. The apostle also knew full well that it would take courage to face death with the proper attitude. **Eagerly expect** is the translation of a unique word. It describes straining one's neck to catch a glimpse of something that is ahead. (*Apokaradokia,* a noun, is used only here and in Rom. 8:19.) Paul's concern was not what would happen to him but what testimony would be left for his Lord. Release would allow him to continue preaching Christ. But martyrdom would also advance the cause of Christ.

1:21. Paul's main purpose in living was to glorify Christ. Christ was the essence of his life. Yet Paul knew that if he were martyred, Christ would be glorified through the promotion of the gospel which would result from his testimony in death. And Paul himself would benefit, for death would result in his being with Christ (v. 23). The words **to die** suggest the act of dying, not the state of death.

1:22-24. The apostle's seeming frustration of mind is apparent in these verses. He knew if he could **go on living** there would certainly be fruit from his labor (v. 22). God would bless his work and continue to use him as He had in the past. Yet if Paul had a choice between going on living or dying for Christ, he was at a loss as to how to decide. He simply did not know which to choose. Of course the choice was really not up to him anyway.

Paul was distressed. He was hardpressed to know which would bring the most glory to God and therefore be to everyone's advantage in the long run. His personal desire was **to depart and be with Christ** (v. 23). This he knew would be **better by far** for him since it would mean his release from the persecutions and other hardships that he suffered. But he also knew that the Philippians needed him. For them it was **more necessary** that he **remain in the body,** or stay alive (v. 24). Paul's selfless attitude is revealed here by his placing his friends' needs above his own desires.

1:25-26. New confidence of his release appears to have come to Paul. (The word **convinced** is the same word rendered "being confident" in v. 6.) By his release and return to them they would **progress . . . in the faith** and would experience great **joy** (v. 25).

The rejoicing of the Philippians would **overflow** (v. 26; the same word is rendered "abound" in v. 9), and that exulting would be **in Christ Jesus,** the source of true joy for all believers. ("Joy" in v. 26 is the word "exulting" [*kauchēma*] which differs from the more common word for "joy" used more often in Phil., including v. 25.) They would exult because the one who had taught them about Christ would be with them again.

3. SOLEMN EXHORTATIONS (1:27-30)

1:27. The apostle had the believers in Philippi on his heart. Regardless of what would happen to him—release from bonds or martyrdom—he wanted them to honor and glorify Christ. The words **conduct yourselves** translate a political word which would mean much to the

Philippian believers. Literally it means "live as citizens." Because Philippi was a Roman colony, the Christian inhabitants of the city would appreciate Paul's use of that verb. To live in a way that is **worthy of the gospel of Christ** (cf. Eph. 4:1) is indeed the responsibility of every child of God. This Paul exhorted the Philippians to do.

The saints embraced a common cause, for they each shared in the same body of Christ. Therefore Paul was burdened that they **stand firm** (cf. Phil. 4:1) **in one spirit** and contend **as one man** (lit., "in one soul") **for the faith of the gospel,** the body of truth (cf. "faith," Jude 3). Their **contending** (*synalthountes*) for the faith suggests a joint effort, like that of an athletic team.

1:28. Paul wanted his readers to live courageously for Christ in the midst of opposition and persecution. True, they would be opposed but this should not frighten them **in any way.** Instead they were to be reminded at such times that their own victorious Christian response would be a sign that their opposers would eventually be destroyed. At the same time it would be **a sign** that the saints of God would be delivered **by God** Himself. This assurance would doubtless be the Holy Spirit working in their hearts.

1:29-30. So that being opposed would not come as a surprise, he gave them a reminder. Both believing on **Christ** and suffering **for Him** had been **granted to** them (v. 29). Suffering for Christ was not to be considered accidental or a divine punishment. Paul referred to a kind of suffering that was really a sign of God's favor. The Greek word *echaristhē,* translated "granted," is derived from a word which means "grace" or "favor." Believing on Christ and suffering for Him are both associated with God's grace.

Paul and his readers shared a similar **struggle** (v. 30). So Paul encouraged them as they had him. They wanted to know how he fared in Rome. He told them, so they could also be encouraged as they faced hardships.

II. Examples for Living the Christian Life (2:1-30)

A. *The Son of God whose attitude the believer is to share (2:1-18)*

This passage is a continuation of the exhortation begun in 1:27-30. The entire section (1:27–2:18) states what Paul called the saints at Philippi to do. It includes the famous *kenōsis* or self-emptying passage (2:5–11), in which the Son of God Himself is set forth as the One whose attitude the believer should share.

1. THE DECLARATION (2:1)

2:1. In 1:27 Paul had written about living the Christian life in harmony with the message on which it is based. He followed that message with a call to show forth spiritual unity. This unity is possible because of the reality of the four qualities mentioned in 2:1. The "if" clauses, being translations of first-class conditions in Greek, speak of certainties. So in this passage "if" may be translated "since." Paul wrote here about realities, not questionable things. Paul appealed on the basis of (a) **encouragement from being united with Christ . . .** (b) **comfort from His love . . .** (c) **fellowship with the Spirit . . .** (d) **tenderness and compassion.**

"Encouragement" is from a Greek word related to the one Christ used in referring to the Holy Spirit as "the Counselor" (John 14:16; "Comforter," kjv). It may also be translated "exhortation" in the sense of either rebuke or comfort. Since each believer had received this work of the Spirit, Paul used it as a basis to appeal for their spiritual unity.

Also they each had "comfort from His [God's] love." God's love in people's hearts produces spiritual unity in their lives.

"Fellowship with the Spirit" is a result of the Spirit's permanent indwelling ministry (cf. 1 Cor. 6:19). This may refer, however, to fellowship that comes *from* the Holy Spirit, just as encouragement comes *from* Christ and comfort comes *from* love.

Paul also spoke of "tenderness (*splanchna*; cf. Phile. 7, 20) and compassion." One of the Spirit's ministries is to produce within each believer a concern and love for other members of God's family. This may be received or rejected by a believer, but the Spirit's work is a reality and is a basis for spiritual unity.

2. THE EXHORTATIONS (2:2-4)

2:2. On the basis of what was presented in verse 1, Paul exhorted his readers to show in practical ways the unity which was theirs in Christ. Their expres-

sion of that spiritual unity would make his joy complete. Corresponding to the four realities in verse 1 are four specific ways in which their spiritual unity would be realized. They would be **like-minded**, have **the same love**, be **one in spirit** (*sympsychoi*), and be one in **purpose.**

2:3-4. Paul gave further exhortations, also based on the declaration of the fourfold reality expressed in verse 1. The terms the apostle used reveal an underlying problem in the church at Philippi. The situation Paul addressed evidently was prompted by self-centeredness among certain Christians.

Nothing was to be done **out of selfish ambition** (v. 3). The same word (*eritheian*) appears in 1:17 to describe the attitude of those who opposed Paul. Without question such behavior is of the flesh and not the Spirit (cf. Gal. 5:20, which uses the same word). **Vain conceit**, meaning "empty glory," was probably the root cause of their selfish ambition.

The two negatives are followed by a positive exhortation: **in humility consider others better than yourselves. But**, a word of contrast, introduces these words. Humility before God and man is a virtue every child of God needs to strive for. A spirit of pride in human relations indicates a lack of humility before God. Paul exhorted the Philippians to consider others before themselves (cf. 1 Peter 5:5-6). "This will go far toward removing disharmony" (Homer A. Kent, Jr., "Philippians," in *The Expositor's Bible Commentary*, 11:122).

Paul explained how humility can be expressed (Phil. 2:4). Instead of concentrating on self, each believer should be concerned for **the interests of others** in the household of faith (cf. Rom. 12:10). Preoccupation with oneself is sin.

3. THE HUMILIATION OF CHRIST (2:5-8)

Christ is the supreme example of humility and selfless concern for others (vv. 5-8). These verses, along with verses 9-11, constitute a grand statement on Christology.

2:5. Believers are exhorted to have the same attitude—selfless humility—Christ exhibited in His humiliation and condescension. The word here translated **attitude** is translated "like-minded" in verse 2.

2:6-8. The word translated **nature**

(*morphē*) in verses 6 and 7 is a crucial term in this passage. This word (trans. "form" in the KJV and NASB) stresses the inner essence or reality of that with which it is associated (cf. Mark 16:12). Christ Jesus, Paul said, is of the very essence (*morphē*) of God, and in His incarnation He embraced perfect humanity. His complete and absolute deity is here carefully stressed by the apostle. The Savior's claim to deity infuriated the Jewish leaders (John 5:18) and caused them to accuse Him of blasphemy (John 10:33).

Though possessing full deity (John 1:14; Col. 2:9), Christ did not consider His **equality with God** (Phil. 2:6) as **something to be grasped** or held onto. In other words Christ did not hesitate to set aside His self-willed use of deity when He became a man. As God He had all the rights of deity, and yet during His incarnate state He surrendered His right to manifest Himself visibly as the God of all splendor and glory.

Christ's humiliation included His making **Himself nothing,** taking the **very nature** (*morphē*) **of a servant,** and **being made in human likeness** (v. 7). These statements indicate that Christ became a man, a true human being. The words "made Himself nothing" are, literally, "He emptied Himself." "Emptied," from the Greek *kenoō,* points to the divesting of His self-interests, but not of His deity. "The very nature of a servant" certainly points to His lowly and humble position, His willingness to obey the Father, and serve others. He became a man, a true human being. "Likeness" suggests similarity but difference. Though His humanity was genuine, He was different from all other humans in that He was sinless (Heb. 4:15).

Thus it is seen that Christ, while retaining the essence of God, was also human. In His incarnation He was *fully* God and *fully* man at the same time. He was God manifest in human flesh (John 1:14).

Some have wrongly taught that the phrase, **being found in appearance as a man** (Phil. 2:8), means that He only *looked* human. But this contradicts verse 7. "Appearance" is the Greek *schēmati,* meaning an outer appearance which may be temporary. This contrasts with *morphē* ("very nature") in verses 6 and 7, which speaks of an outer appearance that reveals permanent inner quality.

The condescension of Christ included not only His birth—the Incarnation in which He became the God-Man—but also His **death.** And it was the most cruel and despicable form of death—**even death on a cross!** (v. 8) This form of capital punishment was limited to non-Romans and the worst criminals.

No better example of humiliation and a selfless attitude for believers to follow could possibly be given than that of Christ. With this example before them, the saints at Philippi should be "likeminded" (v. 2) and live humbly before their God and each other.

4. THE EXALTATION OF CHRIST (2:9-11)

God the Father is the subject in these verses, whereas in verses 6-8 God the Son was the subject. Christ's obedience was followed by the Father's exaltation of Him to the place of highest honor. God exalted and honored the One men despised and rejected.

2:9. Christ's exaltation and His receiving a **name that is above every name** was the answer to His high-priestly prayer (John 17:5). The exaltation refers to His resurrection, ascension, and glorification at the Father's right hand (Acts 2:33; Heb. 1:3). His "name" is not merely a title; it refers to His person and to His position of dignity and honor.

2:10. In keeping with Christ's exaltation and high **name . . . every knee** will one day **bow** and acknowledge Him for who He really is. Paul stressed the same truth in his letter to the Romans (Rom. 14:11). Both instances reflect Isaiah's prophecy (Isa. 45:23) of the singular greatness of the God of Abraham, Isaac, and Jacob. The extent of Christ's sovereign authority is delineated in the threefold phrase, **in heaven and on earth and under the earth.** No intelligent being—whether angels and saints in heaven; people living on the earth; or Satan, demons, and the unsaved in hell—in all of God's universe will escape. All will bow either willingly or they will be made to do so.

2:11. What all will **confess** is that **Jesus Christ is Lord.** This, the earliest Christian creed, meant that Jesus Christ is Yahweh-God. One day all will be made to acknowledge that Jesus Christ is all He claimed to be—very God of very God. Unfortunately, for many it will be too late for the salvation of their souls. The exalted place the Savior now occupies and the universal bowing in the future in acknowledgement of His lordship is all **to the glory of God the Father.**

5. THE EXHORTATIONS CONTINUED (2:12-18)

In these verses Paul returned to the exhortations which he began earlier in verses 2-4.

2:12-13. Therefore connects these verses with what immediately precedes them. Christ obeyed the Father and carried out His plan even to death on the cross (v. 8). The Philippian Christians needed to obey, to follow Paul's instruction which was drawn from Christ's example.

The exhortation was direct and pointed, but tempered with love, for he called the believers **my dear friends.** This tender expression doubtless reminded them of the experiences they shared with the apostle and Silas when they first came to Christ and established their church (Acts 16:19-40). When Paul was with them, they followed his instructions willingly and quickly. He reminded them of this before he asked them to do the same at the present time, even though he was far from them. He had earlier spoken of his absence (Phil. 1:27).

The special request he had for them, in view of their needs and in view of the example of Christ, is stated forcefully—**continue to work out your salvation with fear and trembling.**

It is commonly understood that this exhortation relates to the personal salvation of the saints at Philippi. They were told to "work out," to put into practice in their daily living, what God had worked in them by His Spirit. They were not told to work *for* their salvation but to work *out* the salvation God had already given them. In view of the apparent problems of disunity and pride among those believers this interpretation seems correct. Some were not doing their work selflessly and with the interests of others ahead of their own (cf. 2:3-4).

Some writers understand Paul's challenge to refer to the corporate life of the whole assembly in Philippi. Those who hold this view find support in the imme-diate context where Paul argued against their looking exclusively to their own needs (cf. v. 4). In this view "salvation" refers to the whole assembly's deliverance from disunity, pride, and selfishness.

Perhaps it is best to see *both* the outworking of personal salvation and the corporate salvation or deliverance of the whole assembly from whatever held them back from experiencing God's best.

This outworking was to be done "with fear and trembling," with a complete trust in God and not in themselves.

The only way this could be realized was through **God** who would enable them to do it (v. 13). Paul told the Philippian saints that God worked in them so that they could do His good pleasure and accomplish **His good purpose.** Both divine enablement and human responsibility are involved in getting God's work done. Believers are partners with God, laboring together with Him. The verb **works** (v. 13) means "energizes" or "provides enablement." God makes His own both willing and desirous to do His work.

2:14-16. These verses give specific instructions on how to work out God's "good purpose" (v. 13) in relation to daily Christian living.

Everything was to be done **without complaining or arguing** (v. 14). The order of the Greek words here places emphasis on everything a believer does. The present tense of the verb **do** suggests that this was to be done continually. "Complaining" is the translation of a word which reflects a bad attitude expressed in grumbling. The apostle may have had in mind the behavior of the Israelites who often complained to Moses and in turn to God (cf. 1 Cor. 10:10). "Arguing" reflects a legal connotation of disputing and may refer, at least in part, to the practice of going to civil courts to settle their differences (cf. 1 Cor. 6:1-11).

The importance of the kind of behavior called for is set forth in Philippians 2:15-16. Before their testimony for Christ could ever be effective in the community where they lived, the Philippians needed to set some things straight in their own assembly.

Evidently the believers were complaining (to God and each other) and arguing (with each other). As a result they were not **without fault** among the unregenerate; they were not shining **like stars** in their world (2:15). The Philippian assembly needed to show themselves as united and as one in Christ. Non-Christians were not being attracted to Him by the saints' strifes and contentions. **Blameless** (*amemptoi*, v. 15) means "above reproach." This does not mean sinless perfection. The corporate testimony of the church is in view. All believers are called on to live out the salvation God has worked in them—to progress in their spiritual maturity. The people were to live so that those outside of Christ could not rightfully point an accusing finger at them. **Pure** translates *akeraioi*, a word that was used of wine which had not been diluted and of metal which had not been weakened in any way. Jesus also used the word when He told the Twelve to be "innocent" as doves (Matt. 10:16). The Greek words for "blameless" and "pure" here (Phil. 2:15) differ from those translated "blameless" and "pure" in 1:10 (see comments on 1:10).

The Philippians lived **in a crooked and depraved generation** (2:15). Again it seems that Paul had the unbelieving Israelites in mind. Moses had used similar words to describe Israel who had gone astray (cf. Deut. 32:5). Peter used the same terminology ("corrupt generation," Acts 2:40) that Christ did ("perverse generation," Matt. 17:17).

The world today, like theirs, is unscrupulous and perverted. Most people have turned their backs on God and truth. In this kind of world God's people are to "shine like stars" (Phil. 2:15; cf. Matt. 5:14-16). They are to be **children of God without fault.**

A child of God is in God's family, but the unregenerate are alienated from Him. They are His enemies. God's sovereign plan is to use His Word, administered by God's people, to transform His enemies into His friends by the regenerating work of God's Spirit. The Greek word *epechontes,* **hold out** (v. 16) means either "hold forth" or "hold firmly." The former fits better here. It was used in secular Greek of offering wine to a guest at a banquet. As the Philippian saints held out (or offered) **the word of life** to others, Paul would then be able to **boast** (glory) **on the day of Christ** that he had not labored in vain with them. The "day of Christ" refers to the Rapture

when the Savior returns and meets His own in the air (1 Thes. 4:13-18). This boasting was not a selfish ambition of Paul's; he was concerned with God's honor.

2:17-18. Paul's stated desire to be able to rejoice when he would see Christ and to be sure he had not labored in vain for the Philippians is followed by a statement about his joy in the midst of suffering. The apostle knew that death as a martyr was a real possibility for him.

Paul viewed himself as **being poured out like a drink offering** on behalf of the Philippians (v. 17). But instead of sorrowing he rejoiced. "Poured out" is from the Greek word *spendomai,* used of a drink offering given as a sacrifice to God. The possibility of release from prison was not uppermost in Paul's mind as it had been before (cf. 1:24-26). He now viewed his death as imminent. Later, near the actual time of his death, he used this same language (2 Tim. 4:6).

The sacrifice and service (perhaps this could be understood as "sacrificial service") stemmed from their faith. Paul used the same word for sacrifice (*thysia*) in Romans 12:1. There the sacrifice the believer-priest offers is his body. "Service" (*leitourgia*) is the same word translated "ceremonies" in Hebrews 9:21 (cf. Phil. 2:25, 30). This means that the work the Philippians did for God was considered an act of worship. All of this brought rejoicing to the apostle's heart even though it resulted in his facing imminent death.

Paul wanted his friends at Philippi to experience the same joy he had (2:18) and to **be glad and rejoice with** him.

B. *The servants of God whose manner of life the believer is to follow (2:19-30)*

In chapter 2 Paul first discussed the fact that the attitude of Christ, who humbled Himself and became obedient to death, should be shared by believers (vv. 1-18). Then Paul pointed out (vv. 19-30) that choice servants of God also provide examples for others to follow.

1. TIMOTHY AND PAUL (2:19-24)

Paul's incarceration had made it impossible for him to visit the saints at Philippi. He had referred to this fact earlier (v. 12). His deep and abiding concern for his friends' spiritual welfare prompted him to send Timothy to visit and to minister in his place. Timothy was at the time Paul's companion (1:1), though evidently not a prisoner. The letter would be delivered by Epaphroditus and Timothy's visit would follow.

2:19. The concern Paul demonstrated in sending Timothy was an example for the Philippians and all believers to follow. Not only did Paul give them the gospel and lead them to Christ, but he also wanted to be sure they were growing spiritually. His genuine interest in them continued.

Not certain of his own future, the apostle prefaced his desire with the words **I hope in the Lord Jesus.** This was an unusual way to speak of Timothy's proposed journey. Paul was especially aware that his release or death could come at any time.

The intent of Timothy's visit was clearly stated—**that I also may be cheered.** Both Paul's letter and Timothy's visit would certainly encourage the believers at Philippi. But the apostle also wanted to be encouraged as Timothy returned with good news from them.

Another lesson to be learned from Paul's sending Timothy is the need for selflessness. Timothy was close to Paul and dear to his heart. If Paul ever needed Timothy, it was while he was there in Rome under house arrest. Yet he was willing to sacrifice Timothy's companionship so that others could be helped.

2:20. Paul's young son in the faith had a deep interest and concern for the Philippians. In fact, Paul had **no one else** in Rome who was **like him.** Timothy's interest in their **welfare** was unexcelled. He was an excellent example of one who was selfless, more concerned about others than himself (cf. 2:3-4). The believers in the Philippian assembly needed to share Timothy's sincere interest in the welfare of others. The words "no one else like him" are literally "no one of equal soul" (*isopsychon*; cf. "one in spirit," *sympsychoi*, in 2:2).

2:21. This verse appears to make a rather broad claim. Did Paul mean to include everybody he ever knew? Or did he mean that of all who were near him in Rome, none compared to Timothy? Did Paul mean all others whom he might have

contacted to run the errand were more interested in their **own interests** than in those of Christ's? The second suggestion seems correct. Timothy stood out as a rare gem in a world of self-seekers (cf. 1:15, 17).

2:22. The Philippians knew Timothy, so they knew that what the apostle said about him was true. From the start, when he worked with Paul in Philippi, Timothy was faithful (cf. Acts 16). He had been closely associated with Paul since Paul's second missionary journey. The man had often been tested and **proved.** Paul was Timothy's spiritual **father,** and Timothy worked with him as his **son.** Together they both served the Lord as slaves **in the work of the gospel.**

Timothy's qualities were unexcelled. His whole life stands as an example for every child of God. Those in the Philippian assembly who were deficient in any of these qualities must have been pricked in conscience as they read Paul's letter, even as believers are today.

2:23-24. After his grand commendation of Timothy, Paul reaffirmed his intention to send him to them (v. 23). Just as soon as Paul knew how things were going, he would **send him.** Apparently Paul was waiting for some decision in his legal case.

In view of verse 24, Paul must have expected release from his chains. Significantly Paul's confidence was now **in the Lord** (cf. "in the Lord Jesus," v. 19). This phrase may be rendered "if the Lord wills."

Though the Scriptures include no specific statement about Paul's release, it must have occurred since he was imprisoned again in Rome during which time he wrote his last letter, 2 Timothy. Though there is no record of Paul's revisiting Philippi, he may have returned there after his release.

2. EPAPHRODITUS AND PAUL (2:25-30)

It is uncertain whether Epaphroditus was still with Paul at Rome when Paul wrote Philippians or whether Epaphroditus had already left to return to Philippi. Traditionally Epaphroditus has been viewed as the bearer of this letter to the Philippians. He is mentioned only here and in 4:18.

2:25. Since the church had sent **Epaphroditus** to bring Paul "the gifts" (of money, 4:18) and to discover how things were going with him, they probably intended for him to stay and assist Paul indefinitely. However, the apostle chose to send him back to them. But Paul wanted to be doubly sure the believers knew how highly he thought of Epaphroditus. He called him **my brother, fellow worker . . . fellow soldier,** and **messenger.** He shared Paul's spiritual life, labors, and dangers. He willingly took the role of a servant to assist Paul. What an exemplary lifestyle for every believer to follow. This man, whose name means "charming," served the Lord while he served others. The words **take care** translate the noun *leitourgon* ("serve as a priest"), which is related to the word "service" (*leitourgia*) in verse 17 (cf. v. 30). Epaphroditus' ministry to Paul was a priestly kind of service (cf. 4:18).

2:26-27. Epaphroditus had a deep concern for his friends in Philippi. He longed for all of them. He was **distressed because** he knew they had **heard he was ill.** His longing for the Philippians was exactly like Paul's (1:8). And the distress Epaphroditus experienced was similar to the agony Christ experienced in Gethsemane (Matt. 26:37; Mark 14:33).

Whatever illness Epaphroditus suffered was serious because he **almost died** (Phil. 2:27, 30). There is no indication that Paul had the ability to heal him or that he tried to do so. Neither is there any hint that Epaphroditus was sick because of being out of God's will.

Paul praised God for His **mercy** shown to Epaphroditus in restoring him to health and in sparing Paul **sorrow upon sorrow.** Thankfulness filled the apostle's heart. Paul already had sorrow associated with his imprisonment. He loved and needed Epaphroditus, so Epaphroditus' death would have brought Paul additional heaviness.

2:28-30. Paul was indeed selfless. He had the best interests of the Philippian believers and Epaphroditus at heart. They were sorry because their messenger to Paul had been ill and could not do for the apostle what they had hoped. Anticipating what they might think, Paul took full responsibility for sending Epaphroditus home. With haste he arranged for his trip back to Philippi. He did so for two reasons: He wanted them to **be glad,** and he

wanted to be relieved of all **anxiety** himself.

The believers in Philippi were not to think wrongly of Epaphroditus for coming home. They were not to think that he had failed when Paul needed him most. He was to be welcomed **in the Lord** and in fact to be honored.

Paul's desire here illustrates how believers ought to relate toward those who may be misunderstood by others. Genuine Christian love, a fruit of the Spirit (Gal. 5:22), is always desirable, for it defends others and overlooks their faults (1 Cor. 13:7).

Paul explained (Phil. 2:30) why the saints should receive Epaphroditus. This messenger from Philippi was so sick he **almost died.** It was while he was serving Christ that he became sick, and if he had died it would also have been for Christ.

The believers from Philippi could not be in Rome helping Paul. Epaphroditus was **risking his life** to do what they **could not** do. He was serving Christ while he served them and Paul. (The word **help** is *leitourgias*, "priestly service," also used in v. 17; cf. v. 25.) As Christians serve Christ, they also serve others. The apostle reminded his readers of this so that they would receive Epaphroditus as they should.

III. Exhortations for Living the Christian Life (3:1-21)

In chapter 1 Paul encouraged the saints at Philippi to go on living the Christian life. In chapter 2 Paul set forth Timothy, Epaphroditus, and himself as examples of how to please God. Exhortations necessary for those who would lead such a life followed in chapter 3.

A. Believers are to have no confidence in the flesh (3:1-14)

1. THE EXHORTATION INTRODUCED (3:1)

3:1. Before stressing the serious danger of placing confidence in the flesh, the apostle called for a spirit of rejoicing in the Lord. His word **finally** was used to introduce a new subject as well as a clue that he had begun to conclude the letter. He used the same phrase again in 4:8. So some feel that chapter 3 is a digression from the author's main theme.

Paul called on believers to **rejoice in the Lord.** The word "rejoice" appears several times in the epistle (1:18 [twice];

2:17-18 [twice]; 3:1; 4:4 [twice], 10). It seems from this repeated emphasis that the Philippian Christians needed this word. Most of God's people need this challenge often. It is easy for believers to let circumstances discourage them. The cure for discouragement is to rivet one's attention on the Lord and rejoice in Him.

It is significant too that a Roman prisoner would beseech people who were free to be joyful in their Savior. It seems that it should be the other way around. Paul learned what every child of God needs to learn—there can be rejoicing in the Lord even when outward circumstances are contrary to a spirit of rejoicing.

Repetition is a vital part of learning. Either orally or in writing (perhaps in 1:27-30) the apostle had given the same truth to the Philippians before. He made no apology for repeating the instruction by writing **the same things to you again.** It was **no trouble** for him to review the essentials again. He felt constrained to do so for their benefit. The instruction was a **safeguard** for them.

2. THE EXAMPLE TO BE AVOIDED (3:2-3)

One particular group in Paul's day was especially guilty of putting confidence in the flesh. These were the Judaizers. They plagued Paul and his converts constantly. Confused about the gospel, they added works of the law to faith in Christ, both for salvation and for Christian living. The Old Testament rite of circumcision was of special concern to them. They insisted that it was necessary for salvation. They did not omit faith in Christ but added works of the flesh. Paul called such men "deceitful workmen" (2 Cor. 11:13).

3:2. Paul also called the Judaizers **dogs, those men who do evil, those mutilators of the flesh.** He considered their work dangerous and not of God. The saints were not to follow these people, but to beware of them, to **watch out** for them.

It was common for some Jews to refer to Gentiles as dogs, which were considered unclean animals. Paul used the term to describe those Jews who mutilated the gospel by insisting on the need to mutilate the flesh in order to be rightly related to God. What they did was

actually evil, even though they may have had good intentions.

3:3. The Old Testament rite of physical circumcision was not only a sign of covenant relationship, but it was also intended to be related to spiritual circumcision of the heart (cf. Deut. 30:6). Writing to Gentiles, Paul made it clear that he and they were the true **circumcision.** This was because they had **no confidence in the flesh** and instead worshiped **by the Spirit of God** and gloried **in Christ Jesus** alone.

Instead of boasting in human accomplishments, as the Judaizers and Jews did, a child of God should glory in Christ Jesus alone. The word **glory** (*kauchōmenoi*) used here means "boast" or "exult" (cf. 1:26; 2:16; 2 Cor. 10:17).

3. THE EXAMPLE TO BE FOLLOWED (3:4-14)

Paul gave some interesting autobiographical facts in these verses. On the surface it appears he was boasting. However, closer examination reveals that this was precisely what he tried to avoid and warn against. To be sure, there was a time when the apostle had confidence in the flesh. But this was no longer true. To stress that he used to have great boldness and pride in his own achievements, Paul reviewed his past for the Philippians. After this he told about his crisis conversion experience on the road to Damascus.

3:4-6. It cannot be emphasized too strongly that Paul did not place any **confidence in the flesh.** He had gained victory over that temptation of the devil. His presentation in these verses was intended to review for the Philippians the things in which he could have placed confidence if he had wanted to. In fact the list included things in which he did place great value and trust before he met Christ. His intention was to show that in the flesh he had more in which he could have boasted than did any of the Judaizers.

The **anyone else** (v. 4) referred to all who place confidence in the flesh. Paul wrote as though he were challenging the Judaizers to a showdown. His preliminary conclusion before he even got specific was that no matter what advantage was brought forth by his opponents, his advantages exceeded theirs (cf. Gal. 1:14).

Seven advantages listed in Philippians 3:5-6 demonstrate what Paul used to have in the flesh but what he later counted as loss for Christ. Two kinds of advantages are enumerated. First are those things which the apostle had by birth, apart from his choice. Four of these are listed—circumcision, of the stock of Israel, of the tribe of Benjamin, and a Hebrew son of Hebrew parents. Next he named those privileges which he voluntarily chose—being a Pharisee, being a persecutor of the church, and having a flawless external record of **legalistic righteousness.**

Circumcision was named first probably because it was a big issue with the Judaizers. Paul's specific time, **the eighth day,** stressed that he was not a proselyte or an Ishmaelite but a pure-blooded Jew. Proselytes were circumcised later in life and Ishmaelites after age 13 (cf. Gen. 17:25-26).

Paul was **of the people of Israel,** which describes his heritage. His parents were both true Jews, unlike some of the Judaizers. He could trace his family lineage all the way back to Abraham. He was a true member of the covenant people (cf. 2 Cor. 11:22).

He was also a Benjamite, from which tribe came Israel's first king (1 Sam. 9:1-2). This tribe had a special place of honor and was viewed with great esteem. Even after the kingdom was disrupted the tribe of Benjamin remained loyal to the house of David.

Hebrew was Paul's native tongue. Unlike some of the Israelites, he did not adopt Greek customs. He knew thoroughly both the language and customs of the people of God. He was a Hebrew son of Hebrew parents.

In regard to the Law, Paul was **a Pharisee,** a member of the strictest sect among his people. In addition to the Law of Moses the Pharisees added their own regulations which in time were interpreted as equal to the Law.

What greater **zeal** for the Jewish religion could anyone boast of than that he persecuted **the church?** Paul did this relentlessly before his conversion to Christ (Acts 9:1-2). No Judaizer could match such zeal.

In "legalistic righteousness" Paul also excelled. In fact in his own eyes he was **faultless** (*amemptos;* the same word is used in Phil. 2:15 where it is rendered "blameless").

3:7-9. Any of those who troubled the saints at Philippi would have loved to have been able to list to his credit those things Paul did. On the human side these were reasons to have religious self-confidence. But all those things enumerated in verses 5-6 the apostle considered **loss for the sake of Christ** (v. 7).

Consider means to "think through or reflect on." After reflection he considered them loss. This he did at a point in time in the past and that decision was still in effect when he wrote, as connoted by the use of the Greek perfect tense. Doubtless Paul considered his life-transforming conversion on the Damascus Road as the time when he switched from confidence in the flesh to confidence in Christ alone.

It would be hard to find a more forceful refutation of human effort to please God than what Paul presented here (v. 8). Four Greek particles (*alla menoun ge kai*) are translated **what is more** and introduce the strong statements of verse 8. Paul considered as **loss** not only the things already listed (vv. 5-6), but **everything** (v. 8). In exchange for confidence in the flesh Paul gained the **surpassing greatness of knowing Christ Jesus** personally. Christ was now his **Lord.**

His former "gains" (*kerdē,* v. 7) he considered "rubbish" (which can mean food scraps or dung) so that he might **gain** (*kerdēsō*) **Christ.** Nothing else really mattered to him any longer. Having Christ as his Savior and Lord so far surpassed anything he had in Judaism.

Those who "gain Christ" (v. 8) are those **found in Him** (v. 9). Christ is in the believer and the believer is in Christ. Paul wanted his life to demonstrate these truths. Being in Christ, he was not clinging to any **righteousness** of his own doing associated with Law-keeping. Such a righteousness is viewed by God as no righteousness at all but rather as "filthy rags" (Isa. 64:6). The righteousness which saves and in which Paul rested is **through** (*dia*) **faith in Christ.** This is the only kind which **comes from God and is by** (*epi*) **faith.** When a believing sinner responds in faith to the Spirit's work in his heart, he is clothed in the righteousness of Christ (Rom. 3:24-26). In this position he is "accepted in the Beloved" (Eph. 1:6, KJV). Thus robed, the believing sinner stands complete in Christ.

3:10-11. These verses contain an open and honest confession to the Philippians. Paul already knew Christ as his Savior. But he wanted to know Him more intimately as his Lord. **To know** (v. 10) means "to know by experience" (*gnōnai*). The noun (*gnōseōs*) is used in verse 8. The "surpassing greatness of knowing Christ" is now elaborated in verses 10-11. This is how Paul wanted to know Him. More of what he desired in his Christian life follows.

To experience **the power of His resurrection** was also the apostle's goal. The power which brought Christ forth from the dead now operates in believers' lives since they have been "raised with Christ" (Col. 3:1). "Power" (*dynamis*, also used in Acts 1:8; Rom. 1:16) means ability to overcome resistance. By setting forth his own goals and ambitions Paul gave the Philippians an example to follow. His example was, of course, in stark contrast to the Judaizers whose example they were not to follow.

Paul also longed to share in the fellowship of Christ's sufferings and in so doing to become **like Him in His death** (Phil. 3:10). These sufferings were not Christ's substitutionary sufferings on the cross. Paul knew that those could not be shared. But he did desire to participate with Christ, since he was one of His, in suffering for the sake of righteousness (cf. 1:29). God had used Ananias to tell Paul that this is precisely what he would do as a servant of Christ (Acts 9:16). The apostle did indeed suffer for Christ because he represented Him so openly and truly (cf. Rom. 8:36; 2 Cor. 4:10).

The words "becoming like Him" translate *symmorphizomenos*, which means "being conformed inwardly in one's experience to something" (cf. Phil. 3:21), in this case, to Christ's death. As Christ died *for* sin, so a believer has died *to* sin (Rom. 6:2, 6-7; Col. 3:3). He should exhibit that cutting off from his former sinful way by daily being set apart from sin (Rom. 6:1-4, 11-14) and living a new life by means of Christ's resurrection power (Rom. 6:4).

"Resurrection" (Phil. 3:11) is the translation of *exanastasin*, a Greek word used nowhere else in the New Testament. It means a partial resurrection out from among other corpses, literally an "out-re-surrection." But why did Paul say he wanted **somehow, to attain to the** (out-) **resurrection from the dead?** Did he doubt he would be raised from the dead? Hardly. Perhaps he was using this word to refer to the Rapture, thus expressing the hope that the Lord would return during his lifetime.

3:12-14. Though Paul was a spiritual giant in the eyes of the Philippian saints, he wanted them to know that he had not yet attained the goals stated in verse 10. He was still actively pressing on toward them. He had by no means reached the final stage of his sanctification.

Paul's salvation experience had taken place about 30 years before he wrote to the Philippians. He had won many spiritual battles in that time. He had grown much in those years, but he candidly confessed he had not **obtained all this,** nor was he yet **made perfect** (v. 12). He still had more spiritual heights to climb. This testimony of the apostle reminded the saints at Philippi—and it serves to remind believers today—that there must never be a stalemate in their spiritual growth or a plateau beyond which they cannot climb.

Paul pursued Christlikeness with the enthusiasm and persistence of a runner in the Greek games. Unlike the Judaizers, whose influence was prevalent among the Philippians, the apostle did not claim to have attained spiritual maturity. He was still pressing on, pursuing **that for which Christ Jesus took hold of** him. Nor had he yet **taken hold of it,** that is, he had not yet attained perfection or ultimate conformity to Christ. But he was determined that he would forget the past and, like a runner, press on toward the goal. Paul refused to be controlled or absorbed by his past heritage (vv. 5-7) or his attainments (v. 8).

Vigorously and with concentration Paul sought **to win the prize** to which God had **called** him **heavenward** (v. 14). Again the Greek games must have been on his mind as he wrote of the prize. The winner in those games was called to the place where the judge sat in order to receive his prize. Paul may have referred to ultimate salvation in God's presence, or to receiving rewards at "the judgment seat of Christ" (2 Cor. 5:10).

B. Believers are to have a walk that pleases God (3:15-21)

1. A WALK OF MATURITY (3:15-16)

The second great exhortation in chapter 3 has a positive ring to it—Paul urged Christians to walk, or live lives, pleasing to God (3:15-21). This should first be a mature walk (vv. 15-16).

3:15-16. The apostle called his readers to share with him the pursuit of Christlikeness. What he wanted for himself he also wanted for them. **All of us who are mature should take such a view of things** (v. 15). What view of things? The one he had expressed regarding persistently pressing on toward the goal. One mark of spiritual maturity is a desire to go on with Christ. Paul's appeal here was to maturing believers who shared his ambitions. He trusted God to **make** things **clear** to those who disagreed with him.

No doubt the greatest need among God's people is to live up to what they already have in Christ. Most live far below their exalted position in Christ. Paul's plea to the Philippians was that they **live up to what** they had **already attained,** namely a righteous position in Christ.

2. A WALK OF WATCHFULNESS (3:17-19)

Paul again called on his readers to follow his own example and not that of the Judaizers.

3:17. Having set forth his life ambition to be more Christlike, Paul did not hesitate to tell the Philippians to follow his **example.** He wanted them to imitate him. Surely he did not mean that they should imitate every single area of his life, for he had just stated that he was not sinlessly perfect. But in the matter of relentlessly pursuing after Christlikeness, he did set himself up as an example. Those Philippians who followed him would **join with others** who were already doing so.

3:18-19. These verses give the reasons for the exhortations in verse 17: **many live as enemies of the cross of Christ.** Believers should be able to determine truth from error (cf. 1 John 4:6). Paul was so concerned about the Philippians' spiritual welfare that he warned them often and wept as he did so.

As enemies of God these false teachers were destined for **destruction.** Those Paul warned against were perhaps profligates in incipient Gnosticism who trusted in their own attainments and not in the sufficiency of Christ alone. All who do so are not children of God, so they await destruction. This word (*apōleia*) does not mean annihilation but rather ruination by separation from the presence of God in eternal judgment.

Three further descriptions of these false teachers follow. First, **their god is their stomach.** They had in mind only their own physical desires and unrestrained gluttony (cf. Rom. 16:18).

Second, **their glory is in their shame.** Instead of giving glory to God these teachers heaped praise on themselves. Ironically they prided themselves in the things they should have been ashamed of.

Third, **their mind is on earthly things.** It is certainly not wrong for God's people to care about their earthly affairs. But those Paul warned against here were depending on earthly things to gain merit with God. The apostle frequently alerted the people of God against such a lifestyle (cf. Gal. 4:3, 9-11; Col. 2:21-22).

3. A WALK COMPLETED (3:20-21)

3:20-21. The people of Philippi were living there as colonists while their citizenship was in Rome. Similarly Christians, while living on earth, have their **citizenship** elsewhere—**in heaven.** This contrasts with those in verse 19 whose minds are exclusively on earthly things.

The believer looks with keen anticipation for his Savior's return from heaven. **Eagerly await** translates a word (*apekdechometha*) that suggests a tiptoe anticipation and longing. This word is also used in Romans 8:19, 23, 25; 1 Corinthians 1:7; Galatians 5:5; Hebrews 9:28.

At the Rapture of the church, Christ **will transform** (*metaschēmatisei,* "change the outward form of") **our lowly bodies so that they will be like** (*symmorphon,* "identical in essential character"; cf. the participle *symmorphizomenos* in Phil. 3:10) **His glorious body.** Then every child of God will be made like the Son of God (1 John 3:2), that is, all Christians will receive glorified bodies like His. No more will they have the limitations they now experience in their "lowly" bodies, which are humbled by disease and sin. Their resurrected bodies will be like Christ's, and their sanctification will be completed.

IV. Enablement for Living the Christian Life (4:1-23)

A. Christ at the center (4:1-7)

Paul's love for the Philippians, which is evident throughout this letter, is especially apparent in the opening verses of chapter 4. One of his chief concerns was that these people would be characterized by the fruit of the Spirit. Love, joy, and peace were uppermost in his heart and mind for them. In order to experience these Christian graces Christ must be at the center of a believer's life. Paul made this plain as he wrote to the saints at Philippi.

1. STANDING FAST IN HIM (4:1-3)

In these verses the apostle first gave a general plea for unity and steadfastness and then a specific plea to two women.

4:1. **Therefore** introduces this exhortation and applies what he wrote in chapter 3 about sanctification and glorification. The apostle's affection for this congregation is revealed by his love and longing for them and his calling them his **brothers** (cf. "brothers" in 1:12; 3:1, 13, 17; 4:8), his **joy and crown** (*stephanos*, the runner's wreath or victor's crown; cf. 1 Thes. 2:19-20), and his **dear friends** (cf. Phil. 2:12). These saints were to their spiritual father what victory wreaths were to runners in the Greek races. The believers were exhorted to **stand firm in the Lord** (cf. 1:27, where Paul urged the same steadfastness).

4:2. Two women, **Euodia** and **Syntyche**, did not live up to the meanings of their names. "Euodia" means a "prosperous journey." "Syntyche" means a "pleasant acquaintance." Since Paul pleaded with these two **to agree with each other in the Lord**, it seems that they were causing dissension in the assembly. This helps explain Paul's earlier plea for unity (2:1-4).

4:3. At one time Euodia and Syntyche **contended** at Paul's **side in the cause of the gospel.** But as he wrote they were not in harmony with each other. They were contentious, rather than content.

The exact identity of Paul's **loyal yokefellow** is not known. Some say "yokefellow" (*syzyge*) is a proper name. Paul knew he could count on him to work

with the women and bring them back to fellowship with each other and with the Lord. **Clement** and other **fellow workers** had also contended for the gospel with these women. (This is more likely than supposing the words "along with Clement and the rest of my fellow workers" go with "help," as though Paul were enlisting Clement and others to help Syzygus unite the women.)

2. REJOICING IN HIM (4:4)

4:4. Sometimes the trials and pressures of life make it almost impossible to be happy. But Paul did not tell his readers to be happy. He encouraged them to **rejoice in the Lord.** In fact, he said it twice in verse 4 (cf. 3:1; 1 Thes. 5:16). Christ is the One in whom the sphere of rejoicing was to take place. Surely there are many circumstances in which Christians cannot be happy. But they can always rejoice in the Lord and delight in Him. Paul himself was an excellent example of one who had inner joy when external circumstances—such as persecution, imprisonment, the threat of death—were against him.

3. LIVING IN THE LIGHT OF HIS PRESENCE (4:5-7)

4:5. In addition to joy, believers are to have **gentleness,** which is to **be evident to all.** *Epieikes* ("gentleness") suggests a forbearing, nonretaliatory spirit. Joy, an inner quality in relation to circumstances, may not always be seen; but the way one reacts to others—whether in gentleness or harshness—will be noticed. Why be gentle? Because **the Lord is near.** This probably refers to the Rapture, not to His presence with His own at all times.

4:6-7. Joy and gentleness (vv. 4-5), accompanied with an awareness of Christ's imminent return, should dispel anxiety. Paul's appeal to the Philippians is **do not be anxious about anything.** But this was not a call to a carefree life. To care and be genuinely concerned is one thing. To worry is another. Paul and Timothy cared for the people they ministered to (2 Cor. 11:28; Phil. 2:20), yet they retained trust in God. Jesus warned against worry which obviously eliminates trust in God (Matt. 6:25-33).

Paul exhorted the Philippians to prayer instead of anxiety. Praying with thanksgiving involves trusting God. Four words are used here to describe a believer's communion with God. **Prayer** (*proseuchē*) describes a believer's approach to God. **Petition** (*deēsei*) emphasizes requesting an answer to a specific need. **Thanksgiving** (*eucharistias*) is an attitude of heart which should always accompany one's prayers. **Requests** (*aitēmata*) speak of definite and specific things asked for.

When the exhortations of verses 4-6 are heeded, **the peace of God** (v. 7) will flood one's troubled soul. The Lord Jesus Christ is a believer's peace (Eph. 2:14), and every child of God has peace *with* God through justification by faith (Rom. 5:1). But the peace *of* (or from) God relates to the inner tranquility of a believer's close walk with God.

This peace of God **transcends all understanding,** that is, it is beyond man's ability to comprehend. This peace guards the believers. **Guard** (*phrourēsei*, also used in 1 Peter 1:5) translates a military term which means "to protect or garrison by guarding." Like soldiers assigned to watch over a certain area, God's peace garrisons the **hearts and . . . minds,** that is, the emotions and thoughts, of God's children.

B. God's presence with believers (4:8-9)

1. THINKING WORTHY THOUGHTS (4:8)

4:8. By the word **finally** Paul indicated he was about to conclude the section. Six items are mentioned as objects of a wholesome thought life, and each one is introduced with **whatever.** In the Greek "whatever" is plural, which suggests that several things could be included under each heading.

True (*alēthē*) things are of course the opposite of dishonest and unreliable things (cf. Eph. 4:15, 25). **Noble** refers to what is dignified and worthy of respect (this word *semna* is used in the NT only here and in 1 Tim. 3:8, 11; Titus 2:2). **Right** refers to conformity to God's standards. **Pure** (*hagna*) refers to what is wholesome, not mixed with moral impurity. **Lovely** (*prosphilē*, occurring only here in the NT) speaks of what promotes peace rather than conflict. **Admirable** (*euphēma*, also used only here) relates to what is positive and constructive rather than negative and destructive.

These six objects of thought are then described as **excellent** (*aretē*) and **praiseworthy** (*epainos*).

2. DOING WORTHY DEEDS (4:9)

4:9. The Christian life involves proper thinking (v. 8), but it also includes doing righteous deeds.

Since the Philippians knew Paul well, he could ask them to follow his example. They had **learned . . . received** and **heard from** him, and they had even **seen** the apostle's conduct. As they **put** these things (from Paul's teaching and living) **into practice,** they would enjoy the presence of **the God of peace** (cf. "the peace of God," v. 7).

C. God's supply of human needs (4:10-20)

Epaphroditus was the messenger the Philippians sent to bring their gift to Paul (4:18). It appears that Paul wrote this letter as both a thank-you note and as a word of greeting and exhortation. The apostle could certainly testify that God does supply His people's needs.

1. THE LESSON OF CONTENTMENT (4:10-13)

4:10-13. Paul's heart was made glad (**I rejoice greatly in the Lord**) because of the continued interest the Philippian Christians showed in him. They had not forgotten him; through them God had met his needs. Even before they sent Epaphroditus they were concerned but **had no opportunity to show it.**

Paul did not beg God's people to help him in his work. He just placed the need before them and trusted God to meet it. Too, he had learned the lesson of contentment. Changing circumstances did not affect the inner contentment he enjoyed. The word **content** (*autarkēs*) means "self-sufficient." The Stoics used this word (which occurs only here in the NT) to mean human self-reliance and fortitude, a calm acceptance of life's pressures. But Paul used it to refer to a *divinely* bestowed sufficiency, **whatever the circumstances.**

At times Paul experienced definite financial and material needs, and at other times he had an abundance (v. 12). He learned how to cope with both **need** and plenty. The words **I have learned the secret** translate *memyēmai* (from *myeō*), which occurs only here in the New Testament. In the mystery religions it was a technical term meaning "to initiate (into the mysteries)." Paul used it here to suggest a kind of "initiation" (by his experiences) into being content when either **well fed or hungry,** and either **in plenty or in want.**

Paul said he could **do everything**—including handling poverty and living in abundance—**through Him who** gave him **strength.** This was not an expression of pride in his own abilities but a declaration of the strength provided by Christ.

2. THE BLESSING OF GIVING AND RECEIVING (4:14-20)

4:14-16. Though Paul was content no matter what the circumstances, he was nevertheless grateful for the help the Philippians sent with Epaphroditus.

Because they gave of their means they shared with the apostle in his **troubles;** they did something about his problem.

In the very beginning of their Christian experience (Acts 16) when Paul left Macedonia they alone shared with him in **the matter of giving and receiving.** And again when Paul was in Thessalonica on his second missionary journey (Acts 17:1) and experienced definite need, the Philippians **sent** him **aid** twice.

4:17-20. Others were always uppermost in Paul's mind. He was not **looking for a gift** simply to satisfy his own needs. He wanted credit to come to the **account** of the Philippians.

Since these people had already helped him so much, Paul did not want them to think he was still looking for more from them. He had received from the Philippians full payment, all the money they had sent, so he was then abounding and was **amply supplied.** What they had sent with Epaphroditus (2:25-30) had an effect on both him and God, for the gifts were a **fragrant offering, an acceptable sacrifice, pleasing to God.** The term "fragrant offering" was used in Leviticus (in the LXX) for an offering that pleased God. It also was used in Ephesians 5:2 of Christ's offering of Himself.

God would reciprocate to the Philippians. They had met Paul's needs and now God would meet theirs. God would not only bless them *out of* or *from* His bounty but also *in accordance with* (*kata*) it: **according to His glorious riches in Christ Jesus.**

To our God—his heavenly Father and theirs—the apostle gave thanks and praise.

D. Conclusion (4:21-23)

4:21-23. Final greetings came to the Philippians from Paul, from his fellow workers, and from other believers.

The apostle sent his greetings from **all the saints** (v. 21). He addressed "all the saints" (1:1) in writing the epistle. The **brothers** who were with Paul also sent greetings. Timothy was certainly included in this group. **The saints** (v. 22) who sent greetings were those in the church in Rome (Rom. 16:1-15).

Those who belong to Caesar's household (Phil. 4:22) were probably those who had come to Christ as a result of Paul's house arrest. They probably included soldiers and relatives of Caesar's household. No wonder Paul could say that what had happened to him had advanced the gospel (1:12).

As was his usual practice Paul gave great prominence to Christ's marvelous **grace** as he concluded his letter (cf. Phile. 25).

BIBLIOGRAPHY

Berry, Harold J. *Studies in Philippians. Gems from the Original,* vol. 3. Lincoln, Neb.: Back to the Bible, 1978.

Boice, James Montgomery. *Philippians: An Expositional Commentary.* Grand Rapids: Zondervan Publishing House, 1971.

Getz, Gene A. *A Profile of Christian Maturity.* Grand Rapids: Zondervan Publishing House, 1976.

Gromacki, Robert G. *Stand United in Joy.* Grand Rapids: Baker Book House, 1980.

Hendriksen, William. *Exposition of Philippians.* New Testament Commentary. Grand Rapids: Baker Book House, 1962.

Kent, Homer A., Jr. "Philippians." In *The Expositor's Bible Commentary*, vol. 11. Grand Rapids: Zondervan Publishing House, 1978.

Lightfoot, J.B. *Saint Paul's Epistle to the Philippians*. Reprint. Grand Rapids: Zondervan Publishing House, 1953.

Martin, R.P. *The Epistle of Paul to the Philippians: An Introduction and Commentary*. Tyndale New Testament Commentaries. Grand Rapids: Wm. B. Eerdmans Publishing Co., 1959.

Meyer, F.B. *The Epistle to the Philippians*. Grand Rapids: Baker Book House, 1952.

Pentecost, J. Dwight. *The Joy of Living: A Study of Philippians*. Grand Rapids: Zondervan Publishing House, 1973.

Tenney, Merrill C. *Philippians: The Gospel at Work*. Grand Rapids: Wm. B. Eerdmans Publishing Co., 1956.

Vincent, Marvin R. *A Critical and Exegetical Commentary on the Epistle to the Philippians and to Philemon*. International Critical Commentary. Edinburgh: T. & T. Clark, 1897.

Walvoord, John F. *Philippians: Triumph in Christ*. Chicago: Moody Press, 1971.

Wiersbe, Warren W. *Be Joyful: A Practical Study of Philippians*. Wheaton, Ill.: SP Publications, Victor Books, 1974.

Wuest, Kenneth. *Philippians in the Greek New Testament*. Grand Rapids: Wm. B. Eerdmans Publishing, Co., 1951.

COLOSSIANS

Norman L. Geisler

INTRODUCTION

The Book of Colossians was written by the Apostle Paul about A.D. 60–62, while he was imprisoned in Rome. One purpose was to correct the heresy that had sprung up in the Asian city of Colosse.

Author. The Pauline authorship of Colossians is supported by abundant evidence both in and out of the book. Colossians has three personal references to Paul in the first person (1:1; 1:23; 4:18) and numerous references to Paul's associates, such as Tychicus (4:7), Onesimus (4:9), Aristarchus (4:10), Mark (4:10), Justus (4:11), Epaphras (4:12), Luke (4:14), Demas (4:14), and Archippus (4:17). The style and content of Colossians is similar to Ephesians, written about the same time and probably alluded to as "the letter from Laodicea" (4:16).

While 34 Greek words are unique to Colossians, they are characteristic of the theme of the book and fit the thoughts of Paul. Words in this category include "visible" (1:16), "supremacy" (1:18), "fill up" (1:24), "philosophy" (2:8), and "Deity" (2:9).

The conclusion of Ephesians confirms that Tychicus was the carrier of both it and Colossians (Eph. 6:21; cf. Col. 4:7). This helps confirm Paul as the author of the Colossian epistle.

The external evidence for Paul's authorship is strong, despite the claim of some that the heresy combated in the book is second-century Gnosticism. But there is good reason to believe that the heresy addressed in Colossians (at least in its incipient form) had appeared already in Paul's lifetime. And in view of Paul's other encounters with heresies, in books which are unquestionably his, it seems clear that he authored Colossians (cf. 1 Cor. 15; Gal. 1–2; 2 Thes. 2).

Colossians includes some stylistic differences such as unusual genitival combinations: "the hope of glory" (Col. 1:27), "body of . . . flesh" (2:11, NASB), "growth . . . from God" (2:19, NASB), "reward of . . . inheritance" (3:24, NASB). However, as Donald Guthrie correctly observed, "stylistic differences are generally attributable to changing circumstances or subject matter" (*New Testament Introduction*. Downers Grove, Ill.: Inter-Varsity Press, 1973, p. 553).

One of the strongest lines of evidence that Colossians is a first-century work of the Apostle Paul is its close link to the Book of Philemon, the authenticity of which is virtually impeccable. (1) Both books include Timothy's name with Paul's in the opening greeting (Col. 1:1; Phile. 1). (2) Greetings are sent in both books from Aristarchus, Mark, Epaphras, Luke, and Demas (Col. 4:10-14; Phile. 23-24). (3) Archippus' ministry is referred to in both books (Col. 4:17; Phile. 2). (4) Onesimus the slave is mentioned in both books (Col. 4:9; Phile. 10).

Date and Place of Writing. Colossians was written from Rome during Paul's (first) imprisonment there, as recorded in Acts 28:30. At the same time Paul wrote Ephesians and Philemon (ca. A.D. 60–62). In Philemon 1, 9 Paul referred to himself as "a prisoner of Christ Jesus." Ephesians also contains references to Paul being a "prisoner" (Eph. 3:1; 4:1). And Ephesians refers to Tychicus carrying the epistles from Paul to their destinations (Eph. 6:21; cf. Col. 4:7). Since the record of Acts ends around A.D. 60–62, Colossians was probably written during this two-year imprisonment. And since neither Colossians, Ephesians, nor Philemon mention the outcome of Paul's trial, anticipated in Philippians 1:19-21, it can be assumed that Colossians was written before Philippians.

Colosse was in the Lycus Valley,

about 100 miles east of Ephesus in Asia Minor. Its name is possibly derived from *Colossus,* a large statue, which in turn may have been named for the unusual shape of stony deposits there. Colosse is about 12 miles from Hierapolis and Laodicea, the other two cities of that valley (see the location of these three on the map between Acts and Rom.). The area was rich in mineral deposits and was also subject to frequent earthquakes. Rich pasturelands were nearby. Several references in Colossians indicate that Paul had not visited the city (Col. 1:7; 2:1; 4:12).

Occasion. The circumstance which prompted the writing of Colossians seemed to be the special heresy that arose there. This false teaching seemed to be the beginning of what later (in the second century) developed into Gnosticism. It contained several characteristics. (1) It was Jewish, stressing the need for observing Old Testament laws and ceremonies. (2) It was philosophical, laying emphasis on some special or deeper knowledge (*gnōsis*). (3) It involved the worship of angels as mediators to God (2:18). (4) It was exclusivistic, stressing the special privilege and "perfection" of those select few who belonged to this philosophical elite. (5) It was also Christological. But this seminal Gnosticism denied the deity of Christ, thus calling forth one of the greatest declarations of Christ's deity found anywhere in Scripture (1:15-16; 2:9).

Purposes. Three purposes seem to have been in Paul's mind as he wrote Colossians. First, he sought to show the deity and supremacy of Christ in the face of the Colossian heresy (1:18; 2:9). Second, he wanted to lead believers into spiritual maturity (1:28; 2:6-7). Third, he wanted to inform them about his state of affairs and elicited their prayers on his behalf (4:2-8).

Contents. The epistle may be summarized as follows: "Greetings, brothers (1:1-2). We thank God for your faith and love (1:3-8). And we ask God to fill you with the knowledge of His will. We pray this so that you will be fruitful for Christ who has redeemed you (1:9-14). For Christ, our Creator and Head, is supreme in all things (1:15-20). And through Christ's death God has reconciled you

who were aliens and enemies (1:21-23). So I rejoice that I can suffer for the church so that God's fullness can be known by the Gentiles (1:24-27). To this end we labor that everyone may be perfect in Christ (1:28-29). For all true wisdom and knowledge is found in Christ (2:1-5). Therefore, brothers, just as you began with Christ, continue in Him (2:6-7).

"Now don't be deceived: God's fullness is in Christ alone and not in vain human philosophy (2:8-10). And since you have been identified with Christ in your baptism, you have no need to live under Jewish laws (2:11-17). And don't let anyone rob you of your prize by forsaking Christ your Head (2:18-19). For you died with Christ, so you need not submit to worldly (legalistic) rules (2:20-23). And since you were raised with Christ, you should set your hearts on heavenly things above (3:1-4). So put to death your sinful worldly practices (3:5-11). And clothe yourself with Christ's virtues (3:15-17).

"In view of your new exalted identity with Christ, I exhort wives to submit to their husbands; husbands to love their wives; children to obey their parents; fathers not to embitter their children; slaves to obey their masters; and masters to be fair with their slaves (3:18-4:1).

"Brothers, pray for me that I may preach this message effectively and clearly, and you live wisely toward outsiders (4:2-6). My coworkers in the gospel send greetings to you (4:7-15). Exchange letters with the Laodiceans and exhort Archippus to complete his ministry (4:16-18)."

OUTLINE

COMMENTARY

I. Doctrinal: Deeper Life in Christ (1:1–2:7)

A. Greetings (1:1-2)

1:1-2. In all but his two earliest epistles (1 and 2 Thes.) and his personal letter to the Philippians, **Paul** began by designating himself as **an apostle** (see the chart, "Paul's Introductions to His Epistles," near Rom. 1:1-7). He was not one of the 12 Apostles (Acts 1:21-26) who were with Christ from the beginning of His earthly ministry (Acts 1:22; Luke 1:2; John 15:27). Nevertheless he did see the risen **Christ** (1 Cor. 9:1; 15:8-9), and he did possess special miraculous powers given to authenticate apostles (2 Cor. 12:12; cf. Heb. 2:3-4).

Timothy was with Paul here as he often was (cf. 2 Cor. 1:1; Phil. 1:1; 2 Thes. 1:1). Timothy had a Gentile father (Acts 16:1) but his mother and grandmother were godly Jewesses (2 Tim. 1:5) from whom he had learned the Old Testament Scriptures from childhood (2 Tim. 3:15). Paul picked up Timothy on his second missionary journey at Lystra where the "brothers . . . spoke well of him" (Acts 16:2). Paul spent much time discipling Timothy and wrote two of his last letters to him.

Paul addressed the Colossian believers as **the holy and faithful brothers in Christ.** This phrase marks them as holy people, chosen and set apart for **God.** It parallels the Ephesian introduction to "the saints . . . the faithful in Christ Jesus" (Eph. 1:1). Paul's characteristic greeting, **grace and peace** includes *charis* ("grace"), a variation of the normal Greek salutation, *chaire* ("Greetings"; cf. Luke 1:28). *Chaire* probably suggested the similar-sounding but richer *charis.* His greeting also includes the normal Jewish salutation, "peace." So Paul wished for them God's favor (grace) and a healthy condition of life (peace).

B. Thanksgiving (1:3-8)

1:3-4. Giving continual thanks to God was characteristic of Paul's prayers (Rom. 1:8; 1 Cor. 1:14; Eph. 1:6; etc.), though he omitted this praise in Galatians and 2 Corinthians. Here **God** is recognized as the cause of goodness in His people. This thanks, Paul said, is rendered **when we pray.** And thanksgiving was given **because** Paul had **heard** (from Epaphras, Col. 1:7; cf. 4:12) about their growing **faith in Christ Jesus and** their **love . . . for all the saints.** Prayer here is the broader, more inclusive act of worship including thanksgiving and intercession (cf. Matt. 6:7; Acts 16:25).

1:5. Paul thanked God for their **faith and love that spring from . . . hope.**

This trilogy of virtue—faith, love, and hope—is a favorite of Paul's (cf. 1 Cor. 13:13; 1 Thes. 1:3) and Peter's (1 Peter 1:3, 5, 22). Faith is the soul looking *upward* to God; love looks *outward* to others; hope looks *forward* to the future. Faith rests on the past work of Christ; love works in the present; and hope anticipates the future. Even though "without faith it is impossible to please God" (Heb. 11:6), and "hope does not disappoint us" (Rom. 5:5), nevertheless "the greatest of these is love" (1 Cor. 13:13). The Colossians' love extended to "all the saints" (Col. 1:4), or all believers, probably not only at Colosse but everywhere (cf. 1 Thes. 1:7-8 for a similar commendation).

Faith and love "spring from" (*dia,*

lit., are "on account of") "hope," confidence in what God will do in the future. This confidence led to a greater trust in God and a deeper love for others. This confident expectation of Christ's return, called "the blessed hope" (Titus 2:13), influences believers' conduct (cf. 1 Thes. 4:13-18; 1 John 3:3).

This hope is **stored up . . . in heaven** because Christ, the essence of this hope, is there. Without Christ's Ascension to heaven (Acts 1:10-11) and His present intercession there on behalf of believers (Heb. 7:25; 1 John 2:1), they would have no hope (cf. 1 Cor. 15:16-19). This message is **the Word of truth** (cf. Eph. 1:13; 2 Tim. 2:15; James 1:18), **the gospel** as Paul defines it here and elsewhere (cf. 1 Cor. 15:1-3; Rom. 10:9-10).

1:6. Paul thanked God because the **gospel** was spreading **all over the world.** In fact, in an obvious hyperbole, Paul wrote in verse 23 that the gospel was being "proclaimed to every creature under heaven" (cf. Rom. 1:8). But Paul stressed not only the universality of the gospel but also its practicality, for it was **producing fruit and growing.** As a tree bears fruit and grows in size, so the gospel produces spiritual "fruit" in believers' lives (cf. "the fruit of the Spirit," Gal. 5:22-23; "the fruit of righteousness," Phil. 1:11) and spreads to and influences others (cf. the same words "bearing fruit" and "growing" in Col. 1:10). Heresies (such as the one at Colosse) are local and harmful; but truth is universal and helpful. One of the unmistakable characteristics of the true gospel is **God's grace in all its truth.** Some preach a "different gospel—which is really no gospel at all" (Gal. 1:6-7). This is because it is a gospel of grace plus works, or faith plus works. But the true gospel is one of grace alone (Rom. 11:6; Eph. 2:8-9; Titus 3:5-7).

1:7. The Colossians **learned it,** the gospel, **from Epaphras** who apparently founded the church at Colosse (cf. 4:12). Paul called him a **dear fellow servant,** a humble description from a great apostle, **and a faithful minister of Christ,** as opposed, no doubt, to those unfaithful ones who here and elsewhere were disturbing the faith of God's flock (cf. 2 Cor. 11:15; 2 Peter 2:1-3, 12-19). Paul also called Tychicus "a faithful minister and fellow servant in the Lord" (Col. 4:7).

Epaphras was in Rome with Paul, for Paul called him "my fellow prisoner" (Phile. 23). "Epaphras" is a shortening of "Epaphroditus," referred to in Philippians 2:25 and 4:18. These could be the same person or different persons since both names were common.

Epaphras, said Paul, ministered **on our behalf,** probably as Paul's representative (cf. Phil. 2:25; 4:18 for a similar situation). This implies, of course, that Paul had not visited Colosse himself (cf. Col. 2:1). But even though Epaphras was sent by Paul, he was primarily a "minister of Christ."

1:8. Not only did Epaphras carry the good news of Christ to Colosse, but he also brought back to prisoner Paul the good news about their **love in the Spirit** for Christ. Believers are in the Spirit and the Spirit is in them (Rom. 8:9). Thus their "love . . . for all the saints" (Col. 1:4; cf. v. 5) stemmed from the indwelling Holy Spirit. Elsewhere Paul urged that by "the love of the Spirit" (Rom. 15:30) believers manifest the "fruit of the Spirit" (Gal. 5:22).

C. Petition (1:9-14)

1:9. For this reason, because Paul had heard this good report of them from Epaphras, he continued to pray for them. Paul's ceaseless prayer (**we have not stopped praying for you;** cf. 1 Thes. 5:17) does not mean that he prayed without ever stopping but that he never forgot to pray for them when he daily and regularly prayed (cf. Acts 20:31; Eph. 1:16). "Praying" (Col. 1:9) is the general word for prayer (proseuchomenoi), also used in v. 3; and **asking** is the word for petitioning or requesting (aitoumenoi).

Paul's primary petition was that **God** would **fill** them **with the knowledge of His will.** Paul used two key words, "fill" (plēroō) and "knowledge" (epignōsis, also used in v. 10 and 3:10). The first suggests a filling out to completeness, and the latter suggests a full, deep understanding. Such knowledge of God's will does not come from a fleshly mind (which "puffs up, " 1 Cor. 8:1), but from the Holy Spirit who enlightens a believer's inner person (1 Cor. 2:5-6, 13), and from the Word of God. God's will, revealed in the Bible, is made known to believers by the Holy Spirit's teaching ministry. To this Paul added, **through all spiritual wisdom** (*sophia*; used six times in Col. 1:9, 28; 2:3, 23; 3:16; 4:5), that is, practical know-how which comes from God (James 1:5; 3:15), **and understanding** (*synesei*; also used in Col. 2:2), which speaks of clear analysis and decision-making in applying this knowledge to various problems. By contrast, the false teachers offered only "an appearance of wisdom" (*sophia*; 2:23), which captivated their minds and lives in legalistic regulations. But true spiritual wisdom is both stabilizing and liberating (Eph. 4:14). Knowledge (or understanding or intelligence) and wisdom are often connected in Scripture (cf. Ex. 31:3 ["skill" in the NIV is the Heb. word for wisdom]; Deut. 4:6; Isa. 11:2; 1 Cor. 1:19). And the fear of the Lord is the beginning of both (cf. Prov. 1:7; 9:10).

1:10. Paul's aim in this petition was practical: **in order that you may live a life worthy of the Lord.** A genuine knowledge of Christ reveals itself in transformed character (cf. Eph. 4:1; 1 Thes. 2:12), in Christlikeness. *Axiōs,* "worthy," means "of equal weight." Believers are to equal the Lord's standards, to be holy as He is holy (cf. 1 Peter 1:15). The aim of believers in all their worthy conduct should be to **please Him in every way,** to anticipate and do His wishes in every aspect of life (cf. Eph. 5:10). Merely pleasing people is incompatible with being a servant of Christ (Gal. 1:10; Eph. 6:6; Col. 3:22; 1 Thes. 2:4). Indeed, Paul made it the ambition of his life to please God (2 Cor. 5:9). Four things, given in participles, result from such a God-pleasing life: "bearing fruit" and "growing" (Col. 1:10), "being strengthened" (v. 11), and "giving thanks" (v. 12). The first two are related: **bearing fruit** and **growing in the knowledge** (*epignōsei*) **of God** (Paul used these same words "bearing fruit" and "growing," trans. "producing," in v. 6). As one manifests the fruit of faith (cf. Matt. 7:16; Gal. 5:22-23), he grows in faith himself (cf. Eph. 4:13). He comes to a deeper "knowledge" (*epignōsis;* cf. Col. 1:9) of God. As Augustine put it, "Faith is understanding's step, and understanding is faith's reward."

1:11. Spiritual strength is a third factor that results from knowing God's will and pleasing Him. **Being strengthened with all power according to His glorious might** includes three

words for strength: "being strengthened" is *dynamoumenoi;* "power" is *dynamei,* spiritual vitality; and "might" is *kratos* ("power that overcomes resistance"; used only of God in the NT). This God-given strength produces **great endurance and patience.** This endurance (trans. "perseverance" in James 1:3) was exemplified by Job (James 5:11). To this endurance Paul added "patience," a word generally connected with gentleness and calm sweetness (as in 1 Cor. 13:4). Endurance and patience are often associated (cf. 2 Cor. 6:4, 6; 2 Tim. 3:10; James 5:10-11). Endurance (*hypomonē,* lit., a "remaining under") implies not easily succumbing under suffering; and patience (*makrothymia,* lit., "long temper"; cf. Col. 3:12) means self-restraint which does not hastily retaliate. A lack of endurance often results in despondency or losing heart, whereas a lack of patience often leads to wrath or revenge (cf. Prov. 15:18; 16:32).

All this is according to God's "glorious might" (lit., "might of His glory"). Glory means manifest excellence. It is an outward manifestation of God's inner character. In Ephesians 1:19-20 Paul wrote of God's "great power" (*dynamis*) and "the working (*energeian*) of His mighty (*kratous*) strength (*ischyos*)," which raised Christ from the dead.

1:12-13. Such patient-producing power should be accompanied by "joyfully," not begrudgingly, **giving thanks to the Father** from whom comes every good and perfect gift (James 1:17).

Thankfulness, a fourth result of following God's will and pleasing Him, is a keynote in the spiritual life. Believers are urged elsewhere by Paul, "Give thanks in all circumstances" (1 Thes. 5:18) and to come before God "in everything, by prayer and petition, with thanksgiving" (Phil. 4:6). Four other times in Colossians (3:15-17; 4:2) Paul enjoined believers to be grateful. Joyfulness too is part of the fruit of the Spirit (Gal. 5:22), made possible by the gospel (cf. Isa. 29:19; John 16:20; Acts 13:52). Here Paul centered thanksgiving on the fact that God has **qualified you** (lit., "made you competent"; cf. 2 Cor. 3:6) **to share in the inheritance of the saints** (i.e., the kingdom treasures that belong to believers; cf. Eph. 1:7). In short, though believers are unfit in themselves, God has fitted them to share in the inheritance of His holy people. This "inheritance" (tēn merida tou klērou, lit., "the parcel of the lot") is reminiscent of the way the inheritance of the land of promise was given to the Israelites under Joshua (Josh. 14:2). This inheritance is in the . . . light (cf. 2 Cor. 4:6; 1 Peter 2:9). (The NIV, supplying the words "kingdom of," which are not in the Gr., reads "in the kingdom of light.") This light is the spiritual sphere to which believers have been transferred from the dominion of darkness (Luke 22:53; Acts 26:18; Eph. 6:12). From this dominion (exousias, "power, authority") of darkness (cf. John 3:19-20) believers have been rescued, delivered. Through Christ they were brought from a rebel kingdom and placed under the sovereignty of their rightful King. The sovereign Christ is here called the Son He loves (lit., "the Son of His love"; cf. 1 John 4:8, 16). J. B. Lightfoot says this means the Son who embodies and manifests God's love (St. Paul's Epistles to the Colossians and to Philemon, p. 142). But H.C.G. Moule says it signifies the Son who is "the blessed Object of the Father's love . . . the supremely Beloved One" (The Epistles of Paul the Apostle to the Colossians and to Philemon, p. 75). This seems preferable (cf. Eph. 1:6).

1:14. Through Christ, God's "Loved One," Christians have redemption, the forgiveness of sins. The parallel passage (Eph. 1:7) adds "through His blood" (as do some mss.) here. "Redemption" (apolytrōsin) means "to rescue by ransom" (see the chart, "New Testament Words for Redemption," at Mark 10:45), and "forgiveness" (aphesin) means "remission" by the Redeemer. This emancipation is enjoyed only because of the tremendous cost Christ paid on the cross (cf. Rom. 3:24-26).

D. Exaltation of Christ (1:15-20)

From Paul's petition that the Colossians be enlightened about God's redemptive working in their lives, he moved naturally into his epistle's main emphasis—the exaltation and preeminence of Christ. In this paragraph (vv. 15-20) Paul mentioned seven unique characteristics of Christ, which fittingly qualify Him to have "the supremacy" (v. 18). Christ is: (1) the image of God, (2) the Firstborn over Creation, (3) Creator of

the universe, (4) Head of the church, (5) Firstborn from the dead, (6) the fullness of God, and (7) the Reconciler of all things. No comparable listing of so many characteristics of Christ and His deity are found in any other Scripture passage. Christ is the supreme Sovereign of the universe!

1:15. First, Christ is the image of the invisible God. Besides the obvious meaning of likeness (cf. 2 Cor. 4:4), "image" implies representation and manifestation. Like the head of a sovereign imprinted on a coin, so Christ is "the exact representation of [the Father's] being" (Heb. 1:3). As Jesus said, "Anyone who has seen Me has seen the Father" (John 14:9). Anyone who saw Christ, the visible manifestation of the invisible God, has thereby "seen" God indirectly. For "no one has ever seen God, but God the only Son . . . has made Him known" (John 1:18). Paul wrote of the "invisible" God (1 Tim. 1:17), but Christ is the perfect visible representation and manifestation of that God. Though the word "image" (eikōn) does not always denote a perfect image (cf. 1 Cor. 11:7), the context here demands that understanding. Indeed, like the word "form" (morphē; trans. "nature" in Phil. 2:6-7), eikōn means the very substance or essential embodiment of something or someone. In Hebrews 10:1 "shadow" and "the very image" (eikōn), which is Christ, are contrasted (cf. Col. 2:17). So Christ's supremacy is first shown in His relationship with God the Father. Christ is the perfect resemblance and representation of God.

Second, Christ's supremacy is shown in His relationship to Creation. He is the Firstborn over all Creation. Though it is grammatically possible to translate this as "Firstborn in Creation," the context makes this impossible for five reasons: (1) The whole point of the passage (and the book) is to show Christ's superiority over all things. (2) Other statements about Christ in this passage (such as Creator of all [1:16], upholder of Creation [v. 17], etc.) clearly indicate His priority and superiority over Creation. (3) The "Firstborn" cannot be part of Creation if He created "all things." One cannot create himself. (Jehovah's Witnesses wrongly add the word "other" six times in this passage in their New World Translation. Thus they suggest that Christ created all other things after He was created! But the word "other" is not in the Gr.) (4) The "Firstborn" received worship of all the angels (Heb. 1:6), but creatures should not be worshiped (Ex. 20:4-5). (5) The Greek word for "Firstborn" is *prōtotokos*. If Christ were the "first-created," the Greek word would have been *prōtoktisis*.

"Firstborn" denotes two things of Christ: He preceded the whole Creation, and He is Sovereign over all Creation. In the Old Testament a firstborn child had not only priority of birth but also the dignity and superiority that went with it (cf. Ex. 13:2-15; Deut. 21:17). When Jesus declared Himself "the First" (*ho prōtos*; Rev. 1:17), He used a word that means "absolutely first." "Firstborn" also implies sovereignty. The description "firstborn" was not a fairly common Old Testament designation of the Messiah-God. "I will also appoint Him My Firstborn, the most exalted of the kings of the earth" (Ps. 89:27). While this regal psalm refers to David, it also designates the Messiah, as seen in Revelation 1:5, where Christ is called "the Firstborn from the dead (cf. Col. 1:18) and the Ruler of the kings of the earth." So "Firstborn" implies both Christ's priority *to* all Creation (in time) and His sovereignty *over* all Creation (in rank).

1:16-17. The third characteristic of Christ is that **by Him all things were created.** In fact **all things were created by Him** (*di' autou*, instrumental Cause) **and for Him** (*eis auton*, final Cause), and **in Him** (*en autō*) they **hold together** (He is the constituting or conserving Cause). Christ is not only the One through whom all things came to be, but also the One by whom they continue to exist. Two other New Testament verses parallel this description of Christ: "Through Him all things were made" (John 1:3), and Christ the Son is the One "through whom [the Father] made the universe" (Heb. 1:2). The Father, then, is the ultimate Source (efficient Cause), and the Son is the mediating Cause of the world. The Son was the "master Workman" of Creation, "the beginning (*archē*) of the Creation of God" (Rev. 3:14, NASB).

The Son's Creation includes "all" **things in heaven and on earth, visible and invisible.** These indicate the *entire* universe, both material and immaterial. The hierarchy of angelic beings—**thrones** (*thronoi*) **or powers** (*kyriotētes*) **or rulers** (*archai*) **or authorities** (*exousiai*)—indicate a highly organized dominion in the spirit world, a sphere in which the Colossians were engaged in the worship of angels (Col. 2:18) and over which Christ reigns supreme (cf. Eph. 1:21; 3:10; 6:12; Phil. 2:9-10; Col. 2:10, 15).

1:18. Fourth, Christ **is the Head of the body, the church.** Besides being the Lord of the universe He is also the church's Head (cf. Eph. 1:22-23; 5:23). The reference here is to the invisible or universal church into which all believers are baptized by the Holy Spirit the moment they believe in Christ (1 Cor. 12:13). This work of the Spirit began on the day of Pentecost (Acts 1:5; 2:1-2; 11:15-16). It is a special body in which there is "neither Jew nor Gentile" (Gal. 3:28) but a whole new creation of God (Eph. 2:15). The church is a "mystery . . . which was not made known to men in other generations" (Eph. 3:4-5; cf. Rom. 16:25-26; Col. 1:26).

Fifth, Christ **is the Beginning** (*archē*) **and the Firstborn from among the dead** (cf. Rev. 1:5). Christ was the first to rise in an immortal body (1 Cor. 15:20), and as such He heads a whole new order as its Sovereign (cf. "Firstborn" in Col. 1:15). Also Christ's resurrection marked His triumph over death (Heb. 2:14; 1 John 3:8). He was the "Firstfruits" of those who die (1 Cor. 15:20) since, unlike others, He rose never to die again. He "was declared with power to be the Son of God by His resurrection from the dead" (Rom. 1:4). So He continues to live "on the basis of the power of an indestructible life" (Heb. 7:16). All this is **so that in everything He might have the supremacy.** Christ is given first place over all Creation. He is preeminent. The same eternal *Logos* (John 1:1) who "became flesh" (John 1:14) and "humbled Himself" (Phil. 2:8) is now "exalted" by God the Father "to the highest place" and has been given "the name that is above every name" (Phil. 2:9).

1:19. The sixth description of the exalted Christ is that **all God's fullness dwell[s] in Him.** Later Paul wrote, "In Christ all the fullness of the Deity lives in bodily form" (2:9). Colossians 1:19 is one of the most powerful descriptions of Christ's deity in the New Testament (cf. Heb. 1:8). "Fullness" (*plērōma*), a key word in Colossians, is used in 1:19 and 2:9. (The verb *plēroō* is used in 1:9, 25; 2:10; and 4:17.) The noun means "completeness" and is used of a wide range of things including God's being (Eph. 3:19), time (Gal. 4:4), and grace in Christ (John 1:16). This full and complete Deity is said to "dwell" (*katoikēsai*, "abide lastingly or permanently") in Christ.

1:20. The seventh feature of Christ is that He is the Reconciler. Through Christ God will **reconcile to Himself all things.** The phrase "all things" is limited to good angels and redeemed people since only **things on earth** and **things in heaven** are mentioned. Things "under the earth" (Phil. 2:10) are not reconciled. On God's restoring of nature, see comments on Romans 8:19-21; and on the reconciling of sinners, see comments on Romans 5:10-11 and 2 Corinthians 5:17-20. It is important to note that people are reconciled to God ("to Himself") not that God is reconciled to people. For mankind has left God and needs to be brought back to Him. In 2 Corinthians 5:19 "reconciliation" was used by Paul in a judicial (vs. an actual) sense in which the whole "world" is made savable through Christ's death. Paul spoke of "the many" (i.e., "those who receive God's abundant provision of grace") being "made righteous" through the Cross (Rom. 5:19). To make **peace through His blood** means to cause God's enemies (Rom. 5:10; Col. 1:21) to become, by faith, His friends and His children (cf. Eph. 2:11-19).

E. Reconciliation by Christ (1:21-23)

1:21. Having struck the note of reconciliation as the seventh characteristic of the exalted Christ, Paul then developed that theme. Reconciliation is necessary because people are **alienated** ("cut off, estranged") **from** life and **God** (Eph. 2:12; 4:18). Before conversion the Colossian believers also **were enemies** or hostile to God **in** their **minds** as well as in their behavior, internally and externally. Sin begins in the heart (Matt. 5:27-28) and manifests itself in overt deeds (Gal. 5:19). ("In the sphere of your evil deeds" is better than NIV's **because of your evil behavior.** People are not inwardly hostile vs. God because of their outward acts of sins; they commit sins because they are inwardly hostile.)

1:22. Reconciliation of sinners to

God is **by Christ's physical body through death.** The Gnostic tendency of the Colossian heresy, with its Platonic orientation, denied both Christ's true humanity and His true deity. As John explained, it is necessary to confess "that Jesus Christ has come in the flesh" (1 John 4:2). Spirits cannot die, and "without the shedding of blood there is no forgiveness" (Heb. 9:22). In order to redeem humans, Christ Himself must be truly human (cf. 1 Tim. 2:5; Heb. 2:17). Thus Christ's real physical body and death were necessary for man's salvation (cf. Rom. 7:4; Heb. 10:10).

The result of Christ's death is redemptive—**to present you holy in His sight.** This may mean judicially perfect as to a believer's position, or spiritually perfect as to his condition. Ultimately God envisions both for believers, and Christ's death is the basis for judicial justification (Rom. 3:21-26), progressive sanctification (Rom. 6-7), and even ultimate glorification (Rom. 8). As Paul wrote the Ephesians, "He chose us in Him before the Creation of the world to be holy and blameless in His sight" (Eph. 1:4). Christians are **without blemish** (*amōmous*; correctly translated "blameless" in Eph. 1:4 and Phil. 2:15; cf. "without . . . blemish" in Eph. 5:27 and "without fault" in Jude 24) in Christ, and also are **free from accusation** (*anenklētous*). This latter Greek word is used five times in the New Testament and only by Paul (here and in 1 Cor. 1:8; 1 Tim. 3:10; Titus 1:6-7). It connotes one who is unaccused, free from all charges. Satan is "the accuser of the brethren" (Rev. 12:10, KJV), but Christ is their "Advocate" (1 John 2:1, KJV) or "Defense" (1 John 2:1, NIV) before the Father. Therefore by the merits of Christ believers are free from every charge (cf. Rom. 8:33). In Christ the accused are unaccused and the condemned are freed.

1:23. This reconciliation in Christ comes only by an abiding faith—**if you continue in your faith.** The Colossians had a settled faith—**established** (i.e., "grounded" like a building on a strong foundation) **and firm** (*hedraioi*, "seated or settled"; cf. 1 Cor. 7:37; 15:58), so Paul did not doubt that they would continue. In fact he spoke of **the hope** (confident expectation) which this **gospel** of reconciliation provides not only to them but also to the whole world—**to every creature under heaven.** This is obviously a figure of speech indicating the universality of **the gospel** and its proclamation, not that every person on the globe heard Paul preach. In Acts 2:5 this phrase describes a wide range of people from various countries without including, for example, anyone from North or South America (cf. also Gen. 41:57; 1 Kings 10:24; Rom. 1:8).

F. Revelation of the mystery of Christ (1:24-27)

1:24. This reconciliation by Christ of Jews and Gentiles to God in one body is a mystery revealed only in Christ. Paul rejoiced that he was able to suffer for them **what** was **still lacking in regard to Christ's afflictions.** By this he did not mean that Christ's suffering on the cross was insufficient (cf. Rom. 3:21-26; Heb. 10:10-14). He was speaking not of salvation but of service. Christ's suffering alone procures salvation (1 Peter 1:11; 5:1; Heb. 2:9). But it is a believer's privilege to suffer for Christ (2 Tim. 3:11; 1 Peter 3:13-14; 5:9; Heb. 10:32). The word "affliction" (*thlipsis*)—never used in the New Testament of Christ's death—means "distress," "pressure," or "trouble" (which Paul had plenty of; 2 Cor. 11:23-29). Ordinarily it refers to trials in life, not the pains of death. Christ does indeed continue to suffer when Christians suffer for Him. He asked Saul (later called Paul) on the Damascus Road, "Why do you persecute Me?" (Acts 9:4) Since the church is Christ's body, He is affected when it is affected. For the sake of Christ's body Paul willingly suffered (Phil. 1:29).

1:25-26. He was a God-ordained servant of the precious truth of **the Word of God in its fullness** (cf. 1:9; 2:9). The Colossian heresy boasted of a "fullness" of knowledge possible only through their mystical experience. But Paul declared that the fullness of **the mystery** is found only in Christ. By "mystery" he meant something once concealed but then revealed. This contrasted with the Colossian heretics' notion that a mystery was a secret teaching known only to an exclusive group and unknown to the masses. The church was unknown in the Old Testament because it had **been kept hidden for ages and generations.** In fact,

said Paul, it is only **now disclosed to the saints.** Since the church is Christ's body, resulting from His death on the cross, it could not possibly have been in existence in the Old Testament. Indeed, Jesus, when on earth, said it was yet future (Matt. 16:16-18). Since the church is Christ's body, welded together by the baptism of the Holy Spirit (1 Cor. 12:13), the church's birthday occurred when this baptism took place (Acts 1:5; 2). Soon Saul recognized that this mysterious body of Christ, the church, was in existence and that he was persecuting it (Acts 9:4; cf. Gal. 1:13).

The "mystery" of the church, however, does not mean that Gentile salvation and blessing was unforeseen before Christ (cf. Luke 2:29-32; Amos 9:11-12). The mystery was not *that* Gentiles would be saved but *how* they could be "fellow-heirs" (Eph. 3:6, KJV), on the same level with Jews, with no middle wall of partition between them (Eph. 2:12-14). In the Old Testament Gentiles who believed and became a part of Judaism were still considered lower than Jews. This special union in which there "is neither Jew nor Greek" (i.e., Gentile, Gal. 3:28) was nonexistent before Christ died and the Spirit descended to baptize all believers into this new body. (For a list of other NT "mysteries" see the chart near Matt. 13:10-16.)

1:27. God has chosen to make known this mystery to New Testament saints. He willed in His sovereign mercy to reveal His eternal purpose with all its **glorious riches** (i.e., divine effulgence or blazing splendor). The amazing thing is that this is now revealed **among the Gentiles,** whereas previously God's special revelation was to the Jews (Rom. 2:17; 3:1-2; 9:4). Now those "who once were far away have been brought near through the blood of Christ" (Eph. 2:13). Those "without hope and without God" (Eph. 2:12) have been given a glorious hope **which is Christ in you** (i.e., in you Gentiles; Col. 1:27). Because of "the glorious riches" (lit., "the riches of the glory"), believers are indwelt by Christ, **the hope of glory.** They are thus "in Christ" (2 Cor. 5:17; Eph. 1:4), and Christ is in them (cf. Rom. 8:10; 2 Cor. 13:5). Because of Christ, believers look forward to sharing His glory (Col. 3:4; Rom. 5:2;

8:18, 30; 2 Cor. 4:17; Gal. 5:5; 1 Peter 5:10; also cf. Rom. 8:24).

G. Perfection in Christ (1:28-29)

1:28-29. Paul, in proclaiming this Christ who now also dwells in Gentile believers was **admonishing** (*nouthetountes*, "counseling") **and teaching** (*didaskontes*, "instructing") **everyone** (cf. 3:16). No doubt he did this "admonishing" and instructing because of the false teaching about Christ in Colosse. He did so wisely (cf. 4:5-6) since his purpose was not to drive them into the hands of the heretics but to **present everyone perfect** (*teleion*, "mature"; cf. James 1:4) **in Christ.** Paul was interested in believers not remaining spiritual babies (cf. 1 Cor. 3:1-2) but in becoming spiritually mature (cf. Heb. 5:11-14). Elsewhere Paul prayed for complete sanctification of believers (1 Thes. 5:23). Paul preached the "fullness" of the gospel so that believers could have the fullness of life Jesus promised (John 10:10). **To this end** Paul expended all his God-given strength. Developing maturity in believers took great **labor** (*kopiō*) or wearisome toil (cf. 1 Cor. 15:10, 58; Gal. 4:11; 1 Thes. 1:3) and even **struggling** (*agōnizomenos*; cf. Col. 2:1; 4:12) or agonizing like an athlete in an arena (cf. 1 Cor. 9:25; 1 Tim. 6:12). The power for this struggle came from Christ (cf. Phil. 4:13).

H. Education (wisdom) in Christ (2:1-5)

2:1. Paul's labor (*agōna*, **struggling;** cf. 1:29; 4:12) of love was not limited to those he personally knew; it extended to **all who** had **not met him personally.** This is a clear indication that Paul had not started this or other churches in the Lycus Valley. The mention of **Laodicea** (cf. 4:16) indicates that the heresy had spread there too, though it was probably centered in Colosse.

2:2-3. Paul's stated **purpose** was that **they** might **be encouraged in heart and united in love.** Confidence and strength of conviction as well as cohesive unity yield a full understanding of the truth. There is no full knowledge apart from moral commitment. **Complete understanding** (*syneseōs*, "insight") results from complete yielding. And this understanding is Christocentric. This insight into God's ways enables believers to **know** (*epignōsin*) Christ fully. **Christ,** as the true

mystery of God, reveals God to man (cf. John 1:18; Heb. 1:2-3). For in Him **are hidden** (cf. Col. 1:26) **all the treasures of wisdom** (*sophia*, cf. 1:9) **and knowledge.** Knowledge is the apprehension of truth; wisdom is its application to life. Knowledge is prudent judgment and wisdom is prudent action. Both are found in Christ (cf. Rom. 11:33; 1 Cor. 12:8) whose wisdom is foolishness to the world (1 Cor. 1:21-25), but who is the power of God by which a believer receives "righteousness, holiness, and redemption" (1 Cor. 1:30).

2:4-5. Only this full knowledge and wisdom of Christ can keep a believer from being deceived **by fine-sounding arguments** (*pithanologia*, occurring only here in the NT, is lit., "persuasive speech" that uses plausible but false arguments). Truth and persuasion do not always correlate. Error can persuade, and truth can be compelling at times. It all depends on whether one has the *full* truth and a complete *commitment* to it. Hence even **though** Paul was **absent from** the Colossians, he delighted in **how orderly** (cf. 1 Cor. 14:40) **and how firm** (steadfast, solid) their **faith in Christ** was.

I. Exhortation to live in Christ (2:6-7)

2:6-7. These two verses conclude the argument begun in 1:15. Paul's point may be summarized thus: Divine exaltation belongs to Christ (1:15-20); in Him are found (a) reconciliation to God (1:21-23), (b) the revelation of the mystery of Christ (1:24-27), (c) believers' perfection (1:28-29), and (d) education (wisdom) (2:1-5). Therefore believers should continue to live in Him (vv. 6-7).

The Christian life continues as it commenced: **just as you received Christ Jesus as Lord, continue to live in Him.** Paul gave the same kind of exhortation to others (cf. 2 Cor. 11:4; Gal. 1:6). Since their faith initially laid hold decisively on the apostolic gospel, Paul exhorted them not to forsake its divine authority for any human sophistry. For with these divine roots (**rooted . . . in Him**) that began in the past they can be continually **built up** (edified) and **strengthened in the faith.** If they did so they would not be blown to and fro with every wind of doctrine (Eph. 4:14). As believers are "built up" in Christ, they become more grateful and are **overflowing with thankfulness** (cf. Col. 1:12).

II. Polemical: Higher Life in Christ (2:8-23)

After exhorting believers to continue in Christ (2:6-7)—in whom is the fullness of God and who brought complete redemption—Paul then condemned the Colossian heresy that was diverting them from Christ.

A. "Gnosticism" is wrong: deity is in Christ (2:8-10)

2:8. Paul was concerned that no false teacher take the Colossian believers **captive through hollow and deceptive philosophy** (cf. v. 4). He wrote here not against all philosophy but against *false* philosophy, as the Bible also speaks against false religion (James 1:26). The particular false philosophy at Colosse was "hollow" (*kenēs*, "empty"), "deceptive," and based **on human tradition . . . rather than on Christ.** True Christian philosophy "take[s] captive every thought to make it obedient to Christ" (2 Cor. 10:5). Philosophy is the love of wisdom, but if one loves wisdom that is not Christ (the Sum of all wisdom, Col. 2:3), he loves an empty idol. Such a one will be "always learning but never able to acknowledge the truth" (2 Tim. 3:7). This kind of philosophy is based on the world's **basic principles** (*stoicheia*, "elementary principles" or "elemental spirits" [rsv]; cf. Col. 2:20; Gal. 4:3, 9). This may refer to the evil spirits who inspire such heresy and over whom Christ triumphed (cf. 2 Cor. 4:3-4; Eph. 6:11-12). Such a philosophy is demonic and worldly, not godly or Christlike. Unless believers are careful, such philosophy may ensnare them, taking them "captive."

2:9. There is no "fullness" (*plērōma*) in philosophy based on vain human reasoning. **For in Christ all the fullness of the Deity lives.** Hence only in Christ can one have fullness. Apart from Him is emptiness. As philosopher Jean Paul Sartre put it, "Life is an empty bubble on the sea of nothingness" (cf. Ecc. 1:14-18). The word for "Deity" is *theotētos*, a strong word (used only here in the NT) for Christ's essence as God. The full deity of Christ is nonetheless **in bodily form**—a full humanity (cf. Col. 1:22). Both Christ's deity and humanity were challenged by this early Gnostic-like heresy. Those heretics diminished Christ to an angel

whose "body" was only apparent, not real. Paul affirmed here that Christ is both fully God and truly man (cf. 1 John 4:1-6).

2:10. Not only is all the "fullness" (*plērōma*) of God in Christ (v. 9), but also believers **have been given fullness in Christ.** Their fullness of life comes from Christ's fullness. They partake of the divine nature through Christ (2 Peter 1:4), for "from the fullness of his grace we have all received" (John 1:16). This, of course, does not mean believers *become* God but simply share in Him. They *have* or share in the goodness of the nature which He *is.* They share in the body of Him **who is the Head** (cf. Col. 1:18) **over every power** (*archēs*, "ruler") **and authority** (*exousias*, "ruling power") (cf. 1:16; 2:15), including those who would talk the Colossians into living according to the world instead of according to Christ.

B. Legalism is wrong: reality is in Christ (2:11-17)

2:11-12. Paul turned from the theological errors of the false teachers to their practical errors—from "Gnosticism" to legalism. The Gentile Christians in Colosse had no need to conform to Jewish rules and regulations, such as **circumcision.** For in Christ they had been **circumcised.** This spiritual "circumcision" was **done by Christ,** not by man. It was in fact a crucifixion or putting off of the body, a circumcision of the heart (cf. Rom. 2:29; Eph. 2:11). Their **sinful nature** (lit., "the body of the flesh"; cf., lit., "the mind of the flesh," Col. 2:18) was decisively put off by Christ's death and resurrection. What people were in Adam—sinful, fallen, and corrupt—was destroyed by Christ. Now "in Christ" a believer is a new creation (2 Cor. 5:17). And having a new Head a believer has a new authority for his life—not the Law of Moses but the life of Christ.

The words **putting off** are from the noun *apekdysei* ("total breaking away from"), which occurs only here in the New Testament. This putting off of the old life occurs at the moment of salvation, when a believer is **buried with** Christ **in baptism** by the Spirit (cf. 1 Cor. 12:13) **and is raised with Him** to new life. This co-burial and co-resurrection is pictured in baptism. In water baptism, immersion portrays burial with Christ, and coming out of the water depicts the resurrection by **the power of God** to "live a new life" (Rom. 6:4).

2:13-14. Before a person is liberated to this new life in Christ, he is **dead in** his **sins and in** his **sinful nature** (cf. comments on the "earthly nature" in 3:5 and the "old self" in 3:9). Death means separation, not annihilation. Even the unsaved still bear the image of God (Gen. 9:6; James 3:9), but they are separated from God. Cut off from spiritual life, they still have human life. But now **God made you alive with Christ** (cf. Eph. 2:1-6). The same "power" (*energeias;* cf. "energy" in Col. 1:29) that raised Christ from the dead (2:12) resurrects believing sinners to spiritual life (v. 13).

This new life came when God **forgave us all our sins** for He **canceled the written code.** Before God's written Law, His "written code," people **stood** condemned (cf. Rom. 3:19), so it worked **against** them and **opposed** them. But in Christ the Law is fulfilled (Rom. 8:2) and done away with (Gal. 3:25; Heb. 7:12). Legalism is wrong because believers are dead to the Law in Christ. He fulfilled its demands in His life and by His death, and Christians are *in* Him.

This written code, the Law, was like a handwritten "certificate of debt" (NASB). Since people cannot keep the Law, it is like a bill of indebtedness. So people, unable to pay the debt, are criminals. But Jesus **took . . . away** this criminal charge, this certificate of indebtedness, by His death. It is as if He were **nailing it to the cross** with Him, showing He paid the debt. He wiped the slate clean. As Krishna Ral put it: "Jesus for thee a body takes, thy guilt assumes, thy fetter breaks, discharging all thy dreadful debt; and canst thou then such love forget?"

2:15-17. By fulfilling the demands of the Law, Christ **disarmed the** demonic **powers and authorities** (cf. 1:16; 2:10), **triumphing over them** (cf. 2 Cor. 2:14). As a result believers are delivered from these evil powers which inspire legalistic rules about foods and festivals. No one should **judge you by what you eat or drink** because Christians are free from the Law's legalistic requirements (such as those in Lev. 11; 17; Deut. 14). God does not condemn those who eat everything (Rom. 14:1-4). In fact, God says that all foods may be eaten since they were "created to be received with thanksgiving

by those who believe and who know the truth" (1 Tim. 4:3). The teaching that forbids this, Paul wrote, is "taught by demons" (1 Tim. 4:1) whom Christ has disarmed (Col. 2:15). This liberation of believers pertains also to festivals such as **a New Moon celebration or a Sabbath Day** (cf. Gal. 4:10). Those who would bring Christians under the bondage of the Law make artificial distinctions between the "ceremonial" and "moral" law, and so they say the Sabbath has not passed away. That this is false can be seen from the following: (1) The Sabbath command is the only one of the Ten Commandments not repeated in the New Testament. (2) The early believers, following Christ's resurrection and appearance on Sunday (Mark 16:1; John 20:1), met on Sundays (Acts 20:7; 1 Cor. 16:2). (3) The Bible nowhere distinguishes between the so-called "moral" and "ceremonial" laws (this distinction was not made before the 13th century A.D.) (4) This Colossian passage explicitly condemns those who command Sabbath obedience. (5) As Paul put it, the Old Testament Law (including the Sabbath) was only **a shadow of the things that were to come. The reality** or "substance" (*sōma,* lit., "body"), **however, is** to be **found in Christ** (cf. Heb. 8:5; 10:1). What the Old Testament foreshadowed, Christ fulfilled (cf. Matt. 5:17; Rom. 8:3-4). A "shadow" (*skia*) is only an image cast by an object which represents its form. Once one finds Christ, he no longer needs to follow the old shadow.

C. Mysticism is wrong: headship is in Christ (2:18-19)

2:18. Those who turn believers from the reality in Christ to the shadow of the Law **disqualify** them **for the prize.** That is, they rob (*katabrabeuetō,* "to decide against"; cf. *brabeuetō* in 3:15) believers of their spiritual rewards. As a judge disqualifies those who turn the wrong way in a race, so believers who turn from faithfully following Christ will be "robbed" of their rewards from Him (cf. 1 Cor. 3:10-15). Some heretics who turn believers away from faithful service have a **false humility,** which is only "a form of godliness but denying its power" (2 Tim. 3:5) that is in Christ (Rom. 8:3-4). This artificial godliness of legalists was connected with **the worship of angels**

which Scripture forbids (Ex. 20:3-4; cf. Rev. 22:8-9). In fact, legalism is a teaching inspired by fallen angels (1 Tim. 4:1) who as "elemental spirits" (Gal. 4:3, RSV) would bring men into slavery by their mystical meditations. These legalistic mystics dwell on what they have seen (in visions), which Paul called idle notions (*eikē*, "vain, to no avail"; cf. Gal. 3:4). This phrase may have occasioned the variant (but less preferable) translation "which he hath *not* seen" (KJV). Far from being humble, such a person's unspiritual mind (lit., "the mind of the flesh"; cf., lit., "the body of the flesh," v. 19) is puffed with pride in his visions.

2:19. While believing that his mysticism brings him in touch with some "higher" reality, a legal mystic has actually lost connection with the Head (Christ) who alone supplies life for it to grow as God causes it to grow (cf. John 15:1-5). True spirituality does not come by compliance with laws (which are only a shadow) but by connection with the Life (who is the reality). Without a vital connection to its Head, the body of Christ cannot grow. Using a parallel image, Jesus said, "I am the Vine; you are the branches. If a man remains in Me and I in Him, he will bear much fruit; apart from Me you can do nothing" (John 15:5).

D. *Asceticism is wrong: immunity is in Christ (2:20-23)*

2:20-21. A concomitant of legalism and mysticism is asceticism. It is the pseudo-spiritual position that revels in rules of physical self-denial. Do not handle! Do not taste! Do not touch! These prohibitions increase from not handling to not even touching. This same legalism was manifest in Eve's carnal exaggeration, "You must not touch it, or you will die" (Gen. 3:3; cf. Gen. 2:16-17). Asceticism arises out of guilt. But Christ has taken away all human guilt by His death (Col. 2:13-14). So since believers died with Christ to the basic principles (*stoicheia*; cf. comments on v. 8) of this world, they are no longer obligated (by fleshly inclinations) to obey them. Only those alive to sin (Rom. 6:2-7) need obey it as master. Worldliness is living by the world's rules, including those that have a show of humility and some alleged "angelic" source. Spirituality is living by the power of the Spirit in union with

Christ by whom the believer has died to sin. "For we know that our old self was crucified with Him so that the body of sin might be rendered powerless" (Rom. 6:6).

2:22-23. Asceticism is a man-made system of rules (often taken out of context from God's Law) based on human commands and teachings. The persistent example of legalism in the New Testament was the Old Testament command of circumcision which God intended for the Jews as a *sign* of faith (Rom. 4:11) but which the legalists wanted to make a *condition* of grace (Gal. 2:21). Living by such regulations or self-made religion has a certain appearance of wisdom (*sophias*; cf. Col. 1:9; 2:3, 4:5), but it has absolutely no value in restraining sensual indulgence. "Sensual indulgence" is literally "the flesh" (*sarkos*; cf. 2:11, 18). For denying the body its desires merely arouses them, as is well known by many who have tried to lose weight by sticking to rigid diets. Neglecting the body, Paul argued, does not nourish the spirit.

III. Spiritual: Inner Life in Christ (3:1-17)

Knowing that all wisdom is in Christ (2:1-5), Paul urged the Colossian Christians to continue in Him (2:6-7), not being deceived by vain philosophies (2:8-10). Since believers are identified with Christ, they are not to live under Jewish laws (2:11-17), for that would only rob them of their rewards (2:18-19). They have died with Christ and hence need not submit to legalistic rules (2:20-23).

Furthermore, they have also been raised with Christ. So they should set their hearts on heavenly things (3:1-4), put to death sinful worldly practices (3:5-11), and clothe themselves with Christ's virtues (3:12-17). Stated in another way, believers are to seek spiritual values (3:1-4), put off the sins of the old life (3:5-11), and put on the virtues of the new life (3:12-17). This in turn should affect their relationships with other members of their families and society (3:18–4:1).

A. *Seeking spiritual values (3:1-4)*

3:1. Since believers have not only died with Christ but have also been raised with Christ (cf. Rom. 6:8-10; Col. 2:12-13), they should set their hearts on things above. That is, believers' lives should be dominated by the pattern of heaven, bringing heavenly direction to their earthly duties. "Set" (*zēteite*) means "to seek or strive for earnestly" (cf. Rev. 9:6; 1 Cor. 7:27). Fixing their attention decisively toward "things above" involves centering their lives on the ascended (Eph. 4:10), glorified (John 17:5; Phil. 2:9) Christ, who is seated at the right hand of God (Ps. 110:1; Luke 22:69; Acts 2:33; 5:31; Rom. 8:34; Eph. 1:20; Heb. 1:3, 13; 8:1; 10:12; 12:2; 1 Peter 3:22). This is His seat of divine authority because He has defeated the forces of evil and death (Heb. 2:14-15).

3:2. Also Paul wrote, Set your minds on things above, not on earthly things. That is, concentrate your concern on the eternal, not the temporal. "Fix [your] eyes not on what is seen, but on what is unseen. For what is seen is temporary, but what is unseen is eternal" (2 Cor. 4:18). The similarity of the two commands in Colossians 3:1-2 reinforces their impact. "Set your hearts on things above" is *ta anō zēteite,* and "Set your minds on things above" is *ta anō phroneite.* The first suggests striving; the second suggests concentrating.

Paul was not enjoining an otherworld asceticism; he had just condemned that (2:20-23). He was saying that life *in this world* will be better if it is lived by a power *beyond this world,* the power of the resurrected, ascended, glorified Christ. The "earthly things" (*ta epi tēs gēs,* lit., "things upon the earth," 3:2; the same Gr. words are used in v. 5) to be avoided are moral, not physical (cf. immorality, impurity, lust, etc., in v. 5). Paul was not encouraging a kind of Gnostic disdain for material things. Every physical thing God created, including the body and sex, is good (cf. Gen. 1:27-30; 1 Tim. 4:1-4). However, since having a physical body does give occasion for the works of the (moral) flesh (cf. Rom. 7:4-6), Paul warned against setting one's affections in this area and perverting God's purpose for them.

3:3-4. At the moment of his salvation, a Christian died to the evil of the "flesh," the sin nature (Rom. 6:3-8; Col. 2:11), and his life is now hidden with Christ in God. "Hidden" implies both concealment and safety; both invisibility and security. He is not yet glorified, but

he is secure and safe in Christ. In fact, Christ is his very life. Christ said He was going where "the world will not see Me anymore" (John 14:19).

But when He will appear at the Rapture (1 Thes. 4:16-18), believers will appear with Him and will be glorified. As John put it, "We know that when He appears, we shall be like Him, for we shall see Him as He is" (i.e., believers will be glorified as He is glorified; 1 John 3:2; cf. 1 Cor. 13:12; Col. 1:27). So Paul added a new direction to the believers' focus of attention: they should look *upward* to Christ's reign over them in heaven and also *forward* to His return for them in the clouds.

B. Putting off the sins of the old life (3:5-11)

3:5-6. Paul's imagery moved from death and life to putting clothes on and off. Put to death . . . whatever belongs to your earthly nature. The Greek tense in this command suggests a decisive action, as if Paul said, "Mortify it! Do it now! Do it resolutely!" Of course, God has already done it, but Christians are to *know* this, *count* it to be true, and *act* accordingly (Rom. 6:5-14). In other words, they are not to go on living as though they are still alive to sin when in actuality they are not. They are to put away that old life, which springs from their earthly natures. "Whatever belongs to your earthly nature" is literally "the members that are upon the earth" (*ta melē ta epi tēs gēs*). These contrast with the "things above" (Col. 3:1; *ta epi tēs gēs* is also used in v. 2). This "earthly nature" is the "old self" (or "sinful nature" [2:13], or "old man" [KJV]; Eph. 4:22; Col. 3:9). Some take this to mean the persons Christians were before conversion, whereas others take it (more likely) to refer to the evil tendencies in believers today (i.e., their "old natures"). Even if it means the former, the net effect is the same: they should not live as they did before, because they are new creations in Christ (2 Cor. 5:17).

The list of evil activities flowing from man's earthly nature includes immorality (*porneia,* "fornication"), impurity (a wider perversion), lust (*pathos,* "uncontrollable passion"), evil desires ("illicit craving"), and greed (or coveting), which is idolatry (because it seeks satisfaction in things below and not above). Similar lists of sins appear often in Paul's writings (Rom. 1:29-31; 1 Cor. 5:11; 6:9; Gal. 5:19-21; Eph. 5:3-5). Paul added that **because of these** evils **the wrath of God is coming.** The words "is coming" render the present tense *erchetai* (lit., "comes"). This suggests that God's wrath has already begun (cf. John 3:36). It will, of course, culminate in His future climactic visitation on evil (Rom. 2:5; 2 Thes. 1:7-9).

3:7-9. Though the Colossian Christians **used to walk** [live] **in these** evil **ways,** before they came to know Christ, Paul commanded that they do so no more. **Now you must rid yourselves of all such things.** The word "rid" (*apothesthe*) means "to put off" like a suit of clothes. In its ethical use here it means "throw it off like a dirty shirt" (cf. Rom. 13:12; Eph. 4:22, 25; Heb. 12:1; James 1:21; 1 Peter 2:1). In the Bible, behavior is often likened to a garment (e.g., Job 29:14; Ps. 35:26; Isa. 11:5; Rom. 13:12; 1 Thes. 5:8).

Repulsive habits—**anger, rage, malice, slander, and filthy language**—do not fit or suit Christians. They are unbecoming to believers (cf. Eph. 4:17, 31). "Anger" (*orgēn*) is a chronic attitude of smoldering hatred, whereas "rage" (*thymon*) is an acute outburst. *Thymos* elsewhere is rendered "outbursts of anger" (2 Cor. 12:20), "fits of rage" (Gal. 5:20), and "rage" (Eph. 4:31). "Malice" (*kakian*, the vice that lies below anger and rage as their root) is forbidden, as is "slander" (*blasphēmian*, "railing or evil speaking"). "Filthy language" (*aischrologian*) is shameful or abrasive speech. Neither should Christians **lie** (cf. Eph. 4:25) for truthfulness is essential in followers of the One who is "the Truth" (John 14:6).

Lying and all other vices are inappropriate for a Christian for at salvation he discarded his **old self** (lit., "the old man," i.e., the former sinful way of living, characteristic of the unregenerate; Col. 2:11, 13a) **with its practices** (cf. "died" in 2:20; 3:3).

3:10. A Christian is to **put on** (cf. v. 12) **the new self** (new way of life or disposition). Hence his conduct should be in accord with his new position. This "new self" needs constant renewal or refreshing—it **is being renewed** (pres. tense), in order to keep it victorious over sin. Paul also expressed this idea of continual renewal in 2 Corinthians 4:16 ("Though outwardly we are wasting away, yet inwardly we are being renewed day by day"); in Romans 12:2 (being "transformed by the renewing of your mind"); and in Ephesians 4:23 ("to be made new in the attitude of your minds").

This renewal of the new self is **in knowledge** (*eis epignōsin;* cf. Col. 1:9; 2:2). It takes place as a believer comes to a personal, deep knowledge of and fellowship with Christ. And the renewal is **in** (*kat'*, "according to") **the image of its Creator;** its goal is to make believers like Him, for the "new self [was] created to be like God" (Eph. 4:24). Adam was created in the image of God (Gen. 1:27), which included a moral and intellectual likeness to God. Though this image was not erased (but only effaced) by the Fall (Gen. 9:6; James 3:9), yet it was corrupted and needs to be repaired and renewed. Christians become increasingly like the Lord as they refresh their new natures, yielding to the Holy Spirit's sanctifying work. And in the resurrection believers "shall bear the likeness of the Man [Christ] from heaven" (1 Cor. 15:49). Then the task of restoring God's image will be complete, for "we shall be like Him" (1 John 3:2).

3:11. In Christ distinctions are removed. These include national distinctions (**Greek or Jew;** Jews called all those outside their nation Greeks; cf. Gal. 3:28); religious distinctions (**circumcised or uncircumcised**); cultural distinctions (anyone foreign to Greek culture was a **barbarian,** and a **Scythian** was a wild, savage nomad); and economic or social distinctions (**slave or free**). If a Greek, an uncircumcised person, a barbarian, a Scythian, or a slave became a believer, he was a "new creation" (2 Cor. 5:17), a "new self" (Col. 3:10), just like a Jew or free person who became a Christian. For **Christ is all, and is in all.** That is, normal human distinctions are overruled and transfigured by one's union in Christ.

All barriers are destroyed in Christ, and all believers are truly "created equal." So it is to be expected that each believer—regardless of his nationality, former religion, culture, or economic standing—should do away with his former sinful practices and should live in accord with his "new self."

C. Putting on the virtues of the new life (3:12-17)

Because of their new lives in Christ all believers are called on to clothe themselves in virtue, letting Christ's peace rule their hearts. His Word should dwell in them richly, and they should do everything in the name of the Lord Jesus.

3:12. Again Paul called on believers to take a decisive action: **Clothe yourselves** (*endysasthe*). Because they have "put on (*endysamenoi*) the new self" (v. 10), they should live accordingly, with appropriate attributes and attitudes. In verses 8-9 Paul listed six vices (anger, rage, malice, slander, filthy language, and lying). Now in contrast to them, Christians—**as God's chosen people** (cf. Rom. 8:33; Titus 1:1), **holy** ("separated to God"; cf. Col. 1:2) **and dearly loved** (cf. Rom. 5:8; 1 John 4:9-11, 19)—are to have several virtues. These include **compassion** (*splanchna oiktirmou*, lit., "tender sympathy of heartfelt compassion"—an unusually touching expression; in Phil. 2:1 Paul joined these two nouns with "and"), **kindness** (benevolence in action; cf. 2 Cor. 6:6), **humility** (a lowly attitude toward God; cf. Phil. 2:3; 1 Peter 5:5), **gentleness** (*prautēta*), meekness, a lowly attitude toward others, **and patience** (*makrothymian*, self-restraint, a steady response in the face of provocation; cf. Col. 1:11). The last three of these are mentioned in the Greek in the same order in Ephesians 4:2; and Galatians 5:22-23 in the Greek includes three of them: patience and gentleness, as well as kindness.

3:13. Furthermore, believers are to **bear with each other** (i.e., "put up with each other") with the attitudes just mentioned in v. 12. Also they are to **forgive whatever grievances** (complaints) **they may have against** others. How? By forgiving **as the Lord forgave** them, graciously and freely (Eph. 4:32). Grudges have no place in a Christian's life for they may lead to the sins mentioned in Colossians 3:8-9.

3:14. But **over all these virtues** Christians are to **put on love.** As Paul wrote elsewhere, "The greatest of these is love" (1 Cor. 13:13). In one's catalog of virtues love should be the cover, because it is of supreme importance and is the perfect bond, holding **them all together in perfect unity.**

3:15. Believers are also to **let the peace of Christ rule in their hearts** because they are **called to peace** as **members of one body.** The closer believers are to Christ (and His likeness), the closer they are to each other. In interpersonal relationships "peace" (transcendent, God-given tranquility) should rule (*brabeuetō*, "arbitrate, decide every debate"; a word used only here in the NT; cf. *katabrabeuetō*, "decide against," 2:18). Christ's followers who have put on the virtues Paul listed (3:12-14), are concerned about being arbitrated in every trying circumstance by His peace, not by their wrangling. Also Christians are to **be thankful** (cf. Phil. 4:6; Col. 1:12; 3:16-17; 4:2; 1 Thes. 5:18). An attitude of gratitude contributes to an enjoyment of spiritual tranquility, whereas grumbling makes for inner agitation.

3:16. The new life Christians must "put on" is one in which **the Word of Christ** dwells **richly.** Christ's words were recorded by Spirit-guided apostles (cf. John 14:26; 16:13; 20:31). The words of the Bible, God's written Word, are to **dwell in** believers. That is, by study, meditation, and application of the Word, it becomes a permanent abiding part of one's life. When the words of Christ become part of a believer's nature, they spring forth naturally and daily in **psalms** (songs from the Book of Psalms), **hymns** (other songs of praise), **and spiritual songs** (as opposed to secular odes) **with gratitude** (*en tē chariti*; lit., "in grace"). This can mean either (a) God's grace, (b) graciousness in Christian singing, or (c) Christian thanks. As suggested by the NIV it probably has the third meaning. Such joyful singing is not only to please oneself or others but is to be praise **to God.** Through this Spirit-filled kind of life (cf. Eph. 5:18-19), Christians can **teach** (instruct) **and admonish** ("counsel") **one another** (Col. 3:16; cf. "admonishing and teaching" in 1:28) if it is done **with all wisdom** (*sophia*; cf. 1:9; 2:3; 4:5) and not tactlessly (cf. Gal. 6:1).

3:17. Whatever one does (cf. v. 23)—for there is no sacred-secular split in God's eyes; He is Sovereign over all—**whether in word or deed** (by lip or life) should **all** be done **in the name of the Lord Jesus** (i.e., for His glory; cf. 1 Cor. 10:31) and with a thankful spirit (cf. Phil. 4:6; 1 Thes. 5:18). Three times in three verses Paul mentioned thankfulness: "be thankful" (Col. 3:15) "sing . . . with gratitude" (v. 16), and give thanks to God the Father (v. 17).

IV. Practical: Outer Life in Christ (3:18–4:18)

In this last section Paul turned to practical interpersonal relations that should flow from a believer's position in Christ. First, he exhorted each member in human families to perfect (mature in) his *private* life (wives, husbands, children, fathers, slaves, masters; 3:18–4:1). He then reminded believers to perfect their *prayer* lives (4:2-4) and their *public* lives (4:5-6). Then he shared his concern for perfecting the *personal* lives of all the Colossian believers (4:7-18).

A. Perfecting one's private life (3:18–4:1)

In accordance with the theme of Colossians—maturity in Christ (1:28)—Paul exhorted believers to become mature in their private home relationships.

3:18. Wives are to **submit to** their **husbands as** their heads. This command was not limited to Paul's day, as is obvious from two reasons he gave elsewhere: (1) the order of Creation (man was created first, then woman; 1 Tim. 2:13); (2) the order within the Godhead (Christ submits to the Father; 1 Cor. 11:3). Submission or subordination does not mean inferiority; it simply means that the husband, not the wife, is head of the home. If he may be thought of as the "president," she is the "vice-president."

Of course there are moral limits to this submission; it is only **as is fitting in the Lord.** Just as obedience to government is commanded (Rom. 13:1; Titus 3:1; 1 Peter 2:13) but only insofar as government takes its place under God (Ex. 1; Dan. 3; 6), even so a wife's submission to her husband is only "in the Lord." That is, she is not obligated to follow her husband's leadership if it conflicts with specific scriptural commands.

3:19. Husbands are responsible to **love their wives** (as Christ loved the church; Eph. 5:28-29). So they are to exercise loving leadership, not dictatorial dominion. Perhaps husbands need this reminder to be tender and loving as much or more than wives need the reminder not to usurp authority over their hus-

bands. Assuming absolute authority will only embitter one's wife, not endear her. The words **be harsh** translate *pikrainesthe,* which is more literally, "make bitter." (A different word is used in Col. 3:21; see comments there.) Wives, like tender and sensitive flowers (cf. 1 Peter 3:7), may wilt under authoritarian dominance but blossom with tender loving care. So in a maturing marriage the husband exercises compassionate care and his wife responds in willing submission to this loving leadership.

3:20. Children are to **obey** their **parents in everything.** Disobedience to parents is designated in the Old Testament as rebellion against God and was severely punished (Ex. 21:17; Lev. 20:9). Jesus set an example for children by obeying Joseph and His mother Mary (Luke 2:51). Obedience to parents **pleases the Lord.** This does not suggest that obeying one's parents merits salvation for a child. Rather, obedience reflects God's design for order in the home. As Paul wrote elsewhere, "It is right" (*dikaion,* "just" or "proper") for children to obey their parents (Eph. 6:1).

3:21. Fathers (and mothers; cf. Prov. 1:8; 6:20) should not presume on this obedience and **embitter** (*erethizete,* "provoke or irritate") their **children** by continual agitation and unreasonable demands. Paul wrote, "Fathers, do not exasperate (*parorgizete*) your children" (Eph. 6:4). This will only make them **become discouraged.** Praise for well-doing rather than constant criticism will, along with loving discipline (cf. Heb. 12:7), help rear children in "the training and instruction of the Lord" (Eph. 6:4).

3:22-25. Slaves are exhorted to **obey** (the same word is directed to children in v. 20) their **earthly masters.** "Earthly" is literally "according to the flesh"; only Christ is master of the *spirits* of believing slaves. This obedience is to be **with sincerity of heart,** not simply when their masters are watching them or **to win their favor.** Also slaves are to work with **reverence for the Lord.** Working with an awareness of God's character and presence enhances the dignity of the labor of even slaves. In fact, **whatever** (cf. v. 17) slaves do should be **with all their heart**[s] (lit., "out of the soul," i.e., genuine and from within, not merely by outward pretense) and **for the Lord, not for men.**

While slavery was certainly undesirable, Paul's goals did not include restructuring social institutions (cf. 1 Cor. 7:17-24). Principles in Colossians 3:22-25 for Christian slaves may be applied today to Christian employees. If more Christian employees today served their employers with genuine concern and as though they were serving God, quality and productivity would increase dramatically! **It is the Lord Christ** whom all Christians **are serving.** (This is the only place in the NT where the term "the Lord Christ" is used.) After all, the final "payday" (**an inheritance . . . as a reward**) is coming **from the Lord** (cf. 2 Cor. 5:10). He will judge without **favoritism** (cf. Rom. 2:9; Eph. 6:9), that is, in full justice, repaying wrongdoers and rewarding those who serve Him.

In these verses (Col. 3:22-25) Paul made numerous points about the motives, attitudes, and conduct of Christian slaves. Such instruction was remarkable in a master-slave society.

4:1. On the other hand **masters** were to **provide** ("give deliberate care") for their **slaves with what is right** (*dikaion*) **and fair** (*isotēta*, "equitable"). After all, masters themselves are responsible to the Lord, their **Master in heaven,** who treats them fairly. If employers of nonslaves today manifested this kind of compassionate and impartial care for their employees, certainly their employees' motivation to work would radically improve.

B. Perfecting one's prayer life (4:2-4)

4:2. Paul not only practiced a mature prayer life (cf. 1:3-12) but he also prescribed it for all believers. They should **devote** themselves to (lit., "persist, continue in"; cf. Rom. 12:12) **prayer.** Prayer is not a spiritual luxury; it is essential for growth. Prayer—as vital to one's spiritual health as breathing is to one's physical health—should be continual (1 Thes. 5:17), not casual. In his praying, a Christian should be **watchful** ("alert, aware") against spiritual drowsiness caused by attention to the world (Matt. 24:42; Acts 20:31; 1 Cor. 16:13; 1 Thes. 5:6) and/or by the wiles of the devil (Eph. 6:16; 1 Peter 5:8). Being **thankful** should always accompany prayer (Phil. 4:6; Col. 1:12; 3:16-17;

1 Thes. 5:18), for it places a believer in the proper attitude before God (cf. Rom. 1:21).

4:3-4. Pray for us was a request Paul often made of his readers (Rom. 15:30; Eph. 6:19; 1 Thes. 5:25; 2 Thes. 3:1). His request was not selfish; it was for an **open . . . door** (cf. 1 Cor. 16:9; 2 Cor. 2:12) through which he could clearly minister the gospel **message . . . the mystery of Christ** (cf. Eph. 3:4; 6:19; Col. 1:26-27; 2:2), **for which** he was **in chains** (cf. Phil. 1:7, 13-14, 16; Col. 4:18; Phile. 1, 9-10, 13). He desired not only an opportunity to preach but also clarity in preaching: **that I may proclaim it clearly, as I should** (i.e., "as I am obligated to"; cf. Rom. 1:14-15).

C. Perfecting one's public life (4:5-6)

4:5-6. Completion or perfection in Christ includes not only one's private (and prayer) life but also one's public life. To perfect this dimension of one's life in Christ, Paul told believers to **be wise in the way they act.** This wisdom (*sophia*; cf. 1:9; 28; 3:16), which is God's, not man's (cf. James 3:13, 17), should be evident to **outsiders,** that is, those outside the "household of faith" (cf. 1 Cor. 5:12; 1 Thes. 4:12; 1 Tim. 3:7). Also Paul's readers should **make the most of every opportunity** (lit., "buy up [*exagorazomenoi*] the time"). They should be ready "in season and out of season" (2 Tim. 4:2) to proclaim Christ. In addition, their **conversation** (*logos*, "word, discourse, talking") should **be always full of** (lit., "in") **grace** ("gracious, pleasing"; cf. Col. 3:8-9) and yet **seasoned with salt** (i.e., pure and penetrating; 4:6). In this way they could **answer everyone** who asked "the reason for the hope" (1 Peter 3:15) they had.

D. Perfecting one's personal life (4:7-17)

Paul set an example for mature interpersonal relations. Besides remembering his friends and companions, he expressed genuine concern for them.

4:7-8. Tychicus (a leader in the church and bearer of this letter) was **a dear brother, a faithful minister** (cf. Eph. 6:21), **and a fellow servant** with Paul in the ministry. He was from the province of Asia (Acts 20:4) and was mentioned by Paul also in 2 Timothy 4:12 and Titus

3:12. Paul sent him to Colosse **for the express purpose** of informing them about his state of affairs to **encourage** them.

4:9. Onesimus (a converted runaway slave of Philemon) was also a **faithful and dear brother** (cf. Phile. 16) to Paul and a fellow Colossian: **one of you** (cf. Col. 4:12). He would accompany Tychicus and also report on Paul's circumstances.

4:10. Aristarchus was a Thessalonian who accompanied Paul on his third missionary journey (Acts 19:29; 20:4; 27:2). Being Paul's **fellow prisoner** meant either that Aristarchus attended Paul, or more likely, that he was incarcerated with Paul (probably also for preaching the gospel). Paul also called him a fellow worker (Phile. 24).

Mark, the cousin of Barnabas, was a companion on Paul's first missionary journey (Acts 12:25). He was later Peter's associate ("my son," 1 Peter 5:13; cf. Acts 12:12-13). Though Mark deserted Paul on the first missionary journey (Acts 15:37-39), Paul here commended him (cf. Phile. 24), as he did later (2 Tim 4:11).

4:11. Jesus was a common Jewish name. This companion of Paul's was also **called Justus** ("righteous"), also a common name (Acts 1:23; 18:7). These three—Aristarchus, Mark, and Justus—were **Jews** (lit., "of the circumcision") by either birth or conversion (proselytism). These three **fellow workers for the kingdom of God** comforted or consoled Paul by their loving loyalty to him. **Comfort** is the unusual word *parēgoria* ("relief, consolation"), found only here in the New Testament.

4:12-13. Epaphras, like Onesimus (v. 9), was a Colossian (**one of you**) whom Paul depicted as **a servant of Christ Jesus** who was **always wrestling** (*agōnizomenos;* cf. 1:29) **in prayer** (as Jacob did with the angel; Gen. 32) **for the Colossians.** His concern was that the Colossians would **stand firm in** God's **will . . . mature** (*teleioi,* "perfected") **and fully assured** (Rom. 4:21; 14:5) or fulfilled. This fits the overall theme of Colossians: that believers be mature, perfected in Christ. Epaphras' prayerful concern went to the point of **working hard** (lit., "has much pain"; *ponon,* "pain or distress," is used only here and in Rev. 16:10-11). His painful labor was for all the believers in the Lycus Valley—those in Colosse,

Laodicea, and Hierapolis (see the location of these three on the map between Acts and Rom.).

4:14. Luke, Paul's **dear friend** and **doctor,** stood firm not only in this earlier imprisonment but also in Paul's latter imprisonment, by which time **Demas** (here with Paul) had forsaken him (2 Tim. 4:10). Luke is the author of the Third Gospel and of Acts (cf. Acts 1:1). By tradition he was one of the 72 (Luke 10:1). Some also suggest he was the anonymous disciple on the Emmaus Road (Luke 24:13). Since the only men with Paul who were "of the circumcision" were Aristarchus, Mark, and Jesus (Justus), Luke may have been a Gentile.

4:15. Paul asked that his **greetings** be given **to the brothers at Laodicea and to Nympha** in whose **house** the **church** met. Churches meeting in homes was a common practice then before there were church buildings (Rom. 16:5; 1 Cor. 16:19; Phile. 2).

4:16. Paul urged an exchange of epistles; once they had read Colossians they should send it to Laodicea and **read the letter** (coming) **from Laodicea.** This "Laodicean letter" may be the letter to the Ephesians, which was written about that time, and sent to the same general vicinity.

4:17. Archippus, probably the son of Philemon (cf. Phile. 2), was ministering in Colosse, possibly in Epaphras' absence. Paul exhorted his readers to **tell** Archippus to **see to** (*blepe,* "look out" for dangers in) **it that** he **complete the work** (lit., "the ministry") God had given him. Whatever his problem, he was not fulfilling (completing) his work. This was another example of Paul's concern that the Colossians be complete in Christ.

E. Salutation (4:18)

4:18. As was Paul's custom and sign of authenticity, he signed a **greeting** with his **own hand** (cf. 1 Cor. 16:21; Gal. 6:11; 2 Thes. 3:17; Phile. 19). He then asked that his readers **remember** (in prayerful support) his imprisonment (**chains;** cf. Col. 4:3). As with so many of his epistles, his closing was a benediction, a prayer that God's **grace** (cf. 1:2) **be with** them (see the chart, "Paul's Concluding Benedictions in His Epistles" near Rom. 16:20).

BIBLIOGRAPHY

Barry, Alfred. "The Epistle to the Colossians." In *Ellicott's Commentary on the Whole Bible*. Reprint (8 vols. in 4). Grand Rapids: Zondervan Publishing House, 1959.

Calvin, John. "Commentaries on the Epistles of Paul to the Galatians and Ephesians." In *Calvin's Commentaries*, vol. 21. Translated by William Pringle. Reprint. Grand Rapids: Baker Book House, 1981.

Carson, Herbert M. *The Epistle of Paul to the Colossians and Philemon*. The Tyndale New Testament Commentaries. Grand Rapids: Wm. B. Eerdmans Publishing Co., 1960.

Erdman, Charles R. *The Epistle of Paul to the Colossians and to Philemon*. Philadelphia: Westminster Press, 1933.

Gromacki, Robert G. *Stand Perfect in Wisdom: An Exposition of Colossians and Philemon*. Grand Rapids: Baker Book House, 1981.

Kent, Homer A., Jr. *Treasure of Wisdom*. Grand Rapids: Baker Book House, 1978.

Lightfoot, J.B. *St. Paul's Epistle to the Colossians and to Philemon*. London: Macmillan & Co., 1879. Reprint. Grand Rapids: Zondervan Publishing House, 1959.

Moule, H.C.G. *Studies in Colossians and Philemon*. 1893. Reprint. Grand Rapids: Kregel Publications, 1977.

Peake, A.S. "The Epistle to the Colossians." In *The Expositor's Greek Testament*, vol. 3. Grand Rapids: Wm. B. Eerdmans Publishing Co., 1951.

Simpson, E.K., and Bruce, F.F. *Commentary on the Epistles to the Ephesians and the Colossians*. The New International Commentary on the New Testament. Grand Rapids: Wm. B. Eerdmans Publishing Co., 1957.

Thomas, W.H. Griffith. *Studies in Colossians and Philemon*. Grand Rapids: Baker Book House, 1973.

Vaughan, Curtis. "Colossians." In *The Expositor's Bible Commentary*, vol. 11. Grand Rapids: Zondervan Publishing House, 1978.

————. *Colossians: Bible Study Commentary*. Grand Rapids: Zondervan Publishing House, 1973.

Wiersbe, Warren W. *Be Complete*. Wheaton, Ill.: Scripture Press Publications, Victor Books, 1981.

1 THESSALONIANS

Thomas L. Constable

INTRODUCTION

The City of Thessalonica. The city of Thessalonica flourished for hundreds of years, partly because of its ideal location. It was situated on the banks of a hospitable harbor in the Thermaic Gulf near the northwest corner of the Aegean Sea. In the Apostle Paul's day it was the chief seaport of the Roman province of Macedonia. Thessalonica ranked with Corinth and Ephesus, the main ports of the provinces of Achaia and Asia, as a great shipping center.

Thessalonica also enjoyed another advantage. The Egnatian Way, the main Roman road from Rome to the Orient via Byzantium (modern Istanbul), passed through the city. This put Thessalonica in direct contact with many other important cities by land as well as by sea. It was one of the most important centers of population in Paul's day, occupying a strategic location both governmentally and militarily.

Estimates of the population of Thessalonica in New Testament times place it at near 200,000 (Everett F. Harrison, *Introduction to the New Testament*, Grand Rapids: Wm. B. Eerdmans Publishing Co., 1964, p. 245). Most of the inhabitants were native Greeks, but many Romans also lived there. Orientals and Jews likewise populated the city. Wherever commerce flourished in the ancient world one would find Jewish businessmen. The Jewish synagogue in Thessalonica was influential; many Greek proselytes were present when Paul preached there (Acts 17:4).

First Thessalonians reflects the moral climate of the city. The pagan Greek religion of the largest segment of the population produced many forms of immorality but whetted the appetites of some for spiritual reality. Evidently the higher standards of Judaism attracted disillusioned Greeks, Romans, and Orientals to the synagogue.

Thessalonica was built by Cassander in 315 B.C. near the site of an ancient city called Therma, named for the hot springs in the area. He chose this place for its excellent location and named it after his wife, Thessalonica, who was a half sister of Alexander the Great. Cassander was a Greek general under Alexander.

Many years later, when the Romans conquered the area (168 B.C.), they divided Macedonia into four districts and named Thessalonica the capital of one of these. In 146 B.C. the Romans reorganized Macedonia and made Thessalonica the capital of the new province which encompassed all four of the older districts. In 42 B.C. Thessalonica received the status of a free city from Anthony and Octavian (later called Caesar Augustus) because the Thessalonians had helped these men defeat their adversaries, Brutus and Cassius. The Romans ruled Thessalonica with a loose hand; though the Roman proconsul (or governor) lived there, no Roman troops were garrisoned in the city. The citizens were allowed to govern themselves, as in a Greek city-state, which they did through a group of five or six politarchs, a senate, and a public assembly.

In World War I the Allies based soldiers in Thessalonica, and during the Second World War the Nazis extracted 60,000 Jews from the city and executed them. Thessalonica still exists today with a population near 300,000. It is called Salonica (or Thessaloniki).

The Evangelization of the City. The Apostle Paul first preached the gospel in Thessalonica during his second missionary journey. Having revisited the churches in the province of Asia where Paul and Barnabas had preached on their first journey, Paul, Silas, Timothy, Luke, and perhaps others made their way to

Troas, after unsuccessfully attempting to travel in other directions. In Troas Paul received his vision of a man of Macedonia calling for help. Responding to this call the party crossed into Europe and preached at Philippi, a major city of Macedonia. Through a series of circumstances the missionaries were led to leave Philippi and press on about 100 miles westward along the Egnatian Way to the next major population center, Thessalonica (Acts 17:1-9).

As was his custom, Paul visited the Jewish synagogue in Thessalonica where he knew he would find people who held much in common with him: respect for the Old Testament, theological concepts, and cultural practices. Since Paul was a well-trained teacher, he was allowed to speak in the synagogue. His message, as Luke summarized it, consisted of two points: the Old Testament taught a suffering, dying, resurrected Messiah; and these predictions were fulfilled in Jesus of Nazareth. Though Luke did not say so, Paul also may have taught that Jesus Christ would return to fulfill the remaining messianic prophecies (Acts 17:7). In the Thessalonian Epistles Paul sought to answer questions that had arisen from his teaching. As a result of Paul's preaching several people were converted including (a) some Jews, (b) several Gentile Greeks who had come to the synagogue because they had placed faith in or were interested in more information about the Jews' God, and (c) the wives of some prominent Thessalonian citizens (17:4).

The length of Paul's stay on this occasion is a matter of minor disagreement among students of the Thessalonian Epistles. Some believe that the reference to Paul's presence in the synagogue on three Sabbath Days (17:2) means that he was in Thessalonica for only about 21 days (e.g., James E. Frame, *A Critical and Exegetical Commentary on the Epistles of St. Paul to the Thessalonians*, p. 7). Others feel that Paul was probably there for a longer period of time, perhaps as long as six months (e.g., Richard B. Rackham, *The Acts of the Apostles*, London: Metheun & Co., 1901, p. 296). Those who hold the latter opinion base it on the implications of other passages that may hint at Paul's experiences in Thessalonica during this visit. For example, Paul apparently worked at his craft of tentmaking while in Thessalonica (1 Thes. 2:9; 2 Thes. 3:8). These references may imply a prolonged stay, but they do not require it. Some interpreters contend that Philippians 4:16 suggests that the Philippians sent two gifts to Paul while he was in Thessalonica and that would be unlikely, they say, if he were there just three weeks. Other commentators insist that this verse only says that the Philippians sent two gifts; they claim it does not explicitly say that Paul was in Thessalonica when he received both of them.

The length of Paul's stay is significant because of the doctrinal background of his readers which the Thessalonian Epistles reveal. Of course knowledge of what went on in the Thessalonian church after Paul left as well as while he was there is sketchy at best. But it seems that Paul fed these new believers a rich diet of doctrinal instruction in a fairly brief period of time. Also, Paul wrote as though he left Thessalonica before he really wanted to. Perhaps a stay of a few months in Thessalonica is fairly accurate.

Quite possibly Paul continued his teaching and evangelizing out of Jason's house after the Jews opposed him (Acts 17:5-10). His adversaries regarded Paul's message as a threat to Judaism, as Jews have done since the gospel was first preached in Jerusalem. The non-Christian Jews in Thessalonica resorted to a strategy to get rid of Paul that was similar to that employed by Jesus' enemies and Stephen's accusers. They hired troublemakers and put false accusations in their mouths. Storming Jason's house, but failing to find the missionaries, the mob dragged Jason before the politarchs. The Jews charged Jason with harboring revolutionaries who were promoting treason by teaching the people to disobey Roman law and to follow a king other than Caesar. Though this was a serious charge, especially in a city whose free status could be withdrawn by Rome if it were true, the city rulers saw through the motives of these jealous Jewish zealots. The rulers only required Jason to guarantee that Paul and his friends would not disturb the city's peace any longer. This made it necessary for the missionaries to leave Thessalonica. The Christians who remained continued to feel the heat of Jewish persecution, however, not only from the Jews themselves, but also from the Gentiles whom the unbelieving Jews influenced (1 Thes. 2:14; 2 Thes. 1:4).

The Occasion of the Letter. When Paul and Silas left Thessalonica, they proceeded about 40 miles west along the Egnatian Way to Berea. There they ministered for a short time until the hostile Thessalonian Jews, hearing of Paul's preaching in Berea, tracked down the missionaries and incited the Berean Jews to expel Paul from their city. Paul made his way south to Athens while Silas and Timothy remained in Berea. Paul sent a message to these two companions as soon as he reached Athens, asking them to join him, which they did (Acts 17:10-15; 1 Thes. 2:1-5). The plight of the new Thessalonian converts so concerned Paul that he sent Timothy back to Thessalonica to check on the church's welfare. Timothy rejoined Paul at the next stop, Corinth, with encouraging news (Acts 18:1, 5; 1 Thes. 3:6-7). This led Paul to write 1 Thessalonians.

Some students of this epistle believe that Paul wrote not only to commend the Thessalonian believers for their steadfastness in persecution, but also to answer questions they sent to him through Timothy. Though there is no external evidence for the existence of a document containing these questions, it is obvious from the text that Paul wrote answers to some of their questions (cf. 1 Thes. 4:9; 5:1). These questions may have been relayed orally by Timothy. Another reason for Paul's writing was to correct misinformation and false accusations that circulated after Paul left Thessalonica. Paul also wrote to exhort them to go forward in their faith.

The Purpose of the Letter. Specifically, the Holy Spirit led Paul to pen this inspired epistle in order to meet several needs. He encouraged his children in the faith to persevere despite their persecution. He refuted false charges made by the local enemies of the gospel: that the missionaries had preached in order to fatten their wallets and gain other personal benefits; that Paul had left Thessalonica hurriedly and had not returned because he was a coward and a hypocrite. Paul also wrote to correct some errors that had cropped up in the church: an inclination to moral laxity and laziness, and a tendency not to respect the church's spiritual leaders. Paul gave instruction too on the subject of what would happen to Christians who would die before the Lord's return.

The Place and Date of Writing. References in Acts 17 and 18 as well as in 1 Thessalonians make it clear that Paul wrote this epistle from Corinth.

Evidently the letter was written shortly after Paul arrived in Corinth (Acts 17:1-10; 18:1). The references to Gallio's proconsulate in Corinth (cf. 18:12) on ancient secular inscriptions make it possible to date Paul's stay in Corinth fairly accurately—in the early 50s (Jack Finegan, *Light from the Ancient Past,* Princeton, N.J.: Princeton University Press, 1969, p. 282). Conservative scholars date 1 Thessalonians between A.D. 50 and 54. This would make the epistle one of Paul's earliest inspired writings, probably his second (after Galatians).

The Authenticity of the Epistle. The Pauline authorship for 1 Thessalonians is not questioned by scholars who take the statements of the book at face value. During the last century objections to Paul's authorship were raised by critics, but these have now been answered satisfactorily (see, e.g., A. Robert and A. Feuillet, eds., *Introduction to the New Testament,* New York: Desclée Co., 1965, p. 390).

OUTLINE

COMMENTARY

I. Salutation and Greeting (1:1)

1:1. Letters written in first-century Greco-Roman culture began with three statements which are found in the opening verse of 1 Thessalonians: the name(s) of the writer(s), the name(s) of the addressee(s), and a word of formal greeting.

The Apostle **Paul** was the writer of this epistle. His name appears first and he spoke of himself in the singular elsewhere in the letter (e.g., 3:5). He was Saul of Tarsus whose Hebrew name means "asked for." His Roman name, Paul, by which he was known more commonly, means "little." **Silas and Timothy** joined Paul in sending 1 Thessalonians; that is, Paul wrote for them as well as for himself. Perhaps Silas served as Paul's amanuensis, or secretary. Frequently in 1 Thessalonians Paul wrote "we" so he was either including these brethren in his thoughts (e.g., 1:2; 2:1; etc.) or using an editorial "we." Silvanus is the Roman form of Silas which Paul used consistently in his writings, as did Peter (1 Peter 5:12). Luke called the same person Silas (Acts 15:22; etc.). Silas was Paul's primary associate on the second missionary journey (Acts 15:40). Timothy, of course, was a young man Paul led to faith in Jesus Christ (1 Tim. 1:2), probably during

Paul's visit to Asia Minor on his first missionary journey (Acts 13–14). Timothy's name (which means "honored by God" or "God-honorer") was doubtless given in faith by his God-fearing mother Eunice (2 Tim. 1:5). His father may have been a pagan Greek when Timothy was born (Acts 16:1). This young man had recently returned to Paul from a trip to Thessalonica with news of conditions in that church (1 Thes. 3:1-2, 6). These three men were undoubtedly the best-known and most highly respected Christian missionaries by the believers in Thessalonica.

The addressees are grouped together in the salutation as **the church of the Thessalonians.** A local church is a group of people called out by God from the mass of humanity to a life of separation to Him. The definite article before "Thessalonians" is not found in some ancient copies of 1 Thessalonians. If this is the correct wording, the text further emphasizes the distinction between those in the church and others in the city.

The church is described as being **in God the Father and the Lord Jesus Christ.** To Paul, the Lord Jesus Christ was as much God as the Father. He preached this in Thessalonica (Acts 17:3) and affirmed it again in this epistle. The description of God as Father connotes security, love, and strength. Paul balanced this picture with a reminder that God the Son is also Lord; He is the Sovereign who is to be obeyed. "Jesus" is the Lord's human name, the Greek form of Joshua, "Savior." "Christ" is the Greek translation of the "Messiah" of the Old Testament and means "Anointed One."

The shortened greeting customary in the Pauline Epistles appears here. **Grace** was the common Greek salutation meaning "greetings" or "rejoice." In Greek **peace** is equivalent to the Hebrew šālôm meaning "favor," "prosperity," and "well-being." It is interesting that those two words of salutation always occur in this order in the New Testament. Theologically God's grace is the basis for and leads to man's peace.

II. Personal Commendations and Explanations (1:2–3:13)

In general the first three chapters of 1 Thessalonians are personal in nature, and the last two are practical.

A. Thanksgiving for the Thessalonians (1:2-10)

This first chapter deals primarily with the subject of salvation. Several aspects of the Thessalonians' salvation elicited Paul's thanksgiving to God in these verses.

1. SUMMARY STATEMENT (1:2-3)

In these two verses Paul expressed his gratitude to God and set forth in a brief statement why he was thankful for the Thessalonians.

1:2. Paul, Silas, and Timothy rejoiced together in what God had done in their converts' lives. They continually and frequently gave thanks; the Thessalonians were a constant source of joy to them. Whenever these missionaries prayed for the Thessalonians, they gave thanks to **God** for them. Rather than being a source of grief these Christians evoked gratitude. In this they served as models for all Christians.

1:3. Three characteristics of these believers stood out in Paul's mind. First, they had performed an important **work produced by** (lit., "of") **faith** in Christ. Verse 9 mentions that they had turned to the true God from idols. Faith in Christ had produced true repentance. Second, they performed **labor** (*kopou*, "toil") **prompted by** (lit., "of") **love** for Christ. This consisted in their serving the living and true God (v. 9) in the midst of persecution (v. 6). Third, they had **endurance** (*hypomonēs*, lit., "a bearing up patiently under a heavy load"; cf. 2 Thes. 1:4) **inspired by** (lit., "of") **hope in Christ.** Specifically they were waiting for God's Son from heaven (1 Thes. 1:10). These three cardinal virtues that should mark every Christian—faith, love, and hope—stood out in the Thessalonian believers' lives (cf. 1 Cor. 13:13). Each of these virtues found its object in Jesus Christ, and each produced praiseworthy behavior. The Thessalonians had exercised saving faith in Christ in the past when they had believed the gospel, they were loving Christ in the present, and they were hoping for His return in the future. Their lives were certainly focused on Jesus Christ. No wonder Paul and his companions gave thanks for them.

2. SPECIFIC REASONS (1:4-10)

1:4. The Thessalonians' response to the preaching of the gospel in their midst constituted indisputable proof of their salvation. Paul rehearsed their response in this verse as he expanded on the idea he had just introduced.

Characteristically Paul addressed his fellow Christians as **brothers.** He used this term (*adelphoi*) 15 times in this one brief epistle (1:4; 2:1, 9, 17; 3:7; 4:1, 10, 13; 5:1, 4, 12, 14, 25-27), and 7 times in 2 Thessalonians (1:3; 2:1, 13, 15; 3:1, 6, 13). He did not claim superiority over them but recognized the equality of all the redeemed in the sight of their heavenly Father, as he taught elsewhere (e.g., 1 Cor. 12:14-27) and as the Lord taught (Matt. 23:9; etc.). Paul had come a long way from being a proud Pharisee to the place where he could consider Gentiles his equals before God. He reminded his readers that they were beloved by God. Even Paul's incidental statements throb with the warm realization of God's presence (1 Thes. 1:3) and love.

The proof of God's love for the Thessalonians was His choice of them unto salvation. From the word translated **chosen** (*eklogēn*) comes the English "election." That God has chosen to bless some individuals with eternal life is clearly taught in many places in both the Old and New Testaments (e.g., Deut. 4:37; 7:6-7; Isa. 44:1-2; Rom. 9; Eph. 1:4-6, 11; Col. 3:12; 2 Thes. 2:13). Equally clear is the fact that God holds each individual personally responsible for his decision to trust or not to trust in Jesus Christ (cf. John 3; Rom. 5). The difficulty in putting divine election and human responsibility together is understanding how both can be true. *That* both are true is taught in the Bible. *How* both can be true is apparently incomprehensible to finite human minds; no one has ever been able to explain this antinomy satisfactorily. This task transcends human mental powers, much as seeing angels transcends human visual powers and hearing very high-pitched sounds transcends human auditory powers. The Thessalonians' response to the gospel message proved that God had chosen them for salvation.

1:5. The response of his converts was a supernatural work of God, not a natural response to a clearly delivered sermon. When Paul preached to them, he did not just share human opinion and philosophy (cf. 1 Cor. 2:1-5). Rather, his message was marked by the **power** of God (cf. Rom. 1:16). **The Holy Spirit** brought it home to their hearts with **deep conviction** (John 16:8). Paul's message was marked by his own certainty that this message would change their lives as it had radically changed his.

Not only did Paul and his traveling companions preach a convincing message, but they also lived lives consistent with that message when they were in Thessalonica. The Thessalonians were fully aware of their teachers' manner of life and that their motive was to benefit the Thessalonians. The message Paul preached—the **gospel** of the grace of God—had entered into the minds and hearts of these Macedonians and they had been saved. From their belief beautiful lives had blossomed.

1:6. The outstanding fruit of faith in the gospel was the Thessalonians' change of behavior. They **became imitators** of their spiritual parents, the missionaries. This is normal Christian experience. But they also went on to imitate **the Lord.** This too is natural, and the order is true to life as well. A new Christian first looks to other believers as his pattern, but then as he matures he realizes that Jesus Christ is his best "model" (cf. 1 Peter 2:21).

Despite **severe suffering** the Thessalonians **welcomed the message.** The Jews among them must have felt the hatred of their unbelieving brothers in the flesh who, as has been pointed out, were especially antagonistic to the gospel in that city. The Gentile converts must have had to swim against the swift current of paganism that flowed like a torrent through the conduit of commercial Thessalonica. And the city's chief men's wives, who had become Christians, had to go home to unbelieving husbands who would not have appreciated their newly sensitized consciences. Yet **in spite of** trials without, the Thessalonian believers possessed **joy** within, the joy of sins forgiven. It is interesting that Christians who have tribulations in their daily walks often seem to have greater joy in the Lord than those who live in more comfortable spiritual climates. A Christian's joy should be determined not by his circumstances but by his relationship with Christ. This was

true of the Thessalonians. The source of their joy was the indwelling **Holy Spirit.**

1:7. The testimony of these Christians did not burn brightly merely at home; it also shone abroad to other people in other parts of **Macedonia,** reaching even to **Achaia,** the neighboring province to the south. Having become imitators of the missionaries and their Lord (v. 6) they in turn became the object of imitation by other believers. When Paul wrote to the Corinthians he pointed to these Macedonians as **a model** (*typon;* cf. 2 Thes. 3:9) of sacrificial giving (2 Cor. 8:1-8). He wrote that they had given money to help other believers even though they themselves were poor. One of the most revealing evidences of a Christian's true spirituality is the way he manages his money. In this revealing test the Thessalonians emerged as gold tried in the fire.

1:8. This verse explains how the Thessalonians became examples to other Christians. Having received the gospel (v. 5) they passed it on to others. The word *exēchētai,* translated **rang out,** could be rendered "reverberated." Paul saw the Thessalonians as amplifiers or relay stations that not only received the gospel message but sent it farther on its way with increased power and scope. Paul's preaching in Thessalonica had the effect of speaking into a public address microphone; his words were received and repeated by many different "speakers" in many remote places where his unaided voice could not have reached.

Apparently it was not through an organized evangelistic campaign that their witness went forth, though Paul's preaching in Thessalonica and elsewhere illustrates this approach. But it was through the personal lives and testimonies of these transformed individuals that neighbors heard about their **faith in God.** As they went the gospel was heard **everywhere,** so an apostolic missionary campaign was not needed.

1:9. Other people were telling Paul what had happened after he had preached the gospel in Thessalonica. The events of his visit had become well known in that part of the world, not because Paul had spread the word, but because of the outspoken Thessalonian believers' witness. Their boldness should challenge every true child of God.

These believers had **turned to God,**

the only true God, **from idols.** This strongly suggests that many of those believers had been pagan Gentiles. The Jews, of course, abhorred idolatry. Someone has observed that humans have the freedom to choose who their master will be, but they do not have the freedom to choose **no** master. The Thessalonians had chosen to **serve the living and true God** rather than God's creatures or satanic powers (cf. Rom. 1:18-23). The fact that God is a living Person was precious to the Jews and to Paul; this is the characteristic by which God is most often distinguished from so-called gods in the Old Testament. He is the only living God; all other gods are not alive and therefore not worthy objects of worship.

1:10. Not only had the Thessalonians turned to God in repentance and begun to serve Him, but they were also awaiting the return of **His Son from heaven.** Paul may have had in mind the "heavens" (pl.) through which Jesus Christ passed when He ascended from the earth (Acts 1:9-11), rather than the seat of His heavenly rule at the right hand of the Father in "heaven" (sing., Rev. 4:2-11). If so, he said that the Thessalonians were looking for Jesus' coming through the clouds, literally, "out of the heavens."

But it was not the clouds, or the signs of His coming, or His deliverance which interested these believers; it was the person of **Jesus,** the Son of the living God. He was the object of their hope, the focus of their attention. May Jesus Himself, rather than anything that will accompany Him or characterize His return, always fill the hopes of His saints!

This reference to "Jesus," His human name, is a strong claim to Jesus of Nazareth's deity. He is further described as the Son of God, the One risen from the dead by the living God. The fact of the Resurrection is indisputable proof (cf. 1 Cor. 15:14-19) of the deity of Jesus.

The return of Jesus is a source of hope for Christians for several reasons, but the reason which Paul mentioned here was Jesus' deliverance of the saints **from the coming wrath** of God. The wrath of God will be poured out on unrighteous people because of their failure to trust in Christ (John 3:36; Rom. 1:18). This happens at many times and in many ways, the great white throne judg-

ment being the most awful occasion (Rev. 20:11-15). But the "time of trouble for Jacob" (Jer. 30:4-7), also called "the Great Tribulation" (Rev. 7:14), will be a period in history during which God's wrath will be poured out on the earth as never before (cf. Rev. 6–19).

Was Paul thinking of a specific time in which God's wrath would be poured out (1 Thes. 1:10), or was he referring to the outpouring of God's wrath on unbelievers in a more general sense? Paul, the Thessalonian believers, and Christians today will escape all aspects of God's wrath, general and specific, including the Tribulation period. The clear implication of this verse is that Paul hoped in the Lord's imminent return. Otherwise Paul would have told his readers to prepare for the Tribulation.

In the phrase "from the coming wrath" the word translated "from" means that Christians are kept from it, not taken out of it. The same verb **(rescues)** and preposition **(from)** are used in 2 Corinthians 1:10 where Paul said he was delivered from a deadly peril. Obviously this does not mean Paul died and was resurrected. Christians will be kept away from God's wrath, not just kept safe through it (cf. comments on Rev. 3:10).

This chapter, like every chapter in this epistle, closes with a reference to the return of Jesus Christ (1 Thes. 1:10; 2:19; 3:13; 4:13-18, 5:23).

B. Reminders for the Thessalonians (2:1-16)

Paul's thoughts, led by the Holy Spirit, turned from the Thessalonians' response to his preaching to other events of his recent visit.

1. HOW THE GOSPEL WAS DELIVERED (2:1-12)

The first part of this chapter records Paul's comments about his visit to Thessalonica. His words suggest that people outside the church were charging him with unworthy motives and improper conduct.

2:1. In verses 1-6 Paul reminded his readers of his actions among them and clarified his motives. All of chapter 2 constitutes an expansion of 1:9. **You** is emphatic in the Greek; Paul called on his readers to remember carefully the facts of his **visit** to them. Thinking back, they would recall that Paul's visit was not in vain. It **was not a failure.** Paul had not come merely to give speeches. Changes in the Thessalonian believers' lives testified to the value and success of his visit.

2:2. Paul and his companions were not on a vacation trip. They had come to Thessalonica after having **suffered, been insulted,** beaten, and imprisoned for preaching the gospel **in Philippi** (Acts 16:22-24). This mission had cost them dearly, but God gave them uncommon boldness to stand up in the synagogue at Thessalonica and preach the same message that had brought them persecution in Philippi. And when opposition broke out in Thessalonica the missionaries kept on preaching. This is not the reaction of people who are trying to make money or build personal reputations at the expense of their hearers. Paul called on his readers to remember these actions and to recognize the sincerity behind them. The missionaries' boldness amid **strong opposition** was the sign of God at work in His servants and was proof of their genuineness.

2:3. Paul's actions (which the Thessalonians personally observed) demonstrated both his sincerity and his motives (which they could not observe but which Paul explained here). Paul denied three allegations: (a) his *message* was not deceptive; it was truth, not **error;** (b) his *motivation* was not **impure,** but was clean; (c) his *method* was not to **trick,** mislead, or deceive them, but was straightforward.

2:4. In strong contrast to these improprieties, Paul said he spoke out of the best motives, realizing that God had put his heart to the test. He and his companions spoke **not . . . to please men, but God.** Having been **approved** (*dedokimasmetha,* "shown by testing to be genuine"**) by God,** He **entrusted** them **with the gospel.** Paul used the word "gospel" five times in 1 Thessalonians (1:5; 2:2, 4, 8; 3:2). Paul and his fellow missionaries were veterans; they had been tried and tested for years. God would not have blessed their work if their motivation had not been right. Paul saw himself as a steward entrusted by God to carry His message of salvation to lost men and women (cf. 1 Cor. 9:17). Paul did not choose his work; God selected him for the high calling of proclaiming the gospel. This responsibility was most significant to Paul, who viewed himself as under God's constant scrutiny. So he would not dare serve with the wrong motives.

2:5. Paul's preaching to the Thessalonians was not aimed at making a favorable impression on them. He asked them to remember how he spoke. He never wore a false face, preaching to gain something for himself. Because they could not know this, Paul appealed to **God** as the **witness** of his motives.

2:6. The missionaries were **not** seeking the **praise** of any man but the praise of God. Traveling philosophers and orators were common in the Roman Empire. They itinerated from place to place, entertaining and seeking a personal following for fame and fortune. Paul and his companions had nothing in common with such men! Rather than seeking something for themselves they delighted in giving to others freely.

2:7. In verses 7-9 Paul shifted the emphasis somewhat from the preachers' activities to the hearers' responses. Paul, Silas, and Timothy rightfully could have expected their converts to support them financially and could have called on them to do so (cf. 1 Tim. 5:18). Certainly they had a right to expect esteem. But they chose to minister rather than to be ministered to for the sake of the Thessalonian converts. Paul and his companions cared for their converts as a nursing **mother** gently cares **for her little children.** This instructive illustration provides a good example for all who are responsible for the care of new believers. If a nursing mother does not feed herself, she cannot feed her baby. If she eats certain foods, her baby will get sick. Similarly the spiritual diet of a parent Christian is vitally important to the health of a newer Christian. The gentleness and unselfishness of Paul as a spiritual parent shines through in this illustration.

2:8. Rather than being greedy (v. 5) the missionaries **were delighted to share with** the Thessalonians. They **not only** gave the message of eternal life, **the gospel of God,** but also imparted their own innermost beings (lit., "our own souls") as well. They gave whatever they had in order to help the beloved Thessalonians. The love of Paul and his companions is evident, for genuine love finds expression in giving to people—not only to their spiritual needs, which are primary, but also to their physical needs.

2:9. Paul ministered to his converts by **toil** (*kopon*; cf. the same word for "toil" in 1:3) and suffering **hardship** (*mochthon*) on their behalf. He **worked night and day** so that he would not **burden** them with his needs (cf. 2 Thes. 3:8). Perhaps he made tents, rising early and staying up late, as he did in other cities (Acts 18:3). Probably he **preached the gospel** and taught as much as he could, both in the daytime and at night.

2:10. Verses 10-12 summarize the appeal to the Thessalonians. The apostles called on their readers and God to bear witness to their behavior in both action and motive. Their inner convictions led to devout (**holy,** *hosiōs*) conduct. With reference to God's objective standard their behavior was **righteous,** measuring up to what God expects and requires. Their conduct was unreproachable (**blameless,** *amemptōs;* cf. 5:23), able to stand their critics' scrutiny because it was right. Both they and **God** were **witnesses** (cf. 2:5) of the truthfulness of Paul's claims.

2:11. Having likened the conduct of the missionaries to the loving, unselfish care of a nursing mother (v. 7), Paul also compared their behavior to that of **a father.** Here the implication is that they trained and instructed the Thessalonians as a responsible father disciplines his children. The word *tekna,* translated **children,** emphasizes the believers' immaturity as well as the apostles' affection. This verse is the fifth time Paul wrote **you know** (cf. 1:5; 2:2, 5).

2:12. The training provided included strong positive appeals (**encouraging,** *parakalountes*), soothing encouragement (**comforting,** *paramythoumenoi*), designed to cheer up and to inspire correct behavior, and solemn, earnest entreaty (**urging,** *martyromenoi*). Such a combination of appeals proved effective in moving the Thessalonians to action by the Holy Spirit's convicting power.

The appeal to lead lives **worthy of God** is the highest of all for those who have tasted God's grace in salvation. Paul heightened his exhortation by reminding his readers that they had been specially called by God, called to enter and be partakers in **His kingdom** and called to glorify and share in God's **glory.**

2. HOW THE GOSPEL WAS RECEIVED (2:13-16)

Paul's attitude of rejoicing continues in this section as indicated by the opening **and,** though now his attention turned from how the gospel came to the Thessalonians to how they welcomed it.

2:13. A second reason for Paul's continual rejoicing is identified in this verse. Not only were the fruits of righteousness manifest in the Thessalonian converts' lives (1:3), but also the way they received the preached **Word of God** warmed the apostles' hearts. The "Word of God" here clearly refers to the message spoken by the missionaries. When the Thessalonians heard it they realized that it was not simply the words of man's wisdom, but a message that had its source in **God** (cf. 1:5). Someone has said that the gospel is not the kind of message that man would invent if he could, nor is it a message that he could invent if he would. The Thessalonian Christians sensed the supernatural truthfulness of the gospel Paul preached as the Holy Spirit brought this conviction home to their hearts. When Christians share their faith, they do not merely give their particular viewpoint on life as one among the endless variety of human theories. They announce the divinely revealed truth of God, a word from God.

The spoken Word of God has an inherent power to change. For this reason the Word of God through the Old Testament prophets was recognized as being powerful and not falling to the ground (i.e., lacking sufficient power to hit its mark and accomplish its purpose; cf. 1 Sam. 3:19). The Word of God has the creative power of God behind it and in it (Gen. 1:3). Paul credited the changes in the Thessalonians to this spoken Word of God. Not only had it effected changes in them in the past, but also it was continuing to change them since they continued to believe it. (The word **believe** is in the Gr. pres. tense, indicating continuing action.) The truth of God, like a good medicine, will continue to heal sin-sick souls so long as people receive it by faith.

2:14. Paul encouraged his readers to recognize this evidence of God's working as being true of all believers by directing their attention to another experience common to all saints. He included himself again, by addressing them as **brothers**

(cf. 1:4; 2:1). Those whose lives are being changed by God often find themselves the objects of criticism and attack by people in whom there is no divine life. Frequently when Christians suffer persecution they are tempted to think God's blessing has departed. Paul countered this lie of Satan by reminding his readers that their experience duplicated that of their elder brothers and sisters in the faith who had become Christians **in Judea.** They also suffered opposition from their neighbors; and their neighbors were Jews too.

2:15. The Thessalonians were not alone in their suffering; they had abundant and worthy company. Their persecutors had **killed the Lord Jesus** Himself **and the** Old Testament **prophets.** They **drove . . . out** their father in the faith, the Apostle Paul, and his fellow missionaries. Though Paul laid guilt for the death of Christ at the feet of the Jews he did not charge them alone with this crime. The Romans who were involved in Jesus' trial and execution were also guilty (1 Cor. 2:8) as was every human being for whose sins Christ tasted death (Heb. 2:9). Most likely Paul mentioned the murder of Jesus first and his own persecutions last because in his mind the first example was much more serious.

Those who persecute believers in Christ antagonize both God and other men. Paul knew whereof he spoke, having been a persecutor of the church himself and one to whom God had revealed that he was fighting against the Lord he sought to serve (Acts 26:14-15). Those who set themselves against God's people also set themselves against God. And they also hurt other non-Christians. The worst thing about unbelief is not that it damns the unbeliever, but that it hinders the salvation of others. Such people seek to extinguish the lamp of truth and in doing so cause others to stumble.

2:16. An unbeliever who is willing to live and let live with respect to personal convictions regarding God is less dangerous than one who not only disbelieves himself but also tries to keep others from hearing the gospel. The unbelieving Jews in Thessalonica were of the latter variety.

Such people's actions hurt themselves as well as others because they **heap up** additional **sins** for which God will judge them. God will only allow an individual or a group of individuals to accumulate so much sin, and then He will judge. He does not judge before this **limit,** which He alone knows, has been reached (cf. Gen. 15:16). The Thessalonians' persecutors were hastening God's judgment on themselves by their actions.

The manifestation of God's **wrath** that Paul had in mind in this verse is debatable. Perhaps he was referring to the destruction of Jerusalem by the Romans in A.D. 70, just a few years in the future, which Paul may have known was as certain to take place as if it had already happened. Or he may have had in mind God's turning from the Jews to create for Himself a unique body of believers made up of both Jews and **Gentiles** who now stand on equal footing before God (Eph. 2:13-16). Or possibly Paul was thinking of the wrath of God that is on every individual who fails to believe in Christ (John 3:36). Or the wrath may refer to the Tribulation which will assuredly **come upon them** because of their rejection of Jesus Christ. This was probably his thought since in other contexts in this epistle where he speaks of the wrath to come he has the Tribulation in mind. Though it is not known for sure which of these thoughts was in Paul's mind—all of them could have been—it is known that the wrath of God has indeed come on unbelievers who hinder gospel preaching in every one of the ways just mentioned. Perhaps Paul chose a general statement rather than a specific one because he had several things in mind. God's wrath had reached its full limit in regard to those individuals.

Why did Paul get so excited about the fate of the Thessalonians' persecutors? It was not out of personal hatred for them (Rom. 9:1-5). Rather it was to emphasize the seriousness of hindering the preaching of the gospel. This message was transforming the Thessalonian believers, and they were heralding it to others far and wide. These verses illustrate how important it is that the gospel reach everybody (Matt. 28:19-20).

C. Concerns for the Thessalonians (2:17–3:13)

At this point the Holy Spirit directed Paul's thoughts from his visit to Thessalonica to more recent developments in his relationship with that church.

1. PAUL'S PLANS (2:17-20)

Quite obviously, from the extent to which he went in explaining his failure to return to Thessalonica, Paul wanted to give a clear and persuasive explanation of his activities. Evidently some people in Thessalonica were questioning or criticizing his conduct.

2:17. But contrasts Paul's experiences, which he was about to relate (3:1-10), with those of the Thessalonian brethren, which he had just narrated.

This verse is most revealing of Paul's feelings for those believers. He used the term of endearment in addressing them again: **brothers.** He described his departure from them as a turning away forced on him by circumstances beyond his control. The verb (*aporphanisthentes*) means literally "to be orphaned" and is used only here in the New Testament. To Paul it was as though his family were being **torn** apart when he left them. He hoped the separation would be brief, but it broke his heart to leave them as infant babes in Christ. Though he had left them physically, they were still prominent in his thoughts; they were not "out of sight, out of mind."

Paul and his companions had tried to return to Thessalonica on several occasions because of the intense longing they felt for their brethren. The care and feeding of new Christians was not just an obligation those missionaries felt toward God; it was something they longed with all their hearts to be able to do, because of the love of Christ, in spite of the personal danger that faced them in Thessalonica.

2:18. Paul blamed **Satan** for his failure to be able to return. Was Satan responsible, or was God, or were other people? Paul's reason for deciding to return was to provide additional spiritual help for the new converts. This by itself is clearly the will of God in any situation. Seen as such, any hindrance becomes opposition to the will of God. Regardless of who was involved on the human level, the ultimate leader of this kind of opposition is Satan. As John Calvin wrote, "Whenever the ungodly cause us trouble, they are fighting under the banner of Satan, and are his instruments for harassing us" (*The Epistles of Paul the Apostle to the Romans and to the Thessalonians*, p.

351). God permitted this to happen, but He is no more responsible for it than He is for any sin which His creatures commit and which He permits.

It is unusual that Paul inserted his name in the letter at this point; he rarely did so in his inspired writings. The reason here may be that he wished to emphasize again in a different way that it was he himself who truly felt this way. He did not try to return just once, but **again and again** he sought ways to get back to Thessalonica.

2:19-20. Paul's affection rose to its climax in this almost lyrical passage. The Philippian believers were the only others who received such warm words of personal love from Paul.

He voiced a rhetorical question to heighten the intensity of his fervor. In effect he asked what would be the greatest blessing he could possibly receive at the judgment seat of Christ. They were! They were everything that was worth anything to Paul. They were his **hope;** their development was what he lived for as a parent lives to see his children grow up to maturity, to produce and reproduce. They were his **joy,** they filled his life with sunshine as he thought of what they used to be, what they had become, and what they would be by the grace of God. They were his **crown;** they themselves were the symbol of God's blessing on his life and ministry. They were his **glory and joy,** and not only his but also the glory and joy of his companions in labor. Paul said in essence, "When life is over and we stand in the presence of our Lord Jesus at His coming, you Thessalonians will be our source of glory and joy; you mean that much to us."

This profession of affection should have removed any thoughts from the Thessalonian Christians' minds that Paul had not returned because he was unconcerned or selfish.

2. TIMOTHY'S VISIT (3:1-5)

The thought begun in 2:17 continues in this section. Paul again stated his sincere concern for the Thessalonians.

3:1. Circumstances prohibited Paul from returning to Thessalonica personally, so he and Silas decided to send Timothy back to encourage the saints. Evidently Paul traveled from Berea to **Athens** without the companionship of

Timothy and Silas. When he reached Athens he sent word back to Berea (by the Berean Christians who had accompanied him) for Timothy and Silas to join him in Athens as soon as possible (Acts 17:15). Apparently Timothy and Silas did so. Their mutual concern for the Thessalonian church led Paul and Silas to dispatch Timothy to Thessalonica (1 Thes. 3:1-2). Silas also returned to Macedonia shortly after Timothy's departure, probably to check on the Philippian church. Silas and Timothy both returned to Macedonia to rejoin Paul in Corinth, Paul's next port of call after Athens (Acts 18:1, 5).

3:2. Paul's description of **Timothy** seems to imply that the young man needed more than Paul's normal endorsement. Perhaps because of his youth Timothy was not as readily recognized and respected as his older fellow missionaries. Paul called Timothy **our brother,** suggesting equality in the Lord's work with Paul and Silas. In relation to the Lord, Timothy was a hardworking servant, suggestive of his zeal and humility. He was a brother-servant in **spreading the gospel of Christ.**

Timothy's mission was to have been a positive blessing and help to the Thessalonian Christians. He was to **strengthen** (*stērizai;* cf. v. 13) them, to make them firm and solid in the faith. He was also sent to **encourage** (*parakalesai;* cf. 2:12) them by providing what they needed to fight the good fight of **faith,** individually and collectively. Much of the ministry of the apostles was devoted to grounding new converts in the faith, a ministry as necessary today as it was in the first century.

3:3. Another purpose of Timothy's visit was that the Christians would not lose their spiritual balance and stability as a result of the **trials** they were experiencing (cf. 2:14). The word *sainesthai,* translated **unsettled,** is used of a dog wagging its tail and paints a picture of the Thessalonians going back and forth because of their persecutions.

Paul added his own stabilizing reminder that trials are not necessarily a sign of God's disfavor, but are part of every Christian's legacy. When trouble comes, Christians often react by doubting that they are where God wants them to be; they often think that they have done

something wrong and that God must be displeased with them. Even some mature Christians react this way, as evidenced by Paul's words of reassurance to Timothy many years later. "Everyone who wants to live a godly life in Christ Jesus will be persecuted" (2 Tim. 3:12). Yet storms often come to believers to make them able to stand firm, rather than to blow them away (cf. 2 Cor. 4:15-16).

3:4. Paul reminded his readers that when he was **with** them he kept telling them to expect persecution. And circumstances had **turned out** just as he had predicted. This reminder would have helped calm them down.

3:5. Returning to his original thought (cf. v. 2) Paul explained that he had sent Timothy back to Thessalonica because he was genuinely concerned for their spiritual welfare. The condition of the believers' **faith** burdened Paul's heart. Were they still trusting in God or had they abandoned Him and returned to paganism? Paul was not concerned that they had lost their salvation; this they could never do (1:4). They could, however, have ceased to walk by faith, not trusting God in all circumstances of life. Paul's concern was that his labor **might have been** in vain, not that their faith had been in vain. Paul's reference to the **tempter** is mindful of Satan's activity in the Garden of Eden (Gen. 3) and in the Judean wilderness (Matt. 4). Paul saw Satan as using the persecution the Thessalonians were undergoing in order to lure them away from what they knew to be God's will, namely, perseverance in the midst of trials. He was concerned that Satan might snatch away the seed Paul had sown before it had a chance to put down stabilizing, fructifying roots.

3. TIMOTHY'S REPORT (3:6-10)

From 2:1 through 3:5 Paul related what had happened in the last few months. Starting with 3:6 he moved to the present.

3:6. But contrasts Paul's previous anxiety with his present relief at the report of **Timothy** who returned to Paul in Corinth. Rather than bringing bad news that the Thessalonians' faith had wavered, Timothy had brought good news that their **faith** was bearing fruit in **love.** This **good news** was as thrilling to

Paul as the gospel; he used the same Greek word for both messages.

The Thessalonians were strong in faith toward God and love toward His apostles (cf. 1:3). Though Paul did not mention their hope explicitly here, he did so implicitly by referring to their desire **to see** the apostles again; they were looking forward to this. The fact that the Thessalonians looked back on the visit of the missionaries with **pleasant memories** and looked forward to seeing them again evidenced their genuine love for the apostles. Paul loved them too, and reminded them by restating his longing **to see** them again.

3:7. Timothy's report came as sweet relief to the anxious missionaries. They were indeed brethren, bound not only by the bonds of life in Christ, but also by the bonds of love for one another. As Paul and more recently Timothy had been sources of encouragement to the Thessalonians in their **persecution,** so now the babes in Christ had provided encouragement to their elder brethren who had been persecuted by fears about that church's condition.

3:8. Nothing filled the apostles with joy like news that their converts were **standing firm in the Lord.** This was the desired result in all their ministry; in this they found their greatest fulfillment. "Standing firm" (*stēkete*; cf. 2 Thes. 2:15) in the faith is really "standing firm in the Lord." Such a relationship strengthens one to withstand the storms of life.

3:9. The force of Paul's rhetorical question is, "We cannot **thank God enough for you** because of **all the joy** you have brought to our hearts by your endurance in these trials." It is noteworthy that Paul thanked *God* for the Thessalonians' behavior; *he* did not take credit for this. Paul acknowledged that their endurance was really a tribute to the work of God in them (cf. Phil. 2:13). He commended the Thessalonians, but also recognized and acknowledged the hand of God at work in their lives.

3:10. News of the Thessalonians' perseverance did not relieve Paul of his desire to return to them. Though they were enduring a trial of their faith they still needed more instruction and more growth. Paul wanted to **supply what** was **lacking** in their **faith.** (The word for "supply" is *katartisai*; cf. Eph. 4:12 where

pros ton katartismon is rendered "to prepare" [NIV] and "for the equipping" [NASB].) The Thessalonians were like tender young plants; their tender roots held them firm against the present storm, but they still needed to grow and mature. This is the first explicit reference to deficiencies in their spiritual condition— deficiencies due more to immaturity than to waywardness. Up till now Paul described them as having the characteristics of new Christians. Now he said they were deficient in certain respects, as a child is deficient in comparison with an adult. In chapters 4 and 5 Paul ministered to some of these deficiencies.

This verse gives another glimpse into the Apostle Paul's private life. He prayed **night and day . . . most earnestly** that God would let him **see** them **again.** That is, he prayed by night and by day, not all night and all day. This and other similar references (cf. 1:2; 2:13) demonstrate the truth of the statement, "It is evident from St. Paul's Epistles that a very large part of his private life was occupied in prayer and thanksgiving to God" (G. W. Garrod, *The First Epistle to the Thessalonians,* London: Macmillan & Co., 1899, p. 89).

4. PAUL'S PRAYER (3:11-13)

The first major section of the epistle, largely personal, closes with a statement in the form of a wish, something for which Paul prayed to God. Verses 11-13 amplify verse 10.

3:11. Paul was praying that he could return to Thessalonica (v. 10); here he expressed the same desire more strongly in a wish before God. **God** was the object of his prayer. He is called the **Father** of Paul and his missionary brethren and the Thessalonian believers. The **Lord Jesus** is addressed equally in prayer with the Father. The fact that Jesus is God is further highlighted by Paul's use of a singular verb (trans. "clear") with a plural subject: "may He **clear the way,** even the Father and Jesus," not "may They clear the way." "One can hardly conceive of a stronger way for Paul to indicate his unquestioning acceptance of the lordship of Jesus and His oneness with the Father" (D. Edmond Hiebert, *The Thessalonian Epistles,* p. 154).

3:12. The Thessalonians were already noted for their **love,** but Paul prayed that it might abound—**increase**

(*pleonasai*) **and overflow** (*perisseusai*)—even more. "Genuine Christian love . . . is the one thing in the Christian life which cannot be carried to excess" (Hiebert, *The Thessalonian Epistles*, p. 155). The image of love overflowing its container suggests that Christian love is something that wells up from within a person naturally. Paul was concerned that it overflow to **everyone**, not just to Christians in the church. His love was their model.

3:13. The Thessalonians needed strengthening by God in their inner beings. The word **strengthen** (*stērizai*), used by Paul in verse 2, describes Timothy's strengthening of the Thessalonians in their faith. Paul did not pray that they would be sinless; that was impossible. He prayed that they would **be blameless** (cf. 2:10), that is, that after they sinned they would deal with it as God requires and so be free from any reasonable charge by their fellowmen. Before God they should be **holy,** separated to **God** in their hearts and habits. Paul longed that when Jesus Christ would return He would find them blameless before men and holy before God. The **holy ones** accompanying Christ at His coming are probably the souls of the saints who have departed this life and gone to be with Christ, whose bodies will be resurrected when He comes (4:16). That is, they are Christians rather than angels.

III. Practical Instructions and Exhortations (4:1–5:24)

Chapters 4 and 5 constitute the second major division of 1 Thessalonians. Whereas chapters 1–3 contain personal messages of commendation for the Thessalonians and explanations of the missionaries' activities and motives, chapters 4–5 record practical instruction in matters of the Thessalonians' deficiencies, plus practical exhortations to proper behavior in view of the truth.

A. Christian living (4:1–12)

This section concerns three aspects of proper Christian living: one general, on conduct; and two specific, about sexual purity and brotherly love.

1. GENERAL CONDUCT (4:1-2)

4:1. The word with which Paul began chapter 4, **Finally,** was not intended to announce the conclusion of the epistle,

as is obvious from all that follows (cf. "Finally" in Phil. 3:1, which is followed by two chapters, as it is here in 1 Thes.). It introduces the final major section of the letter. These chapters deal with "what is lacking in your faith" (3:10). Again Paul reminded his readers of his words to them while in Thessalonica. He moved from their present condition to their next stage of spiritual development. They had responded to Paul's teaching on Christian living. Someone has said that everyone lives to please someone: himself, his spouse, his parents, his child, his God, or someone else. Paul focused motivation for correct living on love for God. Many people regard the Christian life as a set of rules to be obeyed, or a list of prohibitions to avoid; but Paul regarded it as the outworking of a loving desire to **please God** who had chosen him (1:4). His attitude helped prepare his readers to respond positively to his following exhortations.

These instructions were not intended to move the readers to behave differently, but to do more of the same. This conduct was so important that Paul not only asked but urged them to press on (**urge** is *parakaloumen*, also used in v. 10; in 2:12 the participle from the same verb is rendered "encouraging" and in 3:2 and 4:18 the verb is translated "encourage"). Paul added even more power to his exhortation by urging them **in the Lord Jesus** (cf. 2 Thes. 3:12); he wrote in the Spirit and with the authority of Jesus Christ. Paul claimed to speak for Christ in this matter. And he asked them to do so **more and more** (cf. 1 Thes. 4:10).

4:2. So they might not miss this rather subtle emphasis, Paul restated it more clearly here. He said they knew the **instructions** (*parangelias*) he had given them in Jesus' **authority** (cf. v. 1). What he and his fellow missionaries had preached to the Thessalonians they had announced as the gospel of Christ (3:2). The present message came to them with the same authority. Sometimes Christians want to hear new truth when what they need is exhortation to excel still more, to press on to greater experiencing of old truths which they are already practicing to a limited degree.

2. SEXUAL PURITY (4:3-8)

The general exhortation of verses 1-2 is followed by two specific exhortations. The first has to do with sexual purity.

4:3. The will of God is clearly set forth in many places in Scripture, even though Christians often seem to have a great deal of difficulty applying it in everyday decision-making (cf. 5:16-18; 1 Peter 2:15). It is **God's** clear **will** that His people **be holy** (*hagiasmos;* cf. 1 Thes. 3:13). This word can mean a state of being set apart from sin to God, or the process of becoming more dedicated to God. Probably the latter meaning was intended by Paul here. He was not referring to the final state of all Christians when they will be separated from the presence of sin as well as its penalty and power. Rather he probably had in mind the progressive sanctification of his readers by which they were conformed to the image of Christ in daily experiences by proper responses to the Word and the Spirit of God. This is evident by the three statements in verses 3b-6a, each beginning with the word **that.**

The first instruction designed to produce greater holiness is abstinence from **sexual immorality.** Paul called his readers to **avoid** it, implying the need for exercising self-discipline, enabled by God's Spirit. Christians are to avoid and abstain from any and every form of sexual practice that lies outside the circle of God's revealed will, namely adultery, premarital and extramarital intercourse, homosexuality, and other perversions. The word *porneia,* translated "sexual immorality," is a broad one and includes all these practices. The Thessalonians lived in a pagan environment in which sexual looseness was not only practiced openly but was also encouraged. In Greek religion, prostitution was considered a priestly prerogative, and extramarital sex was sometimes an act of worship. To a Christian the will of God is clear: holiness and sexual immorality are mutually exclusive. No appeal to Christian liberty can justify fornication.

4:4. Paul emphasized the same truth in a positive way by expanding on this prohibition. One avoids sexual immorality by learning how to **control his own body** with its passions. Self-control in response to one's sexual desires, Paul

taught, could and must be learned. Christians are not the victims of circumstances or their fleshly passions. Sexual desire can be controlled by the Christian through God's power. Paul did not specify how to control one's passions. He implied that there may be several ways. But the Christian should choose a method that is both **holy** (*hagiasmō*) **and honorable** (*timē*). That is, the action taken as an alternative to sexual immorality must be behavior that is set apart to the Lord in its motivation and recognized by others as intrinsically worthy of respect (cf. 1 Cor. 6:13-20). Each Christian is responsible for his own body and behavior, not his neighbor's (cf. 1 Cor. 10:13). Every young Christian, like the Thessalonians, **should learn** how to deal appropriately with sexual temptations.

4:5. They were not to deal with it as the **heathen** did, by indulging **in passionate lust** (*en pathei epithymias*). Such behavior is a mark of heathenism. A heathen is one who does **not know God.** Here Paul put his finger on the key to overcoming sexual temptations. A Christian can overcome because he knows God; this makes all the difference! Paul did not say that the heathen do not know *about* God. The reason they behave as they do is because they do not know God personally, even though they may know about Him. When a person comes to know God by faith in Jesus Christ, not only do his attitudes toward sex change, but he also discovers that God gives him the ability to act toward sexual temptation as he could not before. Knowing God is basic to living a holy life. This is why maintaining a vital relationship with God is essential to maintaining a clean walk before God.

4:6. In the previous two verses Paul's appeal was based on the importance of sexual purity for the sake of the Christian himself. In this verse Paul appealed on the basis of the other person involved in the immoral act. The **brother** here is most likely another human, not necessarily another Christian male. This seems clear from the fact that this person is a victim of illicit sex. Sexual immorality wrongs the partner in the forbidden act by involving him or her in behavior contrary to God's will and therefore under His judgment. Two or more people practicing sex out of God's will are calling God's wrath down on themselves (Heb. 13:4). The initiator of the act takes advantage of his partner in sin by fanning the fire of passion till self-control is lost.

Paul then cited two reasons (1 Thes. 4:6b-7) why sexual immorality should be avoided. First, sexual immorality is sin, and God will judge all sin (Rom. 6:23a). **All such sins** refers most likely to the various forms of sexual uncleanness not specifically mentioned in the context but covered by the general term "sexual immorality." Everyone who fears the wrath of God should abstain from immorality because judgment follows such sin as surely as day follows night. That God always judges sin is a basic Christian truth which Paul had taught them and **warned** them about when he was in Thessalonica.

4:7. A second reason to avoid sexual immorality is that it goes against God's calling for a Christian. Paul's first reason (v. 6b) looks forward to the prospect of future punishment, but his second reason looks back to the purpose for which God called each Christian to Himself. God's plan for a Christian includes purifying his life. Sexual immorality frustrates the purpose of God's call. Certain pagan cults promoted unclean ceremonies, but Christ's plans for a Christian are to clean him up. A **holy life** demonstrates God's supernatural power at work overcoming what is natural, and it glorifies God. The Greek noun *hagiasmos* ("holiness") occurs here for the fourth time in eight verses (3:13; 4:3-4). (The verb *hagiazō* ["sanctify"] is used in 5:23.)

4:8. In this verse Paul drew a conclusion based on his preceding arguments. Sexual purity is grounded in the revelations of **God** concerning His judgment of sin and His calling to holiness. Sexual purity is simply a practical application of basic doctrine. Paul's attitudes toward sexual uncleanness did not arise from his background or personal preferences. They were the logical consequences of divine revelation. The Thessalonians and later readers of this epistle should realize that to **reject** these instructions is to reject the Person from whom they came originally, that is, God.

Lest anyone feel that God is asking more than is reasonable of weak mortals, Paul concluded this exhortation with a reminder that God has also given believers His indwelling Spirit. This Person of the Trinity is so characterized by holiness that He is called the **Holy Spirit.** The indwelling Holy Spirit has power enough to enable any Christian to learn how to control his own body, even in a pagan, immoral climate. The exhortation is to avoid sexual immorality; the enablement comes from the Holy Spirit.

3. BROTHERLY LOVE (4:9-12)

The second specific exhortation regarding Christian living accentuates the positive. Though sexual impurity is a danger to be avoided (vv. 3-8), loving other Christians is a practice to be cultivated. Both deal with the general subject of loving one's neighbor as himself, the basic horizontal aspect of Christian living.

4:9. Some instructions for Christians come through their brethren in Christ. But other lessons are **taught by God** to His children directly, things that almost intuitively seem right for a Christian to do. Loving other Christians is such a lesson. Christians quickly learn that there is a real kinship between believers, and they relate to other Christians in a way they do not relate to those outside God's family. The Thessalonians had already learned **to love each other** even though they were new Christians. Paul pointed out that God Himself had **taught** them this.

4:10. Paul did not need to write and tell them to love one another, but he did need to write and urge them to do this **more and more** (cf. v. 1). The evidence that they had learned the lesson of brotherly love was their deep, selfless, giving affection for Christians in others parts of their province of **Macedonia.** These were their neighbors in Philippi, Berea, and perhaps other towns where Christians lived. Paul commended believers for their love when he wrote the churches (cf. 2 Cor. 8:1-5). Yet there was still room for improvement, perhaps in the persistence and consistency of their love.

4:11. Everyday habits of living manifest love of the brethren as do more special demonstrations of affection. It is these habits that Paul suggested the Thessalonians ponder in the light of brotherly love. He suggested these goals as worthy objectives for their maturing love. His words may reflect less than ideal conditions in their church.

First, his readers should lead a restful life. The word translated **quiet** (*hēsychazein*) means quiet in the sense of restfulness (cf. Acts 22:2; 2 Thes. 3:12; 1 Tim. 2:2, 11), rather than quiet as opposed to talkativeness (*sigaō;* cf. Acts 21:40; 1 Cor. 14:34). The former means "undisturbed, settled, not noisy," while the latter means "silent." Paul was telling the Thessalonians to be less frantic, not less exuberant. A person who is constantly on the move is frequently a bother to other people as well as somewhat distracted from his own walk with God. The latter can lead to the former. But a Christian who strives to be at peace with himself and God will be a source of peace to his brethren. Such quietude constitutes a practical demonstration of love for others.

Second, Paul recommended minding one's **own business.** The connection with love for the brethren is obvious (cf. Prov. 25:17).

Third, working with one's own hands demonstrates love for the brethren because a self-supporting person is not a burden to others. Paul himself set the example by working **with** his **hands** when he was in Thessalonica (1 Thes. 2:9). Too restful a life can be a problem also, and Paul guarded against that with this instruction. This verse dignifies manual labor. The reference also suggests that many, perhaps most, in the church came out of the working class. The Greeks deplored manual labor and relegated it to slaves as much as possible. But the Jews held it in esteem; every Jewish boy was taught a trade regardless of his family's wealth. Work itself is a blessing, and working with one's hands should never be despised by Christians. A man who is willing to work with his hands demonstrates his love for his brethren by being willing to humble himself to provide for his own needs so that he does not depend on others but provides for himself.

4:12. There are good reasons for these exhortations. Such behavior does **win the respect** of non-Christians and so glorifies the Christian's God. Love of this kind is appreciated by everyone. Paul placed importance on the testimony of Christians before **outsiders,** unbelievers. This kind of behavior also wins the respect of Christians; people appreciate those who do not take advantage of them.

Paul discouraged the Thessalonians from expecting financial favors from the brethren simply because they were fellow Christians. Nor was he promoting a fierce spirit of independence; he was not saying that every Christian must become completely self-sufficient. He was advocating personal responsibility, as is clear from the context. This is a manifestation of mature Christian love for the brethren.

B. The Rapture (4:13-18)

The Apostle Paul turned his attention to another area of deficiency in the Thessalonians' understanding, which had probably come to his attention through Timothy. Though Paul had already mentioned the future in this letter (1:10; 2:12, 19; 3:13), he turned to it again and devoted considerable space to instruction and exhortations dealing with Christ's return (4:13-5:11). The subject of the rest of chapter 4 is the relationship of the Lord's return to believers who had died. This is the classic passage in the Bible on the Rapture of the church.

4:13. Paul introduced these instructions in such a way as to lay no guilt on the Thessalonians for their lack of knowledge. After all, they were new believers. He again called them **brothers,** emphasizing their equality of standing before God despite their knowledge deficiency.

Those who fall asleep are Christians who die. The figure of sleep for death is common in the New Testament (cf. Mark 5:39; John 11:11). This is not sleep of the soul, however, because Paul wrote elsewhere that a Christian who is absent from his body is present with the Lord (2 Cor. 5:8; cf. Phil. 1:23; 1 Thes. 5:10). It is rather the "sleep" of the body in the earth until it is resurrected, changed into a glorious body, and reunited with the soul (1 Cor. 15:35-57; 2 Cor. 5:1-9).

Paul wanted the Thessalonians to be neither ignorant nor grieving **like the rest of men,** that is, like unbelievers, over the death of fellow believers. Christians do grieve over the loss of loved ones; this is a normal human experience which even Jesus shared (John 11:35). But the grief of Christians differs from that of unbelievers, for the latter **have no hope** of bodily resurrection to glory with Christ (1 Thes. 4:16).

4:14. Two reasons why Christians should not grieve like unbelievers are that

Christians have a revelation from God that gives them hope and they have a glorious future with Christ. Just as certainly as **Jesus died and** was resurrected by the Father, so **God will** unite the resurrected dead in Christ with their Savior at His coming.

The death and resurrection of Jesus Christ are among the best-attested facts of history. Since Christians know these events took place, they can be equally certain, Paul said, that the souls of believers who have died will return with Christ when He comes for His living saints. The prophecy of the Rapture is as sure to be fulfilled as the prophecies of Christ's death and resurrection.

4:15. The revelation of this resurrection came from Jesus Christ Himself. How it came to Paul is not known, but perhaps it was a direct revelation. Not only will the souls of the dead in Christ return with Him (v. 14), but their bodies will also be resurrected at His coming. The bodies of dead Christians will be resurrected immediately before living Christians are conveyed upward.

Clearly Paul believed that he and his Thessalonian readers might well be **alive** when the Lord returned. He believed that the Rapture was imminent, that it could take place at any moment (cf. 1:10; 1 Cor. 7:29, "the time is short"; Phil. 4:5, "The Lord is near"). And this truth of imminency brought comfort (1 Thes. 4:18).

4:16. Jesus Christ now sits at the right hand of God in **heaven** (Rom. 8:34; Eph. 1:20; Col. 3:1; Heb. 1:3). He will leave this position and descend to the earth. By the words **the Lord Himself** Paul emphasized that it would be the same Jesus who had ascended through the clouds (cf. Acts 1:11).

The sounds mentioned in this verse—a **loud command, with the voice of the archangel, and with the trumpet call of God**—are difficult to interpret. Who will voice the loud shout? Will it be Jesus Himself (cf. John 11:43), or the archangel Michael (Dan. 10:13; Jude 9), or another angel? Is this a literal trumpet call, or was Paul speaking figuratively in describing the call of God by which He will announce the Advent of His Son? (cf. 1 Cor. 15:52) These three phenomena may all refer to the same thing, but probably they are three separate almost simultaneous announcements heralding

Christ's return. Though one's curiosity about these aspects of the Rapture is not fully satisfied in this passage, one thing is clear: Christ's return for His saints will be announced from heaven forcefully and dramatically.

Then **the dead in Christ will** be resurrected, that is, believers of this dispensation will be raised. Old Testament saints will evidently be raised at the end of the Great Tribulation (Dan. 12:2), for the phrase "in Christ" refers exclusively to Church-Age saints. The bodies of the dead in Christ will **rise** before the living Christians are caught up to meet the Lord in the air (1 Thes. 4:17).

How will God raise the bodies of people who were buried hundreds of years ago? What about the bodies of those Christians who were burned to death and those whose ashes were thrown to the wind, and Christians who perished at sea? The resurrection of the dead poses a great problem to the faith of many. Perhaps that is why Paul stressed that this revelation came from Jesus Christ Himself and that it is as certain of future fulfillment as Jesus' resurrection is a fact of past history. The God who created the universe out of nothing with a word is fully able to reassemble the decayed bodies of all His saints in a moment of time (cf. 1 Cor. 15:35-58).

4:17. Whereas the previous verse explains the future of dead saints at Christ's return, this one deals with what will happen to living believers (cf. 1 Cor. 15:51-52). After the bodies of dead Christians have been raised, those **who are still alive** and have been **left** behind momentarily **will be caught up with them in the clouds to meet the Lord in the air.** Again Paul, by using the word **we** ("we who are still alive and are left"; cf. 1 Thes. 4:15), put himself in the living group; he thought that Christ would probably return in his lifetime, or at least he allowed for its possibility. Only a moment will separate the resurrection of the dead and the translation of the living (1 Cor. 15:51-52). In Latin the word for "caught up" is *rapturo*, from which comes the term "Rapture." This is the Rapture of the church, when Christians are caught up to meet Christ in the clouds (cf. Acts 1:9). The events described here and in the parallel passage, 1 Corinthians 15, differ considerably from those that will accompany Christ's return to the earth to set up His earthly kingdom (Rev. 19:11-21). This difference substantiates the distinction between the Rapture and the Second Coming.

The resurrected or translated bodies of all Christians will be united with Christ and with each other at the Rapture. From that time on and forever thereafter they will be with the Lord. The Lord will take living believers to the place He is presently preparing for them (John 14:2-3). But the place where Christians will be was not so important to Paul as the Person with whom they will be. "The entire content and worth of heaven, the entire blessedness of life eternal, is for Paul embraced in the one thought of being united with Jesus, his Savior and Lord" (Borhemann, quoted by George G. Findlay, *The Epistles of Paul the Apostle to the Thessalonians*, Cambridge: University Press, 1904, p. 103).

4:18. The logical and practical outcome of this revelation is comfort and encouragement. Paul applied his eschatology to life and called on his readers to **encourage** (*parakaleite;* cf. 2:12; 3:2) **each other with these words.** The facts that Christians who have died will be resurrected to join the living saints with the Lord Jesus when He comes, that they will actually precede those who are alive in that day, that those who are alive will be united with them, and that they will all be with the Lord forever, give abundant reasons for rejoicing. Not only do Christians not grieve like unbelievers, but followers of Christ can actually look forward eagerly to that great day. This is the great hope of the church, to see the Lord and be united with Him forever. It is that which every believer in this Age should anticipate. It is a blessed hope (Titus 2:13) with respect to the dead in Christ as well as for the living!

C. Personal watchfulness (5:1-11)

The preceding section (4:13-18) presented a joyful hope; this one gives a solemn warning. The Thessalonians had not heard the first exhortation before (4:18); they had heard this one.

1. THE DAY OF THE LORD (5:1-3)

Paul introduced a new aspect of the subject of the Lord's appearing. His scope of attention broadened from the Rapture to the longer period of history after the Rapture, namely, the day of the Lord. In these verses the emphasis is on the unpredictability of the time of the Lord's return.

5:1. Paul's affectionate tone continues with the word **brothers** again. **Times and dates** refers to the ages (*chronōn*) and events (*kairōn*) preceding the day of the Lord. Paul did not **need to** expound fully on this subject as he had done with the Rapture, since he had already instructed them about the day of the Lord.

5:2. The **day of the Lord** is a future period of time in which God will be at work in world affairs more directly and dramatically than He has been since the earthly ministry of the Lord Jesus Christ. It is a time referred to by many Old Testament prophets (e.g., Isa. 13:9-11; Joel 2:28-32; Zeph. 1:14-18; 3:14-15). As these and other Old Testament verses indicate, the day of the Lord will include both judgment and blessing. That day begins immediately after the Rapture of the church and ends with the conclusion of the Millennium. This day is a major theme of prophecy with its fullest exposition in Revelation 6–19.

This period of history **will come** as a surprise to those on the earth at the time, **like** the visit of **a thief** to a sleeping homeowner (cf. Matt. 24:43-44; Luke 12:39-40). But the thief **in the night** illustration should not be pressed too far. The point is that this day will come unexpectedly, not necessarily that it will take place at night. Obviously it will be night in some parts of the world and daytime in other parts.

5:3. This day will begin when world conditions appear calm rather than calamitous. This peace will come with the signing of the seven-year covenant, predicted in Daniel 9:27. Note that Paul did not include himself and his readers with the group who would see the day of the Lord, as he did when describing the Rapture (1 Thes. 4:15, 17). Evidently **them** refers to those left behind at the Rapture, that is, non-Christians. They will be ignorantly expecting **peace and safety,** but instead **destruction will come on them.** This "destruction" (*olethros;* cf. 2 Thes. 1:9) is not annihilation, but the breaking up of their peace and security through the outpouring of God's wrath on earth in the Great Tribulation. Destruction will come

suddenly. The illustration of the commencement of labor pains suggests both unpredictable suddenness and great personal discomfort (cf. Matt. 24:8; Mark 13:8). The wrath of God that will have been building up over some time will suddenly break forth. The signs of its coming are discernible, even though the moment of its arrival is unpredictable. No more can the world escape the coming wrath of God, when it breaks out on the day of the Lord, than **a pregnant woman** can escape **labor pains.** A strong expression is used in the Greek (a double negative: *ou mē*) to stress that fleeing (*ekphygōsin*) will be futile.

2. CONSEQUENT PREPAREDNESS (5:4-11)

In this section Paul applied the doctrine of the day of the Lord to his readers.

5:4. His readers were not "in the dark" with regard to these things; they had been taught about them before. But Paul meant more than this. His readers were not in the same group who would be surprised by **this day.** Their sphere of life was **not in** the **darkness,** but in the light (cf. Col. 1:13). Instructed Christians should not be surprised by the dawning of **this day** of the Lord; they have been told it is coming. It will not take believers by surprise because they will by then be with the Lord (1 Thes. 4:13-18).

5:5. Christians live in a different sphere of life from non-Christians; it is the difference between day and night (cf. Eph. 5:8). Christians are **sons of the light;** they are also **sons of the day.** That is, they have illumination, and they also live in a realm characterized by light, warmth, and growth. Paul brought himself into the picture (**we**) to prepare for his following exhortation which would be more true to life and readily received if he included himself, than if he directed it only toward the Thessalonians.

5:6. Paul's exhortation was for his readers to behave in keeping with their enlightened condition and to be prepared in view of the day of the Lord. He presented this exhortation as a logical conclusion from what preceded. Besides being logical to behave this way, it is also a necessary duty. Christians should not be indifferent to the reality of the Lord's return; they should not be **asleep** on the job. The word for "asleep" (*katheudōmen;* cf. v. 10) differs from the one used thrice in 4:13-15 where it means death (*koimaō*). Here it means spiritual lethargy and insensitivity. This is the condition of the unsaved, the **others.** Christians, on the other hand, should be watchful and soberly waiting for the Lord's return (1 Cor. 1:7; Titus 2:13; Heb. 9:28; 2 Peter 3:12), and **self-controlled** (1 Thes. 5:6), maintaining self-discipline in view of the great events to come.

5:7. Unbelievers are neither awake nor alert to these spiritual realities. Rather they are asleep and controlled by forces outside themselves—like those who are **drunk**—which render them unable to respond as they should. These are the normal characteristics of those who live in the sphere of **night.**

5:8. In keeping with the sober attitude just described, Paul used the metaphor of a soldier, one of his favorite illustrations of the Christian (Rom. 13:12b; Eph. 6:10-18; 1 Tim. 6:12; 2 Tim. 2:3-4; 4:7a). He based his exhortation on the Christians' position: because they **belong to the day,** they should live accordingly. Standing on the threshold of an event that will mean sudden translation for some and sudden destruction for others, Christians should arm themselves for action with self-control. A Roman **breastplate** covered a soldier from his neck to his waist and protected most of his vital organs (cf. Eph. 6:14). That is what Christians' **faith and love** do. Faith in God protects inwardly and love for people protects outwardly. These two graces cannot be separated; if one believes in God he will also love other people (cf. 1 Thes. 1:3; 3:5). These attitudes equip Christians to stand ready for the Rapture. In addition, **the hope of salvation** guards their heads from attacks on their thinking. The salvation they look forward to is deliverance from the wrath to come when the Lord returns, as is clear from the context. It is not a wishful longing that someday they might be saved eternally. Such a thought is entirely foreign to the New Testament. Followers of Christ have a sure hope; they are not as others who have no hope.

5:9. **For** (*hoti,* "because") introduces another reason why believers should prepare themselves. God's intention for them is not the **wrath** that will come on the earth in the day of the Lord, but the full **salvation** that will be theirs when the

Lord returns for them in the clouds. The wrath of God referred to here clearly refers to the Tribulation; the context makes this apparent. Deliverance from that wrath is God's appointment for believers. This temporal salvation comes through the **Lord Jesus Christ** just as does eternal salvation.

5:10. What did Paul mean by **whether we are awake or asleep?** Did he mean "whether we are alive or dead," or "whether we are spiritually alert or lethargic"? It seems that he meant the latter because he used the same words for "awake" (*grēgorōmen*) and "asleep" (*katheudōmen*) as he used in verse 6, where they clearly mean spiritually alert and spiritually lethargic. If so, then Paul's point is that Christians are assured of life **together with Him,** whether they are spiritually watchful or not. That they might live with Christ was His purpose in dying for them. They *will* escape God's wrath whether they are watchful or not (cf. 1:10). This is a powerful argument for a pretribulational Rapture.

Paul wrote that Christ **died,** not that He was killed. Jesus Christ laid down His life; no man took it from Him (John 10:18). And He died **for us** (cf. 2 Cor. 5:21). This simple statement of the substitutionary nature of the death of Christ required no elaboration for the Thessalonians. Doubtless Paul had emphasized this central doctrine when he first taught them in person; it is foundational.

5:11. The practical exhortation with which Paul concluded this section arose naturally from what he had explained. His readers were to **encourage** and **build up** (edify) **one another.** His own encouragement and edification in this letter were not enough. This new instruction needed constant repetition and reemphasis. It was to be added to the body of truth they already had received, and as they were encouraging each other in their meetings and in private conversations about other revealed truth they were to include this great truth as well. Believers do not need to be hearing something new all the time, but they often do need to remind themselves of what they already know so that they do not forget it. This verse gives some insight into the meetings of the early church. They included opportunity for mutual edification among the believers. Mutual encouragement and edifica-

tion are still needed in every local church. And encouragement and edification with reference to their hope in Christ's return is especially needed.

D. Church life (5:12-15)

In this passage Paul reminded his readers of their present responsibilities as believers in Christ. He turned from instructions regarding the future to exhortations for the present. His cryptic, almost abrupt style in this section may have been intended to bring them back from considerations of the future to the realities of their immediate responsibilities. First he gave them instructions concerning their relationships with their spiritual leaders.

1. ATTITUDE TOWARD LEADERS (5:12-13)

The following directions are addressed to the group as a whole, that is, to all Christians in the church.

5:12. The church leaders are probably the elders of the church in view of how they were described by Paul. These were men who worked **hard** to provide pastoral care for the flock, probably in their spare time since in the early church local church leaders often carried fulltime jobs outside the church. These leaders are further described as being **over you in the Lord.** They had positions of spiritual leadership in the church and were responsible to God for those under their care (cf. Heb. 13:17). This responsibility included providing admonition as needed. Since Paul used the plural **those** to describe their leaders, there was more than one such person in the Thessalonian church, as in other churches to whom Paul wrote (cf. Phil. 1:1).

Paul gave three exhortations to the church regarding their proper attitude toward their leaders. First, they were to **respect** them. This term (*eidenai*) normally means "to know," but here it includes appreciating and respecting them and their work.

5:13. The need to regard leaders highly is further stressed in the second exhortation. Church members are to esteem, value, and respect their leaders for their works' sake. The Greek is strong: **hold them in the highest regard** (*hēgeisthai autous hyperekperissōs*). This should be a continuing attitude. Some church leaders do not command as much personal respect as others, but Paul taught that all should be held in esteem because of the nature of their responsibilities before God. Not just some respect, but the highest respect is due these leaders, and it is to come from an attitude of affection (**in love**) for them, again, **because of their work**, if for no personal reason. Two reasons for this exhortation are the nature of their work and the fact that church leaders do a good service to others.

The third exhortation is to **live in peace with each other.** This results from obeying the former instructions. The idea here is to maintain rather than to initiate peace. Peaceful conditions existed in the Thessalonian church, but they had to continue. The command is imperative. Much dissension in modern churches is traceable to church members disobeying these commands.

2. RELATIONSHIPS AMONG THEMSELVES (5:14-15)

All church members, as well as church leaders, are responsible to minister to each other.

5:14. All Christians have four ongoing and continuous responsibilities to one another: (a) The **idle** need to be warned. Those who neglect their daily duties need to be stirred up to action. (b) The **timid** (*oligopsychous*, lit., "short of soul") need encouragement. These fainthearted people tend to become discouraged and despondent more easily than most. They need cheering up, stimulation to press on, and extra help to live the Christian life. (Interestingly the verbs in these two commands [*parakaloumen* and *paramytheisthe*] are in the same order as the first two participles in 2:12.) (c) The **weak** need **help.** These have not yet learned to lean on the Lord as much as they should for their spiritual needs. Until they do, they need strong support from other believers. Of course all Christians are weak and need the strength that comes from Christian fellowship, but the spiritually weak need it more than most. The fourth responsibility summarizes the preceding three: (d) **Be patient with everyone.** While other Christians are the primary focus of patience in this context, this charge is general enough to include all people. This ability to help others who are in some respect not as strong as

oneself requires nothing short of the love of God produced by the Holy Spirit (1 Cor. 13:4; Gal. 5:22).

5:15. The opposite of patience is retaliation in some form. Retaliation is not an option for a Christian. Even if the wrong done to him is an imposition by a needy brother, or an action springing from evil intent, the offended one never has the right to repay wrong with wrong (cf. Matt. 5:38-48; Rom. 12:17-21; 1 Peter 3:9). One's response should be to show kindness in such instances. Nor is it enough to abstain from evil; one is also to do positive good—**to be kind to each other.** Christians are to do this not in the sense that they will if they can, but in the sense that they earnestly work at it. This kind of response takes effort and must be continued.

E. Holy living (5:16-24)

This final group of instructions contains general exhortations for holy living.

1. PERSONAL LIVING (5:16-18)

These exhortations—dealing with attitudes—are addressed to believers as individuals concerning their personal lives before God.

5:16. God wants His people to **be joyful** and He gives them every reason to be. But Paul knew human nature well enough to sense the need for a reminder to rejoice at all times (cf. Phil. 3:1; 4:4). This is a command. A Christian's joy does not spring from his circumstances, but from the blessings that are his because he is in Christ. "The Christian who remains in sadness and depression really breaks a commandment: in some direction or other he mistrusts God—His power, providence, forgiveness" (A.J. Mason, "The Epistles of Paul the Apostle to the Thessalonians," in *Ellicott's Commentary on the Whole Bible,* vol. 8, p. 145). These two words (*pantote chairete*) constitute the shortest verse in the Greek New Testament.

5:17. Continual prayer is not prayer that prevails without any interruption, but prayer that continues whenever possible. The adverb for **continually** (*adialeiptōs,* also in 1:3) was used in Greek of a hacking cough. Paul was speaking of maintaining continuous fellowship with God as much as possible in the midst of daily living in which concentration is frequently broken.

5:18. The two previous commands deal with one's time ("always" and "continually"); this one deals with his **circumstances.** Christians are to **give thanks** to God in every circumstance of life. The fact that God works everything together for good for those who love Him (Rom. 8:28) is the basis for this entreaty.

These three exhortations in verses 16-18 are not just good advice; they are **God's will for** every Christian. They are not the totality of God's will, but they are a clear and important segment of it. God's will means joy, prayer, and thanksgiving for those who are **in Christ Jesus.**

2. CORPORATE LIVING (5:19-22)

Whereas the preceding verses stress individual responsibility in personal behavior, these deal with life in the assembly of believers. Five commands follow in staccato fashion. Two are negative (vv. 19-20) and three are positive (vv. 21-22).

5:19. The Bible frequently likens the Holy Spirit to a flame (Isa. 4:4; Matt. 3:11; Acts 2:3-4). He warms the heart, enlightens the mind, and empowers people's spirits. It is the effective working of the Holy Spirit that Paul warned against hindering. His **fire** can be diminished or even snuffed **out** if He is resisted. The Holy Spirit's working can be opposed by believers. It is this that Paul warned against. The next verse may give a clue as to how the Spirit was in danger of being quenched by the Thessalonians.

5:20. There may have been a tendency in the early church, and perhaps in the Thessalonian church in particular, to underrate the value of prophetic utterances. The gift of prophecy was the ability to receive and communicate direct revelations from God before the New Testament was completed (1 Cor. 13:8). Sometimes these revelations concerned future events (Acts 11:28), but often they dealt with the present (Acts 13:2). Perhaps people who had not received prophetic revelations were teaching their own views of such things as the Second Advent, with the result that prophetic revelations tended to be evaluated on superficial terms (e.g., the eloquence of the speaker) instead of on the basis of their intrinsic authority.

By way of application, Christians should not disparage any revelation that has come to the church and has been recognized as authoritative and preserved by the Holy Spirit in Scripture. The temptation to put the ideas of men on an equal footing with the Word of God is still present.

5:21. In view of this danger Christians need to **test** what they hear and read, by comparing it with the Word of God, to determine if it is divine in its origin. This is difficult, but it is possible for a spiritual believer (1 Cor. 2:14). Each Christian has the responsibility and ability to do this, though some have more discernment than others (cf. Acts 17:11; 1 John 4:1). What is discovered to be **good** (i.e., in harmony with what has been given by the Holy Spirit in the Word) should be retained.

5:22. On the other hand counterfeit teaching and living should be rejected and avoided. Not only should pseudo-prophecies be discarded but also, as Paul broadened his warning, **every kind** and form **of evil** should be avoided. What may only appear to be bad also falls under this warning. However, "while believers should abstain from actions which will knowingly offend others, it is not always possible to abstain from everything which may appear evil to a narrow and foolish judgment" (Hiebert, *The Thessalonian Epistles,* p. 249).

3. DIVINE ENABLEMENT (5:23-24)

Since these are high requirements, Paul expressed his pious wish that God would enable his readers to attain them.

5:23. To encourage his readers, Paul highlighted God's ability to produce peace. The church at Thessalonica had come to experience peace through the preaching of the gospel. And when Paul wrote this letter, the Thessalonians were enjoying peace with each other. The **God** who had given them **peace** would be their adequate resource for the future as He had been in the past. Paul prayed that God would **sanctify** (set apart) them to Himself in every area of their lives. Paul did not mean they could attain complete sanctification this side of heaven; that is impossible. He also prayed that his readers would be preserved **blameless** (*amemptōs,* i.e., with no legitimate ground for accusation; cf. 2:10) in view of and until the appearing (*parousia*) of the **Lord Jesus Christ** for His saints.

Though Paul spoke of the Christian as **spirit, soul, and body,** man is described elsewhere as having two parts—body and spirit (James 2:26; 2 Cor. 7:1), or body and soul (Matt. 10:28). And man is also said to have a heart, mind, conscience, and other parts. Rather than teaching man as having only three parts, Paul was probably using the three terms here to identify the different aspects of personhood he wished to emphasize. The *spirit* is the highest and most unique part of man that enables him to communicate with God. The *soul* is the part of man that makes him conscious of himself; it is the seat of his personality. The *body*, of course, is the physical part through which the inner person expresses himself and by which he is immediately recognized. Paul was saying then that he desired that the Thessalonians would be kept blameless by God in their relationships with Him in their inner personal lives, and in their social contacts with other people.

5:24. The same God who calls a Christian will perform this by the Holy Spirit who indwells him. God **is faithful** to bring to completion the work He has begun in believers (Phil. 1:6). God does not save a person by grace and then leave him alone to work out his Christian growth by works (Gal. 3:3). As God calls and justifies by grace, He sanctifies by grace too.

IV. Conclusion (5:25-28)

This conclusion is like a postscript to the letter. It contains three more exhortations and a benediction.

A. Personal appeals (5:25-27)

Unlike most of Paul's other epistles, this closing section does not state that it was written by him or by an amenuensis.

5:25. This is the first time in the letter that the greeting **brothers** (used 15 times in 1 Thes.; see comments on 1:4) occurs at the beginning of a sentence in the original. It is emphatic in this position. The force of the present tense here is a strong "keep on praying." Paul's appeal for prayer was to those he regarded as his brothers. Doubtless much of the success of his missionary work could be attributed to the prayers of the Thessalonians and other believers. Paul understood both

his personal insufficiency and God's sufficiency (cf. 2 Cor. 3:5). He requested prayer for his fellow workers as well as for himself.

5:26. It was common in Paul's culture as in many cultures today, to **greet** friends with a kiss on the cheek. The men greeted other men this way, and the women did the same with other women. Such a kiss communicated personal affection, not romantic love. By urging this practice Paul was encouraging an outward physical expression of true Christian love in a form that was culturally acceptable in his day. The kiss was to be **holy,** not passionate or fleshly. An acceptable alternative in Western culture today might be an embrace, a pat on the back, or a handshake. J.B. Phillips paraphrased this verse for 20th-century English readers: "Give a handshake all around among the brotherhood."

5:27. The final exhortation strongly urges that this letter be **read to all the brothers,** probably the whole Thessalonian church. The normal usage of the Greek word for "read" (*anagnōsthēnai*) implies that it should be read aloud. Paul's words are surprisingly strong. He put his readers under oath (*enorkizō hymas*, **I charge you**) to do this, suggesting that God would discipline them if they disobeyed. Were there some problems in the church that Paul wanted to get at by having everyone hear his words? Or did he realize that this epistle was written under divine inspiration and was therefore spiritually valuable? Perhaps he had both motives.

B. Benediction (5:28)

5:28. Paul referred to God's grace in each of his epistolary benedictions. **The grace** of God was Paul's great delight (cf. 1:1). He identified it as the grace that comes through **our Lord Jesus Christ.** In Him Christians have all. Obviously the grace of God is always **with** His children, but Paul's concern was that his readers experience and enjoy this grace. All that one has in Christ is due to His grace.

BIBLIOGRAPHY

Barclay, William. *The Letters to the Philippians, Colossians and Thessalonians.* The Daily Study Bible. Edinburgh: Saint Andrews, 1959.

Calvin, John. *The Epistles of Paul the Apostle to the Romans and to the Thessalonians.* Translated by Ross Mackenzie. Grand Rapids: Wm. B. Eerdmans Publishing Co., 1961.

Ellicott, Charles J. *A Critical and Grammatical Commentary on St. Paul's Epistles to the Thessalonians.* Andover: Warren F. Draper, 1864. Reprint. Grand Rapids: Zondervan Publishing House, 1971.

Frame, James Everett. *A Critical and Exegetical Commentary on the Epistles of St. Paul to the Thessalonians.* The International Critical Commentary. Edinburgh: T. & T. Clark, 1912.

Hendriksen, William. *Exposition of I and II Thessalonians.* New Testament Commentary. Grand Rapids: Baker Book House, 1955.

Hiebert, D. Edmond. *The Thessalonian Epistles.* Chicago: Moody Press, 1971.

Hogg, C.F., and Vine, W.E. *The Epistles of Paul the Apostle to the Thessalonians.* Reprint. Grand Rapids: Kregel Publications, 1959.

Lenski, R.C.H. *The Interpretation of St. Paul's Epistles to the Colossians, to the Thessalonians, to Timothy, to Titus and to Philemon.* 1937. Reprint. Minneapolis: Augsburg Publishing House, 1961.

Lightfoot, J.B. *Notes on the Epistles of St. Paul.* Reprint. Grand Rapids: Zondervan Publishing House, 1957.

Mason, A.J. "The Epistles of Paul the Apostle to the Thessalonians." In *Ellicott's Commentary on the Whole Bible,* vol. 8. Reprint. Grand Rapids: Zondervan Publishing House, n.d.

Milligan, George. *St. Paul's Epistles to the Thessalonians.* Reprint. Grand Rapids: Wm. B Eerdmans Publishing Co., 1952.

Morris, Leon. *The Epistles of Paul to the Thessalonians.* The Tyndale New Testament Commentaries. Grand Rapids: Wm. B. Eerdmans Publishing Co., 1957.

————. *The First and Second Epistles to the Thessalonians.* The New International Commentary on the New Testament. Grand Rapids: Wm. B. Eerdmans Publishing Co., 1959.

Ryrie, Charles Caldwell. *First and Second Thessalonians.* Everyman's Bible Commentary. Chicago: Moody Press, 1968.

Thomas, Robert L. "1 Thessalonians" and "2 Thessalonians." In *The Expositor's Bible Commentary,* vol. 11. Grand Rapids: Zondervan Publishing House, 1978.

Walvoord, John F. *The Thessalonian Epistles.* Grand Rapids: Zondervan Publishing House, 1958.

Wiersbe, Warren W. *Be Ready: A Practical Study of 1 and 2 Thessalonians.* Wheaton, Ill.: SP Publications, Victor Books, 1979.

2 THESSALONIANS

Thomas L. Constable

INTRODUCTION

The Writer of the Epistle. This letter claims to have been written by Paul, who wrote 1 Thessalonians under the inspiration of the Holy Spirit (cf. 1 Thes. 1:1). There are no indications among the writings of the early church fathers who lived during and after Paul's lifetime that anyone questioned the authenticity of this letter's claim. In fact several fathers mentioned the Pauline authorship of this epistle in their writings. Not until early in the 19th century were various questions raised about authorship. They came from rationalistic critics who refused to accept the Bible's claim to divine inspiration. But critical questions have not proven devastating because the authenticity of this and other New Testament books has been demonstrable through the ages.

The Place of Writing. Almost all conservative scholars believe that 2 Thessalonians was written from Corinth. The basis for this conclusion is that Paul, Silas, and Timothy were present together in Corinth (Acts 18:5). They are not referred to in the Bible as being together thereafter, though they might have been. Since 1 Thessalonians was written from Corinth (see *Introduction* to 1 Thes.), and since the topics treated in the second epistle seem to grow out of situations alluded to in the first epistle and reflect a very similar situation in the Thessalonian church, Corinth seems the logical site of composition.

The Date of Writing. For the reasons mentioned above, it appears that 2 Thessalonians was written quite soon after 1 Thessalonians, perhaps within 12 months. This would place the date of composition in the early A.D. 50s and would make this epistle the third of Paul's canonical writings (assuming Galatians was his first).

The Occasion and Purpose for Writing. The epistle gives evidence that Paul had recently heard news about conditions in the church. Probably this information came to him from the messenger who delivered 1 Thessalonians and returned to Corinth. Perhaps other people who had news of the church informed the three missionaries (Paul, Silas, and Timothy) also. Some of the news was good: the Thessalonians were continuing to grow and to remain faithful to Christ in spite of persecution. But some was bad: false teaching concerning the day of the Lord had entered the church and was causing confusion and leading some of the Christians to quit their jobs in expectation of the Lord's return.

In view of these reports Paul felt constrained to write this epistle. He commended his children in the faith for their growth, corrected their doctrinal error about the day of the Lord, and warned of its consequences.

OUTLINE

COMMENTARY

I. Salutation (1:1-2)

1:1. This epistle begins by naming the same three men mentioned in 1 Thessalonians 1:1. As in 1 Thessalonians, **Paul** was the author (directed by the inspiration of the Holy Spirit) for he spoke of himself in the singular (2 Thes. 2:5; 3:17). But **Silas and Timothy** joined him in sending the epistle (Paul frequently used "we": 1:3-4, 11-12, etc.). For more on these three men see the comments on 1 Thessalonians 1:1.

The same assembly of Christians received both letters. **The church** is described as being **in God our Father and the Lord Jesus Christ.** As in so many places in the New Testament Epistles, Jesus Christ is placed on an equal level with God the Father. God is the Father of Christians individually, a revelation given first by Jesus Christ (Matt. 6:9). A church is an assembly of individuals who are in Christ by faith in His atoning death and are therefore the children of God.

1:2. This verse is a word of greeting; the verb "be" must be implied. Paul reminded his readers that they were the recipients of God's **grace and peace,** and he wished that they would experience these blessings in fullest measure. "Grace" is "God's riches at Christ's expense"; it is God's unmerited favor which He freely bestows on all who accept Jesus Christ's substitutionary work for them on the cross by faith. God gives man the opposite of what he deserves: blessing instead of judgment. This is the grace of God. "Peace" is the cessation of hostility which has resulted from Christ's death; God and people can be reconciled because the debt of human sin has been paid by Christ. Christians have peace *with* God through the death of Christ. They also experience the peace *of* God as a result of Christ's work.

Christians can be at peace even in the midst of trials and persecution. This was Paul's desire for the Thessalonians.

Both grace and peace are gifts of God that come to believers through the Lord Jesus Christ.

In both Thessalonian letters Paul gave the greeting "Grace and peace to you," but here (in 2 Thes.) he added **from God the Father and the Lord Jesus Christ.**

II. Commendation for Past Progress (1:3-12)

This section flows smoothly from one subject to the next in a natural, conversational manner. Paul began by thanking God for the spiritual growth the Thessalonian believers had experienced. This led him to encourage them to persevere in their steadfastness. He explained that he and his fellow writers were praying for their spiritual success.

A. Thanksgiving for growth (1:3-4)

The character of, reasons for, and consequences of the apostle's thanksgiving are explained in these verses.

1:3. Paul and his fellow missionaries to Thessalonica had ample reason to **thank God** on behalf of this church, and their thanksgiving was continuous (cf. 1 Thes. 1:2). It was right for them to give thanks because these believers were a cause for thanksgiving. In fact Paul felt obligated to give thanks as though he owed a debt which he paid enthusiastically. Their **faith** had continued to grow (*hyperauxanei*, "to grow exceedingly"; *auxanō* is used in the Gospels of the growth of plants and babies, and in the epistles of spiritual growth [e.g., Eph. 4:15; Col. 1:6, 10], but in the NT *hyperauxanei* is only used here). The faith of Christians should keep **growing** all their lives; they should trust God more consistently and more extensively as they grow older in Christ. Faith in God is not a static thing. Since it is trust in a Person, it is always increasing or decreasing. A growing faith indicates a growing Christian.

Not only were the Thessalonians' relationships with God developing, but so were their relationships with other people. Genuine faith in God is always accompanied by love for others (James 2:14-17). Faith is the root; love is the fruit. The Thessalonians' **love . . . for each other** kept **increasing** (*pleonaxei*). In 1 Thessalonians 3:12 Paul had expressed concern that their love "increase" (*pleonasai*), and now, happily, he said it *was* increasing. Both faith and love were growing like well-fertilized plants, beyond what would have been normally expected. This was an exceptional church.

1:4. Because of such good growth the apostles frequently spoke with justifiable pride to other **churches** about the Thessalonians, using the Thessalonian church as a model to be emulated. In particular, their **perseverance** (*hypomonēs*; cf. 1 Thes. 1:3; 2 Thes. 3:5) in the midst of persecutions was outstanding. The Thessalonians did not react to discomfort the way many Christians do, by running away from their uncomfortable situations. Instead they viewed their circumstances as God's will and determined to brace up under the pressure. Their attitude was not to endure by force of their own strength, however. They had **faith** in God; they looked to Him for grace sufficient to bear up and accepted their circumstances as conditions which He was allowing for His glory. They were patiently **enduring . . . persecutions** (*diōgmois*) from enemies of the gospel who were hostile toward them (cf. 1 Thes. 3:3-4). The **trials** (*thlipsesin*, "pressures, troubles"; cf. 2 Thes. 1:6-7) they were undergoing were painful circumstances that came from both Jewish and Gentile acquaintances (cf. 1 Thes. 1:6; 2:14; Acts 17:5-9). Their persecutions and trials were numerous. Yet, in spite of them all, the Thessalonians kept on standing strong and stable in their faith.

B. Encouragement to persevere (1:5-10)

Paul proceeded to nourish the souls of these beleaguered saints so that they would be able to continue to bear up under the pressures of temptation.

1:5. The present experiences of the Thessalonians, Paul pointed out to them by way of encouragement, illustrated the righteous **judgment** of God, that is, that God is just.

When God would judge the Thessalonians they would be declared **worthy** of God's kingdom. Endurance in trials does not make one worthy of heaven; one does not earn heaven by suffering. But endurance in trials does *demonstrate* one's worthiness. A Christian is made worthy by God's grace, which he receives as a free gift by faith in Jesus Christ. His trials

simply expose what is there already and since the character that emerges through the fire of testing is God-given, God receives all the glory. The grace of God that makes it possible for a Christian to withstand the fires of human experience, which destroy non-Christians, is a Christian's only claim to being worthy of God's kingdom. **The kingdom of God** refers to God's rule over all, which Christians share as His children.

The purpose of the Thessalonians' sufferings was to bring glory to God by manifesting His grace in the way they bore up under their trials. Their **suffering** demonstrated that they were considered worthy of God's kingdom. In another sense they were suffering as soldiers of Christ.

1:6. Paul explained how the Thessalonians' suffering demonstrated the justice of God. He first stated the great truth taught from Genesis through Revelation: **God is just.** God will balance the scales of justice. He will mete out **trouble** (*thlipsin*; cf. v. 4) **to those who** troubled (*thlibousin*) the Thessalonians (cf. Gal. 6:7).

1:7. On the other hand God will give relief from the tensions of trials to those who are unjustly persecuted (lit., "troubled, pressured," *thlibomenois*; cf. vv. 4, 6) by their enemies. The Thessalonians, the apostles, and all other Christians who share in these pressures can look forward to this. **Relief** (*anesin*, "relaxation, rest"; used only five times in the NT: here and in Acts 24:23; 2 Cor. 2:13, 7:5; 8:13) will come at the revelation of Jesus Christ. Paul painted the picture of a veil being removed from in front of Jesus Christ; He will be **revealed in blazing fire** (cf. Ex. 3:2; 19:18; 24:17; Ps. 18:12; Isa. 30:27-30; 66:15; Dan. 7:9-10). This is the **Lord Jesus,** the Man in heaven. He will exercise the power then; the Christians' persecutors do so now. Christ's coming will be **with His powerful angels;** His heavenly servants will be with Him to carry out His bidding. If the Rapture had occurred in Paul's lifetime, the enemies of the Thessalonian believers would have been judged shortly (seven years) thereafter, at Christ's second coming.

1:8. At that time the Lord Jesus Christ will **punish** two classes of people: those who are ignorant of **God** (Rom. 1:18-32), and **those who . . . do not obey the gospel** (cf. John 3:36). The guilt of those in the latter group is the greater because their privilege is greater. God's judgment is perfectly just. Willful rejection of God's revelation spurns God.

1:9. The destruction to befall both groups is stated in this verse. **They will be punished** is literally "they will pay a penalty" (*dikēn tisousin*). For their rejection of God's grace they will experience endless or **everlasting** ruin (*olethron aiōnion*). This is "the most express statement in St. Paul's Epistles of the eternity of future punishment" (Edward Headland and Henry B. Swete, *The Epistle to the Thessalonians*, London: Hatchard, 1863, p. 137). The punishment of the wicked will be neither temporary nor will it be annihilation, but it will continue throughout eternity and those being punished will be conscious. It is eternal death as opposed to eternal life (Matt. 25:46). The nature of the **destruction** follows in the next phrase.

Separation from the Lord's **presence** (lit., "face") is the essence of eternal punishment. On the other hand being in the Lord's presence will make heaven heaven. A Christian's hope is to see and be with the Lord; the judgment of unbelievers is to be eternally inaccessible to His presence (cf. Rom. 1:18; 2:5-9; 6:21; Phil. 3:19; 1 Thes. 1:10; 4:17).

The majesty of His power is the visible splendor of the Lord's presence. The Lord's power will be manifest in a majestic display (cf. Rev. 19:11-16). Unbelievers will be forever **shut out** from the Lord's presence and His power.

1:10. This judgment will take place when the Lord **comes** back to earth and is **glorified** through the lives of believers whom He has transformed by making saints out of sinners. This is not the Rapture (1 Thes. 4:13-18; John 14:2-3), for no judgment accompanies the Rapture. Instead, it is the revelation of Jesus Christ in power and great glory (Ps. 2:1-9; Matt. 25:31), when He will set up His earthly kingdom (Rev. 19:11–20:4). At His return He will destroy the Armageddon armies gathered against Him (Rev. 16:12-16; 19:19-21) and will then judge living Jews (Ezek. 20:33-38) and living Gentiles (Matt. 24:31-46). These judgments are the ones just described (2 Thes. 1:9).

The exact date of His return is not given, of course, but it will be a day of judgment for the lost and a day of glory and marveling for believers. Christ will be "glorified in" (not *by*) His saints, that is, His glory will be mirrored in them. Christians will marvel in that they will admire their Lord for what He has done in them. All believers will marvel—not just those living on the earth and those resurrected when Christ returns, but also those who return to earth with Him, those who had been caught up to be with the Lord at the Rapture.

This group, Paul pointed out, would include the Thessalonian believers to whom he wrote this epistle. Because they **believed** Paul's **testimony** they would share in this great day. Such a hope should strengthen any believer who might be buckling under the pressure of persecution by unbelievers (v. 4). This glimpse into the future undoubtedly encouraged Paul's readers and it should encourage believers in their trials today.

C. Prayer for success (1:11-12)

The preceding revelation moved Paul to pray for his Thessalonian brothers and sisters, that they might live lifestyles that were consistent with their calling and destiny.

1:11. Paul and his colleagues habitually prayed for the Thessalonians. Their spiritual welfare was always on the apostles' hearts.

They prayed that their **God** (the apostles' and the Thessalonians') would reckon or declare the readers **worthy** of the **calling** they had received, to come to God through faith in Jesus Christ (cf. Rom. 8:30; Eph. 4:1; 1 Thes. 4:7). Paul consistently made what God has done for believers the basis of his appeals for them to lead lives in keeping with their destiny. Christians do not live worthily in order to obtain salvation but because they have been granted salvation.

A second request was that God would bring to full expression **every good purpose of** theirs to glorify God, and **every act** motivated by their **faith** in God. Both motives and actions have their source in God (Phil. 2:13); thus they are accomplished **by His power.**

1:12. The ultimate purpose of this prayer is the glory of God. Specifically it was that God's glory might be manifested in and through the Thessalonians, both immediately (v. 12) and at the revelation of Jesus Christ (v. 10). When this happens, the vessels that manifest the glory of God are themselves **glorified** by association with Him. In the Bible **the name** stands for the person named, his character, conduct, reputation, and everything else about him. In praying thus, Paul was asking that God would fully glorify Jesus Christ in these saints. This is in keeping with and springs from the **grace of** God, personalized again by Paul as **our God,** and linked with **the Lord Jesus Christ** as an equal (cf. v. 1; 1 Thes. 1:1). Answers to prayers depend on and are traceable to God's grace. Such lofty requests as these can be fulfilled only by God's grace.

III. Correction of Present Error (2:1-12)

This section of verses contains truths found nowhere else in the Bible. It is key to understanding future events and it is central to this epistle. Paul dealt with a doctrinal error concerning eschatology (the last things) that had crept into the Thessalonian church. In chapter 2 he spoke to the theological error, and in chapter 3 to practical problems in the church that grew out of that error.

A. The beginning of the day of the Lord (2:1-5)

Paul had instructed the Thessalonians from the Old Testament concerning the day of the Lord when he preached to them in person. The day of the Lord is the period of history mentioned repeatedly in the Old Testament during which God will bring judgment and blessing on the people of the earth in a more direct, dramatic, and drastic way than ever before (cf. Isa. 13:6, 9; Zeph. 1:14-16). From other New Testament revelation concerning this period of time it is believed that this will begin after the Rapture of the church, and will include the Tribulation and the Millennium.

In his first letter to the Thessalonians Paul had taught them that the day of the Lord would come as a thief in the night (1 Thes. 5:2). This instruction raised a question in his readers' minds. It must have seemed to some of them that the day of the Lord had already come. After all, the persecutions they were experiencing seemed to be what the prophets had predicted when they wrote about the great calamities coming on God's people and the world in the day of the Lord. The

Thessalonians apparently had received instruction from other teachers to the effect that they were indeed experiencing the judgments of the day of the Lord, that is, the Great Tribulation. But if this were so, how could Paul's previous instruction that they would be caught up and escape the wrath of God coming on the earth be true? Paul wrote this section (2 Thes. 2:1-5) to straighten out the matter.

2:1. The preceding comments concerning the coming of Christ (1:5-10) stimulated the readers' thinking about this subject, but now Paul launched into it more particularly. The **coming** (parousias, "presence") **of our Lord Jesus Christ and our being gathered to Him** refers to the Rapture. "Beseech," though archaic, is perhaps a more effective word than **ask** (erōtōmen) in conveying Paul's attitude of warm personal affection. He lightened their spirits with a reminder that his readers were his **brothers** and sisters in the faith. Paul probably used the full title for God the Son—"our Lord Jesus Christ"—in order to add solemnity to the subject.

2:2. Paul warned his readers against believing the false teaching that was shaking their spiritual equilibrium and triggering their fears. Apparently the theory that they were in **the day of the Lord** was coming to them from several sources (**prophecy, report, or letter**), making the Thessalonians more inclined to accept it as authoritative. Some were saying this teaching had been revealed to them by the Lord. And some were reporting teaching they had heard from others. And the Thessalonians received a letter, which was allegedly from Paul, that taught the same error (cf. 3:17). No wonder the new converts were shaken.

The erroneous message which all these voices echoed was that the day of the Lord had arrived; the Thessalonians were in it. But if this were so, the believers were wondering, how could Paul speak of the Lord's return as preceding the day of the Lord? (1 Thes. 1:10) And what about those promises that they would not see God's wrath? (1 Thes. 1:10; 5:9) It is clear that Paul had taught them a pretribulational Rapture. Their confusion arose because they could not distinguish their present troubles from those of the day of the Lord.

2:3. Having stated the issue and

identified the sources of the false teaching, Paul proceeded to warn his readers against being deceived. The Thessalonians must not be deceived by any person, no matter how credible he might appear to be, or by the way anyone might present his teaching, claiming the authority of God or godly men. New Christians tend to be gullible because they are not yet grounded in the truth of God's Word (cf. Eph. 4:14). But all Christians can be misled by impressive personalities and spectacular appeals. The antidote to poisonous heresy is a good strong dose of the truth which Paul proceeded to administer.

He referred to three events which must occur before the judgments of the day of the Lord took place. They are the apostasy (2 Thes. 2:3), the revealing of the man of lawlessness (vv. 3-4, 8), and the removal of restraint against lawlessness (vv. 6-7). (These are not necessarily given in strict chronological order. See the following comments on vv. 3 and 7.)

One major event is the rebellion (lit., "the falling away," hē apostasia, from whence comes the English word "apostasy"). This is a revolt, a departure, an abandoning of a position once held. This rebellion, which will take place within the professing church, will be a departure from the truth that God has revealed in His Word. True, apostasy has characterized the church almost from its inception, but Paul referred to a specific distinguishable apostasy that will come in the future (cf. 1 Tim. 4:1-3; 2 Tim. 3:1-5; 4:3-4; James 5:1-8; 2 Peter 2; 3:3-6; Jude). He had already told his readers about it (2 Thes. 2:5).

Some interpreters have taken this "departure" as a reference to the Rapture of the church (e.g., E. Schuyler English, *Rethinking the Rapture*, New York: Loizeaux Brothers, 1954, pp. 67-71), but this is not too probable. D. Edmond Hiebert refutes this view that *apostasia* here refers to the Rapture (*The Thessalonian Epistles*, p. 306). Some scholars believe that this apostasy (called by Paul "the" apostasy) will consist of people turning from God's truth to worship the Antichrist, who will set himself up in God's temple and claim to be God (v. 4). If this is so, then the judgments of the day of the Lord will occur in the second half of the seven-year period preceding Christ's second coming.

Another event that must take place before the judgments of the day of the Lord occur is the revelation of "the man of lawlessness" (*ho anthrōpos tēs anomias*). Paul used a tense for the verb is revealed which indicates that this revelation will be a decisive act that will take place at a definite moment in history (cf. vv. 6, 8). He will be fully associated with and characterized by "lawlessness" (or "sin," as some mss. and the κjν have it). He is also described as the man doomed to destruction (lit., "the son of perdition," κjν). The destruction to which he is destined is the opposition of salvation; it is everlasting torment. It seems probable that the man of sin will be identified by some people living then when he makes a covenant with Israel at the beginning of the 70th week of Daniel (Dan. 9:27a); but when he breaks the covenant three and a half years later (Dan. 9:27b), he will be widely recognized for who he really is (Charles C. Ryrie, *First and Second Thessalonians*, p. 104). This latter event may be the time Paul had in mind for the "revealing" of the man of lawlessness.

2:4. This man is further described as the adversary of God. He will seek to replace the worship of the true God and all false gods with the worship of himself, and will proclaim himself to be God. The beast will tolerate the worship of no one or nothing but himself (cf. Rev. 13:5-8). He will set himself up on God's throne in the inner sanctuary of God's temple. This probably refers to a literal temple, but some suggest that it is a figurative reference to his occupying the most holy place in human worship, which rightfully belongs only to God. The early church fathers and several good modern-day commentators accept the literal view. This man is also called the "beast coming out of the sea" (Rev. 13:1-10), "a scarlet beast" (17:3), and simply "the beast" (17:8, 16; 19:19-20; 20:10). He is the Antichrist (1 John 2:18), a pseudo-Christ hostile to the Savior. He will be a real human being, not a principle or a system or a succession of individuals. Such a person has not yet been spotlighted on the stage of human history.

2:5. This teaching was nothing new to the Thessalonians; Paul had taught them about the day of the Lord when he was with them in Thessalonica. He called on them to recall those lessons. For the first time in this epistle Paul wrote that he personally (sing.) had taught them. He said this in order to emphasize the truth of his message, as he was the chief spokesman in Thessalonica. Paul did not regard prophetic truth as too deep or unimportant or controversial for new Christians. He believed it was a vital part of the whole counsel of God, so he taught it without hesitation or apology.

B. The mystery of lawlessness (2:6-12)

The Apostle Paul continued his correction by giving more information about the man of lawlessness in relation to the removal of the One who now partially restrains lawlessness. This removal constitutes a third event referred to by Paul that must take place before the day of the Lord will begin. The theme of lawlessness pervades this whole section of the epistle.

2:6. **And** (kai) connects what precedes with what follows; the same subject continues, but the emphasis shifts to what is presently restraining the revelation of the man of sin. Paul said the Thessalonians knew what it was, but he did not identify it here. Perhaps he had told them in person. Something or Someone is holding back the culmination of lawlessness. Part of the purpose of this restraint is to keep the man of sin from being revealed prematurely.

2:7. This verse explains and expands on verse 6. Paul reminded his readers that **the secret power of lawlessness** was **already at work.** The "secret power" (mystērion, whence "mystery") is one of the mysteries of the New Testament (Rom. 16:26; 1 Cor. 2:6-12; Eph. 1:9; 3:3-5; Col. 1:25-27). A mystery in the New Testament is a new truth previously unknown before its revelation in the present dispensation. In this case the mystery is the revelation of a future climax of lawlessness in the world. Then and now a movement against divine law directed by Satan was and is operative. But it is being restrained somewhat, and this restraining will continue until the time appointed for revealing the man of sin and the climax of lawlessness.

Who or what is restraining the satanically empowered movement against God's law and is postponing the revelation of the man of sin? Some say it is the Roman Empire. But the empire has long vanished and "the holder back" is not yet

revealed. Another suggestion is that this is Satan, but it is difficult to see why he would hold back sin. Others suggest that human governments are holding back sin and the revealing of the Antichrist. But human governments will not end prior to the Antichrist's unveiling. Nor do all governments restrain sin; many encourage it!

The Holy Spirit of God is the only Person with sufficient (supernatural) power to do this restraining. Some object to this being the Holy Spirit on the grounds that to katechon in 2 Thessalonians 2:6 is neuter ("what is holding back"). But this is no problem for two reasons: (a) The neuter is sometimes used of the Holy Spirit (John 14:26; 15:26; 16:13-14). (b) In 2 Thessalonians 2:7 the words are masculine: ho katechōn, **the one who . . . holds it back.** How does He do it? Through Christians, whom He indwells and through whom He works in society to hold back the swelling tide of lawless living. How will He be **taken out of the way?** When the church leaves the earth in the Rapture, the Holy Spirit will be taken out of the way in the sense that His unique lawlessness-restraining ministry through God's people will be removed (cf. Gen. 6:3). The removal of the Restrainer at the time of the Rapture must obviously precede the day of the Lord. Paul's reasoning is thus a strong argument for the pretribulational Rapture: the Thessalonians were not in the Great Tribulation because the Rapture had not yet occurred.

2:8. After the removal of restraint the world will plunge headlong into lawlessness and the man of sin will be revealed (see comments on v. 3). This man's name is never given in the Bible, but he will be known by his actions. He is the same person referred to in verse 3. He is also spoken of in Daniel 9:26-27 and 11:36-12:1. Paul was conscious of the spiritual forces behind this individual, and for this reason described his revelation as something that will take place by the power of another, not himself.

This powerful person will be destroyed by the mere **breath** of **the Lord Jesus.** Antichrist may control mankind, but he will be no match for Messiah. Jesus is Lord indeed. "The very breathing of the glorified Jesus will slay the lawless one like the blast of a fiery furnace" (Hiebert, *The Thessalonian Epistles*, p.

315). He will be killed and his work will be destroyed, brought to nothing. The shining forth of Christ's presence when He comes to earth will immobilize the Antichrist's program as certainly as the revelation of the glorified Christ on the Damascus Road stopped Saul in his tracks and terminated his program of fighting against God.

This verse (2 Thes. 2:8), spans the seven-year career of the Antichrist from the time he makes a covenant with Israel soon after the Rapture, till his **overthrow** by Christ at **His** second **coming** at the end of the Tribulation.

2:9. The career of this **lawless** leader is described in more detail in verses 9-12. His career will be empowered by **Satan** (cf. Rev. 13:2b) and characterized by Satan's method: counterfeiting. Satan's desire to **counterfeit** God's miracles in the world can be traced from Genesis through Revelation. Paul employed three terms to describe the supernatural power this man will demonstrate. **Miracles** (*dynamei*) emphasizes the inherent power behind the works he will perform. **Signs** (*sēmeiois*) refers to the fact that they will have significance. **Wonders** (*terasin*) indicates the attitude of awe that they will evoke when people behold them. He will, in short, perform such powerful miracles that it will be evident to all that he has supernatural power, and people will stand in awe of him. One such miracle and the people's awe are mentioned in Revelation 13:2b-4 and 17:8.

2:10. His miracles are not the only thing that will deceive people into thinking he has divine power. Everything he does will mislead people, especially those whose minds are blinded to the truth of who he is and what he is doing because they do not believe God's Word. The meaning of this verse is not that everything he does will be perceived as **evil** by people, but that it will be evil in its essence because it misrepresents **the truth** and leads people away from worshiping God. The same three words used to describe his miracles in verse 9 (miracles, signs, wonders) were used of the miracles of Jesus Christ (Acts 2:22) and the apostles (Heb. 2:4). It will appear to unbelievers living on the earth at that time that he is indeed God. He will be able to pass himself off as God and receive worship as God.

Those who are being deceived by the man of sin **are perishing** (*apollymenois*, pres. part.; the noun "destruction" [*apōleias*] in 2 Thes. 2:3 is related to this part.) as the result of their refusal **to love** the truth of God and accept His gift of salvation. Their own choice brings about their condemnation. In spite of the inherent attractiveness of the saving truth of the gospel, these unbelievers refuse it. **To love the truth** of the gospel indicates true acceptance of it and adherence to it; it does not imply a higher requirement than simply believing it. The truth contrasts with the lies of the man of sin. The consequence of believing and loving the truth is salvation. One's responses to the gospel must be a matter of the heart (love), rather than simply of the head.

2:11. God desires that all be saved and come to the knowledge of the truth (1 Tim. 2:4-6). But when people refuse to entertain the truth, He lets them pursue and experience the consequences of falsehood (cf. Rom. 1:18-25). In fact God, as the Judge of men, begins this judgment at the moment of their rebellion and subjects them to the **powerful delusion** (*energeian planēs*) which comes from choosing error over truth. They choose to **believe the lie** and God sends them the delusion that is inherent in their choice. This powerful judgment from God is justified by the unbelievers' decision to refuse the truth. "The lie" is the claim that the man of lawlessness is God.

2:12. The purpose of God in acting thus is to execute justice (cf. 1:6). Eternal condemnation will be the fate of all who on the one hand choose to disbelieve **the truth** and on the other hand delight **in wickedness.** The opposite of believing the truth is delighting in wickedness; a spiritual decision leads to its moral manifestation. This consequence befalls everyone who disbelieves the gospel. Paul's primary concern here is of course unbelievers who will be living when the man of sin will be revealed. But these principles of God's judgment apply in all ages and can be seen in the 20th century.

Is this passage saying that those who do not believe the gospel before the man of sin is revealed—and who are therefore not caught up to meet the Lord at the Rapture but still live on the earth—cannot be saved after the man of lawlessness has been revealed? Or can people who recognize but knowingly reject the truth of the gospel before the Rapture be saved after the Rapture takes place? The "powerful delusion" (v. 11) that God will bring on these individuals in particular suggests that few if any then living on the earth will be saved after the Rapture. This seems to be a special judgment from God that will occur at this one time in history. The many saints which the Book of Revelation indicates will be living on the earth during the Tribulation may thus be people who did not hear and reject the gospel before the Rapture (cf. Rev. 7:4).

In summing up this section, Paul reminded his readers that the trials and persecutions they were experiencing (1:4) did not indicate that they were suffering the judgments of the day of the Lord. They had not missed the Rapture. Before the judgments of the day of the Lord would come, certain identifiable events must occur. These are the apostasy (extensive turning away from the truth of God), the removal of the Restrainer (the Holy Spirit restraining evil in the world as He works through the church He indwells) at the Rapture, and the unveiling of the Antichrist, the man of lawlessness. Since these events had not (and still have not) occurred, the Thessalonians were not experiencing the judgments accompanying the day of the Lord.

IV. Thanksgiving and Prayer (2:13-17)

This section forms a transition between Paul's teaching on the day of the Lord (2:1-12) and his exhortations for present living in view of that day (3:1-15).

A. Thanksgiving for calling (2:13-15)

The character, grounds, and implications of Paul's thanksgiving are included in these verses.

2:13. In contrast to the unbelievers just mentioned, the Thessalonians were a source of joy to the apostles. Paul felt a strong obligation to **thank God** on their behalf continually. They were his **brothers** (cf. vv. 1, 15) and sisters in the faith, **loved by the Lord** though hated and persecuted by their godless neighbors.

The reason for the apostle's joy and gratitude to God was His choice of the Thessalonian believers for eternal salvation. **From the beginning** (cf. "before the Creation of the world," Eph. 1:4) **God**

chose (*heilato*, past tense of *aireō*, "to take or pick," used only here and in Phil. 1:22) them, not on the basis of their love for Him or any merit on their part, but because of His love for them (cf. 1 Thes. 1:4). Paul consistently taught that the initiative in salvation comes from God, not man. The means God uses to effect salvation is the work of His Holy **Spirit** who sets aside chosen individuals for lives of holiness and separation from sin (cf. John 16:7-11). The Holy Spirit regenerates, indwells, and baptizes Christians into the body of Christ. The human aspect of salvation is **belief in the truth** of the gospel. The Holy Spirit then uses the Word of God to purify the believer's life (John 17:17).

That God chooses to save some though He loves all men should lead believers to thank God for His grace on behalf of the elect.

2:14. God **called** the readers to salvation by using the **gospel** as it was proclaimed by the apostolic missionaries in Thessalonica. God's purpose in doing so was that the believers **might** one day **share** the splendor and honor that **Jesus Christ** now enjoys, seated at the right hand of the Father (cf. 1:10-12).

2:15. In view of their calling, the Thessalonian believers were to maintain their present position of faith in God, care for the brethren, and hope in the imminent return of Jesus Christ (cf. 1 Thes. 1:3). They were to **stand firm** (*stēkete*; cf. 1 Cor. 16:13; 1 Thes. 3:8). Christians are in constant danger of being swept downstream by the currents of ungodly culture. They are also prone to let the truths they know and the relationship they enjoy with God grow cold. They need to vigorously **hold to** what they have been taught by God's servants. The Thessalonians were in danger of loosening their grip on the apostles' teachings which they had received (cf. 2 Thes. 3:6) in person from the missionaries and from their letters. They were in danger of slipping backward in their Christian experience because of the pressures of their trials and the daily negative influences of the world, the flesh, and the devil.

B. Prayer for strength (2:16-17)

In the face of the Thessalonians' need for steadfastness Paul prayed that God would give them encouragement and strength (cf. 1 Thes. 3:2, 13; 2 Thes. 3:3).

2:16. Though the Son and Father are both mentioned, They are regarded as One. God's love and **grace** is the foundation for **eternal** (i.e., unending) **encouragement** (*paraklēsin aiōnian*) in the face of any temporary present distress. Also God gives **hope** for the future. And that hope is **good** (*agathēn*, "beneficial") for it assures believers of the return of their victorious Savior.

2:17. Paul had two desires for the Thessalonians: (a) The Thessalonians needed comfort and encouragement (the verb **encourage** [*parakalesai*] suggests both "comfort" and "encourage"; sometimes it means "urge" as in 1 Thes. 4:1, 10; 2 Thes. 3:12) in view of their recent anxiety created by false information concerning the day of the Lord. (b) They needed God's grace to make them firm and stable (**strengthen** is *stērizai*, also used in 1 Thes. 3:2, 13) in every **good deed** ("good" in the sense of being done as unto the Lord) and **in every . . . word** they spoke in defense and confirmation of the gospel.

V. Exhortations for Future Growth (3:1-15)

This last major section of the epistle called on its readers to live in the light of the truth previously revealed and by the grace of God just invoked.

A. Prayer for the apostles (3:1-2)

Paul and his companions requested the prayer support of their Thessalonian brethren for whom they prayed.

3:1. Finally introduces the last major part of the letter. The Thessalonians needed prayer in their temptations, but they also needed to **pray** for others. Assuming a burden of prayer for others lightens one's own load. The apostles were needy too. Prayer was requested for two matters. The apostles acknowledged that the success of their missionary labors was due to God's blessing His Word as they proclaimed it. In particular, the spreading of the gospel was God's work and its reception among those who heard it was due to His preparing hearts. The Thessalonians knew from their experiences how God works in people's hearts to prepare them to receive the gospel; so they could pray with conviction that God

would honor His Word by causing others who heard it to believe it.

3:2. The second request was for deliverance from enemies of the gospel. As the missionaries itinerated from city to city, opponents of Christianity tried to frustrate their efforts. The Thessalonians knew all about this (Acts 17:5-9). The enemies of the gospel were doing something irrational, namely, resisting the free gift of God. They were also being destructive of the spiritual welfare of others. The hostility of these enemies was due to their lack of **faith** in the message of salvation. They were **wicked** (*atopōn*, "perverse") and **evil** (*ponērōn*, "actively harmful"). Verses 1 and 2 show the positive and negative reactions which the preaching of the gospel produce.

B. Confidence of the apostles (3:3-5)

Rather than feeling distraught over the present situation in the Thessalonian church, the apostles were confident.

3:3. The reason for their confidence was the faithfulness of God rather than anything about the Thessalonians. The character of God should be the basis for a Christian's confidence. Because God has promised to supply believers' needs, Paul could rest in the assurance that He would provide strength (cf. 1 Thes. 3:2, 13; 2 Thes. 2:17) to withstand temptation and trials, and protection from the adversary and his emissaries (cf. Phil. 1:6; 1 Thes. 5:24). (Cf. "evil men" in 2 Thes. 3:2 with **the evil one** in v. 3).

3:4. An additional reason for **confidence** was the conviction that the Thessalonians would **continue to** obey the instructions of Paul and his cohorts in this letter. The missionaries were not relying on their readers' inherent power to do what was right; their confidence was that since the believers were **in** Christ, **the Lord** would work in them to react favorably to this epistle.

3:5. This prayer-wish expressed the apostles' petition that Jesus Christ would open up the way for the readers to obey out of a growing appreciation of **God's love** for them and a consequently greater love for God, as well as increasing endurance in the midst of trials which the Lord's example of **perseverance** (*hypomonēn*; cf. 1 Thes. 1:3; 2 Thes. 1:4; Heb. 12:1-2) stimulates within the hearts of believers. Meditation on the love of God and the patient endurance of Christ motivates Christians to obey His Word and to endure trials patiently. The word **direct** (*kateuthynai*) means "clear away the obstacles." It is also used in 1 Thessalonians 3:11.

C. Treatment of the disorderly (3:6-10)

Doctrinal error concerning the day of the Lord had led to disorderly conduct in the church. Paul dealt with the latter problem forcefully in this section. This cause-effect relationship is not stated explicitly in the epistle, but it is a safe deduction.

3:6. That a minority of the church members were misbehaving seems clear in that Paul admonished his readers generally to discipline the erring brethren. The seriousness of the charge is seen in Paul's appeal to **the name of the Lord Jesus Christ.** On behalf of everything that Jesus Christ is, they should do as Paul said. This is a **command,** not a suggestion. When Paul wrote the church earlier, he told them to "warn those who are idle" (1 Thes. 5:14).

Apparently this warning had not been heeded. Now Paul prescribed harsher discipline. Second-degree discipline involved the orderly separating of themselves from the lazy and the disorderly. This may have included excluding them from the life and meetings of the church (cf. 1 Cor. 5:11). This lack of contact would illustrate in a graphic way the spiritual gap that the behavior of the unruly had created. The offense was idleness, deliberate loafing which led some to interfere in the work of others (2 Thes. 3:11) and to expect others to provide for their needs (v. 12). This behavior was in direct disobedience to the apostles' teaching.

3:7. Paul justified this command with the **example** the missionaries had given them while teaching in Thessalonica (vv. 7-10). Paul had commended the church for following his example (1 Thes. 1:6), but when it came to working some were not following it. Quite clearly, Paul regarded the apostles' example as an authoritative model for their converts. They were to imitate behavior as well as to believe teaching. Paul and his associates were never lazy loafers.

3:8. They did not leech off others.

Paul was not saying that they never accepted a gift or a meal from others, but that they were self-supporting. They earned the bread they ate (cf. v. 12). In fact, they **worked** long and hard so as not to be a financial **burden to any of** the Thessalonians (cf. 1 Thes. 2:9).

3:9. The apostles lived this way to give their converts an example (*typon;* cf. 1 Thes. 1:7) of what it means to sacrifice for the good of others. The apostles had every **right to** receive physical **help** for spiritual ministry (cf. 1 Cor. 9:3-14; 1 Tim. 5:18). But they chose to forego this right in order to teach the importance of self-sacrificing love and industry. Paul did not imply that this right should always be sacrificed; he taught elsewhere that it is legitimate, that those who are taught should support their teachers (Gal. 6:6). His point here was that Christians generally should not expect other people to take care of them but should support themselves as much as possible.

3:10. The missionaries had taught the Thessalonians to be industrious as well as giving them a good example. Paul wanted no one to forget exactly what the apostles had said. It was a firm **rule** of Christian conduct. He either quoted it verbatim here or summarized his previous teaching into a single pithy precept. The individuals in view were not those who could **not work** but those who would not work. They were not to be supported by other Christians out of a sense of charity. The loving thing to do for those drones was to let them go hungry so that they would be forced to do right and go to work. No Christian who is able but unwilling to work should be maintained by others who labor on his behalf.

D. Commands for the idle (3:11-13)

Moving from the apostles' example of industry and a general principle to be followed, Paul focused on a specific problem in the church.

3:11. The apostles had heard more than once (this is the force of the pres. tense of **hear,** *akouomen*) that some in the church were not working to support themselves. They were **busybodies** instead of being **busy.** Instead of tending to their own business of earning a living they were meddling in the business of others (cf. 1 Tim. 5:13).

3:12. Paul and his companions both

commanded (*parangellomen*) those in this category and exhorted (*parakaloumen*) them on behalf of their union with **Christ**. With calm and sober minds, in view of what had been written concerning the day of the Lord, they should **settle down** (lit., "be working with quietude" [not noisily or in disorderliness], *hēsychia*; cf. Acts 22:2; 1 Tim. 2:2, 11; and cf. comments on 1 Thes. 4:11) and engage in regular employment to **earn** a living. Then they would earn their own **bread** and not sponge off others. Paul had previously told them to do this (1 Thes. 4:11), but because some disobeyed he gave this sterner command.

3:13. Turning to the faithful majority, Paul urged continuation in doing what they knew to be right regardless of the leeching of the disobedient. When other Christians take easy paths of irresponsibility and seem to prosper in them, it is easy to get discouraged and be tempted to join them. Though one may **tire** *in* **doing what is right,** he should never tire *of* doing what is right. In addressing the diligent as **brothers** and the idle as such people (v. 12), Paul implied that those who disobeyed this word from God were separating themselves by their behavior.

E. Discipline of the disobedient (3:14-15)

These verses contain even stronger words regarding the idle. This was how the rest of the church should relate to them if they would not repent.

3:14. Having been warned twice (1 Thes. 4:11; 5:14) a disobedient person must be given **special** treatment if he failed to repent. Paul regarded his writings as authoritative for the church; they were to be obeyed because he was an apostle and his inspired words were the Word of God. The idle one was to be identified as such by the members of the church and placed in a distinct category as disobedient. This seems to be what each faithful brother should do individually; no mention is made of public identification and discipline in the church (2 Thes. 3:14-15).

The faithful were not to have social contact with an idle person till he repented. The purpose of this social ostracism was to make the offender **feel ashamed** of himself so that he would repent. The design of divine discipline is

always to produce repentance, not division. Social pressure can be effective in helping an erring person come to his or her senses. This is exactly what Paul advocated in this case. Ostracism from the body of believers should help such a person be ashamed and feel his separation from fellowship with the Head of the body, Jesus Christ.

3:15. Concerned that the Thessalonians might overdo the discipline, Paul quickly urged them to treat the offender **as a brother,** not **as an enemy.** An occasion for discipline should not become an occasion for disobedience by those exercising the discipline. They were not to think of the offender as personally antagonistic toward them, nor were they to feel hostile toward him. His objective relationship to them as a brother in Christ should govern their feelings and actions, rather than subjective feelings that might be aroused by his idleness. They were to **warn** (*noutheteite*) **him,** not denounce him. Whereas they were to have no social contact with him they were not to break off *all* contact. They were patiently to admonish him to forsake the error of his ways.

VI. Conclusion (3:16-18)

The epistle closes with a prayer, a final greeting, and a benediction.

3:16. This is Paul's fourth prayer for the Thessalonians in this epistle (cf. 1:11-12; 2:16-17; 3:5). From correction Paul turned to intercession. Without the Lord's working all exhortations would be ineffective. Paul's concern was for **peace** within the church through the unity of all members obeying the truth. The **Lord** is the source of peace (cf. 1 Thes. 5:23) and Paul prayed that He would bestow this on the Christians in Thessalonica. A Christian and a church enjoy peace when they are rightly related to the will of God. Paul prayed that this would be the Thessalonians' condition **at all times** regardless of their circumstances, even in persecution.

In praying that **the Lord** would **be with** them **all,** Paul was not implying that God is with Christians only some of the time (cf. Matt. 28:20). Rather, he was praying that fellowship with Christ (that Christians can enjoy only as they obey His Word) might be the portion of each believer—not just of the obedient but also of those who were presently disobedient through idle living.

3:17. There is good evidence that **Paul** dictated his epistles to an amanuensis who actually wrote them down for him (cf. Rom. 16:22; 1 Cor. 16:21; Col. 4:18). But here Paul wrote a **greeting** with his **own hand.** Probably he wrote something by hand in most of his letters, to guarantee their authenticity to the recipients. In the case of this epistle such a personal salutation was especially needed (cf. 2 Thes. 2:2). His handwriting was undoubtedly distinguishable from his secretary's and was probably recognized by his readers as Paul's own.

3:18. The same benediction is used here as in 1 Thessalonians 5:28 except that **all** is added here. "All" sounds a final appeal for unity in the church through the obedience of each individual to Paul's instruction and admonitions. Such unity can come about only through **the grace of our Lord Jesus Christ.**

BIBLIOGRAPHY

See the Bibliography on 1 Thessalonians.

1 TIMOTHY

A. Duane Litfin

INTRODUCTION

The Pastoral Epistles. "The Pastoral Epistles" is a term used to designate Paul's two letters to Timothy and one letter to Titus. Two things distinguish these three epistles from Paul's other letters: (1) They are among the last things Paul wrote, reflecting the sort of concerns which burdened the apostle near the end of his ministry. (2) They are ostensibly addressed not to a congregation but to two young men who were functioning in pastoral roles. This does not mean, of course, that the letters were not read before congregations. The epistles show clear signs that their author intended them to be used widely. Nor does this mean that the epistles are mere handbooks on pastoral duties. There is much of general interest in the letters. Yet 1 and 2 Timothy and Titus are distinctive among Paul's letters. They are highly personal, practical, and unsystematic in nature; and they deal with matters of church order which Paul had not hitherto addressed except in passing. The evolving need for structure in the churches, combined with Paul's awareness that his own steadying influence would soon be passing from the scene, prompted him to treat certain ecclesiastical and pastoral subjects which have profited the church immensely ever since.

Authorship. Each of the Pastoral Epistles begins with an explicit identification of the Apostle Paul as its author. Until modern times no significant voices questioned their Pauline authorship. However, early in the 19th century liberal scholars attacked the authenticity of the Pastorals, and that concerted attack has gained momentum. Today the majority of liberal scholars hold that the Pastorals were written not by Paul, but by a "Paulinist," that is, a follower of Paul one or two generations removed from the apostle. According to this view the Pastorals actually reflect a perspective characteristic of the early second century rather than the mid-first century and, more importantly, of Paul's later followers rather than the apostle himself.

The attack on the authenticity of the Pastorals is four-pronged: historical, stylistic, ecclesiastical, and theological.

1. Historical arguments. The historical arguments stem from the fact that chronological references in the Pastoral Epistles do not fit comfortably within the historical framework of the Book of Acts. This is in some ways a strange argument since liberal scholars also commonly attack the chronological and historical reliability of Acts. How then can Acts be used as history to undermine the authenticity of the Pastorals? Yet despite this inconsistency in the liberal position, for those who take seriously both the historicity of Acts and the Pauline authorship of the Pastorals, this is a real problem.

Some have attempted to force the Pastorals into the Acts chronology, but the historical obstacles to doing so seem insurmountable. Many liberal scholars have therefore solved the seeming problems by assuming that the letters were written much later with fictitious references designed to make the epistles appear Pauline. A variation of this is the theory that the Pastorals represent fragments of truly Pauline material interspersed with material written by a later editor. In either case, the chronological distance from the events mentioned is assumed to account for the lack of historical "fit" with Acts.

A more satisfactory solution is to assume that the Pastorals do not fit within the Book of Acts at all, but rather describe a period after the end of Acts. The Book of Acts ends with Paul in jail in Rome (A.D. 61–62). Surely if Paul was executed at the end of his imprisonment,

Luke would have mentioned it. On the other hand, it is entirely credible that Paul could have been released (A.D. 62), perhaps for lack of evidence, and left free for another period of ministry. According to this supposition (which is all it can ever be), Paul traveled widely from A.D. 62 to 67 and was eventually recaptured, tried, and executed in Rome in 67. During this period of travel he would have written 1 Timothy and Titus, and during his final imprisonment, 2 Timothy. If this scenario is correct then one ought not expect the Pastorals to fit into the chronology of Acts, which ends with his first Roman imprisonment, and the historical arguments against the Pastorals' authenticity lose their force.

2. *Stylistic arguments.* Another line of argument against the authenticity of the Pastorals grows out of detailed examinations of their vocabulary. The occurrence of unusually high numbers of words used only once in the New Testament (but more regularly by second-century writers), words used by other New Testament writers but never elsewhere by Paul, and the absence or different use of characteristic Pauline words all combine, so the argument goes, to suggest a writing style of someone other than Paul.

But such word-counting cannot support the weight of the critics' conclusions. To begin with, the entire process is scientifically unsound since the available samples of literature are far too small for any such findings to be statistically valid. Furthermore such studies completely overlook the fact that different subject matter, different experiences, advancing age, changes in environment and companions, different recipients and purposes—all these and more affect a writer's vocabulary. When the same word-counting techniques are applied to uncontested Pauline Epistles, much the same results occur. Thus authenticity cannot be determined by merely counting word usage.

3. *Ecclesiastical arguments.* The ecclesiastical arguments against the Pauline authorship of the Pastorals all claim, in one form or another, that the church structure and order evidenced in those epistles did not emerge until well after the Apostolic Age and into the second century. In fact, it is claimed,

Paul's other writings show that he had no interest in church polity at all, so that it would be out of character for him to have written some of the instructions found in the Pastorals.

But once again the critics' arguments are questionable. The polity of the Pastorals can actually be contrasted with that of the second century, when Ignatian-type "bishops" (*episkopoi*) came to be distinguished from and set in hierarchical authority over elders (*presbyteroi*). The Pastorals describe no such differentiation. The two terms are used interchangeably in the Pastorals (cf. Titus 1:5-7) in a typically Pauline fashion (cf. Acts 20:17, 28). Clearly the emergence of the offices of elder-bishop and deacon had already occurred within Paul's lifetime (cf. Phil. 1:1), no doubt at his own instigation. Nothing about those offices in the Pastoral Epistles requires a second-century date.

The same may be said for the so-called "order of widows." While the second-century church did develop almost an "office" in the church for widows, the list of widows mentioned in 1 Timothy represents no such formalized position. From the beginning there had been an awareness of the church's responsibility to needy widows (cf. Acts 6:1-6), and the instructions in the Pastorals represent nothing one would expect to find in an apostolic letter dated two or three decades after the church began.

4. *Theological arguments.* The theological objections to Pauline authorship are two. First, critics argue that the heresy combated in the Pastorals is the well-developed Gnosticism of the second century; and, second, the theological perspective of the author, while admittedly basically Pauline, is in some significant ways unlike the great apostle and much like what one would expect of a second-century follower.

As to the first of these objections, it is widely acknowledged that what became a full-fledged heretical movement called Gnosticism in the second century was already "incipient" during the years of Paul's ministry. He often met and dealt with Gnostic tendencies, preeminently in Colosse. Therefore the fact that the Pastorals contain denunciations of false teaching that shows hints of a Gnostic dualism and asceticism does not require a second-century date. Moreover, on closer inspection, the error addressed in the Pastorals looks less and less like a well-formed Gnosticism. The false teachers described in the Pastorals actually show certain eclectic tendencies, drawing on Jewish influences as well (cf. 1 Tim. 1:7; Titus 1:10, 14; 3:9). Furthermore the essential danger of the error described seemed to lie in its irrelevance and worthlessness, a claim that would not be true of the fully formed second-century Gnosticism. Hence, the objections to Pauline authorship based on presumed references to a full Gnosticism in the Pastorals do not stand up under scrutiny.

As to the theological objection—that the theology of the author is in some ways un-Pauline—the same may be said. This does not stand up under close inspection.

According to this critical view the Pastorals supposedly show a lesser mind at work. They say the material is not anti-Pauline, or even non-Pauline, but merely un-Pauline, or perhaps sub-Pauline. Instead of refuting error, the author simply denounced it. Instead of developing the truth, the author was intent merely on conserving and guarding it. He was concerned with mere religion rather than theology, mere orthodoxy rather than creative thought. Right belief is given too much prominence, goes the argument. So they say Paul would never have written such things. Thus when combined with the fact that some of Paul's favorite ideas are missing, slighted, or reshaped (e.g., the ministry of the Holy Spirit, grace, the believers' mystical position "in Christ"), the conclusion is inevitable, according to the critics: Paul did not write the Pastorals.

Yet such a drastic conclusion is unwarranted. All of Paul's favorite themes do occur in the Pastorals, and any differences in their treatment can be fairly explained by the unique characteristics of the Pastorals. These epistles were written under unique circumstances, to unique audiences (first and foremost Timothy and Titus), for unique purposes. One should not expect them to sound exactly like Paul's other epistles. Arguments built on such subtle and in the end flimsy evidence cannot prove a second-century date.

The Pastorals do reflect, of course, a profound concern on the part of the apostle for the conservation of the truth. Paul was in the best sense of the word a "conservative." Having faithfully done all he could to develop and teach the truths of the gospel throughout his ministry, he was concerned near the end of his life that his faithful disciples not change them, but rather entrust them in turn to other faithful Christians, who would in turn entrust them to still others. He viewed this body of truth as a special stewardship from God, to be managed with great care. Since this truth led to godliness by pointing believers to Jesus Christ, it was the most valuable of treasures. It was to be taught faithfully in the congregation, and all attempts to undermine, pollute, or attack it were to be met with stern resistance.

Such a view of objective propositional truth is in serious conflict with modern existential views of truth. Hence it is not surprising that critics seek to dissociate it from Paul and attribute it to second-century followers. Yet to do so requires an unwarranted a priori assumption about the apostle's view of truth. A more objective assessment is that there is nothing in the theology of the Pastorals which requires a late date or which cannot be explained by the fact that these epistles represent Paul's last instructions to his two faithful representatives, Timothy and Titus.

Date. Paul's missionary journeys occupied approximately the years A.D. 48–56. From 56–60 Paul was slowly making his way through the Roman courts, arriving ultimately at Rome. For two years, 61–62, Paul was held under house arrest in Rome, at the end of which time, it can be surmised, he was released. From 62–67 Paul traveled more or less freely, leaving Timothy in Ephesus and Titus in Crete, and then subsequently writing each of them a letter. Thus the approximate dates for 1 Timothy and Titus are perhaps 63–66. After being recaptured and once again imprisoned, Paul wrote Timothy a second letter, 2 Timothy. Thus 2 Timothy, dated approximately A.D. 67, represents the last Pauline Epistle.

The Recipients. 1. *Timothy.* Timothy was the son of a Greek father and Jewish mother (Acts 16:1). No mention is made of his father being a Christian, but his mother Eunice and grandmother Lois were both known for their sincere faith (2 Tim. 1:5). Timothy was no doubt living at Lystra when Paul visited that city on his first missionary journey (cf. Acts 14:6; 16:1). Whether or not Paul led Timothy to Christ cannot be known with certainty. At any rate Timothy already knew and believed the Old Testament Scriptures, thanks to his mother and grandmother (cf. 2 Tim. 3:15), and Paul took him on as a promising protégé. Paul thus became like a spiritual father to the young man, referring to him as "my true son in the faith" (1 Tim. 1:2) and "my dear son" (2 Tim. 1:2; cf. Phil. 2:22).

Timothy's promise for the ministry was recognized early (1 Tim. 1:18; 4:14; 2 Tim. 4:5). Thus Paul took him on as a companion and he became one of the apostle's most trustworthy fellow-laborers (cf. Rom. 16:21; 1 Cor. 16:10; Phil. 2:19-22; 1 Thes. 3:2). He also became Paul's faithful representative and messenger (Acts 19:22; 1 Cor. 4:17; 2 Cor. 1:19; Phil. 2:19; 1 Thes. 3:2, 6). Six of Paul's epistles include Timothy in the salutations (2 Cor. 1:1; Phil. 1:1; Col. 1:1; 1 Thes. 1:1; 2 Thes. 1:1; Phile. 1; see the chart, "Paul's Introduction to His Epistles" at Rom. 1:1). Timothy had become so dear to Paul that in the apostle's last message was a touching appeal for Timothy to join him in his final days of imprisonment (2 Tim. 1:4; 4:9, 21).

After being released from his first Roman imprisonment Paul, with Timothy by his side, evidently revisited some of the churches in Asia, including Ephesus. On his departure from Ephesus, Paul left Timothy behind to provide leadership to the congregation. Then after an interval Paul wrote Timothy a letter, 1 Timothy, urging him on in that ministry.

Timothy may have been by nature somewhat passive, timid, retiring, and easily intimidated (cf. 2 Tim. 1:7). Thus Paul repeatedly spurred him into action (1 Tim. 1:3; 4:11; 5:7; 6:2; 2 Tim. 3:14; 4:2, 5). He was to let nothing, including his relative youth (1 Tim. 4:12) stand in the way of his performance of duty (2 Tim. 2:1-7; 4:5). Like a good soldier he was to "fight the good fight" (1 Tim. 1:18; 6:12), aggressively protecting and propagating

the gospel, using the full range of his gifts (1 Tim. 4:14; 2 Tim. 1:6).

2. *Titus.* Considerably less is known of Titus than of Timothy. Like Timothy he was one of Paul's converts, or at least a protégé (cf. Titus 1:4), but when or where he became a believer is unknown. Nor is anything known about his family or background, except that he was a Gentile (Gal. 2:3).

It is clear, however, that he was a trustworthy co-laborer with Paul. Titus was given one of Paul's most difficult and delicate assignments—to represent the apostle in troubled Corinth (2 Cor. 2:13; 7:6-7, 13-15; 8:6, 16-17). During the time between his two Roman imprisonments, Paul visited Crete with Titus, whom he left behind to further the work the two had begun (cf. Titus 1:5). Sometime later, during Paul's second imprisonment, Titus left Crete to travel to Dalmatia (2 Tim. 4:10), presumably for evangelistic purposes.

OUTLINE

I. The Salutation (1:1-2)
II. Instructions concerning False Teachers (1:3-20)
   A. Warnings against false teachers (1:3-11)
   B. Paul's experience of grace (1:12-17)
   C. Paul's charge to Timothy (1:18-20)
III. Instructions concerning Conduct in the Church (2:1-3:13)
   A. Instructions concerning prayer (2:1-7)
   B. Instructions concerning men and women (2:8-15)
   C. Instructions concerning elders and deacons (3:1-13)
IV. Instructions concerning Guarding the Truth in the Church (3:14-4:16)
   A. The church and its truth (3:14-16)
   B. Predictions of apostasy (4:1-5)
   C. Responsibilities of a good minister of Christ (4:6-16)
V. Instructions concerning Various Groups in the Church (5:1-6:10)
   A. Concerning various age-groups (5:1-2)
   B. Concerning widows (5:3-16)
   C. Concerning elders (5:17-25)

COMMENTARY

I. The Salutation (1:1-2)

1:1. Paul's typical salutation includes an identification of both author and recipient, combined with a more or less ritualized greeting. Here as in each of his other epistles except Philippians, 1 and 2 Thessalonians, and Philemon, **Paul** identified himself as **an apostle of Christ Jesus.** He no doubt used the term "apostle" in its more restricted sense to refer to those who had been personally commissioned by the risen Christ (cf. 2 Cor. 8:23 ["representatives"]; Phil. 2:25 ["messenger"] for its broader usage). Paul's apostleship was not something he had sought; it had come to him through a heavenly command (Gal. 1:11–2:2; cf. 1 Tim. 2:7). In several of his other epistles Paul commonly made a similar point by stressing his apostolic "calling" according to "the will of God" (1 Cor. 1:1; 2 Cor. 1:1; Eph. 1:1; Col. 1:1; 2 Tim. 1:1). Paul was often in the position of having to defend his authority which came from both God the Father and God the Son. The identification of **God our Savior** has an Old Testament ring to it but is common in the Pastorals (cf. 1 Tim. 2:3; 4:10; Titus 1:3; 2:10; 3:4). **Jesus** is described as **our hope,** a term which directs the reader's attention to the certain fulfillment of God's saving plan in **Christ** (cf. Col. 1:27).

1:2. Though this letter was clearly intended to be read aloud to the congregations in Ephesus and beyond, **Timothy** was identified as its immediate recipient. As Paul's genuine or **true son in the faith,** none could mistake Timothy's special place in Paul's heart. (This is the first of 19 times Paul used the Gr. word *pistis,* "faith," in 1 Tim.) Paul had probably not led him to Christ (cf. 2 Tim. 1:5; 3:15), but he probably had ordained (2 Tim. 1:6) the young minister, and had

great confidence in him. Timothy was issued Paul's fairly standard greeting of **grace, mercy, and peace.**

II. Instructions concerning False Teachers (1:3-20)

A. Warnings against false teachers (1:3-11)

1:3. The moves referred to in this verse cannot be followed clearly. Was Paul leaving **Ephesus** to enter **Macedonia?** Had he given Timothy instructions prior to leaving Ephesus? This is perhaps the best supposition. Timothy was urged, apparently for a second time, to **stay** on in Ephesus, indicating perhaps some inclination on Timothy's part to leave that ministry, perhaps to accompany Paul. Timothy's task in remaining was to stifle **certain men** in the congregation who were teaching **false** (lit., "different"; cf. 6:3) **doctrines**—that is, different from Paul's doctrine (cf. 1:11).

1:4. These false teachers were following after fables (*mythois,* cf. 4:7) and long, involved **genealogies.** Exactly what these fables and genealogies involved is not known. They may have had a Gnostic flavor, but were more likely of Jewish origin (cf. Titus 1:14). Whatever their nature, they were empty of any spiritual value and led only to further speculation, questions, and arguments. Such speculations were to be avoided because they did not further **God's** plan, which is grasped and implemented not by human imaginings, but **by faith.** By contrast, human speculations tend to lead off down endless blind tunnels which serve only to confuse and obscure God's truth.

1:5. Unlike such aimless speculations, the intended result of Paul's instruction to Timothy was **love,** and the purest kind of love at that. It is that love which pours naturally from a cleansed **heart** (cf. 2 Tim. 2:22), untainted **conscience,** and a **sincere** (*anypokritou,* "unhypocritical"; cf. 2 Tim. 1:5) **faith.** Each member of this beautiful trio speaks of a purity and integrity which produces the most exquisite kind of selfless love, seen in its ultimate form in God's love itself. Whereas the false teachers were motivated by worthless curiosity, Paul's instruction was designed to promote the most magnificent of virtues by maintaining the purity of the church's teaching.

God's truth always purifies the human spirit, while error putrifies it.

1:6. Paul no doubt believed that such love should be the goal of all Christian ministry (cf. 1 Cor. 13:1-3). Yet, sadly, though they should have known better, some teachers in the Ephesian congregation had lost sight of this lofty purpose and had wandered away (lit., "missed the aim"; cf. 1 Tim. 6:21; 2 Tim. 2:18) and **turned** aside **to meaningless talk.** Their teaching was *mataiologian,* that is, idle, useless, futile, empty verbiage.

1:7. More specifically, the problem with these false teachers, as is often the case, was a matter of the ego. They wanted to become respected **teachers of the Law.** Yet they were completely incapable of doing so. But instead of recognizing their inadequacies and remaining silent, they went on babbling as if with great authority, never understanding their subject (the Law), or even **what they** were saying about it.

1:8. Paul wanted to be sure that he was not misunderstood. He was not disparaging the Law. Paul viewed the Law as "holy, righteous, and good" (Rom. 7:12). Thus he clarified his point by emphasizing that **the Law is good** provided it is used **properly.** There is an inappropriate, legalistic use of the Law which Paul disavowed; but there is also a proper use of the Law that Paul embraced (cf. Gal. 3:19, 24).

1:9-10. The Law is designed to show people their sinfulness. Thus the Law is not for one who had already recognized his sin and turned to Christ. That person is no longer under the Law but should now walk in the Spirit (Gal. 5:13-26). The Law is intended for those who remain unconvinced of their sin.

Paul provided a striking list of examples which seem to be intentionally based on the Ten Commandments (cf. Ex. 20:3-17). The list begins with three pairs corresponding to the *first* table of the Decalogue dealing with offenses against God: (1) **lawbreakers and rebels,** (2) **the ungodly and sinful,** (3) **the unholy** (*anosiois,* "not devout"; cf. *hosious* in 1 Tim. 2:8) **and irreligious** (*bebēlois,* "profane"; cf. 4:7; 6:20; 2 Tim. 2:16). Paul then listed violators of the first five commandments of the *second* table of the Decalogue: **those who kill their fathers or mothers** represent the ultimate viola-

tion of the fifth commandment, and **murderers** the sixth. **Adulterers and perverts** pertain to the seventh commandment, which was generally broadly interpreted to include all forms of sexual sin. **Slave traders** may correspond to the eighth commandment since kidnapping was viewed as the ultimate act of stealing (Ex. 21:16; Deut. 24:7). **Liars and perjurers** clearly pertain to the ninth commandment. Only the 10th commandment ("You shall not covet") is not included (but cf. Rom. 7:7). Paul concluded this inventory of sinners with an all-inclusive reference to any behavior which **is contrary to sound doctrine** (lit., to "healthy teaching"; cf. 2 Tim. 1:13), including no doubt the very behavior of the false teachers themselves. "Doctrine" here is *didaskalia,* "teaching" or "the content taught," used seven times in this epistle: 1 Timothy 1:10; 4:1, 6, 13, 16; 5:17; 6:1.

1:11. Paul's yardstick for measuring what is and is not sound teaching, of course, was the message of God's great good news in Christ with which he had been **entrusted** (cf. 1 Thes. 2:4; Titus 1:3), and which he had faithfully preached in Ephesus (cf. Acts 20:17-27).

B. Paul's experience of grace (1:12-17)

1:12. At this point Paul's inventory of sinners, of which he knew he was the chief—combined with his remembrance of the gospel with which he had been entrusted—triggered within him a powerful surge of gratitude. Literally, the words "Thanks I have"—with "thanks" in the emphatic position—begins this section. Paul's gratitude stemmed from the fact that God in His grace had provided Paul all necessary enablement (cf. Phil. 4:13) and, considering him trustworthy, had pressed him into a privileged place of **service.**

1:13. The reason this was so striking to the apostle was that he knew so well the pit from which he had been dug. When he said he was **a blasphemer and a persecutor and a violent man,** he was not exaggerating for the sake of effect. (See Acts 22:4-5, 19-20; 26:9-11 for the vivid truth.) Yet Paul **was shown mercy because** his actions were the product of **ignorance.** Willful disobedience triggers God's wrath (cf., e.g., Num. 15:22-31; Heb. 10:26). But God deals gently with the ignorant and misguided (Heb. 5:2). The German philosopher Nietzsche said, "If you could prove God to me, I would believe Him all the less." No such willfulness characterized Paul's unbelief.

1:14. Therefore the apostle received God's mercy, not His wrath. God's **grace** far outpaced even Paul's grievous sin. Where there was once only unbelief, God **poured out . . . faith . . . in Christ.** Where there had been violent aggression against God and His people, now God poured out the **love** of Christ. (See comments on 2 Tim. 2:10.) Everything Paul lacked, God's grace had more than amply supplied. (The verb *hyperepleonasen*, used only here in the NT, means "to be present in great or superabundance.") Here may be seen the full measure of what Paul meant when he spoke of the empowering ministry of Christ (1 Tim. 1:12).

1:15. The central thrust of Paul's personal digression, begun in verse 12, now becomes clear. It is a testimony concerning the purpose of the Incarnation of **Christ. Jesus came** not merely to set an example or to show that He cared. He came to salvage **sinners** from their spiritual destitution—and Paul said he was **the worst** of that lot. There must be no misunderstanding of this most fundamental point. It is a truth that is completely **trustworthy** and deserving of **full acceptance.** (Four other passages include this "trustworthy" phrase: 3:1; 4:9; 2 Tim. 2:11; Titus 3:8.)

1:16. In fact it was just for this purpose—that is, to demonstrate God's plan to save sinners—that Paul himself was saved. As **the worst of sinners** (cf. Paul's other descriptions of himself in 1 Cor. 15:9; Eph. 3:8), Paul represents the extreme **example.** If God was patient and gracious enough to save Paul, He is patient and gracious enough to save anyone. All who follow can look back at Paul as a prototype or pattern ("example," *hypotypōsin*; cf. 2 Tim. 1:13). The ultimate sinner became the ultimate saint; God's greatest enemy became His finest servant. Somewhere between these extremes fall all the rest. In studying Paul's pattern, Christians can therefore learn about themselves.

1:17. This contemplation of God's grace as seen in Paul's case prompted him to one of his typical doxologies. It is filled with awe and adoration of the Lord. **King eternal** (lit., "King of the Ages") emphasizes God's sovereignty over all the ebb and flow of human history. **Immortal** and **invisible** speak of two of the central attributes of God: His eternality and His spiritual essence. **The only God** emphasizes His uniqueness in a typical Jewish monotheistic fashion. To this God alone must all **honor and glory** be ascribed, eternally. **Amen** (cf. 6:16).

C. Paul's charge to Timothy (1:18-20)

1:18. Returning from his brief personal digression (vv. 12-17), Paul got back to the specific matters before Timothy in Ephesus, resuming the charge begun in verse 3. **This instruction** (the same word *parangelian* is translated "command" in v. 5) refers to the teaching about the false teachers mentioned in verse 3. Such instructions were in accord with **the prophecies . . . made** earlier concerning Timothy's call and fitness for service in Ephesus. When and by whom these prophecies were made can only be guessed. It is known that the prophecies reinforced Paul's conviction that Timothy was a fit soldier to conduct the battle against error in the Ephesian church (cf. 6:12; 2 Tim. 4:7 for an athletic rather than military metaphor). Timothy was to remember these prophecies and be inspired by them in the struggle.

1:19. Whereas in Ephesians 6:10-17 Paul spelled out in detail to that church the Christian's equipment for spiritual warfare, here he listed only two items: **faith and a good conscience.** These two always seem to travel together (cf. 1 Tim. 1:5; 3:9). Strength in the one is always combined with strength in the other. So also is failure in the one correlated with failure in the other. Thus **some** who **have rejected** (*apōtheō*, "a strong, deliberate thrusting away"; used elsewhere in the NT only in Acts 7:27; Rom. 11:1-2) a good conscience have also found **their faith** destroyed (cf. 1 Tim. 4:1; 6:10). Theological error is often rooted in moral failure.

1:20. Two in Ephesus who illustrate this principle are **Hymenaeus** (cf. 2 Tim. 2:17) **and Alexander.** Whether this is the same Alexander mentioned in Acts 19:33 and 2 Timothy 4:14 is not clear. Probably it is not. Paul's prescription for these two blasphemers was that they be **handed over to Satan,** a phrase which perhaps refers to excommunication from the congregation (cf. 1 Cor. 5:1-5) and abandonment to realms controlled by Satan (2 Cor. 4:4). Paul viewed the congregation as a haven and protection for believers without which they would suffer painful disadvantage. Thus excommunication was designed to chasten the two apostates. Yet Paul's motive was remedial, not punitive (cf. 2 Cor. 2:5-8; 2 Thes. 3:14-15).

III. Instructions concerning Conduct in the Church (2:1-3:13)

A. Instructions concerning prayer (2:1-7)

2:1. From his concerns about false teachers Paul turned to matters relating to the conduct of the church broadly (cf. 3:14-15). Paul began with what he considered most important: prayer. What too often comes last in a church's priorities should actually come first. Not much weight should be placed on the presumed distinctions between **requests, prayers,** and **intercession.** The terms are more likely designed to build on one another for emphasis. It should be noted, however, that **thanksgiving** should have a prominent place in the church's prayer life.

2:2. The Ephesian church was to pray "for everyone" (v. 1, lit., "all men"), but especially for the leaders of civil government. Paul did not specify here the content of these prayers, but almost certainly he was instructing that requests be made for the salvation of the populace and its governors. This can be seen clearly from the following verses. With Nero's growing resentment toward Christians—which came to full bloom after the fire in Rome in July, A.D. 64—and the general disintegration of the Roman Empire due to Nero's profligacy, Christians began to suffer persecution from the Roman authorities. Having recently been released from his Roman imprisonment, Paul was greatly aware of the deteriorating political atmosphere. Thus he urged prayer for the salvation of all men, but especially rulers, so that the stable, noninterfering environment of previous days might be recovered. This is the minimum requirement if Christians are to live **peaceful and quiet lives in all godliness and holiness.** (This is the first of 10 times Paul used the word *eusebia,*

"godliness." These 10 occurrences are all in the Pastoral Epistles: 2:2; 3:16; 4:7-8; 6:3, 5-6, 11; 2 Tim. 3:5; Titus 1:1. Its five other usages are in Acts 3:12; 2 Peter 1:3, 6-7; 3:11.) Times of political and social upheaval are excellent times in which to die for Christ, but hard times in which to live for Him.

2:3. As in modern times, some in the Ephesian church were prepared to question the validity of a prayer for the salvation of all men. Thus Paul defended his instructions by pointing out that such a prayer **is good, and pleases God our Savior** (cf. 1:1). Literally, the Greek says that such a prayer is "acceptable before" (in the presence of) God. Many prayers are unacceptable to God, but not this one.

2:4. The reason this prayer is acceptable to God is that it is a prayer "according to His will" (1 John 5:14). God, who is by nature a Savior, **wants all men to be saved.** Paul repeated the words "everyone" (1 Tim. 2:1) and "all men" (vv. 3, 6). The same Greek word (*pas,* "all") is used in each case, referring all three times to the same group (cf. 4:10). God desires that no one perish (2 Peter 3:9), that the entire human race come to know the truth through a personal relationship with Jesus Christ, who is the Truth (John 14:6). (Of course not all do come to salvation; Paul was not teaching universalism.)

2:5-6. To further buttress his argument Paul cited the commonly accepted teaching about God and His work in Christ. Verses 5-6 may represent a fragment of a familiar confession of the first century. In any case, Paul cited these unquestioned truths of the gospel: (1) **There is** only **one God.** (2) There is only one way for men to approach Him—through **the Man** who was God in the flesh, **Christ Jesus.** (3) This Jesus **gave Himself** up to die on the cross **as a ransom** (*antilytron;* cf. *lytron,* "ransom" for a slave or prisoner, in Matt. 20:28; Mark 10:45) for the human race. (Cf. the chart, "New Testament Words for Redemption," at Mark 10:45.) This act is a clear **testimony,** offered at just the right **time** (Gal. 4:4-5; Heb. 1:1-2), of God's desire to save **all men** (cf. Titus 1:3).

2:7. The exclusivists in the Ephesian church evidently felt that the gospel was only for Jews. This was a common problem, as seen preeminently in the case of Peter (cf. Acts 10:9-43; Gal. 2:11-13). Thus Paul cited his own commission as **apostle . . . to the Gentiles** as a clincher. Paul had been **appointed a herald** (*kēryx*, "messenger"; cf. 2 Tim. 1:11) to take the gospel to the majority of the human race that the Jews had considered beyond the pale. Thus, as Paul reminded the Ephesians, it can be seen that God desires everyone to be saved. Paul's assurances of his truthfulness were stylistic devices designed to stress the importance of his point (cf. Rom. 9:1; 2 Cor. 11:31; Gal. 1:20).

B. Instructions concerning men and women (2:8-15)

2:8. Undoubtedly Paul wanted all Christians to offer up prayers for a widespread spiritual awakening among the populace and its rulers. Yet in the public assembly Paul specified that **men** (*andras*, lit., "males") **everywhere** are to lead the congregation in **prayer**. Moreover, these prayers were to be offered with lifted **hands**. This was a common Old Testament practice (cf., e.g., 1 Kings 8:22; 2 Chron. 6:13; Ezra 9:5; Pss. 28:2; 141:2; Lam. 2:19). It was also common in the pagan mystery religions of the first century and in the early church. Paintings on the walls of the catacombs in Rome portray this posture. The hands were to be **holy** (*hosious*, "devout, undefiled"), signifying an internal cleanness on the part of these spiritual leaders. Further, such leaders must be men of sound relationships, not characterized by **anger** (*orgēs*, "outbursts of temper") or **disputing** (*dialogismou*). Broken human relationships affect one's ability to pray (cf. Matt. 5:22-24; 6:12; 1 Peter 3:7), which would include leading others in prayer.

2:9. Next Paul turned to the females in the congregation. For their adornment they should not emphasize the external, but the internal. They should dress **modestly, with decency and propriety** (cf. v. 15). These terms stress not so much the absence of sexual suggestiveness, though it is included, but rather an appearance that is simple, moderate, judicious, and free from ostentation. The specifics Paul mentioned (**braided hair or gold or pearls or expensive clothes**) are not wrong in themselves, but become inappropriate when they indicate misplaced values (cf. 1 Peter 3:3). In the

Ephesian church these styles may have been associated with the local temple prostitutes. Christians must be careful about letting a pagan culture set their fashions.

2:10. Instead of stressing external beauty, according to the world's standards, Christian women should manifest a different set of values. They should adorn themselves with (lit., "by means of") **good deeds.** They should depend on their faithful service in the name of Christ to render them attractive to others. This was no plea for women to make themselves unattractive; it was simply an exhortation to reject the world's yardstick for measuring beauty and adopt heaven's standard (1 Sam. 16:7). One should expect nothing less from **women who profess to worship God.**

2:11-12. In emphasizing godly conduct for women, Paul stressed, with Peter, "the unfading beauty of a gentle and quiet spirit, which is of great worth in God's sight" (1 Peter 3:4). The females in the congregation should receive instruction from the male leadership with **quietness and full submission.** They should not attempt to turn the tables by clamoring for the office of congregational teacher or by grasping for **authority over** men. Rather they should, literally, "be in quietness." The word, *hēsychia*, translated "quietness" in 1 Timothy 2:11 and **silent** in verse 12, does not mean complete silence or no talking. It is clearly used elsewhere (Acts 22:2; 2 Thes. 3:12) to mean "settled down, undisturbed, not unruly." A different word (*sigaō*) means "to be silent, to say nothing" (cf. Luke 18:39; 1 Cor. 14:34).

2:13. Why is such a quiet and submissive spirit "of great worth in God's sight"? (1 Peter 3:4) Because it manifests an understanding and acceptance of His design for the human race. As elsewhere (cf. 1 Cor. 11:8-10), Paul here based his view of male/female relationships in the church on the account of Creation recorded in Genesis 2. He made no reference whatever to the so-called "curse" of Genesis 3:16. Rather, the roles Paul spelled out here are a product of God's fundamental design wherein **Adam was formed first, then Eve** (cf. Gen. 2:7-25). More is involved here than mere chronological priority. Paul saw the priority in time as indicative of the leadership given to the male, to which the woman, the "helper suitable for him" (Gen. 2:18), should respond.

2:14. Further, Paul contrasted the experiences of Adam and Eve. **The woman . . . was deceived and became a sinner,** but **Adam was not the one deceived.** Some chauvinists see Paul arguing here that women, as represented in their archetype Eve, are more gullible and thus more susceptible to error, than men. Thus, they say, females should not be in places of teaching or authority in the church. Others believe Paul was saying, in effect, "Look what happens when the Creation order is reversed and the man abdicates the leadership role to the woman." In any case, Paul was emphatically not excusing or absolving Adam of blame for the Fall. Elsewhere Paul put the responsibility squarely on Adam's shoulders (cf. Rom. 5:12-21).

2:15. This is one of the most difficult verses of the New Testament to intepret. The ambiguous words **kept safe through childbirth** have given rise to several diverse interpretations: (a) preserved (physically) through the difficult and dangerous process of childbirth; (b) preserved (from insignificance) by means of her role in the family; (c) saved through the ultimate childbirth of Jesus Christ the Savior (an indirect reference to Gen. 3:15); and (d) kept from the corruption of society by being at home raising children. The interpretation of the verse is further clouded by the conditional clause at the end: **if they,** that is, mothers, **continue in faith, love, and holiness with propriety.** Whatever one understands the first part of the verse to be affirming, it is contingent on a woman's willingness to abide in these four virtues. Hence the second of the preceding options seems most likely. A woman will find her greatest satisfaction and meaning in life, not in seeking the male role, but in fulfilling God's design for her as wife and mother with all "faith, love, and holiness with propriety" (i.e., self-restraint; cf. 1 Tim. 2:9).

C. Instructions concerning elders and deacons (3:1-13)

3:1. Continuing his instructions on how the church should conduct itself, Paul turned to the crucial matter of leadership qualifications. He wanted to encourage respect for the congregation's leaders, so he cited what was apparently a familiar maxim and commended it as a sound one. Two implications emerge: (1) It is valid to aspire to church leadership, and (2) church leadership is **a noble task.** The term **overseer** (*episkopos*), sometimes translated "bishop," is only one of several words used in the New Testament to describe church leaders. "Elders" (*presbyteroi*) is by far the most common. Other terms such as "rulers" (*proistamenoi,* Rom. 12:8; 1 Thes. 5:12), "leaders" (*hēgoumenois,* Heb. 13:17) and "pastors" (*poimenas,* Eph. 4:11; cf. also Acts 20:28; 1 Peter 5:2) are also used. Though each of these terms may describe a different facet of leadership, they all seem to be used interchangeably in the New Testament to designate the same office. This office is different from that of deacons (cf. comments on 1 Tim 3:8).

3:2. More is required of an overseer than mere willingness to serve. In verses 2-7 Paul listed 15 requirements for a church leader: (1) **above reproach.** He must be blameless in his behavior. This Greek word *anepilēmpton,* "above reproach," is used in the New Testament only in this epistle (v. 2; 5:7; 6:14). It means to have nothing in one's conduct on which someone could ground a charge or accusation. It differs slightly in meaning from its synonym *anenklētos* in 3:10 (see comments there). (2) **Husband of but one wife,** literally, a "one-woman man." This ambiguous but important phrase is subject to several interpretations. The question is, how stringent a standard was Paul erecting for overseers? Virtually all commentators agree that this phrase prohibits both polygamy and promiscuity, which are unthinkable for spiritual leaders in the church. Many Bible students say the words a "one-woman man" are saying that the affections of an elder must be centered exclusively on his wife. Many others hold, however, that the phrase further prohibits any who have been divorced and remarried from becoming overseers. The reasoning behind this view is usually that divorce represents a failure in the home, so that even though a man may be forgiven for any sin involved, he remains permanently disqualified for leadership in the congregation (cf. vv. 4-5; 1 Cor. 9:24-27). The most strict interpretation and the one common among the earliest commentators (second and third centuries) includes each of the above but extends the prohibition to *any* second marriage, even by widowers. Their argument is that in the first century second marriages were generally viewed as evidence of self-indulgence. Though Paul honored marriage, he also valued the spiritual benefits of celibacy (1 Cor. 7:37-38) even for those who had lost a mate (1 Tim. 5:3-14). Thus he considered celibacy a worthy goal for those who possessed the self-control to remain unmarried. According to this strict view Paul considered a widower's second marriage, though by no means improper, to be evidence of a lack of the kind of self-control required of an overseer, in much the same way that a similar lack disqualified a widow from eligibility for the list of widows (5:9). Church leaders must also be (3) **temperate** (*nēphalion,* "well-balanced"; used elsewhere only in 3:11; Titus 2:2), (4) **self-controlled** (*sōphrona,* also used in Titus 1:8; 2:5), (5) **respectable,** and (6) **hospitable.** Such characteristics are prerequisites for those who would lead others into these important Christian virtues. The phrase (7) **able to teach** speaks of a leader's ability to handle the Scriptures. He must be able both to understand and to communicate the truth to others, as well as to refute those who mishandle it (cf. Titus 1:9). Not all must necessarily do this publicly, of course; some may conduct this aspect of their ministries more informally in private settings. Yet all leaders must possess an aptitude for handling the Word with skill.

3:3. Four negative phrases follow: (8) **not given to much wine** (cf. Titus 1:7), and (9) **not violent.** His self-control (1 Tim. 3:2) is to extend to his appetites and his anger. By contrast, a church leader must be (10) **gentle,** or forbearing, making room for others. (This word *epieikē* is also used in Phil. 4:5; Titus 3:2; James 3:17; 1 Peter 2:18). Unlike false teachers, an effective church leader is (11) **not quarrelsome** (cf. 1 Tim. 6:4) and (12) **not a lover of money** (cf. 6:5; Titus 1:11). He neither relishes fighting with others nor pursues his ministry for personal gain (cf. 1 Peter 5:2).

3:4. An overseer must (13) **manage his own family well.** Paul's specific focus

here was on the children. The most reliable (though not infallible) means of determining the quality of one's potential leadership is by examining the behavior of his children. Do they respect their father enough to submit to his leadership? **With proper respect** (lit., "with all gravity") may refer, however, not to the children's submission, but to the manner in which the father exercises his authority, that is, without due fuss or clamor.

3:5. A rhetorical question forms a parenthetical support for the validity of the preceding qualification. Paul made an analogy between leadership or management of a home and that in a church (Eph. 2:19; 1 Tim. 3:15). Many of the same skills and qualifications are needed for both. Success in a family may well indicate success in a church; likewise, failure in a home raises a red flag about one's ability to lead in a congregation.

3:6. An overseer **must** (14) **not be a recent convert** (*neophyton,* "neophyte"), lest his rapid advancement to leadership fill him with pride and conceit, and he experience the **same** kind of **judgment** that **the devil** incurred for his pride.

3:7. An overseer **must also** (15) **have a good reputation with outsiders** (cf. Col. 4:5; 1 Thes. 4:12). Paul's thought here seems to be that church leaders, as representatives of the congregation, are constantly susceptible to the snares of the devil (cf. 2 Tim. 2:26). Satan likes nothing better than to **disgrace** God's work and God's people by trapping church leaders in sin before a watching world. It is important therefore that overseers achieve and maintain a good reputation before unbelievers.

3:8. Like overseers, **deacons** (cf. Phil. 1:1) must also be men of quality, even though their function in the congregation is significantly different. The word translated "deacon" (*diakonos*) means literally a "humble servant." The role of the deacons is to carry out, under the elders' oversight, some of the more menial tasks of the church so that the elders can give their attention to more important things. (See Acts 6:1-6 for the prototype of what later became the "office" of deacon in the church.) The qualifications for the office of deacon are almost as stringent as for elder because of their public profile in the church and because the servant nature of their work requires strong qualities of maturity and piety. Deacons must therefore **be men worthy of respect**—that is, serious men of dignity, not clowns. (The same Gr. word is used of women in 1 Tim. 3:11.) They must be **sincere** (*mē dilogous*, lit., "not double-tongued") in the sense of being honest and unhypocritical. Like the overseers (v. 3), deacons must not be heavy **wine** drinkers or greedy chasers after **dishonest gain.**

3:9. Most important of all, deacons **must** be men of spiritual depth (cf. Acts 6:3). Specifically they should be men who understand and **hold** fast **the deep truths of the faith.** By the phrase **with a clear conscience** Paul (cf. "good conscience" in 1 Tim. 1:5) meant that there must be nothing in the conduct of these men that was glaringly inconsistent with their professed beliefs. In other words they must not profess one thing but practice another.

3:10. Moreover, like the overseers, who are to demonstrate their maturity before being placed in a position of responsibility (v. 6), deacons **must** also **first be tested.** Paul's intent here was not to require some formal testing procedure, but rather that these men "prove" their quality over time in the ordinary activities of life and ministry. After they showed themselves "irreproachable," then **let them serve as deacons.** The words **if there is nothing against them** translate two Greek words, *anenklētoi ontes,* "being free from accusation." The word *anenklētos* occurs in the New Testament only in Paul's writings (1 Cor. 1:8; Col. 1:22; 1 Tim. 3:10; Titus 1:6-7). It means one who is unaccused, free from any charge at all. Christlike conduct is required of deacons. (Cf. comments on a synonym, *anepilēmpton,* in 1 Tim. 3:2.)

3:11. Similarly the *gynaikas* ("women" or **wives) are to be worthy of respect,** that is, dignified (the same word, *semnas,* is used of deacons in v. 8), not .slanderers (*diabolous,* from *diaballō* "to slander"; from this verb comes the noun "devil," the chief slanderer) of others, **but** temperate (*nēphalious,* "well-balanced; cf. v. 2; Titus 2:2), **and trustworthy** (lit., "faithful") **in everything.** Who are these *gynaikas* Paul addressed? They were almost certainly not the women of the congregation generally. They were most likely either the wives of the deacons or a group of female deacons (cf. Phoebe, Rom. 16:1). A case can be made for either of these two options, with a slim advantage falling to the first. But being dogmatic about either view is unwarranted by the exegetical data.

3:12. Like the elders, deacons must be "one-women men" (cf. v. 2) and capable managers of their own families. Paul's reasoning behind this latter qualification is spelled out in verses 4-5.

3:13. Though the position of deacon seems by worldly standards to be menial and unattractive, to close followers of Jesus Christ it looks quite different (cf. John 13:11-17; Mark 10:42-45). Those who fulfill their servant roles faithfully **gain** two things: first, **an excellent standing** before fellow Christians who understand and appreciate the beauty of humble, selfless, Christlike service; and second, **great assurance** (*parrēsian,* "confidence, boldness") **in their faith in Christ Jesus.** Humble service, which lacks all the rewards the world deems important, becomes a true test of one's motives. Here one discovers for himself whether or not his efforts are truly prompted by a Christlike spirit of selfless service. When a deacon has indeed "served well" his ministry builds confidence in the sincerity of his own faith in Christ and of his unhypocritical approach to God (cf. Eph. 3:12; Heb. 10:19).

IV. Instructions concerning Guarding the Truth in the Church (3:14–4:16)

A. The church and its truth (3:14-16)

3:14. If Paul had left Timothy at Ephesus to pastor the church (cf. 1:3), he also hoped to rejoin Timothy there soon. In the meantime, in case of delay Paul wanted the Ephesian pastor and congregation to have **these instructions** in hand. The "instructions" no doubt refer to what has come before as well as the exhortations to follow.

3:15. The clearly stated purpose of these instructions is to inform the Ephesian congregation **how people ought to conduct themselves in God's household.** Again Paul used the analogy of the "household" (*oikos*) to refer to the church (*ekklēsia;* cf. v. 5). This merges into an architectural image involving the church as **pillar and foundation of the truth.** The idea of the church as a "building" dedicated to **the living God** is a common one for Paul (cf. 1 Cor. 3:16-17; 2 Cor. 6:16; Eph. 2:20-22). Some people teach that the church as the "foundation of the truth" is the *source* of God's truth, that no one can know the truth unless he depends on the teaching of some organized church or church group. But Paul was simply affirming the crucial role of the universal church as the support and bulwark—not the source—of God's truth. His words should not be stretched beyond this.

3:16. Paul had been discussing proper godly conduct in the church, behavior which is in every way consistent with the truth, rather than "contrary to the sound doctrine" (1:10). In 3:16 he expressed a simple idea which becomes difficult due only to its compactness. This truth about **godliness** being a **mystery** means that it was hidden but now is revealed. Further, it **is a great** (*mega,* "large, important") "mystery" in that it is overwhelmingly large in scope and sublimely important in significance (cf. Eph. 5:32). Paul cited the content of this truth in the form of an excerpt from an early hymn about Christ, who is the essence of the "mystery" (Col. 1:27). Whether the fragment should be divided into two or three parts is disputed. Whichever one chooses, the six elements of the excerpt are as follows: (1) **Appeared in a body** refers to the Incarnation of Christ. (2) **Was vindicated by the Spirit** refers to God's demonstration through the Resurrection (cf. Acts 2:24-36), by the Holy Spirit (cf. Rom. 8:11), that the crucified Jesus is Lord and Messiah. (3) **Was seen by angels** refers to His exaltation before the heavenly realm (cf. Phil. 2:9-11; Col. 2:15; Heb. 1:6). (4) **Was preached among the nations** (cf. Col. 1:23) and (5) **was believed on in the world** refer to the progressive fulfillment of God's redemptive plan through His preordained means (cf. 1 Cor. 1:18-2:5). (6) **Was taken up in glory** refers to the Ascension (Eph. 4:10).

B. Predictions of apostasy (4:1-5)

4:1. As the repository and guardian of the truth, the church must be aware of the strategies of the truth's enemies. It is crucial then for the church to understand what God has revealed about these enemies (cf. 1 Peter 4:1-18; Jude 17-18). By **the Spirit clearly says** Paul was not

necessarily referring to any particular revelation but to the repeated teaching of the Lord (e.g., Mark 13:22), the other apostles (e.g., 2 Peter 3:1-18), and Paul himself (e.g., Acts 20:29; 2 Thes. 2:1-12). According to this teaching the situation will degenerate as Christ's return approaches. **In later times** (cf. 2 Tim. 3:1 for a synonym), which Paul viewed as still future though casting their shadow already, **some** people **will abandon the faith** (cf. 1 Tim. 1:19) to **follow** after the false teaching of **deceiving spirits and . . . demons.** Spiritual error is seldom due to innocent mistakes. It is more often due to the conscious strategies of God's spiritual enemies (cf. Eph. 6:12). The teachings (*didaskaliais*) of demons are false doctrines taught by errorists whose views are instigated by demons.

4:2. But God's spiritual enemies do not directly confront their victims with error. Instead they work through **hypocritical liars** (lit., "men who speak lies in hypocrisy"). This is Satan's standard operating procedure (cf. 2 Cor. 11:13-15). He selects likely representatives and renders their **consciences** beyond feeling (cf. Eph. 4:19), **seared** (from *kaustēriazō,* "to brand, cauterize") **as with a hot iron.** In this condition they are ready to do Satan's bidding.

4:3. The false teachers plaguing the Ephesian church were the forerunners of the Gnostics of the second century. Even at this relatively incipient stage, the strong dualism of the Gnostics is clear: spirit is good; matter is evil. They believed all appetites relating to the body are therefore evil and should be rooted out, including normal desires for sex and food. Thus the false teachers **forbid people to marry and order them to abstain from certain foods** (cf. Col. 2:21). But Paul went to the heart of the dualistic error by stating that matter is not inherently evil; it is rather part of what **God created** (cf. 1 Tim. 6:17b). Hence **those who believe and who know the truth** can gratefully (cf. 4:4) receive and use the things God created, which were designed **to be received** (*eis metalēmpsin,* "for partaking").

4:4. Contrary to the teaching of the errorists, **everything God created is good.** Here Paul echoed God's own verdict (Gen. 1:31). Whereas the false teachers were intent on "forbidding" and "abstaining" (1 Tim. 4:3), Paul said that **nothing is to be rejected**—nothing, that is, that God created. Man can abuse what God has created, as adultery is an abuse of the marital sexual relationship, and gluttony is an abuse of a normal appetite for food. Such abuses should certainly be rejected. But God's creations themselves are all good and should be **received with thanksgiving,** not with taboos.

4:5. All the seemingly "ordinary" things of life can then become extraordinary as they are **consecrated by the Word of God and prayer.** In the light of the Scriptures a Christian recognizes God's good hand behind the things provided, and offers thanksgiving to the Lord. In this way the ordinary things so easily taken for granted (some of which are forbidden by errorists) become sanctified as occasions for worship and praise.

C. Responsibilities of a good minister of Christ (4:6-16)

4:6. From his warning of the apostasy to come Paul turned to Timothy, and exhorted him to pass along these same warnings to others in the church. One of the works of **a good minister of Christ Jesus** is that he is a faithful conduit of the truth to other Christians (cf. 2 Tim. 2:2). To do this, however, Timothy first had to keep himself "nourished" (not **brought up**) by (a) the objective **truths of the faith** which, as Jude 3 puts it, were "once for all entrusted to the saints," and (b) the truths **of the good teaching that you have followed.** This latter phrase probably refers to Paul's own instructions to his young disciple, which Timothy had faithfully carried out (*didaskalia,* "teaching" is also used in 1 Tim. 1:10; 4:1, 13, 16; 5:17; 6:1).

4:7. But since Timothy was to channel God's truth to others, he was to **have nothing to do with godless myths and old wives' tales.** The godless (*bebēlous,* "profane") and the worthless go hand in hand (cf. 1:9; 6:20; 2 Tim. 2:16) and should be shunned. Instead, Timothy was to devote himself to much more manly pursuits. Paul introduced an athletic image with the words **train yourself.** The verb here is *gymnaze,* from which comes the English "gymnasium." But Timothy's training was to be for godliness (cf. 1 Tim. 2:2), not physical fitness. Paul often used athletic analogies to drive home the need for spiritual discipline (cf. esp. 1 Cor. 9:24-27).

4:8. As valuable as **physical** fitness (**training** is *gymnasia,* "exercise," used only here in the NT) may be (and Paul did not disparage it), spiritual fitness, or godliness, is much more valuable. Physical fitness is profitable only, literally, "for a little." **But godliness** is profitable **for all things,** not merely in this **present** transient **life** but in the **life to come,** that is, for eternity. Godliness colors all aspects of temporal and eternal life, bestowing its blessing on all it touches.

4:9. The **trustworthy saying** formula can point forward, as in 1:15, or backward, as in Titus 3:8. Here it is probably best to see it as reinforcing the proverbial impact of 1 Timothy 4:8 (in contrast with the NIV).

4:10. To this end, said Paul, **we labor and strive**—that is, to develop the godliness of verse 8. The word "strive" translates *agōnizometha* ("I agonize"), another athletic term. Paul practiced what he had just preached to Timothy (cf. Col. 1:29). **We have put our hope** renders *ēlpikamen,* a perfect tense denoting an action with the results continuing. The durative quality of Paul's confidence is stressed. Paul knew his struggle was worth it because his hope was set, not on himself, some philosophy of life, other men, or nonexistent gods—but **in the living God, who is the Savior of all men, and especially of those who believe.** The mention of the "living" God picks up the reference in 1 Timothy 3:15; the stress on God as "Savior" picks up 1:1 and 2:3. Again Paul stated that God is the Savior of "all men" (cf. 2:2, 4, 6) since He desires that all be saved and He provided Christ as the ransom (2:6) to make that salvation possible. Yet God is the Savior of those who believe in a special way since only in them has His desire for their salvation come to fruition.

4:11. Timothy, as a young man with perhaps a nonassertive personality, was evidently given to timidity and fear (cf. 1 Cor. 16:10-11). Thus Paul exhorted him to **command** (*parangelle,* "insist on") **and teach these things.** By "these things" Paul usually meant the contents of his instructions in the immediate context, but the term here seems almost intentionally ambiguous (cf. 1 Tim. 3:14; 4:6, 15; 5:7,

21; 6:2, 11). Paul was prodding Timothy to be firm and courageous in his ministry. Paul used the same Greek word *parangelle* in 5:7 and 6:13.

4:12. At first Paul's instruction that Timothy should not **let anyone** "despise" (KJV) his youth might seem impossible to fulfill since Timothy could not control the attitudes of others. Yet when combined with the latter part of the verse, the thrust of Paul's instruction becomes clear. Timothy must not be intimidated by his relative youthfulness or what others might think of it. Instead he was to demonstrate his maturity by living such a godly life that he would become a pattern for other Christians in every area of his life: **speech** . . . **life** (i.e., "behavior or conduct," *anastrophē*; cf. "conduct" in 3:15), **love** . . . **faith, and** . . . **purity.** The word for "purity" (*hagneia*, "moral cleanness") is used only here and in 5:2.

4:13. After referring again to his own movements (cf. 1:3; 3:14-15), Paul exhorted Timothy to attend to his public ministry as well as his private life. This public ministry was to consist of at least three elements: (1) **Public reading of Scripture.** It has always been the practice of God's people to read the Word of God aloud in the congregation (e.g., Ex. 24:7; Deut. 31:11; Josh. 8:35; 2 Kings 23:2; Neh. 8:7-8; Luke 4:16; Acts 15:21; Col. 4:16; 1 Thes. 5:27). (2) **Preaching;** better yet "exhortation" (*paraklēsei*). This term includes the exposition and application of the passages read. (3) **Teaching.** The distinction between this and the former term is by no means clear-cut. The two merge into each other. Yet "teaching" (*didaskalia;* cf. 1 Tim. 1:10; 4:1, 6; 5:17; 6:1) may refer primarily to a more catechetical treatment of the truths of the Christian faith. The two terms occur in Romans 12:7-8 and are there related to spiritual gifts.

4:14. Timothy's image of himself as a minister was evidently deficient, so Paul reminded him of the fact that God had given him the requisite ability for service. Timothy must not ignore or **neglect** this basic factor (cf. 2 Tim. 1:6). If others were not to look down on Timothy, neither was he to look down on himself. His **gift** had come to him **through a prophetic message** which was delivered at the time of his ordination, and the remembrance of this prophecy was designed to strengthen Timothy's confidence. The laying on of **hands** is commonly associated in the Bible with a continuity of leadership (cf. Num. 27:18-23; Deut. 34:9; Acts 6:6; 8:18; 13:3; Heb. 6:2). The phrase **body of elders** renders the Greek *presbyteriou*, which speaks of a group or "board" of elders, or "presbytery." These men together constitute a biblically recognized group. The Bible never speaks of a corresponding group identity for deacons. The notion of deacons functioning as a "board" is never mentioned in the Bible.

4:15. Here is the positive side of Paul's negative ("do not neglect. . . .") exhortation of verse 14. The command **be diligent** (*meleta*, from *meletaō*, "give careful thought to") is the converse of the command in the previous verse (*amelei*, from *ameleō*, "give no thought to"). Timothy was to give his careful attention to Paul's instructions; indeed, he was, literally, "to be in them" (or, with the NIV, to **give** himself **wholly to them**). As he would do so his **progress** would be evident to all observers and his problem of low credibility, implied throughout this section, would be alleviated.

4:16. Watch your life (lit., "yourself") **and doctrine** (lit., "the teaching"; cf. 1:10; 4:1, 6, 13; 5:17; 6:1) **closely** summarizes 4:6-16. Throughout this epistle Paul had been advising Timothy concerning his private life and public ministry. He was to keep a sharp eye on both, persevering in the instructions Paul had offered in the two realms. In so doing, said Paul, **you will save both yourself and your hearers.** Ultimately only God can save, of course; yet in a secondary sense the New Testament speaks of a person "saving" himself (Phil. 2:12) and others (James 5:19-20; Jude 23). Paul's words are a pointed reminder of the awesome burden of responsibility that congregational leaders carry.

V. Instructions concerning Various Groups in the Church (5:1–6:10)

A. *Concerning various age-groups (5:1-2)*

From the above instructions about how Timothy was to conduct his personal life and ministry, Paul turned to advice on how to relate effectively to individuals who make up various groups in the church. Paul's overall advice about how to treat various age-groups was that Timothy handle different people as he would corresponding members of his own family.

5:1-2. Older man translates *presbyteros*, the plural of which is rendered "elders" in 4:14. Here, however, Paul was not referring to those who hold the office of overseer. The word denotes "elderly" men, in contrast with **younger men** (cf. Titus 2:2-3 where the same word is used to contrast "older men" and "older women"). Timothy was to appeal to the older men as he would his own **father**—not with rough rebukes but with gentle exhortations. Young men may be treated somewhat more directly, yet with fraternity as if they were Timothy's own **brothers. Older women** were to receive all the respect Timothy would accord his own mother Eunice (2 Tim. 1:5). **Younger women** were likewise to be treated respectfully, **with** the **absolute purity** (*hagneia*; cf. 1 Tim. 4:12) Timothy would grant his own sister. This would safeguard the young minister from reproach.

B. Concerning widows (5:3-16)

Next Paul offered instruction on how Timothy must deal with the widows in the congregation. Throughout the Old and New Testaments widows, along with aliens and orphans, are viewed as special objects of God's mercy. As such they are to be taken under the wing of the congregation (cf. Deut. 10:18; 14:29; 24:17-21; Acts 6:1-7; James 1:27). As early as Acts 6 the church had established a charitable outreach to widows. Now about 30 years later the ministry to widows, of whom there were no doubt many, showed signs of being a major burden to the congregation. Paul was therefore eager in this passage to identify those who did not truly need help in order to leave enough for those who did.

5:3-4. Timothy was instructed to **give proper recognition to** (lit., "honor") those who were truly widows—that is, **widows who** were **really in need.** These Paul contrasted with widows who had lost their husbands but who had **children or grandchildren** still living. Since in God's economy the first responsibility for caring for the needy falls on the **family** (not the church and surely not the state), **these** family members **should learn first of all to put their religion into practice by**

caring for their own. In so doing, these family members would repay their "forebears" (*progonois;* cf. 2 Tim. 1:3) part of the debt owed them. Such reciprocity **is pleasing to God.** It is "welfare" as God intended it.

5:5. The widow who is really in need and left all alone has nowhere to look for help but to God and His people. Thus one of the marks of a needy widow is that she **puts her hope in God and** therefore **continues** in petition and prayer **night and day.** Such a godly person, dedicated after the death of her husband to the service of the Lord, was deeply respected (cf. the description of the widow-prophetess Anna, Luke 2:37), and was viewed as worthy of the church's support.

5:6. Not all women who became widows gave themselves to such godly service, of course. Some widows used their widowhood to seek after sensual pleasure (**lives for pleasure**); *spatalō,* (used elsewhere in the NT only in James 5:5). Some commentators suggest even the hint of prostitution here. In any case Paul stated that a life devoted to wanton pleasure, in stark contrast to the godly life described in 1 Timothy 5:5, produces a woman who **is dead even while she lives** (cf. Rom. 8:6; Rev. 3:1). One need only witness the spiritual emptiness produced within those who choose such a profligate lifestyle to understand Paul's point. Such women must not be placed on the widows' list.

5:7-8. In 4:11 Paul instructed Timothy to "command . . . these things" (*parangelle tauta*). Now, having added the intervening instructions, Paul repeated the exact words: "Command these things too." Paul wanted Timothy to pass along **these instructions** about the list of widows in order **that no one may be open to blame.** The reference is somewhat ambiguous, but probably refers to the widows in the church. If the wrong women are included on the list their sensual lifestyles (cf. 5:6) will bring reproach on the entire group. But it may also refer to the remaining families of the widows. Failure to **provide** (*pronoei* means "to think ahead, to provide by seeing needs in advance") **for** these family members gives the lie to any claim to know God (cf. Titus 1:16) and becomes de facto a denial of **the faith.** Indeed, such a failure renders the defaulting family member **worse than an unbeliever,** since even many non-Christians understand and fulfill their familial responsibilities.

5:9-10. The "proper recognition" of verse 3 is here made specific. Widows **may be put on the list** if they meet three primary qualifications. What exactly this list involved is not known. It may have been an official order for service in the congregation; more likely it was merely a roll of those **widows** who were to receive assistance from the congregation. In any case, to qualify a woman had to meet these qualifications: (1) She must be **over 60.** Though the age of 60 was more advanced in that day, Paul had his reasons for keeping the younger widows off the rolls (cf. vv. 11-15). (2) She must have **been faithful to her husband.** The Greek here is literally "a one-man woman," the mirror image of the stipulation for both the overseer-elder (cf. 3:2; Titus 1:6) and the deacon (1 Tim. 3:12), and for the same reason (cf. comments on 3:2). The NIV, to be consistent with its renderings of 3:2, 12 and Titus 1:6, should have adopted its footnote reading, "has had but one husband." The translation, "has been faithful to her husband," points to the view that the words merely prohibit promiscuity. (3) **She must be well-known for her good deeds.** As illustrations of the kinds of things he had in mind, Paul cited five examples, which characterize godly women (cf. 1 Tim. 2:10). The examples span the realms of home, church, and community, and include child-raising, **hospitality, washing** saints' **feet** (humble service; cf. comments on John 13:1-15) **helping people in trouble,** and various other **kinds of good deeds.** The women on the widows' roll must be those whose reputations for godly living are well known.

5:11-12. **Younger widows,** on the other hand, were **not** to be **put** on the list. Paul's reasoning for this was twofold: First, unlike the older women whose active sexual lives would presumably be behind them, the younger women might be faced with normal sexual **desires** which would **overcome their dedication to Christ.** As a result they would **want to** remarry, bringing **judgment on themselves, because they** had **broken their**

first pledge. The pledge Paul referred to was probably a more or less formal commitment, taken on joining the list of widows, wherein the woman vowed to serve Christ entirely without thought of remarriage. In this way she could devote herself without distraction to the Lord (cf. 1 Cor. 7:34-35). Remarriage would involve breaking this vow and a broken vow would incur judgment (cf. Num. 30:2; Deut. 23:21; Ecc. 5:4-5).

5:13-15. Second, younger and more energetic widows would have a more difficult time resisting the temptations connected with idleness. With the congregation supporting them, their time normally given to maintaining a living would be free. Instead of giving this time to the service of Christ in visitation and counseling, **younger widows** would be more susceptible to **going about from house to house** and becoming **idlers . . . gossips** (*phlyaroi,* used only here in the NT; the verb *phlyareō* is used in 3 John 10) **and busybodies, saying things they ought not to.** Too much time with not enough to do is dangerous for anyone except those too old to get into trouble. Hence Paul's **counsel** was that younger widows should not take the vow and be added to the list; instead they should marry, raise a family, **manage their homes,** and by being thus occupied **give the enemy no opportunity for slander.**

The "enemy" here may refer to the church's adversaries who looked for every chance to tear others down (cf. 1 Cor. 16:9), or to the opposition of the devil himself (cf. 1 Tim. 5:15). Perhaps Paul did not see much difference between the two (cf. 4:1). The importance of Paul's counsel was buttressed by the fact that it came too late to preserve the congregation from some who had **in fact already turned away to follow Satan.** No doubt Paul was aware of specific cases in the churches where younger women had been placed on the list and then had broken their vows.

5:16. Paul wanted to be certain that the instructions of verse 8 were understood to include well-situated women as well as men. The men would be the obvious objects of Paul's directions in verse 8, but not necessarily the women. So, as a closing note to his discussion of **widows,** Paul specified that any believing **woman** who possessed the means bore the same responsibilities for widows in her family as would a man in similar circumstances. This would relieve the congregation of the responsibility so that the church could help those widows who were really in need.

C. Concerning elders (5:17-25)

5:17. The elders (presbyteroi) refer here, not merely to elderly men (cf. v. 1), but to those who occupy official positions of leadership in the church (cf. 3:1-7; Titus 1:5-9; Acts 20:17-38). The task of the elders is to direct the affairs of the church. Elders have the oversight of the affairs of the congregation, with the deacons providing their helpful support wherever appropriate. For their oversight all elders received a stipend; but those who excelled in this ministry of leadership were to be considered worthy of double honor, or twice the remuneration as the rest. Especially was this true of those who labored in preaching and teaching. While the leadership needs of a congregation extend far beyond the preaching and teaching of the truth, these are at the core of the ministry and are perhaps most important, which should be reflected by the double value given them by the congregation.

5:18. To support his point—that elders should be paid, and certain ones paid double—Paul quoted two Scripture passages: (1) Do not muzzle the ox while it is treading out the grain (Deut. 25:4; cf. also 1 Cor. 9:9). (2) The worker deserves his wages probably refers to passages such as Leviticus 19:13 and Deuteronomy 24:15, or perhaps to the teaching of the Lord Jesus Himself (cf. Matt. 10:10; Luke 10:7). Though Paul reserved the right not to receive support from a congregation (cf. 1 Cor. 9:15-23; 1 Thes. 2:9), he clearly believed and repeatedly taught that a congregation did not have the right not to offer it (cf. Gal. 6:6; 1 Cor. 9:14).

5:19-20. Paul was deeply aware of opposition to the ministry. He had already spoken of the need to guard the congregation from the reproach of slanderers (cf. 3:2, 7), and would do so again (6:1). Here he stipulated the procedure for separating valid accusations from false ones. It is the venerable approach of both the Old Testament (cf. Deut. 19:15) and the New (cf. Matt. 18:16; John 8:17; 2 Cor. 13:1), wherein an accusation should be considered only if two or three witnesses swear to it. When such accusations would then prove to be true, Timothy was to rebuke the offenders publicly, that is, before the entire congregation. In this way the remaining members could take warning (lit., "have fear"). Fear of the discipline of God, in this case administered through the congregation, is a healthy thing in a Christian, especially for those in places of leadership. Modern congregations that ignore church discipline do so at the peril of both the offender and themselves.

5:21. Why Paul punctuated his instructions with this strong charge can only be guessed. Had Timothy passively avoided unpleasant confrontations, or had he taken a strong stand in some cases but not others? For whatever reasons, Paul strongly adjured the young minister to follow through on (keep is lit., "guard") these instructions without partiality (lit., "prejudging," used only here in the NT) or favoritism (prosklisin, lit., "inclination toward someone," used only here in the NT). The strength of Paul's charge is underlined by his invocation of the authority of God and Christ Jesus (cf. 2 Tim. 4:1), and the elect angels, all of whom are associated with righteous judgment (cf. Matt. 25:31; Mark 8:38; Luke 9:26; Rev. 14:10).

5:22. One way to avoid painful situations involving the disciplining of an elder is to be careful about who is ordained in the first place. Thus Paul counseled Timothy to a judicious reluctance in the laying on of hands (cf. 4:14; 2 Tim. 1:6). The words do not share in the sins of others may be merely advice for Timothy to guard his own conduct generally (cf. 1 Tim. 4:16; Acts 20:28). But more likely, in light of the context, this is a warning about the implications of hasty ordinations. Those who take part in the premature ordination of an errant elder share some of the blame for the negative consequences to their church. Whichever is the case, Timothy was to keep himself free from sin. One cannot deal with sin in another if one's own life is not pure (hagnon).

5:23. This verse may be only a somewhat disjointed bit of personal advice to Timothy or it may flow more naturally from the reference to purity in verse 22. Perhaps Timothy was inclined to an asceticism which associated purity with total abstention (cf. 4:3-5), which in turn led in Timothy's case to **stomach ailments** and **frequent illnesses,** perhaps due to the poor quality of the **water** he drank. Paul thus qualified his exhortation to purity by encouraging Timothy to drink **a little wine** (*oinō oligō*) for his stomach's sake, because of his "frequent illnesses." This instruction applies only to using wine for medicinal purposes, of course, and therefore contributes little or nothing to either side of the debate over the use of wine as a beverage.

5:24-25. The meaning of these two verses, though at first glance obscure, proves on closer examination to be profound. Verse 23 is a parenthesis. Thus verse 24 picks up the advice of verse 22 and carries the thought forward. All people are heading toward **judgment,** carrying with them either their **sins** or their **good** works. For some, their **sins** or good works go before **them** and **are obvious** to all observers. For others their sins or good works **trail behind,** hidden from view, becoming known only after the individual has passed. Thus Paul emphasized the difficulties inherent in choosing qualified candidates for the ordination. Hasty, superficial assessments, whether positive or negative, are sometimes inaccurate, leading to the enlistment of unqualified men or the overlooking of those whose fine qualities are less obvious. With time, however, a man's true colors will emerge to an astute observer. Thus the perceptive observations of verses 24-25 are designed to underline the warning of verse 22: do not rush to ordain someone.

D. Concerning slaves and masters (6:1-2)

6:1. Under normal circumstances slaves and masters had no associations outside the institution **of slavery.** With the advent of the gospel, however, these two groups found themselves thrown together in the congregation in new ways, creating problems the apostles were forced to address repeatedly (cf. 1 Cor. 7:20-24; Gal. 3:28; Eph. 6:5-9; Col. 3:22-25; Phile.; 1 Peter 2:13-25). Paul's instructions here correspond entirely with what is taught elsewhere in the New Testament on the subject, with one major exception: in this passage he addresses

only slaves. Usually his exhortations to submit to authority were immediately buttressed by warning **masters** against abusing their authority (cf. Eph. 6:5-9; Col. 3:22-4:1).

The matter of the uses and abuses of authority is first and foremost a problem of attitude. Thus Paul wrote repeatedly of how slaves and masters should see themselves and one another. Here he wrote that slaves are to view their masters as **worthy of full respect** (*timēs,* "honor"). The same word is used of God in 1 Timothy 1:17 and 6:16, and of elders in 5:17. Such honor or respect should be granted lest **God's** reputation and the Christian faith (*hē didaskalia,* "the teaching"; cf. 1:10; 4:1, 6, 13, 16; 5:17) **be slandered** (lit., "be blasphemed"). Social goals should always be subordinate to spiritual values.

6:2. Paul's thought here is totally foreign to the world, and can be fully appreciated only by those who view their lives through the eyes of Jesus Christ (cf. Mark 10:42-45). Christian slaves whose **masters** are also believers should redouble rather than reduce their service. This should stem purely from the realization that the one who is receiving the benefits is a beloved brother or sister in Christ. The attitude undergirding this instruction is complete nonsense to anyone who does not understand the Lord Jesus, but it is the genius of Christlikeness and the ultimate source of all meaning and joy in life to those who have eyes to see (cf. John 13:4-17; 15:9-14). Thus Timothy was commanded once again to **teach and urge . . . these things** on the congregation (cf. 1 Tim. 4:6, 11; 5:7).

E. Concerning the heretical and greedy (6:3-10)

6:3. The last group Paul discussed are those with whom he began (cf. 1:3-11): false teachers. Here, like a physician diagnosing a sick patient, Paul described the characteristics of their disease. The objects of Paul's attention show three overlapping symptoms: (1) those who teach **false doctrines** (lit., "anyone who teaches differently"; 1:3 has the same word); (2) those who do **not agree to the sound instruction of our Lord Jesus Christ;** with the word "sound" Paul reintroduced a medical analogy (cf. also 2 Tim. 2:17); he spoke of, literally, the "healthy words or sayings" (*hygiainousin logois*) of Christ; (3) those who do not consent **to godly teaching** (lit., "the teaching which corresponds to godliness," *tē kat' eusebian didaskalia*). The correspondence between truth and godliness, and error and moral deficiency, is one of the recurrent themes in the Pastoral Epistles.

6:4-5. Doctrinal error is seldom merely a case of being innocently mistaken. There is almost always some degree of culpability. The false teachers in Ephesus were **conceited** (lit., "puffed up"), with inflated egos (cf. 1:7). Such a one **understands nothing.** Picking up the medical analogy again, Paul described them as "diseased with" (*nosōn peri*) **controversies** (*zētēseis*, "debates," perhaps on theological problems; cf. 2 Tim. 2:23; Titus 3:9) **and arguments** (*logomachias*, "battles of words"), out of which come only **envy, quarreling, malicious talk, evil suspicions, and constant friction.** This contrasts strikingly with the *telos* or "end" of Paul's instruction (1 Tim 1:5; cf. also the similar contrast in Gal. 5:16-24). Such evil fruits seem the inevitable external products of false teachers once one understands their true inner motives (Matt. 7:13-23). They are **men:** (1) whose minds have been corrupted (cf. 2 Tim. 3:8); (2) **who have been robbed of the truth** by Satan (cf. Luke 8:5, 12, and the culpability of being "hard ground" rather than "good ground"); (3) **who think that godliness is a means to financial gain.** Greed was their core motivation (cf. Titus 1:11; Jude 12). In that day the stipends associated with ministry were attractive, so that even the best men had to be warned against letting personal gain creep into their motivation (cf. 1 Peter 5:2). Congregational leaders were to be chosen from those known for their "freedom from the love of money" (cf. 1 Tim. 3:3, 8; Titus 1:7). By contrast the moral corruption so often associated with false teaching (cf. Jude 4-16 for the most graphic description in the NT) produced just the opposite.

6:6. Picking up on the words "godliness" and "gain," Paul shifted their meaning in a characteristically Pauline fashion (cf. 1 Cor. 2:5-6 for a similar shift) from the erroneous to the truthful. **Godliness** does not *give* financial gain (1 Tim. 6:5); it itself *is* gain when

accompanied with **contentment.** *Autarkeias* literally means "self-sufficiency." Yet the sufficiency of oneself is due to the sufficiency of God (cf. 2 Cor. 9:8; Phil. 4:11, 13 for other uses of the same word). Godliness combined with that inner God-given sufficiency which does not depend on material circumstances (the opposite of the false teachers' greed) is indeed of great gain.

6:7-8. Paul supported his point with a common Jewish and Christian idea (cf. Job 1:21; Ecc. 5:15; Luke 12:16-21) about the complete transiency of material things. They should freely be used and enjoyed to the glory of God if one has them (cf. 1 Tim. 4:3-4; 6:17), but in no way do they contribute to godliness. Christians do have basic material needs for **food and clothing,** of course, like everyone else; but when these are met a godly Christian can be satisfied (cf. Heb. 13:5-6). Paul knew whereof he spoke (Phil. 4:10-13).

6:9-10. Paul contrasted the proper attitude of contentment with its opposites: The craving **to get rich** and **the love of money,** two sides of the same coin. The history of the human race, and perhaps especially that of modern Western societies, cries out in support of Paul's point. The grasping after riches leads to: (1) **temptation,** (2) **a trap,** and (3) **many foolish and harmful desires that plunge men into ruin and destruction.** Though not an end in itself, greed **is** actually **a root of all kinds of evil.** It is a crucial chink through which other vices gain access. To illustrate his point Paul referred indirectly to **some people,** undoubtedly known to Timothy, who had fallen into the trap Paul was discussing. **Eager for money,** they **wandered from the faith.** This may mean that they had fallen into heretical teaching (cf. 2 Tim. 2:17-18) or simply that their spiritual fruitfulness had been choked off (cf. Luke 8:14) by their concern for riches. In either case, they had suffered for it, causing themselves to be **pierced . . . with many griefs** (lit., "pains").

VI. Final Charge to Timothy (6:11-21)

A. Exhortation to godliness (6:11-16)

6:11. Paul began this concluding section of the epistle by turning directly to Timothy. The words **but you** are an emphatic contrast with "some people" of verse 10, who chase after riches. Timothy, as a **man of God,** was to do the opposite—to **flee from all this,** but chase instead after personal virtues that are of eternal value: **righteousness, godliness** (*eusebeian;* cf. 2:2; 3:16; 4:7-8; 6:3, 5-6; 2 Tim. 3:5; Titus 1:1), **faith, love, endurance** (*hypomonēn,* "steadfastness under adversity"), **and gentleness.** This list may be compared to both the fruit of the Spirit (Gal. 5:22-23) and the qualifications of elders (1 Tim. 3:1-3).

6:12. Fight the good fight is the language of athletic contests. In 1:18 the same English words translate Greek words that refer to a military conflict. Timothy was to give his best effort to this most worthwhile of struggles, the struggle to further **the faith.** This would involve the complete appropriation (cf. "take hold" in v. 19) at all times of the fact that he possessed eternal life. (Paul's words, **Take hold of . . . eternal life** in no way suggest that Timothy could gain eternal life by his own efforts.) To Paul, Christ's life is the possession of each Christian, not only throughout eternity, but now (cf. 2 Cor. 4:10-12). It is this new life in Christ (2 Cor. 5:17) to which every Christian is **called** and which Christians confess by baptism (Rom. 6:4) and by word (Rom. 10:9-10). Timothy's **good confession in the presence of many witnesses** could refer to his ordination but more likely speaks of his baptism.

6:13. Repeatedly in this letter Paul directly addressed Timothy with personal charges, the second strongest of which is found in 5:21. But here is Paul's strongest, most solemn charge of all (**I charge you,** *parangellō;* cf. 1:3; 4:11; 5:7; 6:14) conjuring up images of perhaps a familiar baptismal formula triggered by the reference in verse 12. **While testifying before Pontius Pilate** is translated by some, "who testified in the time of Pontius Pilate." If translated this way, the qualifying clause is designed to fix the Crucifixion in time, as in the Apostles' Creed. Both translations are possible.

6:14. The content of Paul's charge is that Timothy **keep this commandment without spot or blame.** The "commandment" is probably broader than any single law. It refers to the entire body of sound teaching Paul had been describing throughout the letter. Timothy, by his

own godly life and by his faithful ministry, was to preserve this body of truth from stain or reproach **until the appearing** (cf. 2 Tim. 1:10; 4:1, 8; Titus 2:13) **of our Lord Jesus Christ.** Then and only then will the struggle (1 Tim. 6:12) be over.

6:15-16. Early in his ministry Paul was convinced that Christ would return soon. Now near the end of his ministry he showed both an awareness that Christ might not return before he died and a desire to encourage Timothy to leave the timing of this great event up to the Lord. Hence Paul stressed that **God will bring about** Christ's appearing **in His** (or "its") **own time.** The section ends with an inspiring doxology to the **God** who is the cause and object of it all: the ultimate **Ruler** of the universe, **the King of kings and Lord of lords** (cf. Rev. 17:14; 19:16), the only eternal One, who dwells where no man can survive or approach or even see (cf. John 1:18). Such a Lord deserves an awesome reverence combined with complete humility (cf. Job 42:1-6). **To Him be honor and might forever. Amen** (cf. 1 Tim. 1:17).

B. Instructions for the rich (6:17-19)

6:17. Paul had dealt with those who did not possess wealth, but who deeply desired it (vv. 3-10). Now he addressed those who had it, and instructed them as to what their attitude should be toward it. They are **not to be arrogant** as if their wealth is deserved (1 Cor. 4:7-8; 1 Sam. 2:7). Nor must they **put their hope in wealth, which is so uncertain** and transient. This is perhaps the greatest temptation to wealthy Christians, into which category most modern Western believers fit. Christians should **put their hope in God,** who is the Source of material things. Again material possessions are among those things God has given **for our enjoyment.**

6:18-19. Yet Christians must not merely consume material possessions selfishly. Possessions are to be shared with those who have less. Thus Timothy was to charge the well-off **to do good, to be rich,** not ultimately in money, but **in good deeds.** The wealthy should make every effort **to be generous and willing to share** what they have. If they do this **they will lay up treasure for themselves** in heaven. This undoubtedly refers to the sayings of Jesus (cf. Matt. 6:19-21; Luke 12:33-34; 18:22) wherein the transient is exchanged for the eternal. Such eternal treasure becomes **a firm foundation for** the future, recalling in a mixed metaphor perhaps another of the Lord's teachings (cf. Matt. 7:24-27; Luke 6:47-49). Wealthy Christians should invest their riches for eternity. "He is no fool who gives what he cannot keep to gain what he cannot lose" (Jim Elliot). Paradoxically it is in this giving away of the possessions which the world considers the key to the good life that a Christian **may take hold of** (cf. 1 Tim. 6:12) **the life that is truly life.** The alluring but vain and plastic substitutes for life, supplied by an unhealthy attachment to material things, pale into worthlessness when compared with that life which is found in Jesus Christ (cf. Matt. 16:24-26), who is Himself the Life (John 14:6) and whom to know is life everlasting (John 17:3).

C. Exhortations to remain faithful (6:20-21)

6:20-21. One final time Paul exhorted **Timothy** to **guard** (cf. *phylaxon,* "keep," in 5:21) the "deposit" or "trust" Paul had passed on to him (*parathēkēn,* used elsewhere only in 2 Tim. 1:12, 14), a reference to the body of Christian truth which in some way was under attack in Ephesus. Paul was concerned that Timothy give himself wholly to the truth and reject even the subtle inroads of error. Thus Timothy must **turn away from godless chatter** (lit., "profane empty utterances"; cf. 2 Tim. 2:16), and from **opposing ideas** (*antitheseis,* "counterassertions"*) of what is falsely called knowledge.** Such knowledge was the supposed key to the mystery religions which were already aborning and which would mature into a full-fledged Gnosticism during the next century. Their influence was already being felt in Ephesus, so much so that Paul could say that some had gotten so caught up in professing their esoteric *gnōsis* that they **wandered from the faith** (lit., "concerning the faith missed the aim"; cf. 1 Tim. 1:6; 2 Tim. 2:18). This does not suggest that true believers lose their salvation but that some believers turn to false doctrines, from the content of their faith. With these exhortations Paul seemed to

have come full circle, back to his concerns in 1 Timothy 1:3-6.

Paul closed his letter with the simple benediction, **Grace be with you.** "You" is in the plural, however, no doubt indicating Paul's awareness that this letter would be read widely in the churches (cf. Col. 4:18; 2 Tim. 4:22; Titus 3:15).

BIBLIOGRAPHY

Barrett, C.K. *The Pastoral Epistles.* Oxford: Clarendon Press, 1963.

Blaiklock, E.M. *The Pastoral Epistles.* Grand Rapids: Zondervan Publishing House, 1972.

Dibelius, Martin, and Conzelmann, Hans. *The Pastoral Epistles.* Translated by Philip Buttolph and Adela Yarbro. Edited by Helmut Koester. Philadelphia: Fortress Press, 1972.

Getz, Gene A. *A Profile for a Christian Life Style: A Study of Titus.* Grand Rapids: Zondervan Publishing House, 1978.

Guthrie, Donald. *The Pastoral Epistles.* Grand Rapids: Wm. B. Eerdmans Publishing Co., 1957.

Hendriksen, William. *Exposition of the Pastoral Epistles.* New Testament Commentary. Grand Rapids: Baker Book House, 1957.

Hiebert, D. Edmond. *First Timothy.* Chicago: Moody Press, 1967.

————. *Titus and Philemon.* Chicago: Moody Press, 1957.

Jensen, Irving L. *1 and 2 Timothy and Titus: A Self-Study Guide.* Chicago: Moody Press, 1973.

Kelly, J.N.D. *A Commentary on the Pastoral Epistles.* London: Adam and Charles Black, 1963. Reprint. Grand Rapids: Baker Book House, 1981.

Kent, Homer A. *The Pastoral Epistles.* Chicago: Moody Press, 1958.

Knight, George W. *The Faithful Sayings in the Pastoral Epistles.* Grand Rapids: Baker Book House, 1979.

Lock, Walter. *A Critical and Exegetical Commentary on the Pastoral Epistles.* The International Critical Commentary. Edinburgh: T. & T. Clark, 1924.

Stott, John R.W. *Guard the Gospel: The Message of 2 Timothy.* Downers Grove, Ill.: InterVarsity Press, 1973.

Wiersbe, Warren W. *Be Faithful.* Wheaton, Ill.: Scripture Press Publications, Victor Books, 1981.

2 TIMOTHY

A. Duane Litfin

INTRODUCTION

Paul was a prisoner in a Roman dungeon when he wrote this, the last of his epistles, to Timothy (cf. 2 Tim. 1:8, 16; 4:6-13). The date, as best it can be established, was approximately A.D. 67. Not long afterward, according to tradition, the apostle was beheaded. (For a more detailed discussion of the authorship and dating of the Pastoral Epistles see the *Introduction* to 1 Tim.)

The purpose of 2 Timothy was to encourage Timothy in his ministry at Ephesus. The primary theme of the letter is the need for faithfulness in the face of hardship.

OUTLINE

COMMENTARY

I. Salutation (1:1-2)

1:1-2. In his typical fashion **Paul** began this letter identifying himself as **an apostle of Christ Jesus,** a reminder Timothy hardly needed. No doubt this is another indication that Paul knew he was writing first to Timothy but ultimately to a much wider audience. In his first letter to the young pastor Paul said his apostleship was "by the command of God" (1 Tim. 1:1). Here Paul said it was **by the will of God.** The two are essentially synonymous. The words **according to the promise of life that is in Christ Jesus** are intentionally vague. They relate to Paul's apostleship (not the will of God), but did they refer to a promise of life Paul personally received, or to a promise he was to proclaim to others? In other words was his apostleship "because of" the promise or "in conformity to" the promise? The Greek word *kata* (here ambiguously trans. "according to") allows the two to merge. The promise of life in Christ, the gospel, was the reason for and the yardstick of Paul's apostleship (cf. Titus 1:2-3). **To Timothy, my dear son** (lit., "child") once again (cf. "my true son" in 1 Tim. 1:2) emphasizes the close fatherly relationship Paul maintained with his protégé, if not his convert. The remainder of the greeting duplicates 1 Timothy exactly (cf. 1 Tim. 1:2). (See the chart, "Paul's Introductions to His Epistles" at Rom. 1:1-7.)

II. Call to Faithfulness (1:3-18)

A. Thanksgiving for Timothy (1:3-7)

1:3. In 1 Timothy Paul expressed thanks for his own salvation and ministry (1 Tim 1:12); here he began by expressing thanks for Timothy's salvation and ministry. In passing, Paul referred to his own upbringing, just before he turned to Timothy's (2 Tim. 1:5). The apostle viewed his own faith in Christ, not as a break with his Jewish forefathers, but in continuity with their faith. (Cf. **a clear conscience** with 1 Tim. 1:5, "a good conscience.") As Paul prayed for Timothy **night and day,** his gratitude for Timothy kept welling up anew. Sitting chained in a Roman prison there was little else Paul could do but pray; and Timothy, perhaps Paul's closest companion, ministering to the church that Paul probably knew best, was no doubt the single most common object of his petitions.

1:4. Paul remembered Timothy's **tears** on their last parting, possibly at Paul's second Roman arrest. In this letter he would ask Timothy to join him in Rome (cf. 4:9, 21). Paul had longed for Timothy's companionship which was such a **joy** to him. Even the great apostle at times became lonely, discouraged, and in need of support from fellow Christians.

1:5. So many, it seems, had opposed or deserted Paul (cf. 1:15; 2:17; 3:1-9, 13; 4:3-4, 10-21) that Timothy's **sincere** (*anypokritou,* "unhypocritical"; cf. 1 Tim. 1:5) **faith** stood out in bold relief. Paul attributed Timothy's faith to the influence of his Jewish **mother Eunice** and **grandmother Lois,** both of whom were believers (cf. Acts 16:1). Timothy's father was a Gentile and probably an unbeliever; hence no mention of him is made here. According to this verse, Paul seems to attribute Timothy's conversion to his mother and grandmother (cf. 2 Tim. 3:15). References to Timothy as Paul's son in the faith (cf. 1:2; 2:1; 1 Tim. 1:2) could therefore probably be understood to mean a mentor-protégé relationship.

1:6. Because Paul was persuaded that Timothy possessed true faith (v. 5), something he often refused to take for granted in others (e.g., 1 Thes. 3:5), he urged the young minister **to fan into flame** (or perhaps, "keep at full flame")

his God-given ability for ministry. God's gifts must be used if they are to reach and maintain their full potential. In Timothy's case, Paul wrote (1 Tim. 4:14) that his **gift** (*charisma*) had come "through" (*dia*) a prophetic message, "with" (*meta*) the laying on of the elder board's hands. Here Paul stated that the gift came "through" (*dia*) **the laying on of** his own **hands.** The language is highly imprecise and may reflect nothing more in the apostle's thinking than a general association between Timothy's ordination (which involved both a prophetic message and the laying on of hands by Paul and the elders) and the young man's awareness of his own abilities. Surely the language does not bear the weight of any detailed conclusions about how spiritual gifts are bestowed, much less full-blown theories of apostolic succession or of ordination as a means of grace.

1:7. Why Timothy needed this reminder of his ordination, and the confidence in his own gifts he developed as a result of it, is not clear. In 1 Timothy the reference to Timothy's ordination is associated with problems stemming from his youthfulness (cf. 1 Tim. 4:12). Perhaps he had become somewhat intimidated by the opposition to both Paul and the gospel, even in some ways threatened, defensive, and ashamed (cf. 2 Tim. 1:8) at having to defend a prisoner (cf. 2:9) and the "foolishness" which they both preached about a despised and crucified Jesus (cf. 1 Cor. 1:18–2:5). But such **timidity** (*deilias,* lit., "cowardice," used only here in the NT) has no place in God's service. Instead **God** gives **a spirit of power** (cf. 1 Cor. 2:4), **of love** (cf. 1 Tim. 1:5), **and of self-discipline** (cf. 1 Tim. 4:7). These three virtues, each supplied by the Holy Spirit, should characterize Timothy.

B. Call to courage (1:8-12)

1:8. If Timothy's ministry were marked by power, love, and self-discipline, he would be able to stand tall against his opponents, and would **not be ashamed to testify about our Lord** (cf. 1 Cor. 1:6), **or ashamed of** Paul **His prisoner.** Though Paul was held in a Roman prison (cf. 2 Tim. 1:16; 2:9), yet he called himself Christ's prisoner—that is, a prisoner for Christ's sake and purpose (cf. Eph. 3:1; Phil. 1:12-14; Phile. 1, 9). With this reminder of his own condition, which was far graver than Timothy's, Paul exhorted Timothy to join courageously with him in suffering for the gospel (cf. 2 Tim. 2:3), for it is just in such circumstances that the power of God is made manifest (cf. 2 Cor. 12:9-10).

1:9-10. Having mentioned the gospel, Paul spelled out some of its most important details. God **saved us and called us to a holy life.** This is an accomplished fact, not something yet to come. Timothy could therefore count on God's power in his daily ministry. Moreover, this salvation had nothing to do with a believer's merits **but** was purely **because of His own purpose** (*prothesin*; cf. Rom. 8:28; 9:11; Eph. 1:11; 3:11) **and grace** (cf. 1 Tim. 1:14). This is the very core of the gospel (cf. Eph. 2:8-10). **Before the beginning of time** Christians were granted this unmerited favor, but were only made aware of it **through the appearing** (*epiphaneias*; 2 Thes. 2:8; 1 Tim. 6:14; 2 Tim. 4:1, 8; Titus 2:13) **of our Savior, Christ Jesus.** Here and in Titus 1:4; 2:13; and 3:6 *Christ* is called Savior; in 1 Timothy 1:1; 2:3; 4:10; Titus 2:10; and 3:4 *God* is titled Savior (cf. 2 Peter 1:1 with 3:18). Clearly both are in different senses true. Christ the Son embodied God the Father's saving purpose and plan, by which **death,** the product of sin (cf. Gen. 2:17; Rom. 5:12; 6:23), would be **destroyed** (1 Cor. 15:26), and **life and immortality** (lit., "incorruptibility"; cf. 1 Peter 1:4) would be brought into view.

1:11-12. Little wonder that Paul called this **gospel** "glorious" (1 Tim. 1:11). It is the most important message ever told. Paul had been **appointed** to serve as **a herald and an apostle and a teacher** of this message (cf. 1 Tim. 2:7), three roles which merely reflect different facets of the stewardship entrusted to him (1 Tim. 1:11). Carrying out his stewardship had brought Paul much **suffering,** including his present imprisonment. In the eyes of the world he was a common criminal (cf. 2 Tim. 2:9). Yet he was able to say, **I am not ashamed.** He was trusting his own destiny to the same One who had **entrusted** him with the stewardship of the gospel. Thus, even though he was suffering abuse and humiliation, he was confident of God's complete vindication in the end (cf. 1:18; 4:8). Throughout, of course, Paul was using his own example to bolster Timothy's perhaps flagging courage.

C. Call to guard the truth (1:13-14)

1:13. From the example of his life, Paul turned to the example or **pattern** (*hypotypōsin*; cf. 1 Tim. 1:16) of his teaching. Timothy was to view what he had **heard from** Paul as the essential outline or sketch of **sound teaching** (lit., "healthy doctrine"; cf. 1 Tim. 1:10) and was to **keep** or maintain it. Timothy was to hold the truth **with faith and love in Christ Jesus.** To be balanced, a commitment to the truth always requires faith and love, virtues which ultimately come only from being "in Christ" (1 Tim. 1:14).

1:14. Paul used the notion of a "trust" (*parathēkēn*; cf. 1 Tim. 5:21; 6:20) in two ways in the Pastorals. First, he had been given a trust or stewardship from God (cf. 1 Tim. 1:11); second, he had in turn **entrusted** himself and his destiny to God (2 Tim. 1:12). Here Paul spoke of the first of these two. The stewardship of the truth he had received had now been passed along into the hands of Timothy, who was to pass it on yet again to other faithful Christians, who were to pass it on to still others (2:2). While it was in Timothy's possession, however, he was to **guard** (*phylaxon*; cf. 1 Tim. 5:21; 6:20) it **with the help of the Holy Spirit who lives in us.** It was Timothy's responsibility to preserve sound teaching from becoming corrupted through distortion, dilution, deletion, and addition. Heretical teaching was not only a possibility to Paul; it was a constant threat to be guarded against. Moreover, Timothy could count on the assistance of the indwelling Spirit of God (cf. 1 John 3:24; 4:13) who desires to promote the truth about Christ (John 16:13).

D. Examples of unfaithfulness and faithfulness (1:15-18)

1:15. Nothing is known of **Phygelus and Hermogenes** beyond this single reference. It is fair to conjecture that theirs may have been the most unexpected defections among the group represented by **everyone in the province of Asia,** of which Ephesus was the leading city. (See the location of Asia and of Ephesus on the map between Acts and Rom.) Perhaps they were leaders of some sort. Timothy certainly knew their situation well, in any case, and Paul singled them out. It is unnecessary to assume either that (a) that "everyone" means literally every Christian, or (b) that their failure consisted of a total defection from the faith. Verses 16-18 suggest rather that there was a general failure to support the apostle in his personal time of need.

1:16-18. From these sad examples of unfaithfulness, Paul turned to the sparkling instance **of Onesiphorus** (mentioned elsewhere only in 4:19), who had supported Paul not only **in Ephesus** but also **in Rome.** Repeatedly he had gone out of his way to help Paul, even to the point of following him to Rome and painstakingly seeking out his whereabouts. There, despite Paul's imprisonment and the stigma attached to it, Onesiphorus remained unfazed, continuing his faithful ministry without hesitation. For all of this Paul commended him, twice invoking God's **mercy** (1:16, 18) on both the faithful servant and his **household.**

The contrast between the faithful and the unfaithful, the strong and the weak, the trustworthy and the unreliable, is striking. The many in Asia (v. 15) portray the very things Paul had been warning Timothy against—cowardice, shame, self-indulgence, infidelity. Onesiphorus, on the other hand, demonstrated the characteristics Paul had been recommending to Timothy—courage, love, self-discipline, boldness, and faithfulness. Clearly the negative and the positive examples were designed to strengthen Timothy's resolve to be counted among those who were willing to stand shoulder to shoulder with the apostle.

III. Challenge to Endurance (2:1-13)

A. Enduring hardship for Christ (2:1-7)

2:1. After the reminders of Timothy's ordination, his own example, and that of others, Paul addressed Timothy with a direct application: **You then, my son** (teknon, "child," an endearing term), **be strong** (lit. "be empowered"; cf. Eph. 6:10). Yet Timothy's strength was not his own; it was a divine "gift" (**grace,** charis) found only **in Christ** (Phil. 4:13).

2:2. Traveling with Paul, Timothy had **heard** the apostle address scores of diverse audiences. Among all those groups the essence of Paul's message had not changed. It was the same body of truth Paul had taught Timothy personally. Now, with the apostle nearing the end of his own ministry, what Timothy had heard from Paul he was in turn to **entrust** (cf. 1:14) **to reliable men who will also be qualified to teach others** (cf. 1 Tim. 3:2; Titus 1:9). This has come to be called "the ministry of multiplication," and it is God's method for propagating the good news of Jesus Christ.

2:3-4. Such faithfulness to God's truth would inevitably involve Timothy in suffering, even as it had Paul. Thus without varnishing Timothy's prospects the mentor once again called his protégé to share in **hardship** or suffering (cf. 1:8 for the same word used only in these two places: synkakopathēson, "to suffer hardship with someone"; also cf. 4:5) for the sake of Christ (cf. John 15:18-20). Paul introduced three common illustrations to emphasize his point (cf. 1 Cor. 9:7, 24 for the same three): **a . . . soldier,** an athlete, and a farmer (2 Tim. 2:3-6). Military images were common in Paul's thought (cf. 1 Tim. 1:18), no doubt because the word pictures were familiar to his readers (cf. Rom. 6:13 ["instruments" can be trans. "weapons"]; Rom. 7:23; 1 Cor. 9:7; 2 Cor. 6:7; Eph. 6:11-18; Phil. 2:25; Phile. 2). A Roman soldier's single-minded purpose, rigorous discipline, and unquestioning obedience to **his commanding officer** combine to make the figure of a soldier an apt one for a servant of the gospel.

2:5. With a quick change of metaphor Paul switched to **an athlete.** The thought here is similar to 1 Corinthians 9:24-27 (and Heb. 12:1-2). **According to the rules** translates nomimōs (lit., "lawfully"). The metaphor clearly draws on athletic games such as the Olympics, but do "the rules" refer to the regulations governing each event or to those governing the training of those qualified to take part? Competitors in the Olympic games, for example, were required to swear that they had trained diligently for at least 10 months. Though the second is in some ways easier to explain, the first is required by Paul's grammar, which suggests that the issue is not whether one is qualified to compete but, among those competing, who will win the **crown.** Every athletic event has its boundaries, its rules; moreover, all who fail to discipline themselves to observe these rules are disqualified. Paul wanted Timothy to run so as to win the crown (cf. 2 Tim. 4:7-8) and not be disqualified. This requires a Christian to have strong qualities of discipline, self-control, endurance, and a certain toughness.

2:6. The final image is that of a **farmer.** The language puts an emphasis on the word **hardworking,** in contrast with idle, lazy workers. The diligence Paul has just described in each case has its reward (cf. vv. 11-12): A diligent soldier gains the approval of his commanding officer; a diligent athlete wins the victory; a diligent farmer wins **the first . . . share of the crops.** The three illustrations have in common the point that success is achieved through discipline (cf. 1:7), hard work, and single-mindedness.

2:7. Paul appealed to Timothy to **reflect on what I am saying,** confident that with meditation and contemplation **the Lord** would grant the young man the **insight** (*synesin,* lit., "understanding") **into** the wisdom of Paul's instructions (cf. James 1:5).

B. Christ's example of endurance (2:8-10)

2:8. Paul rather abruptly introduced the ultimate example of endurance leading to success: **Jesus Christ** (cf. Heb. 12:2-3). The words **raised from the dead, descended from David** may represent a fragment of some familiar creed or catechetical formula (cf. Rom. 1:3-4). The purpose of the fleeting reference is not to expound, but simply to suggest to Timothy a rich subject for his meditation (2 Tim. 2:7), the place of suffering in the life of God's servant (cf. 1 Peter 2:19-24). The quick reference to Jesus' identity (via His ancestral line) and resurrection represents only a portion of Paul's **gospel,** of course, but a central one. The Gospel writers and the messages of the apostles in Acts address both Christ's lineage and His resurrection in great detail.

2:9-10. Preaching the good news about the crucified but resurrected Son of David was what had landed Paul in a Roman jail. Much of the Book of Acts catalogs Paul's suffering for the cause of Christ (cf. 2 Cor. 11:23-33 for a sum-

mary). With every move as he wrote or dictated this letter, the clinking iron reminded him that he was **chained like a criminal** (*kakourgos,* lit., "evildoer"). But though he was chained, **God's Word is not chained** (Paul equated "my gospel" with "God's Word"; cf. 1 Thes. 2:13; 2 Thes. 3:1). God would continue to use it through Timothy, and those to whom Timothy entrusted it. Paul's apparent shame and impotence should be no cause for alarm, discouragement, or faintheartedness. God's Word accomplishes its purpose of calling out God's people, **the elect, that they too may obtain the salvation that is in Christ Jesus, with eternal glory.** If this process required **suffering** from Paul, so be it. He was willing to **endure** (*hypomenō,* "be steadfast under"; cf. 2 Tim. 2:12) **everything for the sake of** "the chosen ones" (*tous eklektous;* cf. Col. 3:12; Titus 1:1). The contrast with Paul's original, natural sentiments could not be more stark (cf. Acts 22:4; 26:9-11; 1 Tim. 1:13), giving full meaning to the apostle's words in 1 Timothy 1:14. The greatest enemy of the saints became their greatest friend, all as a result of the gracious outpouring of Christ's love into his heart.

C. A faithful saying (2:11-13)

2:11-13. Once more Paul used the trustworthy-saying formula, so common in the Pastorals (cf. 1 Tim. 1:15; 3:1; 4:9; Titus 3:8), to introduce a quotation. The formula serves to place Paul's stamp of approval on the content of the quotation, which may have been part of a baptismal ceremony. The quotation sets forth four couplets, the first two of which are positive: (1) **If we died with Him, we will also live with Him** expresses the idea so powerfully portrayed in the rite of baptism and explained in Romans 6:2-23. The reference is not to martyrdom for Christ, but rather to a believer's mystical identification with the death and life of Christ (cf. Col. 3:3). (2) **If we endure** (*hypomenomen;* cf. 2 Tim. 2:10), **we will also reign with Him** furthers the believer's identification with Christ. In the previous couplet the focus is on the contrast between death and life; here the parallel contrast is between suffering and glorification (Rom. 8:17). Christ endured and will one day reign (1 Cor. 15:25), and those saints who endure will one day reign with Him (Rev. 3:21). The last two couplets are negative: (3) **If we disown Him, He will also disown us** speaks of the possibility of apostasy (cf. 1 Tim. 4:1; Heb. 10:38-39; 2 John 9) and the Lord's ultimate rejection of those who professed Christ only temporarily (cf. Matt. 10:33). Instead of identifying with Christ, the apostate finally dissociates himself with Christ. (4) **If we are faithless, He will remain faithful** speaks not of the apostate, but of a true child of God who nevertheless proves unfaithful (cf. 2 Tim. 1:15). Christ **cannot disown Himself;** therefore He will not deny even unprofitable members of His own body. True children of God cannot become something other than children, even when disobedient and weak. Christ's faithfulness to Christians is not contingent on their faithfulness to Him. The significance of these couplets could hardly have been lost on Timothy.

IV. Marks of a Good Workman (2:14-26)

A. Faithfulness in ministry (2:14-19)

2:14. The instruction of the previous verses was not for Timothy only. Timothy was to **keep reminding** others of **these things.** The verb is a present imperative, which means that this was to be Timothy's regular practice. The bulk of preaching to a knowledgeable audience frequently consists of reminding them of what they already know. In the case of the Christians at Ephesus, they were to be solemnly charged in the presence of God (cf. 1 Tim. 5:21) to avoid **quarreling about words** (cf. 1 Tim. 1:3-4; 4:7; 6:4; 2 Tim. 2:23; Titus 3:9), a tendency in the early church (cf. Acts 18:15). Such wrangling **is of no value,** but worse, actually **ruins those who listen** (cf. 2 Tim. 2:16, 18; 3:6), The destructiveness, but especially the worthlessness, of false teaching is a recurrent note in the Pastorals.

2:15. As for Timothy, he was to **do his best** (lit., "be zealous") to be sure he would meet with God's approval, a "laborer" (*ergatēn*; cf. Matt. 20:1, 8) **who does not need to be ashamed.** Paul had spoken of shame before men (2 Tim. 1:8, 12, 16); far worse is shame before God. Timothy need not fear such shame if he would **correctly** handle **the Word of truth**

(cf. Eph. 1:13; Col. 1:5; James 1:18), which for him included both Old Testament Scripture and what he had heard orally from Paul. The Greek *orthotomounta,* "correctly handling," found only here and in the Septuagint in Proverbs 3:6 and 11:5, means literally "to cut straight," but just what image Paul had in mind here is uncertain. Stone masons, plowers, road builders, tentmakers, and (least likely of all) surgeons have all been suggested, but a firm conclusion remains elusive. What is clear is that the shame of God's disapproval awaits those who mishandle His Word.

2:16-18. Timothy was to **avoid godless chatter** (lit., "shun profane empty utterances"; cf. 1 Tim. 6:20) which only advances ungodliness like **gangrene** (*gangraina*). (Such godless chatter contrasts with "the Word of truth" [2 Tim. 2:15] and "the truth" [v. 18].) The medical image is striking. Participating with those who engage in such profane speculations will only, literally, "give their words a feeding place like gangrene." They must be amputated instead. Two who deserved such treatment were **Philetus** about whom nothing is known, and **Hymenaeus,** whom Paul had already "delivered over to Satan" for chastisement (1 Tim. 1:20). These two had **wandered away from the truth** (lit., "concerning the truth missed the mark"; cf. 1 Tim. 1:6; 6:21) regarding the crucial doctrine of **the resurrection.** Greek philosophers typically viewed the soul as immortal and the body as its temporal prison. The idea of the physical resurrection of the body, both Christ's and the Christians', was therefore foreign and difficult for them to grasp. Hence there was a natural tendency toward heresies which rejected bodily resurrection (1 Cor. 15; Acts 17:32). The heresy of Philetus and Hymenaeus probably involved the idea that resurrection was a purely spiritual affair which occurred at conversion or baptism. But bodily resurrection is the keystone of Christian doctrine, as Paul showed (1 Cor. 15). Without it, the entire edifice of the gospel collapses. Little wonder then that Paul said that these two false teachers **destroy the faith of some** (cf. 1 Tim. 1:19).

2:19. Yet the defection of these two, and their followers, must not shake

Timothy's confidence. **God's solid foundation** (i.e., the church; cf. 1 Cor. 3:10-15; Eph. 2:19-22; 1 Tim. 3:15) **stands firm,** with two inscriptions as a "seal" to indicate the structure's authenticity and integrity (cf. Rom. 4:11; 1 Cor. 9:2). The first is a reference to the rebellion of Korah in which the Lord differentiated between the true and the false (Num. 16:5; cf. Jude 11). The second inscription is possibly a loose reference to Numbers 16:26 or more likely some other Old Testament passage such as Isaiah 52:11. The two inscriptions emphasize respectively both God's sovereign control over the church and every Christian's responsibility to turn away from evil. Thus Timothy did not need to fear for the destiny of God's work, but he was to make every effort to keep himself free from the contamination of the false teachers.

B. A clean instrument (2:20-21)

2:20-21. Paul furthered his point about noncontamination by introducing a new but similar metaphor. The image changes from a building to a household (cf. 1 Tim. 3:5, 15). In a **large** and varied household are all sorts of containers. Some are made **of gold and silver** and others **of wood and clay.** More importantly, **some are for noble purposes and some for ignoble.** Clearly the reference so far is to the faithful and the unfaithful within the church. But Paul then shifted the metaphor slightly to show how one can **be an instrument for noble purposes,** by cleansing **himself from the** ignoble vessels. The metaphor is somewhat mixed (one would usually think of cleansing from corruption, not cleansing from the corrupted vessels), but the apostle's point is clear: Timothy was to have nothing to do with the false teachers. In this way he would be a vessel: (1) "for noble purposes" ("unto honor," *timēn*), (2) **made holy** ("set apart"), (3) **useful** ("serviceable") **to the Master, and** (4) **prepared to do any good work** (cf. 2 Tim. 3:16). What is clean and set apart for special use can easily get contaminated and be rendered unusable through contact with the corrupt. Paul was concerned that Timothy, his choicest disciple, keep himself in a usable condition for the Lord.

C. Faithfulness in conduct (2:22-26)

2:22-23. Timothy was still a young man (cf. 1 Tim. 4:12), and even though he was probably mature beyond his years, he might have still displayed some of the characteristics and passions of the young: impatience, intolerance, love of argument, self-assertion, partiality. Timothy was to **flee the evil desires of youth** (probably Paul did not have sexual passions in mind here, at least not primarily), **and pursue** the opposite virtues: **righteousness, faith, love** (cf. 1 Tim. 6:11 for the same trio), **and peace.** The NIV wrongly places a comma after "peace"—the phrase should read straight through: "peace" **along with those who call on the Lord out of a pure heart** (cf. "pure heart" in 1 Tim. 1:5). While Timothy must oppose the false teachers, he was to be at peace with his brethren who were honest before God. The clear implication is that the false teachers were dishonest before God (cf. 1 Tim. 1:5; 4:2; 6:3-5). Timothy must refuse to get caught up in **foolish and stupid arguments** (*zētēseis,* "debates"; cf. 1 Tim. 6:4; Titus 3:9) which only **produce quarrels.**

2:24-26. False teaching will always be divisive, but **the Lord's servant** should **not be** a fighter but a promoter of unity, by being **kind** ("gentle") **to everyone** (cf. 1 Thes. 2:7), **able** or ready **to teach** (cf. 1 Tim. 3:2) those who are willing to learn, and forbearing in the face of differences (*anexikakon,* lit., "ready to bear evil treatment without resentment"; used only here in the NT). He must treat even his opponents with gentle instruction characterized by "meekness," **in the hope that God will grant them repentance** ("a change of heart and conduct") **leading them to a knowledge** (*epignōsin,* "full knowledge"; cf. Col. 1:9; 2 Tim. 3:7) **of the truth.** The goal is always remedial, never punitive, when dealing with brethren (cf. 2 Thes. 3:6, 15). The purpose must always be to edify Christ's body, not tear it down (cf. 1 Cor. 14:26). Thus when brethren fall into false teaching they must be treated with gentleness and Christian love in the hope **that they will come to their senses and escape from the trap of the devil** (cf. Gal. 5:1; 1 Tim. 3:7; 6:9) **who has taken them captive to do his will.** False teaching and all its negative consequences in the church are always the handiwork of Satan, but God in His grace often salvages the situation through the Christlike ministry of His servants.

V. Predictions of Faithlessness (3:1-9)

3:1-5. As in his previous letter, Paul warned Timothy about the collapse predicted for **the last days** (cf. 1 Tim. 4:1-3), a term which includes the entire period between the first century and Christ's return. During this interim, according to the prediction, the world will see **terrible times** of societal degeneration. Paul gave an extraordinary list (cf. Rom. 1:28-32) of 19 general characteristics believers should expect. **People will be:** (1) **lovers of themselves** (*philautoi*, "self-centered, narcissistic"); (2) **lovers of money** (*philargyroi*; cf. 1 Tim. 6:9-10); (3) **boastful**—the outward manifestation of the fact that inwardly they are (4) **proud** ("arrogant"); (5) **abusive** toward others, which translates *blasphēmoi* ("blasphemers"). Several of the words which follow begin in the Greek with the prefix *a-*, meaning "without" (as in moral-amoral, theist-atheist), signifying absence of the designated virtue. Thus people will be (6) **disobedient** (*apeitheis*) **to their parents;** (7) **ungrateful** (*acharistoi*); (8) **unholy** (*anosioi*); (9) **without love** (*astorgoi*, trans. "heartless" in Rom. 1:31, the only other place it is used in the NT); (10) **unforgiving** (*aspondoi*). *Diaboloi*, a word usually translated "devil" (cf. 1 Tim. 3:6-7; 2 Tim. 2:26), is used here with the root meaning (11) **slanderous;** (12) **without self-control** (*akrateis*); (13) **brutal** (*anēmeroi*, lit., "untamed," the opposite of civilized); (14) **not lovers of the good** (*aphilagathoi*; cf. Titus 1:8; Pss. 15:4; 19:8). The next two characteristics begin in the Greek with the prefix *pro-*, indicating an aggressive inclination toward vice: (15) **treacherous** (*prodotai*, "disposed toward betrayal"); (16) **rash** (*propeteis*, "disposed toward recklessness"). The final three characteristics are (17) **conceited** (lit., "puffed up"; cf. 1 Tim. 3:6; 6:4); (18) **lovers of pleasure** (*philēdonoi*) **rather than lovers of God** (*philotheoi*; the Gr. prefix *phil-* here and in characteristics 1, 2, and 14 above signifies "lovers of . . ."); (19) **having a form** (*morphōsin*, "outward shape," used only here and in Rom. 2:20) **of godliness but denying its power** (cf. Titus 1:16).

Though these characteristics are cataloged under the auspices of a prediction about "the last days," it is clear that Paul considered them to be already present in Ephesus. Though they would intensify with time, Timothy had to beware of such people and **have nothing to do with them.** No doubt Paul had in mind here Timothy's official associations, since he had already instructed Timothy to be kind to everyone (cf. 2 Tim. 2:24).

3:6-7. Paul focused on the specific situation in Ephesus. It was from the increasingly large group in society who displayed the preceding characteristics that the false teachers had emerged to plague the church. Their methods were insidious. They would **worm their way into homes and gain control over** those they knew were vulnerable and gullible. In the case of Ephesus the false teachers had crept in via a group of **weak-willed women who** were, literally, "heaped with sin and fed by various lusts." Once more Paul connected false teaching with moral deficiency. Their carnality and immaturity rendered them easy targets for the false teachers (cf. Eph. 4:14). Out of a so-called "openness to learn" they evidently embraced as a fad whatever new heresy came along. Their problem was that they could not recognize the truth when they saw it. (**To acknowledge the truth** is, lit., "to come to a full knowledge of the truth"; cf. 2 Tim. 2:25.)

3:8-9. The reference to **Jannes and Jambres** and their opposition to **Moses** draws not on the Old Testament but on a widespread Jewish legend about two of Pharaoh's magicians who competed against Moses and lost (cf. Ex. 7:11; 9:11). The comparison between the false teachers and the Egyptians, and implicitly therefore Timothy and Moses, must have encouraged the young minister. The opponents were **men of depraved** (lit., "corrupt"; cf. 1 Tim. 6:5) **minds** who **oppose the truth** and were therefore **rejected** (*adokimoi*, "disapproved") by God in regard to any claim to be teaching **the faith** (cf. 1 Tim. 3:9). Consequently, while their influence was temporarily a serious matter in the church, in the long run they would **not get very far.** Like Jannes and Jambres, eventually **their folly** would **be clear to everyone** (cf. 1 Tim. 4:15; 5:24-25).

VI. Challenge to Faithful Preaching (3:10–4:8)

A. Faithfulness in the face of opposition (3:10-13)

3:10-11. Paul returned (cf. 1:8, 12; 2:10) to his own example of endurance and faithfulness in another of his direct exhortations to Timothy (cf. 2:1). The contrast with the false teachers is a strong one: **You, however.** . . . Timothy knew intimately of Paul's **teaching** (*didaskalia*, "content") **way of life . . . purpose, faith, patience, love, endurance** (cf. 2:10; 12), **persecutions, sufferings** (cf. 1 Tim. 6:11), along with his various missionary experiences and deliverances, and the elderly apostle was not ashamed to lift them up before his young disciple as exemplary. The references to **Antioch** (of Pisidia), **Iconium, and Lystra** must have stirred Timothy's earliest memories of Paul (cf. Acts 13:14, 51; 14:6, 21; 16:1).

3:12-13. It was important for Timothy, as for all Christians, to realize that persecution awaits **everyone who wants to live a godly life in Christ** (cf. John 15:18-21)—hence Paul's reminder of his own past experience. Yet with the last days again in mind Paul wrote that Timothy could actually expect the situation to get worse and the pressure to intensify. False teaching would increase as **evil men and impostors** (lit., "magicians," but here with the connotation of "charlatans") **go from bad to worse** (lit., "advance further"), **deceiving and being deceived.** Error feeds on itself.

B. Faithfulness to God's Word (3:14–4:5)

3:14-15. Again the strong direct address, **But as for you.** . . . begins this section (cf. 2:1; 3:10; 4:5). The exhortation is to **continue** in the things Timothy had **learned** and **become convinced of** (cf. 1 Cor. 15:1-2). These things had come from two sources, which Paul set side by side as of equal importance: his own testimony, and **the Holy Scriptures,** which at that time of course consisted of the Old Testament. Timothy's complete confidence in both sources would be enough to prevent any slippage in his commitment to the truth. Again these verses seem to imply that Timothy's salvation occurred prior to his acquaintance with Paul (cf. 1 Tim. 1:2; 2 Tim. 1:2,

5; Acts 16:1). The Scriptures bring **salvation** only when one places his **faith in Christ Jesus.**

3:16-17. Paul had just noted that the Scriptures are able to make one wise with regard to salvation, a lesson Timothy had learned long before. But now Paul wanted to reemphasize to Timothy the crucial role of God's inscripturated revelation in his present ministry. Thus Paul reminded Timothy that **all Scripture is God-breathed** (*theopneustos,* "inspired"), that is, God's words were given through men superintended by the Holy Spirit so that their writings are without error. This fact was virtually taken for granted by the Jews. Then Paul asserted the "usefulness" of the Word. For each aspect of Timothy's ministry, whatever it might be—**teaching** (instructing believers in God's truths), **rebuking** those in sin (cf. 1 Tim. 5:20; 2 Tim. 4:2), **correcting** those in error (cf. 2 Tim. 2:25; 4:2), **and training** (*paideian,* lit., "child-training") **in righteousness** (guiding new believers in God's ways)—for all of these and more the written Word of God is profitable. With it **the man of God** (one who must provide spiritual leadership to others) is *artios*—"complete, capable, proficient in the sense of being able to meet all demands." To drive home his point still more emphatically Paul added **equipped** (*exērtismenos,* "furnished") **for every good work** (cf. 2:21). Paul placed heavy burdens of ministry on his young disciple in this letter, but he did not do so irresponsibly. He was confident of Timothy's commitment to and dependence on the Scriptures, and he was even more confident of God's ability to supply all Timothy's needs through the Word.

4:1. It would be difficult to see how Paul could have made his **charge** to Timothy any more weighty (cf. 1 Tim. 5:21; 6:13). He adjured Timothy, not only **in the** name of **God and of Christ,** but in the light of the coming judgment, Christ's return (*epiphaneian,* **appearing;** cf. 1 Tim. 6:14; 2 Tim. 4:8; Titus 2:13), and the establishment of **His** millennial **kingdom.**

4:2. The content of Paul's charge represents the central thrust of every minister's task: Timothy was to **preach the Word.** All the weight of verse 1 bears on this entreaty. Paul could hardly have emphasized the matter more strongly.

423

2 TIMOTHY

Because the Word is inspired and profitable for all aspects of the ministry, proclaiming that Word was to be Timothy's business **in season and out of season,** that is, he was to stand by this duty whether the opportunity seemed ripe or not. Those in error he was to **correct** (cf. 2:25); those who were sinning he was to **rebuke** (1 Tim. 5:20; 2 Tim. 3:16; Titus 1:13; 2:15); those who were doing well he was to **encourage.** These are the facets of public ministry: proclamation, correction, rebuke, and encouragement—all of which must be done **with great patience and careful instruction.**

4:3-4. The reason Paul's charge to Timothy is so solemn is that **the time will come**—and no doubt was already partially present, in the apostle's opinion—**when men will not put up with sound** (lit., "healthy"; cf. 1 Tim. 1:10; 6:3; 2 Tim. 1:13; Titus 1:9, 13; 2:8) **doctrine. Instead . . . they** would seek out (lit. "heap up") **teachers,** of whom many are always available, who would tell them what they wanted to hear rather than face them with the truth (cf. Rom. 1:18-32). Such teachers merely "tickle the ear" so that they **turn** people **away from the truth** on the one hand and toward **myths** (*mythous*; cf. 1 Tim. 1:4) on the other. Paul's main focus in this passage was on the inclinations of the audience rather than, as was more his custom (but cf. 2 Tim. 3:6-7), the evil intent of the false teachers. For error to flourish both sides of the transaction must cooperate. This is the sixth time Paul used "truth" in this epistle (cf. 2:15, 18, 25; 3:7-8). (He referred to truth five times in 1 Tim. [2:4, 7; 3:15; 4:3; 6:5] and twice in Titus [1:1, 14].) Obviously he was concerned about the dangers of heresies diverting people from God's truth.

4:5. Again Paul used the strong contrast **But you . . .** (cf. 3:10, 14). Timothy must remain cool-headed in the face of difficulties. He must be ready to **endure hardship** (cf. 2:3) as the pressure mounted. He must **do the work of an evangelist,** proclaiming the gospel at every opportunity. (There is no reason to assume, as some suggest, that Timothy was without the gift of evangelism). In every way, Paul wrote, fulfill **your** ministry (*diakonian,* the word for voluntary "service" from which comes "deacon").

C. Faithfulness of Paul (4:6-8)

4:6. What had overshadowed the entire epistle is now stated explicitly: Paul was about to die. The apostle's strong charge in the previous verses takes on added weight with this reminder. The "But you" of verse 5 must therefore be seen in contrast not only with the false teachers of verses 3-4 but also with the **For I** of verse 6. Paul viewed his death now as certain; he was **already being poured out like a drink offering** (cf. Phil. 2:17). This refers to the libation connected with the daily offerings of the lambs (cf. Num. 28:4-7). Paul knew, sitting in a Roman jail, that there would be no release. **The time** had **come for** his **departure** (*analyseōs,* a traveler's term commonly used as a euphemism for death).

4:7. Looking back over his life, the apostle offered a remarkable description few could honestly echo. He had **fought the good fight** (cf. 1 Tim. 6:12) **finished the race** (cf. Acts 20:24), and **kept the faith** (cf. 1 Tim. 6:20). The first two are common Pauline athletic images (cf. 1 Cor. 9:24-27), while the third draws again on the image of faithfulness in one's stewardship of Christian truth (cf. 2 Tim. 1:14).

4:8. As a result of his faithfulness to duty Paul had no fear of facing **the Lord, the righteous Judge,** but only anticipation of reward in the form of a **crown** (*stephanos,* the laurel wreath of the athletic games) **of righteousness which** was already waiting **in store for** him. "Crown of righteousness" can mean either that righteousness itself is the crown or reward, or that this crown is the reward *for* righteousness (cf. 2 Tim. 3:16). In favor of the first view is the fact that James 1:12 and Revelation 2:10 seem to say that the "crown of life" means that life *is* the crown, not that a crown is given because one has life. In either case Paul expected to receive his reward **on that day** (a reference to Christ's return, not Paul's death), side by side with the rest of the faithful **who have longed for His appearing** (cf. Phil. 3:20-21; Titus 2:13).

VII. Reminder of God's Faithfulness in Paul's Adversity (4:9-18)

A. Paul's enemies and friends (4:9-16)

4:9. In this last section of the epistle

Paul twice urged Timothy to join him in Rome (vv. 9, 21). The emphasis is on speed since Paul did not know how much longer he would be allowed to live. The delivery of the epistle, followed by Timothy's travel, would occupy some months as it was; any delay on Timothy's part could make his arrival too late. Paul evidently had reason to believe that his execution was imminent (cf. v. 6).

4:10. Paul's need for Timothy was intensified by the defection of **Demas** who, instead of loving the Lord's appearing (v. 8), **loved this world.** Previously mentioned among Paul's fellow workers (though, perhaps significantly, not commended) in Colossians 4:14 and Philemon 24, Demas **deserted** the apostle to embrace the safety, freedom, or comfort of **Thessalonica.** It should not be surprising that Paul would long for his most faithful disciple Timothy at such a time (cf. Phil. 2:20-22; 2 Tim. 1:4). Of **Crescens** nothing is known. He and **Titus** had evidently been dispatched to the Lord's work elsewhere, Crescens to **Galatia** and Titus to **Dalmatia,** now Yugoslavia. Unlike Demas, there is no hint of any defection on their part.

4:11. Of all Paul's close associates, **only** the "beloved physician" **Luke** (cf. Col. 4:14) was **with** Paul. He had accompanied Paul on many of his travels and had shared the first Roman imprisonment with him (cf. Col. 4:14; Phile. 24). In joining the two of them, Timothy was to pick up **Mark** along the way. It is not known where Mark might have been located. But this one whom Paul had once considered untrustworthy (Acts 15:36-40) was now considered **helpful to** Paul **in** his **ministry.** Barnabas' concern (in opposition to Paul's wishes) to salvage the young John Mark was now paying dividends to Paul himself (cf. Col. 4:10).

4:12. Tychicus, another of Paul's faithful traveling companions (cf. Acts 20:4) and messengers (Eph. 6:21-22; Col. 4:7-9) had been **sent . . . to Ephesus.** The reference is cryptic and evidently self-explanatory to Timothy. Perhaps Tychicus delivered the letter; perhaps he was even, by prior arrangement, to relieve Timothy temporarily (cf. Titus 3:12). In any case Tychicus was another of Paul's absent companions.

4:13. Again little is known of **Carpus** or **the cloak . . . scrolls,** or **parchments** mentioned here. Such glimpses into the daily life of the apostle are intriguing, but any attempts to suggest what the documents might have contained, for example, are purely speculative. Paul may have needed the cloak because winter was coming on and his prison was cold, but even this is uncertain.

4:14-15. Alexander the metalworker may be the same man named in Acts 19:33-34, or more likely, the person in 1 Timothy 1:20. But since the name Alexander was common, one cannot be certain. The Alexander referred to here was well known to Timothy and had done **a great deal of harm** to Paul by opposing his **message.** The apostle had no desire for personal revenge, as may be seen by his reference to Psalm 62:12: **The Lord will repay him for what he has done** (cf. Rom. 12:19). Yet Paul was concerned lest Timothy run afoul of Alexander's attacks. Hence his warning to **be on your guard against him.**

4:16. Paul's **first defense** evidently refers, not to his first Roman imprisonment, about which Timothy would have already known, but to a preliminary hearing leading up to his present trial. At such trials it was common to hear advocates for the accused, but in Paul's case **no one came to** his **support, but everyone deserted** him. The widespread desertion of the apostle may be explained by the fact that, unlike the period of his first imprisonment, it had now become dangerous to be a Christian in Rome. As early as A.D. 59-60 Roman Jews had informed Paul "that people everywhere are talking against this sect" (Acts 28:22). But the situation had gotten far worse after the fire of Rome in July of A.D. 64. Nero made the Christians scapegoats and many were tortured and died. The intensity of the anti-Christian pressure must have eased somewhat by A.D. 67, but the thought of identifying themselves with the fearless and outspoken apostle must have been more than the Roman Christians and even Paul's companions could face. In fact Paul was understanding toward their unfaithfulness, and he expressed the hope that **it not be held against them** (cf. Christ's words on the cross, Luke 23:34).

B. Paul's deliverance by the Lord (4:17-18)

4:17. Paul's courage in proclaiming the gospel was not dampened by the weakness of those around him. The secret to his ministry was his dependence on the strength of God (Phil. 4:13; 1 Tim. 1:12). Though nobody remained with him Paul said, **The Lord stood at my side and gave me strength.** The apostle to the Gentiles had long before discounted his own life for the sake of preaching the gospel (cf. Acts 20:24). This was simply the latest episode of many wherein Paul put his own life on the line **so that through him the message might be fully proclaimed and all the Gentiles might hear it.** And once again, at least for the time being, he had been **delivered from the lion's mouth.** Some have seen in this last phrase a metaphorical reference to Nero or a literal reference to the wild animals in the Roman Coliseum. More likely Paul is drawing on a biblical image (cf. Ps. 22:21; Dan. 6:22).

4:18. Paul knew that his fate in the Roman courts was sealed (cf. vv. 6-8), and he was ready to die. Yet he saw his death not as a victory for Rome but as a **rescue** of the Lord. Despite **every evil attack,** he had complete confidence that God would **bring** him **safely to His heavenly kingdom** (cf. v. 1). For this Paul, even in the face of his own death, could do nothing but praise God: **To Him be glory forever and ever. Amen** (cf. Eph. 3:21; 2 Peter 3:18).

VIII. Final Greetings (4:19-22)

4:19-20. Prisca (NIV marg.; elsewhere called **Priscilla) and Aquila,** the well-known couple who taught Apollos in Ephesus (cf. Acts 18:2, 18, 26; Rom. 16:3; 1 Cor. 16:19), **and the** faithful **household of Onesiphorus** (cf. 2 Tim. 1:16) were singled out by the apostle for greeting. **Erastus** was an old associate of Timothy (Acts 19:22) and his whereabouts would presumably be of interest; the same would be true of the information about **Trophimus** (cf. Acts 20:4; 21:29), an Ephesian.

4:21. The appeal in verse 9 is repeated with the addition of the words **before winter.** Paul may have desired his cloak before the weather turned cold (v. 13), but he was more likely concerned about the sailing conditions on the Adriatic Sea. Of the four individuals listed, **Eubulus . . . Pudens, Linus,** and **Claudia,** nothing is known. Though "everyone" had deserted Paul at his first defense, still, in the spirit of forgiveness expressed in verse 16, Paul had not cut the Roman Christians off. The greeting is from **all the brothers.**

4:22. Paul's closing benediction is first directed to Timothy (**your spirit,** sing.) and then to his other readers (**you,** pl.), once again demonstrating that the epistle was designed to be read widely (cf. 1 Tim. 6:21; Titus 3:15). If 2 Timothy were penned during Paul's second Roman imprisonment, these are the last words of the apostle to have survived.

BIBLIOGRAPHY

See Bibliography on 1 Timothy.

TITUS

A. Duane Litfin

INTRODUCTION

Titus was a Gentile convert (Gal. 2:3) who had served and traveled with the Apostle Paul (Gal. 2:1-3). Titus had also functioned as a faithful emissary to the troubled church in Corinth (2 Cor. 7:6-7; 8:6, 16).

In approximately A.D. 63–64, sometime after they left Timothy behind in Ephesus, Paul and Titus traveled on to Crete. After a brief visit Paul then left Titus behind to help provide leadership for the Cretan churches (Titus 1:5). Subsequently the apostle wrote this epistle and had it delivered to Titus. The exact time and place of writing is unknown. (See the *Introduction* to 1 Timothy for a more detailed discussion of the authorship and dating of the Pastoral Epistles.)

The purpose of the epistle to Titus was to instruct him about what he should do and teach in the Cretan churches. A special theme of the letter is the role of grace in promoting good works among God's people (Titus 2:11–3:8).

Paul hoped to join Titus again in Nicopolis for the winter (3:12), but there is no way of knowing whether that meeting ever took place. Titus was last mentioned by Paul (2 Tim. 4:10) as having gone to Dalmatia (Yugoslavia). Tradition has it that Titus later returned to Crete and there served out the rest of his life.

OUTLINE

COMMENTARY

I. Salutation (1:1-4)

1:1. Paul began by identifying himself as **a servant of God.** Usually, no doubt as a result of his Damascus Road experience (Acts 9:1-9), Paul called himself a "servant of Christ Jesus." Only here did he use the term "servant of God." On the other hand **apostle of Jesus Christ** is standard. Both of these titles ("servant" and "apostle") focus on Paul's two main concerns: **the faith of God's elect** (cf. Rom. 8:33; Col. 3:12) **and the knowledge of the truth that leads to godliness** (cf. 1 Tim. 2:4; 2 Tim. 2:25; 3:7). God was using Paul to call out a people for Himself (e.g., 1 Thes. 1:2-10) and to teach them the truth which is conducive to godly living (cf. 1 Tim. 6:3). In other words Paul's ministry was aimed at both the salvation and sanctification of God's people.

1:2-3. In the NIV the **faith and knowledge** (already mentioned in v. 1) are said to be **resting on the hope of eternal life.** "Resting on" is from the single Greek word *epi.* But it is better to understand this word as "with a view to," as in Ephesians 2:10. Thus Paul's thought

427

is that all of his ministry is "with a view to" eternal life. This hope was promised to the elect from eternity past (2 Tim. 1:9) by God, who cannot default on His word. Only in the latter days, however, has the full understanding of that word come to light in the message God gave Paul to preach. As is common in the Pastorals, the apostle referred to God as Savior (cf. 1 Tim. 1:1; 2:3; 4:10; Titus 2:10; 3:4). God's eternal plan to salvage a people for Himself, rather than any this-worldly agenda to liberate social structures or institutions, formed the primary focus of Paul's ministry.

1:4. Titus was the ostensible recipient of the letter even though this epistle, like 1 and 2 Timothy, was designed to be read widely. Titus was called **my true son,** indicating possibly that Paul was responsible for Titus' conversion. The same phrase was also used of Timothy (1 Tim. 1:2). Or the term may denote a mentor-protégé relationship, or both concepts. The greeting **grace and peace from God the Father and Christ Jesus our Savior** is typical (cf. 1 Tim. 1:2; 2 Tim. 1:2) except for the last term which was applied earlier (Titus 1:3) to God the Father. Paul used the term *Savior* in Titus' letter interchangeably for the first two Members of the Godhead (cf. 2:10 and 13; 3:4 and 6).

II. Qualifications of the Elders (1:5-9)

1:5. As with Timothy in Ephesus (1 Tim. 1:3), Paul had left Titus behind to provide leadership to the fledgling church in Crete. Now the apostle reiterated his previous instructions, both for Titus' sake and for the congregation's. The organization of the Cretan church was **unfinished** due to the brevity of Paul's visit. Thus Titus was to **straighten out** (lit., "set in order") the situation by appointing **elders in every town.** Titus was now acting as an apostolic agent (cf. Acts 14:23) in Paul's absence. His authority in the Cretan church was an extension of Paul's own. Such authority ended with the close of the Apostolic Age.

1:6. As in 1 Timothy 3:2-7 Paul listed the qualifications for elders (cf. comments on 1 Tim. 3:1). There the list numbered 15; here 17. Yet both lists cover essentially the same qualities: (1) the elder must be **blameless** (*anenklētos,*

"unreprovable"). In 1 Timothy 3:10 Paul used this same word of deacons, while in 1 Timothy 3:2 he used *anepilēmpton* to express the same thought of the elders. (2) **Husband of but one wife** probably means that the elder should have been married only once (see comments on 1 Tim. 3:2). (3) The elder must have his own household under control. This involves not only the matter of discipline (1 Tim. 3:4-5), but also positive spiritual influence as well. His children must be believers who **are not open to the charge of being wild and disobedient.** The apostle had explained why this requirement is important (1 Tim. 3:5).

1:7. Here Paul switched from the term "elder" (*presbyteros*) to **overseer** (*episkopos,* commonly trans. "bishop"). The two words are plainly interchangeable in the apostle's thinking, referring to the same church office. The term "overseer" is singular here, but this certainly does not mean that there must be only one *episkopos* per congregation. Rather the word is used here in a generic sense. Paul was simply affirming that these qualifications are required of all overseers. The need for blamelessness is repeated from verse 6. The reason this quality is so important is that an overseer serves as a steward of God. Damage to a church leader's reputation is damage to God's reputation. Then Paul resumed his list with five vices which must not characterize an overseer: (4) **not overbearing,** not arrogant and self-willed; (5) **not quick-tempered** (cf. James 1:19-20); (6) **not given to much wine;** (7) **not violent** (cf. 1 Tim. 3:3 for this and the previous vice); (8) **not pursuing dishonest gain** (cf. comments on 1 Tim. 6:5).

1:8. Whereas verse 7 lists negative characteristics to avoid, verse 8 lists positive qualities to be sought. The elder must be (9) **hospitable** (cf. 1 Tim. 3:2); (10) **one who loves what is good** (cf. Ps. 15); (11) **self-controlled,** or temperate and sensible (*sōphrona;* cf. Gal. 5:23; 1 Tim. 3:2; Titus 2:2, 4); (12) **upright** (*dikaion,* "just"); (13) **holy** (these last two are, with blamelessness, two of the characteristics Paul himself had modeled [cf. 1 Thes. 2:10], but neither is mentioned in 1 Tim. 3); and (14) **disciplined** (in contrast to the vices of Titus 1:7; cf. 1 Tim. 4:7-8).

1:9. Not only must an overseer meet moral and spiritual standards in his personal life, but he must also be a reliable man of the Word. **(15) He must hold firmly to the trustworthy message as it has been taught.** This last clause, "as it has been taught," actually comes first in the Greek, for emphasis. According to Paul, an elder is a conservator of the truth, one who must understand it, hold it fast; (16) **encourage others** by teaching it; and (17) **refute those who oppose it.** To be qualified as an elder a man must be a capable handler of the truth (cf. comments on 1 Tim. 3:2).

III. Characteristics of the False Teachers (1:10-16)

1:10. Having mentioned those who oppose the truth, Paul then described them for Titus and offered advice on how to handle them. He noted their three most prominent characteristics: they are **rebellious** (cf. Jude 8), **mere talkers,** and **deceivers.** All three characteristics were also present in Timothy's opponents in Ephesus (cf. 1 Tim. 1:3-11; 6:3-10; 2 Tim. 2:14-18); but in Crete, Titus faced a Jewish element (the **circumcision group,** cf. Acts 11:2; Gal. 2:12) in whom these characteristics stood out prominently.

1:11. These false teachers **must be silenced** because of the damage they were doing to the families of the congregation (cf. 2 Tim. 3:6). No doubt Titus' method of silencing was to be the same as Timothy's: the false teachers were to be instructed not to teach certain things lest they be excommunicated (cf. 1 Tim. 1:3-4; 2 Tim. 3:5). Again Paul condemned the motives of the false teachers—they were interested in **dishonest gain** (cf. comments on 1 Tim. 6:5).

1:12. To emphasize his point Paul quoted from Epimenides, a Cretan poet and philosopher from the sixth century B.C. who was widely believed to be a religious prophet. Though the quotation may originally have referred to a particular lie (viz., that Zeus was buried in Crete, which was especially offensive to those who believed Zeus was still alive), by Paul's day the saying had become a proverb which merely emphasized the low reputations of Cretans generally. So little did others think of the Cretans that the verb *krētizō* was invented to mean "to lie." Of course many noble Christians were in the congregations in Crete, but Paul was frontal in his assertion that the

false teachers possessed these baser Cretan tendencies.

1:13-14. How the congregations reacted to Paul's forthright use of this quotation is not known, but they certainly could not have missed his point: **This testimony is true.** The false teachers fit the Cretan stereotype. Thus their negative influence must be remedied, if at all possible, by salvaging the false teachers themselves. Titus was to **rebuke them sharply, so that they will be sound** ("healthy"; cf. 1 Tim. 1:10; 6:3-4) **in the faith.** The ultimate goal of discipline should be to recover the one who is in error (Gal. 6:1; 2 Thes. 3:14-15). In the present case Paul hoped that Titus' severe rebuke would be enough to bring the errorists around so that they would cease paying **attention to Jewish myths** and **to the commands of those who reject the truth.**

1:15-16. The "commands" of verse 14, especially in light of the Jewish and possibly Gnostic influences, undoubtedly included ascetic rules about eating, drinking, and purification (cf. Col. 2:20-23; 1 Tim. 4:1-5). Paul set the matter straight by reminding his readers of the Lord's teaching that purification is largely a matter of the internal rather than the external (cf. Mark 7:15; Luke 11:39-41). Nothing outside can corrupt one who is internally pure; but someone who is internally impure corrupts all he touches. The problem with the false teachers was that on the inside, in their **minds and consciences,** they were impure. As a result, even though they claimed to know and follow God, their corrupt actions belied their true natures (cf. 1 John 2:4). Their impure interiors thus rendered them externally **detestable** (lit., "abominable") to God, **disobedient** (cf. Titus 1:10), and **unfit** (*adokimoi,* "disapproved"; cf. 1 Cor. 9:27) **for doing anything good** (cf. 2 Tim. 3:17). Once again Paul connected theological error with moral deficiency.

IV. Godly Behavior for Different Groups (2:1-10)

A. Older men (2:1-2)

2:1. Returning to his instructions to Titus, Paul established a strong contrast with the false teachers he had just discussed. **You** translates *sy de,* which should probably be rendered more strongly: "But as for you. . . ." Titus was to teach in the congregation **what is in accord with sound doctrine,** or more literally, "healthy teaching." The notion of healthy teaching is common in the Pastorals (cf. 1 Tim. 1:10; 6:3; 2 Tim. 1:13; 4:3; Titus 1:9, 13; 2:2). So also is the idea that certain behavior befits sound doctrine, and other behavior does not (cf. 1 Tim. 1:10; 6:3). The victims of false teachers (cf. Titus 1:16) were out of harmony with sound doctrine; but now Paul would describe the right sorts of behavior.

2:2. Paul addressed several groups, the first being the **older men.** Titus was to teach them to manifest the characteristics of maturity. Older men are to be **temperate** (*nēphalious;* cf. 1 Tim. 3:2), **worthy of respect** (*semnous,* "serious-minded," i.e., not clowns), and **self-controlled** (*sōphronas,* cf. 1 Tim. 3:2; Titus 1:8; 2:4). These marks of maturity should be complemented by marks of godliness, the three central Christian virtues of **faith . . . love,** and **endurance** (*hypomonē*). This last one may seem to have replaced the familiar virtue "hope" in the trio, but the two are closely aligned (cf. Rom. 5:4; 15:4, 1 Thes. 1:3), especially for those who have lived long lives.

B. Older women (2:3)

2:3. Titus was likewise to teach the **older women** to behave reverently, in a way suitable to sound doctrine. They were **not to be slanderers** (cf. 1 Tim. 3:11) **or addicted to much wine** (cf. 1 Tim. 3:8). Both were real possibilities for women whose families were grown and who may have had too much idle time on their hands (cf. 1 Tim. 5:13-14). Titus was to encourage these older women to develop a ministry of teaching younger women **what is good.** Younger women with children were to keep their primary focus at home (see Titus 2:4-5), but the older women would do well to reach outside their homes and share what they had learned with those who would profit from it most.

C. Younger women (2:4-5)

2:4-5. Paul specified here what he meant by his general reference to "what is good" in verse 3. Older women could help the **younger women** in at least seven areas, a list that no doubt represents the apostle's understanding of a young wife

and mother's proper priorities. This list emphasizes, in the original, first what young wives and mothers are to be, and then only secondarily what they are to do. They are to be (1) lovers of their **husbands;** (2) lovers of their **children;** (3) **self-controlled;** (4) **pure;** (5) **busy at home,** that is (cf. 1:8; 2:2) "domestic" (*oikourgous,* lit., "working at home"); (6) **kind;** and (7) **subject to their husbands.** By (*agathas,* "good") manifesting these qualities, Paul wrote, young Christian wives and mothers would earn the respect of outsiders and thereby prevent God's Word from being maligned. Today, though the opposite is often true, Christian wives and mothers can still be sure that the Lord will honor those who value what He values, and that He will ultimately vindicate both His Word and those who are faithful to it.

D. Younger men (2:6-8)

2:6. Titus was to **similarly** encourage the **young men** to exercise self-control, a virtue in which many young men are deficient. Paul used some form of the word here translated "self-control" with each of the four groups of people (vv. 2, 4, 5, 6). Various forms of the word are prominent in the Pastorals, indicating for all Christians the importance of moderation, sensibleness, and self-restraint.

2:7-8. Titus qualified as a young man too, and so received some direct advice from the apostle. He must strive to "show himself" **an example** (*typos,* "pattern") to all (but esp. to the other young men) in every good work (cf. 1 Tim. 4:15-16). In his public ministry of teaching Titus must show an **integrity, seriousness, and soundness of speech that cannot be condemned.** Paul was always concerned lest **those who oppose** be provided ammunition for their attacks. Far better, said the apostle, that they **be ashamed because they have nothing bad to say about us.** They would not cease their attacks, of course, but they might at least be embarrassed by having to make up their own false accusations.

E. Slaves (2:9-10)

2:9-10. Slaves too, who made up a significant portion of first-century congregations, were responsible to honor God with their lives (see comments on 1 Tim.

6:1). Paul listed five qualities which were to characterize Christians who found themselves serving others. Titus was to teach them (1) **to be subject to their masters in everything;** (2) **to try to please them;** (3) **not to talk back to them;** (4) **not to steal from them;** (5) **to show that they can be fully trusted.** From the world's perspective a slave should not owe any of these things to his master, but from a Christian's perspective the situation looks different. A Christian slave is in fact serving, not his earthly master, but the Lord Christ who will vindicate him in the end (Col. 3:23-24). In the meantime he must avoid giving offense, and must concentrate on following Christ's example in every way (cf. 1 Peter 2:18-25). In this way his life will prove to be an adornment to **the teaching about God our Savior.** Thus Paul drove home again what had been the theme of this entire section (Titus 2:1-10): a believer's behavior is to be in accord with or befitting sound doctrine.

V. Role of Grace in Promoting Godly Behavior (2:11–3:11)

A. The educating power of grace (2:11-14)

2:11-12. Paul had been exploring the affirmation that godly living is demanded by God's truth. Now he changed his focus to explore that central aspect of God's truth which demands godly living: grace. The word **for** (*gar*) suggests that here is the theological foundation for what the apostle had just written.

When fully understood, it is the gospel of **the grace of God** which teaches Christians how to live. This grace has brought salvation to all men, i.e., it is universally *available.* The NIV, however, states that God's grace **that brings salvation has appeared to all men,** thus suggesting a universal *appearance.* The question is whether "to all men" goes with "appeared" (as in the NIV) or with the adjective *sōtērios* ("that brings salvation"). Grammatically "to all men" can be taken either way, but the latter makes better sense and correlates with the clear teaching of 1 Timothy 2:4, 6; 4:10. In each case the reference to God as Savior (cf. 1 Tim. 2:3; 4:10; Titus 2:10) prompted Paul to affirm the universal availability of salvation through Christ. To side with the NIV, on the other hand,

introduces an idea foreign to the New Testament and to common sense, since the gospel itself has patently not "appeared" to all men (unless "all men" means all kinds of people and not every single person). The message of God's grace, when its full implications are seen, leads Christians, negatively, **to say "No" to ungodliness and worldly passions** (cf. Heb. 11:24-26), and positively, **to live self-controlled, upright, and godly lives in this present Age.** All the specific instructions of Titus 2:1-10 can fit into these two negative and positive categories.

2:13-14. The gospel of grace affects one's present behavior, on the one hand, by focusing on God's unmerited favor in the past (see the Lord's parable in Matt. 18:23-35 for the dynamics of how this should work). But the Gospel also promotes godly living by focusing on the future. Christians look forward to **the blessed hope—the glorious appearing of our great God and Savior, Jesus Christ** (cf. 2 Tim. 4:8). It is crucial, moreover, to see that this One whom Christians look forward to meeting is the same One **who gave Himself for us to redeem** (*lytrōsētai,* "set free by payment of a price"; cf. Luke 24:21; 1 Peter 1:18) **us from all wickedness and to purify for Himself a people that are His very own, eager to do what is good.** A holy people was His purpose in paying such a fearful price. Therefore, knowing what all He has done and why He has done it, a Christian who truly loves Christ and looks forward to His return will pay any price to bring his life into conformity with his beloved Lord's will, lest he disappoint Him at His return. This was the Apostle John's thought when he wrote about the hope of Christ's appearing: "Everyone who has this hope in him purifies himself, just as He is pure" (1 John 3:3). A full understanding of these things leads inexorably to godly living. Conversely, ungodly living in a Christian is a clear sign that either he does not fully understand these things or he does not actually believe them.

B. The gracious behavior that results from grace (2:15–3:2)

2:15. Turning again to Titus, Paul told him to teach **these . . . things,** i.e., the specific aspects of godly behavior listed in verses 1-10 and referred to more crypti-

TITUS

cally in the last phrase of verse 14, "what is good." Like Timothy (e.g., 1 Tim. 4:12; 2 Tim. 4:2), Titus was told to step out aggressively in his public ministry, encouraging those who were doing well, rebuking those who needed to be corrected, being intimidated by no one.

3:1-2. A large part of any pastor's public ministry is reminding people of what they already know. Titus was to **remind** the Christians on Crete to be good citizens within their communities, a virtue in which Cretans were notoriously deficient. Though Paul did not repeat it here, his thought was no doubt that this behavior, like that of a Christian slave, will adorn the gospel and make it attractive to others (cf. 2:10). Paul listed seven qualities expected of Christian citizens: (1) **to be subject to rulers and authorities;** (2) **to be obedient** (cf. Rom. 13:1-7); (3) **to be ready to do whatever is good** (cf. Eph. 2:10; 2 Tim. 3:17); (4) **to slander no one;** (5) **to be peaceable and** (6) **considerate; and** (7) **to show true humility toward all men.** A Christian citizen should be an influence for good in the community in every way, demonstrating the loveliness of Christ to all through courteous and gracious behavior. This is precisely the lifestyle that results from understanding God's grace. In other words the instructions in Titus 2:15–3:2 must be seen as concrete examples of the behavior required of one who understands God's grace (2:11-14).

C. Grace as a motivation for godly living (3:3-8)

3:3. Paul never forgot the sinful condition from which he and his converts had been salvaged (cf. 1 Cor. 6:9-11; Eph. 4:17-24; Col. 3:6-7), and he reminded them of it once more. Instead of the gracious, Christlike people he was encouraging them to be, they once were just the opposite, being **foolish** instead of sensible, **disobedient** instead of submissive, **deceived and enslaved by all kinds of passions and pleasures** instead of self-disciplined and ready for every good work. Far from being peaceable, considerate, and humble, they were characterized by **malice and envy, being hated and hating one another.** Such is the brutish existence of people apart from God. While a veneer of civilization often obscures the bleak truth, the slightest

crack in the surface of society reveals the reality behind the facade. The painful truth is that apart from God people degenerate into little more than animals wrangling over bones.

3:4. But all of that changed **when the kindness and love** (philanthrōpia, lit., "love for man") **of God our Savior appeared.** The contrast is startling. In verse 3 man is the actor, but in verses 4-7 man is merely the recipient, and God becomes the actor. What man could in no wise do for himself, God initiated for him. (On the reference to God as Savior, see comments on 1 Tim. 1:1.)

3:5. God in His grace saves those who believe, not because of any righteousness in them (cf. Rom. 3:21-24; Eph. 2:8-9; 2 Tim. 1:9), but **because of His mercy.** The three words, "kindness," "love," and "mercy" (Titus 3:4-5) all represent aspects of God's grace. The dual means of grace through which He accomplished this salvation are (1) the **rebirth** spoken of as a **washing** from the filth of sin, and (2) the **renewal by the Holy Spirit** (cf. 2 Cor. 5:17). No mention is made here of the role of faith in the process because Paul's entire focus was on what God has done, not on human response.

3:6-7. God **poured out** the Holy Spirit on the world **generously through Jesus Christ our Savior.** Jesus was the Mediator of the Spirit (cf. Acts 2:33). The language intentionally conjures up images of the day of Pentecost (Acts 2:17). God's purpose in pouring out the Holy Spirit was **so that, having been justified by His grace,** believers **might become heirs having the hope of eternal life.** The ministry of the Holy Spirit is intimately involved, the New Testament explains, with bringing to fruition God's gracious purposes to save (cf. Rom. 8:15-17; Gal. 4:6-7; Eph. 1:13-14). What God in His grace began, God in His grace will see to the end, through His Spirit.

3:8. The **trustworthy saying** formula so common in the Pastorals (cf. 1 Tim. 1:15; 3:1; 4:9; 2 Tim. 2:11) introduces Paul's return to direct address. Because what he had just been saying is trustworthy, Titus should **stress these things** in order to promote godly behavior in his listeners. Twice before Paul had instructed Titus to teach these things in accordance with sound doctrine (Titus

432

2:1, 15), and this exhortation is his final reiteration of what is probably the central thrust of the entire epistle. Paul was deeply concerned that God's people **devote themselves to doing what is good** because **these things are excellent and profitable for everyone.** Titus was to promote good works, for they go hand in hand with sound doctrine.

D. Behavior inconsistent with grace (3:9-11)

3:9. If sound teaching is profitable for everyone, **foolish controversies and genealogies and arguments and quarrels about the Law . . . are unprofitable and useless.** This is a repeated theme in the Pastorals (cf. 1 Tim. 1:4; 6:4; 2 Tim. 2:23; Titus 1:14). Titus was to **avoid** (lit., "turn away from") such things.

3:10-11. As to the people who are advocating these useless things and thereby exerting a divisive and otherwise destructive influence in the church (cf. 1:11), Paul's instructions to Titus were direct and specific. He was to give such a person two warnings. If that did not work, he was to **have nothing to do with him.** The assumption is that a failure to respond to two warnings is a clear sign that the offender is **warped and sinful,** and **self-condemned.** Paul's thought here is similar to the Lord's instructions (Matt. 18:15-17), when He taught that after giving an offender three chances to repent, he is then to be cut off (but cf. 2 Thes. 3:14-15).

VI. Final Instructions and Greetings (3:12-15)

3:12. As usual, Paul ended his letter with some personal allusions. Though it is not known where Paul was when he wrote this epistle, he was planning to winter at **Nicopolis** on the Adriatic coast of Greece. Paul exhorted Titus to do his best to join him there as soon as **Artemas**

or **Tychicus** arrived. Evidently Paul intended to send one of the two to relieve Titus in Crete. Of Artemas nothing is known. (On Tychicus, see comments on 2 Tim. 4:12.)

3:13. Zenas the lawyer is mentioned nowhere else in the New Testament, and nothing is known about him, not even whether he was Jewish or Roman. But **Apollos** was a familiar fellow worker. The apostle's instructions seem to suggest that both Zenas and Apollos were in Crete and that Titus was in a position to **see that they have everything they need.** Servants of Christ who are called to travel from place to place have always received support from the churches (cf. 3 John 6-8).

3:14. Some have suggested that the Cretan Christians may have manifested some of their countrymen's traits (cf. 1:12) and were therefore unable to **provide for daily necessities,** much less be of use to anyone else. This is probably behind Paul's reference to **unproductive lives.** In any case Paul had been stressing the need for good works, not to earn salvation but to serve others, and he pointedly reiterated it here. He expressed the same thought to the Ephesian congregation (Eph. 4:28).

3:15. It is not known who was included in the phrase **everyone with me. Those who love us in the faith** obviously excluded the false teachers who opposed Paul. The closing greeting, **grace be with you all,** is similar to that in both 1 and 2 Timothy. The plural word **you** indicates an awareness on Paul's part that he was addressing a broader audience than just Titus.

BIBLIOGRAPHY

See Bibliography on 1 Timothy.

PHILEMON

Edwin C. Deibler

INTRODUCTION

Concerning the authenticity of this most personal of Paul's epistles, there has been no question. John Knox wrote, "The genuineness of the letter is so well established as to require little discussion" (*Philemon among the Letters of Paul*, p. 32).

Authorship. Among the church fathers, Ignatius, Tertullian, Origen, and Eusebius give evidence of the canonicity of this brief book. It was also included in the canon of Marcion and in the Muratorian fragment.

Three times in the epistle the author refers to himself as Paul (vv. 1, 9, 19). The style and language remind one of Paul (cf. v. 4 with Phil. 1:3-4). Paul in the introductions of his epistles commonly used the terms "love" and "faith." And these are used here also, in Philemon 5. Too, there is a close association with Colossians, for both epistles mention Archippus, Epaphras, Aristarchus, Demas, and Luke (cf. Col. 4:10, 12, 14, 17).

Date and Place of Writing. Paul was a prisoner when he wrote Philemon (vv. 1, 9). This epistle is therefore included among the so-called "prison epistles," and was written during his first Roman imprisonment, A.D. 61-63. Because Onesimus accompanied Tychicus, who carried the letter to Colosse, it is evident the two epistles were written at about the same time, probably in the summer of A.D. 62.

Destination. Philemon was the recipient. Judging by his ownership of slaves and the size of his home (large enough to house the local church referred to in v. 2), Philemon was a wealthy resident of Colosse. Though it is not known when Philemon first heard Paul, evidently Philemon was a convert of the apostle (v. 19b). It is likely that the two became friends during Paul's three-year ministry

in Ephesus (Acts 19). It is commonly believed that Apphia (Phile. 2) was Philemon's wife, and Archippus his son, though this cannot be asserted dogmatically.

Included among the first readers were the members of "the church that meets in [Philemon's] home" (Phile. 2). Possibly Archippus was an official in this church, and Philemon served as a lay worker (vv. 1-2; contrast the terms "fellow worker" and "fellow soldier"). Lightfoot suggests that Archippus was an elder or was on a missionary charge, either of which was an important responsibility in the church. Some suggest that Archippus may have been the pastor. It is possible that Archippus had some official capacity at Colosse (Col. 4:17).

Occasion and Purpose. The occasion for writing is almost identical with the story of the epistle itself. Onesimus, a slave of Philemon, had run away, having evidently robbed his master (Phile. 18). His travels somehow brought him to Rome where, in the providence of God, he came in contact with Paul. Through this contact Paul led Onesimus to know the Savior. Then Onesimus in some way became useful to Paul (vv. 12-13).

But Paul realized that Onesimus had a responsibility to Philemon and should make restitution for his thievery. Thus Paul deemed it right to return Onesimus to Philemon. Tychicus was given the responsibility of carrying Paul's letter from Rome to the Colossians, and Onesimus evidently traveled back with him (Col. 4:7-9).

In this letter to Philemon Paul explained his situation and asked Philemon to treat Onesimus not as a runaway, thieving slave, but now as a beloved brother in Christ (Phile. 15-16; cf. Col. 4:9). In so doing, the apostle gave not only some insight into the institution of slavery in the Apostolic Age but also his

Christian response to it. The reality of Galatians 3:28 becomes evident here in Philemon: "There is neither . . . slave nor free . . . in Christ Jesus." Paul also gave a brilliant cameo of gospel truth in the words, "Charge that to my account" (Phile. 18, NASB).

OUTLINE

COMMENTARY

I. The Salutation of the Letter (vv. 1-7)

A. The writer (v. 1a)

V. 1a. This is the only one of Paul's epistles in which he referred to himself in the salutation as **a prisoner of Christ Jesus.** In seven of his epistles he called himself "an apostle"; in two of them (1 and 2 Thes.) he used no appellation, and in three he referred to himself as Christ's "servant."

Probably Paul refrained from calling himself an apostle here because this epistle is one of entreaty and request, not one of commands that would necessitate its readers' awareness of his apostolic authority. Paul was a prisoner of the Roman Empire, but actually his imprisonment was because of his witness for the Savior. Paul called himself "a prisoner of Christ Jesus" (Phile. 9). Epaphras was his "fellow prisoner" (v. 23).

Adding the words **and Timothy our brother** strengthened the weight of Paul's sympathy and love. Timothy's name was also joined with Paul's in the salutations to five of Paul's other epistles (2 Cor., Phil., Col., 1 and 2 Thes.).

B. The readers (v. 1b-2)

V. 1b. About all that is known of Philemon in the New Testament is disclosed in the words, **To Philemon our dear friend and fellow worker.** He was loved by Paul ("dear friend" is the rendering of *agapētō*, lit., "loved" or "beloved"; cf. v. 16); and Paul considered Philemon on his level as a "fellow worker" (cf. the pl. "fellow workers," v. 24). Philemon was a well-to-do Christian of the Apostolic Age, in whose home at Colosse the church met. "Fellow worker" does not necessarily suggest that Paul and Philemon labored together; more likely, Philemon worked to build up the church in Colosse while Paul served in nearby Ephesus (see "Destination" under the Book of Philemon's *Introduction*). Paul also addressed Philemon as "brother" in verses 7 and 20.

V. 2. Apphia our sister was most likely the wife of Philemon. She may have possibly served in a semi-official position in the church in their home. "She is as much a part of the decision as her husband, because according to the custom of the time, she had day-to-day responsibility for the slaves" (Arthur A. Rupprecht, "Philemon," in *The Expositor's Bible Commentary*, 11:458).

Some have surmised that **Archippus our fellow soldier** was Philemon's son. He may likely have been a mission-pastor in Colosse, for Paul gave a brief instruction for the Colossians to pass on to Archippus (Col. 4:17). Perhaps Archippus, because of his position, could have exerted additional influence on Philemon.

The church that meets in your home could also put pressure on Philemon to heed Paul's request. If Paul had not included this church in his salutation, they might have gossiped when they saw Onesimus had returned. The practice of churches meeting in private homes for worship was common up to A.D. 200. Not until the third century did churches meet in separate buildings. Home churches were also mentioned by Paul in Romans 16:5 and Colossians 4:15. The words "your home" may refer, some say, to Archippus' home ("your" is the sing. *sou*), but it is better to take it as referring to Philemon's home since he is addressed first in the salutation. The singular "you" in Philemon 4, 6-8, 10-12, 16, 18-21, 23 obviously refers to Philemon. "You" and "your" is plural only in verses 22 and 25.

C. The salutation (v. 3)

V. 3. This salutation—**Grace to you and peace from God our Father and the Lord Jesus Christ**—is the usual Pauline greeting. It is almost identical in wording to the greeting in six of his other epistles (Rom., 1 and 2 Cor., Gal., Eph., Phil.); the salutation in Paul's six other epistles have only slight variations (Col., 1 and 2 Thes., 1 and 2 Tim., Titus). (See chart, "Paul's Introductions to His Epistles" at Rom. 1:1.)

It is important to note the word order. The word "peace" expresses a spiritual state denoting a proper relationship between God and man; it is the effect of only one cause: the "grace" of God. There can be no peace apart from grace. Peace *with* God, a judicial matter, comes by means of faith (Rom. 5:1). The peace *of* God, an experiential condition, results from the infilling ministry of the Holy Spirit (Eph. 5:18; Gal. 5:22-23). Paul concluded the letter with a similar prayer regarding the "grace of the Lord Jesus Christ" (Phile. 25).

D. The commendation (vv. 4-7)

1. THANKSGIVING (VV. 4-5)

V. 4. Every letter of Paul's except Galatians includes an expression of thanksgiving in the opening. This follows the custom, in both pagan and Christian first-century correspondence, of including a word of thanks in the salutation. The words **I always thank my God as I remember you in my prayers** are almost the same ones Paul used in his other prison epistles (see Eph. 1:15-16; Phil. 1:3-4; Col. 1:3-4). Paul told *when* he gave thanks ("always"), and *to whom* ("God"), and *for whom* ("you," i.e., Philemon).

V. 5. Paul also told *why* (**because I hear about your faith in the Lord Jesus and your love for all the saints**). The coupling of faith in Christ and love for the saints was also true of the Ephesians (Eph. 1:15), the Colossians (Col. 1:4), the Thessalonians (1 Thes. 1:3; 2 Thes. 1:3).

Paul may have heard about Philemon's faith in Christ and love for the saints from Onesimus and Epaphras. Philemon's faith in Christ produced love for all the saints. Since Philemon loved "all" the saints, he surely should include Onesimus, now a saint, in his love!

2. PRAYER (V. 6)

V. 6. Having commended Philemon's faith and love (v. 5) Paul expanded on Philemon's faith (v. 6) and his love (v. 7). Paul's prayer was that Philemon (**you** is sing.) would be **active in sharing his faith** (lit., "active in *the* sharing," *hē koinōnia*). The relationship of the second clause to the first is difficult to translate. The NIV suggests that the second is a *result* of the first: **so that you will have a full understanding of every good thing we have in Christ.** Philemon's sharing of his faith would then lead to a full understanding of his spiritual blessings. However, the NIV words "so that you will have" are simply the one Greek word *en* ("in"). This hints that the first clause results from the second. As Philemon would gain a fuller understanding of his blessings in Christ he would become more active in sharing Him. He would share Christ *in* (i.e., in the sphere of) his full understanding of his blessings. The more a believer comes to comprehend all he has in Christ the more eager he is to share Him with others. The "full understanding" is *epignōsei*, mentioned in Paul's prayers in each of the other prison epistles (Eph. 1:18; Phil. 1:9; Col. 1:9).

3. TESTIMONY (V. 7)

V. 7. Philemon's **love** (cf. vv. 5, 9) resulted in **joy and encouragement** for

Paul, for Philemon had **refreshed the hearts of the saints.** "Refreshed" (*anapepautai*, cf. v. 20) is the word the Lord used in Matthew 11:28, "Come to Me, all you who are weary and burdened, and I will give you rest" (*anapausō*, "I will refresh you"). Philemon, having been spiritually "refreshed" by Christ, could refresh others. "Hearts" is not the normal Greek word *kardia* for heart, but is *splanchna* (lit., "inner parts of the body"). The emotions stemmed from the inner parts, according to some Greeks. Thus this is a deep emotional term. Paul used it again in Philemon 12 and 20 (cf. Phil. 2:1, KJV).

II. The Body of the Letter (vv. 8-21)

A. The plea (vv. 8-12, 17)

Paul then gave his recommendations regarding the runaway slave Onesimus. Throughout this plea the apostle's words were courteous, and yet they bore a note of authority and earnestness. He revealed a double truth. Onesimus was now a *son* in the faith to Paul (v. 10), and Onesimus was now a *brother* to Philemon (v. 16). The latter forms a Christian reply to the horrible institution of slavery. Onesimus, in the lowest social status in the Roman world—a slave with no rights—was on a spiritual plane equal with his owner Philemon and with the leading apostle!

1. A PLEA, NOT A COMMAND (V. 8)

V. 8. Therefore introduces the application of Paul's prior words (vv. 4-7). Philemon's love, demonstrated to all the saints, should now include Onesimus. As an apostle Paul said he **could be bold and order you to do what you ought to do,** but he refrained. The word "bold" is *parrēsian*, rendered "courage" and "confidence" in Hebrews (3:6; 10:19, 35).

2. A PLEA FOR LOVE'S SAKE (V. 9)

V. 9. Paul's **appeal** was **on the basis of love,** probably Philemon's love (cf. vv. 5, 7). To receive back and forgive Onesimus would be a laudable expression of Philemon's love to both Onesimus and Paul. Further motivation for heeding Paul's plea was that Paul was both **an old man and now also a prisoner of Christ Jesus** (cf. v. 1). Being an "old man" (*presbytēs*) meant that Paul had authority (since older men in those days were considered wise and thus authoritative) and also that Paul's position as an *impris-*

oned old man greatly restricted what he himself could do for Onesimus. Also, the reminder that Paul was imprisoned might appeal to Philemon's sympathy. Thus Onesimus' restitution depended on Philemon. Paul's calling himself an old man undoubtedly was in contrast to Onesimus rather than to Philemon.

3. A PLEA FOR A SPIRITUAL SON (VV. 10-11)

V. 10. The verb **I appeal** (*parakalō*) was repeated from verse 9, thus giving it special force. This plea was for Paul's **son** (*tou emou teknou*, lit., "my own child"), a term of endearment, which Paul used elsewhere only of Timothy and Titus (1 Tim. 1:2; 2 Tim. 1:2; Titus 1:4). Onesimus, having escaped from his owner, somehow met Paul in Rome. Led to the Savior by Paul, Onesimus **became** Paul's **son while** he **was in chains.** Since the slave was converted while Paul was in prison, their relationship was probably stronger. What an encounter it must have been between that slave and that prisoner! But the slave-prisoner relationship became spiritually a son-father relationship. Paul thought of himself as a father to those he won to the Lord (1 Cor. 4:15; cf. 1 Tim. 1:2; 2 Tim. 1:2). A special bond of Christian affection exists between a believer and the person God used to bring him to Christ.

In Greek, the word **Onesimus** is last in Philemon 10, evidently withheld deliberately in order to render Philemon's heart more tender.

V. 11. Onesimus, a common name for slaves, means "useful." But this slave, by running away, had become the opposite of his name. He was then of no use to his owner. The words **but now** suggest a change resulting from his new birth. He who **was useless** (*achrēston*) had **become useful** (*euchrēston*) **both to you and to me.** "St. Paul seems to say, 'He belied his name in days past; he will more than deserve it now' " (Alfred Barry, "The Epistle to Philemon," in *Ellicott's Commentary on the Whole Bible,* 4:273). Onesimus was then doubly useful, to Paul as well as Philemon. This clever play on words on the slave's name no doubt strengthened the force of the apostle's request.

4. A PLEA FROM THE HEART (V. 12)

V. 12. Paul passed the problem on to Philemon: **I am sending him . . . back to**

you. Philemon would not have opportunity to think over Paul's request before seeing Onesimus. Instead, facing Onesimus, the slave owner would need to decide right then. Since this converted slave was, as Paul wrote, **my very heart** (*splanchna*, "emotions"; cf. vv. 7, 20), how could Philemon refuse his friend Paul? The apostle certainly knew the art of friendly persuasion! This verse suggests that Onesimus himself was the bearer of the letter.

5. A PLEA FROM A PARTNER (V. 17)

V. 17. Earlier Paul wrote that his appeal was "for" Onesimus (v. 10), and that Philemon could "have him back for good" (v. 15). But not until verse 17 did Paul explicitly state his request: **welcome him.**

Since Philemon considered Paul a **partner,** he certainly should welcome Onesimus as if he were welcoming Paul himself. The bond between the apostle and the slave owner was that kind of unity which draws fellow workers in the gospel to each other. "Partner" is *koinōnon.* This is from *koinōnia* ("fellowship or partnership"), which Paul used in verse 6. If Philemon rejected Onesimus, it would be like rejecting the apostle, his friend (v. 1), fellow worker (v. 1), brother (vv. 7, 20), and even partner (v. 17). Such would of course be unthinkable.

B. The relationship (vv. 13-16)

1. THE PRESENT BROTHERHOOD BETWEEN PAUL AND ONESIMUS (V. 13)

V. 13. Paul's estimate of this Christian slave placed the latter on equal footing with Philemon. If Onesimus were kept by Paul—which Paul **would have liked** — Onesimus would have served in **place** of (*hyper*) Philemon. Both were equally capable of helping Paul. And being **in chains for the gospel,** incarcerated because of his testimony for Christ (cf. "prisoner" in vv. 1, 9), Paul could have used some assistance. But duty erased his wish. Knowing that a slave was his master's property, Paul had no choice but to send him back.

2. THE PAST BROTHERHOOD BETWEEN PAUL AND PHILEMON (V. 14)

V. 14. Retaining a slave could be done only with the owner's **consent.** Though Paul probably could have talked

Philemon into letting him keep Onesimus in Rome, he did not want to take undue advantage of their relationship. Paul preferred that such permission would be **spontaneous** (*hekousion,* "voluntary," used only here in the NT). No one knows whether Philemon freed Onesimus and sent him back to minister to Paul in Rome, but it is an interesting thought.

3. THE FUTURE BROTHERHOOD BETWEEN ONESIMUS AND PHILEMON (VV. 15-16)

V. 15. Philemon's temporary loss **(for a little while** is lit., "to an hour") of his slave resulted in his having him returned permanently. Some slaves were able to stay undetected in large cities or isolated areas, never to be returned to their owners. The words **for good,** which translate *aiōnion* (normally rendered "forever"), may mean either permanently in this life or forever in heaven.

V. 16. Paul also contrasted Onesimus' status **as a slave** with his new relationship to Philemon **as a dear brother,** thus placing all three men on the same level. Paul also called Onesimus "dear brother" in Colossians 4:9. The slave was dear to Paul but should be even more so to Philemon (cf. Phile. 11, "useful both to you and me"). For Philemon to take Onesimus back **no longer as a slave but better than a slave** may suggest emancipation (cf. v. 21). On the other hand some say that Philemon's receiving him **as a man** (lit., "in flesh") may point to a retaining of the master-slave relationship along with their new spiritual relationship **in the Lord.** Or these phrases may indicate just the opposite, with "as a man" referring to a person-to-person relationship, not a master-slave relationship.

(The commentary for v. 17 appears after that for v. 12.)

C. The pledge (vv. 18-21)

1. PHILEMON TO CHARGE ONESIMUS' DEBT TO PAUL (VV. 18-19A)

V. 18. Though Paul did not name Onesimus' offense, it probably involved a monetary loss for Philemon. Onesimus may have stolen some money or goods when he escaped from his owner, or the absence of Onesimus' services may have involved Philemon in financial loss. Paul did not castigate Onesimus for some crime; he simply wrote **if he has wronged you or owes you anything.**

Paul asked Philemon to charge (*el-loga*, an accounting term) Onesimus' financial obligation to Paul. This generous act compares in a small way with Christ's substitutionary work on the cross. As Onesimus was in debt to Philemon, so sinners are in debt; they must pay for their sins against God. As Paul was not involved in any way with Onesimus' guilt, so Christ was sinless, separate from sinners (Heb. 4:15; 7:25). And as Paul assumed Onesimus' debt, so Christ took on Himself the sins of the world (Isa. 53:6; John 1:29; Heb. 7:27; 9:26, 28).

V. 19a. Paul stated that he was writing these words with [his] **own hand** (cf. Gal. 6:11), thus placing himself under legal obligation to carry out his commitment. His ability to **pay it back** may have come from the gifts sent to him from Philippi (cf. Phil. 4:14-19).

2. PHILEMON TO CONSIDER HIS OWN DEBT TO PAUL (V. 19B)

V. 19b. You owe me your very self hints that Philemon may have been won to the Lord by Paul, and was thus obligated to him spiritually. If so, this was further evidence that Onesimus and Philemon were on the same spiritual plane; they had both been led to the Savior by the apostle. Such a debt could in one sense cover Onesimus' obligations. And yet Paul chose not to dwell on that fact.

3. PHILEMON TO REFRESH PAUL (V. 20)

V. 20. Receiving and restoring Onesimus would give **some benefit** to Paul **in the Lord** (cf. "in the Lord," v. 16) and would **refresh** his **heart in Christ.** The words "some benefit" translate the Greek *onaimēn*, which is obviously related to the word "Onesimus." Paul was saying in effect, "Let me find in you, as I have found in him, a true Onesimus." "Refresh" (*anapauson*) and "heart" (*splanchna*) recall the words of verse 7. Philemon, who refreshed the hearts of other saints, could hardly refrain from doing the same for Paul.

4. PHILEMON TO GO BEYOND PAUL'S REQUEST (V. 21)

V. 21. Paul was sure that Philemon would heed his request. **Obedience** is stronger than Paul's other more tactful and less direct appeals. Paul was also confident that Philemon would do **even**

more than he asked. What Paul had asked was that Onesimus be welcomed and forgiven. What could be "more than" that? Onesimus' freedom seems to be in mind (cf. v. 16, "no longer as a slave"). Or it may refer to Philemon's returning Onesimus to Paul; but had he not asked already for that, though subtly? (v. 13) If Onesimus were released, this shows an effect of Christianity on slavery through a recognition of true brotherhood in Christ.

III. The Conclusion of the Letter (vv. 22-25)

A. The comfort (v. 22)

V. 22. Paul then requested something for himself: **Prepare a guest room for me,** likely in Philemon's home. The prospect of a visit from the apostle would comfort Philemon but would also spur him to respond quickly to Paul's plea for Onesimus. The "guest room" points to Philemon's financial status. Like Paul, many Christian workers have been encouraged and assisted in their ministries by such provisions.

Paul knew that many were praying for his release (cf. Phil. 1:25-26). (How could Philemon pray for Paul's release and yet refuse to release Onesimus?) By using the plural **you** and **your,** Paul referred back to those mentioned in Philemon 1-2: Philemon, Apphia, Archippus, and all the believers with them.

B. The fraternal greetings (vv. 23-24)

Vv. 23-24. Those who sent greetings to Philemon (**you** in v. 23 is sing.) are five of the six people also mentioned in Colossians 4:10-14, though in a different order: **Epaphras . . . Mark, Aristarchus, Demas, and Luke.** In Colossians Paul also added "Jesus, who is called Justus." In Colossians 4:12-13 Paul highly commended Epaphras, who in Philemon 23 is called **my fellow prisoner for Christ Jesus.**

C. The benediction (v. 25)

V. 25. Paul concluded all 13 of his epistles with a one-sentence benediction similar to the one here: **The grace of the Lord Jesus Christ be with your spirit.** "Your" is plural, pointing back to those addressed in verses 1-2. These believers were already enjoying the grace that brought them salvation, but here and in verse 3 Paul was concerned that they be encompassed with God's enabling grace for their daily walk before others. "Spirit" (cf. "your spirit" in the Gal. 6:18 and 2 Tim. 4:22 benedictions) refers to one's inner spiritual self. What a gracious way for Paul to conclude this touching intimate epistle.

BIBLIOGRAPHY

Barnes, Albert. *Barnes' Notes on the New Testament*. Grand Rapids: Kregel Publications, 1966.

Barry, Alfred. "The Epistle to Philemon." In *Ellicott's Commentary on the Whole Bible*. Reprint (8 vols. in 4). Grand Rapids: Zondervan Publishing House, 1959.

Carson, Herbert M. *The Epistles of Paul to the Colossians and Philemon*. Tyndale New Testament Commentaries. Grand Rapids: Wm. B. Eerdmans Publishing Co., 1960.

Gromacki, Robert G. *Stand Perfect in Wisdom: An Exposition of Colossians and Philemon*. Grand Rapids: Baker Book House, 1981.

Hendriksen, William. *Exposition of Colossians and Philemon*. New Testament Commentary. Grand Rapids: Baker Book House, 1964.

Hiebert, D. Edmond. *Titus and Philemon*. Chicago: Moody Press, 1957.

Jamieson, Robert; Fausset, A.R.; and Brown, David. *A Commentary Critical, Experimental and Practical on the Old and New Testaments*. Grand Rapids: Wm. B. Eerdmans Publishing Co., 1974.

Knox, John. *Philemon among the Letters of Paul*. Chicago: University of Chicago Press, 1935. Reprint. New York: Abingdon Press, 1959.

Lightfoot, J.B. *St. Paul's Epistles to the Colossians and Philemon*. London: Macmillan & Co., 1879. Reprint. Grand Rapids: Zondervan Publishing House, 1979.

Lohse, Eduard. *Colossians and Philemon*. Translated by William R. Poehlmann and Robert J. Harris. Philadelphia: Fortress Press, 1971.

Moule, H.C.G. *The Epistles of Paul the Apostle to the Colossians and to Philemon*. Cambridge Bible for Schools and Colleges. Cambridge: At the University Press, 1906.

Muller, Jacobus J. *The Epistles of Paul to the Philippians and to Philemon*. The New International Commentary on the New Testament. Grand Rapids: Wm. B. Eerdmans Publishing Co., 1955.

Oesterly, W. E. "The Epistle to Philemon." In *The Expositor's Greek Testament*. Grand Rapids: Wm. B. Eerdmans Publishing Co., 1951.

Rupprecht, Arthur A. "Philemon." In *The Expositor's Bible Commentary*, vol. 11. Grand Rapids: Zondervan Publishing House, 1978.

At David C Cook, we equip the local church around the corner and around the globe to make disciples. Come see how we are working together—go to **www.davidccook.com**. Thank you!